Problems and Materials
on Consumer Law

ASPEN PUBLISHERS

PROBLEMS AND MATERIALS ON CONSUMER LAW
Fifth Edition

Douglas J. Whaley
Professor of Law Emeritus
The Ohio State University

Wolters Kluwer
Law & Business

AUSTIN   BOSTON   CHICAGO   NEW YORK   THE NETHERLANDS

Aspen Publishers
Attn: Permissions Department
76 Ninth Avenue, 7th Floor
New York, NY 10011-5201

To contact Customer Care, e-mail customer.care@aspenpublishers.com,
call 1-800-234-1660, fax 1-800-901-9075, or mail correspondence to:

Aspen Publishers
Attn: Order Department
PO Box 990
Frederick, MD 21705

Printed in the United States of America.

1 2 3 4 5 6 7 8 9 0

ISBN 978-0-7355-7711-4

Library of Congress Cataloging-in-Publication Data

Whaley, Douglas J.
    Problems and materials on consumer law / Douglas J. Whaley. — 5th ed.
        p. cm.
    Includes bibliographical references and index.
    ISBN 978-0-7355-7711-4
    1. Consumer protection—Law and legislation—United States. I. Title.
    KF1609.W48 2009
    343.7307′1—dc22

                                                                2009019570

About Wolters Kluwer Law & Business

Wolters Kluwer Law & Business is a leading provider of research information and workflow solutions in key specialty areas. The strengths of the individual brands of Aspen Publishers, CCH, Kluwer Law International and Loislaw are aligned within Wolters Kluwer Law & Business to provide comprehensive, in-depth solutions and expert-authored content for the legal, professional and education markets.

CCH was founded in 1913 and has served more than four generations of business professionals and their clients. The CCH products in the Wolters Kluwer Law & Business group are highly regarded electronic and print resources for legal, securities, antitrust and trade regulation, government contracting, banking, pension, payroll, employment and labor, and health-care reimbursement and compliance professionals.

Aspen Publishers is a leading information provider for attorneys, business professionals and law students. Written by preeminent authorities, Aspen products offer analytical and practical information in a range of specialty practice areas from securities law and intellectual property to mergers and acquisitions and pension/benefits. Aspen's trusted legal education resources provide professors and students with high-quality, up-to-date and effective resources for successful instruction and study in all areas of the law.

Kluwer Law International supplies the global business community with comprehensive English-language international legal information. Legal prac-titioners, corporate counsel and business executives around the world rely on the Kluwer Law International journals, loose-leafs, books and electronic products for authoritative information in many areas of international legal practice.

Loislaw is a premier provider of digitized legal content to small law firm practitioners of various specializations. Loislaw provides attorneys with the ability to quickly and efficiently find the necessary legal information they need, when and where they need it, by facilitating access to primary law as well as state-specific law, records, forms and treatises.

Wolters Kluwer Law & Business, a unit of Wolters Kluwer, is headquartered in New York and Riverwoods, Illinois. Wolters Kluwer is a leading multinational publisher and information services company.

This book is dedicated to Lorraine S. Latek
and Arthur F. Greenbaum

Summary of Contents

Contents

Acknowledgments

I began teaching Consumer Law in 1973, just as it became a hot topic. This was early in my teaching career, and I needed a lot of help to keep current on the developments in this fast-changing field. Professor Gerald Bepko (former Chancellor of Indiana University, Purdue University at Indianapolis), who was then also teaching this subject, helped me develop an embryonic version of these materials in the mid-1970s. Undoubtedly some of his sentences are still in the text, and his influence remains throughout. We spent a good deal of time parsing out the meaning of these statutes. I am very grateful for all I have learned from him.

My research assistants through the years have done a great deal to supply the background materials I needed to put this book together. I would especially like to thank my research assistants here at Ohio State who gave me significant help in assembling the various editions: John Walker (Class of 1988), Peter Larsen (Class of 1990), Gene Crawford (Class of 2003), and Hyatt Shirkey (Class of 2010). Barbara Shipek, my personal manager, also did her usual splendid job in straightening out the complications life throws in the path of anyone trying to get a book written and published.

The good people at Aspen Law & Business continue to have my thanks and appreciation for the professionalism they constantly display. This is my seventh Aspen casebook, and I have never wavered in my admiration for those who take my jumbled manuscript and turn it into a real book. I am, as ever, in their debt.

Finally, I want to thank the many students who have studied this subject under me. Every year since 1973, these materials were rewritten, and the students who took the course had to cope with unpublished materials filled with errors, hard-to-read reproductions of various items, and an unpolished text. They caught many of the errors, made suggestions, and coped with it all gracefully. I learned a lot from them as we explored these statutes (some of which were hot off the press) together. May their practices flourish and their clients be happy.

Douglas J. Whaley

Introduction to the Practice of Consumer Law

Consumer law is not quite respectable. It deals not with the great issues of our day, but with the petty ones—issues so small as to be mostly ignored by traditional law. Were consumers duped about the terms of the deal? *Caveat emptor*. Was the contract filled with unfair terms? *Laissez-faire*. (Doesn't someone who signs a contract have a duty to read?) Did the car fall apart? Did the interest rate prove to be deceptive? Was the credit report wrong? *De minimis non curat lex*. The courts should not bother with such trifles. Our system cannot bear litigating the annoyances of day-to-day life. The floodgates would open and horrors would wash ashore.

The problem with this attitude is that consumer issues really do matter. Moreover, they matter to everyone because everyone is a consumer. To the consumer with a problem, that problem is more important than most issues of daily life. The resolution of the problem often greatly affects any subsequent musings on the fairness of our legal system. The American sense of fair play is badly injured by the outrages practiced daily upon consumers: incidents of rapacious plundering too much for any law to ignore.

Before there was much legislation on point, consumer law was handled by tort theories: fraud, defamation, invasion of privacy, assault, and conversion. In these suits, a sympathetic judge could do much to redress the wrong: grant damages as large as possible and pile punitive damages on top of these. In some states, the successful plaintiff in a fraud suit is awarded attorney's fees in addition to other damages, in spite of the standard American rule that makes a party bear the expenses of lawyering, win or lose. In class actions, the prevailing plaintiffs collected a pot of money from which the attorney could be paid.

Starting in this century, legislation was enacted at both the state and federal levels giving rights to the consumer in each of the three major areas covered by this book: deceptive practices, product quality, and the granting of credit. The ascension of the baby boomers to societal power in the late 1960s and 1970s resulted in the passage of a massive amount of pro-consumer legislation, particularly by the federal government. Suddenly the consumer not only had rights, the consumer had *great* rights. All the consumer had to do in the usual case was get to an attorney who understood the law (not always an easy task), and the typical result was immediate victory as soon as the statute was pointedly explained to the other side. In 1981, the dawning of the Reagan era brought pro-consumer activity to an abrupt halt. The federal agencies, formerly as tenacious as pit bulls in assaulting creditor misbehavior, saw their funds slashed to starvation levels and their boards filled with appointees who did not believe in the basic mission of the agency. The Federal Trade Commission, for example, which had been a whirlwind of activity during the 1970s, issued almost nothing in the nature of pro-consumer regulation in the entire decade of the 1980s. The temper of the times changed throughout the legal world. Law students stopped taking the Consumer Law course, so law professors stopped teaching it. Lawyers graduated from law school with no ability to recognize a violation of the consumer laws if they saw one or with no interest in prosecuting it even if they were cognizant of the relevant rules. The vigorous consumer litigation of the 1970s and early 1980s dwindled to nothing, or almost nothing. However, in the early part of this new century, predatory lending, the mortgage foreclosure crisis, and payday lending have sparked a new interest in consumer law, and a number of statutes have been enacted to regulate these matters; consumer lawsuits are once again booming.

Moreover, the earlier laws remain on the books, real laws with teeth and bite. Consumers still have legal rights; what they don't have are many lawyers to represent them, and, alas, courts are often unsympathetic to their complaints. From the standpoint of the harmed consumer it sometimes seems that no one cares.

You are about to study those laws. Is it worth it?

Well, knowledge is almost never wasted, particularly this kind of knowledge. You are a consumer, and you are about to become a dangerous one. Before this course is over you will likely have made use of the things (tricks?) you will have learned, in addition to impressing the relatives and friends who, as consumers themselves, will be bringing you their problems, believing that you can help and hoping that you care about truth and justice even with respect to their small difficulties. If you think you can avoid practicing consumer law, think again. It will come up over and over throughout your life. Keep this book.

What if you decide to practice consumer law as a larger part of your professional enterprise?

Of course, you may have no choice. Become a lawyer representing a bank and, willy-nilly, you are going to have learn all about the consumer credit laws. Defense work in consumer law is a major part of the practice of numerous attorneys across the land.

As a plaintiff's attorney, the practice of consumer law is more problematic. Such a lawyer has to keep up with changes in a lot of complex statutes and know how to wield them as weapons on clients' behalf. What's more, the consumer law attorney has to battle the attitude described at the beginning of this Introduction: consumer law is so trivial it is not worth the time and trouble of anybody—litigant, court clerk, lawyer, or judge. You, the plaintiff's attorney, will be accused of conduct that is vaguely unethical for daring to raise matters no other attorney ever mentions.

How do you combat this mind-set? My advice is to ignore it. The laws are on the books. Even though the other lawyer, or even the judge, may wish they were not, that wish will not be granted. The statutes are real, the statutes are clear, the statutes say that the plaintiff wins. To the conservative, strict constructionist judge, the plaintiff's lawyer argues that it is not the place of the judiciary to choose which laws to enforce. Any plea to change the law should be made to the legislature, the appropriate body for legal reform.

Does the other side argue that your client was not really hurt? Rather than conceding that (a major mistake), focus on the fact that the law does not (in the typical consumer protection statute) require proof of actual harm (which the legislators recognized was often too difficult to establish), but awards automatic punitive damages (frequently modest in amount). Stress again and again that instead of creating yet another governmental bureaucracy to police the offending conduct, the legislature decided to invest the consumer plaintiff with the status of a "private attorney general," selflessly bringing litigation to forward the goals of the state toward the protection of its citizens.

Most of the statutes we will study provide for the awarding of attorney's fees. How easily are such fees recovered? As an attorney whose family, friends, neighbors, and former clients phone with such issues ("You are the only attorney I know"), you may approach this question as a business proposition. The answer is that getting paid is not very easy, but it is possible. And the more you take consumer cases and learn to wield the statutes as the awesome weapons they are, the more often your fees will be paid by the other side. There is no sweeter fee than the one you receive from opposing counsel's client.

Judges are often reticent to award fees, so you will have to use your most persuasive arguments supporting fee awards. The battle for attorney's fees is often as tough as the actual case. To help make *your* case, start the moment the client comes in the door. Look for all possible statutory violations, exploring all the interlocking statutory schemes. Tack together as many attorney's fee—granting statutes as you can find to apply—even more than you might need to prevail in the actual case. When you can point out to the judge that all three statutory schemes violated by the seller provide for attorney's fees, the judge is hard-pressed not to award them.[1]

Make sure you research your state's technical requirements for justifying the amount of the attorney's fee. If you can't find consumer law examples, look to other statutory awards of attorney's fees. Civil rights cases, for example, are often a rich source of information on the time records you need to keep (*always* contemporaneously with the performance of the work, and as detailed as possible) and the type of contract you should sign with your client (*always* in writing). Remember at all steps of the litigation that you will have to live up to your promises made in justifying the fee during the trial itself. Therefore keep complete records, and save all correspondence so that you can make a "settlements efforts" chart showing what the parties offered each other (be particularly careful to save the time-wasting letters and discovery requests the other side generated). You may want to create a graph showing all the time you expended on this complicated case.

However, since few cases are actually litigated, you will also need to try to get your fees paid out of any settlement. This is akin to getting the other attorney to tell his client that the attorney's fees just doubled. Defending parties are loath to pay your fees. Suggest to the other attorney that fees just be "lumped" into the general settlement, or designate them by a more palatable name such as "other" or "multiplier" damages. As you negotiate, keep your fees in mind and never let opposing counsel forget that payment of your fees must be part of the settlement. This will not sit well and may bring negotiations to a screeching halt—literally. At this point you will either have to give in on your fees or stand fast and be ready to go to trial. Few attorneys are ever actually prepared to go to trial. If you are ready, willing, and even anxious to go to trial, never let opposing counsel forget that.

---

1. Many states have "reciprocal fee" statutes providing for the consumer to recover attorney's fees if the contract awards them to the other side. See 11 Ark. Code §16-22-308; Cal. Civ. Code §1717; Conn. Gen. Stat. §42-150bb; Fla. Stat. Ann. §57.105(7); Haw. Rev. Stat. §607-14; Mont. Code Ann. §28-3-704; N.H. Rev. Stat Ann. §361-C:2; N.Y. Gen. Oblig. Law §5-327; Or. Rev. Stat. §20.096; Utah Code §78-27-26.5; Wash. Rev. Code §4.84.330. Idaho allows attorney's fees to be paid to the prevailing party in a breach-of-contract action; Idaho Code §12-120(3). Missouri does this for the enforcement of credit agreements; Mo. Stat. Ann. §408.092.

Every step in a consumer case includes maneuvering for your fees. Remind opposing counsel that you enjoy "wearing the white hat" and "can't wait to get this case in front of the jury." Remember (and point this out to opposing counsel) that every member of the jury is a consumer, but there won't be any representatives of the defendant's interests (such as used car dealers, bankers, or insurance brokers) in the jury box. Establish your reputation as someone who knows the law and who is ready to take consumer abuse to the jury, and things will get better. If the other side chooses to stall (the usual tactic of attorneys for defendants), remind them forcefully that this leads to increasingly accumulating fees that their client will eventually have to pay.

One valuable ploy in the successful representation of consumers is the initial *threat letter*. This letter, addressed to the offending future defendant, should do the following things:

1. Clearly state what happened (featuring prominently the equities in favor of your client).

2. Explain the violations of the law, giving citations.

3. Explain the penalties provided by law to rectify the difficulty, highlighting not only the actual damages incurred, but also any punitive damages and, especially, attorney's fees (the amount to date of which you might include in the letter).

4. State a date by which you expect an answer and further state what action you will take if a satisfactory response is not forthcoming. (Remember also that it is unethical to threaten an action you have no intention of taking.) Urge settlement.

5. Send a copy to your client, who will love it. (You should mail your client copies of all the paperwork you generate. Doing so reassures the client that you are on the job.)

To help you, the future consumer attorney, fight your consumer law battles, I have included throughout the book my favorite quotations under the heading "Quotes for the Attorney's Arsenal." Save these. They can provide significant, eloquent help in arguing the points of law involved. Things that are well said invite respect.

One final topic for this Introduction: how to read a consumer law statute. This book will cover an enormous number of statutes and regulations, many of them quite detailed. The preparation required for your class would be overwhelming if you had to read every sentence and be ready to parse out its meaning for your instructor. Instead, recognize that your goal is to get an *overview* of the statute/regulation, with the details to be filled in only as necessary to answer the Problems posed or the Questions asked by the text. Skim the relevant material to get its general idea. As time goes on this will get easier. A lot of these statutes are copied in part from others (the "bona fide error" defense, for example, is almost word for word the same on all levels, state and federal). Only when a real, live client has come into your life is it necessary to make sure that you have overlooked no details of the relevant law.

Problems and Materials
on Consumer Law

PART 1

Fraud and Deceptive Practices

Human civilization depends on cooperation, not just among friends but strangers as well. Where any given individual is not only uncooperative, but also manipulative of another's trust for personal advantage, people react with outrage. It is no surprise that our laws condemn most strongly those who practice rapacious deceit on others. If you, the attorney, can prove that the defendant fits this category, the rest is almost easy; everyone in the courtroom will be eager to punish this violator of civilized norms. In this Part of the book, we will explore what kind of conduct merits punishment, and the remedies imposed on the wrongdoers.

CHAPTER 1
Fraud

FISCHER v. DIVISION WEST CHINCHILLA RANCH
United States District Court, District of Minnesota, 1970
310 F. Supp. 424

NEVILLE, District Judge.

At various dates in late 1966 and early 1967 the seven co-plaintiffs in this action, after listening to and being motivated by defendant's television advertisements, each paid or obligated themselves to pay $2,150 or more for one male and six female chinchillas together with an additional sum for cages, pumice (for baths), feed and supplies.[1] Each contemplated becoming a chinchilla rancher on the representations that "Chinchilla ranching can be done in basements, spare rooms, closed in porches and out buildings with minor modifications..." the chinchilla being "odorless and practically noiseless.... A profitable pastime that can explode into a FIVE FIGURE INCOME... requiring only about 30 minutes per day... interesting and inexpensive... costs only $3.75 per year per animal." All plaintiffs alleged that the promises and representations made to them and on which they relied were false and fraudulent. None have had any financial success with their ranches in a period now of approximately three years....

The case was tried to the court at Duluth, Minnesota on January 8, 9, and 19, 1970 with jury waived. It now has become clear that each of the suits is in effect one for a rescission. The court perceives no basis for assessing punitive damages,[2] and any substantial claim for loss of profits, even as to the three plaintiffs who are State of Wisconsin residents is so remote and speculative as to prevent any substantial recovery therefor.

None of the plaintiffs are sophisticated businessmen nor highly educated and are respectively a medical photographer; a millwright and carpenter; a

---

1. Plaintiff Ida Mae Dayton purchased 12 females and 2 males at double the cost.
2. Even in plaintiffs' post trial brief, their counsel does not assert nor urge any recovery for punitive damages.

mechanic employed by the railroad; a farmer engaged partly in construction work; a paper mill hand; a widow; and a housewife. All responded independently to defendant's television ads and soon thereafter were called upon by one of defendant's salesmen.

Although the actual representations made to each individual plaintiff vary somewhat, the general pattern was the same. In addition to the representations mentioned above, all plaintiffs were told, either in the literature or by the defendant's salesman that the average price of a pelt would be $20 or more up to $40 and if desired defendant would purchase the pelts from the ranchers; chinchillas are substantially disease free; the average number of young which each female will have in one litter is one to three and each female is capable of producing three litters per year; defendant would provide eight consultation meetings at each plaintiff's home with one of its experts who would inspect the herd and render advice; that defendant would arrange a general meeting with other chinchilla ranchers thus affording an opportunity to talk to experienced persons; no special skill or knowledge would be required to become a successful chinchilla rancher; income would progress yearly as the herds grew and after five years a rancher could expect in excess of $5,000 annual profit based on a mathematical progression formula.

The court finds that each of the plaintiffs relied on the fore-mentioned representations in entering into their contracts with defendant. To date none have ever sold or been able to sell any of the chinchillas for pelts, though some plaintiffs made real efforts so to do. The court finds that the pelts because of their size, inferior quality and color cannot be sold commercially or profitably. None of the plaintiffs as of the time of the trial had profited or had income from their venture by any amount.

It is true that the contracts which each of the plaintiffs signed in purchasing the chinchillas specifically disclaimed all written or oral warranties except as the same were reduced to writing and included in the actual sales contracts. The present suits however in reality are not brought for breach of contract or to enforce contractual rights, but are bottomed on fraudulent inducement by the defendant to purchase the chinchillas upon the faith of the various representations. Such actions sound in tort rather than in contract and thus are not controlled in any event by the terms of the contract between plaintiffs and defendant.

While it may be argued that none of the representations made by the defendant, when viewed in isolation amount to fraud per se, the court finds that when considered as a whole the various statements and the entire plan worked a fraud on plaintiffs. Defendant created the impression in its potential customers including plaintiffs that chinchilla ranching was an easy undertaking and that there was no requirement for any special skills, experience, knowledge or special facilities in order to become a successful chinchilla rancher. This court is convinced that it was fraudulent for defendant to sell the chinchillas to people whom they knew or well should have known most likely would be unable successfully to raise chinchillas for profit because of their lack of skills, proper environment and/or experience. The defendant's own witness testified that the raising of chinchillas is to some extent an art and that the environment in which they are raised must be carefully controlled as to temperature, humidity and noise. Throughout the trial it became readily apparent that a large number of the chinchillas were "chewers" and chewed their own fur so as to make such unmarketable as a pelt. The expert testimony received at trial indicated that while the exact cause of this "chewing" is not known, in some instances it can be controlled and even eliminated by proper control of the environment. By adjusting the temperature and the humidity in the room where the chinchillas are caged the desire for chewing can be lessened. Each plaintiff testified that at the time of the sale the defendant's salesman told them that his particular basement or room where he planned to raise the chinchillas would be "ideal" and that no changes in the area would be necessary. Defendant's vice president Shafer was a witness and asserted he was a successful home rancher, but that in his basement he had a humidifier, an air conditioner and an exhaust fan. He testified these were advisable. None of plaintiffs were told of this desirability. Another of defendant's witnesses examined several of plaintiffs' herds the day before trial and was critical of their locale and environment even though plaintiffs were told the contrary originally. The conclusion is inescapable that defendant knew or should have known that each of the plaintiffs was doomed to or at least seriously risking failure in the business of raising chinchillas and that to sell seven chinchillas for $2,150 or more to each plaintiff under these circumstances constituted a fraud.

Plaintiffs presented no direct evidence as to the reasonable value or cost of a chinchilla animal. The only evidence is that of witness Denzler who raised chinchillas from 1963 to 1969. He testified he purchased an original herd of 21 animals for a price of $900 and later bought a male at a price which he considered a bargain for $80.00 who sired 117 offspring. It is not an unwarranted conclusion however that a great portion of the price paid by the plaintiffs is attributable to the promised service visits of experts and other advisory aspects.

Plaintiffs' expert witness viewed the animals of three of the plaintiffs the day before he took the witness stand, and had previously viewed plaintiff Dayton's animals. The court finds from his testimony that of plaintiff Fischer's 78 animals, none were of salable quality due to a small neck, small size, light color and not being fully veiled. Of the Bauers' 18 animals, the court finds they had a value at best of $7.50 per pelt because of light color, chewing and medium size. The 30 Dayton animals had been put under a grading light and the court finds proved to be yellowish and thus not commercially valuable. This plaintiff actually tanned some pelts and was unable to sell them, though she had installed a humidifier, air conditioner and had revamped the room in which the animals were kept. Much the same general opinion was given as to the Symiczek animals and the court finds them to be commercially valueless.

Plaintiff Gruper's animals all died long prior to the trial despite his efforts to determine the cause thereof through a veterinarian and by freezing one dead animal as instructed and returning to defendant for analysis. The court finds they were felled by a disease.

Plaintiff Christensen has but 12 animals left after three years. Plaintiff Bauman has but five animals left and no male. She determined the animals to be sick and requested defendant to take them back but was refused. Those she tried to market were "chewed" and not salable.

All of the above would support at least an inference if not an actual finding that the quality of the animals sold to plaintiffs was inferior and they were not capable of producing pelts anywhere near the $20 and up to $40 value promised and held out to plaintiffs as attainable nor the number thereof promised. . . .

Thus in applying the substantive law in this case the court must look to Wisconsin law for the three plaintiffs who reside in that state and must examine Minnesota law as to the four residents of Minnesota. Nebraska law becomes immaterial. As to whether or not there was fraud practiced upon the plaintiffs there appears to be no significant difference between Minnesota and Wisconsin law, Hartwig v. Bitter, 29 Wis. 2d 653, 139 N.W.2d 644, 16 A.L. R.3d 1303 (1966). The measure of damages may differ somewhat however as between the law of the two states. It is a well established principle that fraud cannot be predicated upon the mere expression of an opinion, when it is understood as being only such. Kennedy v. Flo-Tronics, Inc., 274 Minn. 327, 143 N.W.2d 827 (1966). Similarly representations as to profits to be made in the future usually are deemed expressions of opinion upon which an action for fraud ordinarily will not lie. Kennedy v. Flo-Tronics, supra. The elements constituting fraud in Minnesota were clearly set forth in Hanson v. Ford Motor Co., 278 F.2d 586 (8th Cir. 1960), where the Eighth Circuit Court of Appeals reviewed the decisions of the Minnesota Supreme Court and defined the eleven or more elements of fraud.

Upon examination of the cases apposite to the instant situation it becomes readily observable that courts in the past have examined the disparity in knowledge and experience between buyer and seller and have held that it is fraudulent to sell something to a person who is obviously not able to use it because of his lack of experience or skills. In Spiess v. Brandt, 230 Minn. 246, 41 N.W.2d 561, 27 A.L.R.2d 1 (1950), two brothers, who were 21 and

26 years of age, bought a resort from the defendant. Neither had any previous experience in operating a resort, either large or small, whereas defendants who sold the resort were mature men of considerable experience in the resort as well as other business enterprises. In holding that the transaction was fraudulent on the part of defendants the court stated in part:

> Although the element of disparity in business experience is not of itself a sufficient ground for relief, nevertheless, the law does not ignore such disparity. . . . Disparity may under some circumstances be a factor of considerable importance when we keep in mind that the question is not whether the representation would deceive the average man. . . . [T]he question is whether the representations were of such a character and were made under such circumstances that they were reasonably calculated to deceive, not the average man, but a person of the capacity and experience of the particular individual who was the recipient of the representations. . . . 41 N.W.2d at 566-567.

The Minnesota case most apposite to the instant one and almost a "cranberry" is Hollerman v. F. H. Peavey & Co., 269 Minn. 221, 130 N.W.2d 534 (1964), where the plaintiffs entered into a contract with certain defendant corporations for the purchase of the defendants' products and services, all of which have to do with on the farm feeding, production and processing of chicken broilers. The plaintiffs raised three flocks of chickens with an extremely high death and disease rate in each flock and very few of the chickens were able to be sold commercially. Prior to entering the contractual arrangements with the various defendants the plaintiffs received a brochure about the chicken raising business the contents of which are strikingly similar to the brochure used by the defendant in the present case. It read in part:

> "The plan and programs described here will return to the careful broiler raiser an income roughly equal to half as much as is obtained from an average size farm in the Midwest—and it will do so for about 6 hours of one person's attention daily." . . .
> "Your success with this plan is virtually assured, if you follow the plan as described. . . . " The grower is assured that he is "always going to get paid at least the minimum, or advance price." . . .
>   "This is a solid substantial program which combines the elements of security and success for the broiler raisers who become affiliated with them." 130 N.W.2d at 537.

The Minnesota court held these representations went beyond mere "puffing" or "salesman's talk." In noting that the parties in that case were not "on an equality" the court stated:

> Defendants had superior knowledge, or an opportunity for knowledge, of the problems which might be encountered in the conduct of the business. Because of their ignorance and inexperience in regard to matters concerning which material representations were made, plaintiffs had a right to rely upon the superior knowledge of defendants. 269 Minn. at 228, 130 N.W.2d at 540.

The court concluded that based upon the "highly colored" and "overly optimistic" representations made to the defendants there was sufficient basis to find fraud and misrepresentation citing Vulcan Metals Co. v. Simmons Mfg. Co., 248 F. 853, 856 (2d Cir. 1918) which stated (Judge Learned Hand):

> When the parties are so situated that the buyer may reasonably rely upon the expression of the seller's opinion, it is no excuse to give a false one . . . it makes much difference whether the parties stand "on an equality." For example, we should treat very differently the expressed opinion of a chemist to a layman about the properties of a composition from the same opinion between chemist and chemist, when the buyer had full opportunity to examine.

Upon examination of the evidence presented in this case there can be but one conclusion. Selling each of the respective plaintiffs in this case a number of chinchillas to start a chinchilla ranch, for the price of $2,150 or more when none of the plaintiffs had any previous experience in chinchilla ranching taken together with all of the other representations made contemporaneously is an act of fraud upon these plaintiffs. So to sell a laborer a complicated computer, a blue-collar worker life insurance for an amount of premium which he could not possibly afford, a non-high school graduate a set of William James' Philosophy . . . is to sell a person something that he cannot use and that is of little, if any, value to him; and to do so by representing that it is readily and easily understandable and that there are no serious problems involved with the product and that there are substantial profits in the offing is to mislead. The plan here was neither economically feasible nor commercially profitable.

In determining the measure of damages to be awarded each respective plaintiff, the court is cognizant of two conflicting rules in actions for fraudulent representations inducing a contract. The first, which is said to be the majority rule, allows the plaintiff the "benefit of his bargain," that is, it allows him to recover what he would have received had the representations relied upon been true. The minority rule allows plaintiff only the amount which he is "out of pocket," that is, the difference in value between what he gave as consideration and what he actually received.

It is clear that Minnesota follows the minority rule, that is, the "out of pocket rule." Lehman v. Hansord Pontiac Co., 246 Minn. 1, 74 N.W.2d 305 (1955); General Corporation v. General Motors Corp., 184 F. Supp. 231 (D. Minn. 1960). Under this rule plaintiffs cannot recover anticipated profits. General Corp. v. General Motors Corp., supra. In *Lehman*, supra, the Minnesota court stated that the measure of damages under the "out-of-pocket rule" is as follows:

> [It] is the loss naturally and proximately resulting from the fraud, and it will usually be the difference between what the plaintiff parted with and what he got. . . . It is therefore not a question of what the plaintiff might have gained through the transaction but what he lost, by reason of defendant's deception. 74 N.W.2d at 311.

This court holds it appropriate in all seven cases at bar to grant relief as for rescission. Each plaintiff should give back what he still retains of his herd, whether increased or decreased in number, his cages and any supplies on hand, and should recover what he has paid in cash on his or her contract with defendant, be released from paying any claimed balance due thereon and recover in addition his cash, out-of-pocket outlay and expenses as provided hereinafter.

Under both the "loss of bargain" and the "out-of-pocket" rules an award can only be made for damages resulting directly and proximately from the fraud. General Corporation v. General Motors Corp., supra, 184 F. Supp. at 240. The court does not believe all of the damages claimed by plaintiffs are or were directly and proximately caused by the fraudulent activities of the defendant. The court makes the following findings:

A claim is made on behalf of each plaintiff for the labor which he or she expended in his or her chinchilla ranching venture. The rate of two dollars per hour was applied in each instance and the respective claims ranged from $970 to $3,630. None of the plaintiffs testified during trial that he gave up his regular employment or shortened the hours which he could spend at his regular vocation because of the time spent on the chinchillas. The time so spent came from the plaintiffs' leisure time and did not directly cause any of them any economic loss. Admittedly the plaintiffs had less leisure time for other hobbies or activities but the court under the "out-of-pocket" theory or otherwise cannot ascribe any monetary value to this. So the court disallows plaintiffs' claim for damages based upon time spent in working with the chinchillas.

Plaintiff Bauers testified that he built an additional room onto his house to accommodate his chinchilla business and that he expended $1,200 for this construction. This room certainly will not lose its value to plaintiff upon termination of his chinchilla business. To allow plaintiff to recover this amount from defendant would be unjustly to enrich him. Thus the claim of plaintiff Bauers for the $1,200 for construction costs is denied.

The same reasoning as used above is apropos to the claim made by plaintiff Dayton as to her expenditure for heaters and fans in the amount of $360, and as to plaintiff Bauman for an item of $130 for a heater. Both of these claims are hereby denied.

Each plaintiff claims damages for the cost of heat and electricity. The court was not presented with any evidence to support a finding that each plaintiff would not have heated the rooms where he or she caged the chinchillas had he or she not purchased them and thus holds that these expenses are not directly and proximately caused by the fraudulent activities of defendant.

The court finds that the expenditures made by each plaintiff for supplies, cages, food, etc. are legitimate claims as they were made as the direct and proximate result of the fraudulently induced contract. Absent such contracts these appropriations would not have been made and so recovery for the aforementioned claims is allowed.

The automobile costs claimed by each plaintiff involved traveling to meetings with other chinchilla ranchers and to get feed and supplies. While defendant argues that the figures included for said expense are extremely high, it offered no evidence to contradict the same and the court will allow full recovery for such costs since they are directly and proximately the result of the defendant's fraud.

The principal remaining claim made by each plaintiff is for the "loss of 3 year Bargain." By this claim plaintiffs presumably seek to recover the profits which they would have made had defendant's representations in fact been true. A chart was shown to some of the plaintiffs by defendant's salesmen which diagramed the estimated future income which a chinchilla rancher could expect over a given amount of time. This indicated an income (not necessarily net profit) of $721 during the third year of ranching. Presumably expenses would be deducted from this figure of income which is based on a purported National average of $21.60 per pelt.[3] To those to whom the chart was not shown, the salesman made similar representations. As above indicated such a claim may not be allowed as to those transactions which occurred in Minnesota.

As to the three plaintiffs who reside in Wisconsin, i.e., Gruper, Bauman and Christensen, and considering that Wisconsin is committed to the majority, or "benefit of the bargain" rule (Anderson v. Tri-State Home Improvement Co., 268 Wis. 455, 67 N.W.2d 853 (1955)), and even though the court regards these as essentially rescission actions, the court will allow $200 to each. In any event, no great profits were expected or promised until after the fifth year and such are remote, contingent and speculative. See 13 A.L.R.3d 875 for an exhaustive annotation on the general subject of the majority and minority rules.

Defendant sought at the trial to introduce a Federal Trade Commission consent decree entered in a civil proceeding whereby defendant agreed to cease and desist from certain claims, representations and advertising. This consent decree was entered into by defendant after the occurrence of the fraudulent activities involved in the present suit. The court did not and does

---

3. Plaintiffs' Exhibit 3, p.2.

not now allow the consent agreement nor the accompanying order to go into evidence, analogizing the situation to one in which courts have consistently disallowed the introduction of Federal Trade Commission consent decrees in civil antitrust suits. Perhaps a better basis for its non admission however is that since the Federal Trade Commission order was entered after the fraudulent activities complained of in these lawsuits, the actions of the defendant in relation to each of the plaintiffs did not go towards showing bad faith in violating this decree, nor was any reference in the consent agreement made to the events involved in this case. Thus the findings of the court herein expressed in no way reflect or are influenced by the findings of the Federal Trade Commission in said order. The court's findings are based entirely upon the evidence presented before the court.

The following schedule represents the amount of damage allowed to plaintiffs in each case. Since plaintiffs' claims were unliquidated, plaintiffs are entitled to interest only from date of entry of judgment herein.

1. ADOLPH FISCHER:

Payments on Contract	$1,405.00
Supplies	340.71
Food	239.58
Car Costs	300.00
TOTAL	$2,285.29

2. GLEN CHRISTENSEN:

Payments on Contract	$1,564.00
Supplies	93.94
Feed	61.65
Car Costs	179.00
Loss of Bargain	200.00
TOTAL	$2,098.59

3. JOHN SYMICZEK:

Payments on Contract	$1,675.31
Supplies	134.15
Food	195.52
Cages and Other Supplies	95.00
Car Costs	150.00
TOTAL	$2,249.98

4. IDA MAE DAYTON:

Payments on Contract	$2,659.60
Feed	175.62
Pens	53.40
Veterinarian	10.00
Car Expenses	150.00
TOTAL	$3,048.62

5. JANICE BAUMAN:

Payments on Contract	$1,037.00
Feed	100.00
Supplies	190.00
Car Expenses	150.00
Loss of Bargain	200.00
TOTAL	$1,677.00

6. BRUCE N. GRUPER:

Payments on Contract	$2,175.00
Supplies	137.00
Feed	35.00
Loss of Bargain	200.00
TOTAL	$2,547.00

7. GENE R. BAUERS:

Payments on Contract	$1,075.00
Feed and Hay	139.10
Supplies	75.17
Car Expenses	74.30
TOTAL	$1,363.57

It is ordered that each plaintiff have judgment for the amount of money set after his or her name and be released from any further liability to defendant.

It is further ordered that contemporaneously with and at the time of payment of the judgments, defendant may take possession of and title to, at its own expense and at and from the respective plaintiffs' homes or locations of the chinchilla, all animals, cages and supplies on hand and in possession of each plaintiff. This opinion shall be in lieu of findings of fact as required by Rule 52(a) of the Federal Rules of Civil Procedure. Plaintiffs may tax costs.

Let judgment be entered accordingly.

QUESTIONS

1. The consumers' attorney apparently was unaware of Uniform Commercial Code §2-721. If that section had been called to the attention of the judge, would it have changed the result in the case?
2. Were the plaintiffs in this case consumers?

Fraud is the civil action for the punishment of lying. While innocent misrepresentations may lead to rescission or damages, and are sometimes grouped by the courts under the heading of fraud, the basic concept of true fraud deals with lies and liars. Perhaps you can remember the early battles about lying that you fought with your parents (and lost): Is a half-truth a lie? Is the telling of the "literal" truth a lie? Etcetera. Those same battles have been waged, with identical results to your childhood skirmishes, in courtrooms where the defendant is charged with fraud. For a discussion of the legal principles at issue, see Fleming James & Oscar Gray, Misrepresentation, 37 Md. L. Rev. 286 (Part I) and 488 (Part II) (1977-1978).

While negligent or innocent misrepresentation can be actionable (and is sometimes called "constructive fraud"), the more typical fraud lawsuit is aimed at redressing damages caused by deliberate misrepresentations. The courts identify the following elements as necessary predicates to a successful fraud suit: the misrepresentation of an existing fact, scienter (meaning that the defendant either knew that the statement was a lie or had a reckless disregard for the truth), justifiable reliance, and actual damages.

PROBLEM 1

The sales personnel at Facade Motors had a bet that no one on the staff could sell "The Red Bomb," their affectionate name for a

1995 vehicle that had been returned twice for nonperformance. When Nancy Student came onto the used car lot looking for a car that would suit her needs during college, one of the salesmen decided that she could be talked into purchasing The Red Bomb. He told Nancy not to be deceived by appearances; the car was dependable and wouldn't cause her significant mechanical problems for two years. He also told her that if anything went wrong Facade Motors would fix it instantly. He then had her sign a contract of purchase, and she failed to notice that the contract contained a disclaimer of warranties, a merger clause, and a statement that the car was being sold "AS IS." The car suddenly blew up in Nancy's driveway a week later when she tried to start it. Nancy was not hurt, but she was plenty angry when the salesman at Facade Motors denied making any statements about the car and took refuge in the contract language. Nancy sued and produced a witness who had offered to buy The Red Bomb two days before Nancy purchased it, but who was steered onto another vehicle when the same salesman told him that The Red Bomb was a "piece of junk, dangerous to drive." The evidence at the trial also established that Facade Motors never did repair work and did not have the capacity to do maintenance of any kind. Facade's lawyer argued to the court that fraud must consist of the knowing misrepresentation of an existing fact and that statements of opinion and promises of future performance do not so qualify. How should this come out? See Vulcan Metals Co. v. Simmons Mfg. Co., 248 F. 853 (2d Cir. 1918); Langford v. Sloan, 833 N.E.2d 331 (Ohio App. 2005).

QUOTES FOR THE ATTORNEY'S ARSENAL: "OPINIONS AS FACTS"

There must be a misstatement of an existing fact; but the state of a man's mind is as much a fact as the state of his digestion. It is true that it is very difficult to prove what the state of a man's mind at a particular time is, but if it can be ascertained it is as much a fact as anything else. A misrepresentation as to the state of a man's mind is, therefore, a misstatement of fact.

Lord Bowen in Edginton v. Fitzmaurice, 29 Ch. Div. 459, 483 (1882).

VON HOFFMANN v. PRUDENTIAL INSURANCE CO. OF AMERICA[4]

United States District Court, Southern District of New York, 2002
202 F. Supp. 2d 252

CHIN, District Judge.

In 1987, plaintiff Ladislaus Von Hoffmann ("Von Hoffmann") purchased $30 million worth of "vanishing premium" life insurance from defendant The Prudential Insurance Company of America ("Prudential"). Defendant Alexander & Alexander, Inc. ("A & A") was the broker. Premiums were to "vanish" after seven years because the first seven years worth of premiums were expected to generate sufficient dividends to eliminate the need for Von Hoffmann to pay any further premiums. Prudential and A & A were careful to provide disclaimers; they advised Von Hoffmann that the seven-year premium feature was based on expected investment returns and that they could not guarantee future performance. They specifically noted that if investments did not perform as predicted, additional premiums would be required. They provided illustrations to show how the process would work, and represented that actual dividends paid on life insurance policies had exceeded the illustrated dividends for the prior twenty years.

In fact, the premiums did not "vanish" after seven years, and to date the cost of the policies has exceeded the originally projected premiums by more than $3.3 million. Von Hoffmann and his wife, Beatrix Von Hoffmann (the "Von Hoffmanns"), brought this action for, inter alia, common law fraud, alleging that Prudential and A & A engaged in a scheme of marketing fraud. The Von Hoffmanns' claims against Prudential have been settled, but plaintiffs' claims against A & A remain. A & A moves pursuant to Fed. R. Civ. P. 56 for summary judgment dismissing plaintiffs' claims for common law fraud, negligent misrepresentation, negligence, and violation of New York Insurance Law §2123. A & A also moves to dismiss Prudential's cross-claims for indemnification and contribution as moot.

Although certain of the Von Hoffmanns' claims are time-barred and must be dismissed, their principal claims, including the claim of fraud, survive, for a reasonable jury could find that A & A failed to disclose a critical fact—Prudential had changed its methodology for calculating dividends, and thus the twenty-year history of dividends touted by A & A and Prudential was no longer applicable. Although A & A and Prudential had provided certain disclaimers, including a statement that future dividend rates could not be guaranteed, a reasonable jury could surely find that the failure to disclose the

---

4. Footnotes in this case have been renumbered for clarity.

change in methodology constituted a material omission. Accordingly, A & A's motion for summary judgment is granted in part and denied in part. A & A's motion to dismiss Prudential's cross-claims for indemnification and contribution is granted, as it has not been opposed.

BACKGROUND

A. FACTS

The facts set forth below are drawn from the parties' motion papers and supporting materials, and are construed in the light most favorable to the Von Hoffmanns for purposes of this motion.

In 1986, Von Hoffmann sold one of his businesses, Omicron Holdings, Inc., which carried three life insurance policies on his life totaling $50,000,000. (Von Hoffmann Decl. ¶2). In deciding what to do with the policies once the business was sold, Von Hoffmann had his company's controller, Albert Lopez, consult with A & A, the insurance broker Von Hoffmann had relied on since 1977. (Id. ¶¶1-3). Under this arrangement, Von Hoffmann retained authority over whether to purchase a policy, and Lopez relayed any information or documents he received from A & A to Von Hoffmann. (Id. ¶3).

Concerned with cost, Von Hoffmann advised A & A that he wanted to pay the premiums on any policy he purchased as quickly as possible. (Id. ¶5; Lopez Decl. ¶5). A & A responded that a single-premium policy was not feasible. (Von Hoffmann Decl. ¶5). Instead, A & A encouraged Von Hoffmann to purchase whole life policies with a "vanishing premium" or "abbreviated payment plan" option, where Von Hoffmann would make only seven cash premium payments, and after that, the premiums would "vanish" or "abbreviate."[5] (Id. ¶6; Am. Compl. ¶47; Lopez Decl. ¶6). Between December 1986 and June 1987, A & A provided "illustrations" concerning the policies, i.e., written promotional material used to "illustrate" how a policy would perform, which Lopez delivered to Von Hoffmann. (Lopez Decl. ¶7). Von Hoffmann asserts that each illustration was accompanied by either a cover letter or fax cover sheet representing that premiums would "abbreviate" in seven years. (Von Hoffmann Decl. ¶8; Lopez Decl. ¶7).

In 1987, Von Hoffmann "question[ed A & A] about the credibility of Prudential's dividend scales," whether the illustrated dividends were likely to

---

5. Prudential describes this type of policy as follows: "When a policy 'abbreviates', it has reached the point where enough premiums have been paid in cash so that future projected dividends, plus those already used to purchase paid-up additional insurance, are sufficient to pay the remaining premiums on an annual mode." (Lopez Decl. Ex. 8).

be paid, and if so, what the basis was for such expectation. (Pls.' 56.1 Statement ¶28; Von Hoffmann Decl. ¶10). A & A responded by letter dated June 12, 1987, enclosing a marketing brochure and other materials intended to "support the strong record of Prudential over a very long period of time." (Lopez Decl. Ex. 6). These illustrations explained that the policyholder would make only seven out-of-pocket cash premium payments, and that the remaining premium payments were to be paid out of funds accumulated in the policies. (Von Hoffmann Decl. ¶12; Lopez Decl. ¶¶10, 12). In addition, they showed that Prudential's actual dividends on life insurance policies had exceeded the illustrated dividends for the previous twenty years. (Von Hoffmann Decl. ¶10; Lopez Decl. ¶13 & Ex. 6). The illustrations also stated that premium payments were required for every year of the policy, and that "Annual payments are assumed." (Von Hoffmann Decl. ¶12; Lopez Decl. Ex. 6). A & A did not disclose that the illustrated dividends for the twenty-year period were based on an outdated method of crediting dividends that was no longer applicable. (Pls.' Opp'n Summ. J. at 3-4). A & A did not disclose that similar results could not be expected under the new method of crediting dividends.

Von Hoffmann claims that A & A withheld information from him, including a particular five-page illustration concerning his policies. (Id.). Specifically, Von Hoffmann claims that even though A & A received the complete five-page illustration from Prudential, A & A always removed page five (and also erased the page numbers) before forwarding the illustrations to Von Hoffmann. (Pls.' Opp'n Summ. J. at 3; Lopez Decl ¶17). Page five was entitled "Explanation of the Abbreviated Payment Plan," and disclosed that cash premium payments might be required for more years than illustrated. (Pls.' Opp'n Summ. J. at 3). Von Hoffmann also claims that A & A removed page three on a number of occasions. (Id.). Page three stated that "Annual payments are assumed," and also, that dividend amounts are "not guarantees or estimates for the future" and illustrated dividends are "likely to change as current interest rates change." (Lopez Decl. Ex. 6). Von Hoffmann admits that he received page three on this occasion, however, included with the illustrations attached to A & A's June 12, 1987 letter. (Pls.' 56.1 Statement ¶57; Lopez Decl. Ex. 6).

Based on A & A's advice, Von Hoffmann decided to convert the three life insurance policies that Omicron Holdings, Inc. had carried on his life into whole life insurance trusts for his daughters worth $30 million. (Von Hoffmann Decl. ¶3). The Von Hoffmanns signed the insurance applications in July of 1987 and the policies were issued in August of 1987 (id. ¶11), creating two life insurance trusts with Mrs. Von Hoffmann as trustee. (Id. ¶3). Von Hoffmann acknowledges that the front covers of both policies state that "Premiums are payable throughout the Insured's lifetime."

(Id. ¶12 & Ex. 1). In addition, the policies provide that the policy and the application form the entire contract, and that modifications may only be made by a Prudential officer in writing. (Von Hoffmann Decl. Ex. 1). Von Hoffmann asserts, however, that on the applications for the policies, A & A typed "Abbreviated Payment Plan" under the section entitled "State any special request." (Id. ¶13 & Ex. 1; Lopez Decl. ¶16). Von Hoffmann understood this phrase as referring to the illustrations he received, which showed that annual premiums would vanish after seven premium payments were made. (Von Hoffmann Decl. ¶13).

On or about October 7, 1987, on request from Von Hoffmann, Prudential prepared materials for Von Hoffmann to illustrate Prudential's "projection of values for future years." (Lopez Decl. Ex. 8). The illustrations included the complete five-page illustration referred to above. (Id. ¶17 & Ex. 8). Von Hoffmann asserts that this was the first time he received the complete five-page illustration. (Pls.' Mem. Opp'n Summ. J. at 4; Von Hoffmann Decl. ¶28). As mentioned above, page three explained, under the heading "Explanatory Notes," that dividend amounts are "not guarantees or estimates for the future"; illustrated dividends assume that current rates of investment earnings will continue each year into the future; and illustrated dividends are therefore "likely to change as current interest rates change." (Lopez Decl. Ex. 8). Page Five, "Explanation of the Abbreviated Payment Plan," provided: "[t]he dividends used in this illustration are based on the current scale and are not guaranteed. The possibility exists that cash premium payments may be required for more or fewer years than the period illustrated." (Id.). This was the first time the Von Hoffmanns saw page five.

Prudential also attached a cover letter and a form called the "Abbreviated Payment Plan Authorization" with the illustrations. (Lopez Decl. ¶17 & Ex. 8). The letter informed Von Hoffmann that "[b]ased on [Prudential's] projections, [the Von Hoffmanns'] policies will have the premiums 'vanish' or 'abbreviate' after seven annual payments." (Lopez Decl. Ex. 8). It also explained that the enclosed "authorization to proceed on [the Abbreviated Payment Plan] basis will be sent to the trustee when the eighth premium is due." (Id.). The authorization itself provided that Prudential would begin paying premiums on the policies by "surrendering paid-up additional coverage and/or withdrawing accumulated dividends" when it determined that the dividends would be sufficient to pay future premiums. (Id.). It also stated that continuation of the present rates "is not guaranteed. . . . " (Id.). Finally, the authorization explained that if Prudential determined that dividend accumulation and the cash value of paid-up additional coverage were not sufficient to pay a premium when due, the agreement would end. (Id.). Lopez states that he asked A & A about the meaning and effect of the explanatory notes and authorization form, and that A & A assured him that these items were "boilerplate," i.e., automatically generated whenever a policy was issued. (Id. ¶17). Lopez reported this information to Von Hoffmann. (Id.).

On or about January 8, 1992, A & A first informed Von Hoffmann, in writing, that ten premium cash payments would be required on his policy instead of seven. (Von Hoffmann Decl. ¶14; Lopez Decl. ¶21 & Ex. 10). Von Hoffmann requested an explanation. (Von Hoffmann Decl. ¶14). By letter dated February 5, 1992, Prudential provided detailed information regarding the major elements of the dividend formula, as well as information concerning "the recent dividend changes." (Defs.' 56.1 Statement Ex. 19). In his letter to A & A of March 4, 1992, Von Hoffmann acknowledged receipt of this information, and posed additional questions concerning whether to continue his payments under the policies. (Id. Ex. 20). Von Hoffmann also requested a meeting with a representative from Prudential, and on April 24, 1992, Jim Avery met with Von Hoffmann in his home. (Von Hoffmann Decl. ¶17).

Avery testified that, at the meeting, Von Hoffmann asked numerous questions regarding "why dividends had done what they had done on his policy" and that "[h]e wanted to understand the investment generation method." (Avery Dep. 46:5-8). Avery also testified that he and Von Hoffmann "went through tremendous detailed conversations about dividends, dividend determination, how to view this, investment generation, company policy, who determines dividends." (Id. at 47:12-17). Avery stated that Von Hoffmann "quite frankly, drilled me for two and a half hours nonstop." (Id.).

Von Hoffmann admits he understood that the exact amount of future dividends was not guaranteed, and that interest rates in the economy were not guaranteed. (Pls.' 56.1 Statement ¶54). He claims that he believed, however, that the illustrated dividends for his policy were "actuarially sound," which he based, in part, on Prudential's history of paying high dividends. (Id.). He also admits that he "may have suspected there was a risk that more than seven cash payments might be needed." (Id. ¶55). He claims that he did not know, however, that the dividend payments could decrease to the extent that the abbreviated payment plan could not be sustained. (Von Hoffmann Decl. ¶9). He also claims that A & A did not inform him that Prudential had recently changed its method of calculating dividends to a new method that was much more volatile. (Id. ¶10). He also contends that Prudential and A & A refused to provide specific information as to how Prudential credited dividends to its policies and A & A and Prudential also did not explain the differences between the new and old methods for crediting dividends or their effect on the dividend illustrations. (Id. ¶¶15-16).

From 1992 through 1995, Lopez and Von Hoffmann exchanged correspondence with A & A and Prudential, whereby Von Hoffmann sought further explanation as to why his policies did not abbreviate. (Id. ¶19). He states that he received little information in response. (Id.). In the summer of 1996, Von Hoffmann received a copy of a report entitled "The Multi-state Life Insurance Task Force and Multi-State Market Conduct Examination of The Prudential Insurance Company of America" (the "Task Force Report"), drafted by the Examiners of The Multi-state Life Insurance Task Force From Several State Departments of Insurance and other State Regulatory Agencies. (Id. ¶20 & Ex. 2). The report revealed, among other things, that Prudential had "changed its method of allocating interest to dividends," making transactions appear more beneficial to customers. (Id. Ex. 2). It also reported that some of Prudential's agents had engaged in abusive sales practices. (Id.). Von Hoffmann claims that when he read the Task Force Report, he suspected for the first time that Prudential and A & A had committed fraud. (Id. ¶22).

B. PRIOR PROCEEDINGS

The Von Hoffmanns filed the complaint in this action on June 18, 1997. On September 9, 1997, the case was transferred to the United States District Court for the District of New Jersey, by order of the Judicial Panel on Multidistrict Litigation. The Von Hoffmanns filed an amended complaint in the District of New Jersey on November 17, 1997. The parties engaged in discovery. On January 22, 2001, again by order of the Judicial Panel on Multidistrict Litigation, the case was remanded to this Court. On January 8, 2002, A & A filed this motion for summary judgment dismissing the first, fourth, fifth, and ninth causes of action, and dismissing the cross-claims for indemnification and contribution as moot.

DISCUSSION

The Von Hoffmanns have asserted claims against A & A for common law fraud, negligent misrepresentation, negligence, and violation of New York Insurance Law §2123. A & A moves for summary judgment dismissing the claims on the grounds that they are time-barred; with respect to the fraud claim, A & A argues in the alternative that the Von Hoffmanns fail to state a cause of action. I discuss the merits first and the statute of limitations defense second.

A.   THE MERITS

1.   Applicable Law

To state a claim for fraudulent inducement in an insurance context, a plaintiff must allege a misrepresentation or material omission by the defendant that induced the plaintiff to purchase the policies, as well as scienter, reliance, and injury. Gaidon v. Guardian Life Ins. Co. of Am., 94 N.Y.2d 330, 704 N.Y.S.2d 177, 185, 725 N.E.2d 598 (1999) (*"Gaidon II"*) (citing New York Univ. v. Continental Ins. Co., 87 N.Y.2d 308, 639 N.Y.S.2d 283, 289, 662 N.E.2d 763 (1995)). Claims for fraud in the inducement cannot be based on a "mere unfulfilled promissory statement," but may be grounded on a "promise made with the preconceived and undisclosed intention that the promise will not be performed." United Safety of Am., Inc. v. Consol. Edison Co. of N.Y., Inc., 213 A.D.2d 283, 623 N.Y.S.2d 591, 593 (1st Dep't 1995) (citations omitted). Additionally, the elements of fraud are "narrowly defined, requiring proof by clear and convincing evidence." *Gaidon II*, 704 N.Y.S.2d at 186, 725 N.E.2d 598.[6]

2.   Application

The Von Hoffmanns argue that A & A committed fraud in four respects:

First, A & A falsely represented that premiums would "vanish" after seven years;

Second, A & A modified Prudential's sales illustrations to delete information that might have cast doubt on the seven-year schedule;

Third, A & A provided no illustrations showing longer payment periods or using lower rates; and

Fourth, A & A failed to disclose that the illustrations and representations as to twenty years of performance were based on an out-of-date method for crediting dividends—a method that was no longer applicable to the policies A & A was trying to induce the Von Hoffmanns to buy—that likely predicted more optimistic results.

---

6. A & A argues that the Von Hoffmanns may not rely on the policy illustrations as evidence of fraud because they are not part of the policies and the policies contain merger clauses. (Defs.' Mem. Supp. Summ. J. at 11). This argument is inapplicable. Under New York law, a general merger clause declaring a writing to be the entire agreement between the parties will not bar admission of parol evidence to establish fraud in the inducement of the contract. First Nationwide Bank v. 965 Amsterdam, Inc., 212 A.D.2d 469, 623 N.Y.S.2d 200, 202 (1st Dep't 1995) (citing Sabo v. Delman, 3 N.Y.2d 155, 164 N.Y.S.2d 714, 717, 143 N.E.2d 906 (1957)).

Resolving all conflicts in the evidence and drawing all reasonable inferences in favor of the Von Hoffmanns, I conclude that, standing alone or together, the first, second and third alleged misrepresentations do not form a basis for a fraud claim as a matter of law, for the "vanishing premium" feature was not guaranteed. The fourth alleged misrepresentation is sufficient, however, to support a claim for fraud; considering all the evidence, I conclude that genuine issues of material fact exist as to whether A & A fraudulently withheld material information to induce the Von Hoffmanns to purchase the Prudential policies.

(a) Vanishing Premiums

The Von Hoffmanns claim that A & A fraudulently induced them to purchase Prudential insurance policies based on the first, second, and third misrepresentations set forth above. In light of the New York Court of Appeals' decision in *Gaidon II*, discussed below, to the extent the fraud claim is based on these alleged misrepresentations, it fails because the Von Hoffmanns cannot establish the "threshold element" for a claim of fraud, namely, misrepresentation or material omission. *Gaidon II*, 704 N.Y.S.2d at 186, 725 N.E.2d 598.

In *Gaidon II*, the court addressed claims of fraud similar to those at issue here, arising out of the sale of "vanishing premium" life insurance policies. The plaintiffs there alleged, essentially, that they purchased their life insurance policies relying on misleading illustrations and the defendants' false representations that the premium payments on the policy would "vanish" after eight years. Id. at 179, 725 N.E.2d 598. They argued that the illustrations were based on dividend projections that the insurer "knew or should have known were untenable." Id. The court considered the illustrations, noting that limitations accompanying each illustration disclosed: "Figures depending on dividends are neither estimated nor guaranteed, but are based on the [current year's] dividend scale," and "[a]ctual future dividends may be higher or lower than those illustrated depending on the company's future experience." Id. at 179-80, 725 N.E.2d 598. In addition, the defendants argued that the projections were based on the "continuation of an existing state of affairs and cannot be construed or characterized as guarantees." Id. at 186, 725 N.E.2d 598. The court ultimately found that "[b]y stating that the illustrated dividend/interest rates are not guaranteed and that they may be higher or lower than depicted, defendants made a partial disclosure." Id. at 186, 725 N.E.2d 598. It also observed, however, that the defendants "failed to reveal that the illustrated vanishing dates were wholly unrealistic." Id. at 187, 725 N.E.2d 598. Nevertheless, the court held that the insureds had not established the misrepresentation element required to state a claim for fraudulent inducement, and that the disclaimers were sufficient to "absolve [the defendants] of fraud." Id. at 186, 725 N.E.2d 598.

See also Heslin v. Metro. Life Ins. Co., 287 A.D.2d 113, 733 N.Y.S.2d 753, 755-56 (3d Dep't 2001) (relying on *Gaidon II* and affirming dismissal of fraud count for failure to state a claim in vanishing premium context).

In this case, as in *Gaidon II*, A & A gave the Von Hoffmanns illustrations representing that the out-of-pocket cash premiums would "vanish" after seven years. The Von Hoffmanns claim that A & A knew or should have known that their payments would not actually vanish as represented in the illustrations. As in *Gaidon II*, the illustrations here contained express disclaimers. In fact, Von Hoffmann admits that he received one such illustration before he purchased the policies, which stated: "Illustrated dividends on permanent policies assume that current rates of investment earnings . . . will continue each year into the future. Thus illustrated dividends are likely, to change as current interest rates change." (Pls.' 56.1 Statement ¶57; Lopez Decl. Ex. 6). Another disclaimer explicitly stated "[t]he dividends used in this illustration are based on the current scale and are not guaranteed. *The possibility exists that cash premium payments may be required for more or fewer years than the period illustrated.*" (Lopez Decl. Ex. 8) (emphasis added). Accordingly, even if A & A had removed certain pages and deleted page numbers from the illustrations before forwarding them to the Von Hoffmanns, the illustrations it did provide nevertheless contained the disclaimers just described. In light of the Court of Appeals' conclusion in *Gaidon II*, I conclude that the first, second, and third alleged misrepresentations are not sufficient to sustain plaintiffs' claim for fraud.

(b) Material Omissions

Although the Von Hoffmanns cannot reasonably argue that they were defrauded into believing the premiums were sure to vanish in seven years or that the rates would not change, a reasonable jury could conclude that A & A committed fraud by omitting material information in an effort to induce the Von Hoffmanns to purchase the policies. For example, if the Von Hoffmanns' allegations are true, A & A used Prudential's favorable twenty-year performance history to induce them to buy the policies, knowing that Prudential had changed its methodology for crediting dividends, and knowing that the information was therefore misleading. The old method— which generated the twenty years worth of favorable results—was no longer applicable, and A & A and Prudential knew that the new method would generate different results. A reasonable jury could certainly conclude that this omitted information was material, and that a reasonable investor would have wanted to know that the method used to generate the twenty years worth of results was no longer being used and that a new, perhaps less favorable method was going to be used instead.

In addition, for purposes of this motion, I assume that A & A consistently omitted certain pages from the illustrations. A reasonable jury could rely on these omissions in considering whether the failure to disclose the change in dividend methodology was material and deceitful. Although some of the information apparently was provided on one or two occasions, a reasonable jury could still conclude that the overall effect was to mislead the Von Hoffmanns. Moreover, A & A has not disputed that it earned more than $1 million in commissions on these sales; a jury could reasonably find scienter, or, an intent to defraud, from A & A's omission of material information. (Pls.' Opp'n Summ. J. at 1). Finally, the fact that the Von Hoffmanns understood that the "vanishing premium" feature was not guaranteed does not change the result. A reasonable jury could find that information concerning Prudential's change in methodology was critical to a decision whether to purchase the policies—information A & A purposefully withheld to induce the Von Hoffmanns to purchase the policies.

An issue of fact also exists as to what was discussed at the 1992 meeting. A & A points to Jim Avery's deposition testimony that suggests that the different methodologies were discussed, but Von Hoffmann has submitted sworn statements attesting to the fact that Prudential's change in methods and the ramifications thereof were not fully disclosed. For purposes of this motion, I must accept Von Hoffman's version as true.

Von Hoffmann asserts that in 1996, when he received the Task Force Report, he suspected for the first time that Prudential and A & A had committed fraud. The "Task Force" was formed by the New Jersey Insurance Commissioner in April of 1995, in response to "widespread allegations of improper sales and marketing activity of life insurers." (Von Hoffmann Decl. Ex. 2). The report states, "[i]n the wake of lawsuits and publicity about Prudential, the Task Force's first objective was to review allegations of improper sales practices regarding the company. . . . " (Id.). It concluded, inter alia, that Prudential had "changed its method of allocating interest to dividends," making transactions appear more beneficial to customers, and that some of Prudential's agents had engaged in abusive sales practices. (Id.). For all these reasons, I conclude that genuine issues of material fact exist as to whether A & A fraudulently withheld material information to induce the Von Hoffmanns to purchase Prudential insurance policies. . . .

CONCLUSION

For the reasons set forth above, A & A's motion to dismiss the Von Hoffmanns' claims is denied in part and granted in part; Prudential's cross-claims for indemnification and contribution are dismissed, as moot. The parties shall appear for a pre-trial conference on June 7, 2002 at 2:00 p.m.

SO ORDERED.

Superior Knowledge. As many cases illustrate, the courts have deemed fraudulent the opinions of a misrepresentor who has superior knowledge of a situation. For instance, while ordinarily a misrepresentation of the rules of law is not fraudulent, it is actionable when the statement is made by an attorney, Ward v. Arnold, 52 Wash. 2d 581, 328 P.2d 164 (1958), or by someone pretending to have legal expertise, Sorenson v. Gardner, 215 Or. 355, 334 P.2d 471 (1959).

PROBLEM 2

Hans Toothpick told Gerald Gullible that he (Hans) owned the Brooklyn Bridge, and Gerald agreed to buy it for $40,000. He gave Hans a $4000 down payment. When Hans proved to lack title, Gerald sued to recover the down payment, asking punitive damages for the fraud. Hans defended by stating that Gerald's reliance was not reasonable, since no reasonable person would have believed that Hans owned the Brooklyn Bridge. Is this a good defense?

QUOTES FOR THE ATTORNEY'S ARSENAL: "UNREASONABLE RELIANCE"

No rogue should enjoy his ill-gotten plunder for the simple reason that his victim is by chance a fool.

Chamberlin v. Fuller, 59 Vt. 247, 256, 9 A. 832, 836 (1887)

The fact that a false statement may be obviously false to those who are trained and experienced does not change its character, nor take away its power to deceive others less experienced. There is no duty resting upon a citizen to suspect the honesty of those with whom he transacts business. Laws are made to protect the trusting as well as the suspicious. The best element of business has long since decided that honesty should govern competitive enterprises, and that the rule of caveat emptor should not be relied upon to reward fraud and deception.

Justice Hugo L. Black in Federal Trade Commn. v. Standard Educ. Socy., 302 U.S. 112, 116 (1937)

That a more cautious buyer might not have relied, might have smelled a rat, does not defeat liability. There is no defense of contributory negligence to an intentional tort, including fraud.

Judge Richard Posner in Ampat/Midwest, Inc. v. Illinois Tool Works, Inc., 896 F.2d 1035, 1041 (7th Cir. 1990).

In fraud as well as elsewhere, the law will go only so far. If the victim signs up for a foolish venture having full knowledge of the facts that include *no misrepresentations*, an action in fraud will not lie. See Ellis v. Newbrough, 6 N.M. 181, 27 P. 490 (1891) (no relief for believer who gave all his property to a "Land of Shalam" commune in the desert).

PROBLEM 3

In the most terrible incident in the history of the city of Sleepy Falls, John Brown went berserk one night and murdered his wife and three small children, killing himself as the police stormed the residence. His parents inherited the house in which this had all occurred, and they moved into the house two months later. They were disturbed on the first night by the sound of screams—horrible screams—that were repeated every night thereafter as soon as the house became silent. Police were called, scientific experts were summoned, but no one seemed able to explain the phenomenon, except to note that nothing happened when trained observers were on the scene with their equipment. Eventually the whole thing was put down to "nerves" of the spooked individuals. John Brown's father had to be sent to a home for the disturbed, and John Brown's mother sold the house to Frank and Nancy Yuppie, to whom she said only that the house had once belonged to her son, now deceased. The Yuppies moved in with their own two children and were quite happy with the house until helpful neighbors told them all. Frank Yuppie calls you, his lawyer and cousin, for advice. Can he claim that Mrs. Brown tricked him when she failed to mention that the house came complete with ghosts? Is this a matter for the doctrine of caveat emptor ("let the buyer beware") or is there relief in the law of fraud? See Stambovsky v. Ackley, 169 App. Div. 254, 572 N.Y.S.2d 672 (1991).

Silent Fraud. The "rule" of Peek v. Gurney, 6 H.L. 377, 1861-73 All Eng. Rep. 116 (1873), is that there is never a duty of disclosure no matter how morally censurable silence may be. Some courts still adhere to this, Swinton v. Whitinsville Sav. Bank, 311 Mass. 677, 42 N.E.2d 808 (1942) (termites). Others disagree, Obde v. Schlemeyer, 56 Wash. 2d 449, 353 P.2d 672 (1960), following the suggestion of a well-known article by Dean Page Keeton that an action for "silent fraud" lies whenever "justice, equity, and fair dealing demand it," Keeton, Fraud—Concealment and Non-Disclosure, 15 Tex. L. Rev. 1, 31 (1936), as is obviously the case when a dangerous condition exists; see Annot., 22 A.L.R.3d 972. In some states silent fraud may violate the deceptive practices statutes, considered in the next chapter; see, e.g., Benik v. Hatcher, 750 A.2d 10 (Md. 2000).

When the defendant takes affirmative steps to conceal a problem, more than mere silence is involved, and a "misrepresentation" occurs, Lindberg Cadillac Co. v. Aron, 371 S.W.2d 651 (Mo. App. 1963) (used car's engine spray-painted black to look shiny), as it does when the defendant knows that under no circumstances would plaintiff have gone through with the transaction had the truth been known, Jewish Center v. Whale, 397 A.2d 712 (N.J. Super. 1979) (rabbi failed to mention his past criminal record and disbarment as an attorney when hired by synagogue).

Remedies. Fraud is a ground for rescinding the contract, an equitable remedy, and forcing the defendant to return any property belonging to the plaintiff. It may be possible to have the court declare a *constructive trust* as to such property, finding that the defendant holds it as trustee for its return to the plaintiff. (However, if the defendant files for bankruptcy, the recognition of a constructive trust by the federal courts is problematic; see In re Omegas Group, Inc., 16 F.3d 1443 (6th Cir. 1994). Fraud also is a reason for reformation of the contract. Reformation is an equitable action by which the court rewrites the contract to eliminate the effect of fraud, and then the court enforces the contract as rewritten.

Punitive Damages. When the conduct of the defendant involves either actual malice or a reckless disregard for the consequences of the action taken, the court may award punitive (sometimes called "exemplary") damages to punish the defendant and deter repetition of the condemned conduct. The amount of punitive damages is not always tied to the amount of actual damages and, indeed, may in appropriate cases far exceed them. When punitive damages are obviously called for, the court may permit discovery of the defendant's financial records so that plaintiff has a basis for determining the amount of punitive damages that will really pinch the defendant. Iola State Bank v. Bolan, 679 P.2d 720 (Kan. 1984); Manning v. Lynn Immke Buick, Inc., 28 Ohio App. 203, 276 N.E.2d 253 (1971). Of course, the threat of such discovery frequently promotes a harmonious atmosphere for settlement of the dispute.

The United States Supreme Court has held that punitive damages greatly exceeding the compensatory damages are unconstitutional as violating the Due Process Clause of the Fourteenth Amendment; see State Farm Mut. Auto. Ins. Co. v. Campbell, 538 U.S. 408 (2003) (punitive damages of $145 million excessive where actual damages were $1 million); BMW of N. Am., Inc. v. Gore, 517 U.S. 559 (1996) (punitive damages of $2 million excessive where actual damages were $4,000); Phillip Morris USA v. Williams, 549 U.S. 346 (2007) (punitive damages used to punish injury to nonparties violates Due Process Clause). State courts have also struggled with this issue; see Parrot v. Carr Chevrolet, Inc., 331 Or. 537, 17 P.3d 473 (2001) (jury award of $1 million punitive damages upheld in lemon used car sale where the actual damages were $11,496).

Attorney's Fees. Although attorney's fees generally are not recoverable as consequential damages in lawsuits, there are exceptions to the rule. First, if the lawsuit is brought pursuant to statute, the statute itself may award attorney's fees to the prevailing party (this is particularly true of statutes protecting consumers). Second, the contract may provide that in the event of a legal dispute, attorney's fees must be paid. And third, in intentional fraud suits, the courts frequently have been willing to award the defrauded party the attorney's fees incurred (in addition to assessing punitive damages; see the next case); see Annot., 44 A.L.R.4th 776.

JOYNER v. ALBERT MERRILL SCHOOL[7]
Civil Court of the City of New York, 1978
411 N.Y.S.2d 988, 97 Misc. 2d 568

MARGARET TAYLOR, Judge.

Plaintiff, Michael Joyner, was born in Mexico in 1919. His formal education was limited to completing the sixth grade of primary school in Mexico. He never attended high school nor did he obtain a high school equivalency certificate. He speaks English with a pronounced accent. He has been employed at the same job for twenty-two years as a factory worker, earning less than $5,000 per year.

In June, 1969, as a result of reading subway advertisements and seeing television commercials offering a promising career at a good salary, plaintiff visited defendants' school to inquire about obtaining training as a computer programmer. He was interviewed at that time by a representative of defendants, a Mr. Pardes. In the course of that interview plaintiff informed Mr. Pardes of his correct age and limited education. Despite plaintiff's limited educational background and difficulty with the English language, Mr. Pardes administered a so-called "aptitude" test. Plaintiff was

---

7. Footnotes in this case have bean renumbered for clarity.

unable either to understand or complete this test during the time usually allotted and it was necessary that he be given additional time by the tester.

Following his "testing" by defendants' representative, plaintiff was given a "B+" score on the aptitude test. The significance of this score and the validity of the test as a measure of an applicant's "aptitude" for computer programming/data processing could not be determined inasmuch as defendants failed to produce the test questions, although a notice had been served by plaintiff's counsel requesting, among other things, the production at the trial of "all of the original records maintained by defendants pertaining to plaintiff's schooling."

After advising plaintiff that he had scored a "B+" on his "aptitude test" defendants' representative told plaintiff that "he had a good head, worth a $10,000 job." Plaintiff was further assured that the school would place him in such a job following his completion of the course. Plaintiff told Mr. Pardes that his only purpose in taking the course was to get a job.

The "aptitude" test answer sheet, reviewed by Mr. Pardes, also contains notes made by the person who corrected plaintiff's test. These notes indicate that plaintiff was a high school graduate, when, in fact, plaintiff had advised Mr. Pardes of his limited grade school education, and, further, that plaintiff was a loan applicant.

Following this conversation and the testing, plaintiff completed an "Application for Admission" to an IBM Data Processing/Computer Programming Course offered by defendants. All plaintiff had to do was print his name, address and date of birth and then sign on an indicated line on the *front* of the document. Plaintiff did not read this "application." He just signed it. Significantly, he never received a complete copy of the "application" but only a photocopy of the *front* portion.

On the reverse side of the "application" (defendants' Exhibit A) the following appears, *inter alia*:

> 1. I understand that this application, if accepted by the school, constitutes a binding contract.
> 2. I understand that this application contains all the terms of the contract. . . .
> 9. I understand that upon successful completion of the course, I will be eligible for the services of the school's placement department for free job counseling. I further understand that this is not a guarantee of a job or an offer of employment.

By signing the application, plaintiff enrolled himself in a $1,468.90 course offered by defendant in data processing/computer programming consisting of "360 class hours in the theory and practical operation of IBM tabulation machines; (29 Card Punch, 82 Sorter, 85 Collator, 514 Reproducer, 548 Interpreter, 403 Accounting Machine) and the programming of IBM

Computers (1401 Data Processing System and IBM System/360)" (Defendants' Exhibit A).

Plaintiff began school in July of 1969. Shortly thereafter, on two separate occasions, a representative of the defendants asked him to leave the evening classes he was attending and presented him with documents to sign. Plaintiff signed the documents but was not given an opportunity to read them nor any explanation as to what they contained or their general import. Subsequently, plaintiff was informed by Mr. Pardes and the school Director at graduation that by signing the documents he had applied for $1,500 in New York State tuition loans but that these loans would not become due until he had obtained the position promised him by defendants in the computer programming industry. Copies of the agreements were never provided to the plaintiff nor were they produced by defendants at the trial although called for by the Notice to Produce served by plaintiff's attorney.

Plaintiff attended over 360 hours in classes offered by defendants without any absence. During these classes he repeatedly informed his instructors and other representatives of defendants that he was unable to comprehend the subject matter of the courses. He told them that "he wanted to quit and didn't want to lose money." The school director, however, discouraged plaintiff from exercising his contractual right to withdraw from the course and obtain a refund, advising him "not to panic; everybody here graduates." Plaintiff was repeatedly assured that his concern was unfounded, that it was only necessary that he complete the course and defendants would then place him in a good job with a high salary.

Plaintiff completed defendants' regular course in April, 1970, although he never comprehended the tests administered to him. The students were given open book tests, during which they were permitted to copy from other students' examination papers, in the presence of a teacher. Upon completion of the course, plaintiff still could not understand the computer programming/data processing field, and arrangements were made for him to attend supplemental classes through the Spring of 1971.

After completion of both the regular and supplementary courses, and extending through the Spring of 1975, plaintiff visited defendants' placement office seeking the job that was promised him. A resume was prepared for him by that office. The resume contained a false date of birth, 1931, rather than 1919. Plaintiff was advised by representatives of defendants that he could not obtain employment in the computer industry unless he was under forty years of age. The resume, *prepared by defendants' placement office,* also indicates, erroneously, that plaintiff completed two years of high school and a bookkeeping course, and, further, presents a blatantly distorted description of plaintiff's present employment (Plaintiff's Exhibit 2).

During the five years following completion of the data processing/computer programming course, plaintiff went on fifty to sixty job interviews. *At no time could he pass any of the tests administered by prospective employers and received no job offers.*

This bubble of false promises and misplaced expectations was not burst until the Spring of 1975 when defendants finally advised plaintiff that no jobs could be found for him. A default judgment on his tuition loan was entered against him in Supreme Court, Albany County, and his life savings of $500 was seized. Threatened with an attachment on his meager salary, plaintiff, to avoid the possible loss of his job, made monthly payments to the Sheriff of New York County.

Convinced that he had been deceived, plaintiff then sought legal assistance. He obtained counsel who instituted this action for breach of contract for failing to find the employment which defendants promised, for fraud and misrepresentation in inducing the plaintiff to enter into the contract for training, and for punitive damages.

Defendants produced no witnesses and no documents except for the "Application for Admission." They relied initially on their claim that plaintiff's action was barred by the statute of limitations. Defendants' reliance on the statute of limitations is not well founded. An action based on fraud does not accrue until six years from the date of the fraud, or two years from the date the fraud is discovered or could, with reasonable diligence, be discovered. C.P.L.R. §§213(8); 203(f). Plaintiff can use "whichever date is longer." Siegel, New York Practice §43 (West 1978); Azoy v. Fowler, 57 A.D.2d 541, 393 N.Y.S.2d 173 (App. Div. 2d Dept. 1977); Klein v. Shields, 470 F.2d 1344 (2d Cir. 1972). Similarly, a cause of action based on breach of contract does not accrue until the alleged breach has occurred.

The record clearly establishes that defendants continued plaintiff in their program through the Spring of 1971 and repeatedly misled him as to his employment prospects until at least the Spring of 1975. Defendants did not disillusion plaintiff as to his promised job opportunities until that time.

Based on the testimony at trial and an evaluation of the credibility of plaintiff, the only witness called, the court finds that the plaintiff did not and could not have discovered the fraud until the Spring of 1975. Thus, both under plaintiff's cause of action for fraud and for breach of contract, plaintiff's claims are timely. Both causes of action accrued either in the Spring of 1971 when plaintiff completed his schooling or in the Spring of 1975. Suit was commenced in February, 1977, less than six years after he completed his schooling and less than two years after defendants finally admitted to him that they could not place him in a job in the computer industry.

It is necessary to determine, therefore, whether plaintiff has established his claims of breach of contract and fraud and misrepresentation. Our courts and legislatures recognize the need for close scrutiny of commercial consumer transactions to guard against predatory practices calculated to take advantage of the unwary consumer. The doctrine of *caveat emptor* has given way, at least in part, to the doctrine of *caveat venditor* in recognition of the fact that many consumers, by reason of their lack of education, lack of experience, and limited bargaining power, are not in equal bargaining positions with the vendors with whom they deal. Albert Merrill School v. Godoy, 78 Misc. 2d 647, 357 N.Y.S.2d 378 (Civil N.Y. 1974); Educational Beneficial, Inc. v. Reynolds, 67 Misc. 2d 739, 324 N.Y.S.2d 813 (Civil N.Y. 1971).

The court finds, on the record before it, and on the facts set forth above, that the defendants fraudulently induced plaintiff to enter into a data processing/computer programming course by admitting him to their program and by falsely promising to place him in a job in the data processing/computer programming industry at a salary of $10,000 per year upon completion of the course. The high grade given to plaintiff on defendants' so-called "aptitude" test was clearly calculated to mislead and deceive him. In spite of his repeated statements to his instructors and other representatives of defendants that he did not understand the training, plaintiff was encouraged to remain in the program with defendants promising to find him employment once he completed the course. Plaintiff made it clear he would not have entered or continued in defendants' program if they had not promised him a job.

Defendants argue that the statement contained on the reverse side of its "application" that the job counseling it offers "is not a guarantee of a job or an offer of employment" bars recovery in spite of the promise made by its representatives. However, it was uncontroverted at trial that plaintiff did not read the application and that he was not given a copy of the back of the application containing defendants' alleged "merger" and "immunity" clauses. Assuming, *arguendo*, that plaintiff did read and was given a copy of the back of defendants' application, it is a well-established principle of law that fraud vitiates the parol evidence rule. E.g., Danann Realty Corp. v. Harris, 5 N.Y.2d 317, 184 N.Y.S.2d 599, 157 N.E.2d 597 (1959); Suburban Lawn Service v. Allstate Insurance Co., 68 Misc. 2d 1010, 328 N.Y.S.2d 583 (Dist. Ct. Suffolk Cty. 1971). The court finds therefore that despite the language contained on defendants' form "application," defendants did promise plaintiff a job in the data processing/computer programming industry as an inducement for him to enter into the contract. Further, the court finds that defendants' conduct in enrolling plaintiff in the program, discouraging him from withdrawing and continuing, until 1975, to encourage in him false hopes of a "good job and salary" was calculated to induce plaintiff not to exercise his contractual right to terminate the contract or his right to take legal recourse against the defendants.

The general merger clause contained in defendants' "application," " . . . I understand that this application contains all the terms of the contract," may not be invoked to exclude evidence of fraudulent oral statement by defendants. Sabo v. Delman, 3 N.Y.2d 155, 164 N.Y.S.2d 714, 143 N.E.2d 906 (1957); Barash v. Pennsylvania Term Real Estate Corp., 26 N.Y.2d 77, 308 N.Y.S.2d 649, 256 N.E.2d 707 (1970). A limited rule evolved in this jurisdiction in 1959 to the effect that where a merger clause recites that a specific representation has not been made orally and that the buyer has not relied on any representation other than those appearing in the contract and, further, where the buyer has had the opportunity to discover the true facts, there is a specific disclaimer and a plaintiff cannot prove reliance on the oral representation in a cause of action for fraud. See, e.g., Danann Realty Corp. v. Harris; Wittenberg v. Robinov, 9 N.Y.2d 261, 213 N.Y.S.2d 430, 173 N.E.2d 868 (1961); Cohen v. Cohen, 1 A.D.2d 586, 151 N.Y.S.2d 949 (App. Div. 1st Dept. 1956).

The general merger clause contained in defendants' "application" combined with the statement contained in paragraph 9 of that application:

> 9. I understand that upon successful completion of the course I will be eligible for the services of the school's placement department for free job counseling. I further understand that this is not a guarantee of a job or an offer of employment.

does not come under the rule stated in *Danann*. This language fails to constitute a specific disclaimer by plaintiff of reliance upon defendants' fraudulent misrepresentation. Absent a sufficiently specific disclaimer which would negate the element of reliance, plaintiff cannot be barred from asserting his claim of fraud against defendants. Galgani v. Fleming, 56 A.D.2d 644, 391 N.Y.S.2d 892 (App. Div. 2d Dept. 1977). Accord, United States v. Amrep Corp., 560 F.2d 539 (2d Cir. 1977); Crowell-Collier Publishing Co. v. Josefowitz, 9 Misc. 2d 613, 170 N.Y.S.2d 373 *aff'd* 6 A.D.2d 791, 175 N.Y.S.2d 560 *aff'd* 5 N.Y.2d 998, 184 N.Y.S.2d 859, 157 N.E.2d 730 (1959); Zamzok v. 60 Park Avenue Corp., 80 Misc. 2d 573, 363 N.Y.S.2d 868 (Sup. Ct. N.Y. Cty. 1974).

Even if a specific disclaimer of reliance were contained in defendants' contract, plaintiff's cause of action for fraud would not be barred unless he also had an opportunity to discover the true facts. Danann Realty Corp. v. Harris. In this way sellers cannot, by careful drafting immunize themselves against claims of fraud. See Crowell-Collier Publishing Co. v. Josefowitz.

Proper emphasis must be placed on the factual background surrounding plaintiff's entry into the contractual relationship with the defendants. Plaintiff was fifty-two years old and had a sixth-grade education at the time he signed the "application." Plaintiff obviously had difficulty with English as his second language. It was necessary for him to use an interpreter during the trial. The "application" was printed and prepared by defendants with no input by plaintiff as to its terms. Plaintiff acted at all times in reliance upon the defendants' expertise in the computer industry and education field. At no time was plaintiff on an equal footing with defendants. In this posture no consumer can be said to have an opportunity to discover the true facts.

The court finds, therefore, by a preponderance of the credible evidence, that defendants fraudulently induced plaintiff into a contract for vocational education, knowing, that plaintiff was not by training, education or background capable of absorbing or using their particular training program.[8] As a result, plaintiff was damaged in the amount of $1,486.90.

The court will now deal with the issue of punitive damages. Punitive damages are recoverable in fraud actions where the fraud is gross and involves high moral culpability. Walker v. Sheldon, 10 N.Y.2d 401, 223 N.Y.S.2d 488, 179 N.E.2d 497 (1961). Punitive damages are not only available in cases of wanton and malicious fraud directed at a specific individual but in cases of consumer fraud. The Court of Appeals in *Walker* established the principle that the assessment of exemplary or punitive damages serves the purpose of deterring fraudulent consumer sales. Walker v. Sheldon; Star Credit v. Ingram, 75 Misc. 2d 299, 347 N.Y.S.2d 651 (Civil N.Y. 1973). And if punitive damages are to be awarded to protect the public from continuation of a fraudulent consumer scheme, they must be taxed in an amount which will accomplish that purpose. Id.; Nitti v. Credit Bureau of Rochester, Inc., 84 Misc. 2d 277, 375 N.Y.S.2d 817 (Sup. Ct. Monroe Cty. 1975).

---

8. It should be clearly understood that this court is in no way suggesting that plaintiff should not have the opportunity to attend a computer programming school or improve his education, career or salary. But defendants enrolled plaintiff in their program without giving any consideration to his possibilities for success. Whereas some colleges and universities have embarked on "open enrollment" programs in which unprepared students are placed in courses specially tailored to their educational needs, there is no evidence that defendants made any perceivable effort to provide unprepared students with special assistance. Had plaintiff been given an aptitude test that accurately measured his potential for success in the computer industry, had admissions officers provided him with an honest assessment of his chances of successfully completing the courses and obtaining employment, and had he been offered special educational and supportive services or, in the alternative, been advised that none were available but that other educational options existed, perhaps plaintiff's realistic hopes of improving his position and salary would have been actualized.

The facts here show that defendants admitted plaintiff despite his obvious lack of educational qualifications. Plaintiff was induced to enroll in defendants' course with a false promise of employment. Defendants knowingly continued to mislead plaintiff with a promise of a $10,000 a year job in the computer programming/data processing industry despite defendants' knowledge that by virtue of plaintiff's age, lack of education and the state of the job market, plaintiff could never secure such employment.

Punitive damages are necessary here to prevent defendants in the future from defrauding those similarly seeking to improve their training and employment. As a consequence of defendants' deceptive practices, plaintiff wasted his valuable time and, to him, a considerable sum of money. Plaintiff seeks only $2,500 in punitive damages. The court is restricted to that demand and accordingly, punitive damages are hereby assessed at $2,500. The court would, however, have been willing to assess a greater sum to serve as a more convincing deterrent to the defendants and to discourage them from engaging in the future in the deceptive sale of courses neither suited to an applicant's needs nor the job market.[9]

The clerk is directed to enter judgment in favor of the plaintiff against the defendants in the amount of $3,968.90, together with appropriate interest, costs and disbursements.

NOTE

For a discussion of proprietary schools and their regulation by federal and state authorities and private actions, see Patrick F. Linehan, Dreams Protected: A New Approach to Policing Proprietary Schools' Misrepresentations, 89 Geo. L.J. 753 (2001).

---

9. The abuses revealed by the record in this case were subsequently specifically prohibited by various statutes and regulations and examined in detail by State and Federal Authorities. See, e.g. N.Y. Educ. Law §5002 (McKinney Suppl. 1978) (eff. July 1, 1973) (requiring *inter alia* a high school diploma or Certificate of Equivalency for admission to vocational school); N.Y.C. Dept. of Consumer Affairs Regs. Nos. 5 (eff. November 23, 1970) and 19 (eff. January 14, 1972) (regarding vocational school advertising and aptitude tests); 8 N.Y.C.R.R. §§126.3 and 126.7 (eff. April 16, 1973) (regarding vocational school advertising and enrollment agreements). See, also, report of the New York State Consumer Protection Board of July 20, 1978 entitled "The Profits of Failure: The Proprietary Vocational School Industry in New York State" and Federal Trade Commission Report entitled "Proprietary Vocational and Home Study Schools" (December 10, 1976) and the proposed regulations published therein.

CHAPTER 2
Deceptive Practices

I. ODOMETERS

In explaining the need for a federal statute regulating odometer tampering, Congress put the following at the beginning of the statute:

(a) Congress finds that—
(1) buyers of motor vehicles rely heavily on the odometer reading as an index of the condition and value of a vehicle;
(2) buyers are entitled to rely on the odometer reading as an accurate indication of the mileage of the vehicle;
(3) an accurate indication of the mileage assists a buyer in deciding on the safety and reliability of the vehicle; and
(4) motor vehicles move in, or affect, interstate and foreign commerce.
(b) Purposes.—The purposes of this chapter are—
(1) to prohibit tampering with motor vehicle odometers; and
(2) to provide safeguards to protect purchasers in the sale of motor vehicles with altered or reset odometers.

49 U.S.C. §32701

Odometer rollback is a very profitable, $3-billion-a-year enterprise. It is estimated that for every 10,000 miles taken off the odometer, the value of a used car increases $300 to $500. Moreover, it is physically quite easy to accomplish the task: on older cars a bent paper clip will often do the trick.

The Act makes it a crime to change automobile odometers, §32709(b). Section 32704 provides that if the odometer is incorrect, a notice to that effect must be posted in the left door frame. Section 32710 states that for any violation of the Act with intent to defraud, a civil suit may be brought and the plaintiff may recover three times the actual damages or $1500, whichever is greater, plus costs and reasonable attorney's fees. The court in Evans v. Paradise Motors, Inc., 721 F. Supp. 250, 252 (N.D. Cal. 1989), concluded that the minimum $1500 award recompenses the "time plaintiff spent in negotiations or the emotional harm of her embarrassment or anger." The statute confers federal jurisdiction without an amount limitation, but creates a two-year statute of limitations. Relevant portions of the statute are reprinted below.

The Secretary of Transportation has authority to make disclosure rules. These rules can be found at 49 C.F.R. §580 and are reprinted below.

FEDERAL ODOMETER ACT
49 U.S.C. §§32701 et seq.

* * *

§32702. Definitions

In this chapter—

(1) "auction company" means a person taking possession of a motor vehicle owned by another to sell at an auction.

(2) "dealer" means a person that sold at least 5 motor vehicles during the prior 12 months to buyers that in good faith bought the vehicles other than for resale.

(3) "distributor" means a person that sold at least 5 motor vehicles during the prior 12 months for resale.

(4) "leased motor vehicle" means a motor vehicle leased to a person for at least 4 months by a lessor that leased at least 5 vehicles during the prior 12 months.

(5) "odometer" means an instrument for measuring and recording the distance a motor vehicle is driven, but does not include an auxiliary instrument designed to be reset by the operator of the vehicle to record mileage of a trip.

(6) "repair" and "replace" mean to restore to a sound working condition by replacing any part of an odometer or by correcting any inoperative part of an odometer.

(7) "title" means the certificate of title or other document issued by the State indicating ownership.

(8) "transfer" means to change ownership by sale, gift, or any other means.

§32703. Preventing tampering

A person may not—

(1) advertise for sale, sell, use, install, or have installed, a device that makes an odometer of a motor vehicle register a mileage different

from the mileage the vehicle was driven, as registered by the odometer within the designed tolerance of the manufacturer of the odometer;

(2) disconnect, reset, alter, or have disconnected, reset, or altered, an odometer of a motor vehicle intending to change the mileage registered by the odometer;

(3) with intent to defraud, operate a motor vehicle on a street, road, or highway if the person knows that the odometer of the vehicle is disconnected or not operating; or

(4) conspire to violate this section or section 32704 or 32705 of this title.

§32704. Service, repair, and replacement

(a) Adjusting mileage. A person may service, repair, or replace an odometer of a motor vehicle if the mileage registered by the odometer remains the same as before the service, repair, or replacement. If the mileage cannot remain the same—

(1) the person shall adjust the odometer to read zero; and

(2) the owner of the vehicle or agent of the owner shall attach a written notice to the left door frame of the vehicle specifying the mileage before the service, repair, or replacement and the date of the service, repair, or replacement.

(b) Removing or altering notice. A person may not, with intent to defraud, remove or alter a notice attached to a motor vehicle as required by this section.

§32705. Disclosure requirements on transfer of motor vehicles

(a) Disclosure requirements.—(1) Under regulations prescribed by the Secretary of Transportation that include the way in which information is disclosed and retained under this section, a person transferring ownership of a motor vehicle shall give the transferee the following written disclosure:

(A) Disclosure of the cumulative mileage registered on the odometer.

(B) Disclosure that the actual mileage is unknown, if the transferor knows that the odometer reading is different from the number of miles the vehicle has actually traveled.

(2) A person transferring ownership of a motor vehicle may not violate a regulation prescribed under this section or give a false statement to the transferee in making the disclosure required by such a regulation.

(3) A person acquiring a motor vehicle for resale may not accept a written disclosure under this section unless it is complete.

(4)(A) This subsection shall apply to all transfers of motor vehicles (unless otherwise exempted by the Secretary by regulation), except in the case of transfers of new motor vehicles from a vehicle manufacturer jointly to a dealer and a person engaged in the business of renting or leasing vehicles for a period of 30 days or less.

(B) For purposes of subparagraph (A), the term "new motor vehicle" means any motor vehicle driven with no more than the limited use necessary in moving, transporting, or road testing such vehicle prior to delivery from the vehicle manufacturer to a dealer, but in no event shall the odometer reading of such vehicle exceed 300 miles.

(5) The Secretary may exempt such classes or categories of vehicles as the Secretary deems appropriate from these requirements. Until such time as the Secretary amends or modifies the regulations set forth in 49 CFR 580.6, such regulations shall have full force and effect.

(b) Mileage statement requirement for licensing.—(1) A motor vehicle the ownership of which is transferred may not be licensed for use in a State unless the transferee, in submitting an application to a State for the title on which the license will be issued, includes with the application the transferor's title and, if that title contains the space referred to in paragraph (3)(A)(iii) of this subsection, a statement, signed and dated by the transferor, of the mileage disclosure required under subsection (a) of this section. This paragraph does not apply to a transfer of ownership of a motor vehicle that has not been licensed before the transfer.

(2)(A) Under regulations prescribed by the Secretary, if the title to a motor vehicle issued to a transferor by a State is in the possession of a lienholder when the transferor transfers ownership of the vehicle, the transferor may use a written power of attorney (if allowed by State law) in making the mileage disclosure required under subsection (a) of this section. Regulations prescribed under this paragraph—

(i) shall prescribe the form of the power of attorney;

(ii) shall provide that the form be printed by means of a secure printing process (or other secure process);

(iii) shall provide that the State issue the form to the transferee;

(iv) shall provide that the person exercising the power of attorney retain a copy and submit the original to the State with a copy of the title showing the restatement of the mileage;

(v) may require that the State retain the power of attorney and the copy of the title for an appropriate period or that the State adopt alternative measures consistent with section 32701(b) of this title, after considering the costs to the State;

(vi) shall ensure that the mileage at the time of transfer be disclosed on the power of attorney document;

(vii) shall ensure that the mileage be restated exactly by the person exercising the power of attorney in the space referred to in paragraph (3)(A)(iii) of this subsection;

(viii) may not require that a motor vehicle be titled in the State in which the power of attorney was issued;

(ix) shall consider the need to facilitate normal commercial transactions in the sale or exchange of motor vehicles; and

(x) shall provide other conditions the Secretary considers appropriate.

(B) Section 32709(a) and (b) applies to a person granting or granted a power of attorney under this paragraph.

(3)(A) A motor vehicle the ownership of which is transferred may not be licensed for use in a State unless the title issued by the State to the transferee—

(i) is produced by means of a secure printing process (or other secure process);

(ii) indicates the mileage disclosure required to be made under subsection (a) of this section; and

(iii) contains a space for the transferee to disclose the mileage at the time of a future transfer and to sign and date the disclosure.

(B) Subparagraph (A) of this paragraph does not require a State to verify, or preclude a State from verifying, the mileage information contained in the title.

(c) Leased motor vehicles.—(1) For a leased motor vehicle, the regulations prescribed under subsection (a) of this section shall require written disclosure about mileage to be made by the lessee to the lessor when the lessor transfers ownership of that vehicle.

(2) Under those regulations, the lessor shall provide written notice to the lessee of—

(A) the lessee's mileage disclosure requirements under paragraph (1) of this subsection; and

(B) the penalties for failure to comply with those requirements.

(3) The lessor shall retain the disclosures made by a lessee under paragraph (1) of this subsection for at least 4 years following the date the lessor transfers the leased motor vehicle.

(4) If the lessor transfers ownership of a leased motor vehicle without obtaining possession of the vehicle, the lessor, in making the

disclosure required by subsection (a) of this section, may indicate on the title the mileage disclosed by the lessee under paragraph (1) of this subsection unless the lessor has reason to believe that the disclosure by the lessee does not reflect the actual mileage of the vehicle.

(d) State alternate vehicle mileage disclosure requirements.—The requirements of subsections (b) and (c)(1) of this section on the disclosure of motor vehicle mileage when motor vehicles are transferred or leased apply in a State unless the State has in effect alternate motor vehicle mileage disclosure requirements approved by the Secretary. The Secretary shall approve alternate motor vehicle mileage disclosure requirements submitted by a State unless the Secretary decides that the requirements are not consistent with the purpose of the disclosure required by subsection (b) or (c), as the case may be.

(e) Auction sales.—If a motor vehicle is sold at an auction, the auction company conducting the auction shall maintain the following records for at least 4 years after the date of the sale:

(1) the name of the most recent owner of the motor vehicle (except the auction company) and the name of the buyer of the motor vehicle.

(2) the vehicle identification number required under chapter 301 or 331 of this title.

(3) the odometer reading on the date the auction company took possession of the motor vehicle.

(f) Application and revision of State law.—(1) Except as provided in paragraph (2) of this subsection, subsections (b)-(e) of this section apply to the transfer of a motor vehicle after April 28, 1989.

(2) If a State requests, the Secretary shall assist the State in revising its laws to comply with subsection (b) of this section. If a State requires time beyond April 28, 1989, to revise its laws to achieve compliance, the Secretary, on request of the State, may grant additional time that the Secretary considers reasonable by publishing a notice in the Federal Register. The notice shall include the reasons for granting the additional time. In granting additional time, the Secretary shall ensure that the State is making reasonable efforts to achieve compliance.

§32706. Inspections, investigations, and records

(a) Authority to inspect and investigate.   Subject to section 32707 of this title, the Secretary of Transportation may conduct an inspection or investigation necessary to carry out this chapter or a regulation prescribed or order issued under this chapter. The Secretary shall cooperate with State and local officials to the greatest extent possible in conducting an inspection

or investigation. The Secretary may give the Attorney General information about a violation of this chapter or a regulation prescribed or order issued under this chapter.

(b) Entry, inspection, and impoundment. (1) In carrying out subsection (a) of this section, an officer or employee designated by the Secretary, on display of proper credentials and written notice to the owner, operator, or agent in charge, may—

(A) enter and inspect commercial premises in which a motor vehicle or motor vehicle equipment is manufactured, held for shipment or sale, maintained, or repaired;

(B) enter and inspect noncommercial premises in which the Secretary reasonably believes there is a motor vehicle or motor vehicle equipment that is an object of a violation of this chapter;

(C) inspect that motor vehicle or motor vehicle equipment; and

(D) impound for not more than 72 hours for inspection a motor vehicle or motor vehicle equipment that the Secretary reasonably believes is an object of a violation of this chapter.

(2) An inspection or impoundment under this subsection shall be conducted at a reasonable time, in a reasonable way, and with reasonable promptness. The written notice may consist of a warrant issued under section 32707 of this title.

(c) Reasonable compensation. When the Secretary impounds for inspection a motor vehicle (except a vehicle subject to subchapter II of chapter 105 of this title) or motor vehicle equipment under subsection (b)(1)(D) of this section, the Secretary shall pay reasonable compensation to the owner of the vehicle or equipment if the inspection or impoundment results in denial of use, or reduction in value, of the vehicle or equipment.

(d) Records and information requirements. (1) To enable the Secretary to decide whether a dealer or distributor is complying with this chapter and regulations prescribed and orders issued under this chapter, the Secretary may require the dealer or distributor—

(A) to keep records;

(B) to provide information from those records if the Secretary states the purpose for requiring the information and identifies the information to the fullest extent practicable; and

(C) to allow an officer or employee designated by the Secretary to inspect relevant records of the dealer or distributor.

(2) This subsection and subsection (e)(1)(B) of this section do not authorize the Secretary to require a dealer or distributor to provide information on a regular periodic basis.

(e) Administrative authority and civil actions to enforce.   (1) In carrying out this chapter, the Secretary may—

(A) inspect and copy records of any person at reasonable times;

(B) order a person to file written reports or answers to specific questions, including reports or answers under oath; and

(C) conduct hearings, administer oaths, take testimony, and require (by subpoena or otherwise) the appearance and testimony of witnesses and the production of records the Secretary considers advisable.

(2) A witness summoned under this subsection is entitled to the same fee and mileage the witness would have been paid in a court of the United States.

(3) A civil action to enforce a subpoena or order of the Secretary under this subsection may be brought in the United States district court for any judicial district in which the proceeding by the Secretary is conducted. The court may punish a failure to obey an order of the court to comply with the subpoena or order of the Secretary as a contempt of court.

(f) Prohibitions.   A person may not fail to keep records, refuse access to or copying of records, fail to make reports or provide information, fail to allow entry or inspection, or fail to permit impoundment, as required under this section.

§32707. Administrative warrants

(a) Definition.   In this section, "probable cause" means a valid public interest in the effective enforcement of this chapter or a regulation prescribed under this chapter sufficient to justify the inspection or impoundment in the circumstances stated in an application for a warrant under this section.

(b) Warrant requirement and issuance.   (1) Except as provided in paragraph (4) of this subsection, an inspection or impoundment under section 32706 of this title may be carried out only after a warrant is obtained.

(2) A judge of a court of the United States or a State court of record or a United States magistrate may issue a warrant for an inspection or impoundment under section 32706 of this title within the territorial jurisdiction of the court or magistrate. The warrant must be based on an affidavit that—

(A) establishes probable cause to issue the warrant; and

(B) is sworn to before the judge or magistrate by an officer or employee who knows the facts alleged in the affidavit.

(3) The judge or magistrate shall issue the warrant when the judge or magistrate decides there is a reasonable basis for believing that probable cause exists to issue the warrant. The warrant must—

(A) identify the premises, property, or motor vehicle to be inspected and the items or type of property to be impounded;

(B) state the purpose of the inspection, the basis for issuing the warrant, and the name of the affiant;

(C) direct an individual authorized under section 32706 of this title to inspect the premises, property, or vehicle for the purpose stated in the warrant and, when appropriate, to impound the property specified in the warrant;

(D) direct that the warrant be served during the hours specified in the warrant; and

(E) name the judge or magistrate with whom proof of service is to be filed.

(4) A warrant under this section is not required when—

(A) the owner, operator, or agent in charge of the premises consents;

(B) it is reasonable to believe that the mobility of the motor vehicle to be inspected makes it impractical to obtain a warrant;

(C) an application for a warrant cannot be made because of an emergency;

(D) records are to be inspected and copied under section 32706(e)(1)(A) of this title; or

(E) a warrant is not constitutionally required.

(c) Service and impoundment of property. (1) A warrant issued under this section must be served and proof of service filed not later than 10 days after its issuance date. The judge or magistrate may allow additional time in the warrant if the Secretary of Transportation demonstrates a need for additional time. Proof of service must be filed promptly with a written inventory of the property impounded under the warrant. The inventory shall be made in the presence of the individual serving the warrant and the individual from whose possession or premises the property was impounded, or if that individual is not present, a credible individual except the individual making the inventory. The individual serving the warrant shall verify the inventory. On request, the judge or magistrate shall send a copy of the inventory to the individual from whose possession or premises the property was impounded and to the applicant for the warrant.

(2) When property is impounded under a warrant, the individual serving the warrant shall—

(A) give the person from whose possession or premises the property was impounded a copy of the warrant and a receipt for the property; or

(B) leave the copy and receipt at the place from which the property was impounded.

(3) The judge or magistrate shall file the warrant, proof of service, and all documents filed about the warrant with the clerk of the United States district court for the judicial district in which the inspection is made.

§32708. Confidentiality of information

(a) General. Information obtained by the Secretary of Transportation under this chapter related to a confidential matter referred to in section 1905 of title 18 may be disclosed only—

(1) to another officer or employee of the United States Government for use in carrying out this chapter; or

(2) in a proceeding under this chapter.

(b) Withholding information from Congress. This section does not authorize information to be withheld from a committee of Congress authorized to have the information.

§32709. Penalties and enforcement

(a) Civil penalty. (1) A person that violates this chapter or a regulation prescribed or order issued under this chapter is liable to the United States Government for a civil penalty of not more than $2,000 for each violation. A separate violation occurs for each motor vehicle or device involved in the violation. The maximum penalty under this subsection for a related series of violations is $100,000.

(2) The Secretary of Transportation shall impose a civil penalty under this subsection. The Attorney General shall bring a civil action to collect the penalty. Before referring a penalty claim to the Attorney General, the Secretary may compromise the amount of the penalty. Before compromising the amount of the penalty, the Secretary shall give the person charged with a violation an opportunity to establish that the violation did not occur.

(3) In determining the amount of a civil penalty under this subsection, the Secretary shall consider—

(A) the nature, circumstances, extent, and gravity of the violation;

(B) with respect to the violator, the degree of culpability, any history of prior violations, the ability to pay, and any effect on the ability to continue doing business; and

(C) other matters that justice requires.

(b) Criminal penalty. A person that knowingly and willfully violates this chapter or a regulation prescribed or order issued under this chapter shall be fined under title 18, imprisoned for not more than 3 years, or both. If the person is a corporation, the penalties of this subsection also apply to a

director, officer, or individual agent of a corporation who knowingly and willfully authorizes, orders, or performs an act in violation of this chapter or a regulation prescribed or order issued under this chapter without regard to penalties imposed on the corporation.

(c) Civil actions by Attorney General. The Attorney General may bring a civil action to enjoin a violation of this chapter or a regulation prescribed or order issued under this chapter. The action may be brought in the United States district court for the judicial district in which the violation occurred or the defendant is found, resides, or does business. Process in the action may be served in any other judicial district in which the defendant resides or is found. A subpoena for a witness in the action may be served in any judicial district.

(d) Civil actions by States. (1) When a person violates this chapter or a regulation prescribed or order issued under this chapter, the chief law enforcement officer of the State in which the violation occurs may bring a civil action—

(A) to enjoin the violation; or

(B) to recover amounts for which the person is liable under section 32710 of this title for each person on whose behalf the action is brought.

(2) An action under this subsection may be brought in an appropriate United States district court or in a State court of competent jurisdiction. The action must be brought not later than 2 years after the claim accrues.

§32710. Civil actions by private persons

(a) Violation and amount of damages. A person that violates this chapter or a regulation prescribed or order issued under this chapter, with intent to defraud, is liable for 3 times the actual damages or $1,500, whichever is greater.

(b) Civil actions. A person may bring a civil action to enforce a claim under this section in an appropriate United States district court or in another court of competent jurisdiction. The action must be brought not later than 2 years after the claim accrues. The court shall award costs and a reasonable attorney's fee to the person when a judgment is entered for that person.

§32711. Relationship to State law

Except to the extent that State law is inconsistent with this chapter, this chapter does not—

(1) affect a State law on disconnecting, altering, or tampering with an odometer with intent to defraud; or

(2) exempt a person from complying with that law.

FEDERAL ODOMETER REGULATIONS[1]
49 C.F.R. Part 580

§580.1 Scope

This part prescribes rules requiring transferors and lessees of motor vehicles to make written disclosure to transferees and lessors respectively, concerning the odometer mileage and its accuracy as directed by sections 408(a) and (e) of the Motor Vehicle Information and Cost Savings Act as amended, 15 U.S.C. §1988(a) and (e). In addition, this part prescribes the rules requiring the retention of odometer disclosure statements by motor vehicle dealers, distributors and lessors and the retention of certain other information by auction companies as directed by sections 408(g) and 414 of the Motor Vehicle Information and Cost Savings Act as amended, 15 U.S.C. 1990(d) and 1988(g).

§580.2 Purpose

The purpose of this part is to provide purchasers of motor vehicles with odometer information to assist them in determining a vehicle's condition and value by making the disclosure of a vehicle's mileage a condition of title and by requiring lessees to disclose to their lessors the vehicle's mileage at the time the lessors transfer the vehicle. In addition, the purpose of this part is to preserve records that are needed for the proper investigation of possible violations of the Motor Vehicle Information and Cost Savings Act and any subsequent prosecutorial, adjudicative or other action.

§580.3 Definitions

All terms defined in sections 2 and 402 of the Motor Vehicle Information and Cost Savings Act are used in their statutory meaning. Other terms used in this part are defined as follows:

"Lessee" means any person, or the agent for any person, to whom a motor vehicle has been leased for a term of at least 4 months.

"Lessor" means any person, or the agent for any person, who has leased 5 or more motor vehicles in the past 12 months.

"Mileage" means actual distance that a vehicle has traveled.

---

1. These regulations were written for the original version of the statute, but since the changes made by the rewrite were neither extensive nor substantive the regulations have not changed, even though they still refer to the numbering of the original statute.—ED.

"Secure printing process or other secure process" means any process which deters and detects counterfeiting and/or unauthorized reproduction and allows alterations to be visible to the naked eye.

"Transferee" means any person to whom ownership of a motor vehicle is transferred, by purchase, gift, or any means other than by the creation of a security interest, and any person who, as agent, signs an odometer disclosure statement for the transferee.

"Transferor" means any person who transfers his ownership of a motor vehicle by sale, gift, or any means other than by the creation of a security interest, and any person who, as agent, signs an odometer disclosure statement for the transferor.

§580.4 Security of title documents and power of attorney forms

Each title shall be set forth by means of a secure printing process or other secure process. In addition, power of attorney forms issued pursuant to §§580.13 and 580.14 and documents which are used to reassign the title shall be issued by the State and shall be set forth by a secure process.

§580.5 Disclosure of odometer information

(a) Each title, at the time it is issued to the transferee, must contain the mileage disclosed by the transferor when ownership of the vehicle was transferred and contain a space for the information required to be disclosed under paragraphs (c), (d), (e) and (f) of this section at the time of future transfer.

(b) Any documents which are used to reassign a title shall contain a space for the information required to be disclosed under paragraphs (c), (d), (e) and (f) of this section at the time of transfer of ownership.

(c) In connection with the transfer of ownership of a motor vehicle, each transferor shall disclose the mileage to the transferee in writing on the title or, except as noted below, on the document being used to reassign the title. In the case of a transferor in whose name the vehicle is titled, the transferor shall disclose the mileage on the title, and not on a reassignment document. This written disclosure must be signed by the transferor, including the printed name. In connection with the transfer of ownership of a motor vehicle in which more than one person is a transferor, only one transferor need sign the written disclosure. In addition to the signature and printed name of the transferor, the written disclosure must contain the following information:

(1) The odometer reading at the time of transfer (not to include tenths of miles);

(2) The date of transfer;

(3) The transferor's name and current address;

(4) The transferee's name and current address; and

(5) The identity of the vehicle, including its make, model, year, and body type, and its vehicle identification number.

(d) In addition to the information provided under paragraph (c) of this section, the statement shall refer to the Federal law and shall state that failure to complete or providing false information may result in fines and/or imprisonment. Reference may also be made to applicable State law.

(e) In addition to the information provided under paragraphs (c) and (d) of this section,

(1) The transferor shall certify that to the best of his knowledge the odometer reading reflects the actual mileage, or:

(2) If the transferor knows that the odometer reading reflects the amount of mileage in excess of the designed mechanical odometer limit, he shall include a statement to that effect; or

(3) If the transferor knows that the odometer reading differs from the mileage and that the difference is greater than that caused by odometer calibration error, he shall include a statement that the odometer reading does not reflect the actual mileage, and should not be relied upon. This statement shall also include a warning notice to alert the transferee that a discrepancy exists between the odometer reading and the actual mileage.

(f) The transferee shall sign the disclosure statement, print his name, and return a copy to his transferor.

(g) If the vehicle has not been titled or if the title does not contain a space for the information required, the written disclosure shall be executed as a separate document.

(h) No person shall sign an odometer disclosure statement as both the transferor and transferee in the same transaction, unless permitted by §§580.13 or 580.14.

§580.6 [Redesignated]

§580.7 Disclosure of odometer information for leased motor vehicles

(a) Before executing any transfer of ownership document, each lessor of a leased motor vehicle shall notify the lessee in writing that the lessee is required to provide a written disclosure to the lessor regarding the mileage. This notice shall contain a reference to the federal law and shall state that failure to complete or providing false information may result in fines and/or imprisonment. Reference may also be made to applicable State law.

(b) In connection with the transfer of ownership of the leased motor vehicle, the lessee shall furnish to the lessor a written statement regarding the mileage of the vehicle. This statement must be signed by the lessee and, in addition to the information required by paragraph (a) of this section, shall contain the following information:

(1) The printed name of the person making the disclosure;

(2) The current odometer reading (not to include tenths of miles);

(3) The date of the statement;

(4) The lessee's name and current address;

(5) The lessor's name and current address;

(6) The identity of the vehicle, including its make, model, year, and body type, and its vehicle identification number;

(7) The date that the lessor notified the lessee of disclosure requirements;

(8) The date that the completed disclosure statement was received by the lessor; and

(9) The signature of the lessor.

(c) In addition to the information provided under paragraphs (a) and (b) of this section,

(1) The lessee shall certify that to the best of his knowledge the odometer reading reflects the actual mileage; or

(2) If the lessee knows that the odometer reading reflects the amount of mileage in excess of the designed mechanical odometer limit, he shall include a statement to that effect; or

(3) If the lessee knows that the odometer reading differs from the mileage and that the difference is greater than that caused by odometer calibration error, he shall include a statement that the odometer reading is not the actual mileage and should not be relied upon.

(d) If the lessor transfers the leased vehicle without obtaining possession of it, the lessor may indicate on the title the mileage disclosed by the lessee under paragraph (b) and (c) of this section, unless the lessor has reason to believe that the disclosure by the lessee does not reflect the actual mileage of the vehicle.

§580.8 Odometer disclosure statement retention

(a) Dealers and distributors of motor vehicles who are required by this part to execute an odometer disclosure statement shall retain for five years a photostat, carbon or other facsimile copy of each odometer mileage statement which they issue and receive. They shall retain all odometer disclosure statements at their primary place of business in an order that is appropriate to business requirements and that permits systematic retrieval.

(b) Lessors shall retain, for five years following the date they transfer ownership of the leased vehicle, each odometer disclosure statement which they receive from a lessee. They shall retain all odometer disclosure statements at their primary place of business in an order that is appropriate to business requirements and that permits systematic retrieval.

(c) Dealers and distributors of motor vehicles who are granted a power of attorney by their transferor pursuant to §580.13, or by their transferee pursuant to §580.14, shall retain for five years a photostat, carbon, or other facsimile copy of each power of attorney that they receive. They shall retain all powers of attorney at their primary place of business in an order that is appropriate to business requirements and that permits systematic retrieval.

§580.9 Odometer record retention for auction companies

Each auction company shall establish and retain at its primary place of business in an order that is appropriate to business requirements and that permits systematic retrieval, for five years following the date of sale of each motor vehicle, the following records:

(a) The name of the most recent owner (other than the auction company);

(b) The name of the buyer;

(c) The vehicle identification number; and

(d) The odometer reading on the date which the auction company took possession of the motor vehicle.

§580.10 to §580.16 [Omitted.]

§580.17 Exemptions

Notwithstanding the requirements of §§580.5 and 580.7:

(a) A transferor or a lessee of any of the following motor vehicles need not disclose the vehicle's odometer mileage:

(1) A vehicle having a Gross Vehicle Weight Rating, as defined in §§571.3 of this title, of more than 16,000 pounds;

(2) A vehicle that is not self-propelled;

(3) A vehicle that was manufactured in a model year beginning at least ten years before January 1 of the calendar year in which the transfer occurs; or

Example to paragraph (a)(3): For vehicle transfers occurring during calendar year 1998, model year 1988 or older vehicles are exempt.

(4) A vehicle sold directly by the manufacturer to any agency of the United States in conformity with contractual specifications.

(b) A transferor of a new vehicle prior to its first transfer for purposes other than resale need not disclose the vehicle's odometer mileage.

(c) A lessor of any of the vehicles listed in paragraph (a) of this section need not notify the lessee of any of these vehicles of the disclosure requirements of §580.7.

APPENDIX B TO PART 580—DISCLOSURE FORM FOR TITLE
Odometer Disclosure Statement

Federal law (and State law, if applicable) requires that you state the mileage in connection with the transfer of ownership. Failure to complete or providing a false statement may result in fines and/or imprisonment.

_____

I state that the odometer now reads _____ (no tenths) miles and to the best of my knowledge that it reflects the actual mileage of the vehicle described herein, unless one of the following statements is checked.

_____ (1) I hereby certify that to the best of my knowledge the odometer reading reflects the amount of mileage in excess of its mechanical limits.

_____ (2) I hereby certify that the odometer reading is NOT the actual mileage. WARNING—ODOMETER DISCREPANCY.

_____

(Transferor's Signature)

_____

(Transferee's Signature)

_____

(Printed name)

_____

(Printed name)

Date of Statement: _____

Transferee's Name: _____

Transferee's Address: _____
                                          (Street)

_____

(City)   (State)   (ZIP Code)

PROBLEM 4

a. On her eighteenth birthday, Portia Moot was delighted to learn that her father planned to give her his two-year-old automobile. If he does so, must he give her an odometer mileage statement? See the Regulation at §580.3. If he does not do so because he was unaware of this requirement, can she sue him for at least $1,500?

b. Detroit Motor Company manufactures automobiles. Must it give odometer statements on each of them to the retailers to whom it sells the cars? See §580.17(b).

c. At an automobile show, John Visor sold his restored 1967 Mustang convertible to an eager buyer but failed to give an odometer mileage statement. Is he liable to suit? See §580.17(a)(3).

For an Annotation collecting all the cases arising under the Federal Odometer Act, see 28 A.L.R. Fed. 581. A commentary on the statute and its application can be found in Automobile Fraud (National Consumer Law Center 1998, with supplements to date).

DELAY v. HEARN FORD

United States District Court, District of South Carolina, 1974 373 F. Supp. 791

HEMPHILL, District Judge.

Plaintiff seeks relief in this forum under the provisions of Subchapter IV, of the Motor Vehicle Information and Cost Savings Act, 15 U.S.C.A. §§1981-1991, Public Law 92-513, 86 Stat. 947 (1972). This court's jurisdiction over this action is found in 15 U.S.C.A. §1989(b). This case appears to be among the first to be brought under this statute, the cause of action allegedly arising the first day after the effective date of the statute.

STATEMENT OF FACTS

On December 23, 1972, plaintiff purchased a 1973 Ford automobile from the defendant, Hearn Ford, a new and used car dealer. At the time of the transaction he traded in his 1967 Chevrolet, serial number 1648Y176476. At the time he traded the Chevrolet to Hearn Ford, its odometer read approximately 72,000 miles.

Thereafter, because the new Ford had to be fixed or repaired daily, Mr. Delay felt the purchase was unsatisfactory. Hearn Ford replaced this car with a second new Ford which also proved unsatisfactory to plaintiff. He sold the second new Ford to Kenneth E. Jones, the used car manager at Hearn Ford, and repurchased from defendant the same 1967 Chevrolet which he had traded in originally.

The repurchase was made on January 19, 1973 for cash. After completing the transaction, plaintiff drove the car away and en route home noticed that the odometer then read less than 49,000 miles. Upon reaching his home, plaintiff called Jones who could not explain the difference in mileage.

Jones presented an affidavit to the court in which he swore, to the best of his knowledge, that, prior to January 18, 1973, the effective date of the statute in question, the 1967 Chevrolet automobile which was resold to plaintiff on January 19, 1973, was delivered to the lot from Shillinglaw's Clean-Up Shop and that the mileage reading on the odometer of the car was not altered, changed, or reset in any manner subsequent to the delivery of the automobile to the used car lot, and more particularly, on or after January 18, 1973. No statement was made as to any possible alteration after the initial trade-in of the 1967 Chevrolet by plaintiff on December 23, 1972 and before the delivery of the car to Shillinglaw's Clean-Up Shop.

Roddey Caskey, a policeman employed by the town of Fort Mill, South Carolina, and a son-in-law of plaintiff, submitted an affidavit in which he stated that he has had frequent occasions to drive plaintiff's 1967 Chevrolet and that he knows, of his own knowledge, that, prior to the trading of the car to Hearn Ford, the mileage on the automobile's odometer read at least 65,000 miles. After plaintiff repurchased the car on January 19, 1973, Caskey, at the request of plaintiff, observed that the odometer on the same vehicle read less than 49,000 miles.

Plaintiff filed his complaint on March 19, 1973, seeking judgment against defendant for $1,500, reasonable attorney's fees, and costs of the action. Defendant moved for summary judgment and the court heard oral arguments on March 1, 1974.

THE APPLICABLE STATUTE

The basic Congressional intent of Subchapter IV, Odometer Requirements, is set forth in the first section of the subchapter, 15 U.S.C.A. §1981. It is obvious that Congress took a dim view of anyone who tampered with an odometer in order to make a used car appear to be a more attractive purchase to the prospective buyer. In effect, this statute, for that reason, outlaws odometer tampering.

The act became law on October 20, 1972. Public law 92-513, §412, provided: "This title . . . shall take effect ninety calendar days following the date of enactment of this Act." Thus, the effective date of this statute was January 18, 1973.

The present action is based on 15 U.S.C.A. §1989(a). This subparagraph provides for treble damages or $1,500, whichever is greater, together with reasonable attorney's fees, as determined by the court, and the costs of the action, if a seller of a motor vehicle, with intent to defraud, violates any requirements imposed under the subchapter.

Plaintiff contends that both 15 U.S.C.A. §1984 and §1988 have been violated by defendant through its agents.

ANALYSIS

The court finds that the actions shown to have occurred are sufficient to prove an intentional act to defraud prospective purchasers in violation of the statutes in question. The affidavits presented to the court clearly establish that the car in question was previously owned by plaintiff and that it was traded in to Hearn Ford on December 23, 1972. At that time it had approximately 72,000 miles on the odometer. Plaintiff subsequently repurchased the same car on January 19, 1973 from Hearn Ford. As he was driving the car home, he discovered that the odometer then read less than 49,000 miles.

From these facts a reasonable inference arises that sometime between December 23, 1972 and January 19, 1973, the roll back of the odometer was done by or for defendant through its agents. This would only seem logical since, during the entire time in which plaintiff claimed the alteration in mileage took place, the car was under the dominion and control of defendant. Such a conclusion is compelled, absent a showing by defendant as to when such roll back occurred and by whom it was done. Defendant is in a far better position than anyone else to make such information available to this court. At first reading it appears defendant has violated 15 U.S.C.A. §1984.

Defendant also appears to have violated 15 U.S.C.A. §1988 by its failure to disclose to plaintiff that the odometer reading was known by defendant to be different from the number of miles that the vehicle had actually traveled. The failure to disclose to the purchaser may be evidence of an intent to defraud, absent a showing by defendant that the change was unintentional or was made with an intent other than an intent to defraud. Such a requirement might be satisfied by a showing that the change was accidental, malicious mischief, mistake by a third party, etc.

Defendant's claim of ignorance as to the cause of the change is not satisfactory to avoid the finding of an intent to defraud. During the term of defendant's dominion over the car, defendant was the only party which had anything to gain by rolling back the odometer. The only other party to have possession, Shillinglaw's Clean-Up Shop, as defendant's third party independent contractor, had nothing to gain by changing the mileage reading.

The fact that the purchaser was the prior owner is not sufficient to avoid the requirement that the disclosure of the mileage change had to be made to plaintiff. To reiterate, 15 U.S.C.A. §1989(a)(1) states:

> Any person who, *with intent to defraud*, violates any requirement imposed under this subchapter shall be liable in an amount equal to the sum of three times the amount of actual damages sustained or $1,500, whichever is greater. . . . (Emphasis added.)

The statute prohibits violations of any requirement imposed under the subchapter upon sellers, with intent to defraud. The statute does not require that, additionally, a purchaser must be hurt. Nevertheless, if a purchaser is hurt, he or she may recover treble actual damages. If a purchaser is not hurt, he or she may obtain the alternative recovery of $1,500. The purchaser in this case was not actually hurt, so therefore, he has pursued his remedy in the alternative. To construe the statute to require actual damage to the purchaser would effectively gut the statute of its alternative remedy. Indeed, it appears that under the statute, as it is presently written, this case presents one of the few situations in which a purchaser could have knowledge of the actual mileage so as to determine whether there has been any tampering with the odometer.

All that is required of a purchaser before recovery will be allowed is that a change in the odometer reading has occurred and that the seller has failed to disclose the change. An intent to defraud arises from the proof of the foregoing in the absence of an explanation of the odometer change.

The purpose of the statute is to punish odometer tamperers by imposing civil penalties upon them and to reward purchasers who discover such tampering and bring it to the attention of the federal courts.

In keeping with the stated Congressional purpose in enacting these statutes, this court will not permit defendant to avail itself of the argument that the odometer was rolled back prior to the actionable date of the statute. It is manifest from the Congressional statement of intent that the ninety day waiting period was only for the purpose of the dissemination of information to those most affected by the law and was not intended by Congress to give those who sold used cars a ninety day period in which to alter such odometers as they wished without having to disclose that fact after January 18, 1973, the effective date of the statute on which such conduct became actionable. The tampering statute, §1984, and the disclosure statute, §1988, meshed at the end of the ninety day period. After January 18, 1973, the seller must disclose the actual mileage and any prior tampering or be responsible for the failure to so state.

The court has searched in vain for law review articles and other periodicals discussing the statutes involved herein. The court's interpretation is therefore based solely on the statute's legislative history expressing the Congressional intent as it appears in 3 U.S. Code Cong. & Admin. News, 3960, 3970-72 (1972).

Being without prior case law as a guide, the court must resort to a practical analogy. The statutes herein prohibit tampering with an odometer and the failure to disclose the tampering, committed with an intent to defraud the purchaser. Akin to this offense, would be an assault with a deadly weapon. The tampering in §1984 is akin to loading the weapon to make it "deadly." The weapon, like the car with the tampered odometer, may lay around unused for some time. When the weapon is used to assault someone, like the sale of the car with the tampered odometer to a purchaser with a failure to disclose the tampering, the damage is done and the conduct becomes actionable. Here, there was no damage done until the car was sold on January 19, 1973, even though the tampering occurred at some unknown time between December 23, 1972 and January 19, 1973. If the sale had been made on January 17, 1973, there would have been no cause of action stated herein because the statute did not become effective until the next day.

This court, upon full reflection, concludes that there are potential, and contested, issues of fact as to the following:

CONCLUSIONS

1. Whether defendant has violated 15 U.S.C.A. §1984 by altering the odometer of a 1967 Chevrolet, serial number 164877Y176476, with the intent to change the number of miles indicated thereon, sometime between December 23, 1972 and January 19, 1973.

2. Whether defendant has violated 15 U.S.C.A. §1988(a)(2) and (b) by failing to disclose to the purchaser that the odometer reading is known to it, as the transferor-seller, to be different from the number of miles the vehicle has actually traveled.

3. Whether plaintiff is entitled to $1,500 under 15 U.S.C.A. §1989(a)(1) and, in the event of the successful action to enforce the foregoing liability the costs of the action together with such attorney fee, as will be determined to be reasonable by this court, pursuant to 15 U.S.C.A. §1989(a)(2).

Defendant's motion for summary judgment is denied.

And it is so ordered.

QUESTION

Is it just to give plaintiff a remedy under the statute when he knew the true mileage, and so was not harmed by the alteration?

PROBLEM 5

In 2011, Jay Eastriver bought a 2006 used car. The car dealership, relying on the odometer statement given to it by the auto auction where it had purchased the car, gave Eastriver an odometer statement stating that the car had only 49,016 miles on it. The car dealership convinced the court that it had no actual knowledge that the odometer was in error and that only an elaborate investigation would have revealed that the car had to have been driven more than 49,016 miles given its current condition. Is the car dealership nonetheless liable to Eastriver? See Jones v. Hanley Dawson Cadillac Co., 848 F.2d 803 (7th Cir. 1988).

NIETO v. PENCE
United States Court of Appeals, Fifth Circuit, 1978
578 F.2d 640

GODBOLD, Circuit Judge.

Plaintiff in this case seeks to invoke civil liability under the Motor Vehicle Information and Cost Savings Act, 15 U.S.C. §§1981-1991, against an automobile dealer who sold her a motor vehicle and did not have actual knowledge, but may have had constructive knowledge, that the odometer reading on the vehicle was less than the number of miles it actually had traveled, and who failed to disclose that the mileage was unknown. The district court held that actual knowledge was required for liability. We conclude that constructive knowledge is sufficient, and reverse.

In 1975 plaintiff purchased in Texas from defendant,[2] used car dealer or dealers, for $600, a 10-year-old pickup truck with an odometer reading of 14,736 miles. Pursuant to the Act, defendant furnished to plaintiff an odometer mileage statement disclosure form. The Act requires that, pursuant to rules promulgated by the Secretary of Transportation, any transferor must give the following written disclosure to the transferee in connection with the transfer of ownership of a motor vehicle:

(1) Disclosure of the cumulative mileage registered on the odometer.

---

2. We use the singular "defendant" and the pronoun "he" for simplicity.

(2) Disclosure that the actual mileage is unknown, if the odometer reading is known to the transferor to be different from the number of miles the vehicle has actually traveled.

15 U.S.C. §1988(a). The Act also provides,

It shall be a violation of this section for any transferor to violate any rules under this section or to knowingly give a false statement to a transferee in making any disclosure required by such rules.

15 U.S.C. §1988(b).

Defendant stated on the disclosure form that the odometer reading at the time of sale was 14,736 miles. Defendant did not check the box on the form that says: "I further state that the actual mileage differs from the odometer reading for reasons other than odometer calibration error and that the actual mileage is unknown." Defendant had purchased the truck from another used-car dealer who certified the odometer reading at the time of transfer as 14,290 miles and did not state that the actual mileage was unknown. That dealer had bought the truck from another dealer who had certified the odometer reading at the time of transfer at 14,290 miles and had not stated that the actual mileage was unknown.

Plaintiff sued under 15 U.S.C. §1989 which provides that:

Any person who, with intent to defraud, violates any requirement imposed under this chapter shall be liable. . . .

The district court found that defendant had no actual knowledge that the odometer reading differed from the actual mileage and also that defendant did not intend to defraud plaintiff. The court made no finding whether defendant had constructive knowledge that the odometer reading differed from the actual mileage. There was evidence tending to establish that defendant reasonably should have known that the odometer reading differed from the actual mileage. The odometer reading was very low for a 10-year-old truck, and defendant Pence admitted he would be suspicious of an odometer reading of 14,000 miles on a truck that old. Pence had been in the auto business approximately 12 years.

The legislative history indicates that a transferor who lacks actual knowledge that the odometer reading is incorrect may still have a duty to state that the actual mileage is unknown. The Senate Report addressed the very situation this case presents:

[Section 1988] makes it a violation of the title for any person "knowingly" to give a false statement to a transferee. This section originally allowed a person to rely completely on the representations of the previous owner. This original provision created a potential loophole, however. For example, a person could have purchased a vehicle knowing that the mileage was false but received a statement from the transferor verifying the odometer reading. Suppose an auto dealer bought a car with a 20,000 mile odometer verification but any mechanic employed by that auto dealer could ascertain that the vehicle had at least 60,000 miles on it. The bill as introduced would have permitted the dealer to resell the vehicle with a 20,000 mile verification. In order to eliminate this potential loophole the test of "knowingly" was incorporated so that the auto dealer with expertise now would have an affirmative duty to mark "true mileage unknown" if, in the exercise of reasonable care, he would have reason to know that the mileage was more than that which the odometer had recorded or which the previous owner had certified.

1972 U.S. Code Cong. & Admin. News pp. 3971-72. Thus defendant had a duty to disclose that the actual mileage was unknown if, in the exercise of reasonable care, he would have had reason to know that the mileage was more than that which the odometer had recorded or the previous owner had certified.

The legislative history makes clear that, if defendant had constructive knowledge that the odometer reading was incorrect, he violated §1989. A separate question is whether defendant can be civilly liable for the violation. Because §1989 requires intent to defraud, a violation does not automatically lead to civil liability.

Several district courts have considered whether a transferor can be civilly liable for a failure to disclose that a vehicle's actual mileage is unknown when he lacked actual knowledge that the odometer reading was incorrect. One district court has held that a transferor can be found to have had the requisite intent to defraud only if he had actual knowledge that the odometer reading was incorrect. Mataya v. Behm Motors, Inc., 409 F. Supp. 65, 69-70 (E.D. Wis. 1976). Other district courts have held that a transferor may have intended to defraud even if he lacked actual knowledge that the odometer reading was incorrect. Pepp v. Superior Pontiac GMC, Inc., 412 F. Supp. 1053, 1055-56 (E.D. La. 1976) (intent to defraud may be inferred from gross negligence); Jones v. Fenton Ford, Inc., 427 F. Supp. 1328, 1333-36 (D. Conn. 1977) (intent to defraud inferred from recklessness); Kantorczyk v. New Stanton Auto Auction, Inc., 433 F. Supp. 889, 893 (W.D. Pa. 1977) (intent to defraud found in reckless disregard); see Stier v. Park Pontiac, Inc., 391 F. Supp. 397 (S.D. W. Va. 1975) (court held that transferors with constructive knowledge may be liable without discussing intent to defraud); Duval v. Midwest Auto City, Inc., 425 F. Supp. 1381, 1387 (D. Neb. 1977) (court held transferor with constructive knowledge liable without discussing intent to defraud).[3]

---

3. District courts have also inferred intent to defraud in cases where the defendant was charged with tampering with a vehicle's odometer yet claimed ignorance. Delay v. Hearn Ford,

We hold that a transferor who lacked actual knowledge may still be found to have intended to defraud and thus may be civilly liable for a failure to disclose that a vehicle's actual mileage is unknown. A transferor may not close his eyes to the truth. If a transferor reasonably should have known that a vehicle's odometer reading was incorrect, although he did not know to a certainty the transferee would be defrauded, a court may infer that he understood the risk of such an occurrence.[4]

Moreover, unless a violation of the Act can lead to civil liability the Act is toothless. The district court holding there could be no intent to defraud in the absence of actual knowledge countered this obvious argument by noting that the U.S. Attorney General can petition for injunctive relief even when the transferor lacks an intent to defraud. *Mataya*, supra, 409 F. Supp. at 69-70; see 15 U.S.C. §1990. But see *Jones*, supra, 427 F. Supp. at 1333. But such relief, although theoretically available, is unlikely. Private prosecution is needed to make the Act effective. . . .

Vacated in part, reversed in part and remanded.

II. UNFAIR OR DECEPTIVE SALES PRACTICES

A. *Unordered Merchandise*

POSTAL REORGANIZATION ACT OF 1970
39 U.S.C.A. §3009 Mailing of unordered merchandise

(a) Except for (1) free samples clearly and conspicuously marked as such, and (2) merchandise mailed by a charitable organization soliciting contributions, the mailing of unordered merchandise or of communications prohibited by subsection (c) of this section constitutes an unfair method of

---

373 F. Supp. 791 (D.S.C. 1974); see Klein v. Pincus, 397 F. Supp. 847 (E.D.N.Y. 1975). Absent an explanation, a defendant's sole dominion of a vehicle tends to show his responsibility for an altered odometer, and his failure to disclose that the odometer reading is incorrect is evidence of intent to defraud. In tampering cases, however, the inferences courts have drawn go to show that the defendant tampered with the odometer, and thus the inferences tend to show actual knowledge as well as intent to defraud.

4. Our conclusion is rooted in the facts of this case. The Senate Report suggests that auto dealers should adopt business practices reasonably calculated to uncover incorrect odometer readings. Plaintiff presented no evidence that defendant had not adopted such business practices, and defendant offered no evidence that he had. Thus we do not need to decide whether a court might infer from the failure to adopt such practices that a dealer knew his practices would work to defraud some of the people with whom he would deal or conversely whether a court might infer from the adoption of such practices that a dealer lacked constructive knowledge or intent to defraud.

competition and an unfair trade practice [under §5 of the Federal Trade Commission Act].

(b) Any merchandise mailed in violation of subsection (a) of this section, or within the exceptions contained therein, may be treated as a gift by the recipient, who shall have the right to retain, use, discard, or dispose of it in any manner he sees fit without any obligation whatsoever to the sender. All such merchandise shall have attached to it a clear and conspicuous statement informing the recipient that he may treat the merchandise as a gift to him and has the right to retain, use, discard, or dispose of it in any manner he sees fit without any obligation whatsoever to the sender.

(c) No mailer of any merchandise mailed in violation of subsection (a) of this section, or within the exceptions contained therein, shall mail to any recipient of such merchandise a bill for such merchandise or any dunning communications.

(d) For the purposes of this section, "unordered merchandise" means merchandise mailed without the prior expressed request or consent of the recipient.

PROBLEM 6

How does the above statute affect the following situations?

(a) Joseph Armstrong signed a contract with the Book-of-the-Month Club, whereby BOMC monthly sends him a notice describing the next selection and, if it hears no objection from its customer, it then mails out the book (and bill, of course). Is such a "negative option plan," as it is called, in conflict with the above statute? (Negative option plans are regulated by the Federal Trade Commission, 16 C.F.R. Part 425.)

(b) Rudolph Longhair opened his door one day to find a carton of country music CDs from the Hard Rock Music Club. It was their introductory package (thereafter one need buy only a CD a month for six months at regular rates). Longhair had not ordered the CDs; it turned out that a friend (who was an accomplished practical joker) had ordered them in Longhair's name. Longhair likes only classical music. Must he pay for these or any CDs he did not order?

(c) Tim Wilkerson was annoyed to find on his doorstep a package he had not ordered labeled "Learn French While You Sleep," which purported to teach language skills subliminally by means of a device placed under one's pillow at night. The package, which was accompanied by a bill for $39.99, had been left on his doorstep by United Parcel Service. What should Tim do about this unwanted item?

While the Postal Reorganization Act allows recipients of unordered merchandise to keep the merchandise with no obligation to pay, courts have held that there is no affirmative cause of action for damages available under the statute. See Wisniewski v. Rodale, Inc., 510 F.3d 294 (3rd Cir. 2007).

B. *The Federal Trade Commission*

The Federal Trade Commission was established in 1914 pursuant to an act of Congress, 15 U.S.C. §41. It was given broad powers affecting all United States businesses.

Section 5 of the Federal Trade Commission Act, 15 U.S.C. §45, permits the FTC to condemn "unfair and deceptive acts or practices" in or affecting interstate commerce. The FTC has interpreted this power broadly and uses §5 as the basis for the condemnation of a multitude of selling practices at all levels, including advertising. Consumers often have been the beneficiaries of FTC actions. The FTC has a web site containing information and statistics about fraud (particularly Internet fraud) and identity theft: www.consumer. gov/sentinel. It lists the more than 300,000 consumer complaints filed with the FTC during the past several years. The Commission also maintains a hotline to call in the event of suspected violations: (877) FTC-HELP (383-4357).

IN RE ARTHUR MURRAY STUDIO OF WASHINGTON, INC.
Federal Trade Commission, 1971 78 F.T.C. 401, *aff'd,*
458 F.2d 622 (5th Cir. 1972)

By DIXON, Commissioner.

This matter is before the Commission on cross appeals of respondents and counsel supporting the complaint from an initial decision holding that respondents had violated Section 5 of the Federal Trade Commission Act.

The complaint charges four corporations and two individuals with numerous unfair and deceptive practices in connection with the sale of dance instruction courses. The alleged unlawful conduct includes the following practices: obtaining leads to prospective purchasers of dance instruction by awarding gift certificates for such instruction either through the use of so-called "contests" in which all participants can win or by falsely representing that a person has been "selected" to receive a free course of instruction; failing to provide the full number of "free" hours of dance instruction promised but instead devoting much of the time to promoting the sale of dancing lessons; representing that certain clubs sponsored by respondents are bona fide adult social clubs when in fact such clubs are devices used to obtain leads to prospective students and to lure prospects into respondents' studios where a sales presentation could be made; using sham "dance analysis tests" where all prospective students are given passing grades regardless of dancing ability, aptitude or proficiency; using "relay salesmanship" which involves successive efforts by a number of different salesmen in a single day to persuade a prospective student to sign a contract for dancing instruction; and using "intense, emotional, and unrelenting" sales pressure to persuade a prospective student to sign a contract for a substantial number of dancing lessons without affording the prospect a reasonable opportunity to consider and comprehend the scope and extent of the contractual obligations involved. . . .

After briefs had been filed and oral argument held, the hearing examiner on December 19, 1969, ordered that the record be closed for the reception of evidence. On January 5, 1970, complaint counsel moved to reopen the record for the reception of evidence in support of the order provision placing a $1500 limitation on respondents' contracts for dance instruction. This motion stated in part:

> Complaint counsel will introduce evidence through consumer and expert witnesses to demonstrate the unconscionable nature of respondents' contracts in excess of $1500. Evidence will be adduced from members of the dance industry to show that $1500 is a fair balance between the practical business need of an operator of a dance studio and the equitable and fair amount which a person should be indebted for dance instruction.

The examiner granted this motion over respondents' objection and the Commission subsequently denied respondents' application for permission to file an interlocutory appeal from the examiner's order reopening the record. Hearings were then held to permit counsel supporting the complaint to introduce evidence supplementing the stipulation of facts in support of the requested prohibition against contracts in excess of $1500.

The hearing examiner, in an initial decision based upon the stipulated facts and the evidence adduced in support of the $1500 contractual limitation, found that the charges in the complaint had been sustained and issued his order to cease and desist. . . .

In their appeal from the initial decision respondents do not contest the examiner's findings or his conclusions that the challenged practices are illegal. They address themselves only to two aspects of the order to cease and desist. The first and by far the more important of the two major issues raised by their appeal is whether the order may properly prohibit respondents from entering into contracts for an amount in excess of $1500 for dance instruction or any other service provided by respondents' dance studios.

Respondents argue in this connection that counsel supporting the complaint did not prove either the unconscionability of respondents' contracts in excess of $1500 or the fairness of such a limitation when the economics of operating the dance studio are balanced against a "fair amount which a person should be indebted for dance instruction." In the absence of proof of the illegality of such contracts, according to respondents, the Commission has no authority to issue an order banning their use. Respondents further contend that the hearings added very little, if anything, to the case-in-chief in support of the complaint—that respondents had stipulated to all facts upon which the essential findings of the initial decision were based. . . .

We agree with respondents that most of the evidence adduced by counsel supporting the complaint does not go beyond the facts originally stipulated by counsel. Certainly much of this evidence is redundant. We also agree that counsel supporting the complaint did not prove that all contracts for dance instruction in excess of $1500 are unconscionable. We do not agree however that the evidence adduced is not relevant to the question of whether a $1500 contractual limitation should be imposed; nor do we agree that the record does not support the imposition of such a limitation.

It should be emphasized first of all, contrary to the arguments advanced by respondents, that the Commission's remedial powers under Section 5 are not restricted to the prohibition of only those acts and practices found to be unlawful. The purpose of a Commission order is to prevent the continuance of such practices but, to accomplish this end, the Commission may, if it deems necessary, forbid acts lawful in themselves. In Jacob Siegel Co. v. Federal Trade Commission, 327 U.S. 608 (1946) the Supreme Court held that the Commission has wide discretion in determining what remedy is necessary to eliminate unfair or deceptive practices which have been disclosed, and in Federal Trade Commission v. Ruberoid Co., 343 U.S. 470, 473 (1952) the Court stated that "if the Commission is to attain the objectives Congress envisioned, it cannot be required to confine its road-block to the narrow lane the transgressor has traveled; it must be allowed effectively to close all roads to the prohibited goal, so that its order may not be by-passed with impunity." The Court also upheld the Commission's order suppressing the use of a "lawful device" for the purpose of preventing the continuation of a price fixing conspiracy in Federal Trade Commission v. National Lead, 352 U.S. 419, 510 (1959) concluding that "the Commission was justified in its determination that it was necessary to include some restraint in its order against the individual corporations in order to prevent a continuance of the unfair competitive practices found to exist."

It is apparent from a review of the initial decision that the hearing examiner believed that the $1500 limitation should be imposed, not because contracts in excess of that amount are unconscionable or per se illegal, but because a restriction of this type would be necessary to prevent a recurrence of unfair acts and practices employed by respondents to induce members of the public to execute long-term contracts. Having found that the order without the $1500 limitation "does not eradicate the root of the evil," he concluded that such a limitation "is a necessary and reasonable safeguard to forestall and stop in their incipiency the respondents' unfair and deceptive acts and practices before their purposes become fulfilled." . . .

We agree with this conclusion. Without the $1500 limitation the order will not, in our opinion, effectively deter respondents from engaging in many of the unfair practices which they have used to sell dancing lessons. It is important to note, in this connection, that the order contained in the initial decision does not specifically prohibit all the practices alleged as unfair in the complaint, as respondents contend. The complaint charges in Paragraph 13 that respondents have used "intense, emotional and unrelenting sales pressure" to persuade a prospect or student to sign a long-term contract and that "such person is insistently urged, cajoled, and coerced to sign such a contract hurriedly and precipitatedly through use of persistent and emotionally forceful sales presentations which are often of several hours' duration." The record fully supports this charge. The unfair pressure tactics used by respondents to persuade students to sign contracts for dance instruction are disclosed in the testimony of students and former employees of respondents' studios. However, except for "relay salesmanship," these unfair pressure tactics, some of which are described below, are not prohibited either specifically or in general terms.

A former employee of respondents' Baltimore studio testified with respect to a procedure used routinely by respondents to exert pressure on the prospective student. This witness testified that in his capacity as interviewer and dance analyst he would attempt to gain the confidence of a student for the purpose of obtaining information about the student's past which could be used to persuade her to sign a contract. According to him, the sales approach or technique used by respondents assumed that many of the people who come to dance studios do so for some more deep-seated reason than simply a desire to learn to dance. Respondents referred to this reason as the "X-Factor" and assigned to the interviewer the task of discovering it. This factor could be loneliness, marital difficulties, or some unpleasant experience or unhappiness in the prospect's past which could be exploited for the purpose of selling dance instructions. The information obtained by the interviewer would be passed on to the studio manager, who would sometimes eavesdrop on the interview and instruct the interviewer by telephone how to conduct the interrogation. Thereafter, the student would be given a sham dance analysis test and then brought to a small room where the studio manager would close the deal. Prior to closing, members of the staff would attempt to make the student as nervous and confused as possible. Also prior to closing, the interviewer would extract a promise from her that she would not tell the studio manager that she needed or wanted time to think about signing the contract. The interviewer would then stand beside the student at the closing, sometimes holding her hand, and would pretend to speak in her behalf, leading her to believe that he was persuading the studio manager to accept her as a student. By making this feigned appeal to the manager and by appearing extremely solicitous of her welfare, the interviewer would attempt to bring the student to a highly emotional state. Often the student would break down and cry and on one occasion a young woman actually "dropped down on one knee and asked the studio manager to please let her enroll." . . .

To apply additional pressure to the more recalcitrant students the studio manager would falsely state at the closing that the decision to enter into the contract must be made immediately and that the student would not be permitted to sign after a specified hour. Sometimes the studio manager would block the door to prevent the student from leaving, and once respondent Mara pushed a chair in front of the door. In some cases, the closing would last three to four hours.

Even after a student had obligated herself for lessons costing thousands of dollars she was still constantly harassed and badgered to sign up for more hours. One student, a woman 62 years old, who had over 300 unused hours of dance instruction testified that she was under considerable pressure to take a test to determine whether she would qualify to join respondents' "Tiffany Club" which would cost an additional $8000. She testified that she had no intention of buying more hours but that she took the test because she had learned that a student was "practically ostracized at the studio" . . . if she refused to do so. Although she "insisted through the entire thing that [she] was not going to make any further investment" she nevertheless signed a contract for the additional lessons "to relieve the pressure."

Another student described her closing experience as follows:

I tried to say no and get out of it and I got very, very upset because I got frightened at paying out all that money and having nothing to fall back on. I remember I started crying and couldn't stop crying. All I thought of was getting out of there.

So finally after—I don't know how much time, Mr. Mara said, well, I could sign up for 250 hours, which was called the 500 Club, which would amount to $4300.

So I finally signed it. . . .

Another testified, "I was confused, I was confounded, I was beset, I was frantic, I didn't want it, and I couldn't get out of it, and I signed this contract and practically went off the deep end after it. . . ." She further stated that she had "begged and pleaded with these people to leave [her] alone."

The difficulty in fashioning an order which will effectively stop respondents from engaging in practices of the type described above is apparent. Respondents suggest that "The remedy . . . is clearly to outlaw the pressure." But this is not easily done. An order which would enjoin the particular acts and practices previously used by respondents could be avoided by a change in tactics, and one which would prohibit generally the use of excessive or unfair pressure would be virtually impossible to enforce. Since the selling practices involved here almost invariably take the form of oral representations made privately to a student, violations of an order addressed to such practices would be extremely difficult to discover and prove. In view of respondents' demonstrated proclivity to utilize such sales methods, we have no doubt that they would continue to use them if they believed they could do so without detection. They would, however, have considerably more difficulty circumventing an order which would prohibit them from entering into contracts in excess of $1500.[5]

Respondents argue, however, that there is no reasonable relation between the prohibition and the practice found to be unlawful—that a bar on contract size bears no reasonable relationship to the unfair and deceptive practices used to secure such contracts. We do not agree. Human nature being what it is, we think that respondents are far more likely to apply excessive pressure to secure a large contract than a small one. The greater the gains or rewards respondents will reap, the greater their incentive will be to engage in these practices or to devise new and more elaborate methods to accomplish the desired end. There is, moreover, testimony in the record indicating that such is the case. As one witness testified, "As a rule of thumb, I would say that every single contract for a sizable sum was entered into under extreme pressure . . ." and that "The more sizable ones would have, in my interpretation, more pressure than the lesser size." But if we are wrong on this point, and we later learn that respondents are engaging in the objectionable practices despite the $1500 limitation, we can consider at that time what monetary limitation will have the desired effect on their behavior.

Respondents also contend that the public is adequately protected by the provision in the order which requires them to include in all contracts a

---

5. There is other evidence of record which strongly supports an order imposing a monetary limitation on respondents' contracts with students. Several witnesses testified that after a student had executed a long-term contract the quality of service provided by respondents to that student deteriorated. The prohibition may well have the added salutary effect therefore of deterring respondents from taking advantage of "captive" students.

statement to the effect that the student may rescind the agreement for any reason by submitting written notice of their intention to do so within seven days from the date of execution thereof. While this provision will of course be of value, we have no reason to believe that all students who succumb to respondents' unfair practices will demand within seven days to be released from the contract merely because there is a notation in the contract that they may do so. Moreover, it is quite apparent from the testimony that many of the students are in such a confused and highly emotional state when they execute the contract that it is unlikely that they are even aware of the notation.

We turn next to respondents' contention that the prohibition under consideration will impose upon them dire economic hardship. The hearing examiner, having found that the prohibition is necessary to prevent unfair practices, held that whether or not respondents can operate profitably under this provision of the order is beside the point—that "Economic feasibility does not act to insulate or excuse the respondents' challenged acts and practices from the requirements of the law nor allow the respondents to obtain the ill-gotten gains of their unfair and deceptive acts and practices." (Initial decision, p. 36) We find no error in this ruling. As the Supreme Court stated in United States v. E.I. du Pont de Nemours & Co., 366 U.S. 316, 327, with respect to an order requiring divestiture, "the Government cannot be denied the latter remedy because economic hardship, however severe, may result. Economic hardship can influence choice only as among two or more effective remedies."

In any event we find no substance to respondents' contention that the evidence shows that the imposition of a contractual limitation is tantamount to denying the individual respondents the opportunity to engage in the dance business in the future. Testimony of studio owners called by respondents that they could not exist without long-term contracts is for the most part based on the assumption that they would lose all the income they were receiving from students under such contracts. This is of course an unfounded assumption since there is no reason to believe that this income would be lost if the students were released from the long-term contracts or if they had not signed them in the first place.

Other witnesses called by respondents failed to give a plausible explanation of why it is necessary to the successful operation of a dance studio for the student to be *obligated* to take hundreds of hours of dancing instruction. The principal advantage to the studio may well be that the student who has executed a long-term contract is less likely to drop out, even though he may desire to do so, than one who has not so obligated himself. Understandably, respondents do not make this argument. . . .

The appeals of respondents and counsel supporting the complaint are denied. The hearing examiner's initial decision is adopted as the decision of the Commission. An appropriate order will be entered.

When the FTC investigates a troublesome area and decides that §5 has been violated, it can take a number of actions. If the violator agrees to abandon the offending practice, a voluntary compliance affidavit is signed. If the alleged violator is not so cooperative, a complaint is filed, with the matter to be heard by an administrative law judge (ALJ). If the matter is settled, a consent order is entered. If not, the matter proceeds to trial before the ALJ, using the procedures specified at 16 C.F.R. §§1.1-4.2 (the FTC is not generally governed by the Administrative Procedures Act). If the ALJ decides a violation has occurred, a cease and desist order is entered.

Appeal from the decision of the ALJ is to the five-person Federal Trade Commission itself, and from the FTC's decision to the circuit court in which the act occurred or where the respondent resides.

The penalty for violation of a voluntary compliance affidavit, a consent order, or a cease and desist order of the ALJ is $10,000 per violation.

Though the original thrust of §5 was the prosecution of antitrust policies affecting interstate commerce, the FTC was quick to use its powers to regulate a broad spectrum of business behavior, see Millstein, The Federal Trade Commission and False Advertising, 64 Colum. L. Rev. 439 (1964). In the field of advertising, for example, the FTC has promulgated complex rules and interpretive guides designed to make sure that advertising is not false and misleading. (A "guide" does not have the force of law, but is, as the name suggests, a mere index to the criteria the FTC staff will use in deciding whether to assess a violation.) The word "free" is given FTC "guide" treatment so that it is judged by what the public thinks the word means: free, 16 C.F.R. §251. The FTC has frequently required advertisers to prove to the satisfaction of the Commission that its advertised statements about its product are true (this is called "ad substantiation"). If the FTC decides that prior advertising has been deceptive, it may order offenders to engage in "corrective advertising" ("We lied to you in our prior ads. Our product will not, as we suggested, cure the common cold."). In 1999, for example, the FTC ordered the manufacturer of Doan's Pills to stop advertising that its product was more effective than other brands for the relief of back pain, and ordered corrective advertising in all its advertising until it had expended $8 million, stating therein: "Although Doan's is an effective pain reliever, there is no evidence that Doan's is more effective than other pain relievers for back pain." In recent years, the FTC has been policing consumer fraud on the internet. See, e.g., F.T.C. v. Trustsoft, Inc., 2005 WL 1523915 (S.D. Tex. 2005) (court ordered the freezing of the assets of a company that was selling a phony spyware removal product).

Perhaps more important for attorneys (both for consumers and the regulated businesses), the FTC has promulgated a host of rules and regulations (having the force of law since they interpret §5 of the FTC Act) affecting many areas of commerce. To solve the next Problem, use the FTC regulation that follows it.

PROBLEM 7

When her husband was killed in a tragic automobile accident, Mrs. Shoe was so devastated that she was barely able to function. Her husband's body was taken to the Rest In Price Funeral Home, where it was embalmed, placed in a very expensive casket, displayed for viewing, taken to the cemetery, and buried in an elaborate ceremony. Mrs. Shoe was even more devastated when she received a bill for *$32,000!* She calls you, her attorney-cousin, and asks if she has to pay this outrageous amount. You ask a few questions and she tells you that she never requested an embalming (which is not required by state law), nor did she receive any price quotations. The bill includes the cost of an "outer burial container" ($4,000), which means that the casket itself was placed in another container prior to burial at the cemetery. What do you advise?

F.T.C. REGULATION OF FUNERAL INDUSTRY PRACTICES
16 C.F.R. Part 453

§453.1 Definitions.

(a) Alternative container. An "alternative container" is an unfinished wood box or other non-metal receptacle or enclosure, without ornamentation or a fixed interior lining, which is designed for the encasement of human remains and which is made of fiberboard, pressed-wood, composition materials (with or without an outside covering) or like materials.

(b) Cash advance item. A "cash advance item" is any item of service or merchandise described to a purchaser as a "cash advance," "accommodation," "cash disbursement," or similar term. A cash advance item is also any item obtained from a third party and paid for by the funeral provider on

the purchaser's behalf. Cash advance items may include, but are not limited to: cemetery or crematory services; pallbearers; public transportation; clergy honoraria; flowers; musicians or singers; nurses; obituary notices; gratuities and death certificates.

(c) Casket. A "casket" is a rigid container which is designed for the encasement of human remains and which is usually constructed of wood, metal, fiberglass, plastic, or like material, and ornamented and lined with fabric.

(d) Commission. "Commission" refers to the Federal Trade Commission.

(e) Cremation. "Cremation" is a heating process which incinerates human remains.

(f) Crematory. A "crematory" is any person, partnership or corporation that performs cremation and sells funeral goods.

(g) Direct cremation. A "direct cremation" is a disposition of human remains by cremation, without formal viewing, visitation, or ceremony with the body present.

(h) Funeral goods. "Funeral goods" are the goods which are sold or offered for sale directly to the public for use in connection with funeral services.

(i) Funeral provider. A "funeral provider" is any person, partnership or corporation that sells or offers to sell funeral goods and funeral services to the public.

(j) Funeral services. "Funeral services" are any services which may be used to:

(1) Care for and prepare deceased human bodies for burial, cremation or other final disposition; and

(2) Arrange, supervise or conduct the funeral ceremony or the final disposition of deceased human bodies.

(k) Immediate burial. An "immediate burial" is a disposition of human remains by burial, without formal viewing, visitation, or ceremony with the body present, except for a graveside service.

(l) Memorial service. A "memorial service" is a ceremony commemorating the deceased without the body present.

(m) Funeral ceremony. A "funeral ceremony" is a service commemorating the deceased with the body present.

(n) Outer burial container. An "outer burial container" is any container which is designed for placement in the grave around the casket including, but not limited to, containers commonly known as burial vaults, grave boxes, and grave liners.

(o) Person. A "person" is any individual, partnership, corporation, association, government or governmental subdivision or agency, or other entity.

(p) Services of funeral director and staff. The "services of funeral director and staff" are the basic services, not to be included in prices of other categories in §453.2(b)(4), that are furnished by a funeral provider in arranging any funeral, such as conducting the arrangements conference, planning the funeral, obtaining necessary permits, and placing obituary notices.

§453.2 Price Disclosures

(a) Unfair or deceptive acts or practices. In selling or offering to sell funeral goods or funeral services to the public, it is an unfair or deceptive act or practice for a funeral provider to fail to furnish accurate price information disclosing the cost to the purchaser for each of the specific funeral goods and funeral services used in connection with the disposition of deceased human bodies, including at least the price of embalming, transportation of remains, use of facilities, caskets, outer burial containers, immediate burials, or direct cremations, to persons inquiring about the purchase of funerals. Any funeral provider who complies with the preventive requirements in paragraph (b) of this section is not engaged in the unfair or deceptive acts or practices defined here.

(b) Preventive requirements. To prevent these unfair or deceptive acts or practices, as well as the unfair or deceptive acts or practices defined in §453.4(b)(1), funeral providers must:

(1) *Telephone price disclosure.* Tell persons who ask by telephone about the funeral provider's offerings or prices any accurate information from the price lists described in paragraphs (b)(2) through (4) of this section and any other readily available information that reasonably answers the question.

(2) *Casket price list.*

(i) Give a printed or typewritten price list to people who inquire in person about the offerings or prices of caskets or alternative containers. The funeral provider must offer the list upon beginning discussion of, but in any event before showing caskets. The list must contain at least the retail prices of all caskets and alternative containers offered which do not require special ordering, enough information to identify each, and the effective date for the price list. In lieu of a written list, other formats, such as notebooks, brochures, or charts may be used if they contain the same information as would the printed or typewritten list, and display it in a clear and conspicuous manner.

Provided, however, that funeral providers do not have to make a casket price list available if the funeral providers place on the general price list, specified in paragraph (b)(4) of this section, the information required by this paragraph.

(ii) Place on the list, however produced, the name of the funeral provider's place of business and a caption describing the list as a "casket price list."

(3) Outer burial container price list.

(i) Give a printed or typewritten price list to persons who inquire in person about outer burial container offerings or prices. The funeral provider must offer the list upon beginning discussion of, but in any event before showing the containers. The list must contain at least the retail prices of all outer burial containers offered which do not require special ordering, enough information to identify each container, and the effective date for the prices listed. In lieu of a written list, the funeral provider may use other formats, such as notebooks, brochures, or charts, if they contain the same information as the printed or typewritten list, and display it in a clear and conspicuous manner. Provided, however, that funeral providers do not have to make an outer burial container price list available if the funeral providers place on the general price list, specified in paragraph (b)(4) of this section, the information required by this paragraph.

(ii) Place on the list, however produced, the name of the funeral provider's place of business and a caption describing the list as an "outer burial container price list."

(4) *General price list.*

(i)(A) Give a printed or typewritten price list for retention to persons who inquire in person about the funeral goods, funeral services or prices of funeral goods or services offered by the funeral provider. The funeral provider must give the list upon beginning discussion of any of the following:

(1) The prices of funeral goods or funeral services;

(2) The overall type of funeral service or disposition; or

(3) Specific funeral goods or funeral services offered by the funeral provider.

(B) The requirement in paragraph (b)(4)(i)(A) of this section applies whether the discussion takes place in the funeral home or elsewhere. Provided, however, that when the deceased is removed for transportation to the funeral home, an in-person request at that time for authorization to embalm, required by §453.5(a)(2), does not, by itself, trigger the requirement to offer the general price list if the provider in seeking prior embalming approval discloses that embalming is not required by law except in certain special cases, if any. Any other discussion during that time about prices or the selection of funeral goods or services triggers the requirement under paragraph (b)(4)(i)(A) of this section to give consumers a general price list.

(C) The list required in paragraph (b)(4)(i)(A) of this section must contain at least the following information:

(1) The name, address, and telephone number of the funeral provider's place of business;

(2) A caption describing the list as a "general price list"; and

(3) The effective date for the price list;

(ii) Include on the price list, in any order, the retail prices (expressed either as the flat fee, or as the price per hour, mile or other unit of computation) and the other information specified below for at least each of the following items, if offered for sale:

(A) Forwarding of remains to another funeral home, together with a list of the services provided for any quoted price;

(B) Receiving remains from another funeral home, together with a list of the services provided for any quoted price;

(C) The price range for the direct cremations offered by the funeral provider, together with:

(1) A separate price for a direct cremation where the purchaser provides the container;

(2) Separate prices for each direct cremation offered including an alternative container; and

(3) A description of the services and container (where applicable), included in each price;

(D) The price range for the immediate burials offered by the funeral provider, together with:

(1) A separate price for an immediate burial where the purchaser provides the casket;

(2) Separate prices for each immediate burial offered including a casket or alternative container; and

(3) A description of the services and container (where applicable) included in that price;

(E) Transfer of remains to funeral home;

(F) Embalming;

(G) Other preparation of the body;

(H) Use of facilities and staff for viewing;

(I) Use of facilities and staff for funeral ceremony;

(J) Use of facilities and staff for memorial service;

(K) Use of equipment and staff for graveside service;

(L) Hearse; and

(M) Limousine.

(iii) Include on the price list, in any order, the following information:

(A) Either of the following:

(1) The price range for the caskets offered by the funeral provider, together with the statement: "A complete price list will be provided at the funeral home."; or

(2) The prices of individual caskets, disclosed in the manner specified by paragraph (b)(2)(i) of this section; and

(B) Either of the following:

(1) The price range for the outer burial containers offered by the funeral provider, together with the statement: "A complete price list will be provided at the funeral home."; or

(2) The prices of individual outer burial containers, disclosed in the manner specified by paragraph (b)(3)(i) of this section; and

(C) Either of the following:

(1) The price for the basic services of funeral director and staff, together with a list of the principal basic services provided for any quoted price and, if the charge cannot be declined by the purchaser, the statement: "This fee for our basic services will be added to the total cost of the funeral arrangements you select. (This fee is already included in our charges for direct cremations, immediate burials, and forwarding or receiving remains.)". If the charge cannot be declined by the purchaser, the quoted price shall include all charges for the recovery of unallocated funeral provider overhead, and funeral providers may include in the required disclosure the phrase "and overhead" after the word "services"; or

(2) The following statement: "Please note that a fee of (specify dollar amount) for the use of our basic services is included in the price of our caskets. This same fee shall be added to the total cost of your funeral arrangements if you provide the casket. Our services include (specify)." The fee shall include all charges for the recovery of unallocated funeral provider overhead, and funeral providers may include in the required disclosure the phrase "and overhead" after the word "services." The statement must be placed on the general price list together with the casket price range, required by paragraph (b)(4)(iii)(A)(1) of

this section, or together with the prices of individual caskets, required by (b)(4)(iii)(A)(2) of this section.

(iv) The services fee permitted by §453.2(b)(4)(iii)(C)(1) or (C)(2) is the only funeral provider fee for services, facilities or unallocated overhead permitted by this part to be non-declinable, unless otherwise required by law.

(5) *Statement of funeral goods and services selected.*

(i) Give an itemized written statement for retention to each person who arranges a funeral or other disposition of human remains, at the conclusion of the discussion of arrangements. The statement must list at least the following information:

(A) The funeral goods and funeral services selected by that person and the prices to be paid for each of them;

(B) Specifically itemized cash advance items. (These prices must be given to the extent then known or reasonably ascertainable. If the prices are not known or reasonably ascertainable, a good faith estimate shall be given and a written statement of the actual charges shall be provided before the final bill is paid.); and

(C) The total cost of the goods and services selected.

(ii) The information required by this paragraph (b)(5) may be included on any contract, statement, or other document which the funeral provider would otherwise provide at the conclusion of discussion of arrangements.

(6) *Other pricing methods.* Funeral providers may give persons any other price information, in any other format, in addition to that required by §453.2(b)(2), (3), and (4) so long as the statement required by §453.2(b)(5) is given when required by the rule.

§453.3 Misrepresentations

(a) Embalming provisions.

(1) Deceptive acts or practices. In selling or offering to sell funeral goods or funeral services to the public, it is a deceptive act or practice for a funeral provider to:

(i) Represent that state or local law requires that a deceased person be embalmed when such is not the case;

(ii) Fail to disclose that embalming is not required by law except in certain special cases, if any.

(2) Preventive requirements. To prevent these deceptive acts or practices, as well as the unfair or deceptive acts or practices defined in §§453.4(b)(1) and 453.5(2), funeral providers must:

(i) Not represent that a deceased person is required to be embalmed for:

(A) Direct cremation;

(B) Immediate burial; or

(C) A closed casket funeral without viewing or visitation when refrigeration is available and when state or local law does not require embalming; and

(ii) Place the following disclosure on the general price list, required by §453.2(b)(4), in immediate conjunction with the price shown for embalming: "Except in certain special cases, embalming is not required by law. Embalming may be necessary, however, if you select certain funeral arrangements, such as a funeral with viewing. If you do not want embalming, you usually have the right to choose an arrangement that does not require you to pay for it, such as direct cremation or immediate burial." The phrase "except in certain special cases" need not be included in this disclosure if state or local law in the area(s) where the provider does business does not require embalming under any circumstances.

(b) Casket for cremation provisions.

(1) Deceptive acts or practices. In selling or offering to sell funeral goods or funeral services to the public, it is a deceptive act or practice for a funeral provider to:

(i) Represent that state or local law requires a casket for direct cremations;

(ii) Represent that a casket (other than an unfinished wood box) is required for direct cremations.

(2) Preventive requirements. To prevent these deceptive acts or practices, as well as the unfair or deceptive acts or practices defined in §453.4(a)(1), funeral providers must place the following disclosure in immediate conjunction with the price range shown for direct cremations: "If you want to arrange a direct cremation, you can use an alternative container. Alternative containers encase the body and can be made of materials like fiberboard or composition materials (with or without an outside covering). The containers we provide are (specify containers)." This disclosure only has to be placed on the general price list if the funeral provider arranges direct cremations.

(c) Outer burial container provisions.

(1) Deceptive acts or practices. In selling or offering to sell funeral goods and funeral services to the public, it is a deceptive act or practice for a funeral provider to:

(i) Represent that state or local laws or regulations, or particular cemeteries, require outer burial containers when such is not the case;

(ii) Fail to disclose to persons arranging funerals that state law does not require the purchase of an outer burial container.

(2) Preventive requirement. To prevent these deceptive acts or practices, funeral providers must place the following disclosure on the outer burial container price list, required by §453.2(b)(3)(i), or, if the prices of outer burial containers are listed on the general price list, required by §453.2(b)(4), in immediate conjunction with those prices: "In most areas of the country, state or local law does not require that you buy a container to surround the casket in the grave. However, many cemeteries require that you have such a container so that the grave will not sink in. Either a grave liner or a burial vault will satisfy these requirements." The phrase "in most areas of the country" need not be included in this disclosure if state or local law in the area(s) where the provider does business does not require a container to surround the casket in the grave.

(d) General provisions on legal and cemetery requirements.

(1) Deceptive acts or practices. In selling or offering to sell funeral goods or funeral services to the public, it is a deceptive act or practice for funeral providers to represent that federal, state, or local laws, or particular cemeteries or crematories, require the purchase of any funeral goods or funeral services when such is not the case.

(2) Preventive requirements. To prevent these deceptive acts or practices, as well as the deceptive acts or practices identified in §§453.3(a)(1), 453.3(b)(1), and 453.3(c)(1), funeral providers must identify and briefly describe in writing on the statement of funeral goods and services selected (required by §453.2(b)(5)) any legal, cemetery, or crematory requirement which the funeral provider represents to persons as compelling the purchase of funeral goods or funeral services for the funeral which that person is arranging.

(e) Provisions on preservative and protective value claims. In selling or offering to sell funeral goods or funeral services to the public, it is a deceptive act or practice for a funeral provider to:

(1) Represent that funeral goods or funeral services will delay the natural decomposition of human remains for a long-term or indefinite time;

(2) Represent that funeral goods have protective features or will protect the body from gravesite substances, when such is not the case.

(f) Cash advance provisions.

(1) Deceptive acts or practices. In selling or offering to sell funeral goods or funeral services to the public, it is a deceptive act or practice for a funeral provider to:

(i) Represent that the price charged for a cash advance item is the same as the cost to the funeral provider for the item when such is not the case;

(ii) Fail to disclose to persons arranging funerals that the price being charged for a cash advance item is not the same as the cost to the funeral provider for the item when such is the case.

(2) Preventive requirements. To prevent these deceptive acts or practices, funeral providers must place the following sentence in the itemized statement of funeral goods and services selected, in immediate conjunction with the list of itemized cash advance items required by §453.2(b)(5)(i)(B): "We charge you for our services in obtaining: (specify cash advance items)," if the funeral provider makes a charge upon, or receives and retains a rebate, commission or trade or volume discount upon a cash advance item.

§453.4 Required purchase of funeral goods or funeral services

(a) Casket for cremation provisions.

(1) Unfair or deceptive acts or practices. In selling or offering to sell funeral goods or funeral services to the public, it is an unfair or deceptive act or practice for a funeral provider, or a crematory, to require that a casket be purchased for direct cremation.

(2) Preventive requirement. To prevent this unfair or deceptive act or practice, funeral providers must make an alternative container available for direct cremations, if they arrange direct cremations.

(b) Other required purchases of funeral goods or funeral services.
(1) Unfair or deceptive acts or practices. In selling or offering to sell funeral goods or funeral services, it is an unfair or deceptive act or practice for a funeral provider to:

(i) Condition the furnishing of any funeral good or funeral service to a person arranging a funeral upon the purchase of any other funeral good or funeral service, except as required by law or as otherwise permitted by this part;

(ii) Charge any fee as a condition to furnishing any funeral goods or funeral services to a person arranging a funeral, other than the fees for: (1) Services of funeral director and staff, permitted by §453.2(b)(4)(iii)(C); (2) other funeral services and funeral goods selected by the purchaser; and (3) other funeral goods or services required to be purchased, as explained on the itemized statement in accordance with §453.3(d)(2).

(2) Preventive requirements.

(i) To prevent these unfair or deceptive acts or practices, funeral providers must:

(A) Place the following disclosure in the general price list, immediately above the prices required by §453.2(b)(4)(ii) and (iii): "The goods and services shown below are those we can provide to our customers. You may choose only the items you desire. If legal or other requirements mean you must buy any items you did not specifically ask for, we will explain the reason in writing on the statement we provide describing the funeral goods and services you selected." Provided, however, that if the charge for "services of funeral director and staff" cannot be declined by the purchaser, the statement shall include the sentence: "However, any funeral arrangements you select will include a charge for our basic services" between the second and third sentences of the statement specified above herein. The statement may include the phrase "and overhead" after the word "services" if the fee includes a charge for the recovery of unallocated funeral provider overhead;

(B) Place the following disclosure in the statement of funeral goods and services selected, required by §453.2(b)(5)(i): "Charges are only for those items that you selected or that are required. If we are required by law or by a cemetery or crematory to use any items, we will explain the reasons in writing below."

(ii) A funeral provider shall not violate this section by failing to comply with a request for a combination of goods or services which would be impossible, impractical, or excessively burdensome to provide.

§453.5 Services provided without prior approval

(a) Unfair or deceptive acts or practices.   In selling or offering to sell funeral goods or funeral services to the public, it is an unfair or deceptive act or practice for any provider to embalm a deceased human body for a fee unless:

(1) State or local law or regulation requires embalming in the particular circumstances regardless of any funeral choice which the family might make; or

(2) Prior approval for embalming (expressly so described) has been obtained from a family member or other authorized person; or

(3) The funeral provider is unable to contact a family member or other authorized person after exercising due diligence, has no reason to believe the family does not want embalming performed, and obtains subsequent approval for embalming already performed (expressly so described). In

seeking approval, the funeral provider must disclose that a fee will be charged if the family selects a funeral which requires embalming, such as a funeral with viewing, and that no fee will be charged if the family selects a service which does not require embalming, such as direct cremation or immediate burial.

(b) Preventive requirement. To prevent these unfair or deceptive acts or practices, funeral providers must include on the itemized statement of funeral goods and services selected, required by §453.2(b)(5), the statement: "If you selected a funeral that may require embalming, such as a funeral with viewing, you may have to pay for embalming. You do not have to pay for embalming you did not approve if you selected arrangements such as a direct cremation or immediate burial. If we charged for embalming, we will explain why below."

§453.6 Retention of documents

To prevent the unfair or deceptive acts or practices specified in §453.2 and §453.3 of this rule, funeral providers must retain and make available for inspection by Commission officials true and accurate copies of the price lists specified in §§453.2(b)(2) through (4), as applicable, for at least one year after the date of their last distribution to customers, and a copy of each statement of funeral goods and services selected, as required by §453.2(b)(5), for at least one year from the date of the arrangements conference.

§453.7 Comprehension of disclosures

To prevent the unfair or deceptive acts or practices specified in §453.2 through §453.5, funeral providers must make all disclosures required by those sections in a clear and conspicuous manner. Providers shall not include in the casket, outer burial container, and general price lists, required by §§453.2(b)(2)-(4), any statement or information that alters or contradicts the information required by this Part to be included in those lists.

§453.8 Declaration of intent

(a) Except as otherwise provided in §453.2(a), it is a violation of this rule to engage in any unfair or deceptive acts or practices specified in this rule, or to fail to comply with any of the preventive requirements specified in this rule;

(b) The provisions of this rule are separate and severable from one another. If any provision is determined to be invalid, it is the Commission's intention that the remaining provisions shall continue in effect.

(c) This rule shall not apply to the business of insurance or to acts in the conduct thereof.

§453.9 State exemptions

If, upon application to the Commission by an appropriate state agency, the Commission determines that:

(a) There is a state requirement in effect which applies to any transaction to which this rule applies; and

(b) That state requirement affords an overall level of protection to consumers which is as great as, or greater than, the protection afforded by this rule;

then the Commission's rule will not be in effect in that state to the extent specified by the Commission in its determination, for as long as the State administers and enforces effectively the state requirement.

In 1999, the FTC began reviewing the Funeral Rule to decide whether to expand it to include cemeteries, mortuaries, monument dealers, and casket sellers.

In its only pro-consumer activity of the 1980s, the Federal Trade Commission promulgated its Credit Practices Rule, 16 C.F.R. §444 (effective March 1, 1985).[6]

Use the rule (which is in your statute book) to resolve the following Problem.

PROBLEM 8

Natty Bumpo went to the Cooper Loan Company to get a loan so that he could finance a hunting trip. The company offered him a $2,200 loan if he would sign a promissory note with the following provisions:

a. If he failed to pay the loan as scheduled, and the Cooper Loan Company was forced to file suit against him, he (and any surety signing the note) hereby authorized the Cooper Loan Company to

---

6. As it is required to do by law, the Federal Reserve Board then adopted a similar regulation applicable to banks (the FTC has no jurisdiction over banks), 12 C.F.R. §227.11 (effective January 1, 1986).

hire an attorney for him, who would confess that he owed the judgment requested.

b. He hereby waived the right to claim any exemption state law would otherwise give him from creditor process.

c. He hereby gave the Cooper Loan Company a security interest in his champion cocker spaniel dog, his new living room suite, his snowmobile, his collection of Whistler watercolors, and the television set he had bought for his bedroom.

d. He hereby assigned to Cooper Loan Company his paychecks as security for any missed payments.

The company also required him to get a surety who would sign the promissory note, so Natty asked his Uncle Mohawk to do this service for him. The loan officer assured the very nervous uncle that this was all a formality and that the chances were small that the loan company would ever contact Uncle Mohawk again. Thirty seconds before the uncle signed the promissory note, the loan company gave him a sealed envelope containing the notice found in §444.3(c) of the FTC rule. The loan officer explained that the sealed envelope contained some legal papers the uncle might want to read later.

Natty paid the first three installments on time, but the fourth installment was paid four days late. The loan company assessed a $10 late charge against the account. The next month Natty paid the usual amount on time, but the loan company took $10 of this payment and used it to pay the prior month's late charge. This meant that the new payment was now $10 short, so the company assessed a new late charge of $10 because of the underpayment. The company did this for the next four payments that Natty made on time, thereby salting away an extra $10 each month.

When Natty defaulted on the loan, the loan company filed suit against him and Uncle Mohawk in the local trial court, using the authorization in the promissory note to have an attorney appear for the defendants and confess judgment. The loan officer then sent Natty and Uncle Mohawk a letter stating that unless the judgment was immediately paid, the company was going to have the sheriff seize all the collateral and place a garnishment on both Natty's paycheck and Uncle Mohawk's checking account at a nearby bank.

Frantic, Natty and Uncle Mohawk call you, a lawyer friend of theirs. Is there anything you can do? What relief does the FTC Credit Practices Rule provide?

C. State Statutes

Your course in Contracts will likely have spent some time discussing the issue of unconscionability, reflected in §2-302 of the Uniform Commercial Code and in similar statutes, so this course will not repeat those lessons other than to remind you that unconscionability is a powerful weapon to use when consumers have been victimized by rapacious practices. Instead, we turn to other state statutes that may give relief.

Since there is typically no private civil remedy for violations of §5 of the FTCA, consumers injured by deceptive practices must turn to state law for relief. Most states have enacted statutes forbidding deceptive selling practices, modeling some on the language of §5 of the FTCA. Many of these statutes specifically provide that violations of the FTCA are prima facie violations of the state statute.[7]

The model statute on point is the Uniform Consumer Sales Practices Act. Use it (or your state statute, if available) to resolve the following Problems.

PROBLEM 9

Happy Harold, the appliance dealer, was forever holding "sales" for his products, so much so that they were almost never sold for the routine price that was put on tags attached to the items. Most of his sales were for mundane reasons, such as "Fourth of July" or "Christmas," but occasionally he would pretend to have sales for allegedly pressing reasons, such as "Liquidation Sale," "Lost Our Lease—Everything Must Go," and "Fire Sale." Is there any harm in this practice? If so, what? If a customer purchases an item at such a sale and then discovers, for example, that Happy Harold did not in fact lose his lease, has a deceptive or unconscionable practice occurred? What remedies are available to the consumer who cannot prove any actual damages from the alleged deception?

---

7. Some consumer sales practices acts (including those in Maryland, North Carolina, and Ohio) specifically exempt lawyers from being covered, but other state versions have no such exemption and have been interpreted to cover lawyers and their consumer clients. See a state-by-state discussion in Oberst, Shysters, Sharks, and Ambulance Chasers Beware: Attorney Liability Under CUTPA, 11 Bridgeport L. Rev. 97 (1990).

PROBLEM 10

Happy Harold's Appliance Store ran an advertisement in the newspaper touting the virtues of the "Uneeda Dishwasher," which was regularly sold at $250, but was "a mere $150 this week only!" Harold instructed his sales force to disparage the Uneeda Dishwasher if customers came in asking for it, telling them that studies by consumer groups showed that it was subject to sudden unexplained fires. The customers were then to be shown pricier dishwashers, guaranteed to be safe from fire hazard. If the customers persisted in examining the Uneeda, the salespersons were instructed to say that the store was sold out of them except for the one demonstrator on the floor. (In fact, the floor sample was the only Uneeda Dishwasher in the whole inventory.) May a consumer who buys one of the more expensive dishwashers prevail in a lawsuit charging Happy Harold with a deceptive practice? For the FTC Guides on Bait Advertising, see 16 C.F.R. §238.

CARLILL v. CARBOLIC SMOKE BALL COMPANY[8]
Queen's Bench, 1892
2 Q.B. 484, *aff'd*, 1 Q.B. 256 (Court of Appeals, 1893)

The defendants, who are the proprietors and vendors of a medical preparation called "The Carbolic Smoke Ball," inserted in the Pall Mall Gazette of November 13, 1891, the following advertisement: "100*l.* reward will be paid by the Carbolic Smoke Ball Company to any person who contracts the increasing epidemic influenza, colds, or any disease caused by taking cold, after having used the ball three times daily for two weeks, according to the printed directions supplied with each ball. 1000*l.* is deposited with the Alliance Bank, Regent Street, shewing our sincerity in the matter.

"During the last epidemic of influenza many thousand carbolic smoke balls were sold as preventives against this disease, and in no ascertained case was the disease contracted by those using the carbolic smoke ball.

"One carbolic smoke ball will last a family several months, making it the cheapest remedy in the world at the price, 10*s.* post free. The ball can be refilled at a cost of 5*s.* Address:

"Carbolic Smoke Ball Company,

"27, Princes Street, Hanover Square, London, W."

---

8. Footnotes in this case have been renumbered for clarity.

The plaintiff, a lady, having read that advertisement, on the faith of it bought one of the defendants' carbolic smoke balls, and used it as directed three times a day, from November 20 till January 17, 1892, when she was attacked by influenza. She thereupon brought this action against the defendants to recover the 100*l.* promised in their advertisement.

The defendants pleaded that there was no contract between the plaintiff and the defendants that the defendants should pay 100*l.* in the event which happened; and that if there was such a contract it was void, either under 8 & 9 Vict. c.109, as being a contract by way of wagering, or under 14 Geo. 3, c.48, s.2, as being a contract of insurance not made in accordance with the provisions of that section, or as being contrary to public policy. The action came on for trial before Hawkins, J., and a jury; but the facts not being in dispute, the learned judge reserved the case for further consideration on the points of law raised in the defence.

Asquith, Q.C. (*Loehnis*, with him), for the defendants. First, there was no contract between the parties. The advertisement was a mere representation of what the advertisers intended to do in a certain event. The defendants did not by issuing it mean to impose upon themselves any obligation enforceable by law. That this was so is shewn by the wide terms in which it is couched, for the reward is offered to any one who contracts influenza "after having used the ball"; but they could not have meant to bind themselves to pay the money to persons who contracted the complaint years after they had ceased to use the ball. . . .

Secondly, if there was a contract it was void, as being a contract by way of wagering, within the meaning of 8 & 9 Vict. c.109. A wagering contract is one the liability to perform which depends on events beyond the control of the parties. This case is similar to Brogden v. Marriott,[9] where an agreement by which the defendant sold the plaintiff a horse, on the terms that the price should be 200*l.* if within one month after the date of the agreement it trotted eighteen miles in an hour, but one shilling if it failed to do so, was held to be a wager, and void as such, under 9 Anne, c. 14. So, too, in Rourke v. Short,[10] a contract for the sale and purchase of goods at a price to be regulated by ascertaining a past fact unknown to the parties at the time of the contract was held to be void as a wager. In Taylor v. Smetten,[11] where the defendant sold at a fixed price packets containing a pound of tea and a coupon entitling the purchaser to a prize the amount of which was not

---

9. 3 Bing. N.C. 88.
10. 5 E. & B. 904.
11. 11 Q.B.D. 207.

determined till after the sale, it was held that the transaction was a gaming transaction, and an offence against the Lottery Act.

Thirdly, if there was a contract, and it was not a wagering contract, then it was a contract by way of insurance, and void under s.2 of 14 Geo. 3, c.48, which provides that, "It shall not be lawful to make any policy or policies on the life or lives of any person or persons, or other event or events, without inserting in such policy or policies the person or persons, name or names, interested therein, or for whose use, benefit, or on whose account such policy is so made or underwrote."

W. Graham, (*Murphy, Q.C.*, and *Bonner*, with him), for the plaintiff. The transaction between the parties amounted to a contract of warranty of prevention of disease with liquidated damages in the event of breach. The advertisement which was issued by the defendants was an offer by them to enter into such a contract, which offer was accepted and converted into a contract upon any person performing the conditions of the advertisement. . . .

July 4. HAWKINS, J., delivered the following written judgment: The facts not being in dispute, I was requested to hear the legal objections discussed on further consideration, and to enter the verdict and judgment as I thought right. I have done so, and I proceed now to deliver my judgment.

Four questions require consideration in determining this case.

1st. Was there a contract of any kind between the parties to this action?

2nd. Was such contract, if any, wholly or partly in writing so as to require a stamp?

3rd. Was the contract a wagering contract?

4th. Was it a contract of insurance affected by statute, 14 Geo. 3, c.48, s.2.

As regards the first question, I am of opinion that the offer or proposal in the advertisement, coupled with the performance by the plaintiff of the condition, created a contract on the part of the defendants to pay the 100*l.* upon the happening of the event mentioned in the proposal. It seems to me that the contract may be thus described. In consideration that the plaintiff would use the carbolic smoke ball three times daily for two weeks according to printed directions supplied with the ball, the defendants would pay to her 100*l.* if after having so used the ball she contracted the epidemic known as influenza.

The advertisement inserted in the Pall Mall Gazette in large type was undoubtedly so inserted in the hope that it would be read by all who read that journal, and the announcement that 1000*l.* had been deposited with the Alliance Bank could only have been inserted with the object of leading those who read it to believe that the defendants were serious in their proposal, and would fulfil their promise in the event mentioned; their own words, "*shewing our sincerity* in the matter," state as much. It may be that,

CARBOLIC SMOKE BALL

WILL POSITIVELY CURE

COUGHS Cured in 1 week	**CATARRH** Cured in 1 to 3 months.	**HOARSENESS** Cured in 12 hours.	**THROAT DEAFNESS** Cured in 1 to 3 months.	**INFLUENZA** Cured in 24 hours.	**CROUP** Relieved in 5 minutes.
COLD IN THE HEAD Cured in 12 hours.	**ASTHMA** Relieved in 10 minutes.	**LOSS OF VOICE** Fully restored.	**SNORING** Cured in 1 week.	**HAY FEVER** Cured in every case.	**WHOOPING COUGH** Relieved the first application.
COLD ON THE CHEST Cured in 12 hours.	**BRONCHITIS** Cured in every case.	**SORE THROAT** Cured in 12 hours.	**SORE EYES** Cured in 2 weeks.	**HEADACHE** Cured in 10 minutes.	**NEURALGIA** Cured in 10 minutes.

As all the Diseases mentioned above proceed from one cause, they can be Cured by this Remedy.

£100 REWARD

WILL BE PAID BY THE
CARBOLIC SMOKE BALL CO.

to any Person who contracts the increasing Epidemic,

INFLUENZA,

Colds, or any Diseases caused by taking Cold, after having used the **CARBOLIC SMOKE BALL** according to the printed directions supplied with each Ball.

£1000 IS DEPOSITED

with the ALLIANCE BANK, Regent Street, shewing our sincerity in the matter.

During the last epidemic of **INFLUENZA** many thousand **CARBOLIC SMOKE BALLS** were sold as preventives against this disease, and in no ascertained case was the disease contracted by those using the **CARBOLIC SMOKE BALL**.

Free Trials at our Consulting Rooms.
For Inhalation Only.

Free Trials at our Consulting Rooms.
For Inhalation Only.

THE CARBOLIC SMOKE BALL,

TESTIMONIALS.

The DUKE OF PORTLAND writes: "I am much obliged for the Carbolic Smoke Ball which you have sent me, and which I find most efficacious."

SIR FREDERICK MILNER, Bart., M.P., writes from Kew, March 7, 1890: "Lady Milner and my children have derived much benefit from the Carbolic Smoke Ball."

Lady MOSTYN writes from Carshalton, Cory Caravel, Torquay, Jan. 10, 1890: "Lady Mostyn believes the Carbolic Smoke Ball to be a certain check and a cure for a cold, and will have great pleasure in recommending it to her friends. Lady Mostyn hopes the Carbolic Smoke Ball will have all the success its merits deserve."

Lady ERSKINE writes from Sproxton Hall, Northampton, Jan. 1, 1890: "Lady Erskine is pleased to say that the Carbolic Smoke Ball has given every satisfaction; she considers it a very good invention."

Mrs. GLADSTONE writes: "She finds the Carbolic Smoke Ball has done her a great deal of good."

Madame ADELINA PATTI writes: "Madame Patti has found the Carbolic Smoke Ball very beneficial, and the only thing that would enable her to rest well at night when having a severe cold."

AS PRESCRIBED BY
SIR MORELL MACKENZIE, M.D.

HAS BEEN SUPPLIED TO

H.I.M. THE GERMAN EMPRESS.

H.R.H. The Duke of Edinburgh, K.G.
H.R.H. The Duke of Connaught, K.G.
The Duke of Fife, K.T.
The Marquis of Salisbury, K.G.
The Duke of Argyll, K.T.
The Duke of Westminster, K.G.
The Duke of Richmond and Gordon, K.G.
The Duke of Manchester.
The Duke of Newcastle.
The Duke of Norfolk.
The Duke of Rutland, K.G.
The Duke of Wellington.
The Marquis of Ripon, K.G.
The Earl of Derby, K.G.
Earl Spencer, K.G.
The Lord Chancellor.
The Lord Chief Justice.
Lord Tennyson.

TESTIMONIALS.

The BISHOP OF LONDON writes: "The Carbolic Smoke Ball has benefited me greatly."

The MARCHIONESS DE SAIN writes from Pedworth House, Reading, Jan. 12, 1890: "The Marchioness de Sain has daily used the Smoke Ball since the commencement of the epidemic of Influenza, and has not taken the Influenza, although surrounded by those suffering from it."

Dr. J. RUSSELL HARRIS, M.D., writes from 6, Adam Street, Adelphi, Sept. 24, 1891: "Many obstinate cases of post-nasal catarrh, which have resisted other treatment, have yielded to your Carbolic Smoke Ball."

A. GIBBONS, Esq., Editor of the Lady's Pictorial, writes from 172, Strand, W.C., Feb. 11, 1890: "During a recent sharp attack of the prevailing epidemic I had some of the unpleasant and dangerous catarrh and bronchial symptoms. I attribute this entirely to the use of the Carbolic Smoke Ball."

The Rev. Dr. CHICHESTER A. W. READE, LL.D., D.C.L., writes from Hamstead Downs, Surrey, May 1890: "My duties in a large public institution have brought me daily, during the recent epidemic of influenza, in close contact with the disease. I have been perfectly free from any symptom by having the Smoke Ball always handy. It has also wonderfully improved my voice for speaking and singing."

The Originals of these Testimonials may be seen at our Consulting Rooms, with hundreds of others.

One **CARBOLIC SMOKE BALL** will last a family several months, making it the cheapest remedy in the world at the price—10s. post free.

The **CARBOLIC SMOKE BALL** can be refilled, when empty, at a cost of 5s., post free. Address:

CARBOLIC SMOKE BALL CO., 27, PRINCES ST., HANOVER SQ., LONDON, W.

of the many readers of the advertisement, very few of the sensible ones would have entertained expectations that in the event of the smoke ball failing to act as a preventive against the disease, the defendants had any intention to fulfil their attractive and alluring promise; but it must be remembered that such advertisements do not appeal so much to the wise and thoughtful as to the credulous and weak portions of the community; and if the vendor of an article, whether it be medicine smoke or anything else, with a view to increase its sale or use, thinks fit publicly to promise to all who buy or use it that, to those who shall not find it as surely efficacious as it is represented by him to be he will pay a substantial sum of money, he must not be surprised if occasionally he is held to his promise.

I notice that in the present case the promise is of 100*l. reward*; but the substance of the offer is to pay the named sum as compensation for the failure of the article to produce the guaranteed effect of the two weeks' daily use as directed. Such daily use was sufficient legal consideration to support the promise. . . . [Discussion of the second issue omitted.]

The [next] question is whether the contract I have found to exist is a contract by way of gaming or wagering within the meaning of statute 8 & 9 Vict. c.109, s.18, which renders such contracts null and void, and, therefore, not enforceable by action. I think it is not. It is not easy to define with precision what amounts to a wagering contract, nor the narrow line of demarcation which separates a wagering from an ordinary contract; but, according to my view, a wagering contract is one by which two persons, professing to hold opposite views touching the issue of a future uncertain event, mutually agree that, dependent upon the determination of that event, one shall win from the other, and that other shall pay or hand over to him, a sum of money or other stake; neither of the contracting parties having any other interest in that contract than the sum or stake he will so win or lose, there being no other real consideration for the making of such contract by either of the parties. It is essential to a wagering contract that each party may under it either win or lose, whether he will win or lose being dependent on the issue of the event, and, therefore, remaining uncertain until that issue is known. If either of the parties may win but cannot lose, or may lose but cannot win, it is not a wagering contract.

It is also essential that there should be mutuality in the contract. For instance, if the evidence of the contract is such as to make the intentions of the parties material in the consideration of the question whether it is a wagering one or not, and those intentions are at variance, those of one party being such as if agreed in by the other would make the contract a wagering one, whilst those of the other would prevent it from becoming so, this want of mutuality would destroy the wagering element of the contract and leave it

enforceable by law as an ordinary one: see Grizewood v. Blane;[12] Thacker
v. Hardy;[13] Blaxton v. Pye.[14] No better illustration can be given of a purely
wagering contract than a bet on a horse-race. A. backs Tortoise with B. for
100*l*. to win the Derby. B. lays ten to one against him—that is, 1000 to 100.
How the event will turn out is uncertain until the race is over. Until then,
A. may win 1000*l*. or he may lose 100*l*., B. may win 100*l*. or he may lose
1000*l*.; but each must be a winner or a loser on the event. Under the wager
neither has any interest except in the money he may win or lose by it. True it
is that one or both of the parties may have an interest in the property of the
horse; but that interest is altogether apart from the bet, and each party is in
agreement with the other as to the nature and intention of his engagement. If
any one desires to read more upon the subject of wagers he will find the
subject fully and clearly treated in Mr. Stutfield's able and learned book.
One other matter ought to be mentioned, namely, that in construing a
contract with a view to determining whether it is a wagering one or not, the
Court will receive evidence in order to arrive at the substance of it, and will
not confine its attention to the mere words in which it is expressed, for a
wagering contract may be sometimes concealed under the guise of language
which, on the face of it, if words were only to be considered, might constitute a legally enforceable contract. Such was the case in Brogden v.
Mariott,[15] in which under the guise of a contract for the sale by the defendant to the plaintiff of a horse at a price to depend on the event of a trial
of its speed and staying power, there was concealed a mere bet of the
defendant's horse to 200*l*. that the horse within a month should trot eighteen
miles within an hour. The defendant's horse having failed to accomplish the
task set him, plaintiff claimed the horse at a nominal price of 1*s*. The nature
of this contract was transparent to any person of ordinary intelligence, and
the plaintiff in vain argued that it was a bona fide conditional bargain. The
Court held it to be nothing more nor less than a mere wagering contract
prohibited by the then unrepealed statute 9 Anne, c.14. In that case the
nature of the contract was very clearly to be inferred from the statement of it
in the record. Of course, if in any case it is suggested that a contract good on
the face of it was a mere device to elude the operation of the statute, the
question would be one for a jury to solve: see also Hill v. Fox;[16] Grizewood
v. Blane.[17]

---

12. 11 C.B. 526.
13. 4 Q.B.D. 685.
14. 2 Wils. 309.
15. 3 Bing. N.C. 88.
16. 4 H. & N. 359.
17. 11 C.B. 526.

In the present case an essential element of a wagering contract is absent. The event upon which the defendants promised to pay the 100*l.* depended upon the plaintiff's contracting the epidemic influenza after using the ball; but, on the happening of that event, the plaintiff alone could derive benefit. On the other hand, if that event did not happen, the defendants could gain nothing, for there was no promise on the plaintiff's part to pay or do anything if the ball had the desired effect. When the contract first of all came into existence (i.e., when the plaintiff had performed the consideration for the defendants' promise), in no event could the plaintiff lose anything, nor could the defendants win anything. At the trial it was not even suggested that any evidence could be offered to alter the character of the contract or the facts as deposed to by the plaintiff. I am clearly of opinion that, if those facts established a contract, as I think they did, it was not of a wagering character.

As to the objection that this contract (if any) was one of insurance, and invalid for non-compliance with the statute 14 Geo. 3, c.48, s.2, which enacts that "it shall not be lawful to make any policy or policies on the life or lives of any person, or other event or events, without inserting in such policy or policies the person or persons, name or names, interested therein, or for whose use, benefit, or on whose account such policy is so made or underwrote," it seems to me that the simple answer to that objection is that the section relates only to a policy which is a written document, and cannot apply to a contract like the present, which is created by a written proposal or offer accepted by the fulfilment by the plaintiff of the conditions attached to the offer. I do not feel it necessary to discuss the question whether the contract is one of insurance, which kind of contract Blackburn, J., in Wilson v. Jones,[18] thus describes: "A policy is, properly speaking, a contract to indemnify the insured in respect of some interest which he has against the perils which he contemplates it will be liable to." My present opinion is that it does not amount to such a contract, and certain I am that neither of the parties so intended it.

In the pleadings I find a further defence that the contract was contrary to public policy; but the learned counsel for the defendants was unable to point out to me any grounds for such a contention other than those I have already discussed.

It follows from what I have said that, in my opinion, the plaintiff is entitled to recover the 100*l.* I therefore direct a verdict to be entered for the plaintiff for 100*l.*, and judgment accordingly with costs.

Judgment for the plaintiff.

---

18. Law Rep. 2 Ex. at p. 150.

QUESTIONS

1. Use of the ball resulted in carbolic acid being sprayed up the nose of the user, a very unpleasant experience that caused much sneezing. Given the fact that many people probably used the ball once or twice, disliked it intensely, and stopped using it as directed, how could the company have known that the plaintiff faithfully used the ball as instructed?[19]

2. How do we characterize the amount placed on deposit? Is it a reward? Liquidated damages?

3. The details of this famous case can be found in J. Braun, Advertisements in Court (1965), and Simpson, Quackery and Contract Law: The Case of the Carbolic Smoke Ball, 14 J. Legal Stud. 345 (1985).

QUOTES FOR THE ATTORNEY'S ARSENAL: "PUFFING"

But it was said there was no check on the part of the persons who issued the advertisement, and that it would be an insensate thing to promise £100 to a person who used the smoke ball unless you could check or superintend his manner of using it. The answer to that argument seems to me to be that if a person chooses to make extravagant promises of this kind he probably does so because it pays him to make them, and, if he has made them, the extravagance of the promises is no reason in law why he should not be bound by them.

Lord Justice Bowen in the appellate court opinion, Carlill v. Carbolic Smoke Ball Company, 1 Q.B. 256 (Court of Appeals, 1893).

PROBLEM 11

Pursuant to the state statute on deceptive consumer sales practices, the Attorney General promulgated a rule requiring automobile repair establishments to give car owners the following rights:

a. At the first contact between the parties, the repair shop was to give the consumer an estimate if the cost of repair would be more than $25. This estimate could be given orally or in writing or could be waived in writing.

---

19. The company originally denied Mrs. Carlill any relief for the alleged reason that she had failed to use the ball in their offices, a non-advertised condition to the payment of the reward. This was not seriously argued at the trial level.

b. If the actual repair would exceed the estimate by more than 10 percent, the repair shop could charge no more than 10 percent over the estimate unless the consumer agreed (orally or in writing) to the increased charge.

c. All parts removed from the vehicle had to be returned to the consumer.

On a day when everything else had gone awry, Portia Moot's two-year-old car began emitting smoke, and she had to stop it on the interstate and get out her cell phone. She called Car Hospital, a repair shop near her home, and described the problem. They sent out a tow truck and towed the car to the shop. At the dealership, an employee gave Portia a written estimate of $300 as the cost of repair of her vehicle. When she came to pick it up, they refused to let her have the car unless she paid $450, which she did. This amount included a $35 charge for towing.

A friend of Portia's is an automobile mechanic; he is willing to testify that anyone in the business would have known that the work Portia originally requested would cost at least $400. She is now in your office asking what she can do. Advise her.[20]

PROBLEM 12

Schoolteacher Ralph Rackstraw was losing a lot of his savings making bad decisions in the stock market, so he finally took the advice of a friend and consulted Astrology, Inc., a firm that "read the stars" to give its clients guidance on "all aspects of your life." Astrology, Inc.'s president, John W. Wells, personally took charge of Rackstraw's chart readings and told him that if he followed Wells's advice, "money will pour in." Over a two-year period Rackstraw religiously followed the dictates of the charts as interpreted by Wells, and proceeded to lose every cent of his savings. Disgusted, Rackstraw sued Astrology, Inc. using two theories: fraud and the state deceptive practices statute. Assuming that Rackstraw can produce armies of witnesses who will testify that astrology is superstitious nonsense, and that Wells can produce none who will establish that it has any scientific basis, how should this come out? See Stahl v. Balsara, 587 P.2d 1210 (Haw. 1978).

---

20. For an annotation on point, see Liability of Repairers for Unnecessary Repairs, 23 A.L.R.4th 274.

PELMAN ex rel. PELMAN v. McDONALD'S CORP.[21]
United States Court of Appeals, Second Circuit, 2005
396 F.3d 508

RAKOFF, District Judge.

In this diversity action, plaintiffs Ashley Pelman and Jazlen Bradley, by their respective parents, Roberta Pelman and Isreal Bradley, appeal from the dismissal, pursuant to Rule 12(b)(6), Fed. R. Civ. P., of Counts I-III of their amended complaint. See Pelman v. McDonald's Corp., 2003 WL 22052778 (S.D.N.Y. Sept. 3, 2003), 2003 U.S. Dist. LEXIS 15202 ("*Pelman II*"). Each of these counts purports to allege, on behalf of a putative class of consumers, that defendant McDonald's Corporation violated both §349 and §350 of the New York General Business Law, commonly known as the New York Consumer Protection Act, during the years 1987 through 2002.

Specifically, Count I alleges that the combined effect of McDonald's various promotional representations during this period was to create the false impression that its food products were nutritionally beneficial and part of a healthy lifestyle if consumed daily. Count II alleges that McDonald's failed adequately to disclose that its use of certain additives and the manner of its food processing rendered certain of its foods substantially less healthy than represented. Count III alleges that McDonald's deceptively represented that it would provide nutritional information to its New York customers[22] when in reality such information was not readily available at a significant number of McDonald's outlets in New York visited by the plaintiffs and others. The amended complaint further alleges that as a result of these deceptive practices, plaintiffs, who ate at McDonald's three to five times a week throughout the years in question, were "led to believe[ ] that [McDonald's] foods were healthy and wholesome, not as detrimental to their health as medical and scientific studies have shown, . . . [and] of a beneficial nutritional value," and that they "would not have purchased and/or consumed the Defendant's aforementioned products, in their entire[t]y, or on such frequency but for the aforementioned alleged representations and campaigns." Finally, the amended complaint alleges that, as a result, plaintiffs have developed "obesity, diabetes, coronary heart disease, high blood pressure, elevated cholesterol

---

21. Footnotes in this case have been renumbered for clarity.

22. According to the amended complaint, McDonald's had entered into an agreement in 1987 with the New York State Attorney General to

provide [nutritional] information in easily understood pamphlets or brochures which will be free to all customers so they could take them with them for further study [and] to place signs, including in-store advertising to inform customers who walk in, and drive through information and notice would be placed where drive-through customers could see them.

intake, related cancers, and/or other detrimental and adverse health effects. . . ."

What is missing from the amended complaint, however, is any express allegation that any plaintiff specifically relied to his/her detriment on any particular representation made in any particular McDonald's advertisement or promotional material. The district court concluded that, with one exception, the absence of such a particularized allegation of reliance warranted dismissal of the claims under §350 of the New York General Business Law, which prohibits false advertising. *Pelman II*, 2003 U.S. Dist. LEXIS 15202, at *25-*26. As to the exception—involving McDonald's representations that its French fries and hash browns are made with 100% vegetable oil and/or are cholesterol-free—the district court found that, while the amended complaint might be read to allege implicit reliance by plaintiffs on such representations, see id., at *30, the representations themselves were objectively nonmisleading, see id., at *35. . . .

Plaintiffs' appellate brief does, however, challenge the district court's dismissal of the claims under §349 of the New York General Business Law, which makes unlawful "[d]eceptive acts or practices in the conduct of any business, trade or commerce or in the furnishing of any service in this state." Unlike a private action brought under §350, a private action brought under §349 does not require proof of actual reliance. See Stutman v. Chem. Bank, 95 N.Y.2d 24, 29, 709 N.Y.S.2d 892, 731 N.E.2d 608 (2000). Additionally, because §349 extends well beyond common-law fraud to cover a broad range of deceptive practices, see Gaidon, 94 N.Y.2d at 343, 704 N.Y.S.2d 177, 725 N.E.2d 598, and because a private action under §349 does not require proof of the same essential elements (such as reliance) as common-law fraud, an action under §349 is not subject to the pleading-with-particularity requirements of Rule 9(b), Fed. R. Civ. P., but need only meet the bare-bones notice-pleading requirements of Rule 8(a), Fed. R. Civ. P., [citations omitted].

Although the district court recognized that §349 does not require proof of reliance, the district court nonetheless dismissed the claims under §349 because it concluded that "[p]laintiffs have failed, however, to draw an adequate causal connection between their consumption of McDonald's food and their alleged injuries." *Pelman II*, 2003 U.S. Dist. LEXIS 15202, at *30. Thus, the district court found it fatal that the complaint did not answer such questions as: What else did the plaintiffs eat? How much did they exercise? Is there a family history of the diseases which are alleged to have been caused by McDonald's products? Without this additional information, McDonald's does not have sufficient information to determine if its foods are the cause of plaintiffs' obesity, or if instead McDonald's foods are only a contributing factor. Id. at *33. This, however, is the sort of information that is appropriately the subject of discovery, rather than what is required to satisfy the limited pleading requirements of Rule 8(a), Fed. R. Civ. P. As a unanimous Supreme Court stated in *Swierkiewicz*:

> This simplified notice pleading standard [of Rule 8(a)] relies on liberal discovery rules and summary judgment motions to define disputed facts and issues and to dispose of unmeritorious claims. "The provisions for discovery are so flexible and the provisions for pretrial procedure and summary judgment so effective, that attempted surprise in federal practice is aborted very easily, synthetic issues detected, and the gravamen of the dispute brought frankly into the open for the inspection of the court."

534 U.S. at 512-13, 122 S. Ct. 992 (quoting 5 Charles A. Wright & Arthur R. Miller, Federal Practice and Procedure §1202, at 76 (2d ed.1990)) (internal citations omitted). So far as the §349 claims are concerned, the amended complaint more than meets the requirements of Rule 8(a).

Accordingly, the district court's dismissal of those portions of Counts I-III of the amended complaint as alleged violations of §349 is Vacated, and the case is Remanded for further proceedings consistent with this opinion.

QUESTION

This lawsuit generated a lot of attention in the press and was quite controversial. How do you feel about it? Is there anything to the Complaint?

Deceptive practices often catch the attention of a state's Attorney General, who will typically have a Consumer Frauds Division and will (with varying enthusiasm, depending on the political climate) be interested in stamping out such activity using the power of the state.

KUGLER v. ROMAIN
Supreme Court of New Jersey, 1971
58 N.J. 522, 279 A.2d 640

FRANCIS, J. Acting under the Consumer Fraud Act, N.J.S.A. 56:8-1 et seq., the Attorney General instituted this action in the Superior Court, Chancery Division, against defendant Richard Romain individually and trading as Educational Services Co. Injunctive and other affirmative relief was sought based on charges that in connection with the house-to-house sale of certain so-called educational books defendant had engaged in business practices which violated Section 2 of the Act, N.J.S.A. 56:8-2. Section 2 provides in pertinent part as follows:

> The act, use or employment by any person of any deception, fraud, false pretense, false promise, misrepresentation, or the knowing concealment, suppression, or omission of any material fact with intent that others rely upon such concealment, suppression or omission, in connection with the sale . . . of any merchandise, or with the subsequent performance of such person as aforesaid, whether or not any person has in fact been misled, deceived or damaged thereby, is declared to be an unlawful practice; . . .

The specific authorization for this proceeding appears in N.J.S.A. 56:8-8:

> Whenever it shall appear to the Attorney General that a person has engaged in, is engaging in or is about to engage in any practice declared to be unlawful by this act he may seek and obtain in an action in the Superior Court an injunction prohibiting such person from continuing such practices or engaging therein or doing any acts in furtherance thereof. . . . The court may make such orders or judgments as may be necessary to prevent the use or employment by a person of any prohibited practices, or which may be necessary to restore to any person in interest any moneys or property, real or personal which may have been acquired by means of any practice herein declared to be unlawful.

The Attorney General prayed for (1) injunctive relief barring the specific practices allegedly violative of N.J.S.A. 56:8-2; (2) a declaration that the price of the books printed in the form of contract was a transgression of the statute either because it constituted a fraud within the express terms of N.J.S.A. 56:8-2 or because it was unconscionable under the Uniform Commercial Code, N.J.S.A. 12A:2-302 which he argued is implicitly included within N.J.S.A. 56:8-2; (3) restoration and remedial orders for all persons who were induced to execute such purchase contracts; (4) rescission of all contracts with purchasers listed on a schedule attached to the complaint; (5) imposition of civil penalties against defendant, as provided in the Act, N.J.S.A. 56:8-13, 14; and (6) an order restraining defendant from doing business in New Jersey until he registered his trade name as required by N.J.S.A. 56:1-2.

The relief sought was not limited to the 24 customers whose names were set out in the schedule referred to. The complaint asked for an order enjoining defendant from enforcing or collecting in any manner those obligations arising out of the contracts entered into with those consumers set forth in Schedule A and *those consumers similarly situated*, and an order rescinding any and all obligations arising out of the purported contracts entered into by those consumers set forth in the attached schedule and *those consumers similarly situated.*

After a plenary hearing, the trial court found that defendant violated N.J.S.A. 56:8-2 by using deceptive and fraudulent practices to induce the 24 customers named in the schedule to execute contracts for the purchase of an "educational package" of books and related materials. Accordingly, a judgment was entered in favor of the Attorney General granting certain specified injunctive, restorative and remedial relief which will be discussed more fully hereafter. Believing that the relief granted was not as extensive as the circumstances warranted, the Attorney General appealed from the trial court's judgment. Defendant cross-appealed but abandoned his appeal before argument and limited his participation to a defense of the portions of the judgment attacked by the Attorney General. We certified the cause on our own motion before the appeal was heard in the Appellate Division.

Defendant, a resident and member of the bar of the State of New York, was engaged in the installment sale of so-called educational books and related materials in New York and New Jersey. He operated under the trade name Educational Services Company from an office in New York City. The trade name was not registered in New Jersey as required by N.J.S.A. 56:1-2 as a condition to doing business here.

Sales solicitations were made exclusively through house-to-house canvass by defendant's employees. No advance appointments were made. The solicitors simply descended upon a selected section of a municipality and undertook by house-to-house calls to sell a package of books which was described in large type on the contract presented to the prospective customers as "A Complete Ten Year Educational Program." It was also indicated thereon that the package was the product of the "Junior Institute," and nearby was the plea "Give your child its chance." In engaging his sales personnel, defendant sought persons who were "sales oriented" and extroverted. They were trained by defendant and his sales manager.

The geographical areas to be the subject of sales solicitation were primarily the urban centers of Newark, Paterson, Elizabeth and Rahway. They were chosen by defendant who was familiar with them and the class of people to be sought out by his sales force. With these target areas, the sales solicitations were consciously directed toward minority group consumers and consumers of limited education and economic means. Persons with incomes of less than $5000 a year were favored; some buyers were welfare recipients. Sales among these people were thought to be "easier." Although the canvassing was door-to-door, ordinances in the municipalities involved in this case which required licensing or registration were ignored.

Defendant's educational package consisted of the following books and materials:

1. Questions Children Ask (1 Vol.)
2. Child Horizons (4 Vols.)
3. New Achievement Library (5 Vols.)
4. High School Subjects Self-Taught (4 Vols.)
5. Science Library (1 Vol.)
6. Play-Way French and Spanish Records (2 45 r.p.m. Records)
7. Tell Time Flash Card Set.

Additionally a "bonus" volume—a Negro History, a World Atlas or a Bible—was offered either along with the original package or after completion of payment.

The printed contract form marked "Retail Installment Obligation," which was presented to the customer for signature, consisted of a single sheet covered with printed matter on both sides. The cash and time sale prices were printed on the face of the contract, the former at $249.50, and the latter at $279.95, less a $9 down payment which was obtained whenever possible. Apparently no one paid the cash price. Also printed on the face in small print was the statement: "This order is not subject to cancellation and set is not returnable."

On the reverse side under "Conditions" appeared certain payment acceleration and waiver of defenses clauses, including waiver of all exemptions and right to jury trial.

The trial court found that the wholesale price for the basic package, including the bonus items, was $35 to $40. Thus the cash sale price was six or seven times the wholesale price. Defendant's sales personnel were paid on a commission basis, ranging from $16.50 to $33 per sale; the amount paid depended upon whether (1) he secured the $9 down payment; (2) he obtained the customer's home telephone number; (3) the customer was not self-employed; and (4) the customer had been employed for at least 11½ years. In most cases the commission averaged $16.50. The crew leader also worked on a commission basis and additionally received an over-ride commission of $5 on every approved order of a member of his crew.

The Attorney General offered uncontradicted expert evidence that in view of industry-wide practices the maximum retail price which should have been charged for the entire package was approximately $108-$110. In the witness's opinion, the price charged by defendant was about two and one-half times the retail maximum, and he said that it was exorbitant. The trial court found that the price was exorbitant but held that such exorbitance per se did not constitute a fraud under N.J.S.A. 56:8-2. In its view, proof of deceptive practices was required in addition to the excessive price before a consumer's contract could be vitiated under the statute.

In deciding whether defendant, contrary to the statute, used any deception, fraud, false pretense, or misrepresentation, or whether he concealed, suppressed or omitted any material fact in connection with the sales to book purchasers, the price charged the consumer is only one element to be considered. If the price is grossly excessive in relation to the seller's costs, and if in addition the goods sold have little or no value to the consumer for the purpose for which he was persuaded to buy them and which the seller pretended they would serve, the price paid by the consumer takes on even more serious characteristics of imposition. Here the Attorney General offered persuasive evidence that the books had little or no educational value for the children in the age group and socio-economic position the defendant represented would be benefited by them.

The testimony showed that as to the New Achievement Library, three of the five volumes dealing with Nature, Science and Civilization, represented "very poor, watered-down articles which cover the . . . areas very superficially." They were of "extremely little use" or value as a means of raising the educational level of the children they were supposed to help. Another volume entitled "Getting Acquainted with Your Opportunities in Education" was extremely poor both in quality and content. Although the volume required a tenth grade reading level, it contained articles which the witness characterized as obsolete at the time it was being sold and irrelevant to 98% of its intended readers. "Child Horizons," consisting of four volumes and designed for children 6 to 10 years of age, was said to have no relevance to children whose unfortunate socio-economic conditions did not make them susceptible to the concepts and ideas reflected therein. It was, according to the expert, like giving calculus to a person who had never studied simple algebra. As to "High School Self-Taught," the four volumes were useless not merely for members of a minority group but for basic education for any individual. They might have some value for refreshment purposes for a person who has been through high school, "but for one to self-teach, it is just impossible." Similar comments were made about other books in the package. Defendant offered no contradictory proof on this subject.

The Attorney General's claim was that there was one illegal aspect of the sales contract which was common to every transaction, namely the fixed price. This price for the package of books and materials, which the testimony showed was about two and a half times a reasonable price in the relevant market, was found by the trial court to be exorbitant. As we have already noted, the Attorney General pointed out that in addition to being excessive in relation to defendant's cost, the books had very little and in some cases no value for the purpose for which the consumers were persuaded to buy them. Consequently he urged that under the circumstances the price was unconscionable under Section 2-302 of the Uniform Commercial Code and, as such, was within the proscription of Section 2 of the Consumer Fraud Act. More particularly, he contends that on the uncontradicted and common facts of each transaction, the unconscionable price must be equated with the deception, fraud, false pretense, misrepresentation or knowing material omission condemned by Section 2. If the contention is sound, then it should follow that every consumer who executed the form agreement for the educational package described above at the price fixed by defendant ought to be considered similarly situated, and the Attorney General would therefore be entitled to a judgment invalidating the contract for the entire class of such consumers.

As already noted, however, the trial court declined to hold that the price per se constituted a violation of Section 2 in the absence of some concomitant deceptive practice perpetrated by the seller. The opinion pointed out that the word "unconscionable" did not appear in Section 2 and consequently should not be considered as included therein. Further the court declared that even though enforcement of an unconscionable contract may be denied under Section 2-302 of the Code, the remedy provided thereby is "strictly a matter of private concern" and cannot be asserted or relied upon by the Attorney General in a suit allegedly brought for protection of the consuming public.

Unconscionability is not defined in Section 2-302 of the Uniform Commercial Code, and we agree that it is not mentioned by name in Section 2 of the Consumer Fraud Act. It is an amorphous concept obviously designed to establish a broad business ethic. The framers of the Code naturally expected the courts to interpret it liberally so as to effectuate the public purpose, and to pour content into it on a case-by-case basis.

The standard of conduct contemplated by the unconscionability clause is good faith, honesty in fact and observance of fair dealing. The need for application of the standard is most acute when the professional seller is seeking the trade of those most subject to exploitation—the uneducated, the inexperienced and the people of low incomes. In such a context, a material departure from the standard puts a badge of fraud on the transaction and here the concept of fraud and unconscionability are interchangeable. Thus we believe that in consumer goods transactions such as those involved in this case, unconscionability must be equated with the concepts of deception, fraud, false pretense, misrepresentation, concealment and the like, which are stamped unlawful under N.J.S.A. 56:8-2. We do not consider that absence of the word "unconscionable" from the statute detracts in any substantial degree from the force of this conclusion.

We have no doubt that an exorbitant price ostensibly agreed to by a purchaser of the type involved in this case—but in reality unilaterally fixed by the seller and not open to negotiation—constitutes an unconscionable bargain from which such a purchaser should be relieved under Section 2. If, therefore, in this case the price charged for the educational package is so exorbitant as to be unconscionable, Section 2 makes it unnecessary to decide whether the Attorney General could maintain a class action for all similarly affected consumers based solely upon violation of Section 2-302, the unconscionability clause of the Uniform Commercial Code. Adequate and proper relief for all consumers victimized by an unconscionable price may be obtained by the Attorney General through Section 2 of the Consumer Fraud Act under which his action was brought here.

We are satisfied that the price for the book package was unconscionable in relation to defendant's cost and the value to the consumers and was therefore a fraud within the contemplation of N.J.S.A. 56:8-2. Further, for the reasons stated we are convinced that a view that such price unconscionability gives rise only to a private remedy is an unreasonable limitation on the aim and scope of the Consumer Fraud Act, N.J.S.A. 56:8-1 et seq. The public purpose to be served thereby (and we see the legislative emphasis as being more on public than on private remedies) can be accomplished effectively only by recognizing the authority of the Attorney General to intervene in behalf of all consumers similarly affected by the broadly described fraudulent sales tactics of merchandise sellers.

More specifically here, since the price unconscionability rendered the sales contract invalid as to all consumers who executed it, the Attorney General was entitled to a judgment so holding as to the entire class of such persons. Accordingly, the trial court's order must be modified to the end that such a judgment may be entered. The mechanics of effectuating the judgment with respect to the individuals comprising the class and of accomplishing the necessary restorative relief required by N.J.S.A. 56:8-8 are left to the trial court.

As modified the judgment is affirmed and the cause is remanded for further proceedings consistent with this opinion.

D. Illegality: The Ultimate Penalty

The word "illegal" in contracts law means more than simply criminal (though it does include criminal contracts—for example, an agreement to rob a bank). If a contract or a portion thereof is deemed "illegal," it is void as a matter of public policy. The guilty parties (those *in pari delicto*—of equal fault), are stripped of all legal rights, including quasi-contractual relief. Innocent parties caught up in an illegal contract cannot sue on the contract, but they at least get quasi-contractual relief.

Remembering that guilty parties to an illegal contract are truly outlaws can be a powerful weapon for an attorney's arsenal.

BENNETT v. HAYES
California Court of Appeals, 1975
53 Cal. App. 3d 700, 125 Cal. Rptr. 825

THE COURT.

Upon certification by the superior court, we ordered transfer of the appeal in this case, pursuant to section 911 of the Code of Civil Procedure, in order to settle an important question of law, to wit, whether an automobile repair dealer's failure to give his customer a written estimate prior to repair of the customer's automobile, as required by section 984.9 subdivision (a), of the Business and Professions Code, bars any recovery for work performed. With certain additions and modifications, we have adopted the excellent opinion of the appellate department of the superior court, as follows:

"Plaintiff appeals from a judgment for defendant on an action for breach of a written contract and for recovery of an agreed price, entered February 28, 1975 in the Municipal Court. . . .

"On August 24, 1973, defendant-respondent brought his 1964 Jaguar sedan to The European Stable, plaintiff-appellant's foreign car repair shop in Menlo Park, California. In the course of an oral discussion, respondent agreed to pay appellant $70.00 for the repair of one front brake, $100.00 for a radio and $17.00 for lubrication. Although specific sums were mentioned, appellant was unsure of the exact price of all the parts involved. Appellant failed to give respondent a written estimate for this work.

"On September 28, 1973, after appellant had telephoned respondent to say that he had completed the repairs, respondent traveled from his home in San Luis Obispo to Menlo Park to pick up the car. When he arrived, appellant told him the car was inoperable because the rear brakes were in need of repair. When asked to restore the car to its original state, appellant indicated this could not be done without additional cost. Having no other viable alternative, respondent then verbally authorized appellant to repair and replace the rear brakes for $200.00 and returned to his home in San Luis Obispo.

"Respondent did not receive or sign a detailed written description of the work to be performed on his car until it was later delivered to him in San Luis Obispo, where he was billed for $500.00.

"The issue is whether under Business and Professions Code §9884.9 appellant's failure to give respondent a written estimate prior to repairing respondent's car bars any recovery for the work performed.

"Business and Professions Code §9884.9(a) at the time of the instant transaction provided in part as follows:

> The automotive repair dealer shall give to the customer a written estimated price for labor and parts necessary for a specific job and shall not charge for work done or parts supplied in excess of the estimated price without the oral or written consent of the customer which shall be obtained at some time after it is determined that the estimated price is insufficient and before the work not estimated is done or the parts not estimated are supplied. Nothing in this section shall be construed as requiring an automotive repair dealer to give a written estimated price if the dealer does not agree to perform the requested repair.

"It is clear from §9884.9 in August, 1973 and as since amended that if work is done in excess of the written estimate without the consent of the customer, the repairman may not charge for the additional work.

"The Automotive Repair Act became law in 1971 and as yet there are no appellate decisions interpreting the applicable provisions. The Attorney General has stated that 'the purposes of the Act are to foster fair dealing (and) to eliminate misunderstandings.' 55 Opinions of the Attorney General 278 (1972).

"Appellant argues that the Automotive Repair Act sufficiently protects consumers by vesting in the Director of the Bureau of Automotive Repair the discretion to suspend or revoke the licenses of non-complying repairmen. The trial court concluded that allowing appellant to recover despite his failure to provide a written estimate would circumvent the purposes of the Act.

"City Lincoln-Mercury Co. v. Lindsey, 52 C[al.] 2d 267[, 339 P.2d 851] (1959), involved a similar consumer protection statute. The underlying facts are as follows: The defendant purchased a new Lincoln on a conditional sales contract from the plaintiff's company. At the time the defendant signed the sales order, the time price differential and the contract balance were not filled in as required by Subdivision (a) of Section 2982 of the Civil Code. After making two installment payments, the defendant returned the automobile to the seller who in turn resold it and brought an action against the defendant for the deficiency. The defendant answered contending that the contract was illegal and unenforceable.

"The court held that,

The provisions of section 2982(a) . . . [are] for the protection of the purchaser; a violation of the subdivision in this respect makes the contract unenforceable by the seller.

"In the case at bar appellant gave respondent no written estimate and no precise oral estimate of the costs or extent of the repairs to be performed. . . . This violation of B&P Code §9884.9 rendered the contract unenforceable by this appellant-dealer.

"While recognizing the factor of unjust enrichment, the primary purpose of the rule of unenforceability is the discouragement of practices forbidden by law. Because appellant could have easily complied with B&P Code §9884.9, no reason exists for declining to apply this rule in this case.

"Appellant argues he is entitled to quantum meruit equitable relief. However, he failed to advance this theory in his pleadings and offered no evidence at trial as to the reasonable value of his services. This precludes such relief on appeal.

"Even if appellant had presented this issue properly on appeal, he would be denied relief. Tiedje v. Aluminum Taper Milling Co., 46 C[al]. 2d 450[, 296 P.2d 554] (1955), states the general rule that 'the guilty party to an illegal contract cannot bring an action to enforce the contract or to recover on principles of quasi contract the benefits he has conferred under it.' See also Fong v. Miller, 105 C[al]. A[pp]. 2d 411[, 233 P.2d 606] (1951).

"Appellant auto repair dealer has violated B&P Code §9884.9 enacted for the protection of respondent, his customer.

"This violation renders the repair contract unenforceable at law. Equitable relief is granted in such cases only under narrowly drawn exceptions to the general rule designed to discourage such violations by refusing relief. Appellant does not fall within these exceptions."

The judgment of the municipal court is affirmed.

E. Referral Schemes

PROBLEM 13

Suspecting that he had let his "couch potato" status get out of hand, Ralph Video went down to Wonder Spa and inquired about their fitness program. He was told that they had the "best aerobics class in town" and a "full service weight room." They bragged that their "lifetime" program would cost him only $300 a year for three years, payable monthly. But they also informed him that with each new member he recruited, they would take $10 off his monthly payment. Impressed with the facilities, Ralph signed up. The first night that he tried to join the aerobics class it was so crowded that Ralph, a newcomer, was hit in the eye by a fellow classmate, causing him to have to go to the hospital. The next week he decided to try the weight room, but there was no one to help him learn how to use the machines and he strained his back. The following day, lying on the couch in front of the TV, he decided that he wanted out of the contract with Wonder Spa, and he called you, his cousin and therefore favorite attorney, for advice. What can you tell him?

QUOTES FOR THE ATTORNEY'S ARSENAL: "REFERRAL PLANS"

The testimony of Mr. Lyons, the Chief Accountant of the Bureau of Consumer Frauds of the Office of the Attorney General, conclusively proved the mathematical certainty by which the respondents' referral plan was doomed to failure, knowledge of which must be charged to the respondents. He demonstrated that based on respondents' own representations that respondents had converted and could convert every 20 names furnished by each consumer into 12 enrollments, the plan would follow a geometric progression, so that by the seventh stage it would involve millions of people purchasing these items in untold millions of dollars. If carried further it could well exceed the population of the state, nation, and indeed the world.

State ex rel. Lefkowitz v. ITM, Inc., 52 Misc. 2d 39, 47, 275 N.Y.S.2d 303, 315 (1966).

WEBSTER v. OMNITRITION INTERNATIONAL, INC.[23]
United States Court of Appeals, Ninth Circuit, 1996
79 F.3d 776

BEEZER, Circuit Judge:

We consider what constitutes an inherently fraudulent pyramid scheme for purposes of several federal antifraud statutes.

Shaun Webster and Robert Ligon represent a class of participants (collectively "Webster") in a "multi level marketing" program promoted by Omnitrition International, Inc. ("Omnitrition"). Webster alleges that Omnitrition, Roger Daley, Charles Ragus, James Fobair and Jerry Rubin operated an inherently fraudulent pyramid scheme under both California and federal law. Webster amended the complaint to add as defendants

---

23. Footnotes in this case have been renumbered for clarity.

Omnitrition's outside counsel, Douglas Adkins, and his law firm, Gardere & Wynne, L.L.P. (collectively "Attorney Defendants").

The district court granted summary judgment in favor of all defendants, holding that Omnitrition's program was not a pyramid scheme as a matter of law. The court also held that the federal securities claims against the Attorney Defendants were barred by the statute of limitations.

Webster appeals, claiming that there are disputed issues of material fact as well as errors of law. We have jurisdiction and we affirm in part and reverse in part.

I

Omnitrition is a corporation which operates a "multi level marketing" program, selling nutritional supplements, vitamins and skin care products. Members of Omnitrition's retail sales force are known as "Independent Marketing Associates" ("IMAs").

The first level of IMAs are referred to by Omnitrition as "distributors." There is no charge to become a distributor, and distributors have no quota of products they must purchase or sell. A distributor has the right to buy products at a discount from Omnitrition for use or resale and to recruit others into the program. A distributor can qualify to become a "Bronze Supervisor" by ordering a minimum amount (several thousand dollars) in products, measured by suggested retail price, from Omnitrition in one or two (consecutive) months. In order to remain a supervisor, an IMA must continue to meet the minimum order requirements each month.

Bronze Supervisors are entitled to receive a "Royalty Override Bonus" on up to three generations of "downline" supervisors, i.e. people the supervisor recruits who themselves also meet the minimum monthly order requirements to be supervisors. The "Royalty Override Bonus" gives the Bronze Supervisor a 1 to 4% commission on orders placed by downline supervisors. Supervisors and those they recruit must continue to purchase a minimum amount of products each month from Omnitrition to qualify the supervisor for commissions. Beyond the Bronze Supervisor level are Silver, Gold, and Diamond supervisors, who can recruit more supervisors into the program and earn the right to royalties on up to six levels of downline supervisors. Omnitrition has three policies which are supposed to encourage retail sales. First, to order products, IMAs must certify that they have sold at least 70% of products previously purchased. This requirement can be met either by retail sales to end users or by sales to downline IMAs. Second, to qualify to earn commissions on downline orders, supervisors must certify that they have made sales to ten retail customers in the past month. It is undisputed that Omnitrition randomly calls some customers listed by supervisors to confirm that the sales have occurred. Third, if an IMA resigns from the program, Omnitrition will buy back unsold inventory for 90% of invoice price, with the caveat that Omnitrition will only repurchase consumable products that are less than three months old.

Fobair, Daley and Ragus are corporate officers of Omnitrition. Rubin, now deceased but appearing by the executor of his estate, was alleged to be involved in the creation and promotion of the marketing program. Adkins, a partner at Gardere & Wynne, is outside counsel and Assistant Secretary of Omnitrition. Adkins appears in a promotional videotape produced by Omnitrition, in which he states that Omnitrition is "not a pyramid scheme," gives advice on how to sell the nutritional products within the constraints of FDA guidelines, and makes other promotional statements concerning Omnitrition.

Webster and Ligon are former Omnitrition IMAs. Each filed class actions, Ligon in the Southern District of Texas and Webster in the Northern District of California, on behalf of all IMAs in Omnitrition's program who lost money. The two actions were consolidated in the Northern District of California and the district court certified the class. Webster's amended complaint alleges that Omnitrition's marketing program is actually a fraudulent pyramid scheme violative of federal securities laws, state unfair sales practice and fraud laws and the Racketeer Influenced and Corrupt Organizations Act ("RICO") (18 U.S.C. §1961 et seq.).

The district court granted summary judgment for all defendants on the ground that Webster had failed to raise a triable issue of fact as to whether Omnitrition's program was a pyramid scheme; the district court held that Omnitrition's policies designed to encourage retail sales took the program outside the definition of fraudulent pyramid schemes. Most of the remainder of the district court's reasons for granting summary judgment depend on this determination.

The district court determined that Omnitrition distributorships were not securities within the purview of the federal securities laws because their return did not depend primarily on the efforts of others. The district court further held that, because the program was not fraudulent, its operation and promotion did not constitute predicate acts under RICO. Finally, the district court determined that Webster had failed to provide evidence of several elements of the state law claims.

The district court granted summary judgment to the Attorney Defendants holding that the limitation period of the statute of limitations had expired on the federal securities claims. Webster timely appeals.

II

* * *

The central issue is whether Omnitrition's marketing program is a pyramid scheme. Operation of a pyramid scheme constitutes fraud for purposes of §12(2) of the Securities Act of 1933, §10 of the Securities Exchange Act of 1934 and various RICO predicate acts. Because the record contains sufficient evidence to present a genuine issue of disputed material fact as to whether Omnitrition promotes a pyramid scheme, we reverse the grant of summary judgment.

A.

Pyramid schemes are said to be inherently fraudulent because they must eventually collapse. See, e.g., S.E.C. v. International Loan Network, Inc., 968 F.2d 1304, 1309 (D.C. Cir. 1992). Like chain letters, pyramid schemes may make money for those at the top of the chain or pyramid, but "must end up disappointing those at the bottom who can find no recruits." In re Koscot Interplanetary, Inc., 86 F.T.C. 1106, 1181 (1975), *aff'd mem. sub nom.* Turner v. F.T.C., 580 F.2d 701 (D.C. Cir. 1978).

The Federal Trade Commission has established a test for determining what constitutes a pyramid scheme. Such contrivances

> are characterized by the payment by participants of money to the company in return for which they receive (1) the right to sell a product *and* (2) the right to receive in return for recruiting other participants into the program rewards which are unrelated to sale of the product to ultimate users.

Id. (emphasis in original). The satisfaction of the second element of the *Koscot* test is the *sine qua non* of a pyramid scheme: "As is apparent, the presence of this second element, recruitment with rewards unrelated to product sales, is nothing more than an elaborate chain letter device in which individuals who pay a valuable consideration with the expectation of recouping it to some degree via recruitment are bound to be disappointed." Id. We adopt the *Koscot* standard here and hold that the operation of a pyramid scheme constitutes fraud for purposes of several federal antifraud statutes.

B.

Omnitrition argues that because it does not charge for the right to sell its products at the "distributor" level, as a matter of law the first *Koscot* element is not met. We disagree.

Omnitrition's argument improperly focuses only on the "distributor" level of Omnitrition's program. The program is unquestionably not a pyramid scheme if only the distributor level is taken into account; the participant pays no money to Omnitrition, has the right to sell products and has no right to receive compensation for recruiting others into the program. The distributor level, however, is only a small part of the entire program. Taking into account the "supervisor" levels, a reasonable jury could conclude the *Koscot* factors are met here.

To become a supervisor, a participant must pay a substantial amount of money to Omnitrition in the form of large monthly product orders. The "payment of money" element of a pyramid scheme can be met where the participant is required to purchase "non returnable" inventory in order to receive the full benefits of the program. In re Amway Corp., 93 F.T.C. 618, 715-16 (1979). In exchange for these purchases, the supervisor receives the right to sell the products and earn compensation based on product orders made by the supervisor's recruits. This compensation is facially "unrelated to the sale of the product to ultimate users" because it is paid based on the suggested retail price of the amount ordered from Omnitrition, rather than based on actual sales to consumers.

On its face, Omnitrition's program appears to be a pyramid scheme. Omnitrition cannot save itself simply by pointing to the fact that it makes some retail sales. See In re Ger-Ro-Mar, Inc., 84 F.T.C. 95, 148-49 (1974) (that some retail sales occur does not mitigate the unlawful nature of pyramid schemes), *rev'd on other grounds*, 518 F.2d 33 (2d Cir. 1975). The promise of lucrative rewards for recruiting others tends to induce participants to focus on the recruitment side of the business at the expense of their retail marketing efforts, making it unlikely that meaningful opportunities for retail sales will occur. *Koscot*, 86 F.T.C. at 1181. The danger of such "recruitment focus" is present in Omnitrition's program. For example, Webster testified that Omnitrition encouraged him to "get to supervisor as quick as [he] could." Ligon states:

> [T]he product sales are driven by enrolling people. In other words, the people buy exorbitant amounts of products that normally would not be sold in an average market by virtue of the fact that they enroll, get caught up in the process, in the enthusiasm, the words of people like Charlie Ragus, president, by buying exorbitant amounts of products, giving products away and get[ting] involved in their proven plan of success, their marketing plan. It has nothing to do with the normal supply and demand in this world. It has to do with getting people enrolled, enrolling people, getting them on the bandwagon and getting them to sell product.

Omnitrition argues that Webster failed to submit sufficient admissible proof that Omnitrition is a pyramid scheme. We disagree. The mere structure of the scheme suggests that Omnitrition's focus was in promoting the program rather than selling the products. When added to statements from Webster's and Ligon's depositions, plaintiffs have produced sufficient evidence to defeat summary judgment.

c.

To rebut the pyramid allegations, Omnitrition relies heavily on In re Amway Corp., 93 F.T.C. 618 (1979), in which the FTC found Amway was not a pyramid scheme because its policies prevented inventory loading and encouraged retail sales. Id. at 715-16. Omnitrition argues that its formal adoption of policies similar to Amway's was sufficient to support summary judgment. We disagree.

The policies adopted by Amway were as follows: (1) participants were required to buy back from any person they recruited any saleable, unsold inventory upon the recruit's leaving Amway, (2) every participant was required to sell at wholesale or retail at least 70% of the products bought in a given month in order to receive a bonus for that month, and (3) in order to receive a bonus in a month, each participant was required to submit proof of retail sales made to ten different consumers. Id. at 716. The Administrative Law Judge ("ALJ") in Amway found as a matter of fact that these policies were enforced by Amway, and, more importantly, that the rules in fact served to encourage retail sales and prevent "inventory loading" by Amway distributors.[24] Id. at 646, 668.

Omnitrition has distribution rules modeled on Amway's. However, the existence and enforcement of rules like Amway's is only the first step in the pyramid scheme inquiry. Where, as here, a distribution program appears to meet the *Koscot* definition of a pyramid scheme, there must be evidence that the program's safeguards are enforced and actually serve to deter inventory loading and encourage retail sales. In *Amway*, the ALJ made that crucial finding of fact, after a full trial. See id. at 631. Our review of the record does not reveal sufficient evidence to establish as a matter of law that Omnitrition's rules actually work.

Further, Omnitrition's rules, while carefully crafted to appear like those in *Amway*, are weaker in operation. The key to any anti-pyramiding rule in a program like Omnitrition's, where the basic structure serves to reward recruitment more than retailing, is that the rule must serve to tie recruitment bonuses to actual retail sales in some way. Only in this way can the second

---

24. "Inventory loading" occurs when distributors make the minimum required purchases to receive recruitment-based bonuses without reselling the products to consumers.

Koscot factor be defeated. Omnitrition has failed to prove that as a matter of law its rules operate in that manner.

First, Omnitrition produced evidence of enforcement only for its ten customer rule. Even assuming that Omnitrition's enforcement measures are effective, it is not clear that these measures serve to tie the amount of "Royalty Overrides" to retail sales. The overrides are paid based on purchases by supervisors. In order to be a supervisor, one must purchase several thousand dollars worth of product each month. That some amount of product was sold by each supervisor to only ten consumers each month does not insure that overrides are being paid as a result of actual retail sales.

Second, Omnitrition produced no evidence of enforcement of its 70% rule. It merely states that, in order to place further orders IMAs must "certify" that they have sold 70% of the product they previously ordered. There is no evidence that this "certification" requirement actually serves to deter inventory loading. Importantly, the requirement can be satisfied by non-retail sales to a supervisor's own downline IMAs. This makes it less likely that the rule will effectively tie royalty overrides to sales to ultimate users, as *Koscot* requires.

In addition, plaintiffs have produced evidence that the 70% rule can be satisfied by a distributor's personal use of the products. If *Koscot* is to have any teeth, such a sale cannot satisfy the requirement that sales be to "ultimate users" of a product.[25]

Third, Omnitrition has not shown that it enforces its buy-back rule, or the extent to which Omnitrition has actually repurchased product from disappointed IMAs. In addition, by Omnitrition's own terms, the rule is weaker than Amway's in two particulars: (1) Omnitrition only refunds 90% of the price of the product and (2) Omnitrition will only repurchase consumable products (the majority of what it sells) if they are less than three months old. The latter fact is very significant. The buy-back rule is only effective if it can reduce or eliminate the possibility of inventory loading by insuring that program participants do not find themselves saddled with thousands of dollars worth of unsaleable products. Omnitrition's rule potentially would not achieve this goal for any person who participated in the program for more than three months.

Omnitrition misreads *Amway* as holding that any "multi level marketing" program employing policies like Amway's is not a pyramid scheme as a matter of law. That was not the FTC's holding. The FTC held that

25. Indeed the record indicates that Omnitrition itself does not treat distributors' use of products as retail sales: distributors who purchase products for personal use are not entitled to the same 30 day money back guarantee that is available to other retail customers.

Amway was not a pyramid scheme as a matter of fact because its policies were enforced and were effective in encouraging retail sales. This ruling does not help Omnitrition at the summary judgment stage.

Omnitrition's *Amway* defense must fail, at least on summary judgment, because the crucial evidence of the actual effectiveness of its anti-pyramiding distribution rules is missing. . . .

V

A.

Whether Omnitrition's program runs afoul of California's laws against false advertising, unfair business practices and fraud is determined under California's statutory definition of "Endless Chain" marketing schemes. California Penal Code §327 makes it a public offense for any person to operate

> any scheme for the disposal or distribution of property whereby a participant pays a valuable consideration for the chance to receive compensation for introducing one or more additional persons into participation in the scheme or for the chance to receive compensation when a person introduced by the participant introduces a new participant. Compensation, as used in this section, does not mean or include payment based upon sales made to persons who are not participants in the scheme and who are not purchasing in order to participate in the scheme.

Cal. Penal Code §327 (West 1995). This definition is equivalent, if not identical, to the *Koscot* test. Because there is sufficient evidence for a jury to conclude the Omnitrition program fails the *Koscot* test, there also is a genuine issue of material fact as to whether it is an "Endless Chain" scheme under §327.

Indeed, at least one of the Omnitrition's *Amway* protections is less salient under the California statute. Omnitrition's "70% Rule" allows supervisors to count products sold at wholesale to their own downlines toward their 70 percent sales requirement. This allows supervisors to be compensated on the basis of sales other than "sales made to persons who are not participants in the scheme and who are not purchasing in order to participate in the scheme." Id. This is expressly prohibited by the California statute, while it is only implicit in the *Amway* "retail sales" defense.

B.

California Business and Professions Code §§17500 et seq. make it unlawful for anyone to use false or deceptive marketing practices. The operation and promotion of an Endless Chain scheme within the meaning of

Penal Code §327 is an inherently deceptive marketing practice, actionable under §17500. People v. Bestline Products, Inc., 61 Cal. App. 3d 879, 132 Cal. Rptr. 767, 789-90 (1976).

California Business and Professions Code §§17200 et seq. create a cause of action for anyone damaged by the defendant's unfair competitive practices. By statutory definition, any illegal business practice is also unfair. Cal. Bus. & Prof. Code §17200 (West 1995). Thus, if Omnitrition's scheme violates Penal Code §327, it is actionable under Business and Professions Code §17200 et seq.

c.

The existence of a triable issue of fact as to Omnitrition's operation of a pyramid scheme raises triable issues of fact as to Webster's cause of action for common law fraud. The familiar elements of a fraud cause of action are (1) misrepresentations of material fact, (2) knowledge of falsity, (3) intent to induce reliance, (4) justifiable reliance and (5) resulting damage. Cicone v. URS Corp., 183 Cal. App. 3d 194, 227 Cal. Rptr. 887, 890 (1986).

Evidence that the defendants operated an illegal, inherently fraudulent pyramid scheme raises a material question of fact going to the first three elements. Misrepresentations, knowledge and intent follow from the inherently fraudulent nature of a pyramid scheme as a matter of law. As to justifiable reliance, the defendants have not carried their burden on summary judgment of showing a lack of evidence to prove this element. To the contrary, defendants argue strenuously that their scheme was not fraudulent, and that plaintiffs were justified in relying upon the statements made in the promotional materials. Further, the very reason for the per se illegality of Endless Chain schemes is their inherent deceptiveness and the fact that the "futility" of the plan is not "apparent to the consumer participant." Bestline, 132 Cal. Rptr. at 788 (quoting Twentieth Century Co. v. Quilling, 130 Wis. 318, 110 N.W. 174, 176 (1907)). Finally, there is a triable issue of fact as to damages. Webster testified that he never made back what he put in to the scheme and Ligon testified that he lost approximately $5,000 in the scheme. . . .

AFFIRMED IN PART, REVERSED IN PART and REMANDED.

NOTE

In an omitted portion of the opinion the court also found that Omnitrition had violated the Racketeer Influenced and Corrupt Organizations Act ("RICO"), 18 U.S.C. §§1961 et seq., a federal statute that we will consider later in this chapter.

There are quite a large number of cases considering pyramid selling schemes, which are used to market many types of items and services. See, e.g., Peterson v. Sunrider Corp., 48 P.3d 918 (Utah 2002) (sale of health and beauty products); Pliss v. Peppertree Resort Villas, Inc., 264 Wis. 2d 735, 663 N.W.2d 851 (Wis. App. 2003) (time shares in condominium).

PROBLEM 14

Attorney Portia Moot received a telephone call one night from her best friend, Sally Greed. Sally invited Portia to join the "Circle of Eight Club," an investment opportunity that worked like this:

a. At the first week's meeting, eight newcomers would each bring $1500 in cash. They would stand in a circle. Inside the circle would be a four-person ring, and inside it would be two persons. In the center would be a single person, and the eight newcomers would give all the money to him or her (a total of $12,000). Each newcomer would be expected to come the next week and bring two additional newcomers.

b. The second week, the previous week's ring would split. Last week's newcomers would advance to the ring of four, getting no money but not having to pay anything either. This week's newcomers would form the outer ring.

c. The third week, the original investors would move to the ring of two.

d. The final week, each of the original investors would be at the center of his or her own ring and would receive $12,000.

Sally told Portia that she herself had been through the ring twice and that it was the best investment she had ever made.

Should Portia join the Circle of Eight? What should Portia tell her friend Sally?

Finally, some mention should be made of Ponzi investment schemes. This scam takes its name from its most famous practitioner, Charles Ponzi, who enjoyed what the United States Supreme Court described as a "remarkable criminal financial career," Cunningham v. Brown, 265 U.S. 1, 7 (1924). Starting in December 1919, when he had capital of but $150, Ponzi issued promissory notes purporting to guarantee that within 90 days he would repay $150 for each $100 loaned him. Boston residents were promised a 400 percent profit! Overall 40,000 people loaned Ponzi a total of $15 million. He told his investors that he was using their money to purchase international postal money coupons and selling them at a great markup from one foreign country to another. In reality, Ponzi was repaying old notes with new borrowings, a situation that of course had a spectacular collapse. (In this it is similar to a check-kiting scheme, in which bad deposited checks are covered by later and larger bad deposited checks, each clearing against accounts in different banks until some bank figures out what is going on and stops paying the checks.) For a book describing Ponzi's life and machinations, see Mitchell Zuckoff, Ponzi's Scheme: The True Story of a Financial Legend (2005).

In 2007 the Albanian government fell because a government-backed Ponzi scheme collapsed and the people of Albania (numbering only 3 million) lost $1.2 billion! Rioting in the streets led to anarchy, and 2,000 people were killed. Rioting also occurred in November 2008 in Bogota, Colombia, when a pyramid scheme promising 70 percent returns fleeced its mostly poor investors out of millions of dollars; angry investors shot one of the alleged perpetrators in the street.

In 2008 the largest Ponzi scheme in history was revealed when Bernard Madoff was found to have deprived his victims of $50 billion! Just like Charles Ponzi, Madoff promised incredible returns, paying the original investors from money received from subsequent ones. As in all such schemes, Madoff's house-of-cards financial structure eventually collapsed, and he was indicted for criminal fraud. Amazingly, his investors included major banks, celebrities, universities, and financial experts. Of course, Madoff's victims should have been suspicious of the incredible return he promised for their original investment, but this is true of most of those who are duped by fraudulent promises. Bunko artists will tell you that an honest and prudent person is much more difficult to cheat than someone who, alas, allows greed to overpower common sense.

F. Telemarketing

Telemarketing is a big business. Many telemarketing concerns are legitimate concerns, but many others are fly-by-night fraud operations that have nothing important to sell but are nonetheless quite skillful at extracting the consumer's money before being exposed.

The Federal Trade Commission has established a national "Do Not Call" registry, and consumers who sign up are put on a list so that telemarketers are forbidden to phone them unbidden. The rules do not prohibit calls from charitable organizations or from businesses with which the consumer has had past volitional contacts. Interestingly enough, attorneys are covered by the rules, and thus are not allowed to make unsolicited calls to those in the registry. Consumers can register online at www.donotcall. gov or can call, toll-free, 1-888-382-1222 (TTY 1-866-290-4236) from the number the consumer wishes to register. Registration is free. The FTC has imposed significant penalties against entities violating the "Do Not Call" registry. For example, in 2005 DirectTV, Inc. was ordered to pay $5.34 million for such a misstep.

In the mid-1990s Congress enacted three statutes governing telemarketing, and the Federal Communications Commission has promulgated regulations under all three. They are the Telephone Consumer Protection Act, 47 U.S.C. §227 (1991—the FCC regulation is at 47 C.F.R. §64.1200), the Telephone Disclosure and Dispute Resolution Act, 47 U.S.C. §228 and 15 U.S.C. §5711 (1992—the FCC regulation is at 47 C.F.R. §64.1500, with a corresponding FTC regulation at 16 C.F.R. §308), and the Telemarketing and Consumer Fraud and Abuse Prevention Act, 15 U.S.C.A. §6101 (its FTC regulation is at 16 C.F.R. §310). The latter statute begins with this:

§6101. Findings

The Congress makes the following findings:

(1) Telemarketing differs from other sales activities in that it can be carried out by sellers across State lines without direct contact with the consumer. Telemarketers also can be very mobile, easily moving from State to State.

(2) Interstate telemarketing fraud has become a problem of such magnitude that the resources of the Federal Trade Commission are not sufficient to ensure adequate consumer protection from such fraud.

(3) Consumers and others are estimated to lose $40 billion a year in telemarketing fraud.

(4) Consumers are victimized by other forms of telemarketing deception and abuse.

(5) Consequently, Congress should enact legislation that will offer consumers necessary protection from telemarketing deception and abuse.

The three statutes and regulations taken together allow consumers to opt out of receiving unwanted calls, ban the use of unsolicited recorded calls and faxes, regulate "900" calls so that consumers do not run up unexpected charges, require telemarketers to tell the truth and to disclose all the material terms of the proposed deal, forbid certain practices (such as harassing the consumer), and regulate how and when a telemarketer is given permission to tap the consumer's checking or savings account.

The defects in the statutes are that either there is no private right of action in favor of injured consumers or the rights of action are limited. The first statute allows suit only in state courts, the second has no private right of action, and the latter allows a private right of action by injured consumers, but only in the federal courts and only if the consumer alleges $50,000 or more as the amount in controversy; the *prevailing party* in the civil suit is entitled to attorney's fees, costs, and witness fees, and the risk of losing and having to bear these expenses will likely mean that it is the rare consumer who will sue under the Act.[26] These statutes will generally be most useful to the federal agencies and the Attorneys General of the various states who are given the right to sue telemarketers that do not comply with the rules (though most are judgment proof or are long gone before any action can possibly be commenced).

This is not to say that some consumers have not been willing to bring suits under these statutes where a private right of action is allowed. Most state courts have permitted actions under the Telephone Consumer Protection Act (TCPA) even without state legislation authorizing such suits. See Joffe v. Acacia Mortg. Corp., 211 Ariz. 325, 121 P.3d 831 (Ariz. App. 2005) (text messages covered by statute); Charvat v. Ryan, 116 Ohio St. 3d 394, 879 N.E.2d 765 (2007) (treble damages available where defendant acted volitionally even though it did not know that its conduct violated the statute); Condon v. Office Depot, Inc., 855 So. 2d 644 (Fla. App. 2003) (13 unsolicited fax advertisements).

REICHENBACH v. CHUNG HOLDINGS, LLC
Court of Appeals, Ohio, 2004
159 Ohio App. 3d 79, 823 N.E.2d 29

PIETRYKOWSKI, Judge.

This case is before the court on appeal from the Toledo Municipal Court, which denied a motion for partial summary judgment filed by appellant Gregory Reichenbach and granted a motion for summary judgment filed by appellee Chung Holdings LLC. Because we find that the trial court erred, we reverse.

This case requires us to consider a federal statute, the Telephone Consumer Protection Act ("TCPA") and its accompanying regulations and to answer these questions: (1) whether the statute provides a private right of action for a single prerecorded or automated telephone call; (2)

---

26. Since many state deceptive practices acts make violation of FTC regulations presumptive violations of the state statute, it may be possible to create a state cause of action for these telemarketing excesses.

whether the prerecorded or automated call that appellant received contained an "unsolicited advertisement," as that term is used in the statute and the regulations; (3) whether a genuine issue of fact exists as to whether appellee placed the prerecorded or automated telephone call to appellee; and (4) whether a genuine issue of material fact exists as to whether appellee violated the statute and regulations by failing to provide appellant with a copy of its "do-not-call" policy.

On November 22, 2002, appellant received a recorded call on his residential phone line from Precision Windshield Repair, a company operated by appellee. Appellee's owner averred in an affidavit that the following prerecorded message was played:

"Hi, this is a message from Precision Windshield Repair. Do you have a crack or chip in the windshield of you[r] car? In most cases the repair is absolutely free. If you would like to speak to a repair specialist please press 1[;] if you would like to leave a message please press 2. If you would like to give us a call, call us at 1-877-244-7349. That's 1-877-CHIP-FIX."

Appellant averred in his affidavit that since the message did not identify the caller, he pressed the button requesting a call back. Within an hour, he received a call from Keith Armbruster of Precision Windshield Repair, and during this call, he also spoke with Hyek "Corey" Chung, who identified himself as the owner of Precision Windshield. Appellant taped part of the prerecorded message and all the second call. During the second call, Armbruster told appellant the address and phone number of Precision Windshield, and he confirmed that a computer had placed the first call. After appellant asked to be placed on the company's do-not-call list, Armbruster put Corey Chung on the line. After appellant and Chung had some discussion about the legality of prerecorded phone calls, appellant again asked to be placed on the company's do-not-call list, and he also asked Chung to send him a copy of the company's do-not-call policy. Not having received the policy, appellant sent a letter to appellee again requesting the policy and demanding $700 for violating both the TCPA and the Ohio Consumer Sales Practices Act ("CSPA"). Later, in an answer to a request for production of documents, appellee admitted that it did not have a do-not-call policy on November 22, 2002. It is undisputed that appellant and appellee do not have a prior business relationship and that appellant did not invite the November 22, 2002, calls. It is also undisputed that appellee is a commercial enterprise and not a tax-exempt, nonprofit organization.

Appellant filed suit against appellee, asserting claims under the TCPA and the CSPA. Subsequently, appellee moved for summary judgment, and appellant moved for partial summary judgment (on all issues "except discretionary damages"). The trial court held a hearing on the motions. The trial court granted appellee's motion and denied appellant's motion but did not issue an opinion explaining its decision. Appellant now appeals. . . .

The first question is whether a private right of action exists when a company causes just one prerecorded phone call to be made. Former Section 227(b), Title 47, U.S. Code provided:

> (b) Restrictions on use of automated telephone equipment
>   (1) Prohibitions. It shall be unlawful for any person within the United States—
>   * * *
>   (B) to initiate any telephone call to any residential telephone line using an artificial or prerecorded voice to deliver a message without the prior express consent of the called party, unless the call is initiated for emergency purposes or is exempted by rule or order by the Commission under paragraph (2)(B).

Former Section 64.1200(a)(2), Title 47, C.F.R. exempted certain phone calls. That section provided:

> (a) No person may: . . .
>   * * *
>   (2) Initiate any telephone call to any residential line using an artificial or prerecorded voice to deliver a message without the prior express consent of the called party, unless the call is initiated for emergency purposes or is exempted by §64.1200(c) of this section. . . .
>   * * *
>   (c) The term "telephone call" in §64.1200(a)(2) of this section shall not include a call or message by, or on behalf of, a caller:
>   (1) That is not made for a commercial purpose,
>   (2) That is made for a commercial purpose but does not include the transmission of any unsolicited advertisement,
>   (3) To any person with whom the caller has an established business relationship at the time the call is made, or
>   (4) Which is a tax-exempt nonprofit organization.

The statute provides a private right of action in state court for violation of Section 227. Section 227(b)(3), Title 47, U.S. Code provides:

> (3) Private right of action. A person or entity may, if otherwise permitted by the laws or rules of court of a State, bring in an appropriate court of that State—
>   (A) an action based on a violation of this subsection or the regulations prescribed under this subsection to enjoin such violation,
>   (B) an action to recover for actual monetary loss from such a violation, or to receive $500 in damages for each such violation, whichever is greater, or
>   (C) both such actions.

Appellee contended in its motion for summary judgment (it did not file an appellate brief) that a different provision applied. Appellee cited Section 227(c)(5), Title 47 U.S. Code, which provides:

> (5) Private right of action. A person who has received more than one telephone call within any 12-month period by or on behalf of the same entity in violation of the regulations prescribed under this subsection may, if otherwise permitted by the laws or rules of court of a State bring in an appropriate court of that State—
>   (A) an action based on a violation of the regulations prescribed under this subsection to enjoin such violation,
>   (B) an action to recover for actual monetary loss from such a violation, or to receive up to $500 in damages for each such violation, whichever is greater, or
>   (C) both such actions.

Thus, according to appellee, appellant does not have a private right of action unless he received two calls in a 12-month period. It is undisputed that appellant received only one such call.

We disagree with appellee. The prohibition against artificial or prerecorded messages is found in Section 227(b)(3). Section 227(b)(3)(A) provides for a private right of action for "a violation of *this subsection* or the regulations prescribed under this subsection." (Emphasis added.) The phrase "this subsection" must be construed to mean subsection (b), which applies to automated or prerecorded calls and facsimile transmissions. See Grady v. Lenders Interactive Servs., 8th Dist. No. 83966, 2004-Ohio-4239, 2004 WL 1799178, at ¶36 (the clear language of Section 227(b) does not require more than one fax transmission to constitute a violation). Section 227 also provides for a separate private right of action under subsection (c)(5), which deals with live telephone calls, not with prerecorded or artificial messages. Under subsection (c), in order to have a private right of action, the recipient must receive more than one phone call in a 12-month period. See In re Rules and Regulations Implementing the Telephone Consumer Protection Act of 1991, 2003 WL 21517853, 2003 FCC LEXIS 3673, at ¶205 (July 3, 2003) (recognizing that Section 227 contains two different private rights of action: one for automated or prerecorded messages and fax transmissions in subsection (b)(3) and one for live telephone calls in (c)(5)). Because the call in question was a prerecorded message, the subsection providing for a private right of action is Section 227(b)(3), which requires only one call. Therefore, appellant has a private right of action in state court for even a single violation of the statute.

Since calls not containing an "unsolicited advertisement" are exempt under Section 64.1200(c)(2), Title 47, C.F.R., the next question is whether appellee's automated message contained an "unsolicited advertisement." Appellant claims that it did. Former Section 227(a)(4), Title 47, U.S. Code and former Section 64.1200(f)(5), Title 47, C.F.R. defined "unsolicited advertisement" as "any material advertising the commercial availability or quality of any property, goods, or services which is transmitted to any person without that person's prior express invitation or permission."

In the trial court, appellee contended that the call did not contain an unsolicited advertisement because the recipient of the call had to do an affirmative act (press 1) in order to hear the actual sales pitch. At least one court in Ohio has rejected this argument, noting that the purpose of the TCPA is to reduce the number of nuisance calls. See Charvat v. Crawford, 155 Ohio App. 3d 161, 2003-Ohio-5891, 799 N.E.2d 661, at ¶18. The Federal Communications Commission has also expressed the opinion that a sale is not required in order for the message to contain an unsolicited advertisement and that offers for "free goods or services that are part of an overall marketing campaign to sell property, goods, or services constitute [an unsolicited advertisement]." In re Rules and Regulations Implementing the TCPA, 2003 WL 21517853, 2003 FCC LEXIS 3673, at ¶140. The FCC stated:

> Therefore, a prerecorded message that contains language describing a new product, a vacation destination, or a company that will be in "your area" to perform home repairs, and asks the consumer to call a toll-free number to "learn more," is an "unsolicited advertisement" under the TCPA if sent without the called party's express invitation or permission. Id. at fn. 477.

The prerecorded message that appellee sent appellant advertised the "commercial availability" of services, see former Section 64.1200(f)(5), Title 47, C.F.R.; Section 227(a)(4), Title 47, U.S. Code, and it closely resembles the type of message defined as an unsolicited advertisement by the FCC. See In re Rules and Regulations at fn 477. We therefore find that the prerecorded message that appellee sent to appellant was an unsolicited advertisement. We also find that no other exemption in Section 64.1200(c), Title 47, C.F.R. applies. Therefore, we find as a matter of law that appellee violated the TCPA by initiating a prerecorded message containing an unsolicited advertisement, and we find that appellant has a private right of action in state court to redress it.

Next, we must decide whether appellee violated the TCPA by failing to provide its do-not-call policy to appellant upon demand. Former Section 64.1200(e)(2), Title 47, C.F.R. provided:

> No person or entity shall initiate any telephone solicitation to a residential telephone subscriber:
>
> (1) Before the hour of 8 a.m. or after 9 p.m. (local time at the called party's location), and,
>
> (2) Unless such person or entity has instituted procedures for maintaining a list of persons who do not wish to receive telephone solicitations made by or on

behalf of that person or entity. The procedures instituted must meet the following minimum standards:

> (i) Written policy. Persons or entities making telephone solicitations must have a written policy, available on demand, for maintaining a do-not-call list. . . .

"Telephone solicitation" was defined in the regulations as:

> the initiation of a telephone call or message for the purpose of encouraging the purchase or rental of, or investment in, property, goods, or services, which is transmitted to any person, but such term does not include a call or message:
>
> (i) To any person with that person's prior express invitation or permission;
>
> (ii) To any person with whom the caller has an established business relationship; or
>
> (iii) By or on behalf of a tax-exempt nonprofit organization.

Former Section 64.1200(f)(3), Title 47, C.F.R.

Since appellee admitted that it did not have a do-not-call policy at the time it made the prerecorded phone call to appellant, that it is not a tax-exempt, nonprofit organization, and that appellant did not give prior consent for the call, appellee has violated the regulations requiring a do-not-call policy that is produced on demand. We therefore find as a matter of law that appellee violated the TCPA in this manner as well.

In sum, we find that appellee, as a matter of law, violated two provisions of the TCPA and that appellant has a private right of action in state court to redress these violations. Therefore, the trial court erred in granting appellee's motion for summary judgment and denying appellant's motion for partial summary judgment, and both of appellant's assignments of error are well taken. The case is reversed and remanded for a determination on damages.

Upon due consideration, we find that substantial justice was not done the party complaining, and the decision of the Toledo Municipal Court is reversed and remanded for a determination on damages. Pursuant to App. R. 24, appellee is ordered to pay the court costs of this appeal.

Judgment reversed.

QUOTES FOR THE ATTORNEY'S ARSENAL: "TELEPHONE SOLICITATIONS"

I'm now convinced that the worst thing a man can do with a telephone without breaking the law is to call someone he doesn't know and try to sell that person something he doesn't want.

Michael Lewis, Liar's Poker 152 (1989).

G. Email Spam

In 2003 Congress passed a statute named the Controlling the Assault of Non-Solicited Pornography and Marketing Act of 2003 (commonly called CAN-SPAM), 15 U.S.C. 7701, to regulate the sending of commercial email. The Federal Trade Commission has power to issue regulations supplementing the Act. Broadly speaking, among other things the statute prohibits untruthful emails, requires senders to be identified, and specifies opt-out provisions. There is no private cause of action for violations of the rules (and in fact those are forbidden), and the statute has been so little enforced that it is widely ignored by spammers (though there have been a few successful criminal prosecutions of major offenders). The truth is that unwanted emails have constantly increased since 2003, reaching 164 billion every day worldwide by the middle of 2008. For a discussion of the Act and its problems, see www.networkworld.com/news/2008/100608-can-spam.html.

H. Home Solicitations

PROBLEM 15

Hardworking Mrs. Smith was depressed that her four children were doing very badly in school. Apparently they couldn't read, though she wasn't sure since she herself was illiterate. One night, five minutes after she got home from her job as a custodian in an office building, she answered the front door to find a salesman selling encyclopedias. When she told him that she was unsure exactly what an encyclopedia was, he informed her that it was the secret to the success of her children in school because it was chock-full of all the information they needed for academic success. He also told her that the sales price would be reduced by $30 for each friend of Mrs. Smith's whom she named and who later consented to a sales pitch for the encyclopedias. Is this last statement illegal? If the statement had been made after Mrs. Smith had signed a contract of purchase, would it be illegal? Assume, instead of the above, that the salesman told Mrs. Smith that he would pay her $10 for each of the names of her friends whom she thought did not own an encyclopedia. Would this offer trigger relief under the consumer statutes?

The Federal Trade Commission, recognizing that people caught in their home by talented salespersons can be talked into buying almost anything, decided to give such consumers a "cooling-off" period (the British call this a "decompression" period) in which to think things over and reconsider the sale. In your statute book read the FTC's Cooling-off Period for Sales Made at Homes or at Certain Other Locations (commonly called the "door-to-door sales" regulation), 16 C.F.R. §429 (effective June 7, 1974), and use it to answer the following Problem.

PROBLEM 16

Say that the salesman from Problem 15 had Mrs. Smith sign the contract on Monday, September 25, leaving her the introductory volume of the encyclopedia set. He had her give him a check for $25 as a down payment on the entire set, which cost $400. He gave her a copy of the FTC door-to-door sales notice as set out in the Regulation.

a. Would the salesman have had to give Mrs. Smith the notice if she had signed up for the encyclopedias not in her own home, but in the home of her next-door neighbor, whom she happened to be visiting when the salesman called?

b. Can the salesman lessen the possibility of her canceling the transaction by burying the FTC notice in all the other paperwork and not calling attention in any way to her right to cancel?

c. Can he avoid the right of rescission by having her sign a waiver of the right to cancel?

d. Would there be a right to cancel if he were selling insurance?[27]

e. How long must the company hold her check?

f. If one of her children were to drop the introductory volume down the incinerator on Tuesday morning, could Mrs. Smith still cancel the sale?

g. Mrs. Smith calls you, her cousin and therefore favorite attorney (and you thought you could escape practicing consumer law), on Thursday morning, September 28. Is it too late for her to cancel? If not, what should she do?

h. Not having heard anything from the encyclopedia company (which never cashed her check), Mrs. Smith sold the introductory

---

27. Laws protecting consumers typically exclude coverage of insurance contracts on the theory that insurance companies are already regulated by state officials, who, of course, would not allow the companies to treat consumers unfairly. For an annotation exploring the applicability of state consumer protection statutes to insurance companies, see 77 A.L.R.4th 991.

volume for 25 cents at a garage sale in early November of that year. Is she allowed to do this?

QUOTES FOR THE ATTORNEY'S ARSENAL: "COOLING-OFF PERIODS"

The proposition that a buyer should have a right to whimsically change his mind with respect to a transaction which has been formalized by an agreement containing all of the elements of a legally binding contract is, indeed, a revolutionary legal concept. This proposal represents an attack upon the basic contractual concepts which are the foundation of the American economic system. It will only be a matter of time before this concept, once accepted, intrudes its way into the entire fabric of American contract law.

Statement of Daniel Blake Burns, Vice President of Grolier, Inc., representing the American Educational Publishers Institute before the National Conference of Commissioners on Uniform State Laws, Special Committee on Retail Installment Sales, January 18, 1968.

QUESTION

Mr. Burns proved to be prophetic. In the 40 or so years since his statement, many consumer statutes enacted at both the federal and state levels contain cooling-off periods. Is this a good idea? As a legislator, would you vote for a statute allowing consumers three days after the signing of a health spa contract in which to perhaps change their minds and avoid the deal?

PROBLEM 17

Suppose your state statute on home solicitation sales differs from the federal rule in two respects:

(1) It exempts the seller from having to give the usual door-to-door sales cancellation notice whenever the buyer initiates the contact between the parties and the seller has a fixed place of business from which it regularly offers the goods for sale.

(2) It covers telephone solicitations initiated by the seller.

Are these state variations in any way affected by the FTC rule? See the rule's §429.2(b).

III. INTERSTATE LAND SALES

In the late 1960s and through the mid-1970s, companies made a lot of money selling undeveloped real estate, sight unseen, to consumers, most of whom were seduced into signing contracts of purchase at dinners where they were wined, dined, and subjected to a brutal sales presentation, typically including classic examples of fraud, misrepresentation, deceptive practices, and out-and-out villainy.

The land being sold was frequently worthless before being purchased by the developer, who would then set prices for resale absurdly high. In Arizona, desert land worth no more than $150 was sold for $5,000. In Hawaii, land next to active volcanoes was resold as a dream retirement spot. In Florida, land that was completely covered by swamp water was the selected realty. Sometimes there was no land at all: a group in Asheville, North Carolina, was indicted for mail fraud in trying to sell 60,000 acres of the Great Smoky Mountains National Park. The FTC found one company "used artificial props including painting the grass and attaching artificial pine cones to trees, in promotional movies to make the subdivisions appear more appealing," FTC News Summary No. 12, at 4 (March 21, 1975).

States responded to this fleecing of the citizenry by enacting statutes regulating the sales practices of developers. Effective in 1969, the Interstate Land Sales Full Disclosure Act, 15 U.S.C. §§1701 et seq., was the congressional answer to the problem.[28] The statute places regulatory jurisdiction in the Department of Housing and Urban Development (HUD). The Act requires developers to create two primary documents: the Statement of Record (a complete description of the project, filed in Washington, D.C., in HUD's Office of Interstate Land Sales Registration—OILSR) and a Property Report (a summary of the Statement of Record that is given to the consumer before he or she signs the contract of purchase).

In the early days of enforcement of the Act, the Statement of Record filed with OILSR was a pretty skimpy document; see §1705 for the bare-bones information required by the statutory language. HUD regulations (24 C.F.R. §§1700 et seq.), however, soon fixed that, requiring massive documentation of the proposed project to be filed with OILSR. Currently, the Statement of Record must also contain the proposed Property Report (the document given to the consumer prior to the consummation of the deal),

---

28. For an excellent analysis of the Act, see Federal Regulation of Interstate Land Sales: The Limitations of Full Disclosure, 11 Colum. J.L. & Soc. Probs. 133 (1975). For the details of land sales fraud, including the unhappy early history of OILSR, see M. Paulson, The Great Land Hustle (1972).

and, as outlined in §1710.100 of the Regulation infra, the Property Report should reveal a great deal about the property under consideration.

Some of the HUD regulations adopted pursuant to the Act are reprinted following the statute. Glance through the statute and regulations to get a general idea of their layout, and then use the specific sections cited in the Problems to explore the law in greater depth.

INTERSTATE LAND SALES FULL DISCLOSURE ACT
(selected sections) 15 U.S.C. §§1701 et seq.

§1701 Definitions

For the purposes of this title the term—

(1) "Secretary" means the Secretary of Housing and Urban Development;

(2) "person" means an individual, or an unincorporated organization, partnership, association, corporation, trust, or estate;

(3) "subdivision" means any land which is located in any State or in a foreign country and is divided or is proposed to be divided into lots, whether contiguous or not, for the purpose of sale or lease as part of a common promotional plan;

(4) "common promotional plan" means a plan, undertaken by a single developer or a group of developers acting in concert, to offer lots for sale or lease; where such land is offered for sale by such a developer or group of developers acting in concert, and such land is contiguous or is known, designated, or advertised as a common unit or by a common name, such land shall be presumed, without regard to the number of lots covered by each individual offering, as being offered for sale or lease as part of a common promotional plan;

(5) "developer" means any person who, directly or indirectly, sells or leases, or offers to sell or lease, or advertises for sale or lease any lots in a subdivision;

(6) "agent" means any person who represents, or acts for or on behalf of, a developer in selling or leasing, or offering to sell or lease, any lot or lots in a subdivision; but shall not include an attorney at law whose representation of another person consists solely of rendering legal services;

(7) "blanket encumbrance" means a trust deed, mortgage, judgment, or any other lien or encumbrance, including an option or contract to sell or a trust agreement, affecting a subdivision or affecting more than one lot offered within a subdivision, except that such term shall not include any lien

or other encumbrance arising as the result of the imposition of any tax assessment by any public authority;

(8) "interstate commerce" means trade or commerce among the several States or between any foreign country and any State;

(9) "State" includes the several States, the District of Columbia, the Commonwealth of Puerto Rico, and the territories and possessions of the United States;

(10) "purchaser" means an actual or prospective purchaser or lessee of any lot in a subdivision; and

(11) "offer" includes any inducement, solicitation, or attempt to encourage a person to acquire a lot in a subdivision.

§1702 Exemptions

(a) Sale or lease of lots generally. Unless the method of disposition is adopted for the purpose of evasion of this title the provisions of this title shall not apply to—

(1) the sale or lease of lots in a subdivision containing less than twenty-five lots;

(2) the sale or lease of any improved land on which there is a residential, commercial, condominium, or industrial building, or the sale or lease of land under a contract obligating the seller or lessor to erect such a building thereon within a period of two years;

(3) the sale of evidences of indebtedness secured by a mortgage or deed of trust on real estate;

(4) the sale of securities issued by a real estate investment trust;

(5) the sale or lease of real estate by any government or government agency;

(6) the sale or lease of cemetery lots;

(7) the sale or lease of lots to any person who acquires such lots for the purpose of engaging in the business of constructing residential, commercial, or industrial buildings or for the purpose of resale or lease of such lots to persons engaged in such business; or

(8) the sale or lease of real estate which is zoned by the appropriate governmental authority for industrial or commercial development or which is restricted to such use by a declaration of covenants, conditions, and restrictions which has been recorded in the official records of the city or county in which such real estate is located, when—

(A) local authorities have approved access from such real estate to a public street or highway;

(B) the purchaser or lessee of such real estate is a duly organized corporation, partnership, trust, or business entity engaged in commercial or industrial business;

(C) the purchaser or lessee of such real estate is represented in the transaction of sale or lease by a representative of its own selection;

(D) the purchaser or lessee of such real estate affirms in writing to the seller or lessor that it either (i) is purchasing or leasing such real estate substantially for its own use, or (ii) has a binding commitment to sell, lease, or sublease such real estate to an entity which meets the requirements of subparagraph (B), is engaged in commercial or industrial business, and is not affiliated with the seller, lessor, or agent thereof; and

(E) a policy of title insurance or a title opinion is issued in connection with the transaction showing that title to the real estate purchased or leased is vested in the seller or lessor, subject only to such exceptions as may be approved in writing by such purchaser or the lessee prior to recordation of the instrument of conveyance or execution of the lease, but (i) nothing herein shall be construed as requiring the recordation of a lease, and (ii) any purchaser or lessee may waive, in writing in a separate document, the requirement of this subparagraph that a policy of title insurance or title opinion be issued in connection with the transaction.

(b) Sale or lease of lots subject to other statutory registration and disclosure requirements.   Unless the method of disposition is adopted for the purpose of evasion of this title the provisions requiring registration and disclosure (as specified in section 1703(a)(1) and sections 1704-1707) shall not apply to—

(1) the sale or lease of lots in a subdivision containing fewer than one hundred lots which are not exempt under subsection (a);

(2) the sale or lease of lots in a subdivision if, within the twelve-month period commencing on the date of the first sale or lease of a lot in such subdivision after the effective date of this subsection or on such other date within that twelve-month period as the Secretary may prescribe, not more than twelve lots are sold or leased, and the sale or lease of the first twelve lots in such subdivision in any subsequent twelve-month period, if not more than twelve lots have been sold or leased in any preceding twelve-month period after the effective date of this subsection;

(3) the sale or lease of lots in a subdivision if each noncontiguous part of such subdivision contains not more than twenty lots, and if the purchaser or lessee (or spouse thereof) has made a personal, on-the-lot

inspection of the lot purchased or leased, prior to signing of the contract or agreement to purchase or lease;

(4) the sale or lease of lots in a subdivision in which each of the lots is at least twenty acres (inclusive of easements for ingress and egress or public utilities);

(5) the sale or lease of a lot which is located within a municipality or county where a unit of local government specifies minimum standards for the development of subdivision lots taking place within its boundaries, when—

(A) (i) the subdivision meets all local codes and standards, and (ii) each lot is either zoned for single family residences or, in the absence of a zoning ordinance, is limited exclusively to single family residences;

(B) (i) the lot is situated on a paved street or highway which has been built to standards applicable to streets and highways maintained by the unit of local government in which the subdivision is located and is acceptable to such unit, or, where such street or highway is not complete, a bond or other surety acceptable to the municipality or county in the full amount of the cost of completing such street or highway has been posted to assure completion to such standards, and (ii) the unit of local government or a homeowners association has accepted or is obligated to accept the responsibility of maintaining such street or highway, except that, in any case in which a homeowners association has accepted or is obligated to accept such responsibility, a good faith written estimate of the cost of carrying out such responsibility over the first ten years of ownership or lease is provided to the purchaser or lessee prior to the signing of the contract or agreement to purchase or lease;

(C) at the time of closing, potable water, sanitary sewage disposal, and electricity have been extended to the lot or the unit of local government is obligated to install such facilities within one hundred and eighty days, and, for subdivisions which do not have a central water or sewage disposal system, rather than installation of water or sewer facilities, there must be assurances that an adequate potable water supply is available year-round and that the lot is approved for the installation of a septic tank;

(D) the contract of sale requires delivery of a warranty deed (or, where such a deed is not commonly used in the jurisdiction where the lot is located, a deed or grant which warrants that the grantor has not conveyed the lot to another person and that the lot is free from encumbrances made by the grantor or any other person claiming by, through, or under him) to the purchaser within one hundred and eighty days after the signing of the sales contract;

(E) at the time of closing, a title insurance binder or a title opinion reflecting the condition of the title shall be in existence and issued or presented to the purchaser or lessee showing that, subject only to such exceptions as may be approved in writing by the purchaser or lessee at the time of closing, marketable title to the lot is vested in the seller or lessor;

(F) the purchaser or lessee (or spouse thereof) has made a personal, on-the-lot inspection of the lot purchased or leased, prior to signing of the contract or agreement to purchase or lease; and

(G) there are no offers, by direct mail or telephone solicitation, of gifts, trips, dinners, or other such promotional techniques to induce prospective purchasers or lessees to visit the subdivision or to purchase or lease a lot;

(6) the sale or lease of a lot, if a mobile home is to be erected or placed thereon as a residence, where the lot is sold as a homesite by one party and the home by another, under contracts that obligate such sellers to perform, contingent upon the other seller carrying out its obligations so that a completed mobile home will be erected or placed on the completed homesite within a period of two years, and provide for all funds received by the sellers to be deposited in escrow accounts (controlled by parties independent of the sellers) until the transactions are completed, and further provide that such funds shall be released to the buyer on demand without prejudice if the land with the mobile home erected or placed thereon is not conveyed within such two-year period. Such homesite must conform to all local codes and standards for mobile home subdivisions, if any, must provide potable water, sanitary sewage disposal, electricity, access by roads, the purchaser must receive marketable title to the lot, and where common facilities are to be provided, they must be completed or fully funded;

(7)(A) the sale or lease of real estate by a developer who is engaged in a sales operation which is intrastate in nature. For purposes of this exemption, a lot may be sold only if—

(i) the lot is free and clear of all liens, encumbrances, and adverse claims;

(ii) the purchaser or lessee (or spouse thereof) has made a personal on-the-lot inspection of the lot to be purchased or leased;

(iii) each purchase or lease agreement contains—

(I) a clear and specific statement describing a good faith estimate of the year of completion of, and the party responsible for, providing and maintaining the roads, water facilities, sewer facilities and any existing or promised amenities; and

(II) a nonwaivable provision specifying that the contract or agreement may be revoked at the option of the purchaser or lessee until midnight of the seventh day following the signing of such contract or agreement or until such later time as may be required pursuant to applicable State laws; and

(iv) the purchaser or lessee has, prior to the time the contract or lease is entered into, acknowledged in writing the receipt of a written statement by the developer containing good faith estimates of the cost of providing electric, water, sewer, gas, and telephone service to such lot.

(B) As used in subparagraph (A)(i) of this paragraph, the terms "liens," "encumbrances," and "adverse claims" do not include United States land patents and similar Federal grants or reservations, property reservations which land developers commonly convey or dedicate to local bodies or public utilities for the purpose of bringing public services to the land being developed, taxes and assessments imposed by a State, by any other public body having authority to assess and tax property, or by a property owners' association, which, under applicable State or local law, constitute liens on the property before they are due and payable or beneficial property restrictions which would be enforceable by other lot owners or lessees in the subdivision, if—

(i) the developer, prior to the time the contract of sale or lease is entered into, has furnished each purchaser or lessee with a statement setting forth in descriptive and concise terms all such liens, reservations, taxes, assessments and restrictions which are applicable to the lot to be purchased or leased; and

(ii) receipt of such statement has been acknowledged in writing by the purchaser or lessee.

(C) For the purpose of this paragraph, a sales operation is "intrastate in nature" if the developer is subject to the laws of the State in which the land is located, and each lot in the subdivision, other than those which are exempt under [subsecs. (a), (b)(6), or (b)(8) of this section], is sold or leased to residents of the State in which the land is located; or

(8) the sale or lease of a lot in a subdivision containing fewer than three hundred lots if—

(A) the principal residence of the purchaser or lessee is within the same standard metropolitan statistical area, as defined by the Office of Management and Budget, as the lot purchased or leased;

(B) the lot is free and clear of liens (such as mortgages, deeds of trust, tax liens, mechanics liens, or judgments) at the time of the signing of the contract or agreement and until a deed is delivered to the purchaser or the lease expires. As used in this subparagraph, the term "liens" does not include (i) United States land patents and similar Federal grants or reservations, (ii) property reservations which land developers commonly convey or dedicate to local bodies or public utilities for the purpose of bringing public services to the land being developed, (iii) taxes and assessments imposed by a State, by any other public body having authority to assess and tax property, or by a property owners' association, which, under applicable State or local law, constitute liens on the property before they are due and payable or beneficial property restrictions which would be enforceable by other lot owners or lessees in the subdivision, or (iv) other interests described in regulations prescribed by the Secretary;

(C) the purchaser or lessee (or spouse thereof) has made a personal on-the-lot inspection of the lot to be purchased or leased;

(D) each purchase or lease agreement contains (i) a clear and specific statement describing a good faith estimate of the year of completion of and the party responsible for providing and maintaining the roads, water facilities, sewer facilities and any existing or promised amenities; and (ii) a nonwaivable provision specifying that the contract or agreement may be revoked at the option of the purchaser or lessee until midnight of the seventh day following the signing of such contract or agreement or until such later time as may be required pursuant to applicable State laws;

(E) the purchaser or lessee has, prior to the time the contract or lease is entered into, acknowledged in writing receipt of a written statement by the developer setting forth (i) in descriptive and concise terms all liens, reservations, taxes, assessments, beneficial property restrictions which would be enforceable by other lot owners or lessees in the subdivision, and adverse claims which are applicable to the lot to be purchased or leased, and (ii) good faith estimates of the cost of providing electric, water, sewer, gas, and telephone service to such lot;

(F) the developer executes and supplies to the purchaser a written instrument designating a person within the State of residence of the purchaser as his agent for service of process and acknowledging that the developer submits to the legal jurisdiction of the State in which the purchaser or lessee resides; and

(G) the developer executes a written affirmation to the effect that he has complied with the provisions of this paragraph, such affirmation to be given on a form provided by the Secretary, which shall include the following: the name and address of the developer; the name and address of the purchaser or lessee; a legal description of the lot; an affirmation that the provisions of this paragraph have been complied with; a statement that the developer submits to the jurisdiction of this title with regard to the sale or lease; and the signature of the developer.

(c) Rules and regulations. The Secretary may from time to time, pursuant to rules and regulations issued by him, exempt from any of the provisions of this title any subdivision or any lots in a subdivision, if he finds that the enforcement of this title with respect to such subdivision or lots is not necessary in the public interest and for the protection of purchasers by reason of the small amount involved or the limited character of the public offering.

§1703 Requirements respecting sale or lease of lots

(a) Prohibited activities. It shall be unlawful for any developer or agent, directly or indirectly, to make use of any means or instruments of transportation or communication in interstate commerce, or of the mails—

(1) with respect to the sale or lease of any lot not exempt under section 1702

(A) to sell or lease any lot unless a statement of record with respect to such lot is in effect in accordance with section 1706;

(B) to sell or lease any lot unless a printed property report, meeting the requirements of section 1708, has been furnished to the purchaser or lessee in advance of the signing of any contract or agreement by such purchaser or lessee;

(C) to sell or lease any lot where any part of the statement of record or the property report contained an untrue statement of a material fact or omitted to state a material fact required to be stated therein pursuant to sections 1704 through 1707 of this title or any regulations thereunder; or

(D) to display or deliver to prospective purchasers or lessees advertising and promotional material which is inconsistent with information required to be disclosed in the property report; or

(2) with respect to the sale or lease, or offer to sell or lease, any lot not exempt under section 1702(a)—

(A) to employ any device, scheme, or artifice to defraud;

(B) to obtain money or property by means of any untrue statement of a material fact, or any omission to state a material fact necessary in order to make the statements made (in light of the circumstances in which they were made and within the context of the overall offer and sale or lease) not misleading, with respect to any information pertinent to the lot or subdivision;

(C) to engage in any transaction, practice, or course of business which operates or would operate as a fraud or deceit upon a purchaser; or

(D) to represent that roads, sewers, water, gas, or electric service, or recreational amenities will be provided or completed by the developer without stipulating in the contract of sale or lease that such services or amenities will be provided or completed.

(b) Revocation of nonexempt contract or agreement at option of purchaser or lessee; time limit. Any contract or agreement for the sale or lease of a lot not exempt under section 1702 may be revoked at the option of the purchaser or lessee until midnight of the seventh day following the signing of such contract or agreement or until such later time as may be required pursuant to applicable State laws, and such contract or agreement shall clearly provide this right.

(c) Revocation of contract or agreement at option of purchaser or lessee where required property report not supplied. In the case of any contract or agreement for the sale or lease of a lot for which a property report is required by this title and the property report has not been given to the purchaser or lessee in advance of his or her signing such contract or agreement, such contract or agreement may be revoked at the option of the purchaser or lessee within two years from the date of such signing, and such contract or agreement shall clearly provide this right.

(d) Additional authority for revocation of nonexempt contract or agreement at option of purchaser or lessee; time limit; applicability. Any contract or agreement which is for the sale or lease of a lot not exempt under section 1702 and which does not provide—

(1) a description of the lot which makes such lot clearly identifiable and which is in a form acceptable for recording by the appropriate public official responsible for maintaining land records in the jurisdiction in which the lot is located;

(2) that, in the event of a default or breach of the contract or agreement by the purchaser or lessee, the seller or lessor (or successor thereof) will provide the purchaser or lessee with written notice of such default or breach and of the opportunity, which shall be given such purchaser or lessee, to remedy such default or breach within twenty days after the date of the receipt of such notice; and

(3) that, if the purchaser or lessee loses rights and interest in the lot as a result of a default or breach of the contract or agreement which occurs after the purchaser or lessee has paid 15 per centum of the purchase price of the lot, excluding any interest owed under the contract or agreement, the seller or lessor (or successor thereof) shall refund to such purchaser or lessee any amount which remains after subtracting (A) 15 per centum of the purchase price of the lot, excluding any interest owed under the contract or agreement, or the amount of damages incurred by the seller or lessor (or successor thereof) as a result of such breach, whichever is greater, from (B) the amount paid by the purchaser or lessee with respect to the purchase price of the lot, excluding any interest paid under the contract or agreement,

may be revoked at the option of the purchaser or lessee for two years from the date of the signing of such contract or agreement. This subsection shall not apply to the sale of a lot for which, within one hundred and eighty days after the signing of the sales contract, the purchaser receives a warranty deed (or, where such deed is not commonly used in the jurisdiction where the lot is located, a deed or grant that warrants at least that the grantor has not conveyed the lot to another person and that the lot is free from encumbrances made by the grantor or any other person claiming by, through, or under him or her).

(e) Repayment of purchaser or lessee upon revocation of all money paid under contract or agreement to seller or lessor. If a contract or agreement is revoked pursuant to subsection (b), (c), or (d), if the purchaser or lessee tenders to the seller or lessor (or successor thereof) an instrument conveying his or her rights and interests in the lot, and if the rights and interests and the lot are in a condition which is substantially similar to the condition in which they were conveyed or purported to be conveyed to the purchaser or lessee, such purchaser or lessee shall be entitled to all money paid by him or her under such contract or agreement.

§1704 Registration of subdivisions

(a) Filing of statement of record. A subdivision may be registered by filing with the Secretary a statement of record, meeting the requirements of this title and such rules and regulations as may be prescribed by the Secretary in furtherance of the provisions of this title. A statement of record shall be deemed effective only as to the lots specified therein.

(b) Payment of fees; use by Secretary. At the time of filing a statement of record, or any amendment thereto, the developer shall pay to the Secretary a fee, not in excess of $1,000, in accordance with a schedule to be

fixed by the regulations of the Secretary, which fees may be used by the Secretary to cover all or part of the cost of rendering services under this title and such expenses as are paid from such fees shall be considered non-administrative.

(c) Filing deemed to have taken place upon receipt of statement of record accompanied by fee.   The filing with the Secretary of a statement of record, or of an amendment thereto, shall be deemed to have taken place upon the receipt thereof, accompanied by payment of the fee required by subsection (b).

(d) Availability of information to public.   The information contained in or filed with any statement of record shall be made available to the public under such regulations as the Secretary may prescribe and copies thereof shall be furnished to every applicant at such reasonable charge as the Secretary may prescribe.

§1705 Information required in statement of record

The statement of record shall contain the information and be accompanied by the documents specified hereinafter in this section—

(1) the name and address of each person having an interest in the lots in the subdivision to be covered by the statement of record and the extent of such interest;

(2) a legal description of, and a statement of the total area included in, the subdivision and a statement of the topography thereof, together with a map showing the division proposed and the dimensions of the lots to be covered by the statement of record and their relation to existing streets and roads;

(3) a statement of the condition of the title to the land comprising the subdivision, including all encumbrances and deed restrictions and covenants applicable thereto;

(4) a statement of the general terms and conditions, including the range of selling prices or rents at which it is proposed to dispose of the lots in the subdivision;

(5) a statement of the present condition of access to the subdivision, the existence of any unusual conditions relating to noise or safety which affect the subdivision and are known to the developer, the availability of sewage disposal facilities and other public utilities (including water, electricity, gas, and telephone facilities) in the subdivision, the proximity in miles of the subdivision to nearby municipalities, and the nature of any improvements to be installed by the developer and his estimated schedule for completion;

(6) in the case of any subdivision or portion thereof against which there exists a blanket encumbrance, a statement of the consequences for an individual purchaser of a failure, by the person or persons bound, to fulfill obligations under the instrument or instruments creating such encumbrance and the steps, if any, taken to protect the purchaser in such eventuality;

(7) (A) copy of its articles of incorporation, with all amendments thereto, if the developer is a corporation; (B) copies of all instruments by which the trust is created or declared, if the developer is a trust; (C) copies of its articles of partnership or association and all other papers pertaining to its organization, if the developer is a partnership, unincorporated association, joint stock company, or any other form of organization; and (D) if the purported holder of legal title is a person other than developer, copies of the above documents for such person;

(8) copies of the deed or other instrument establishing title to the subdivision in the developer or other person and copies of any instrument creating a lien or encumbrance upon the title of developer or other person or copies of the opinion or opinions of counsel in respect to the title to the subdivision in the developer or other person or copies of the title insurance policy guaranteeing such title;

(9) copies of all forms of conveyance to be used in selling or leasing lots to purchasers;

(10) copies of instruments creating easements or other restrictions;

(11) such certified and uncertified financial statements of the developer as the Secretary may require; and

(12) such other information and such other documents and certifications as the Secretary may require as being reasonably necessary or appropriate for the protection of purchasers.

§1706 Effective date of statements of record and amendments thereto [omitted]

§1707 Information required in property report; use for promotional purposes

(a) A property report relating to the lots in a subdivision shall contain such of the information contained in the statement of record, and any amendments thereto, as the Secretary may deem necessary, but need not include the documents referred to in paragraphs (7) to (11), inclusive, of section 1705. A property report shall also contain such other information as the Secretary may by rules or regulations require as being necessary or appropriate in the public interest or for the protection of purchasers.

(b) The property report shall not be used for any promotional purposes before the statement of record becomes effective and then only if it is used in its entirety. No person may advertise or represent that the Secretary approves or recommends the subdivision or the sale or lease of lots therein. No portion of the property report shall be underscored, italicized, or printed in larger or bolder type than the balance of the statement unless the Secretary requires or permits it.

§1708 Certification of substantially equivalent state law [omitted]

§1709 Civil liabilities

(a) Violations; relief recoverable.   A purchaser or lessee may bring an action at law or in equity against a developer or agent if the sale or lease was made in violation of section 1703(a). In a suit authorized by this subsection, the court may order damages, specific performance, or such other relief as the court deems fair, just, and equitable. In determining such relief the court may take into account, but not be limited to, the following factors: the contract price of the lot or leasehold; the amount the purchaser or lessee actually paid; the cost of any improvements to the lot; the fair market value of the lot or leasehold at the time relief is determined; and the fair market value of the lot or leasehold at the time such lot was purchased or leased.

(b) Enforcement of rights by purchaser or lessee.   A purchaser or lessee may bring an action at law or in equity against the seller or lessor (or successor thereof) to enforce any right under subsection (b), (c), (d), or (e) of section 1703.

(c) Amounts recoverable.   The amount recoverable in a suit authorized by this section may include, in addition to matters specified in subsections (a) and (b), interest, court costs, and reasonable amounts for attorneys' fees, independent appraisers' fees, and travel to and from the lot.

(d) Contributions.   Every person who becomes liable to make any payment under this section may recover contribution as in cases of contract from any person who, if sued separately, would have been liable to make the same payment.

§1710 Review of orders; jurisdiction, procedure; conclusiveness of findings; additional evidence; modification of findings by Secretary; stay [omitted]

§1711 Limitation of actions

(a) No action shall be maintained under section 1709 with respect to—

(1) a violation of subsection (a)(1) or (a)(2)(D) of section 1703 more than three years after the date of signing of the contract of sale or lease; or

(2) a violation of subsection (a)(2)(A), (a)(2)(B), or (a)(2)(C) of section 1703 more than three years after discovery of the violation or after discovery should have been made by the exercise of reasonable diligence.

(b) No action shall be maintained under section 1709 to enforce a right created under subsection (b), (c), (d), or (e) of section 1703 unless brought within three years after the signing of the contract or lease, notwithstanding delivery of a deed to a purchaser.

§1712 Contrary stipulations void

Any condition, stipulation, or provision binding any person acquiring any lot in a subdivision to waive compliance with any provision of this title or of the rules and regulations of the Secretary shall be void.

§1713 Additional remedies

The rights and remedies provided by this title shall be in addition to any and all other rights and remedies that may exist at law or in equity.

§1714 Investigations, injunctions, and prosecution of offenses [omitted]

§1715 Administration [omitted]

§1716 Unlawful representations

The fact that a statement of record with respect to a subdivision has been filed or is in effect shall not be deemed a finding by the Secretary that the statement of record is true and accurate on its face, or be held to mean the Secretary has in any way passed upon the merits of, or given approval to, such subdivision. It shall be unlawful to make, or cause to be made, to any prospective purchaser any representation contrary to the foregoing.

§1717 Penalties for violations

Any person who willfully violates any of the provisions of this title, or the rules and regulations prescribed pursuant thereto, or any person who willfully, in a statement of record filed under, or in a property report issued pursuant to, this title makes any untrue statement of a material fact or omits to state any material fact required to be stated therein, shall upon conviction be fined not more than $10,000 or imprisoned not more than five years, or both.

§1718 Rules, regulations, and orders

The Secretary shall have authority from time to time to make, issue, amend, and rescind such rules and regulations and such orders as are necessary or appropriate to the exercise of the functions and powers conferred upon him elsewhere in this title. For the purpose of his rules and regulations, the Secretary may classify persons and matters within his jurisdiction and prescribe different requirements for different classes of persons or matters.

§1719 Jurisdiction of offenses and suits

The district courts of the United States, the United States courts of any territory, and the United States District Court for the District of Columbia shall have jurisdiction of offenses and violations under this title and under the rules and regulations prescribed by the Secretary pursuant thereto, and concurrent with State courts, of all suits in equity and actions at law brought to enforce any liability or duty created by this title. Any such suit or action may be brought in the district wherein the defendant is found or is an inhabitant or transacts business, or in the district where the offer or sale took place, if the defendant participated therein, and process in such cases may be served in any other district of which the defendant is an inhabitant or wherever the defendant may be found. Judgments and decrees so rendered shall be subject to review as provided in sections 1254 and 1291 of title 28, United States Code. No case arising under this title and brought in any State court of competent jurisdiction shall be removed to any court of the United States, except where the United States or any officer or employee of the United States in his official capacity is a party. No costs shall be assessed for or against the Secretary in any proceeding under this title brought by or against him in the Supreme Court or such other courts. . . .

HUD REGULATIONS OF INTERSTATE LAND SALES
(selected sections) 24 C.F.R. §§1700 et seq.

§1710.100 Statement of Record—Format

(a) The Statement of Record consists of two portions; the Property Report portion and the Additional Information and Documentation portion.

(b) General format. The Statement of Record shall be prepared in accordance with the following format:

PROPERTY REPORT

Heading and Section Number

(b) Taxes
(c) Violations and Litigation
(d) Resale or Exchange Program
(e) Unusual Situations
    1. Leases
    2. Foreign Subdivision
    3. Time Sharing
    4. Membership
(f) Equal Opportunity in Lot Sales
(g) Listing of Lots

ADDITIONAL INFORMATION AND DOCUMENTATION

§1710.02 General Instructions for completing the Statement of Record

* * *

(m) Final version of Property Report. On the date that a Statement of Record becomes effective, the Property Report portion shall become the Property Report for the subject subdivision. The version of the Property Report delivered to prospective lot purchasers shall be verbatim to that found effective by the Secretary and shall have no covers, pictures, emblems, logograms or identifying insignia other than as required by these regulations. It shall meet the same standards as to grade of paper, type size, margins, style and color of print as those set herein for the Statement of Record, except where required otherwise by these regulations. However, the date of typing or preparation of the pages and the OILSR number shall not appear in the final version. If the final version of the Property Report is commercially printed, or photocopied by a process which results in a commercial printing quality, and is bound on

the left side, both sides of the pages may be used for printed material. If it is typed or photocopied by a process which does not result in a clear and legible product on both sides of the page or is bound at the top, printing shall be done on only one side of the page. Three copies of the final version of the Property Report, in the exact form in which it is delivered to prospective lot purchasers, shall be sent to this Office within 20 days of the date on which the Statement of Record, amendment, or consolidation is allowed to become effective by the Secretary. If a Property Report in a foreign language is used as required by §1715.25(g), three copies of that Property Report together with copies of the translated documents shall be furnished the Secretary within 20 days of the date on which the advertising is first used. A Property Report prepared pursuant to these regulations shall not be distributed to potential lot purchasers until after the Statement of Record of which it is a part or any amendment to that Statement of Record has been made effective by the Secretary.

§1710.103 Developer obligated improvements

(a) If the developer represents either orally or in writing that it will provide or complete roads or facilities for water, sewer, gas, electricity or recreational amenities, it must be contractually obligated to do so (see §1715.15(f)), and the obligation shall be clearly stated in the Property Report. While the developer may disclose relevant facts about completion, the obligation to complete cannot be conditioned, other than as provided for in §1715.15(f), and an estimated completion date (month and year) must be stated in the Property Report. However, a developer that has only tentative plans to complete may so state in the Property Report, provided that the statement clearly identifies conditions to which the completion of the facilities are subject and states that there are no guarantees the facilities will be completed.

(b) If a party other than the developer is responsible for providing or completing roads or facilities for water, sewer, gas, electricity or recreational amenities, that entity shall be clearly identified in the Property Report under the categories described in §1710.110, §1710.111 or §1710.114, as applicable. A statement shall be included in the proper section of the Property Report that the developer is not responsible for providing or completing the facility or amenity and can give no assurance that it will be completed or available for use.

§1710.105 Cover page

The cover page of the Property Report shall be prepared in accordance with the following directions:

(a) The margins shall be at least 1 inch.

(b) The next 3 inches shall contain a warning, centered, in 1/2 inch capital letters in red type with 1/4 inch space between the lines which reads as follows:

READ THIS PROPERTY REPORT
BEFORE SIGNING ANYTHING

(c) The remainder of the page shall contain the following paragraphs beginning 1/4 inch below the last line of the warning:

> This Report is prepared and issued by the developer of this subdivision. It is not prepared or issued by the Federal Government.
>
> Federal law requires that you receive this Report prior to your signing a contract or agreement to buy or lease a lot in this subdivision. However, NO FEDERAL AGENCY HAS JUDGED THE MERITS OR VALUE, IF ANY, OF THIS PROPERTY.
>
> If you received this Report prior to signing a contract or agreement, you may cancel your contract or agreement by giving notice to the seller any time before midnight of the seventh day following the signing of the contract or agreement.
>
> If you did not receive this Report before you signed a contract or agreement, you may cancel the contract or agreement any time within two years from the date of signing.
>
> Name of Subdivision _____
> Name of Developer _____
> Date of This Report _____

(d)(1) If the purchaser is entitled to a longer revocation period by operation of State law, that period becomes the Federal revocation period and the Cover Page must reflect the requirements of the longer period, rather than the seven days.

(2)(i) If a deed is not delivered within 180 days of the signing of the contract or agreement of sale or unless certain provisions are included in the contract or agreement, the purchaser is entitled to cancel the contract within two years from the date of signing the contract or agreement.

(ii) The deed must be a warranty deed, or where such a deed is not commonly used, a similar deed legally acceptable in the jurisdiction where the lot is located. The deed must be free and clear of liens and encumbrances.

(iii) The contract provisions are:

(A) A legally sufficient and recordable lot description; and

(B) A provision that the seller will give the purchaser written notification of purchaser's default or breach of contract and the opportunity to have at least 20 days from the receipt of notice to correct the default or breach; and

(C) A provision that, if the purchaser loses rights and interest in the lot because of the purchaser's default or breach of contract after 15% of the purchase price, exclusive of interest, has been paid, the seller shall refund to the purchaser any amount which remains from the payments made after subtracting 15% of the purchase price, exclusive of interest, or the amount of the seller's actual damages, whichever is the greater.

(iv) If a deed is not delivered within 180 days of the signing of the contract or if the necessary provisions are not included in the contract, the following statement shall be used in place of any other rescission language:

> Under Federal law you may cancel your contract or agreement of sale any time within two years from the date of signing.

(e) At the time of submission, the developer may indicate its intention to comply with the red printing by an illustration or by a statement to that effect.

(f) The "Date of This Report" shall be the date on which the Secretary allows the Statement of Record to become effective and shall not be entered until the submission has become effective. . . .

§1710.118 Receipt, agent certification and cancellation page

(a) Format. The receipt, agent certification and cancellation page shall be prepared in accordance with the sample printed herein.

RECEIPT, AGENT CERTIFICATION AND CANCELLATION PAGE

PURCHASER RECEIPT

Important: Read Carefully

Name of subdivision_____

OILSR number_____ Date of report_____

We must give you a copy of this Property Report and give you an opportunity to read it before you sign any contract or agreement. By signing this receipt, you acknowledge that you have received a copy of our Property Report.

Received by_____ Date_____

Street address_____

City_____ State_____ Zip_____

If any representations are made to you which are contrary to those in this Report, please notify the:

Office of Interstate Land Sales Registration
HUD Building, 451 Seventh Street, S.W.
Washington, D.C. 20410

AGENT CERTIFICATION

I certify that I have made no representations to the person(s) receiving this Property Report which are contrary to the information contained in this Property Report.

Lot _____ Block _____ Section _____
Name of salesperson _____
Signature _____
Date _____

PURCHASE CANCELLATION

If you are entitled to cancel your purchase contract, and wish to do so, you may cancel by personal notice, or in writing. If you cancel in person or by telephone, it is recommended that you immediately confirm the cancellation by certified mail. You may use the form below.

Name of subdivision _____
Date of contract _____
This will confirm that I/we wish to cancel our purchase contract.
Purchaser(s) signature _____ Date _____

[Sections 1710.208 through 1710.219 omitted.]

SUBPART A—PURCHASERS' REVOCATION RIGHTS

§1715.1 General

The purpose of this subpart is to enumerate the conditions under which purchasers may exercise revocation rights. If more than one document of sale is used in a sale or lease transaction, the revocation period required to be set forth in the document starts at the time of signing of the first document.

§1715.2 Revocation at time of sale or lease

All purchasers have the option to revoke a contract or lease with regard to a lot not otherwise exempt under §§1710.5 through 1710.11 and 1710.14 until midnight of the seventh day following the signing of a contract or agreement. If a purchaser is entitled to a longer revocation period by operation of State law or the Act, that period becomes the Federal revocation period rather than the seven days. All contracts and agreements (including promissory notes) for lot sales and leases must clearly state that the longer revocation period is available to purchasers.

§1715.3 Revocation—Nondelivery of Property Report prior to signing of contract

Purchasers may revoke contracts and agreements (including promissory notes) within two years from the date of signing the contract or agreement if the required Property Report was not given to the purchaser before the signing of the contract or agreement. A statement providing for this right of revocation must be contained in the contract or agreement and any promissory notes.

§1715.4 Contract requirements and revocation

(a) A contract or agreement, including a promissory note, for the sale or lease of a lot not exempt under §§1710.5 through 1710.16 of this chapter may be revoked by a purchaser within two years from the date of signing the contract or agreement if the contract or agreement did not include:

(1) A clear description of the lot in a form acceptable for recording by the appropriate public official responsible for maintaining land records in the jurisdiction in which the lot is located;

(2) A provision requiring the seller to notify a purchaser in writing as to any default or breach of contract or agreement (including promissory notes) for which the purchaser is responsible. The contract must also contain a provision which allows at least 20 days from the date the notice is received for the purchaser to remedy the default or breach of contract or agreement;

(3) A provision which states that if a purchaser has paid at least 15% of the purchase price (excluding any interest owed) at the time of default or breach of contract (including promissory notes) and loses rights and interest in the lot due to that default, the purchaser may be entitled to a refund. The provision must state that the seller must refund to the purchaser whatever amount remains after: (i) Subtracting 15% of the

purchase price of the lot (excluding interest owed) at the time of the default or breach of contract or agreement, or (ii) subtracting the amount of damages incurred by the seller due to the default or breach of contract, whichever is greater.

(b) For the purposes of this section, (1) "Purchase price" means the cash sales price of the lot shown on the contract; (2) "Damages incurred by the seller or lessor" means actual damages resulting from the default or breach as determined by the law of the jurisdiction governing the contract. However, no elements of actual damage may be specified in the contract or agreement. A liquidated damages clause not exceeding 15% of the purchase price of the lot, excluding any interest owed, may be specified.

(c) The contractual requirements of §1715.4 do not apply to the sale of a lot for which, within 180 days after the signing of the sales contract, the purchaser receives a warranty deed or, where warranty deeds are not commonly used, its equivalent under state law.

§1715.5 Reimbursement

If a contract or agreement (including a promissory note) is revoked pursuant to §1715.2, §1715.3 or §1715.4, the purchaser shall be entitled to all money paid under the contract or agreement. The purchaser must tender to the developer an instrument conveying his or her rights and interests in the lot and the lot itself in a condition which is substantially similar to the condition in which they were conveyed or purported to be conveyed to the purchaser. If the purchaser cannot convey the lot in substantially similar condition, the developer may subtract from the amount paid by the purchaser any diminished value in the lot occasioned by the acts of the purchaser.

SUBPART B—SALES PRACTICES AND STANDARDS

§1715.10 General

"Sales practices" means any conduct or advertising by a developer or its agents to induce a person to buy or lease a lot. This subpart describes certain unlawful sales practices and provides standards to illustrate what other sales practices are considered misleading in light of certain circumstances in which they are made and within the context of the overall offer and sale or lease.

§1715.15 Unlawful sales practices—Statutory provisions

In selling, leasing or offering to sell or lease any lot in a subdivision it is an unlawful sales practice for any developer or agent, directly or indirectly, to:

(a) Employ any device, scheme or artifice to defraud.

(b) Obtain money or property by means of any untrue statement of a material fact, or any omission to state a material fact necessary in order to make the statements made (in light of the circumstances in which they were made and within the context of the overall offer and sale or lease) not misleading, with respect to any information pertinent to the lot or the subdivision. It is not necessary for a developer to say everything about the subdivision in each separate contact with the purchaser, but what the developer does choose to say must not omit important facts that would be needed so that a purchaser would not be misled. For example, a Property Report description of a lake or an advertisement for "lakeside property" which omits to state that the lake is dry for six months of the year would be misleading and a likely violation.

(c) Engage in any transaction, practice or course of business which operates or would operate as a fraud or deceit upon a purchaser.

(d) Fail to furnish a purchaser with a printed Property Report (when the subdivision is required to be registered) in advance of the purchaser's signing a contract or agreement.

(e) Use a Statement of Record or Property Report (when the subdivision is required to be registered) which contains an untrue statement of material fact or omits to state a material fact required to be stated therein.

(f) Represent in any manner that roads, sewers, water, gas or electric service, or recreational amenities will be provided or completed by the developer unless there is a contractual provision expressly obligating the developer to provide or complete such services or amenities. Thus, if a developer advertises it will provide roads in the subdivision or shows a purchaser a subdivision master plan and indicates that the developer is providing the road system shown on that plan, there must be a road completion covenant in the contract. If there is no such covenant, the developer may not represent that it will provide the roads.

(1) The contractual covenant to provide or complete the services or amenities may be conditioned only upon grounds that are legally supportable to establish impossibility of performance in the jurisdiction where the services or amenities are being provided or completed.

(2) Contingencies such as Acts of God, strikes, or material shortages are recognized as permissible to defer completion of services or amenities.

(3) In creating these contractual obligations developers have the option to incorporate by reference the Property Report in effect at the time of the sale or lease. If a developer chooses to incorporate the Property Report by reference, the effective date of the Property Report being referenced must be specified in the contract of sale or lease.

(g) Display or deliver to purchasers advertising and promotional material which is inconsistent with information required to be disclosed in the Property Report (when the subdivision is required to be registered).

§1715.20 Unlawful sales practices—Regulatory provisions

In selling, leasing or offering to sell or lease any lot in a subdivision it is an unlawful sales practice for any developer or agent, directly or indirectly, to:

(a) Give the Property Report to a purchaser along with other materials when done in such a manner so as to conceal the Property Report from the purchaser.

(b) Give a contract to a purchaser or encourage him to sign anything before delivery of the Property Report.

(c) Refer to the Property Report or Offering Statement as anything other than a Property Report or Offering Statement.

(d) Use any misleading practice, device or representation which would deny a purchaser any cancellation or refund rights or privileges granted the purchaser by the terms of a contract or any other document used by the developer as a sales inducement.

(e) Refuse to deliver a Property Report to any person who exhibits an interest in buying or leasing a lot in the subdivision and requests a copy of the Property Report.

(f) Use a Property Report, note, contract, deed or other document prepared in a language other than that in which the sales campaign is conducted, unless an accurate translation is attached to the document.

(g) Deliberately fail to maintain a sufficient supply of restrictive covenants and financial statements or to deliver a copy to a purchaser upon request as required by §§1710.109(f), 1710.112(d), 1710.209(g) and 1710.212(i).

(h) Use, as a sales inducement, any representation that any lot has good investment potential or will increase in value unless it can be established, in writing, that:

(1) Comparable lots or parcels in the subdivision have, in fact, been resold by their owners on the open market at a profit, or

(2) There is a factual basis for the represented future increase in value and the factual basis is certain, and

(3) The sales price of the offered lot does not already reflect the anticipated increase in value due to any promised facilities or amenities. The burden of establishing the relevancy of any comparable sales and the certainty of the factual basis of the increase in value shall rest upon the developer.

(i) Represent a lot as a homesite or building lot unless:

(1) Potable water is available at a reasonable cost;

(2) The lot is suitable for a septic tank operation or there is reasonable assurance that the lot can be served by a central sewage system;

(3) The lot is legally accessible; and

(4) The lot is free from periodic flooding.

§1715.25 Misleading sales practices

Generally, promotional statements or material will be judged on the basis of the affirmative representations contained therein and the reasonable inferences to be drawn therefrom, unless the contrary is affirmatively stated or appears in promotional material, or unless adequate safeguards have been provided by the seller to reasonably guarantee the occurrence of the thing inferred. For example, when a lot is represented as being sold by a warranty deed, the inference is that the seller can and will convey fee simple title free and clear of all liens, encumbrances, and defects except those which are disclosed in writing to the prospective purchaser prior to conveyance. The following advertising and promotional practices, while not all inclusive, are considered misleading, and are used to evaluate a developer's or agent's representations in determining possible violations of the Act or Regulations. (In this section "represent" carries its common meaning.)

(a) Proposed improvements. References to proposed improvements of any land unless it is clearly indicated that (1) the improvements are only proposed or (2) what the completion date is for the proposed improvement.

(b) Off-premises representations. Representing scenes or proposed improvements other than those in the subdivision unless

(1) It is clearly stated that the scenes or improvements are not related to the subdivision offered; or

(2) In the case of drawings that the scenes or improvements are artists' renderings;

(3) If the areas or improvements shown are available to purchasers, what the distance in road miles is to the scenes or improvements represented.

(c) Land use representations. Representing uses to which the offered land can be put unless the land can be put to such use without unreasonable cost to the purchaser and unless no fact or circumstance exists which would prohibit the immediate use of the land for its represented use.

(d) Use of "road" and "street." Using the word "road" or "street" unless the type of road surface is disclosed. [All roads and streets shown on subdivision maps are presumed to be of an all-weather graded gravel

quality or higher and are presumed to be traversable by conventional automobile under all normal weather conditions unless otherwise shown on the map.]

(e) Road access and use.   Representing the existence of a road easement or right-of-way unless the easement or right-of-way is dedicated to the public, to property owners or to the appropriate property owners association.

(f) Waterfront property.   References to waterfront property, unless the property being offered actually fronts on a body of water. Representations which refer to "canal" or "canals" must state the specific use to which such canal or canals can be put.

(g) Maps and distances.   (1) The use of maps to show proximity to other communities, unless the maps are drawn to scale and scale included, or the specific road mileage appears in easily readable print.

(2) The use of the terms such as "minutes away," "short distance," "only miles," or "near" or similar terms to indicate distance unless the actual distance in road miles is used in conjunction with such terms. Road miles will be measured from the approximate geographical center of the subdivided lands to the approximate downtown or geographical center of the community.

(h) Lot size.   Representation of the size of a lot offered unless the lot size represented is exclusive of all easements to which the lot may be subject, except for those for providing utilities to the lot.

(i) "Free" lots.   Representing lots as "free" if the prospective purchaser is required to give any consideration whatsoever, offering lots for "closing costs only" when the closing costs are substantially more than customary, or when an additional lot must be purchased at a higher price.

(j) Pre-development prices.   References to pre-development sales at a lower price because the land has not yet been developed unless there are plans for development, and reasonable assurance is available that the plans will be completed.

(k) False reports of lot sales.   Repeatedly announcing that lots are being sold or to make repetitive announcements of the same lot being sold when in fact this is not the case.

(l) Guaranteed refund.   Use of the word "guarantee" or phrase "guaranteed refund" or similar language implying a money-back guarantee unless the refund is unconditional.

(m) Discount certificates.   The use of discount certificates when in fact there is no actual price reduction or when a discount certificate is regularly used.

(n) Lot exchanges.   Representations regarding property exchange privileges unless any applicable conditions are clearly stated.

(o) Resale program. Making any representation that implies that the developer or agent will resell or repurchase the property being offered at some future time unless the developer or agent has an ongoing program for doing so.

(p) Symbols for conditions. The use of asterisks or any other reference symbol or oral parenthetical expression as a means of contradicting or substantially changing any previously made statement or as a means of obscuring material facts.

(q) Proposed public facilities. References to a proposed public facility unless money has been budgeted for construction of the facility and is available to the public authority having the responsibility of construction, or unless disclosure of the existing facts concerning the public facility is made.

(r) Nonprofit or institutional name use. The use of names or trade styles which imply that the developer is a nonprofit research organization, public bureau, group, etc., when such is not the case.

§1715.27 Fair housing

(a) Pursuant to section 804(c) of Title VIII of the Civil Rights Act of 1968, as amended, the Federal Fair Housing law, except as exempted by Section 807, advertising shall not contain any indication of any preference, limitation or discrimination based on race, color, religion, sex or national origin.

(b) All advertising and sales presentations or representation must be consistent with the Advertising Guidelines for Fair Housing published in 37 FR 6700 (4-1-72) and 40 FR 20079 (5-8-75).

(c) Whenever sales activity takes place which is subject to the Fair Housing Law, the HUD approved Fair Housing Poster must be displayed.

§1715.30 Persons to whom Subpart B is inapplicable

Newspaper or periodical publishers, job printers, broadcasters, or telecasters, or any of the employees thereof, are not subject to this subpart unless the publishers, printers, broadcasters, or telecasters—

(a) Have actual knowledge of the falsity of the advertisement or

(b) Have any interest in the subdivision advertised or

(c) Also serve directly or indirectly as the advertising agent or agency for the developer.

SUBPART C—ADVERTISING DISCLAIMERS

§1715.50 Advertising disclaimers; subdivisions registered and effective with HUD

(a) The following disclaimer statement shall be displayed below the text of all printed material and literature used in connection with the sale or lease of lots in a subdivision for which an effective Statement or Record is on file with the Secretary. If the material or literature consists of more than one page, it shall appear at the bottom of the front page. The disclaimer statement shall be set in type of at least ten point font.

> Obtain the Property Report required by Federal law and read it before signing anything. No Federal agency has judged the merits or value, if any, of this property.

(b) If the advertising is of a classified type; is not more than five inches long and not more than one column in print wide, the disclaimer statement may be set in type of at least six point font.

(c) This disclaimer statement need not appear on billboards, on normal size matchbook folders or business cards which are used in advertising nor in advertising of a classified type which is less than one column in print wide and is less than five inches long.

(d) A developer who is required by any state, or states, to display an advertising disclaimer in the same location, or one of equal prominence, as that of the federal disclaimer, may combine the wording of the disclaimers. All of the wording of the federal disclaimer must be included in the resulting combined disclaimer.

PROBLEM 18

Mr. and Mrs. Consumer succumbed to a five-hour sales pitch and signed a contract to purchase land, sight unseen, from the Desert Flower Land Company. If they were handed the Property Report after the contract was signed, how long do they have to rescind the sale? See Act §1703(c). If they received it immediately before signing the contract how long do they have? Act §1703(b). The contract provided that if they missed a payment, Desert Flower could declare an immediate forfeiture and keep all payments made to date as liquidated damages; there was no grace period in which to make up late payments. May the Consumers cancel? Act §1703(d). What if the Consumers discover that they were lied to during the sales pitch (the land is not "green and verdant" but instead is dry and desiccated)? Have they any remedy? Act §§1703(a)(2), 1709, 1711, and 1719.

Exemptions.   The Act does not apply to the sale of realty if the land is "improved," that is, has a home on it, §1702(a)(2). That same section states that even if the land is currently unimproved, the statute does not apply if the developer has made a binding commitment to erect a building on the property within a two-year period. Other than that, as a generality, the Act applies to the sale of 25 or more lots sold to consumers in interstate commerce as part of a common promotional plan, §1702(a). Section 1702(b) partially exempts from statutory coverage certain promotional schemes meeting the guidelines therein listed.

The inclusion/exclusion rules of §1702 are quite complicated. Though the following two cases give some idea of the jurisdictional battlegrounds, in any actual case the attorneys involved must spend some time staring at §1702 carefully.

N & C PROPERTIES v. PRITCHARD
Supreme Court of Alabama, 1988
525 So. 2d 1346

ALMON, Justice.

Plaintiffs, Charles Pritchard, Alton Foster, Donald Johnson, and Kathy Johnson ("investors"), purchased condominium units (prior to the construction of those units) in a project known as East Pass Towers located in Destin, Florida. They sued N & C Properties, Chancellor Land Co., Inc., and Neda, Inc. ("developers"), under the Interstate Land Sales Full Disclosure Act, 15 U.S.C. §§1701-1720 ("ILSFDA" or "the Act"), for failure to provide a written prospectus covering the development. The amended complaint was filed on September 25, 1985, and plaintiffs filed a motion for summary judgment on October 9. A hearing on the motion was set for November 1, but it was stayed pending a decision from the United States Court of Appeals for the Eleventh Circuit regarding whether the ILSFDA applied to condominium sales.

On November 6, 1985, the defendants filed a motion for partial summary judgment, contending that the ILSFDA did not apply to condominium sales. The hearing on the cross-motions was held March 20, 1986, and the court rendered its order on March 28. At the hearing the circuit court granted plaintiffs' motion for summary judgment and denied defendants' application for leave to file post-hearing affidavits dated March 20. On June 20, 1986, the court rendered its final judgment in favor of the plaintiffs, granting them rescission of the condominium purchase agreements and awarding them attorney fees and the amount paid as earnest money.

In October and November of 1983, each of the investors entered into pre-construction purchase agreements with N & C Properties for condominiums in East Pass Towers. The investors deposited letters of credit with N & C Properties, Inc., in the amounts of $27,920, $28,200, and $32,200, respectively. These letters of credit were to serve as security on the purchase price and were to be funded at the closing. The letters were ultimately funded by the investors' bank when the circuit court dissolved the temporary restraining order that had enjoined their payment and denied the investors' request for a preliminary injunction.

Although the condominium project was in accord with applicable Florida laws and administrative regulations, it is undisputed that the project did not comply with the disclosure requirements of the ILSFDA. Title 15 U.S.C. 1703 (1982) states the requirements respecting the sale of lots under the act, as follows:

> (a) It shall be unlawful for any developer or agent, directly or indirectly, to make use of any means or instruments of transportation or communication in interstate commerce, or of the mails—
>> (1) with respect to the sale or lease of any lot not exempt under section 1702 of this title— . . .
>>> (B) to sell or lease any lot unless a printed property report, meeting the requirements of section 1707 of this title, has been furnished to the purchaser or lessee in advance of the signing of any contract or agreement by such purchaser or lessee;

That section essentially requires the developer to furnish a printed prospectus or property report before the purchaser signs the purchase agreement. The Act requires disclosure of the names and addresses of all owners and promoters, the range of selling prices, a description of the land, disclosure of any encumbrances or easements, and other information relevant to the sale. The purpose of the prospectus requirement is to inform the buyer of the details of the offering and prevent fraud in the sale of subdivided real estate.

The developers' initial argument is that the ILSFDA does not apply to condominium sales. The crux of this argument is that a condominium unit is not a "lot" within the meaning of the Act. As can be seen from the quotation above, 15 U.S.C. §1703(a)(1) (1982) makes the act applicable to "the sale or lease of any *lot* not exempt under section 1702 of this title." (Emphasis added.)

The United States Court of Appeals for the Eleventh Circuit has addressed this very issue:

> Congress did not draft the statute to apply solely to raw land, but made it applicable to the sale or lease of lots. The legislative history of the Act indicates that

Congress was concerned with the sale of fairly large numbers of undeveloped lots pursuant to a common promotional plan. Cong. Rep. No. 1785, 90th Cong., 2d Sess. (1968), reprinted in 1968 U.S. Code Cong. & Ad. News 3053, 3066. The legislative history also employs the terms "land" and "real estate." Id. Although Congress may have been primarily concerned with the sale of raw land, it struck a balance by making the statute applicable to *all* lots and providing an exemption, not for all improved land, but for improved land on which a residential, commercial, condominium, or industrial building exists or where the contract of sale obligates the seller to erect such a structure within two years.

The key term that we must construe is "lot" because the sale or lease of any non-exempt lot triggers the provisions of the Act. Lot is not defined anywhere in the ILSFDA. The Secretary of Housing and Urban Development (HUD) has defined lot, as part of a rule making proceeding completed in 1973, as "any portion, piece, division, unit, or undivided interest in land . . . if the interest includes the right to the exclusive use of a specific portion of the land." 24 C.F.R. §1710.1 [1987].

Winter v. Hollingsworth Properties, 777 F.2d 1444 (11th Cir. 1985). (Footnotes omitted.)

That court also explained that the Secretary of Housing and Urban Development ("HUD") intended for the Office of Interstate Land Sales Regulation, the organization designated by the Secretary to administer the ILSFDA, to treat condominiums as the equivalent of subdivisions. The Secretary describes "condominium" as a description of ownership and not a mere structural description. 777 F.2d at 1447, citing 38 Fed. Reg. 23,866 (1973), 44 Fed. Reg. 24,012 (1979). This Court finds this reasoning persuasive, particularly in light of the various forms that condominiums now assume. We also note that §1702 of the ILSFDA exempts "the sale or lease of any improved land on which there is a residential, commercial, condominium, or industrial building, or the sale or lease of land under a contract obligating the seller or lessor to erect such a building thereon within a period of two years." Although the developers do not claim such an exemption, we note in passing that the pre-construction sales contracts did not require construction of the project within two years as required for the statutory exemption. If the Act did not relate to the sale of condominiums, such an exemption would be unnecessary. See *Winter*, 777 F.2d 1444.

The developers contend that, even if the ILSFDA applies, the offering in question was of less than 100 units and was, therefore, exempt under 15 U.S.C. §1702(b)(1). That section exempts from the registration and disclosure requirements of the Act "the sale or lease of lots in a subdivision containing fewer than one hundred lots which are not exempt under subsection (a) of this section." Each of the investors purchased a unit in a development known as East Pass Towers Phase I, a condominium development containing 55 units. The developers contend that this offering was in no way related to East Pass Towers Phase II. They argue that Phase II was never formally offered for sale and that no condominium documents have yet been drafted. It is their contention, as developers of Phase I, that they had a mere option to build Phase II.

The investors, on the other hand, contend that East Pass Towers Phase I and Phase II are part of a common promotional plan and together constitute 101 units, bringing the development within the purview of the Act. A determination of applicability of the Act in the present instance requires a careful reading of the definitions in the Act. Section 1701(3) of the Act defines a "subdivision" as:

> [A]ny land which is located in any State or in a foreign country and is divided or is proposed to be divided into lots, whether contiguous or not, for the purpose of sale or lease as part of a common promotional plan.

Section 1701(4) defines "common promotional plan" as:

> [A] plan, undertaken by a single developer or a group of developers acting in concert, to offer lots for sale or lease; where such land is offered for sale by such a developer or group of developers acting in concert, and such land is contiguous or is known, designated, or advertised as a common unit or by a common name, such land shall be presumed, *without regard to the number of lots covered by each individual offering*, as being offered for sale or lease as part of a common promotional plan. (Emphasis added.)

Section 1701(11) defines "offer" as including "any inducement, solicitation, or attempt to encourage a person to acquire a lot in a subdivision."

The investors' argument below and on appeal is that the developers offered to sell units in Phase I and Phase II as a common plan of development. In support of their argument, they point to the following factors: (1) That Neda, Inc., was formed to promote and sell units in both Phase I and Phase II; (2) The project was advertised, represented, and marketed as a two-phase project consisting of two individual towers adjoining each other, Phase I containing 55 units and Phase II containing 46 units; and (3) The project was advertised and intended by the owners to be a two-phase project containing over 100 units. The investors offered the sworn testimony of Arthur Hill, president of Gulf South Corridor Properties, and Winston Biggs, president of Chancellor Land Company, Inc., in support of their claim during the hearing on March 20, 1986. The testimony of both men was that the development was advertised, represented, and marketed as a two-phase project containing two towers. The towers were to be adjacent to one another, sharing a common lobby and beach front. Mr. Biggs testified that the Johnsons were promised the opportunity to trade their Phase I unit for a nicer unit in Phase II when it was completed. He also testified, and it was undisputed by the appellants, that none of the purchasers in this suit was presented with a prospectus prior to the execution of their pre-construction purchase agreements.

A prospectus covering the development was, however, prepared by the developers, and it was admitted into evidence at the March 20 hearing. It was denominated "East Pass Towers Condominium Declaration," with the cover depicting twin towers on the Destin coast. Phase I of the development was to be completed by June 1, 1992. The maximum number of units in the development was to be 101 "if, in the sole discretion of the developer, Phase II is built." The prospectus also said, "The developer has reserved the right to construct additional apartment buildings . . . as part of this condominium at any time prior to June 1, 2002. . . . The additional units to be constructed will be 46 in number and would be contained in an additional apartment building." Advertising brochures admitted into evidence at the hearing also depicted twin towers joined by a common lobby.

The case of Grove Towers v. Lopez, 467 So. 2d 358 (Fla. 3d Dist. Ct. App.), *cert. denied*, 480 So. 2d 1294 (Fla. 1985), discusses the 100-lot exemption from the disclosure requirements of the ILSFDA. In that case, the developer claimed that its "intent" was to construct only 98 units, while the advertising brochures and the prospectus indicated that 108 units would be built. The Florida court held that mere intent to reserve an option to reduce the number of units in order to accommodate market demand was insufficient grounds to claim exemption under the statute. "As long as appellant wanted the option to build 108 units, it was obligated to comply [with the ILSFDA]." 467 So. 2d at 361.

This is very similar to what occurred in the present case. Here, the developers contend that they did not offer to sell any units in Phase II and, therefore, that the entire development is exempt from the disclosure requirements of the statute. The statute itself defines "offer" as *any* inducement, solicitation, or attempt to encourage a person to acquire a lot. The relevant advertising brochures and sales representations referring to twin towers totaling 101 units are sufficient to constitute offers, inducements, or solicitations for the purposes of the ILSFDA. Such representations necessitated that appellants furnish a prospectus to an investor prior to the execution of any sales agreement.

This Court also agrees with the finding of the circuit court that Phase I and Phase II constitute a "common promotional plan." The statute says that any plan where the land is known, designated, or advertised as a common unit or common name shall be presumed, without regard to the number of lots in a particular offering, to be part of a common promotional plan. 15 U.S.C. §1701(4). The fact that construction on Phase II had not yet begun or that it had not been "formally offered" for sale is irrelevant. The development of Phase II is presumed, under the Act, to be part of a common plan with Phase I. The developers cannot avoid application of the [A]ct simply by breaking the development into two smaller segments. See Eaton v. Dorchester Development, Inc., 692 F.2d 727 (11th Cir. 1982); Dunaway v. Lewis, 554 P.2d 110 (Okla. Ct. App. 1976).

Appellants next contend that the investors purchased the condominiums with the intent to resell them to developers and that the sales are, therefore, exempt from the disclosure requirements under 15 U.S.C. §1702(a)(7). We have searched the record below and have found no evidence whatsoever that the investors here intended to resell to developers. The federal regulations applicable to exemption from the ILSFDA provide, "If a developer elects to take advantage of an exemption, the developer is responsible for maintaining records to demonstrate that the requirements of the exemption have been met." 24 C.F.R. §1710.4(d) (1987). The appellants have offered no evidence in support of their claim and, therefore, we find it without merit.

Affirmed.

SCHATZ v. JOCKEY CLUB PHASE III
United States District Court, Southern District of Florida, 1985
604 F. Supp. 537

SPELLMAN, District Judge.

This is an action brought by condominium purchasers seeking the rescission of a contract for the purchase from Defendant of a condominium unit in the Jockey Club Condominiums, Phase III. The Second Amended Complaint based jurisdiction on section 1719 of the Interstate Land Sales Full Disclosure Act, 15 U.S.C. §§1701-1720, alleging that Jockey Club violated the Act by entering into the contract without providing the purchasers with a printed property report as required by section 1703(c) and section 1707. The Plaintiffs have additionally submitted an affidavit verifying the allegations contained in the Second Amended Complaint. Specifically, Plaintiffs aver that they "never received, and the defendant, Jockey Club Phase III, Ltd., never furnished to them a 'Property Report' of any kind."

Jockey Club has not responded with any evidentiary matter which would tend to refute this point. . . .

In this case, there are no disputed facts. The Jockey Club's position has always been that the instant transaction falls within an exemption to the Act or that the Act is otherwise inapplicable. Jockey Club's arguments will be discussed in turn.

1. *"THE ACT DOES NOT APPLY TO THIS CASE"*

Because this case involves the sale of a condominium unit, Defendant argues that the Interstate Land Sales Full Disclosure Act does not apply in that the Act 'by its terms does not apply to condominium units but only to sales . . . of any lots.' . . .

. . . It has been held that the general purpose of the Act is to prohibit and punish fraud in certain land development enterprises and consequently, it has been said that the Act should be liberally interpreted to attain that end. It should be construed not technically, but flexibly to effectuate its remedial purposes. See McCown v. Heidler, 527 F.2d 204 (10th Cir. 1975). Therefore, to implement this national public policy of protecting the consumer, this Court chooses to accord the Interstate Land Sales Full Disclosure Act a liberal construction. Accordingly, this Court holds that condominiums, or unit properties, are within the application of the federal statute.

2. *"JOCKEY CLUB IS AN EXEMPT PROJECT"*

"[E]ven if the Act were to apply to this transaction," Jockey Club argues, "this action should be dismissed because the Jockey Club condominium project is an exempt project within the terms of the Act." Defendant contends that the instant transaction comes within the exemption which states that the Act's provisions are inapplicable to "the sale or lease of land under a contract *obligating* the seller or lessor to erect such a building thereon within a period of two years." 15 U.S.C. 1702(a)(2) (emphasis added).

Jockey Club asserts that paragraph nine (9) of the contract obligated it to complete the condominium within a period of two years. That paragraph provides, in pertinent part, that:

> The apartment shall be ready for occupancy approximately on the estimated closing date but not later than two (2) years from the date hereof unless delayed by circumstances or conditions [that are] beyond the control of Seller and are legally supportable under Florida law as impossible of performance.

Paragraph nine, however, goes on to limit the purchasers' remedies: "Seller shall not be obligated to make, provide or compensate Buyer for any costs, expenses or losses that may result in a delay in the estimated date of occupancy. Such delays shall not cancel, amend or diminish any of the

Buyer's obligations undertaken." In addition, paragraph seventeen (17) states that "Seller's sole liability and obligation to Buyer in the event Seller fails to complete construction or otherwise fails to close this transaction, is the return of the Buyer's deposits together with interest thereon. No action of specific performance of this agreement shall lie in favor of either party." Finally, paragraph eighteen (18) grants the seller the right to reject the buyer for any reason whatsoever, and if so "this contract shall be terminated and of no further force or effect."

Faced with identical arguments and an identical contract, Judge Eaton in *Inversiones Romar, S.A.* [No. 82-0695-CIV-JE (S.D. Fla. Sept. 18, 1984)] granted summary judgment in favor of the purchasers. Judge Eaton held that "[t]hese provisions of paragraphs 17 and 18 so qualify the seller's promise to erect the unit within two years that it cannot be said that the contract 'obligates' Defendant to do so, within the meaning of the Act." This Court agrees with Judge Eaton. The obligation which a seller must undertake in order to come within §1702(a)(2) is to erect the building within two years. Here, the sole obligation which Jockey Club undertook was to give the purchasers an option to cancel the contract and recover the deposit in the event the condominium unit was not ready for occupancy within two years. This obligation, however, is no different than the obligation that the act itself imposes upon Jockey Club by virtue of its failure to furnish the required property reports to the purchasers.

In Eaton v. Dorchester Development, Inc., No. 81-1615-CIV-EPS (S.D. Fla. November 26, 1984), this Court adopted Judge Daniel Pearson's well-reasoned opinion in Dorchester Development, Inc. v. Burk, 439 So. 2d 1032 (Fla. 3d DCA 1983). Judge Pearson was quoted as follows:

> Where the seller is obligated to complete by a time certain, the purchaser is not limited, as here, to the remedy of rescission, but he may affirm the contract and seek damages. See Marshall v. Karl F. Schultz, Inc. [438 So. 2d 533] (Fla. 2d DCA 1983). . . . Since the Act is to be construed to effectuate its remedial purpose of protecting the land sale consumer, we can hardly conclude that a contract which has the effect of limiting the purchaser's remedies conforms to the requirements of the Act.

Id. at 1034-35 (footnote and citations omitted).

In this case, as in *Burk*, the contract limits the purchasers' ability to enforce the promise to complete the condominium within two years. Therefore, the contract does not comply with §1702(a)(2) which has been interpreted to require an "unconditional commitment" to complete the units within two years. Jockey Club is thus not exempt from the provisions of the Interstate Land Sales Full Disclosure Act by virtue of §1702(a)(2).

3. *"There Is No Claim of a Violation of the Act Which Has Injured Plaintiffs"*

Defendant notes that "Plaintiffs do not claim that they were misled, induced through fraud or 'bilked.' Plaintiffs do not claim that there was a nondisclosure of information which, if disclosed, would have caused them to not enter into the Sales Agreement." Although Defendant is correct, it makes no difference.

Such allegations are not required by the Interstate Land Sales Full Disclosure Act. The Congressional purpose behind the Act was to protect the consumer. This Court is of the opinion that this purpose would be thwarted were this Court to burden the purchaser with the requirement of claiming actual injury when Congress does not require such a claim. See *Inversiones Romar, S.A.* ("because the Act is a remedial statute, the Court finds Defendant's third contention to be without merit.").

The requirements of the Land Sales Full Disclosure Act are clear. And it is Jockey Club, not the purchasers, that must comply with the requirements. Section 1703(c) and section 1707 obligated Jockey Club to provide the purchasers with a printed property report. Since the uncontroverted facts establish that no property report was furnished, the purchasers are entitled to a judgment as a matter of law. Accordingly, Plaintiffs' Motion for Summary Judgment is granted.

PROBLEM 19

When Mr. and Mrs. Consumer sobered up the morning after the dinner at which they had agreed to buy land for a vacation home, they could remember little about the previous night. They did have quite a bit of paperwork that they had dragged home, and within it was something called the Property Report. The cover page had several dire warnings on it, all printed in black ink, one of which stated: "NO FEDERAL AGENCY HAS JUDGED THE MERITS OR VALUE, IF ANY, OF THIS PROPERTY." Mrs. Consumer says that she remembers the salesman telling her that this development was registered with the federal government and had been approved by the Department of Housing and Urban Development, and that similar nearby land had increased in value threefold. Mr. Consumer says that he can't remember much because of the confusion created by the announcer, who was yelling out the lot numbers of property that had just been sold at the dinner. Mr. Consumer is certain that the same lot number was announced as sold more than once. The Consumers cannot afford to go through with this purchase, and they want out. You are Mrs. Consumer's cousin and the only attorney she knows, so two weeks after the dinner, she calls you for help. Look at Regulations §§1710.105, 1715.2, 1715.3, and 1715.10-1715.25 and see if there is any hope for your cousin and her husband.

IV. RICO

The Racketeer Influenced and Corrupt Organizations Act (RICO), 18 U.S.C. §§1961-1968, is directed at "racketeering activity," defined in §1961(1) to encompass, *inter alia,* acts "indictable" under specific federal criminal statutes, including mail and wire fraud. One of RICO's remedial provisions, §1964(c), permits a private civil action to recover *treble* damages in favor of any person injured in his business or property "by reason of a violation of §1962," which in part prohibits conducting or participating in the conduct of an enterprise "through a pattern of racketeering activity."

The statute was designed to be a major weapon against gangster-related activity, but the suits brought under RICO have not been so limited. Perfectly respectable businesses were surprised at being sued under the Act and, having been found to have used the mails to accomplish their aims, forced to pay treble damages to those who could prove injury. Whether RICO was properly employed to punish non-racketeers was an issue that found its way to the United States Supreme Court.

SEDIMA, S.P.R.L. v. IMREX CO.
United States Supreme Court, 1985
473 U.S. 479

Justice WHITE delivered the opinion of the Court.

The Racketeer Influenced and Corrupt Organizations Act (RICO), Pub. L. 91-452, Title IX, 84 Stat. 941, as amended, 18 U.S.C. §§1961-1968, provides a private civil action to recover treble damages for injury "by reason of a violation of" its substantive provisions. 18 U.S.C. §1964(c). The initial dormancy of this provision and its recent greatly increased utilization[29] are

---

29. Of 270 District Court RICO decisions prior to this year, only 3% (nine cases) were decided throughout the 1970's, 2% were decided in 1980, 7% in 1981, 13% in 1982, 33% in 1983, and 43% in 1984. Report of the Ad Hoc Civil RICO Task Force of the ABA Section of Corporation, Banking and Business Law 55 (1985) (hereinafter ABA Report); see also id., at 53a (table).

now familiar history.[30] In response to what it perceived to be misuse of civil RICO by private plaintiffs, the court below construed §1964(c) to permit private actions only against defendants who had been convicted on criminal charges, and only where there had occurred a "racketeering injury." While we understand the court's concern over the consequences of an unbridled reading of the statute, we reject both of its holdings.

I.

RICO takes aim at "racketeering activity," which it defines as any act "chargeable" under several generically described state criminal laws, any act "indictable" under numerous specific federal criminal provisions, including mail and wire fraud, and any "offense" involving bankruptcy or securities fraud or drug-related activities that is "punishable" under federal law. §1961(1).[31] Section 1962, entitled "Prohibited Activities," outlaws the use of income derived from a "pattern of racketeering activity" to acquire an interest in or establish an enterprise engaged in or affecting interstate commerce; the acquisition or maintenance of any interest in an enterprise "through" a pattern of racketeering activity; conducting or participating in

---

30. For a thorough bibliography of civil RICO decisions and commentary, see Milner, A Civil RICO Bibliography, 21 C.W.L.R. 409 (1985).

31. RICO defines "racketeering activity" to mean

(A) any act or threat involving murder, kidnapping, gambling, arson, robbery, bribery, extortion, or dealing in narcotic or other dangerous drugs, which is chargeable under State law and punishable by imprisonment for more than one year; (B) any act which is indictable under any of the following provisions of title 18, United States Code: Section 201 (relating to bribery), section 224 (relating to sports bribery), sections 471, 472, and 473 (relating to counterfeiting), section 659 (relating to theft from interstate shipment) if the act indictable under section 659 is felonious, section 664 (relating to embezzlement from pension and welfare funds), sections 891-894 (relating to extortionate credit transactions), section 1084 (relating to the transmission of gambling information), section 1341 (relating to mail fraud), section 1343 (relating to wire fraud), section 1503 (relating to obstruction of justice), section 1510 (relating to obstruction of criminal investigations), section 1511 (relating to the obstruction of State or local law enforcement), section 1951 (relating to interference with commerce, robbery, or extortion), section 1952 (relating to racketeering), section 1953 (relating to interstate transportation of wagering paraphernalia), section 1954 (relating to unlawful welfare fund payments), section 1955 (relating to the prohibition of illegal gambling businesses), sections 2312 and 2313 (relating to interstate transportation of stolen motor vehicles), sections 2314 and 2315 (relating to interstate transportation of stolen property), section 2320 (relating to trafficking in certain motor vehicles or motor vehicle parts), sections 2341-2346 (relating to trafficking in contraband cigarettes), sections 2421-2424 (relating to white slave traffic); (C) any act which is indictable under title 29, United States Code, section 186 (dealing with restrictions on payments and loans to labor organizations) or

the conduct of an enterprise through a pattern of racketeering activity; and conspiring to violate any of these provisions.[32]

Congress provided criminal penalties of imprisonment, fines, and forfeiture for violation of these provisions. §1963. In addition, it set out a far-reaching civil enforcement scheme, §1964, including the following provision for private suits:

> Any person injured in his business or property by reason of a violation of section 1962 of this chapter may sue therefor in any appropriate United States district court and shall recover threefold the damages he sustains and the cost of the suit, including a reasonable attorney's fee. §1964(c).

In 1979, petitioner Sedima, a Belgian corporation, entered into a joint venture with respondent Imrex Co. to provide electronic components to a Belgian firm. The buyer was to order parts through Sedima; Imrex was to obtain the parts in this country and ship them to Europe. The agreement called for Sedima and Imrex to split the net proceeds. Imrex filled roughly $8 million in orders placed with it through Sedima. Sedima became convinced, however, that Imrex was presenting inflated bills, cheating Sedima out of a portion of its proceeds by collecting for nonexistent expenses.

In 1982, Sedima filed this action in the Federal District Court for the Eastern District of New York. The complaint set out common-law claims of unjust enrichment, conversion, and breach of contract, fiduciary duty, and a

---

section 501(c) (relating to embezzlement from union funds); (D) any offense involving fraud connected with a case under title 11, fraud in the sale of securities, or the felonious manufacture, importation, receiving, concealment, buying, selling, or otherwise dealing in narcotic or other dangerous drugs, punishable under any law of the United States; or (E) any act which is indictable under the Currency and Foreign Transactions Reporting Act. 18 U.S.C. §1961(1) (1982 ed., Supp. III).

32. In relevant part, 18 U.S.C. §1962 provides:

(a) It shall be unlawful for any person who has received any income derived, directly or indirectly, from a pattern of racketeering activity or through collection of an unlawful debt . . . to use or invest, directly or indirectly, any part of such income, or the proceeds of such income, in acquisition of any interest in, or the establishment or operation of, any enterprise which is engaged in, or the activities of which affect, interstate or foreign commerce. . . .

(b) It shall be unlawful for any person through a pattern of racketeering activity or through collection of an unlawful debt to acquire or maintain, directly or indirectly, any interest in or control of any enterprise which is engaged in, or the activities of which affect, interstate or foreign commerce.

(c) It shall be unlawful for any person employed by or associated with any enterprise engaged in, or the activities of which affect, interstate or foreign commerce, to conduct or participate, directly or indirectly, in the conduct of such enterprise's affairs through a pattern of racketeering activity or collection of unlawful debt.

(d) It shall be unlawful for any person to conspire to violate any of the provisions of subsections (a), (b), or (c) of this section.

constructive trust. In addition, it asserted RICO claims under §1964(c) against Imrex and two of its officers. Two counts alleged violations of §1962(c), based on predicate acts of mail and wire fraud. See 18 U.S.C. §§1341, 1343, 1961(1)(B). A third count alleged a conspiracy to violate §1962(c). Claiming injury of at least $175,000, the amount of the alleged overbilling, Sedima sought treble damages and attorney's fees.

The District Court held that for an injury to be "by reason of a violation of section 1962," as required by §1964(c), it must be somehow different in kind from the direct injury resulting from the predicate acts of racketeering activity. 574 F. Supp. 963 (1983). While not choosing a precise formulation, the District Court held that a complaint must allege a "RICO-type injury," which was either some sort of distinct "racketeering injury," or a "competitive injury." It found "no allegation here of any injury apart from that which would result directly from the alleged predicate acts of mail fraud and wire fraud," id., at 965, and accordingly dismissed the RICO counts for failure to state a claim.

A divided panel of the Court of Appeals for the Second Circuit affirmed. 741 F.2d 482 (1984). After a lengthy review of the legislative history, it held that Sedima's complaint was defective in two ways. First, it failed to allege an injury "by reason of a violation of section 1962." In the court's view, this language was a limitation on standing, reflecting Congress' intent to compensate victims of "certain specific kinds of organized criminality," not to provide additional remedies for already compensable injuries. Id., at 494. Analogizing to the Clayton Act, which had been the model for §1964(c), the court concluded that just as an antitrust plaintiff must allege an "antitrust injury," so a RICO plaintiff must allege a "racketeering injury"—an injury "different in kind from that occurring as a result of the predicate acts themselves, or not simply caused by the predicate acts, but also caused by an activity which RICO was designed to deter." Id., at 496. Sedima had failed to allege such an injury.

The Court of Appeals also found the complaint defective for not alleging that the defendants had already been criminally convicted of the predicate acts of mail and wire fraud, or of a RICO violation. This element of the civil cause of action was inferred from §1964(c)'s reference to a "violation" of §1962, the court also observing that its prior-conviction requirement would avoid serious constitutional difficulties, the danger of unfair stigmatization, and problems regarding the standard by which the predicate acts were to be proved.

The decision below was one episode in a recent proliferation of civil RICO litigation within the Second Circuit and in other Courts of Appeals. In light of the variety of approaches taken by the lower courts and the importance of the issues, we granted certiorari. 469 U.S. 1157 (1984). We now reverse.

II.

As a preliminary matter, it is worth briefly reviewing the legislative history of the private treble-damages action. RICO formed Title IX of the Organized Crime Control Act of 1970, Pub. L. 91-452, 84 Stat. 922. The civil remedies in the bill passed by the Senate, S. 30, were limited to injunctive actions by the United States and became §§1964(a), (b), and (d). Previous versions of the legislation, however, had provided for a private treble-damages action in exactly the terms ultimately adopted in §1964(c). See S. 1623, 91st Cong., 1st Sess., 4(a) (1969); S. 2048 and S. 2049, 90th Cong., 1st Sess. (1967).

During hearings on S. 30 before the House Judiciary Committee, Representative Steiger proposed the addition of a private treble-damages action "similar to the private damage remedy found in the anti-trust laws.... [T]hose who have been wronged by organized crime should at least be given access to a legal remedy. In addition, the availability of such a remedy would enhance the effectiveness of title IX's prohibitions." Hearings on S. 30, and Related Proposals, before Subcommittee No. 5 of the House Committee on the Judiciary, 91st Cong., 2d Sess., 520 (1970) (hereinafter House Hearings). The American Bar Association also proposed an amendment "based upon the concept of Section 4 of the Clayton Act." Id., at 543-544, 548, 559; see 116 Cong. Rec. 25190-25191 (1970). See also H.R. 9327, 91st Cong., 1st Sess. (1969) (House counterpart to S. 1623).

Over the dissent of three members, who feared the treble-damages provision would be used for malicious harassment of business competitors, the Committee approved the amendment. H.R. Rep. No. 91-1549, pp. 58, 187 (1970). In summarizing the bill on the House floor, its sponsor described the treble-damages provision as "another example of the antitrust remedy being adapted for use against organized criminality." 116 Cong. Rec. 35295 (1970). The full House then rejected a proposal to create a complementary treble-damages remedy for those injured by being named as defendants in malicious private suits. Id., at 35342. Representative Steiger also offered an amendment that would have allowed private injunctive actions, fixed a statute of limitations, and clarified venue and process requirements. Id., at 35346; see id., at 35226-35227. The proposal was greeted with some hostility because it had not been reviewed in Committee, and Steiger withdrew it without a vote being taken. Id., at 35346-35347. The House then passed the bill, with the treble-damages provision in the form recommended by the Committee. Id., at 35363-35364.

The Senate did not seek a conference and adopted the bill as amended in the House. Id., at 36296. The treble-damages provision had been drawn to its attention while the legislation was still in the House, and had received the endorsement of Senator McClellan, the sponsor of S. 30, who was of the view that the provision would be "a major new tool in extirpating the baneful influence of organized crime in our economic life." Id., at 25190.

III.

The language of RICO gives no obvious indication that a civil action can proceed only after a criminal conviction. The word "conviction" does not appear in any relevant portion of the statute. See §§1961, 1962, 1964(c). To the contrary, the predicate acts involve conduct that is "chargeable" or "indictable," and "offense[s]" that are "punishable," under various criminal statutes. §1961(1). As defined in the statute, racketeering activity consists not of acts for which the defendant has been convicted, but of acts for which he could be. See also S. Rep. No. 91-617, p.158 (1969): "a racketeering activity . . . must be an act in itself *subject* to criminal sanction" (emphasis added). Thus, a prior-conviction requirement cannot be found in the definition of "racketeering activity." Nor can it be found in §1962, which sets out the statute's substantive provisions. Indeed, if either §1961 or §1962 did contain such a requirement, a prior conviction would also be a prerequisite, nonsensically, for a criminal prosecution, or for a civil action by the Government to enjoin violations that had not yet occurred.

The Court of Appeals purported to discover its prior-conviction requirement in the term "violation" in §1964(c). 741 F.2d, at 498-499. However, even if that term were read to refer to a criminal conviction, it would require a conviction under RICO, not of the predicate offenses. That aside, the term "violation" does not imply a criminal conviction. See United States v. Ward, 448 U.S. 242, 249-250 (1980). It refers only to a failure to adhere to legal requirements. This is its indisputable meaning elsewhere in the statute. Section 1962 renders certain conduct "unlawful"; §1963 and §1964 impose consequences, criminal and civil, for "violations" of 1962. We should not lightly infer that Congress intended the term to have wholly different meanings in neighboring subsections.

The legislative history also undercuts the reading of the court below. The clearest current in that history is the reliance on the Clayton Act model, under which private and governmental actions are entirely distinct. E.g., United States v. Borden Co., 347 U.S. 514, 518-519 (1954). The only specific reference in the legislative history to prior convictions of which we are aware is an objection that the treble-damages provision is too broad precisely because "there need *not* be a conviction under any of these laws for it to be racketeering." 116 Cong. Rec. 35342 (1970) (emphasis added). The history is otherwise silent on this point and contains nothing to contradict the import of the language appearing in the statute. Had Congress intended to impose this novel requirement, there would have been at least some mention of it in the legislative history, even if not in the statute.

The Court of Appeals was of the view that its narrow construction of the statute was essential to avoid intolerable practical consequences. First, without a prior conviction to rely on, the plaintiff would have to prove commission of the predicate acts beyond a reasonable doubt. This would require instructing the jury as to different standards of proof for different aspects of the case. To avoid this awkwardness, the court inferred that the criminality must already be established, so that the civil action could proceed smoothly under the usual preponderance standard.

We are not at all convinced that the predicate acts must be established beyond a reasonable doubt in a proceeding under §1964(c). In a number of settings, conduct that can be punished as criminal only upon proof beyond a reasonable doubt will support civil sanctions under a preponderance standard. See, e.g., United States v. One Assortment of 89 Firearms, 465 U.S. 354 (1984); One Lot Emerald Cut Stones v. United States, 409 U.S. 232, 235 (1972); Helvering v. Mitchell, 303 U.S. 391, 397 (1938); United States v. Regan, 232 U.S. 37, 47-49 (1914). There is no indication that Congress sought to depart from this general principle here. See Measures Relating to Organized Crime, Hearings on S. 30 et al. before the Subcommittee on Criminal Laws and Procedures of the Senate Committee on the Judiciary, 91st Cong., 1st Sess., 388 (1969) (statement of Assistant Attorney General Wilson); House Hearings, at 520 (statement of Rep. Steiger); id., at 664 (statement of Rep. Poff); 116 Cong. Rec. 35313 (1970) (statement of Rep. Minish). That the offending conduct is described by reference to criminal statutes does not mean that its occurrence must be established by criminal standards or that the consequences of a finding of liability in a private civil action are identical to the consequences of a criminal conviction. Cf. United States v. Ward, supra, at 248-251. But we need not decide the standard of proof issue today. For even if the stricter standard is applicable to a portion of the plaintiff's proof, the resulting logistical difficulties, which are accepted in other contexts, would not be so great as to require invention of a requirement that cannot be found in the statute and that Congress, as even the Court of Appeals had to concede, 741 F.2d, at 501, did not envision.

The court below also feared that any other construction would raise severe constitutional questions, as it "would provide civil remedies for offenses criminal in nature, stigmatize defendants with the appellation 'racketeer,' authorize the award of damages which are clearly punitive, including attorney's fees, and constitute a civil remedy aimed in part to avoid the constitutional protections of the criminal law." Id., at 500, n.49. We do not view the statute as being so close to the constitutional edge. As noted above, the fact that conduct can result in both criminal liability and treble damages does not mean that there is not a bona fide civil action. The familiar provisions for both criminal liability and treble damages under the antitrust laws indicate as much. Nor are attorney's fees "clearly punitive." Cf. 42 U.S.C. 1988. As for stigma, a civil RICO proceeding leaves no greater stain than do a number of other civil proceedings. Furthermore, requiring conviction of the predicate acts would not protect against an unfair imposition of the "racketeer" label. If there is a problem with thus stigmatizing a garden variety defrauder by means of a civil action, it is not reduced by making certain that the defendant is guilty of *fraud* beyond a reasonable doubt. Finally, to the extent an action under §1964(c) might be considered quasi-criminal, requiring protections normally applicable only to criminal proceedings, cf. One 1958 Plymouth Sedan v. Pennsylvania, 380 U.S. 693 (1965), the solution is to provide those protections, not to ensure that they were previously afforded by requiring prior convictions.

Finally, we note that a prior-conviction requirement would be inconsistent with Congress' underlying policy concerns. Such a rule would severely handicap potential plaintiffs. A guilty party may escape conviction for any number of reasons—not least among them the possibility that the Government itself may choose to pursue only civil remedies. Private attorney general provisions such as §1964(c) are in part designed to fill prosecutorial gaps. Cf. Reiter v. Sonotone Corp., 442 U.S. 330, 344 (1979). This purpose would be largely defeated, and the need for treble damages as an incentive to litigate unjustified, if private suits could be maintained only against those already brought to justice.

In sum, we can find no support in the statute's history, its language, or considerations of policy for a requirement that a private treble-damages action under §1964(c) can proceed only against a defendant who has already been criminally convicted. To the contrary, every indication is that no such requirement exists. Accordingly, the fact that Imrex and the individual defendants have not been convicted under RICO or the federal mail and wire fraud statutes does not bar Sedima's action.

IV.

In considering the Court of Appeals' second prerequisite for a private civil RICO action—"injury . . . caused by an activity which RICO was designed to deter"—we are somewhat hampered by the vagueness of that concept. Apart from reliance on the general purposes of RICO and a reference to "mobsters," the court provided scant indication of what the requirement of racketeering injury means. It emphasized Congress' undeniable desire to strike at organized crime, but acknowledged and did not purport to overrule Second Circuit precedent rejecting a requirement of an organized crime nexus. 741 F.2d, at 492; see Moss v. Morgan Stanley, Inc., 719 F.2d 5, 21 (C.A.2 1983), *cert. denied sub nom.* Moss v. Newman, 465 U.S. 1025 (1984). The court also stopped short of adopting a "competitive injury" requirement; while insisting that the plaintiff show "the kind of economic injury which has an effect on competition," it did not require "actual anticompetitive effect." 741 F.2d, at 496; see also id., at 495, n.40.

The court's statement that the plaintiff must seek redress for an injury caused by conduct that RICO was designed to deter is unhelpfully tautological. Nor is clarity furnished by a negative statement of its rule: standing is not provided by the injury resulting from the predicate acts themselves. That statement is itself apparently inaccurate when applied to those predicate acts that unmistakably constitute the kind of conduct Congress sought to deter. See id., at 496, n.41. The opinion does not explain how to distinguish such crimes from the other predicate acts Congress has lumped together in §1961(1). The court below is not alone in struggling to define "racketeering injury," and the difficulty of that task itself cautions against imposing such a requirement.

We need not pinpoint the Second Circuit's precise holding, for we perceive no distinct "racketeering injury" requirement. Given that "racketeering activity" consists of no more and no less than commission of a predicate act, §1961(1), we are initially doubtful about a requirement of a "racketeering injury" separate from the harm from the predicate acts. A reading of the statute belies any such requirement. Section 1964(c) authorizes a private suit by "[a]ny person injured in his business or property by reason of a violation of §1962." Section 1962 in turn makes it unlawful for "any person"—not just mobsters—to use money derived from a pattern of racketeering activity to invest in an enterprise, to acquire control of an enterprise through a pattern of racketeering activity, or to conduct an enterprise through a pattern of racketeering activity. §§1962(a)-(c). If the defendant engages in a pattern of racketeering activity in a manner forbidden by these provisions, and the racketeering activities injure the plaintiff in his business or property, the plaintiff has a claim under §1964(c). There is no room in the statutory language for an additional, amorphous "racketeering injury" requirement.

A violation of §1962(c), the section on which Sedima relies, requires (1) conduct (2) of an enterprise (3) through a pattern[33] (4) of racketeering activity. The plaintiff must, of course, allege each of these elements to state a claim. Conducting an enterprise that affects interstate commerce is obviously not in itself a violation of §1962, nor is mere commission of the predicate offenses. In addition, the plaintiff only has standing if, and can only recover to the extent that, he has been injured in his business or property by the conduct constituting the violation. As the Seventh Circuit has stated, "[a] defendant who violates section 1962 is not liable for treble damages to everyone he might have injured by other conduct, nor is the defendant liable to those who have not been injured." Haroco, Inc. v. American National Bank & Trust Co. of Chicago, 747 F.2d 384, 398 (1984), *aff'd*, post, p.606.

But the statute requires no more than this. Where the plaintiff alleges each element of the violation, the compensable injury necessarily is the harm caused by predicate acts sufficiently related to constitute a pattern, for the essence of the violation is the commission of those acts in connection with the conduct of an enterprise. Those acts are, when committed in the circumstances delineated in §1962(c), "an activity which RICO was designed to deter." Any recoverable damages occurring by reason of a violation of §1962(c) will flow from the commission of the predicate acts.

---

33. As many commentators have pointed out, the definition of a "pattern of racketeering activity" differs from the other provisions in §1961 in that it states that a pattern *"requires* at least two acts of racketeering activity," §1961(5) (emphasis added), not that it "means" two such acts. The implication is that while two acts are necessary, they may not be sufficient. Indeed, in common parlance two of anything do not generally form a "pattern." The legislative history supports the view that two isolated acts of racketeering activity do not constitute a pattern. As the Senate Report explained: "The target of [RICO] is thus not sporadic activity. The infiltration of legitimate business normally requires more than one 'racketeering activity' and the threat of continuing activity to be effective. It is this factor of *continuity plus relationship* which combines to produce a pattern." S. Rep. No. 91-617, p.158 (1969) (emphasis added). Similarly, the sponsor of the Senate bill, after quoting this portion of the Report, pointed out to his colleagues that "[t]he term 'pattern' itself requires the showing of a relationship. . . . So, therefore, proof of two acts of racketeering activity, without more, does not establish a pattern. . . . " 116 Cong. Rec. 18940 (1970) (statement of Sen. McClellan). See also id., at 35193 (statement of Rep. Poff) (RICO "not aimed at the isolated offender"); House Hearings, at 665. Significantly, in defining "pattern" in a later provision of the same bill, Congress was more enlightening: "[C]riminal conduct forms a pattern if it embraces criminal acts that have the same or similar purposes, results, participants, victims, or methods of commission, or otherwise are interrelated by distinguishing characteristics and are not isolated events." 18 U.S.C. 3575(e). This language may be useful in interpreting other sections of the Act. Cf. Ianelli v. United States, 420 U.S. 770, 789 (1975).

This less restrictive reading is amply supported by our prior cases and the general principles surrounding this statute. RICO is to be read broadly. This is the lesson not only of Congress' self-consciously expansive language and overall approach, see United States v. Turkette, 452 U.S. 576, 586-587 (1981), but also of its express admonition that RICO is to "be liberally construed to effectuate its remedial purposes," Pub. L. 91-452, 904(a), 84 Stat. 947. The statute's "remedial purposes" are nowhere more evident than in the provision of a private action for those injured by racketeering activity. Far from effectuating these purposes, the narrow readings offered by the dissenters and the court below would in effect eliminate §1964(c) from the statute.

RICO was an aggressive initiative to supplement old remedies and develop new methods for fighting crime. See generally Russello v. United States, 464 U.S. 16, 26-29 (1983). While few of the legislative statements about novel remedies and attacking crime on all fronts, see ibid., were made with direct reference to §1964(c), it is in this spirit that all of the Act's provisions should be read. The specific references to §1964(c) are consistent with this overall approach. Those supporting §1964(c) hoped it would "enhance the effectiveness of title IX's prohibitions," House Hearings, at 520, and provide "a major new tool," 116 Cong. Rec. 35227 (1970). See also id., at 25190; 115 Cong. Rec. 6993-6994 (1969). Its opponents, also recognizing the provision's scope, complained that it provided too easy a weapon against "innocent businessmen," H.R. Rep. No. 91-1549, p.187 (1970), and would be prone to abuse, 116 Cong. Rec. 35342 (1970). It is also significant that a previous proposal to add RICO-like provisions to the Sherman Act had come to grief in part precisely because it "could create inappropriate and unnecessary obstacles in the way of . . . a private litigant [who] would have to contend with a body of precedent—appropriate in a purely antitrust context—setting strict requirements on questions such as 'standing to sue' and 'proximate cause.'" 115 Cong. Rec. 6995 (1969) (ABA comments on S. 2048); see also id., at 6993 (S. 1623 proposed as an amendment to Title 18 to avoid these problems). In borrowing its "racketeering injury" requirement from antitrust standing principles, the court below created exactly the problems Congress sought to avoid.

Underlying the Court of Appeals' holding was its distress at the "extraordinary, if not outrageous," uses to which civil RICO has been put. 741 F.2d, at 487. Instead of being used against mobsters and organized criminals, it has become a tool for everyday fraud cases brought against "respected and legitimate 'enterprises.'" Ibid. Yet Congress wanted to reach both "legitimate" and "illegitimate" enterprises. United States v. Turkette, supra. The former enjoy neither an inherent incapacity for criminal activity nor immunity from its consequences. The fact that §1964(c) is used against respected businesses allegedly engaged in a pattern of specifically identified criminal conduct is hardly a sufficient reason for assuming that the provision is being misconstrued. Nor does it reveal the "ambiguity" discovered by the court below. "[T]he fact that RICO has been applied in situations not expressly anticipated by Congress does not demonstrate ambiguity. It demonstrates breadth." Haroco, Inc. v. American National Bank & Trust Co. of Chicago, supra, at 398.

It is true that private civil actions under the statute are being brought almost solely against such defendants, rather than against the archetypal, intimidating mobster.[34] Yet this defect—if defect it is—is inherent in the statute as written, and its correction must lie with Congress. It is not for the judiciary to eliminate the private action in situations where Congress has provided it simply because plaintiffs are not taking advantage of it in its more difficult applications.

We nonetheless recognize that, in its private civil version, RICO is evolving into something quite different from the original conception of its enactors. See generally ABA Report, at 55-69. Though sharing the doubts of the Court of Appeals about this increasing divergence, we cannot agree with either its diagnosis or its remedy. The "extraordinary" uses to which civil RICO has been put appear to be primarily the result of the breadth of the predicate offenses, in particular the inclusion of wire, mail, and securities fraud, and the failure of Congress and the courts to develop a meaningful concept of "pattern." We do not believe that the amorphous standing requirement imposed by the Second Circuit effectively responds to these problems, or that it is a form of statutory amendment appropriately undertaken by the courts.

V.

Sedima may maintain this action if the defendants conducted the enterprise through a pattern of racketeering activity. The questions whether the defendants committed the requisite predicate acts, and whether the

---

34. The ABA Task Force found that of the 270 known civil RICO cases at the trial court level, 40% involved securities fraud, 37% common-law fraud in a commercial or business setting, and only 9% "allegations of criminal activity of a type generally associated with professional criminals." ABA Report, at 55-56. Another survey of 132 published decisions found that 57 involved securities transactions and 38 commercial and contract disputes, while no other category made it into double figures. American Institute of Certified Public Accountants, The Authority to Bring Private Treble-Damage Suits Under "RICO" Should Be Removed 13 (Oct. 10, 1984).

commission of those acts fell into a pattern, are not before us. The complaint is not deficient for failure to allege either an injury separate from the financial loss stemming from the alleged acts of mail and wire fraud, or prior convictions of the defendants. The judgment below is accordingly reversed, and the case is remanded for further proceedings consistent with this opinion.

It is so ordered.

Justice MARSHALL, with whom Justice BRENNAN, Justice BLACKMUN, and Justice POWELL join, dissenting.

The Court today recognizes that "in its private civil version, RICO is evolving into something quite different from the original conception of its enactors." Ante, at 500. The Court, however, expressly validates this result, imputing it to the manner in which the statute was drafted. I fundamentally disagree both with the Court's reading of the statute and with its conclusion. I believe that the statutory language and history disclose a narrower interpretation of the statute that fully effectuates Congress' purposes, and that does not make compensable under civil RICO a host of claims that Congress never intended to bring within RICO's purview.

The Court's interpretation of the civil RICO statute quite simply revolutionizes private litigation; it validates the federalization of broad areas of state common law of frauds, and it approves the displacement of well-established federal remedial provisions. We do not lightly infer a congressional intent to effect such fundamental changes. To infer such intent here would be untenable, for there is no indication that Congress even considered, much less approved, the scheme that the Court today defines.

The single most significant reason for the expansive use of civil RICO has been the presence in the statute, as predicate acts, of mail and wire fraud violations. See 18 U.S.C. §1961(1) (1982 ed., Supp. III). Prior to RICO, no federal statute had expressly provided a private damages remedy based upon a violation of the mail or wire fraud statutes, which make it a federal crime to use the mail or wires in furtherance of a scheme to defraud. See 18 U.S.C. §§1341, 1343. . . .

Once the Court gave its blessing to this use of "civil RICO" actions, the game was on. Obviously RICO, with its treble damages, can be a potent threat as a consumer action.

PROBLEM 20

Music lovers subscribed in large numbers to Internet web site www.InTeensHardRock.com, downloading (for a fee) the latest hits recommended by the site's cyber-disk jockeys. Your teenage son tells you, his attorney/parent, that he has just learned that these cyber-disk jockeys have routinely been taking kickbacks from the record producers to promote unworthy songs. This sort of payola is highly illegal. Does fraud on the Internet trigger RICO? See the definition of "racketeering activity" in the third footnote of the last case.

KENTY v. BANK ONE, COLUMBUS, N.A.
United States Court of Appeals, Sixth Circuit, 1995
67 F.3d 1257

MERRITT, Chief Judge.

Plaintiffs in this class action suit appeal the grant of summary judgment for the defendants by the district court. Each plaintiff contracted with Bank One for a loan to purchase an automobile. The terms of the loan required the plaintiffs to acquire collision and comprehensive automobile insurance, or in the alternative authorized the Bank to purchase the insurance for the plaintiffs. Each of the plaintiffs did not purchase insurance themselves, and the Bank purchased it for them from Transamerica Premier Insurance Company, a co-defendant in this case. The plaintiffs contend that the Bank breached the loan agreement and bought not only the insurance authorized by the agreement, but other coverage as well. Although they do not bring a breach of contract action, the plaintiffs do argue that the Bank violated three federal statutes: the Racketeer Influenced and Corrupt Organizations Act (RICO), 18 U.S.C. §1962(c); the National Bank Act, 12 U.S.C. §85; and the anti-tying provisions of the National Bank Holding Company Act, 12 U.S.C. §1972. The plaintiffs also claim that Transamerica violated RICO. The district court granted summary judgment for the defendants on all of these claims. We affirm the district court's rulings with respect to the National Bank Act and the anti-tying provision of the National Bank Holding Company Act. With respect to the RICO claims, we affirm the district court's ruling in part and reverse in part.

I. FACTS

The plaintiffs in this case individually contracted with the Bank for an automobile loan. The loan contract, which was identical in each case, provided that each plaintiff would purchase collision and comprehensive insurance coverage for the automobile they purchased with the loan proceeds. In the alternative, if a plaintiff did not purchase insurance the agreement provided that the Bank could take out an insurance policy on behalf of that plaintiff and add the charges to the balance of the loan. Specifically the Notice of Requirement to Provide Insurance executed by the plaintiffs stated:

> I understand that the terms of my loan require that:
>
> (a) I provide property insurance against loss or damage (subject to a maximum deductible of $250) on the collateral securing my loan, in an amount sufficient to cover the outstanding balance on my loan, plus any existing liens on the collateral. This coverage is commonly referred to as collision or comprehensive insurance . . . and
>
> (b) The insurance policy contained a loss payable clause endorsement naming BANK ONE as the holder of a lien on the collateral. . . .
>
> I understand that I may obtain the insurance from any agent or company of my choice; if I fail to obtain the required insurance, BANK ONE, at its option but without any obligation to do so, may apply in my name at my expense to purchase limited insurance for the protection of only Bank One for the amount of my loan. I authorize Bank One to add such insurance premiums, and finance charges thereon, to my loan balance. I understand that Bank One will retain a security interest in the collateral securing my loan until the entire balance, including any premiums and finance charges, is paid.

Each of the plaintiffs in the class did not purchase the insurance against loss or damage of their automobile, and the Bank purchased insurance for them from Transamerica.

The policy which the Bank purchased from Transamerica included endorsements which protected the automobiles (the Bank's collateral) from theft and damage that could diminish the value of the automobile. The plaintiffs do not contest these endorsements. In addition, however, the policy purchased from Transamerica also insured the Bank against malfeasance by the plaintiff-borrower and against losses that could be incurred by the Bank even when an automobile was repossessed in undamaged condition ("additional insurance"). For example, in the insurance policy taken out for the class representative, the coverage included protection against "borrower conversion, embezzlement and secretion of the vehicle"; expenses included in "repossessing the vehicle with a prior mechanics lien"; payments for a "loaned insurance premium if borrower defaults and vehicle is repossessed"; "repossession expenses"; "repossessed storage expenses"; "additional coverage to insure vehicle . . . after insurance certificate has been cancelled while the vehicle is being repossessed"; and "waiver of Actual Cash Value to permit recovery of actual amount owed on loan." While the plaintiff was required to provide insurance only against "loss or damage," the Bank argues that these additional types of coverage were permitted under the clause allowing it to buy "limited insurance."

Although each plaintiff received notice that the Bank had purchased insurance from Transamerica in his or her name, the notice they received did not explain that the coverage included any additional coverage beyond protection against "loss or damage." In the case of the class representative, the notice only mentioned "extra endorsements" by number listing "CSI-1, 2, 3, 4, 5, 6, 7, 9, 10, 12, 13, 15." Subsequent notices sent to the plaintiffs included no further suggestion that the insurance coverage included protection of the Bank's loan beyond the value of the collateral in the undamaged automobile. All of the notices included a statement that "This Insurance Protects the Interest of the Lender in the Vehicle."

[T]he premiums were added to the balances on the plaintiffs' loans with the Bank. But, according to the plaintiffs, the Bank received rebates from Transamerica that were not reflected in the price each plaintiff was charged. Thus the Bank did not pass on the rebates to the plaintiffs, and therefore overcharged them for the insurance.

The district court dismissed all three of the plaintiffs' federal claims on a motion for summary judgment. While the case was pending in district court, the plaintiffs filed a similar claim in state court in Ohio on a breach of contract theory, and related state-law grounds. The Ohio Court of Appeals dismissed all the plaintiffs' claims. Recently, however, the Ohio Supreme Court overruled that decision and held that the plaintiffs did state a cause of action under Ohio law sufficient to survive summary judgment. As we read that decision, the Ohio Supreme Court also interpreted Ohio contract law to hold that the Bank breached its contracts with the plaintiffs when it purchased the additional insurance. Kenty v. Transamerica Premium Ins. Co., 72 Ohio St. 3d 415, 650 N.E.2d 863 (1995). Nonetheless, as there is now no final judgment in the Ohio state courts, we are not barred from considering this case under res judicata or collateral estoppel. See State ex rel. Kirby v. S.G. Loewendick & Sons, 64 Ohio St. 3d 433, 596 N.E.2d 460, 463 (1992) (holding that final judgment required for estoppel by judgment and necessary determination needed for collateral estoppel).

* * *

III. RICO

The plaintiffs assert that the Bank and Transamerica violated RICO in two respects. First, plaintiffs argue that the purchase of the additional coverage beyond loss and damage insurance violated RICO. Second, plaintiffs contend that the "kickbacks" that the Bank received from the insurance company also violated RICO.

A violation of RICO under 18 U.S.C. §1962(c) requires (1) conduct (2) of an enterprise (3) through a pattern (4) of racketeering activity. Sedima, S.P.R.L. v. Imrex Co., 473 U.S. 479, 105 S. Ct. 3275, 87 L. Ed. 2d 346 (1985). In order to establish "racketeering activity" the plaintiffs must allege a predicate act. Mail fraud, which the plaintiffs have alleged in this case, is a predicate act. 18 U.S.C. §1961(1)(B).

Mail fraud consists of "a scheme or artifice to defraud and a mailing for the purpose of executing the scheme." Bender v. Southland Corp., 749 F.2d 1205, 1215-16 (6th Cir. 1984). A scheme to defraud consists of "[i]ntentional fraud, consisting in deception intentionally practiced to induce another to part with property or to surrender some legal right, and which accomplishes the designed end." Id. at 1216. To allege intentional fraud, there must be "proof of misrepresentations or omissions which were 'reasonably calculated to deceive persons of ordinary prudence and comprehension.'" Blount Fin. Servs., Inc. v. Walter E. Heller & Co., 819 F.2d 151, 153 (6th Cir. 1987) (citation omitted). Thus, the plaintiffs must allege with particularity a "false statement of fact made by the defendant which the plaintiff relied on." The plaintiff must also allege "the facts showing the plaintiff's reliance on the defendant's false statement of fact." Id. at 152. Alternatively, the plaintiff may allege an omission on which he or she relied. The issue in this case is whether the plaintiffs have sufficiently alleged a misrepresentation or an omission [that] was reasonably calculated to deceive persons of ordinary prudence and comprehension.

A.   STATEMENT AS TO TYPE OF COVERAGE PURCHASED

The plaintiffs argue that every insurance notice sent to them included the statement "This Insurance Protects the Interest of the Lender in the Vehicle." The plaintiffs contend that this statement is a false statement of fact that was reasonably calculated to deceive them. Specifically, the plaintiffs argue that this statement led them to believe that they were only paying for loss and damage insurance when in fact they were also buying insurance that protected the Bank from malfeasance by the plaintiffs and from losses connected to the loan that might occur even if a secured automobile were not damaged or stolen. The plaintiffs stress that the word "Vehicle" is misleading and contend that to be correct the statement should have informed them that the insurance also protected the interest of the Bank in the loan.

This statement is not sufficiently misleading to form the basis of a fraud claim. The "Interest of the Lender" could be read to mean its interest in the vehicle as collateral. When read in this way, all of the insurance coverage can be construed to protect the Bank from diminution in value of its collateral, whether through damage, theft, or other costs incurred because the plaintiffs failed to make their payments (such as the cost of repossession). All of the coverage is designed to insure that the Bank will be fully secured up to the amount of the loan balance. While we recognize that one could read this statement another way, the language is too vague for us to conclude that the statement was "reasonably calculated to deceive" the plaintiffs. Furthermore, the same notice on which this statement appears includes a section which lists by number all of the policy endorsements about which the plaintiff complains. Although the plaintiffs would have had to ask the Bank or Transamerica what these codes stood for, it would have required minimal effort to do so. If the Bank or Transamerica were attempting to deceive the plaintiffs, it is hardly likely that they would have placed all of the endorsements on the notices sent to the plaintiffs. In addition, the presence of these endorsements on the face of the notices undermines the plaintiffs' claims that they reasonably relied on the statement they cite as misleading. A claim of fraud does not inevitably follow from every breach of a contract. Even if the Bank breached the loan agreements here, the plaintiffs still must point to a falsehood that would form the basis for fraud. They have failed to do so. Consequently, the district court properly granted summary judgment for the defendants on this issue because the plaintiffs failed to state with particularity a false statement of fact.

B. INSURANCE REBATES FROM TRANSAMERICA TO THE BANK

The plaintiffs also contend that the Bank and Transamerica entered into an agreement that provided the Bank with rebates or "kickbacks" for placing the insurance with Transamerica. Although the defendants argue that these sums were insurance "commissions" that were paid to an affiliate of the Bank, for the purposes of this review we must interpret the facts in the light most favorable to the plaintiffs.

Irrespective of what type of coverage the plaintiffs believed they were purchasing, they clearly thought that they were being charged what it cost the Bank to buy the insurance. The Notice to Provide Insurance signed by the plaintiffs included the statement: "I authorize Bank One to add such insurance premiums, and finance charges thereon, to my loan balance." If the Bank was receiving a discount on the cost of the insurance that it did not pass on to the plaintiffs, it was engaging in a form of deceit.

In Dana Corp. v. Blue Cross & Blue Shield of Northern Ohio, this Court ruled on similar facts that an allegation of failure to pass on an insurance rebate was sufficient to state a claim under RICO. 900 F.2d 882 (6th Cir. 1990). In that case, the plaintiff corporation hired Blue Cross to provide administrative services only for health insurance. In other words, the company was a self-insurer, but paid Blue Cross to administer payments to health care providers. Under the agreement, Blue Cross would pay its usual 97% of the cost of a medical bill to a health care provider and then bill the plaintiff for that amount. But, Blue Cross received rebates from several hospitals that it never passed on to the plaintiff. It also led the plaintiff to believe that it was passing on all of the rebates. The court held that this failure to pass on rebates was sufficiently fraudulent to state a claim under RICO.

In this case, we may interpret the Bank's failure to pass on the rebates to the plaintiffs as creating either fraudulent omissions or affirmative misrepresentations. The Bank neither informed the plaintiffs that it was receiving these rebates on the insurance, nor that it had an agreement with Transamerica regarding rebates. The plaintiffs had no reasonable possibility of discovering that the agreement existed, or that rebates were being paid. *Cf. Blount,* 819 F.2d at 153 (finding that plaintiffs with "ordinary prudence and comprehension" would have identified any misrepresentation). Consequently, the plaintiffs could not reasonably be expected to know that these rebates were being paid unless either the Bank or Transamerica informed them. Hence, when the facts are construed in the light most favorable to the plaintiffs, this omission can rise to the level of one "reasonably calculated to deceive" the plaintiffs. Furthermore, it is clear that because they were not provided with the information, the plaintiffs acted to their detriment by paying the inflated premiums.

In addition, one can interpret the sums listed on the notices sent to the plaintiffs as affirmative misrepresentations. If the actual cost to the Bank of the insurance was less than the actual sum listed on the notice, then that sum can constitute a misrepresentation "reasonably calculated to deceive" the plaintiffs, particularly given that they had no independent means of ascertaining the actual cost of the insurance to the Bank. Again, the plaintiffs clearly relied to their detriment on the sum presented on the notices. Consequently, we must reverse the district court with respect to this RICO claim as against the Bank. Further factual development will be necessary, however, to determine the precise nature of the agreement between the Bank and Transamerica, and whether the Bank was passing on its actual costs for purchasing the insurance to the plaintiffs. . . .

[Discussion of other issues omitted.]

The judgment of the district is AFFIRMED in part, and REVERSED in part. The case is REMANDED for further proceedings on the remaining portion of the RICO claim.

PART 2

Product Quality and the Consumer

The offending product can be as simple as a pencil or as complicated as a computer program, but if it doesn't work, the task at hand doesn't get done until the problem is solved. Where the product is not only defective, but *dangerous* as well (the car that explodes, the house with defective wiring), even greater interests are at stake. In other courses of study you may have explored some of the law that remedies these difficulties. There is a brief summary of those matters (strict product liability, warranty law, etc.) herein, but to that précis we add a more detailed discussion of the consumer statutes giving extraordinary remedies for defective products.

CHAPTER 3
Product Quality Generally

I. STRICT PRODUCT LIABILITY

As a starter it should be noted that a host of federal and state laws and regulations monitor product quality, and it is the job of an attorney practicing in any given industry to make sure that clients are in compliance with all governmental regulatory measures. For example, at the federal level there are the Food, Drug and Cosmetic Act, 21 U.S.C. §§301 et seq. (since 1938), the Wool Products Labeling Act, 15 U.S.C. §§68 et seq. (1940), the Fur Products Labeling Act, 15 U.S.C. §§69 et seq. (1951), the Textile Fiber Products Identification Act, 15 U.S.C. §§70 et seq. (1958), and the Motor Vehicle Information and Cost Savings Act, 15 U.S.C. §§1901 et seq. (1972), to name only a few.

As far as civil actions go, product quality in this country was originally regulated by actions in tort (chiefly negligence) and contract (chiefly warranty). In time it became obvious that something more was needed. Negligence proved inadequate to protect consumers from dangerous products because the injured plaintiff often has enormous difficulty proving the elements that constitute the tort of negligence (for example, demonstrating exactly what went wrong at the manufacturing stage). Contract theories, such as warranty law (explored below), contain similar difficulties. It is a basic of warranty law, for example, that the injured buyer must give notice of the injury within a reasonable amount of time after learning of the breach or be barred from all remedy. U.C.C. §2-607(3). Injured consumers may or may not think to give this notice, and if they do, they may not give it to all the necessary parties. Contract law, after all, requires privity—legal connection between the parties—before liability arises. This privity requirement presents two difficulties in contractual suits: *vertical privity* (how far back up the distributional chain can the injured buyer sue—for instance, can he or she sue the original manufacturer?) and *horizontal privity* (who, other than the original buyer, can sue the seller—how about the buyer's children, next-door neighbor, mail carrier, etc.?), see U.C.C. §2-318.

A 20th-century revolution in the common law produced the law of strict products liability, described by one renowned commentator as a "freak hybrid born of the illicit intercourse of tort and contract," Prosser, The Assault upon the Citadel, 69 Yale L.J. 1099, 1126 (1960).

Strict products liability avoids the legal minefields that complicate negligence and warranty lawsuits by steering a tight course through the doctrinal difficulties. The basic idea, reflected in Restatement (Second) of Torts §402A (see below), imposes liability on those who distribute into commerce a product with an unreasonably dangerous defect; this liability attaches *even though the seller was not negligent in any way*. The injured party need not be in privity with the defendant.

Full coverage of this exciting area of the law awaits you in other courses. But no discussion of consumer law and product quality can be undertaken without a reminder that strict products liability law is one of the starting points for the consumer-specific statutes we will study later in this section of the book.

RESTATEMENT (SECOND) OF TORTS §402A

§402A Special liability of seller of product for physical harm to user or consumer

(1) One who sells any product in a defective condition unreasonably dangerous to the user or consumer or to his property is subject to liability for physical harm thereby caused to the ultimate user or consumer, or to his property, if

(a) the seller is engaged in the business of selling such a product, and

(b) it is expected to and does reach the user or consumer without substantial change in the condition in which it is sold.

(2) The rule stated in Subsection (1) applies although

(a) the seller has exercised all possible care in the preparation and sale of his product, and

(b) the user or consumer has not bought the product from or entered into any contractual relation with the seller.

Official Comment:

m. "Warranty" . . . The rule stated in this Section is not governed by the provisions of the Uniform Sales Act, or those of the Uniform Commercial Code, as to warranties; and it is not affected by limitations on the scope and content of warranties, or by limitation to "buyer" and "seller" in those statutes. Nor is the consumer required to give notice to the seller of his injury within a reasonable time after it occurs, as is provided by the Uniform Act. The consumer's cause of action does not depend upon the validity of his contract with the person from whom he acquires the product, and it is not affected by any disclaimer or other agreement, whether it be between the seller and his immediate buyer, or attached to and accompanying the product into the consumer's hands. In short, "warranty" must be given a new and different meaning if it is used in connection with this Section. It is much simpler to regard the liability here stated as merely one of strict liability in tort.

LEICHTAMER v. AMERICAN MOTORS CORP.
Supreme Court of Ohio, 1982
67 Ohio St. 2d 456, 424 N.E.2d 568

This litigation arises out of a motor vehicle accident which occurred on April 18, 1976. On that date, Paul Vance and his wife, Cynthia, invited Carl and Jeanne Leichtamer, brother and sister, to go for a ride in the Vance's Jeep Model CJ-7. The Vances and the Leichtamers drove together to the Hall of Fame Four-Wheel Club, of which the Vances were members. The Vances were seated in the front of the vehicle and the Leichtamers rode in the back. The club, located near Dundee, Ohio, was an "off-the-road" recreation facility. The course there consisted of hills and trails about an abandoned strip mine.

While the Vance vehicle was negotiating a double-terraced hill, an accident occurred. The hill consisted of a 33-degree slope followed by a 70-foot long terrace and then a 30-degree slope. Paul Vance drove over the brow of the first of these two slopes and over the first flat terrace without incident. As he drove over the brow of the second hill, the rear of the vehicle raised up relative to the front and passed through the air in an arc of approximately 180 degrees. The vehicle landed upside down with its front pointing back up the hill. This movement of the vehicle is described as a pitch-over.

The speed that the Vance vehicle was travelling at the time of the pitch-over was an issue of dispute. The Leichtamers, who are the only surviving eyewitnesses to the accident, described the vehicle as travelling at a slow speed. Carl Leichtamer described the accident as occurring in this fashion:

" . . . Well, we turned there and went down this trail and got to the top of this first hill. . . . And Paul looked back and make [sic] sure that everybody had their seat belt fastened. That it was fastened down; and he pulled the automatic lever down in low and he put it in low wheel, four wheel, too. . . . And then he just let it coast like over the top of this hill and was using the brake on the way down, too. We came to the level off part. He just coasted up to the top of the second hill, and then the next thing I remember is the back end of the Jeep going over. . . . When we got to the top of the second hill, the front end went down like this (demonstrating) and the back end just started raising up like that (demonstrating)."

John L. Habberstad, an expert witness for American Motors Corporation, testified that the vehicle had to be travelling between 15 and 20 miles per hour. This conclusion was based on evidence adduced by American Motors that the vehicle landed approximately 10 feet from the bottom of the second slope, having traversed about 47 feet in the air and having fallen approximately 23.5 feet.

The pitch-over of the Jeep CJ-7, on April 18, 1976, killed the driver, Paul Vance, and his wife, Cynthia. Carl Leichtamer sustained a depressed skull fracture. The tailgate of the vehicle presumably struck Jeanne Leichtamer. Jeanne was trapped in the vehicle after the accident and her position was described by her brother as follows: "She was like laying on her stomach although her head was sticking out of the jeep and the—she was laying on her stomach like and the tailgate of the jeep like, was laying lower, just a little bit lower or right almost on her shoulders and then the back seat of the jeep was laying on her lower part of her back. . . . [H]er legs were twisted through the front seat." Jeanne Leichtamer is a paraplegic as a result of the injury.

Carl and Jeanne Leichtamer, appellees, subsequently sued American Motors Corporation, American Motors Sales Corporation and Jeep Corporation, appellants, for "enhanced" injuries they sustained in the accident of April 18, 1976. The amended complaint averred that the permanent trauma to the body of Jeanne Leichtamer and the other injuries to her brother, Carl, were causally related to the displacement of the "roll bar" on the vehicle. Appellees claimed that Paul Vance's negligence caused the accident, but alleged that their injuries were "substantially enhanced, intensified, aggravated, and prolonged" by the roll bar displacement.

Paul Vance purchased his Jeep CJ-7 four-wheel drive motor vehicle from a duly-licensed, factory-authorized dealer, Petty's Jeep & Marine, Inc., owned and operated by Norman Petty. Vance purchased the vehicle on March 9, 1976. The vehicle came with a factory-installed roll bar. The entire vehicle was designed and manufactured by Jeep Corporation, a wholly-owned subsidiary of American Motors. American Motors Sales Corporation is the selling agent for the manufacturer. Appellees did not claim that there was any defect in the way the vehicle was manufactured in the sense of departure by the manufacturer from design specifications. The vehicle was manufactured precisely in the manner in which it was designed to be manufactured. It reached Paul Vance in that condition and was not changed.

The focus of appellees' case was that the weakness of the sheet metal housing upon which the roll bar had been attached was causally related to the trauma to their bodies. Specifically, when the vehicle landed upside down, the flat sheet metal housing of the rear wheels upon which the roll bar tubing was attached by bolts gave way so that the single, side-to-side bar across the top of the vehicle was displaced to a position twelve inches forward of and fourteen and one-half inches lower than its original configuration relative to the chassis. The movement of the position of the intact roll bar resulting from the collapse of the sheet metal housing upon which it was bolted was, therefore, downward and forward. The roll bar tubing did not punch through the sheet metal housing; rather the housing collapsed, taking the intact tubing with it. That this displacement or movement of the intact roll bar is permitted by the thin nature of the sheet metal wheel housing to which it is attached and the propensity of the bar to do so when the vehicle lands upside down is central to appellees' case.

The appellants' position concerning the roll bar is that, from an engineering point of view, the roll bar was an optional device provided solely as protection for a side-roll. A side-roll, as opposed to pitch-over, was described by the Court of Appeals as "a roll of the vehicle around its longitudinal axis. A side-roll is simulated when a skewer is run through the plastic model [of the vehicle] front to rear through the center and then rotated so that the sides of the vehicle describe circles about the skewer in the center while the front and rear bumpers spin like propellers." The pitch-over, by way of contrast, was described by the Court of Appeals as "that observed when a skewer is run from side to side through a plastic toy model of the vehicle at the center of it, and then the skewer is rotated so that both the front and rear bumpers move in circles about each other." The roll bar was never tested for this latter eventuality, the pitch-over; appellants assert it was provided solely as protection against the former eventuality, the side-roll.

The other principal element of appellees' case was that the advertised use of the vehicle involves great risk of forward pitch-overs. The accident occurred at the Hall of Fame Four-Wheel Club, which had been organized, among others, by Norman Petty, the vendor of the Vance vehicle. Petty allowed the club to meet at his Jeep dealership. He showed club members movies of the performance of the Jeep in hilly country. This activity was coupled with a national advertising program of American Motor Sales Corporation, which included a multi-million dollar television campaign. The television advertising campaign was aimed at encouraging people to buy a Jeep, as follows: "Ever discover the rough, exciting world of mountains, forest, rugged terrain? The original Jeep can get you there, and Jeep guts will bring you back. . . ."

The campaign also stressed the ability of the Jeep to drive up and down steep hills. One Jeep CJ-7 television advertisement, for example, challenges a young man, accompanied by his girlfriend: "[Y]ou guys aren't yellow, are you? Is it a steep hill? Yeah, little lady, you could say it is a steep hill. Let's try it. The King of the Hill is about to discover the new Jeep CJ-7. . . ." Moreover, the owner's manual for the Jeep CJ-5/CJ-7 provided instructions as to how "[a] four-wheel drive vehicle can proceed in safety down a grade which could not be negotiated safely by a conventional 2-wheel drive vehicle." Both appellees testified that they had seen the commercials and that they thought the roll bar would protect them if the vehicle landed on its top.

Appellees offered the expert testimony of Dr. Gene H. Samuelson that all of the physical trauma to the body of Jeanne Leichtamer were [sic] causally related to the collapse of the roll bar support. These injuries—fractures of both arms, some ribs, fracture of the dorsal spine, and a relative dislocation of the cervical spine and injury to the spinal cord—were described by Samuelson as permanent. He also testified that the physical trauma to the body of Carl Leichtamer was causally related to the collapse of the roll bar.

Appellants' principal argument was that the roll bar was provided solely for a side-roll. Appellants' only testing of the roll bar was done on a 1969 Jeep CJ-5, a model with a wheel base ten inches shorter than the Jeep CJ-7. Evidence of the test was offered in evidence and refused. With regard to tests for either side-rolls or pitch-overs on the Jeep CJ-7, appellants responded to interrogatories that no "proving ground," "vibration or shock," or "crash" tests were conducted.

The jury returned the verdict for both appellees. Damages were assessed for Carl Leichtamer at $100,000 compensatory and $100,000 punitive. Damages were assessed for Jeanne Leichtamer at $1 million compensatory and $1 million punitive. The defendants submitted typed interrogatories to the jury for an explanation of their verdict as to punitive damages. The jury stated the facts from which the defendants were found to have acted, as follows:

"Wilfully suggestive advertising depicting Jeeps going up and down steep and rugged terrain without any risk or warning.

"Grossly neglected to test roll bar support system for foreseeable rollovers and/or foreseeable pitch-overs."

Upon appeal of 15 assignments of error, the Court of Appeals for Stark County affirmed the judgment of the trial court. The Court of Appeals held "the uncontroverted evidence coupled with the admissions of the defendants' agents by way of testimony and responses to pleading interrogatories, establish as a matter of law the following:

"1. That the manufacturer, Jeep Corporation and American Motors Sales Corporation, is chargeable with the actual knowledge of its

Engineering Department that no provision for safety in the event of forward pitch-overs had been designed notwithstanding that the advertisements by American Motors Sales Corporation incite the general public to use the vehicle in such a way as to create a substantial risk of a forward pitch-over.

"2. That the configuration of the Jeep CJ-7 factory installed roll bar is such as to lead a reasonable member of the public and those who might be endangered by the use of this vehicle, to believe that it has been designed and constructed in such a way as to provide safety in the event of a forward pitch-over.

"3. That the intentional, deliberate merchandising of the described product for the advertised use by a corporation whose engineering department knows subjectively that the roll bar configuration will not provide the safety in the event of forward pitch-overs that its appearance reasonably suggests to the consuming public and others, constitutes such a heedless disregard and reckless indifference to the safety of the general public as to constitute, in the absence of any attempt to give warning of that known defect, wilful misconduct and gross negligence for which punitive damages may be awarded; that such conduct is of such a nature to include, swallow up, surpass and exceed negligence and breach of warranty.

"4. That such conduct above described amounts to the making of false representations with corporate knowledge of their falsity with respect to the safety of the vehicle when used in the manner advertised.

"5. The conduct above described renders the defendants Jeep Corporation and American Motors Sales Corporation liable in damages for the trauma to the bodies of the plaintiffs to the extent that the collapse of the roll bar is a proximate cause thereof."

The court further stated that "[w]e believe the evidence on proximate cause as to the enhanced injuries supports in full the verdict of the jury in its entirety, as to both plaintiffs."

The cause is now before this court pursuant to the allowance of a motion to certify the record.

Okey & Casale, Eugene P. Okey and Mark D. Okey, Alliance, for appellees.

Weston, Hurd, Fallon, Paisley & Howely, Andrew P. Buckner and Louis Paisley, Cleveland, for appellants.

WILLIAM B. BROWN, Justice.

I(A)

Appellants' first three propositions of law raise essentially the same issue: that only negligence principles should be applied in a design defect case involving a so-called "second collision." In this case, appellees seek to hold appellants liable for injuries "enhanced" by a design defect of the vehicle in which appellees were riding when an accident occurred. This cause of action is to be contrasted with that where the alleged defect causes the accident itself. Here, the "second collision" is that between appellees and the vehicle in which they were riding.

Appellants assert that the instructions of law given to the jury by the trial court improperly submitted the doctrine of strict liability in tort as a basis for liability. The scope of this review is limited to the question of whether an instruction on strict liability in tort should have been given. For the reasons explained herein, we answer the question in the affirmative.

I(B)

The appropriate starting point in this analysis is our decision in Temple v. Wean United, Inc. (1977), 50 Ohio St. 2d 317, 364 N.E.2d 267. In *Temple*, this court adopted Section 402A of the Restatement of Torts 2d, thus providing a cause of action in strict liability for injury from a product in Ohio. Section 402A provides:

"(1) One who sells any product in a defective condition unreasonably dangerous to the user or consumer or to his property is subject to liability for physical harm thereby caused to the ultimate user or consumer, or to his property, if

"(a) the seller is engaged in the business of selling such a product, and

"(b) it is expected to and does reach the user or consumer without substantial change in the condition in which it is sold.

"(2) The rule stated in Subsection (1) applies although

"(a) the seller has exercised all possible care in the preparation and sale of his product, and

"(b) the user or consumer has not bought the product from or entered into any contractual relation with the seller."

Section 402A was applied to an action in which the plaintiff-appellant was injured while operating a punch press. While she acknowledged the absence of any mechanical malfunction in the press, plaintiff-appellant contended that the punch press was defective in that it was unreasonably dangerous and was placed in the hands of the user without adequate warning. In affirming the granting of a motion for summary judgment in favor of the punch press manufacturer, we found that the record revealed substantial change in the product subsequent to sale, thus removing the cause from Section 402A strict liability analysis. We further considered, and rejected, plaintiff-appellant's claim of negligent design, concluding that in view of the Industrial Commission's Safety Code, the manufacturer had exercised reasonable care in the design of the punch press.

Temple is significant in that it presents two alternate phrasings of the test for recovery under a theory of strict liability in tort. The first is whether a product is "'of good and merchantable quality, fit and safe for . . . [its] ordinary intended use.'" Temple v. Wean United, Inc., supra, at page 321, 364 N.E.2d 267. The other is the "unreasonably dangerous" test of Section 402A of the Restatement of Torts 2d. Id., at paragraph one of the syllabus. We recognized in *Temple*, at page 322, 364 N.E.2d 267, that "there are virtually no distinctions between Ohio's 'implied warranty in tort' theory and the Restatement version of strict liability in tort. . . ." Thus, in Ohio, a product which is unfit and unsafe for its intended use under an "implied warranty in tort" theory, would also be unreasonably dangerous under Section 402A theory. Before moving to an exploration of what would constitute an "unreasonably dangerous" design defect, under the Restatement, it is necessary to address the threshold question of whether Section 402A analysis should apply to design defects involving a "second collision."

Dean Prosser, reporter for the Restatement of Torts 2d, raised a cloud of doubt over the applicability of Section 402A to design cases with his comment: "There are, in addition, two particular areas in which the liability of the manufacturer, even though it may occasionally be called strict, appears to rest primarily upon a departure from proper standards of care, so that the tort is essentially a matter of negligence.

"One of these involves the design of the product, which includes plan, structure, choice of materials and specifications." [Footnotes omitted.] Prosser on Torts (4 Ed.), 644-645, Section 96. See Section 398 of Restatement of Torts 2d, Chattel Made Under a Dangerous Plan or Design, which sets a negligence standard for defective design.

Nevertheless, the vast weight of authority is in support of allowing an action in strict liability in tort, as well as negligence, for design defects. See Annotation, 96 A.L.R.3d 22, Sections 3-6. We see no difficulty in also applying Section 402A to design defects. As pointed out by the California Supreme Court, "[a] defect may emerge from the mind of the designer as well as from the hand of the workman." Cronin v. J. B. E. Olson Corp. (1972), 8 Cal. 3d 121, 134, 104 Cal. Rptr. 433, 501 P.2d 1153. A distinction between defects resulting from manufacturing processes and those resulting from design, and a resultant difference in the burden of proof on the injured party, would only provoke needless questions of defect classification, which would add little to the resolution of the underlying claims. A consumer injured by an unreasonably dangerous design should have the same benefit of freedom from proving fault provided by Section 402A as the consumer injured by a defectively manufactured product which proves unreasonably dangerous.

The doctrine of strict liability evolved to place liability on the party primarily responsible for the injury occurring, that is, the manufacturer of the defective product. Greenman v. Yuba Power Products, Inc. (1963), 59 Cal. 2d 57, 27 Cal. Rptr. 697, 377 P.2d 897. Any distinction based upon the source of the defect undermines the policy underlying the doctrine that the public interest in human life and safety can best be protected by subjecting manufacturers of defective products to strict liability in tort when the products cause harm.

Strict liability in tort has been applied to design defect "second collision" cases. Brandenburger v. Toyota Motor Sales, U.S.A., Inc. (1973), 162 Mont. 506, 513 P.2d 268; Seattle-First Nat. Bank v. Volkswagen of America, Inc. (1974), 11 Wash. App. 929, 525 P.2d 286; Annotation, 42 A.L.R.3d 560. While a manufacturer is under no obligation to design a "crash proof" vehicle, Larsen v. General Motors (C.A. 8, 1968), 391 F.2d 495, an instruction may be given on the issue of strict liability in tort if the plaintiff adduces sufficient evidence that an unreasonably dangerous product design proximately caused or enhanced plaintiff's injuries in the course of a foreseeable use. Dyson v. General Motors Corp. (D.C.E.D. Pa. 1969), 298 F. Supp. 1064. Here, appellants produced a vehicle which was capable of off-the-road use. It was advertised for such a use. The only protection provided the user in the case of roll-overs or pitch-overs proved wholly inadequate. A roll bar should be more than mere ornamentation. The interest of our society in product safety would best be served by allowing a cause in strict liability for such a roll bar device when it proves to be unreasonably dangerous and, as a result, enhances the injuries of the user.

I(C)

We turn to the question of what constitutes an unreasonably dangerous defective product. Section 402A subjects to liability one who sells a product in a "defective condition unreasonably dangerous" which causes physical harm to the ultimate user. Comment *g* defines defective condition as "a condition not contemplated by the ultimate consumer which will be unreasonably dangerous to him." Comment *i* states that for a product to be unreasonably dangerous, "[t]he article sold must be dangerous to an extent beyond that which would be contemplated by the ordinary consumer who purchases it, with the ordinary knowledge common to the community as to its characteristics."

With regard to design defects, the product is considered defective only because it causes or enhances an injury. "In such a case, the defect and the injury cannot be separated, yet clearly a product cannot be considered defective simply because it is capable of producing injury." Kimble & Lesher, Products Liability, at page 80. Rather, in such a case the concept of "unreasonable danger" is essential to establish liability under strict liability in tort principles.

The concept of "unreasonable danger," as found in Section 402A, provides implicitly that a product may be found defective in design if it is more dangerous in use than the ordinary consumer would expect. Another way of phrasing this proposition is that "a product may be found defective in design if the plaintiff demonstrates that the product failed to perform as safely as an ordinary consumer would expect when used in an intended or reasonably foreseeable manner." Barker v. Lull Engineering Co., Inc. (1978), 20 Cal. 3d 413, 429, 143 Cal. Rptr. 225, 573 P.2d 443.[1] As the California Supreme Court pointed out, such a standard is somewhat analogous to the commercial law warranty of fitness and merchantability. Id. As stated, supra, this court has previously recognized a definition of product defect also based upon an analogy to commercial warranty. Lonzrick v. Republic Steel Corp. (1966), 6 Ohio St. 2d 227, at page 235, 218 N.E.2d 185; Temple v. Wean United, supra, 50 Ohio St. 2d, at page 321, 364 N.E.2d 267. This standard reflects the commercial reality that "[i]mplicit in . . . [a product's] presence on the market . . . [is] a representation that it [will] safely do the jobs for which it was built." Greenman v. Yuba Power Products, supra, 59 Cal. 2d, at page 64, 27 Cal. Rptr. 697, 377 P.2d 897.

Moreover, a consumer-expectation test of unreasonable danger recognizes the legitimacy of one of the fundamental values in the law of torts: "the protection of the individuality of persons, by according formal respect for their fairly developed expectations of product safety. . . ." Owen,

---

1. Barker, supra, also provides, 20 Cal. 3d, at page 430, 143 Cal. Rptr. 225, 573 P.2d 443, an alternate test by which a product may be found defective in design even if it satisfies ordinary consumer expectations. Liability would result "if through hindsight the jury determines that the product's design embodies 'excessive preventable danger,' or, in other words if the jury finds that the risk of danger inherent in the challenged design outweighs the benefits of such design." In evaluating a product's design pursuant to the "risk-benefit" standard, a jury is permitted to consider "the gravity of the danger posed by the challenged design, the likelihood that such danger would occur, the mechanical feasibility of a safer alternative design, the financial cost of an improved design, and the adverse consequences to the product and to the consumer that would result from an alternative design." Barker, supra, at page 431, 143 Cal. Rptr. 225, 573 P.2d 443. The court further determined that a manufacturer which seeks to escape liability for an injury proximately caused by its product's design on a risk-benefit theory should bear the burden of persuading the trier of fact that its product should not be judged defective, rather than simply the burden of producing evidence. Id., at pages 431-432, 143 Cal. Rptr. 225, 573 P.2d 443. The appropriateness of this additional test was not raised by either party and we express no position thereon.

Rethinking the Policies of Strict Products Liability, 33 Vanderbilt L. Rev. 681, at page 690.

Thus, we hold a cause of action for damages for injuries "enhanced" by a design defect will lie in strict liability in tort. In order to recover, the plaintiff must prove by a preponderance of the evidence that the "enhancement" of the injuries was proximately caused by a defective product unreasonably dangerous to the plaintiff.

A product will be found unreasonably dangerous if it is dangerous to an extent beyond the expectations of an ordinary consumer when used in an intended or reasonably foreseeable manner.[2]

---

2. The trial judge gave the following instructions:

"Now this leaves for your determination the disputed issue which may be summarized as follows:

"1. Did the defendant breach its implied warranty to the plaintiff that its product was free of defect in design and reasonably safe for the use for which it was intended?

"2. Did the defendant breach its implied warranty to plaintiff in failing to warn the plaintiff that its unit was defective in design and likely to cause harm to persons using it? . . .

"4. Did the defect in design of the product and/or the defendant's failure to warn the plaintiff that its unit was defective and likely to cause harm to persons using it proximately cause or enhance the injury and damage, if any, sustained by the plaintiff? . . .

" . . . The doctrine of 'breach of implied warranty' as charged in the complaint does not depend upon proof of fault. A claim predicated upon breach of implied warranty proceeds upon a legal theory that one who provides a product impliedly represents to consumers or users of that product that it is a good or sound product. In the event it should thereafter develope [sic] that the product was not a sound or good product and a consumer or user thereof sustains an injury due to a defect therein, the manufacturer has breached its implied warranty.

"To recover for a breach of implied warranty, to provide a product free of defect in design and reasonably safe for the use for which it was intended, a plaintiff need not prove that any part of the product broke, fell apart, wore out or malfunctioned. The issue is not the degree of care exercised in the design and manufacture of the product, but rather the degree of safety of the ultimate product itself. I caution you, however, that the issue of breach of implied warranty—sometimes referred to by lawyers as the doctrine of strict liability—does not create absolute liability on the manufacturer of the product. Liability of the manufacturer may not be presumed from the mere happening of an accident. Accidents can happen in the use of any product, be it basically a safe or unsafe one. . . .

"The phrases 'design defect,' 'defective design' and others of like import as used herein is [sic] a fault or imperfection in design, which fault of [sic] imperfection in design exposes the user of a product made from such design to a hazard or danger beyond that which would be contemplated by an ordinary user with the knowledge common to persons using such product as to its characteristics. Thus under this doctrine it is the duty of a manufacturer, such as the defendant, to design a product that is reasonably fit for the use for which it is intended. A product is not considered as reasonably fit for the use for which it is intended if the design thereof makes it unreasonably dangerous to a user who is using it for the purpose for which it is intended. . . .

" . . . A product or device is considered as unreasonably dangerous if it is dangerous to an extent beyond that which would be contemplated by an ordinary user with the knowledge common to persons using such product, or such device as to its characteristics."

II.

Appellants' proposition of law No. 5 asserts, in part, that "[a]n instruction to the jury that the manufacturer's failure to warn is a breach of an implied warranty and renders the manufacturer strictly liable is error." The trial court instructed the jury that appellees had the burden of proving by a preponderance of the evidence that: "Defendant breached its implied warranty to plaintiff in failing to warn plaintiff that its unit was defective in design and likely to cause harm to persons using it; and . . . [t]he defect in the design of the product and the failure to warn the plaintiff as above indicated proximately caused or enhanced the injury and damage, if any, sustained by the plaintiff."

Comment *j* to Section 402A of the Restatement of Torts 2d, in part, states: "In order to prevent the product from being unreasonably dangerous, the seller may be required to give directions or warning on the container, as to its use." Comment *j* further states: "Where warning is given, the seller may reasonably assume that it will be read and heeded; and a product bearing such a warning, which is safe for use if it is followed, is not in defective condition, nor is it unreasonably dangerous."

In light of our adoption of Section 402A "together with its numerous illustrative comments . . . ," Temple v. Wean United, supra, 50 Ohio St. 2d at page 322, 364 N.E.2d 267, an instruction on the duty to warn, in the context of a charge on strict liability, is not reversible error. Civ. R. 61. The absence of a warning does not, without more, provide a basis for liability; rather, evidence of warning is in the nature of an affirmative defense to a claim that a product is unreasonably dangerous. The instruction in the case *sub judice*, however, consistently linked the duty to warn with the duty to keep the product reasonably safe for intended use. Given the repeated emphasis in the jury instructions that the product must be found unreasonably dangerous for its intended use, the jury was not misled as to the proper burden of proof upon appellees.

III.

Appellants in their proposition of law No. 4 contend that it was error for the trial court to have admitted in evidence television commercials which advertised the Jeep CJ-7 as a vehicle to "discover the rough, exciting world of mountains, forests, rugged terrain." Appellants further contend that "a

---

In view of our foregoing formulation of the standard for strict liability in tort for defective design, we find that the trial court's instructions to the jury were a sufficiently accurate statement of the law so that no prejudicial error was committed.

jury may not base its verdict upon such television commercials in the absence of a specific representation contained in the commercials as to the quality or merit of the product in question and in the absence from the plaintiff that the use of the product was in reliance upon such representations."

We held in Part I, supra, that a product is unreasonably dangerous if it is dangerous to an extent beyond the expectations of an ordinary consumer when used in an intended or reasonably foreseeable manner. The commercial advertising of a product will be the guiding force upon the expectations of consumers with regard to the safety of a product, and is highly relevant to a formulation of what those expectations might be. The particular manner in which a product is advertised as being used is also relevant to a determination of the intended and reasonably foreseeable uses of the product. Therefore, it was not error to admit the commercial advertising in evidence to establish consumer expectations of safety and intended use.

IV.

Appellants' sixth proposition of law challenges the award of punitive damages to appellees. The trial court gave the following instructions to the jury on the issue of punitive damages:

" . . . Punitive damages may be awarded only where a party intentionally and with actual malice injured another. Actual malice means anger, hatred, ill-will, hostility against another or a spirit of revenge. . . .

"Before you may award punitive damages in this case, the plaintiff must prove by a preponderance of the evidence that these defendants knew that the design of this rollbar and its support posed a grave danger to its customers and that the defendant's failure to redesign the rollbar and its support structure was intentional, reckless, wanton, willful or gross conduct."

In response to an interrogatory submitted by appellants, the jury explained its verdict as to punitive damages:

"Have you awarded punitive damages to either plaintiff in this action? *Yes*

"If the answer to the preceding question is 'yes' then state those facts from which you have found that the defendant acted:

"(a) Intentionally

"(b) Recklessly

"(c) Wantonly

"(d) Wilfully suggestive advertising depicting Jeeps going up and down steep and rugged terrain without any risk or warning.

"(e) Grossly neglected to test roll bar support system for foreseeable roll-overs and/or foreseeable pitch-overs."

   The Court of Appeals affirmed the award of punitive damages totalling $1.1 million on the basis of "the manufacturer's subjective awareness of the failure to make any plan for the forward pitch-over coupled with the incitement to reckless conduct contained in the advertisements involving clearly foreseeable risks of forward pitch-overs, plus a total failure to exercise any care at all to warn the public about the fact that the roll bar was not as safe as it looked, or as dangerous as the defendant knew it to be, for the advertised use, is, upon the record of this particular case, sufficient to warrant an inference of malice. The flavor of the sales promotion program as an intentional incitement to unlawful conduct permeates the evidence."

   The Court of Appeals relied upon appellants' advertising campaign as conduct from which actual malice could be inferred. Cited as exemplary of this "intentional incitement to unlawful conduct" was the sound track employed in the Jeep television commercials: "My Jeep CJ is the toughest rig around"; "That's Jeep guts—Guts to take you where only the toughest dares to go"; "Jeep guts—will take you places you have never been before"; "CJ-5—will give the young couples the ride of their lives on the dunes and gutsy ground steering"; "All right, which one of you guys is going to climb that big old hill with me? I mean you guys aren't yellow, are you? Is it a steep hill? Yeah, little lady, you could say it's a steep hill. Let's try it. The King of the Hill is about to discover the new Jeep CJ-7"; "That Jeep four-wheel drive is tough enough to go anywhere."

   It is an established principle of law in this state that punitive damages may be awarded in tort cases involving fraud, malice or insult. Roberts v. Mason (1859), 10 Ohio St. 277, paragraph one of the syllabus; Saberton v. Greenwald (1946), 146 Ohio St. 414, 66 N.E.2d 224, paragraph two of the syllabus. Actual malice may be inferred from conduct and surrounding circumstances. Davis v. Tunison (1959), 168 Ohio St. 471, 155 N.E.2d 904, paragraph two of the syllabus. Moreover, intentional, reckless, wanton, willful and gross acts which cause injury to person or property may be sufficient to evidence that degree of malice required to support an award of punitive damages in tort actions. Columbus Finance v. Howard (1975), 42 Ohio St. 2d 178, 184, 327 N.E.2d 654. There must be sufficient evidence of malice, however, before a question of punitive damages will be submitted to the jury. Smithhisler v. Dutter (1952), 157 Ohio St. 454, 105 N.E.2d 868, paragraph one of the syllabus.

   In the case *sub judice*, sufficient evidence of malice is not apparent from the commercial advertising alone. The television commercials relied upon by the Court of Appeals demonstrated an off-the-road use. The commercials are relevant to the foreseeable use of the vehicle and the unreasonable danger of the product when used as intended. But, to characterize the commercials as "intentional incitement to unlawful activity" is to read into them a malicious intent that is not apparent to this court. Mere "suggestive advertising" does not reach the level of "anger, hatred, ill-will, hostility . . . or a spirit of revenge" historically required for a finding of punitive damages under our cases.

The television and commercial advertising considered in conjunction with the evidence pertaining to the testing of the vehicle for roll-overs and pitch-overs is sufficient, however, to support a finding of punitive damages. Although simple negligence is not the basis for recovery of punitive damages in Ohio, Richards v. Office Products Co. (1977), 55 Ohio App. 2d 143, 380 N.E.2d 725, such damages may be awarded where the manufacturer's testing and examination procedures are so inadequate as to manifest a flagrant indifference to the possibility that the product might expose consumers to unreasonable risks of harm. See Owen, Punitive Damages in Products Liability Litigation, 74 Mich. L. Rev. 1258, at page 1340; Annotation, 29 A.L.R.3d 1021.

The manufacturer alone has the ability to screen out many product hazards that are hidden from the consumer. While a manufacturer has no duty to provide a crashproof vehicle, Larsen v. General Motors Corp., supra (391 F.2d 495), the record reveals that these appellants took no steps to ascertain the safety of the roll bar device on the 1976 Jeep CJ-7 vehicles. According to interrogatories answered by appellants, no "proving ground" tests, "vibration or shock" tests, or "crash" tests were performed on a 1976 Jeep vehicle equipped with roll bar assemblies. The record reveals that the only such testing ever done was on a 1969 CJ-5, a model with a wheel base ten inches shorter than the CJ-7, the subject vehicle. This testing was not, however, admitted in evidence.

The commercial advertising clearly contemplates off-the-road use of the vehicle. The salesman's guide to the vehicle described the roll bar in the following terms: "Surround yourself and your passengers with the strength of a rugged, reinforced steel roll bar for added protection. A very practical item, and a must if you run competition with a 4WD club. Adds rugged good looks, too." Given the foreseeability of roll-overs and pitch-overs, the failure of appellants to test to determine whether the roll bar "added protection" represents a flagrant indifference to the probability that a user might be exposed to an unreasonable risk of harm. For appellants to have encouraged off-the-road use while providing a roll bar that did little more than add "rugged good looks" is a sufficient basis for an award of punitive damages. . . .

For the foregoing reasons, the judgment of the Court of Appeals is affirmed.

Judgment affirmed.

[Concurring and dissenting opinions omitted.]

In 1993, the Consumer Product Safety Commission reported that there had been 2,235 fatalities to date related to the use of all-terrain vehicles. Children under age 16 accounted for around 40 percent of hospital emergency room treatments for accidents involving such vehicles.

In 1997, the American Law Institute published a new Restatement (Third) of Torts, Products Liability, designed to update the law in this field. The new promulgation answers a host of questions that had been raised under old Restatement §402A, and is a lot more complicated than its predecessor. The primary change made by Restatement (Third) is that while it retains strict liability for manufacturing defects, it shifts to a negligence standard for design defects and injuries caused by failure to give a proper warning. See Restatement (Third) of Torts, Products Liability §2. For a summary of the new Restatement, see David G. Owen, M. Stuart Madden, & Mary J. Davis, 1 Madden & Owen on Products Liability §§5:10-5.12 (2000).

II. STATE WARRANTY LAW

It is the function of a course in Sales, and not of this book, to teach the law of warranties. Nonetheless, some minimal appreciation of warranty law is necessary to an understanding of the rules that are peculiar to consumer matters. Therefore, you must digest the following outline and be prepared to answer the Problems raised.

A. Types of Warranties

The primary current source for warranty law is Article 2 of the Uniform Commercial Code. In 2003 Article 2 was rewritten, but that revision has proven controversial, and at this writing (the spring of 2009), no state has yet adopted it. Consequently, the discussion that follows refers to the original version of Article 2 (perhaps called the "pre-revision" version in your statute book).

The warranties of quality found in the Code can be divided into two broad categories: express warranties and implied warranties. Express warranties, as the name suggests, arise from seller activity, typically statements the seller makes about the characteristics of the item being sold.

PROBLEM 21

Mr. and Mrs. Consumer went to the showroom of Giant Motors, where the salesman, Howard Glad, sold them a new 2011 automobile. Before he did so he told them that the car that they looked at on the lot was the same as the one they ordered, except that their car would be blue, not red. In answer to a question Mrs. Consumer asked, the salesman told her that the car would get at least 30 miles to the gallon in city driving. He also mentioned that Giant Motors had a complete service department and that if anything went wrong with the car, Giant Motors could fix it. All these statements were oral. The contract they signed contained none of these statements, but did have a merger clause stating that the contract contained all the essential terms of the agreement. It also disclaimed any warranties not contained therein.

a. Look at U.C.C. §2-313 and decide whether there was an express warranty created by the statement that the car delivered would be blue. What about the statement regarding mileage? The statement that the car was a "2011" model? The repair facilities?

b. If the Consumers had seen a TV advertisement for Giant Motors featuring the car they bought and stating it was "wonderful" and "the best car on the road" and "maintenance free," would this ad create express warranties or would this merely be "puffing"?

c. Is it a defense to the car dealer that it did not intend to create any warranties in the sales pitch, nor did it use any formal words such as "warranty" or "guarantee"?

d. Look at U.C.C. §2-316(1) and decide whether the Consumers can get in the evidence of their conversation with Mr. Glad. See also §§2-202 and 2-302.

QUOTES FOR THE ATTORNEY'S ARSENAL: "PUFFING"

[Oliver Wendell Holmes on why words such as "A-ONE" are mere puffs:]

> It is settled that the law does not exact good faith from a seller in those vague commendations of his wares which manifestly are open to difference of opinions,— which do not imply untrue assertions concerning matters of direct observations . . . and as to which "it always has been understood, the world over, that such statements are to be distrusted."

Deming v. Darling, 148 Mass. 504, 505, 20 N.E. 107, 108 (1889).

Implied warranties are created not by the seller but by the legislature of the adopting jurisdiction. They are automatically part of the sale unless the seller (or the circumstances) does something to get rid of them. The philosophy underlying their promulgation is that they reflect the understanding of parties to a typical sale as to what is part of the bargain. Use U.C.C. §§2-314 and 2-315 to answer the following.

PROBLEM 22

Maude bought a new sweater at a clothing store. When she got it home, it unraveled as she took it from the sack. If there were no express warranties made at the time of the sale, can she get her money back? What is her theory? Would we reach the same result if she had bought the sweater at a garage sale?

The implied warranty of merchantability is an enormous warranty; it is the warranty that the product will work (that is, be "fit for the ordinary purpose" in the language of §2-314(2)(c)). When you think about it, this is typically all the warranty the buyer needs. Buyers would be more upset when the warranty is disclaimed if they knew what the word "merchantability" meant. They don't know because we have shrouded the concept (basic buyer protection) with such a strange-sounding legal word. "Merchantability" is so foreboding that most buyers are probably relieved to see it go. Call it the warranty of "suitability" and buyers might ask more questions before agreeing to its disclaimer.

Merchantability is only one of the implied warranties created by the Uniform Commercial Code. The most important of the others is the implied warranty of fitness for a particular purpose.

PROBLEM 23

Having decided to learn about the stars, Robert sent his 10-year-old nephew to the bookstore and told him to get a book about astronomy. The nephew dutifully conveyed this information to the clerk at the bookstore, who said, "We have just what your uncle needs." She then sold him a copy of "Basics of Astrology." When he saw the book, Robert was disgusted and called the bookstore, telling the clerk that she was lamebrained if she thought that astrology was the same thing as astronomy. She slammed down the phone in anger, and now refuses to give Robert back his money, stating that he bought a book that was worth every penny he paid for it, and adding that the book is not defective in any way. How does this come out? See §2-315; cf. §1-103.

PROBLEM 24

You are the attorney for Big Department Store. For the sales of its major appliances, the store wants to avoid warranty liability. Per your advice it has instructed its salespersons to make no express warranties about the products being sold, so the only worry is with implied warranties. Consider the following possibilities.

a. The current contract the store is using (no one is sure who wrote it) has a clause (number 12, on the back of the contract—the front side instructs the reader that important terms of the contract are contained on the back side). The clause, unlike the rest of the type on the page, is entirely in capital letters:

WARRANTY
THERE ARE NO EXPRESS OR IMPLIED WARRANTIES OF
ANY KIND THAT ARE PART OF THIS TRANSACTION
See §§2-316(2) and 1-201(10).

b. The existing contract also contains Clause 13: "The goods are sold as is." See §2-316(3)(a).

c. You may also find Clause 14 interesting: "Buyer is required to inspect the goods before purchase, and either has done so and is satisfied with their condition, or hereby waives the right to such an examination and all that it might reveal." See §2-316(3)(b).

d. What do you advise? Draft a proposed clause and be prepared to read it aloud in class.

Lease of Goods. Article 2 of the Uniform Commercial Code is triggered by the *sale* of goods, defined in §2-106(1) as requiring the "passage of title from the seller to the buyer for a price." What if the transaction is a *lease* of goods? Does the lessor in such a situation make express or implied warranties? Article 2A of the Uniform Commercial Code deals specifically with leases and creates warranty rules copied closely from the existing Article 2 provisions. Leases will be considered in more detail in Chapter 9, and there we will explore Article 2A's interface with other consumer law statutes.

B. Remedies for Breach of Warranty

If the seller does not live up to the warranty—whether express or implied—the Uniform Commercial Code gives the buyer a choice of

remedies. For our purposes, the most important of these is the choice between *acceptance* of the goods (living with the problem plus money for
damages caused) plus relief under §2-714 (the difference between the
product as warranted and the product as delivered), and *rejection* (or revocation of acceptance) with relief being measured under §§2-601, 2-608,
and 2-711. A word about rejection follows.

"Rejection," as that word is used in the UCC, means that the buyer
refuses to take the goods because of some defect in them or in the contract
of sale. Read §2-602. The buyer rejects by giving notice to the seller of the
reason for these actions, and thereafter may even refuse to deliver them
back to the seller if the buyer wants to hold them as collateral ("claim a
security interest in them") for return of the purchase price or any buyer
expenses incurred in connection with the handling of the rejected goods,
§2-711(3). Rejection must be accomplished during a *trial use period*, not
defined in length by the UCC (which says only that it lasts a "reasonable"
period). Once the buyer has done any of the acts that constitute "acceptance" (see §2-606), it is too late for the buyer to "reject."

Now what? What if your client is the consumer purchaser of a lemon
car, as in the next Problem? Say that he or she has clearly "accepted" the
car, but now discovers a serious defect in the vehicle. Is rescission (and
return of the money paid, of course) possible? Yes, is the answer. But to
avoid confusion with the common law meaning of "rescission," the Code
now calls the action "revocation of acceptance" and regulates it in §2-608,
which you should read in order to evaluate the following Problem.

PROBLEM 25

Maria Rose comes to your office to tell you about her troubles with
her new car. Six months ago she bought the car from Facade Motors,
Inc. The car was sold to her by a friend of her father, who is one of the
leading salesmen at Facade Motors. When the car was delivered it
had a chain burn across the top (apparently this car had been
strapped to the top of a trailer carrying lots of new cars) and a smear
of red paint across the otherwise black dashboard. The salesman told
her not to worry—drive the car home, bring it back Monday, and "we'll
fix the chain burn and the dashboard."

On Monday, she took the car to the dealership, reminded them of
these two problems and of their promise (made weeks ago) to install
a luggage rack on the top of the car (this was a bonus to get her to
buy). They assured her that all would be right by 5 p.m., when she
was to pick up the car. She did arrive at that time, paid for the car, and

was annoyed to discover, when she found the car parked on the lot, that the red paint was still on the dashboard. She went back inside and inquired, but was told that the man who worked on the car had gone home and nobody could help her until tomorrow.

The next day Maria called Facade Motors and complained not only about the paint but also about one corner of the new luggage rack, which had popped free. The dealership apologized and told her to bring the car in again soon. Two days later, Maria took time off from work and took the car in to the dealership. When she picked it up, the luggage rack had been fixed, but the red paint was still on the dashboard. They told her that it would take a special solvent to remove it, and, since it was on order, she would have to bring the car in again later.

That weekend it rained and Maria discovered that the windshield wipers wouldn't work. She had a close call on the freeway as a result. When she took time off from work the next day to take the car in, the dealership's employee flipped a switch and the wipers worked beautifully. They told her they still didn't have the paint solvent, but it was on order.

The following week the car stalled in heavy traffic when Maria had her aged mother in the car. The car was towed to Facade Motors, where the personnel told Maria that the car had needed only an adjustment to the carburetor and that it was fine now. They promised her the paint solvent sometime soon.

The next day the car again stalled, and Facade Motors (for the second time at their own expense) towed it to the repair department. They again adjusted the carburetor and put in new spark plugs.

Two weeks later the car stalled in a rainstorm moments after the windshield wipers quit working. Maria was nearly hit by a semi-truck as she flagged down passing cars for help. This time Facade Motors (which had not charged her a penny for all their repair attempts) told her that her car's internal computer had been incorrectly programmed and a specialist was needed to look at it. They smiled brightly as they gave her this news. The specialist was due in town in a week and they would call her and tell her when to bring in her car.

That night she called her sister, who was in her third year of law school, and asked what she should do. The sister told her that it didn't yet sound serious enough to warrant seeing a lawyer.

The specialist did look at her computer the following week, when Maria again took time off from work to have the car repaired. After it was returned to her (red dashboard and all), the car did seem to work well for two months, though the luggage rack again popped free at one corner. At the end of the two-month period, however, the windshield wipers refused to work in a rainstorm and Maria again had to flag down a passing car. The dealership said they had repaired the problem and returned the car to her, but the following week the car stalled in rush-hour traffic and again had to be towed back to the repair department.

Now Maria is in your office. The dealership personnel have had the car for three weeks (to their credit they have given her a "loaner"—a substitute vehicle while her car is in the shop) and have not yet announced when Maria can expect to get it back. She's not sure she wants it—she says she has become afraid of it.

a. Can she still "reject" the car, or had she "accepted" it? See §§2-602 and 2-606.

b. Does she have grounds to reject under §2-602 (note §2-601) or to revoke acceptance under §2-608?

c. If she must revoke acceptance under §2-608, who has the burden of proving whether the car complied with the warranties given at the time of sale? (This can be important—how can anyone prove the "cause" of the wiper's failure or the luggage rack's popping free?) See §2-607(4).

d. If she sues, must she return the car?

e. If they return the car to her (say, for example, she finds it parked in front of her house one morning after she has sent them a notice of rejection/revocation of acceptance), can she sell it and keep the money it brings as damages? See §2-711(3).

f. If she has the car in her possession (for whatever reason), could she continue to drive it without negating her rejection/revocation of acceptance?

g. In her Complaint, must she choose between rejection and revocation, or is she free to advance alternative theories? See your course on Civil Procedure.

h. Can Maria get her lost wages in a revocation of acceptance lawsuit? See §§2-711, 2-608, 2-715.

i. If your state has a "Lemon Car" law (and more than half of the states do have such a statute), how does it answer any of the questions presented?

QUOTES FOR THE ATTORNEY'S ARSENAL: "SHAKEN FAITH"

For a majority of people the purchase of a new car is a major investment rationalized by the peace of mind that flows from its dependability and safety. Once their faith is shaken, the vehicle loses not only its real value in their eyes, but becomes an instrument whose integrity is substantially impaired and whose operation is fraught with apprehension.

Zabriskie Chevrolet, Inc. v. Smith, 99 N.J. Super. 441, 458, 240 A.2d 195, 205 (1968) (permitting a consumer buyer to reject a new car that had to have a new engine installed immediately after delivery).

QUOTES FOR THE ATTORNEY'S ARSENAL: "ENDLESS REPAIRS"

[T]he seller does not have an unlimited time for the performance of the obligation to replace and repair parts. The buyer of an automobile is not bound to permit the seller to tinker with the article indefinitely in the hope that it may ultimately be made to comply with the warranty.

Orange Motors v. Dade County Dairies, Inc., 258 So. 2d 319, 321 (Fla. App. 1972).

QUOTES FOR THE ATTORNEY'S ARSENAL: "THE CAR DEALER'S OBLIGATION"

In passing, we observe that the purchase of an automobile is not only a considerable expenditure, but in this day of mobility, a necessity. When a purchaser answers the inducements made in the tremendous advertising campaigns carried on by the automobile industry and purchases a new automobile, he has the right to expect the automobile to perform properly and as represented. If it does not, through no fault of his, it appears to us that he should be allowed to seek redress. Here, the owner states that he carried the automobile back to the seller at least six times to have the necessary repairs made. The dealer attempts to refute this by saying that upon at least two occasions he did not have an appointment with the service department. We doubt seriously if the dealer required an appointment when the purchaser sought to purchase the automobile.

After a thorough study of the financial transaction involved in this business, we do not believe this opinion will in any way obstruct the free flow of commerce. We do not anticipate that we are placing an undue burden upon the automobile industry in requiring them to shoulder the responsibility of making sure their products perform as they have been represented.

Rehurek v. Chrysler Credit Corp., 262 So. 2d 452, 456 (Fla. App. 1972).

C. Used Cars and Warranties

Effective May 9, 1985, the Federal Trade Commission promulgated a Used Motor Vehicle Trade Regulation Rule, 16 C.F.R. §455, which requires sellers of used cars to post a sticker (called a "Buyer's Guide") in the window of the car explaining the scope of any warranty protection or lack thereof. The sticker must state that "The information on this form is part of any contract to buy this vehicle," and a similar statement must be placed in the contract of sale. The Regulation gives the seller detailed instructions on how to fill out the sticker.

Violation of this Regulation also violates §5 of the FTC Act, but, as we have seen, such a violation gives enforcement rights only to the FTC itself. Most state consumer sales practices statutes, however, incorporate FTC regulations into their coverage and provide that violations thereof give rise to civil actions.

D. *Warranties in Service Contracts*

So far we have focused on warranties in the sale or lease of goods. Absent special statutes on point (which many states have), *service contracts* (such as a contract to repair a car) typically do not give rise to liability in warranty, and are instead handled either as a breach of contract matter or as creating an action in negligence. This is true despite the urgings of a number of commentators who feel that warranty protections should extend to service contracts. See, e.g., Greenfield, Consumer Protection in Service Transactions—Implied Warranties and Strict Liability in Tort, 1974 Utah L. Rev. 661 (1974); Norman, Consumer Service Transactions, Implied Warranties and a Mandate for Realistic Reform, 11 Loy. U. Chi. L.J. 405 (1980); Singal, Extending Implied Warranties Beyond Goods: Equal Protection for Consumers of Services, 12 New Eng. L. Rev. 859 (1977). Some courts have allowed an action for *express warranties* in service contracts, see, e.g., Oak State Prods., Inc. v. Ecolab, Inc., 755 F. Supp. 235, 15 U.C.C. Rep. Serv. 2d 433 (C.D. Ill. 1991), either using the Uniform Commercial Code by analogy or simply making the express warranty part of the contract and allowing damages for its breach.

In some jurisdictions, repairs made pursuant to the sale of an item to a consumer give rise to an implied warranty that the repairs will be made in a good and workmanlike manner; this is usually done under the state Consumer Sales Practices Act. The leading case is Melody Home Mfg. Co. v. Barnes, 741 S.W.2d 349 (Tex. 1987) (using Texas's formidable Deceptive Trade Practices Act); see also Archibald v. Act III Arabians, 755 S.W.2d 84 (Tex. 1988).

III. WARRANTIES AND THE SALE OF HOMES

Warranties in connection with the sale or lease of real property are a comparatively recent development. See Annot., 25 A.L.R.3d 372; J. Sovern, Toward a Theory of Warranties in Sales of New Homes: Housing the Implied Warranty Advocates, Law and Economics Mavens, and Consumer

Psychologists Under One Roof, 1993 Wis. L. Rev. 13; Wendy B. Davis, Corrosion by Codification: The Deficiencies in the Statutory Versions of the Implied Warranty of Workmanlike Construction, 39 Creighton L. Rev. 103 (2006). It should also be noted that several states impose warranties on new residential construction by statute; see Md. Real Prop. Code §10-204(b); N.J. Stat. Ann. §2146:3B-3(b)(3); Va. Code Ann. §55-70.1(E). Many states will look to the rules of the Uniform Commercial Code (by analogy) in deciding warranty issues in the sale of homes. See, e.g., Hicks v. Superior Court, 8 Cal. Rptr. 3d 703(Cal. App. 2004); Board of Managers of Village Centre Condo. Ass'n, Inc. v. Wilmette Partners, 198 Ill. 2d 132, 760 N.E.2d 976 (2001); Brewer v. Poole Constr. Co., 2001 WL 792783 (Mass. Super. 2001).

HUMBER v. MORTON[3]
Supreme Court of Texas, 1968
426 S.W.2d 554

NORVELL, J.

The widow Humber brought suit against Claude Morton, alleging that Morton was in the business of building and selling new houses; that she purchased a house from him which was not suitable for human habitation in that the fireplace and chimney were not properly constructed and because of such defect, the house caught fire and partially burned the first time a fire was lighted in the fireplace. Morton defended upon two grounds: that an independent contractor, Johnny F. Mays, had constructed the fireplace and he, Morton, was not liable for the work done by Mays, and that the doctrine of "caveat emptor" applied to all sales of real estate. Upon the first trial of the case (which was to a jury), Mrs. Humber recovered a judgment which was reversed by the Eastland Court of Civil Appeals and the cause remanded for another trial because of an improper submission of the damage issue. 399 S.W.2d 831 (1966, no writ).

Upon the second trial, defendant Morton filed a motion for summary judgment supported by affidavits, one of which referred to and incorporated therein the statement of the evidence adduced upon the first trial. Plaintiff likewise made a motion for summary judgment. Defendant's motion was granted and that of the plaintiff overruled. Such judgment was affirmed by the Court of Civil Appeals upon the holdings that Mays was an independent contractor and that the doctrine of implied warranty was not applicable to

---

3. Footnotes in this case have been renumbered for clarity.

the case. 414 S.W.2d 765. Mrs. Humber, as petitioner, brought the case here, but we shall refer to the parties by their trial court designations.

It conclusively appears that defendant Morton was a "builder-vendor." The summary judgment proofs disclose that he was in the business of building or assembling houses designed for dwelling purposes upon land owned by him. He would then sell the completed houses together with the tracts of land upon which they were situated to members of the house-buying public. There is conflict in the summary judgment proofs as to whether the house sold to Mrs. Humber had been constructed with a dangerously defective fireplace chimney. Construction engineers who testified under oath for Mrs. Humber, as disclosed by the statement of facts upon the first trial which was made a part of the summary judgment record here, stated that the chimney was defective. Mr. Mays, who built the chimney, denied that his work was substandard or deficient in any way.

While there may be other grounds for holding that Mrs. Humber made a case to go to the jury, such as negligence attributable to Morton, failure to inspect and the like, we need not discuss these theories because we are of the opinion that the courts below erred in holding as a matter of law that Morton was not liable to Mrs. Humber because the doctrine of caveat emptor applied to the sale of a new house by a "builder-vendor" and consequently no implied warranty that the house was fit for human habitation arose from the sale. Accordingly, we reverse the judgments of the courts below and remand the cause to the district court for a conventional trial upon the merits.

Mrs. Humber entered into a contract when she bought the house from Morton in May of 1964 and such house, together with the lot upon which it was situated, was conveyed to her. According to Morton, the only warranty contained in the deed was the warranty of title, i.e. "to warrant and forever defend, all and singular, the said premises unto the said Ernestine Humber, her heirs and assigns, ..." and that he made no other warranty, written or oral, in connection with the sale. While it is unusual for one to sell a house without saying something good about it, and the statement that no warranty was made smacks of a conclusion, we shall assume that such conversation as may have taken place did not involve anything more than mere sales talk or puffing, and that no express warranties, either oral or written, were involved. However, it is undisputed that Morton built the house and then sold it as a new house. Did he thereby impliedly warrant that such house was constructed in a good workmanlike manner and was suitable for human habitation? We hold that he did. Under such circumstances, the law raises an implied warranty.

Preliminary to our discussion of the controlling issue in the case, the applicability of the caveat emptor doctrine, we should notice the reference of the Court of Civil Appeals to Article 1297, Vernon's Ann. Tex. Stats., which incidentally is not set out in the opinion, but is referred to by a quotation from Westwood Development Company v. Esponge, 342 S.W.2d 623 (Tex. Civ. App. 1961, writ ref'd n r e). The statute is not deemed applicable here for a number of reasons. Article 1297 does not say that warranties as to fitness and suitability of structures upon land cannot arise unless expressed in the deed of conveyance. The article relates to covenants which may or may not arise from the use of certain specific words in a conveyance, namely, "grant" or "convey."

This article is part of Title 31, Revised Statutes, relating to conveyances. It relates to covenants of title which arise out of conveyances and not to collateral covenants such as the suitability of a house for human habitation. The presence of a collateral covenant of this type in a deed would be strange indeed. "It is not the office of a deed to express the terms of the contract of sale, but to pass the title pursuant to the contract." 26 C.J.S. Deeds 1, p. 582. The article simply prescribes what covenants may be implied by the use of two designated words, "grant" or "convey." The implied warranty of fitness arises from the sale and does not spring from the conveyance.

It may be that the lower courts were striking at the nonstatutory doctrine of merger under which all prior negotiations with reference to a sale of land are said to be merged in the final transaction between the parties. The doctrine of merger, however, is a matter generally controlled by the intention of the parties. 26 C.J.S. Deeds 91, p.841. For example: A owns Blackacre and agrees with B to construct a house thereon and then conveys the house and lot to B after the house has been completed. There are numerous cases that an implied covenant or warranty to build in a workmanlike manner is not destroyed by the deed. See, e.g., Perry v. Sharon Development Co. [1937] 4 All E.R. 390 (C.A.); Jones v. Gatewood, 381 P.2d 158 (Okla. 1963).

If the passage of a deed does not operate to extinguish a warranty, either expressed or implied, in the case of an uncompleted house, it is difficult to understand how the deed could operate to merge and thus destroy an implied warranty raised by law in the case of a sale of a completed new house. It would be a strange doctrine indeed for the law to raise an implied warranty from a sale and then recognize that such warranty could be defeated by the passage of title to the subject matter of the sale. The issue here is not whether the implied warranty was extinguished by a conveyance, but whether such warranty ever came into existence in the first place.

The cases which give some weight to the doctrine of merger in the implied warranty situation hold that the doctrine of caveat emptor applies to sales of real property, thus reducing the "merger" theory to the status of a "unicorn hunting bow."[4] The merger doctrine implies that there is something to merge.

It might further be pointed out that generally in Texas, the notion of implied warranty arising from sales is considered to be a tort rather than a contract concept. Decker & Sons v. Capp, 139 Tex. 609, 164 S.W.2d 828, 142 A.L.R. 1479 (1942); Putman v. Erie City Mfg. Co., 338 F.2d 911 (5th Cir. 1964). As to warranties implied from contracts and strict liability in tort, see, Epstein, "Strict Liability in Tort—A Modest Proposal," 70 W. Va. L. Rev. 1 (1967).

We return to the crucial issue in the case—Does the doctrine of caveat emptor apply to the sale of a new house by a builder-vendor?

Originally, the two great systems of jurisprudence applied different doctrines to sales of both real and personal property. The rule of the common law—caveat emptor—was fundamentally based upon the premise that the buyer and seller dealt at arm's length, and that the purchaser had means and opportunity to gain information concerning the subject matter of the sale which were equal to those of the seller. On the other hand, the civil law doctrine—caveat venditor—was based upon the premise that a sound price calls for a sound article; that when one sells an article, he implies that it has value. 77 C.J.S. 1159, Sales §315, Sales 275, Sales, 46 Am. Jur. 275, Sales §87.

Today, the doctrine of caveat emptor as related to sales of personal property has a severely limited application. Decker & Sons v. Capp, supra; McKisson v. Sales Affiliates, 416 S.W.2d 787 (Tex. Sup. 1967); Putman v. Erie City Mfg. Co., supra; O. M. Franklin Serum Co. v. C. A. Hoover & Sons, 418 S.W.2d 482 (Tex. Sup. 1967).

In 1884, the Supreme Court of the United States applied the doctrine of implied warranty, the antithesis of caveat emptor, to a real property situation involving false work and pilings driven into the bed of the Maumee River. The case of Kellogg Bridge Company v. Hamilton, 10 U.S. 108, 3 S. Ct. 537, 28 L. Ed. 86, arose in connection with the construction of a bridge. The Supreme Court (the elder Mr. Justice Harlan writing), said:

"Although the plaintiff in error (Kellogg Bridge Company, defendant in the trial court) is not a manufacturer, in the common acceptation of that word, it made or constructed the false work which it sold to Hamilton. The transaction, if not technically a sale, created between the parties the relation of vendor and vendee. The business of the company was the construction of bridges. By its occupation, apart from its contract with the railroad company, it held itself out as reasonably competent to do work of that character. Having

---

4. A broken and inoperative cross-bow which is as effective as a good weapon since no one has seen a unicorn since the time of Noah.

partially executed its contract with the railroad company, it made an arrangement with Hamilton whereby the latter undertook, among other things, to prepare all necessary false work, and, by a day named, and in the best manner, to erect the bridge then being constructed by the bridge company— Hamilton to assume and pay for such work and materials as that company had up to that time done and furnished. Manifestly, it was contemplated by the parties that Hamilton should commence where the company left off. It certainly was not expected that he should incur the expense of removing the false work put up by the company and commence anew. On the contrary, he agreed to assume and pay for, and therefore it was expected by the company that he should use, such false work as it had previously prepared. It is unreasonable to suppose that he would buy that which he did not intend to use, or that the company would require him to assume and pay for that which it did not expect him to use, or which was unfit for use. . . . In the cases of sales by manufacturers of their own articles for particular purposes, communicated to them at the time, the argument was uniformly pressed that, as the buyer could have required an express warranty, none should be implied. But, plainly, such an argument impeaches the whole doctrine of implied warranty, for there can be no case of a sale of personal property in which the buyer may not, if he chooses, insist on an express warranty against latent defects.

"All the facts are present which, upon any view of the adjudged cases, must be held essential in an implied warranty. The transaction was, in effect, a sale of this false work, constructed by a company whose business it was to do such work; to be used in the same way the maker intended to use it, and the latent defects in which, as the maker knew, the buyer could not, by any inspection or examination, at the time discover; the buyer did not, because in the nature of things he could not, rely on his own judgment; and, in view of the circumstances of the case, and the relations of the parties, he must be deemed to have relied on the judgment of the company, which alone of the parties to the contract had or could have knowledge of the manner in which the work had been done. The law, therefore, implies a warranty that this false work was reasonably suitable for such use as was contemplated by both parties. . . ."

In Texas, the doctrine of caveat emptor began its fade-out at an early date. In Wintz v. Morrison, 17 Tex. 369 (1856), involving a sale of personal property, the Texas Supreme Court quoted with approval the following from Story on Sales as to the trend of 19th century decisions:

"[T]he tendency of all the modern cases of warranty is to enlarge the responsibility of the seller, to construe every affirmation by him to be a warranty, and frequently to imply a warranty on his part, from acts and circumstances, wherever they were relied upon by the buyer. The maxim of caveat emptor seems gradually to be restricted in its operation and limited in its dominion, and beset with the circumvallations of the modern doctrine of implied warranty, until it can no longer claim the empire over the law of sales, and is but a shadow of itself. . . . ."

As to the present personal property rule of implied warranties or strict liability in tort, see *Decker*, *Putnam*, *McKisson* and *Franklin*, cited above.

While in numerous common law jurisdictions, the caveat emptor doctrine as applied to the vendor builder—new house situation has overstayed its time, it was said by way of dicta in a Texas Court of Civil Appeals case in 1944 that:

"By offering the (new) house for sale as a new and complete structure appellant impliedly warranted that it was properly constructed and of good material and specifically that it had a good foundation, . . ." Loma Vista Development Co. v. Johnson, Tex. Civ. App., 177 S.W.2d 225, 1 c.227, revd. on other grounds, 142 Tex. 686, 180 S.W.2d 922. This decision has been described as "a preview of things to come."[5]

The rapid sickening of the caveat emptor doctrine as applied to sales of new houses was exposed by the Miller-Perry-Hoye-Weck-Jones-Glisan-Carpenter syndrome.[6] The history of this development is briefly set out in Carpenter v. Donohoe, 154 Colo. 78, 388 P.2d 399 (1964), and in more detail by Professor E. F. Roberts in "The Case of the Unwary Home Buyer: The Housing Merchant Did It," 52 Cornell Law Quarterly 835 (1967). See also, Williston on Contracts (3d Ed. Jaeger) §926A, wherein it is said: "It would be much better if this enlightened approach (implied warranty, Jones v. Gatewood, 381 P.2d 158 [Okla.]) were generally adopted with respect to the sale of new houses for it would tend to discourage much of the sloppy work and jerry-building that has become perceptible over the years." 7 Williston (3d Ed.) p.818: 1 Follmer and Friedman, Products Liability §5.03 [5] [b]; Stewart, "Implied Warranties in the Sale of New Houses," Note, 26 U. Pitt. L. Rev. 862 (1965); Haskell, "The Case for an Implied Warranty of Quality in Sales of Real Property," 53 Geo. L.J. 633 (1965); Gibson and Lounsberry, "Implied Warranties—Sales of a Completed House," Comments, 1 Cal. Western L. Rev. 110 (1965); Smith, "Torts, Implied Warranty in Real Estate, Privity Requirement," Comment, 44 N. Car. L. Rev. 236 (1965); Ramunno, "Implied Warranty of Fitness for

---

5. 52 Cornell Law Quarterly 835, l. c.841.
6. Miller v. Cannon Hill Estates, Ltd. [1931] 1 All E.R. 93 (K.B.); Perry v. Sharon Dev. Co. [1937] 4 All E.R. 390 (C.A.); Hoye v. Century Builders, Inc., 52 Wash. 2d 830, 329 P.2d 474 (1958); Weck v. A. M. Sunrise Construction Co., 36 Ill. App. 2d 383, 184 N.E.2d 728 (1962); Jones v. Gatewood, 381 P.2d 158 (Okla. 1963); Glisan v. Smolenske, 153 Colo. 274, 387 P.2d 260 (1963); and Carpenter v. Donohoe, 154 Colo. 78, 388 P.2d 399 (1964).

Habitation in Sale of Residential Dwellings," 43 Denver L. Rev. 379 (1966).

The *Glisan* case (Glisan v. Smolenske), 153 Colo. 274, 387 P.2d 260 (1963), was factually similar to the hypothetical example heretofore set out in this opinion. Smolenske had agreed to purchase a house from Glisan while it was under construction. The court propounded and answered the implied warranty question, thusly:

"Was there an implied warranty that the house, when completed, would be fit for habitation? There is a growing body of law on this question, which, if followed, requires an answer in the affirmative.

"It is the rule that there is an implied warranty where the contract relates to a house which is still in the process of construction, where the vendor's workmen are still on the job, and particularly where completion is not accomplished until the house has arrived at the contemplated condition— namely, finished and fit for habitation. Weck v. A. M. Sunrise Construction Co., supra [36 Ill. App. 2d 383, 184 N.E.2d 728]; Jones v. Gatewood, supra [381 P.2d 158]; Hoye v. Century Builders, Inc., 52 Wash. 2d 830, 329 P.2d 474; Miller v. Cannon Hill Estates, Ltd., supra [2 K.B. 113]; Perry v. Sharon Development Co., Ltd., supra [4 All E.L.R.]; Jennings v. Tavenner, 2 All E. L.R. (1955) 769; Dunham, Vendor's Obligation as to Fitness of Land for a Particular Purpose, 37 Minn. L. Rev. 108 (1953). Contra: Coutraken v. Adams, 39 Ill. App. 2d 290, 188 N.E.2d 780."

In the next year, 1964, the Colorado Supreme Court in Carpenter v. Donohoe, 154 Colo. 78, 388 P.2d 399, extended the implied warranty rule announced by it in *Glisan* to cover sales of a new house by a builder-vendor. The court said:

"That a different rule should apply to the purchaser of a house which is near completion than would apply to one who purchases a new house seems incongruous. To say that the former may rely on an implied warranty and the latter cannot is recognizing a distinction without a reasonable basis for it. This is pointedly argued in an excellent article, 'Caveat Emptor in Sales of Realty—Recent Assaults upon the Rule,' by Bearman, 14 Vanderbilt Law Rev. 541 (1960-61).

"We hold that the implied warranty doctrine is extended to include agreements between builder-vendors and purchasers for the sale of newly constructed buildings, completed at the time of contracting. There is an implied warranty that builder-vendors have complied with the building code of the area in which the structure is located. Where, as here, a home is the subject of sale, there are implied warranties that the home was built in workmanlike manner and is suitable for habitation."

While it is not necessary for us to pass upon a situation in which the vendor-purchaser relationship is absent, the case of Schipper v. Levitt & Sons, 44 N.J. 70, 207 A.2d 314 (1965), is important as much of the reasoning set forth in the opinion is applicable here. The Supreme Court of New Jersey recognized "the need for imposing on builder-vendors an implied obligation of reasonable workmanship and habitability which survives delivery of the deed." This was a case in which a person other than a purchaser had been injured by a defective water heater which had been installed in a new house by Levitt, the builder-vendor. The opinion cited and quotes from Carpenter v. Donohoe but proceeded upon the theory of strict liability in tort.[7] The court placed emphasis upon the close analogy between a defect in a new house and a manufactured chattel. The opinion states:

"The law should be based on current concepts of what is right and just and the judiciary should be alert to the never-ending need for keeping its common law principles abreast of the times. Ancient distinctions which make no sense in today's society and tend to discredit the law should be readily rejected as they were step by step in Henningsen [v. Bloomfield Motors, 32 N.J. 358, 161 A.2d 69, 75 A.L.R.2d 1 (1960)] and Santor [v. A and M Karagheusian, 44 N.J. 52, 207 A.2d 305, 16 A.L.R.3d 670 (1965)]. . . .

"When a vendee buys a development house from an advertised model, as in a Levitt or in a comparable project, he clearly relies on the skill of the developer and on its implied representation that the house will be erected in reasonably workmanlike manner and will be reasonably fit for habitation. He has no architect or other professional adviser of his own, he has no real competency to inspect on his own, his actual examination is, in the nature of things, largely superficial, and his opportunity for obtaining meaningful protective changes in the conveyancing documents prepared by the builder vendor is negligible. If there is improper construction such as a defective heating system or a defective ceiling, stairway and the like, the well-being of the vendee and others is seriously endangered and serious injury is foreseeable. The public interest dictates that if such injury does result from the defective construction, its cost should be borne by the responsible developer who created the danger and who is in the better economic position

---

7. It is said in the opinion that, "It is true, as Levitt suggests, that cases such as *Carpenter* (388 P.2d 399) involved direct actions by original vendees against their builder vendors and that consequently no questions of privity arose. But it seems hardly conceivable that a court recognizing the modern need for a vendee occupant's right to recover on principles of implied warranty or strict liability would revivify the requirement of privity, which is fast disappearing in the comparable products liability field, to preclude a similar right in other occupants likely to be injured by the builder vendor's default. . . ."

to bear the loss rather than by the injured party who justifiably relied on the developer's skill and implied representation."

In Bethlahmy v. Bechtel, 415 P.2d 698 (Idaho 1966), it appeared that the trial court had rendered judgment in accordance with the 1959 holding of the Supreme Court of Oregon in Steiber v. Palumbo, a much cited case which is relied upon by the defendant here. The specific finding of the trial court was:

"There are no implied warranties in the sale of real property. Steiber v. Palumbo, 219 Oreg. 479, 347 P.2d 978 [78 A.L.R.2d 440] (1959); Annot., 78 A.L.R.2d 446. The sale of this home carried with it, absent an express warranty, no promise that the floor would not leak."

The Idaho court was then called upon to deal with the Oregon decision and the later decisions of the Colorado Supreme Court in *Carpenter* and that of the New Jersey Supreme Court in *Schipper*. After a careful review of many decisions, including the Oregon, Colorado and New Jersey cases mentioned, the court said:

"The *Schipper* decision is important here because: (1) it illustrates the recent change in the attitude of the courts toward the application of the doctrine of caveat emptor in actions between the builder-vendor and purchaser of newly constructed dwellings; (2) it draws analogy between the present case and the long-accepted application of implied warranty of fitness in sales of personal property; and (3) the opinion had the unanimous approval of the participating justices. . . .

"The foregoing decisions all (except the Hoye case) rendered subsequent to the 1959 Oregon decision, relied upon by the trial court, show the trend of judicial opinion is to invoke the doctrine of implied warranty of fitness in cases involving sales of new houses by the builder. The old rule of caveat emptor does not satisfy the demands of justice in such cases. The purchase of a home is not an everyday transaction for the average family, and in many instances is the most important transaction of a lifetime. To apply the rule of caveat emptor to an inexperienced buyer, and in favor of a builder, who is daily engaged in the business of building and selling houses, is manifestly a denial of justice. See also, Loma Vista Development Co. v. Johnson (Tex.) 177 S.W.2d 225 (1943); Appendix to Staff v. Lido Dunes, Inc., 47 Misc. 2d 322, 262 N.Y.S.2d 544, at 553 (1965)."

See also, Waggoner v. Midwestern Development, Inc., 154 N.W.2d 803 (So. Dak. 1967).

In September of 1967, the Houston Court of Civil Appeals handed down its opinion in Moore v. Werner, 418 S.W.2d 918 (no writ), in which, after citing a number of authorities, the court said:

"Many of the authorities cited involve personalty, but we see no reason for any distinction between the sale of a new house and the sale of personalty, especially in a suit between the original parties to the contract, one of whom constructed the house in question. It was the seller's duty to perform the work in a good and workmanlike manner and to furnish adequate materials, and failing to do so, we believe the rule of implied warranty of fitness applies. Hoye v. Century Builders, 52 Wash. 2d 830, 329 P.2d 474, 476; Mann v. Clowser, 190 Va. 887, 59 S.E.2d 78, 84; 13 Am. Jur. 2d, p.29, Sec. 27." . . .

If at one time in Texas the rule of caveat emptor had application to the sale of a new house by a vendor-builder, that time is now past. The decisions and legal writings herein referred to afford numerous examples and situations illustrating the harshness and injustice of the rule when applied to the sale of new houses by a builder-vendor,[8] and we need not repeat them here. Obviously, the ordinary purchaser is not in a position to ascertain when there is a defect in a chimney flue, or vent of a heating apparatus, or whether the plumbing work covered by a concrete slab foundation is faulty. It is also highly irrational to make a distinction between the liability of a vendor-builder who employs servants and one who uses independent contractors. Compare, Conner v. Conejo Valley Development Co., 61 Cal. Rptr. 333 (1967). The common law is not afflicted with the rigidity of the law of the Medes and the Persians "which altereth not," and as stated in Cardozo in "The Nature of the Judicial Process," pp. 150-151 (quoted in 415 P.2d 698):

"That court best serves the law which recognizes that the rules of law which grew up in a remote generation may, in the fullness of experience, be found to serve another generation badly, and which discards the old rule when it finds that another rule of law represents what should be according to the established and settled judgment of society, and no considerable property rights have become vested in reliance upon the old rule. . . ."[9]

---

8. In the vendor-builder situation, Professor Roberts seems inclined to agree with Mr. Bumble's estimate of the law and points out that when caveat emptor is retained with regard to the sale of new houses, the law seemingly concerns itself little with a transaction which may and often does involve a purchaser's life savings, yet may afford relief by raising an implied warranty of fitness when one is swindled in the purchase of a two dollar fountain pen. 52 Cornell L. Rev. 835. Similarly, in 111 Solicitors' Journal 22, l. c.25 (London), it is pointed out that, "the purchaser buying a new house with legal assistance is often less well protected legally than the purchaser buying a chattel without legal assistance." It is further urged that, "The legal profession should have made it their business to insure proper protection for the purchaser without waiting for building societies to take the initiative" for their own protection since most builders "try to do a good job (but) the reputation of all may be injuriously affected by the low standards of a few."

9. See also, Holmes, Collected Legal Papers, p.187, quoted in 16 Baylor L. Rev. 263, 277, viz.: "It is revolting to have no better reason for a rule of law than that it was laid down in the

The caveat emptor rule as applied to new houses is an anachronism patently out of harmony with modern home buying practices. It does a disservice not only to the ordinary prudent purchaser but to the industry itself by lending encouragement to the unscrupulous, fly-by-night operator and purveyor of shoddy work.

The judgments of the courts below are reversed and the cause remanded for trial in accordance with this opinion.

GRIFFIN, J., notes his dissent.

PROBLEM 26

Six months after Mr. and Mrs. Jones had a new roof put on their home, they decided to move to another state. They sold their house to the Browns, telling them at the time of the sale that the roof was new. Two months after the Browns moved in, the roof began to leak due to faulty construction. When the Browns sued the contractor, he responded that any implied warranty he had given ran only in favor of the original purchasers and not to subsequent owners of the house with whom he was not in privity. How should this come out? See Lempke v. Dagenais, 547 A.2d 290 (N.H. 1988).

QUOTES FOR THE ATTORNEY'S ARSENAL: "DISCLAIMING REALTY WARRANTIES"

[O]ne seeking the benefit of such a disclaimer must not only show a conspicuous provision which fully discloses the consequences of its inclusion but also that such was *in fact* the agreement reached. The heavy burden thus placed upon the builder is completely justified, for by his assertion of the disclaimer he is seeking to show that the buyer has relinquished protection afforded him by public policy. A knowing waiver of this protection will not be readily implied.

Crowder v. Vandendeale, 564 S.W.2d 879, 881 n.4 (Mo. 1978) (emphasis in original); see also Tusch Enter. v. Coffin, 113 Idaho 37, 740 P.2d 1022 (1987); commented on in 66 Wash. U. L.Q. 163 (1988).

---

time of Henry IV. It is still more revolting if the grounds upon which it was laid down have vanished long since, and the rule persists from blind imitation of the past."

CHAPTER 4
Federal Quality Control Statutes

I. THE MAGNUSON-MOSS WARRANTY ACT

In 1975 the federal government entered the warranty field with the adoption of the Magnuson-Moss Warranty—Federal Trade Commission Improvement Act, 15 U.S.C. §§2301 et seq. The Act is divided into two Titles. The second Title deals with amendments to the FTC Act and is not relevant to our discussion. Title I, however, makes major changes in state warranty law. Use the statute and the FTC Regulations adopted pursuant thereto (16 C.F.R. §700) to solve the following Problems.

PROBLEM 27

The City of Thebes, Utah, bought a new car for use by the mayor on city business. The car came with a manufacturer's warranty. Does Magnuson-Moss apply to this purchase? See the definitions of "consumer" and "consumer product" in §101 of the Act. Would the Act apply to the *leasing* of a new automobile? See Ryan v. American Honda Motor Co., Inc., 186 N.J. 431, 896 A.2d 454 (2006).

PROBLEM 28

Look at the definition of "written warranty" in the same section and decide whether the following warranties qualify.
a. "Manufacturer warrants that the vehicle being sold is a 2004 model."
b. "Manufacturer promises to repair any defect in the product occurring within one year after sale."
c. "Famous movie star Howard Teeth uses this product every day."

d. "Money back if not satisfied."

The Act never requires a seller to give a warranty, §102(b)(2). It merely regulates the warranty terms if the seller decides to offer a written warranty (note also that the Act does not deal with oral warranties, though, of course, the UCC does). Read §102 of the Act and FTC Reg. §§701.2 and 701.3.

PROBLEM 29

You are the attorney for Sturdy Ladder, Inc., which manufactures ladders for use in the home. The company wants to give a three-year written guarantee on the ladders, but limit the remedy for breach to replacement of the defective ladder. Under no circumstances does the company want to be liable for consequential damages (such as hospital bills) if the consumer is injured while using the ladder. Will Magnuson-Moss allow the warranty to disclaim liability for such damages? See §104. Will state law? See U.C.C. §2-719. What do you advise?

If the product being warranted costs $10 or more, §103 of the Act requires the warranty itself to be labeled as either a "full (statement of duration) warranty" (for example, "full one-year warranty") or simply a "limited warranty." Section 104 then gives some guidance as to what a "full warranty" means, and the FTC Regulations add some flesh to the term. A "limited warranty" means only that the warrantor does not bind itself to meet the standards for a "full warranty." The idea here is that once consumers become aware that they are likely to get better warranty protection with a full warranty than a limited one, the pressure of the marketplace will force warrantors to offer the greater protection of a full warranty. Read §104 of the Act and FTC Reg. §§700.6 and 700.9.

PROBLEM 30

One of your clients manufactures the Spotless Automatic Can Opener, which retails for $20. The client is very proud of its product and wants to offer a warranty on it. The client asks the following questions:

a. The can opener should easily be trouble-free for a two-year period. Should the can opener be covered by a full two-year warranty? A limited warranty?

b. Must the warranty be given to the consumer before he or she purchases the item? See FTC Reg. §702.3.

c. Can the warranty be made contingent on the return of a registration card? See FTC Reg. §§700.7 and 701.4.

d. Can the warranty protection be limited to the first purchaser only? See FTC Reg. §700.6; Haas v. DaimlerChrysler Corp., 611 N.W.2d 382 (Minn. App. 2000).

PROBLEM 31

Mighty Motor Company manufactures snowmobiles and sells them through dealerships all over the United States. You are its corporate counsel, and it has a list of questions for you about the proposed warranty for the snowmobiles.

a. Can it give a full one-year warranty on the engine and no warranty at all on the rest of the snowmobile? See Magnuson-Moss §105.

b. If Mighty Motor Company gives no warranty but offers the consumer an extended service agreement, will that trigger Magnuson-Moss? See §§101(8) and 106 and FTC Reg. §700.11; Ismael v. Goodman Toyota, 106 N.C. App. 421, 417 S.E.2d 290, 18 U.C.C. Rep. Serv. 2d 101 (1992).

c. The company's dealerships will sell the snowmobiles and repair them when necessary, but the dealerships do not want to be liable in any way under the written warranty. Is this possible? See Magnuson-Moss §§107 and 110(f), FTC Reg. §700.4, and U.C.C. §2-316.

d. Mighty Motor Company wants to have complete control over its liability, so it has decided to offer a limited warranty, and it would like to disclaim the implied warranties of merchantability and fitness for a particular purpose that would otherwise arise under the Uniform Commercial Code. Tell the company how to do this. See Magnuson-Moss §108.

e. Mighty Motor Company doesn't like going to court, so it wants to arbitrate any disputes with consumers and make the arbitration binding on both parties. Can it set up its own arbitration panel (staffed by paid employees of Mighty Motors) and make the consumers bring all of their disputes to the panel for resolution? See Magnuson-Moss §110(a) and FTC Reg. §703. There has been a fierce debate in the case law over this issue; compare Borowiec v. Gateway 2000, Inc., 209 Ill. 2d 376, 808 N.E.2d 957 (2004) (nothing in Magnuson-Moss indicates that it lists the only available remedies and strong policy reasons support a binding arbitration clause), with Koons Ford of Baltimore, Inc. v. Lobach, 398 Md. 38, 919 A.2d 722 (2007) (Magnuson-Moss claimants cannot be forced into binding arbitration); see also Jonathan D. Grossberg, The Magnuson-Moss Warranty Act, the Federal Arbitration Act, and the Future of Consumer Protection, 93 Cornell L. Rev. 659 (2008).

f. If Mighty Motor were leasing the car to consumers, would Magnuson-Moss apply at all? See Voelker v. Porsche Cars N. Am., Inc., 353 F.3d 516 (7th Cir. 2003); Szubski v. Mercedes-Benz, U.S.A., L.L.C., 124 Ohio Misc. 2d 82, 796 N.E.2d 81 (Ohio Com. Pleas 2003); but see Parrot v. DaimlerChrysler Corp., 130 P.3d 530 (Ariz. 2006).

UNIVERSAL MOTORS v. WALDOCK
Alaska Supreme Court, 1986
719 P.2d 254, 1 U.C.C. Rep. Serv. 2d 704

COMPTON, Justice.

I. INTRODUCTION

This suit arose over the refusal of a car dealer and manufacturer to authorize repairs on a car under warranty because they concluded that the damage to the car's engine was caused by consumer abuse. The owner filed suit and recovered judgment allowing him to rescind the purchase contract and to receive costs and attorney's fees under the Magnuson-Moss Act. The dealer and manufacturer appeal, claiming that the superior court improperly placed the burden of proof on them to prove that the engine did not fail due to a materials or workmanship defect, and that the award of attorney's fees was an abuse of discretion.

II. FACTUAL AND PROCEDURAL BACKGROUND

Thomas Waldock (Waldock) purchased a 1983 BMW 320i from Universal Motors, Inc. (Universal). It was warranted "to be free of defects in materials or workmanship for a period of three years or 36,000 miles, whichever occurs first." Within the warranty period, the car's engine failed and upon examination was found to have been extensively damaged. Ultimately Dave Pennington, the district service manager of BMW of North America (BMW), denied authorization to repair the car under warranty and Universal was apparently bound by that decision.

BMW denied warranty coverage because it concluded that Waldock damaged the engine by over-revving it. Waldock vehemently disputed BMW's contention. He claimed that while driving the car at a low speed, with the engine at low r.p.m.'s, the engine emitted a gear-crunching noise, ceased operation, and would not restart.

After Universal and BMW (collectively Universal) refused to fix the car under warranty, Waldock filed a complaint against both, alleging that he was entitled to rescind his purchase contract for the BMW because Universal had breached express and implied warranties and had violated the Unfair Trade Practices and Consumer Protection Act and the Magnuson-Moss Act. Further, he alleged that the refusal to repair was outrageous and fraudulent and undertaken with reckless indifference to his rights. Waldock requested either specific performance, damages, or cancellation of the sales contract as well as punitive damages, reasonable costs and attorneys [sic] fees.

Before trial, Universal moved for summary judgment on Waldock's claims for breach of implied warranty, fraud, violation of the Unfair Trade Practices and Consumer Protection Act, and his claims for punitive, incidental and consequential damages. Waldock consented to dismissal of the first three claims. The court ruled that genuine issues of fact existed regarding Waldock's claims for punitive, incidental and consequential damages, thus denying Universal's motion.

At trial, Waldock's expert witnesses testified that the engine failed because of a problem with the engine's timing, caused by a damaged timing tensioner. Universal maintained that the engine damage was caused by consumer abuse, thus specifically excluded from warranty coverage.

The issue on which this appeal turns is solely a question of law concerning the burden of proof in a Magnuson-Moss Act warranty claim. Judge Brian C. Shortell instructed the jury, over Universal's objection, that for Universal to prevail the jury must find it more likely than not that Waldock over-revved the engine and that the over-revving caused the damage to the car. At the jury instruction conference, Judge Shortell stated his reasons for instructing the jury in this manner:

> I'm very troubled by the fact that it seems to me that the [Magnuson-Moss Act] provides that Federal minimum standards for warranty are that the warrantor remedy

the defect in a consumer product within a reasonable time and without charge, and that . . . performance of that duty is only excused if the warrantor can show that the defect, malfunction or failure was caused by damage not resulting from a defect or malfunction while in the possession of the consumer, or unreasonable use.

It seems to me that that's [the] classic burden of proof statement.

The jury returned a verdict for Waldock, and awarded him $15,748.00 for the fair market value of the car and $1,937.80 in incidental damages.[1] Judge Shortell signed the order and awarded reasonable actual attorney's fees of $36,526.00 and reasonable actual costs and expert witnesses fees of $1,987.87 and $6,494.67 respectively, for a total award of $62,684.34. Universal appeals on the burden of proof issue as a matter of law, and on the attorney's fees and costs issue claiming that the trial court abused its discretion.

III. DISCUSSION

A. BURDENS OF PROOF UNDER THE MAGNUSON-MOSS ACT

There are two burdens to be analyzed in this case. According to Waldock, he must show the existence of an express warranty, that it was breached, that the breach proximately caused the loss, and that the product failed to perform in accordance with the warranty terms. If he establishes a prima facie case, the burden shifts to Universal to prove owner abuse.

Judge Shortell correctly noted that the language in the Magnuson-Moss Act relating to consumer abuse is a "classic burden of proof statement." The relevant section of the Magnuson-Moss Act, 15 U.S.C. §2304(c) (1982) provides:

> The performance of the duties under subsection (a) of this section [requiring warrantor to remedy the consumer product in a reasonable time and without charge] shall not be required of the warrantor *if he can show* that the defect, malfunction, or failure of any warranted consumer product to conform with a written warranty, was caused by damage (not resulting from defect or malfunction) while in the possession of the consumer, or unreasonable use (including failure to provide reasonable and necessary maintenance).

---

1. The judgment held Universal jointly liable for the full award without discussion of the issue of privity between consumer and manufacturer. However, it is now common in breach of express warranty actions for the consumer to be able to reach the party that extended the warranty, the manufacturer. Miller & Kanter, Litigation Under Magnuson-Moss: New Opportunities in Private Actions, 13 UCC L.J. 10, 22 (1980). This court has held that privity is not necessary in an action for breach of an implied warranty. Morrow v. New Moon Homes, Inc., 548 P.2d 279, 289 (Alaska 1976). The *Morrow* holding should extend to express warranty cases. Other cases support such an application. Koperski v. Husker Dodge, Inc., 302 N.W.2d 655 (Neb. 1981); Ventura v. Ford Motor Co., 433 A.2d 801 (N.J. Super. App. Div. 1981).

(Emphasis added.) The statute places the burden of proving owner abuse squarely on the warrantor. The crucial question, therefore, is precisely what Waldock had to show to establish a prima facie case and shift the burden to Universal under the Magnuson-Moss Act.

1. Waldock's Burden of Proof

Universal argues that the consumer bears the burden of proof in a breach of warranty case under Alaska's Uniform Commercial Code (UCC) and that the Magnuson-Moss Act was not intended to shift this burden. It further claims that the jury should have been instructed that Waldock had the burden of proving that the [sic] Universal breached its express warranty by selling Waldock a defective automobile. Waldock contends he met his burden as a matter of law, thus the jury instruction requiring Universal to prove consumer abuse by a preponderance of the evidence was not erroneous.

The Magnuson-Moss Act created no new implied warranties upon which consumers can sue; rather it created a new federal cause of action for the breach of consumer warranties. Royal Lincoln-Mercury Sales v. Wallace, 415 So. 2d 1024 (Miss. 1982). An alleged breach of an express warranty can be the basis of two separate claims, one based on the state's UCC and one based on the federal act. "The elements of proof are the same whether the claim is made under the [Magnuson-Moss] act or under state law." *Wallace*, 415 So. 2d at 1026-27; see also Welch v. Fitzgerald-Hicks Dodge, Inc., 430 A.2d 144, 149 (N.H. 1981). Thus to determine Waldock's burden of proof the UCC provisions should be examined, for if it is determined that Waldock established a prima facie case under the UCC, then he has also established a prima facie case under the Magnuson-Moss Act. *Welch,* 430 A.2d at 149.

The parties agree that the BMW warranty in this case is an express warranty as defined in A.S. 45.02.313, a section of the UCC as adopted in Alaska. A.S. 45.02.607(d) provides that "[t]he burden is on the buyer to establish a breach with respect to the goods accepted."

Some courts have held that consumers suing the dealer and manufacturer have a heavy burden of proof. In Arnold v. Ford Motor Co., 566 P.2d 98 (N.M. 1977), the court held that Arnold had the burden of proving four essential elements in a UCC express warranty suit against the dealer and manufacturer: (1) the existence of a defect in the operation of the vehicle, (2) *the defect resulted from factory materials or workmanship*, (3) the plaintiff presented the vehicle to the automobile dealer with a request that the defect be repaired, and (4) the dealer failed or refused to repair the defective parts [emphasis added]. *Arnold*, 566 P.2d at 99.

The warranty in *Arnold*, like the warranty in most car cases, is a standard "repair and replace" warranty providing a remedy if any part is found to be defective in "factory materials or workmanship" within a specified time period. The dispute in *Arnold* focused on whether the consumer had presented sufficient evidence to establish the second element, i.e., the defect resulted from factory materials or workmanship. Although the trial court made no specific findings on the issue, the appellate court held that there was substantial testimony to support the fact that the defects had existed from the time Arnold drove the car from the lot. *Arnold*, 566 P.2d at 99-100.

Likewise, the court in Walker Ford Sales v. Gaither, 578 S.W.3d 23, 25 (Ark. 1979), held that the consumer's burden in an express "repair and replace" warranty case is to show that the defect existed at the time the car was first delivered to the consumer. In *Gaither*, a vibration existed from the date of purchase so the court had no trouble finding that this burden had been met. Id.; see also, Prutch v. Ford Motor Co., 618 P.2d 657, 660 (Colo. 1980) (consumer must establish that the defect arose in the course of manufacturer-distribution and before purchase); Royal Business Machines v. Lorraine Corp., 633 F.2d 34, 44 (7th Cir. 1980) (breach of express warranty occurs only if goods are defective upon delivery and not if goods later become defective through abuse or neglect); Collum v. Fred Tuch Buick, 285 N.E.2d 532, 536 (Ill. App. 1972) (to recover on express warranty theory, consumer must prove that the alleged malfunctioning of the car was caused by a defect in parts or workmanship).[2] In cases such as these, courts have held that circumstantial evidence is enough to support the consumer's burden of proof that the damage was caused by a defect in factory materials or workmanship. See Colorado Serum Co. v. Arp, 504 P.2d 801, 805-06 (Wyo. 1972) (circumstantial evidence permitted to prove that proximate cause of illness of owner's swine herd was manufacturer's defective serum).

The case before us now, however, is more difficult because Waldock experienced a "single incident," total breakdown of his car. Waldock claims that on these facts all he had to prove is that he took his obviously malfunctioning car, then still under warranty, to Universal and that Universal refused to repair it. He argues that a car that will not run does not conform to the warranty. Nonconformance with the warranty is a breach.

Some authorities support Waldock's view. The court in Fargo Machine & Tool Co. v. Kearney & Trecker Corp., 428 F. Supp. 364, 374 (E.D. Mich.

---

2. One primary difference between the case at bar and most other automobile warranty cases is that Waldock's car was in excellent driving condition until it failed one day as Waldock was driving. Most cases involve cars that had major problems from nearly the moment they left the lot. See, e.g., *Gaither*, 578 S.W.2d at 25; *Arnold*, 566 P.2d at 99-100.

1977), held that the burden is not on the consumer of defective goods to show the precise technical explanations behind a malfunction, but rather, he must show that the goods *do not conform* to the warranty.

Likewise, in Osburn v. Bendix Home System, Inc., 613 P.2d 445 (Okla. 1980), a mobile home manufacturer asserted that since the consumer failed to introduce any evidence of a defect in materials or workmanship, he failed in his burden of proof. That court stated:

> [T]he argument advanced is that, as in actions based on the theory of products liability, so in a breach-of-warranty case, the claimant must establish the *presence of a specific defect*. The contention so advanced is without merit. Identification of an existing defect is not essential to recovery upon express warranty. It is sufficient if, as here, the evidence shows, either directly or by permissible inference, that the goods were defective in their performance or function or that they otherwise failed to conform to the warranty.

Osburn, 613 P.2d at 448 (footnote omitted) (emphasis in original). In *Osburn*, the consumer experienced numerous problems soon after moving into his mobile home and the court had no trouble attributing them to defects in materials or workmanship. Id. at 448-49.

On the other hand, in Haas v. Buick Motor Division of the General Motors Corp., 156 N.E.2d 263 (Ill. App. 1959), the court held that a consumer failed to make out a prima facie case against the manufacturer for breach of an express warranty. The court stated that "the burden was on the plaintiff to prove, among other things, that there was some material defect in materials or workmanship." *Haas*, 156 N.E.2d at 266 (citation omitted). The pleadings were silent as to what part failed or was defective in materials or workmanship, thus causing Haas' car to catch on fire. The consumer in *Haas* showed *nothing*, yet expected the manufacturer to go forward with an inspection of the car. Id. at 267. *Haas* is distinguishable from the case before us. Waldock advanced a plausible explanation for an engine failure which can never be conclusively proved, he claims, because of actions by mechanics for Universal. Waldock showed enough to make out a prima facie case of breach of warranty. It was then up to Universal to prove that the damage was caused by consumer abuse. The jury determined that Universal had not proved owner abuse by a preponderance of the evidence.

Problems arise when a consumer is required to prove that there are defects in specific materials or particular workmanship. Furthermore, a requirement that the consumer prove that the defect is caused by materials or workmanship makes the burden of proof language in the Magnuson-Moss Act basically irrelevant. Once the consumer offers credible evidence that the defect is materials or workmanship related, the burden shifts to the warrantor to prove consumer abuse.

Policy reasons also support such a rule. Under the BMW warranty, and according to Universal's witnesses, BMW owners requiring warranty service on their cars may only take the damaged car to the service department of an authorized BMW dealer. Placing the burden on the consumer to prove a precise defect is unfair and unconscionable since the dealer and manufacturer could tamper (whether intentionally or inadvertently) with the evidence. For example, Waldock claims that Universal's work on the engine destroyed evidence of timing problems because the cylinder head was removed.

In a car warranty case, the consumer must offer credible evidence that the defect is materials or workmanship related. Such evidence establishes a prima facie case of breach of an express warranty. The burden then shifts to the dealer or manufacturer to prove consumer abuse. To impose an unreasonably heavy burden on consumers is to deny them a meaningful remedy. *Prutch*, 618 P.2d at 660. We believe this interpretation of the Magnuson-Moss Act best effectuates its intent. . . .

The judgment of the trial court is affirmed.

PROBLEM 32

Your client has purchased a lemon car and now wants to revoke her acceptance of the car and sue. Because you want to get your attorney's fees paid by the other side you frame the lawsuit so that it clearly falls under §110(d) of the Magnuson-Moss Act.

a. Before you sue must you give the car dealership and/or manufacturer notice of the problems involved and a chance to cure the difficulties? See Magnuson-Moss §§104(b) and 110(e) and U.C.C. §2-608.

b. Is it possible to combine a UCC revocation of acceptance action with the relief offered under §110(d)? Compare Mydlach v. DaimlerChrysler Corp., 364 Ill. App. 3d 135, 846 N.E.2d 126 (2005), and Shuldman v. DaimlerChrysler Corp., 1 A.D.3d 343, 768 N.Y.S.2d 214 (2003), with Chaurasia v. General Motors Corp., 212 Ariz. 18, 126 P.3d 165 (Ariz. App. 2006).

c. Can you make this a class action? See Magnuson-Moss §110(d)(3) and Abraham v. Volkswagen of Am., 795 F.2d 238, 1 U.C.C. Rep. Serv. 2d 681 (2d Cir. 1986).

d. If the car was very expensive—say $61,000, as in the next cited case—could you bring the action in federal court? See §110(c)(3)(B) and Golden v. Gorno Bros., Inc., 410 F.3d 879 (6th Cir. 2005).

II. CONSUMER PRODUCT SAFETY ACT

A host of federal and state statutes regulate product quality for hundreds of items, most obviously food, drugs, and cosmetics. These statutes and regulations do not typically provide for a private consumer remedy and are beyond the scope of this course. An attorney whose practice encompasses such products, however, needs to become very familiar with the restrictions imposed in order to keep clients out of trouble with the government.

One federal statute that does provide for a private remedy for violation of its quality standards is the Consumer Product Safety Act, 15 U.S.C. §§2051 et seq. (passed in 1972). The statute was enacted to regulate those products, purchased by consumers, that had substantial risk of injury but that were not regulated by other federal statutes. A 1969 estimate by the Department of Health, Education and Welfare stated that annually such products were causing 30,000 deaths, 110,000 permanently disabling injuries, and 20 million injuries serious enough to require medical treatment. Toys were a particular concern:

> The U.S. Public Health Service estimates that toys injure 700,000 children every year. . . . At least 22 parents are suing the manufacturers of an Etch-a-Sketch toy for lacerations suffered by their children from broken glass panels. In Philadelphia alone, at least 13 children put the wrong end of a Zulu Gun into their mouth and inhaled darts into their lungs. A Little Lady toy oven for young girls had temperatures above 300 degrees Fahrenheit on the outer surface and 600 degrees on the inside. There are no voluntary industrywide safety standards for any of these products.

Report of the National Commission on Product Safety at 30 (1970). In 2005, 73,000 children less than five years old were treated in emergency rooms for toy-related injuries. In 1994, the Commission banned crayons coming from China that contained enough lead to poison a child who ate even a portion of a crayon. In 2001, the Commission went after gun locks, finding only 2 of the 32 studied that were adequate to protect from accidental or deliberate discharge. Also in 2001, the Commission imposed the largest fine in its history: $1.3 million against Cosco, Inc., a maker of baby products, which had failed (as is required by §15 of the statute; see below) to report problems with its baby strollers, car seats, cribs, and high chairs that had led to more than 300 injuries, including two deaths. It was the second fine against Cosco, which had paid $725,000 in 1996 for failing to report dozens of incidents of infants being trapped in toddler beds. In 2008, the Commission worked overtime dealing with multiple products coming from China that contained lead or other injury-producing contaminants.

In addition to having jurisdiction over "consumer products," the Consumer Product Safety Commission (the five-person regulatory body created by Consumer Product Safety Act §4) administers the Federal Hazardous Substance Act, the Poison Prevention Packaging Act, the Flammable Fabrics Act, and the Refrigerator Safety Act. See §2079. A 1988 amendment to the statute banned butyl nitrite (an ingredient in some brands of "poppers," a stimulant used for recreational purposes), §2057a. The Commission has no jurisdiction over tobacco products, motor vehicles, boats, pesticides, firearms, aircraft, drugs, medical devices, or cosmetics. These matters are either unregulated or regulated by other entities.[3] In 2001 the Commission urged Congress to give it jurisdiction over stationary amusement park rides, since in 2000 over 7,000 people (!) ended up in emergency rooms as a result of accidents caused by the rides (the Commission already has jurisdiction over mobile rides that move from place to place, but not permanent ones, which are regulated only by the states in which they are located).

Scan the following statute long enough to get a general idea of its content, and then work through the Problems.

THE CONSUMER PRODUCT SAFETY ACT[4]
(Selected Sections) 15 U.S.C. §§2051 et seq.

§2051 [§2] Congressional findings and declaration of purpose

(a) The Congress finds that—

(1) an unacceptable number of consumer products which present unreasonable risks of injury are distributed in commerce;

(2) complexities of consumer products and the diverse nature and abilities of consumers using them frequently result in an inability of users to anticipate risks and to safeguard themselves adequately;

(3) the public should be protected against unreasonable risks of injury associated with consumer products;

(4) control by State and local governments of unreasonable risks of injury associated with consumer products is inadequate and may be burdensome to manufacturers;

(5) existing Federal authority to protect consumers from exposure to consumer products presenting unreasonable risks of injury is inadequate; and

---

3. For a commentary on the Act's checkered history, see Tobias, Revitalizing the Consumer Product Safety Commission, 50 Mont. L. Rev. 237 (1989).

4. Pub. L. No. 92-573 section numbers are shown in brackets.—ED.

(6) regulation of consumer products the distribution or use of which affects interstate or foreign commerce is necessary to carry out this chapter.

(b) The purposes of this chapter are—

(1) to protect the public against unreasonable risks of injury associated with consumer products;

(2) to assist consumers in evaluating the comparative safety of consumer products;

(3) to develop uniform safety standards for consumer products and to minimize conflicting State and local regulations; and

(4) to promote research and investigation into the causes and prevention of product-related deaths, illnesses, and injuries.

§2052 [§3] Definitions

(a) For purposes of this Act:

(1) The term "consumer product" means any article, or component part thereof, produced or distributed (i) for sale to a consumer for use in or around a permanent or temporary household or residence, a school, in recreation, or otherwise, or (ii) for the personal use, consumption or enjoyment of a consumer in or around a permanent or temporary household or residence, a school, in recreation, or otherwise; but such term does not include—

(A) any article which is not customarily produced or distributed for sale to, or use or consumption by, or enjoyment of, a consumer,

(B) tobacco and tobacco products,

(C) motor vehicles or motor vehicle equipment (as defined by sections 102(3) and (4) of the National Traffic and Motor Vehicle Safety Act of 1966),

(D) pesticides (as defined by the Federal Insecticide, Fungicide, and Rodenticide Act),

(E) any article which, if sold by the manufacturer, producer, or importer, would be subject to the tax imposed by section 4181 of the Internal Revenue Code of 1954 (determined without regard to any exemptions from such tax provided by section 4182 or 4221, or any other provision of such Code), or any component of any such article,

(F) aircraft, aircraft engines, propellers, or appliances (as defined in section 101 of the Federal Aviation Act of 1958),

(G) boats which could be subjected to safety regulation under the Federal Boat Safety Act of 1971 (46 U.S.C. §1451 et seq.) vessels, and appurtenances to vessels (other than such boats), which could be subjected to safety regulation under title 52 of the Revised Statutes or other marine safety statutes administered by the department in which the Coast Guard is operating; and equipment (including associated equipment, as defined in section 3(8) of the Federal Boat Safety Act of 1971) to the extent that a risk of injury associated with the use of such equipment on boats or vessels could be eliminated or reduced by actions taken under any statute referred to in this subparagraph,

(H) drugs, devices, or cosmetics (as such terms are defined in sections 201(g), (h), and (i) of the Federal Food, Drug, and Cosmetic Act), or

(I) food. The term "food," as used in this subparagraph means all "food," as defined in section 201(f) of the Federal Food, Drug, and Cosmetic Act, including poultry and poultry products (as defined in sections 4(e) and (f) of the Poultry Products Inspection Act), meat, meat food products (as defined in section 1(j) of the Federal Meat Inspection Act) and eggs and egg products (as defined in section 4 of the Egg Products Inspection Act).

Such term includes any mechanical device which carries or conveys passengers along, around, or over a fixed or restricted route or course or within a defined area for the purpose of giving its passengers amusement, which is customarily controlled or directed by an individual who is employed for that purpose and who is not a consumer with respect to such device, and which is not permanently fixed to a site. Such term does not include such a device which is permanently fixed to a site. Except for the regulation under this Act or the Federal Hazardous Substances Act of fireworks devices or any substance intended for use as a component of any such device, the Commission shall have no authority under the functions transferred pursuant to section 30 of this Act to regulate any product or article described in subparagraph (E) of this paragraph or described, without regard to quantity, in section 845(a)(5) of title 18, United States Code. See sections 30(d) and 31 of this Act, for other limitations on Commission's authority to regulate certain consumer products.

(2) The term "consumer product safety rule" means a consumer products safety standard described in section 7(a), or a rule under this Act declaring a consumer product a banned hazardous product.

(3) The term "risk of injury" means a risk of death, personal injury, or serious or frequent illness.

(4) The term "manufacturer" means any person who manufactures or imports a consumer product.

(5) The term "distributor" means a person to whom a consumer product is delivered or sold for purposes of distribution in commerce, except that such term does not include a manufacturer or retailer of such product.

(6) The term "retailer" means a person to whom a consumer product is delivered or sold for purposes of sale or distribution by such person to a consumer.

(7)(A) The term "private labeler" means an owner of a brand or trademark on the label of a consumer product which bears a private label.

(B) A consumer product bears a private label if (i) the product (or its container) is labeled with the brand or trademark of a person other than a manufacturer of the product, (ii) the person with whose brand or trademark the product (or container) is labeled has authorized or caused the product to be so labeled, and (iii) the brand or trademark of a manufacturer of such product does not appear on such label.

(8) The term "manufactured" means to manufacture, produce, or assemble.

(9) The term "Commission" means the Consumer Product Safety Commission, established by section 4.

(10) The term "State" means a State, the District of Columbia, the Commonwealth of Puerto Rico, the Virgin Islands, Guam, Wake Island, Midway Island, Kingman Reef, Johnston Island, the Canal Zone, American Samoa, or the Trust Territory of the Pacific Islands.

(11) The terms "to distribute in commerce" and "distribution in commerce" mean to sell in commerce, to introduce or deliver for introduction into commerce, or to hold for sale or distribution after introduction into commerce.

(12) The term "commerce" means trade, traffic, commerce, or transportation—

(A) between a place in a State and any place outside thereof, or

(B) which affects trade, traffic, commerce, or transportation described in subparagraph (A).

(13) The terms "import" and "importation" include reimporting a consumer product manufactured or processed, in whole or in part, in the United States.

(14) The term "United States," when used in the geographic sense, means all of the States (as defined in paragraph (10)).

(b) A common carrier, contract carrier, or freight forwarder shall not, for purposes of this Act, be deemed to be a manufacturer, distributor, or retailer of a consumer product solely by reason of receiving or transporting a consumer product in the ordinary course of its business as such a carrier or forwarder.

§2053 [§4] Consumer Product Safety Commission

(a) Establishment; Chairman.   An independent regulatory commission is hereby established, to be known as the Consumer Product Safety Commission, consisting of five Commissioners who shall be appointed by the President, by and with the advice and consent of the Senate. In making such appointments, the President shall consider individuals who, by reason of their background and expertise in areas related to consumer products and protection of the public from risks to safety, are qualified to serve as members of the Commission. The Chairman shall be appointed by the President, by and with the advice and consent of the Senate, from among the members of the Commission. An individual may be appointed as a member of the Commission and as Chairman at the same time. Any member of the Commission may be removed by the President for neglect of duty or malfeasance in office but for no other cause.

(b) Term; vacancies.   (1) Except as provided in paragraph (2), (A) the Commissioners first appointed under this section shall be appointed for terms ending three, four, five, six, and seven years, respectively, after October 27, 1972, the term of each to be designated by the President at the time of nomination; and (B) each of their successors shall be appointed for a term of seven years from the date of the expiration of the term for which his predecessor was appointed.

(2) Any Commissioner appointed to fill a vacancy occurring prior to the expiration of the term for which his predecessor was appointed shall be appointed only for the remainder of such term. A Commissioner may continue to serve after the expiration of his term until his successor has taken office, except that he may not so continue to serve more than one year after the date on which his term would otherwise expire under this subsection.

(c) Restrictions on Commissioner's outside activities.   Not more than three of the Commissioners shall be affiliated with the same political party. No individual (1) in the employ of, or holding any official relation to, any person engaged in selling or manufacturing consumer products, or (2) owning stock or bonds of substantial value in a person so engaged, or (3) who is in any other manner pecuniarily interested in such a person, or in a substantial supplier of such a person, shall hold the office of Commissioner. A Commissioner may not engage in any other business, vocation, or employment.

(d) Quorum; seal; Vice Chairman.   No vacancy in the Commission shall impair the right of the remaining Commissioners to exercise all the powers of the Commission, but three members of the Commission shall constitute a quorum for the transaction of business, except that if there are

only three members serving on the Commission because of vacancies in the Commission, two members of the Commission shall constitute a quorum for the transaction of business, and if there are only two members serving on the Commission because of vacancies in the Commission, two members shall constitute a quorum for the six month period beginning on the date of the vacancy which caused the number of Commission members to decline to two. The Commission shall have an official seal of which judicial notice shall be taken. The Commission shall annually elect a Vice Chairman to act in the absence or disability of the Chairman or in case of a vacancy in the office of the Chairman.

(e) Offices.   The Commission shall maintain a principal office and such field offices as it deems necessary and may meet and exercise any of its powers at any other place.

(f) Functions of Chairman; request for appropriations.

(1) The Chairman of the Commission shall be the principal executive officer of the Commission, and he shall exercise all of the executive and administrative functions of the Commission, including functions of the Commission with respect to (A) the appointment and supervision of personnel employed under the Commission (other than personnel employed regularly and full time in the immediate offices of commissioners other than the Chairman), (B) the distribution of business among personnel appointed and supervised by the Chairman and among administrative units of the Commission, and (C) the use and expenditure of funds.

(2) In carrying out any of his functions under the provisions of this subsection the Chairman shall be governed by general policies of the Commission and by such regulatory decisions, findings, and determinations as the Commission may by law be authorized to make.

(3) Requests or estimates for regular, supplemental, or deficiency appropriations on behalf of the Commission may not be submitted by the Chairman without the prior approval of the Commission.

(g) Executive Director; officers and employees.

(1)(A) The Chairman, subject to the approval of the Commission, shall appoint as officers of the Commission an Executive Director, a General Counsel, an Associate Executive Director for Engineering Sciences, an Associate Executive Director for Epidemiology, an Associate Executive Director for Compliance and Administrative Litigation, an Associate Executive Director for Health Sciences, an Associate Executive Director for Economic Analysis, an Associate Executive Director for Administration, an Associate Executive Director for Field Operations, a Director for Office of Program, Management, and Budget, and a Director for Office of

Information and Public Affairs. Any other individual appointed to a position designated as an Associate Executive Director shall be appointed by the Chairman, subject to the approval of the Commission. The Chairman may only appoint an attorney to the position of Associate Executive Director of Compliance and Administrative Litigation except the position of acting Associate Executive Director of Compliance and Administrative Litigation.

(B)(i) No individual may be appointed to such a position on an acting basis for a period longer than 90 days unless such appointment is approved by the Commission.

(ii) The Chairman, with the approval of the Commission, may remove any individual serving in a position appointed under subparagraph (A).

(C) Subparagraph (A) shall not be construed to prohibit appropriate reorganizations or changes in classification.

(2) The Chairman, subject to subsection (f)(2) of this section, may employ such other officers and employees (including attorneys) as are necessary in the execution of the Commission's functions.

(3) In addition to the number of positions authorized by section 5108(a) of Title 5, the Chairman, subject to the approval of the Commission, and subject to the standards and procedures prescribed by chapter 51 of Title 5, may place a total of twelve positions in grades GS-16, GS-17, and GS-18.

(4) The appointment of any officer (other than a Commissioner) or employee of the Commission shall not be subject, directly or indirectly, to review or approval by any officer or entity within the Executive Office of the President.

(h) [Omitted]

(i) Civil action against United States. Subsections (a) and (h) of section 2680 of Title 28 do not prohibit the bringing of a civil action on a claim against the United States which—

(1) is based upon—

(A) misrepresentation or deceit on the part of the Commission or any employee thereof, or

(B) any exercise or performance, or failure to exercise or perform, a discretionary function on the part of the Commission or any employee thereof, which exercise, performance, or failure was grossly negligent; and

(2) is not made with respect to any agency action (as defined in section 551(13) of Title 5).

In the case of a civil action on a claim based upon the exercise or performance of, or failure to exercise or perform, a discretionary function, no judgment may be entered against the United States unless the court in which such action was brought determines (based upon consideration of all the relevant circumstances, including the statutory responsibility of the Commission and the public interest in encouraging rather than inhibiting the exercise of discretion) that such exercise, performance, or failure to exercise or perform was unreasonable.

(j) Agenda and priorities; establishment and comments. At least 30 days before the beginning of each fiscal year, the Commission shall establish an agenda for Commission action under the Acts under its jurisdiction and, to the extent feasible, shall establish priorities for such actions. Before establishing such agenda and priorities, the Commission shall conduct a public hearing on the agenda and priorities and shall provide reasonable opportunity for the submission of comments.

§2054 [§5] Product safety information and research

(a) Injury Information Clearinghouse; duties. The Commission shall—

(1) maintain an Injury Information Clearinghouse to collect, investigate, analyze, and disseminate injury data, and information, relating to the causes and prevention of death, injury, and illness associated with consumer products;

(2) conduct such continuing studies and investigations of deaths, injuries, diseases, other health impairments, and economic losses resulting from accidents involving consumer products as it deems necessary;

(3) following publication of an advance notice of proposed rulemaking or a notice of proposed rulemaking for a product safety rule under any rulemaking authority administered by the Commission, assist public and private organizations or groups of manufacturers, administratively and technically, in the development of safety standards addressing the risk of injury identified in such notice; and

(4) to the extent practicable and appropriate (taking into account the resources and priorities of the Commission), assist public and private organizations or groups of manufacturers, administratively and technically, in the development of product safety standards and test methods.

(b) Research, investigation and testing of consumer products. The Commission may—

(1) conduct research, studies, and investigations on the safety of consumer products and on improving the safety of such products;

(2) test consumer products and develop product safety test methods and testing devices; and

(3) offer training in product safety investigation and test methods.

(c) Grants and contracts for conduct of functions.   In carrying out its functions under this section, the Commission may make grants or enter into contracts for the conduct of such functions with any person (including a governmental entity).

(d) Availability to public of information.   Whenever the Federal contribution for any information, research, or development activity authorized by this Act is more than minimal, the Commission shall include in any contract, grant, or other arrangement for such activity, provisions effective to insure that the rights to all information, uses, processes, patents, and other developments resulting from that activity will be made available to the public without charge on a nonexclusive basis. Nothing in this subsection shall be construed to deprive any person of any right which he may have had, prior to entering into any arrangement referred to in this subsection, to any patent, patent application, or invention. . . .

§2056 [§7] Consumer product safety standards

(a) Types of requirements.   The Commission may promulgate consumer product safety standards in accordance with the provisions of section 2058 of this title. A consumer product safety standard shall consist of one or more of any of the following types of requirements:

(1) Requirements expressed in terms of performance requirements.

(2) Requirements that a consumer product be marked with or accompanied by clear and adequate warnings or instructions, or requirements respecting the form of warnings or instructions.

Any requirement of such a standard shall be reasonably necessary to prevent or reduce an unreasonable risk of injury associated with such product.

(b) Reliance of Commission upon voluntary standards.   (1) The Commission shall rely upon voluntary consumer product safety standards rather than promulgate a consumer product safety standard prescribing requirements described in subsection (a) of this section whenever compliance with such voluntary standards would eliminate or adequately reduce the risk of injury addressed and it is likely that there will be substantial compliance with such voluntary standards.

(2) The Commission shall devise procedures to monitor compliance with any voluntary standards—

(A) upon which the Commission has relied under paragraph (1);

(B) which were developed with the participation of the Commission; or

(C) whose development the Commission has monitored.

(c) Contribution of Commission to development cost. If any person participates with the Commission in the development of a consumer product safety standard, the Commission may agree to contribute to the person's cost with respect to such participation, in any case in which the Commission determines that such contribution is likely to result in a more satisfactory standard than would be developed without such contribution, and that the person is financially responsible. Regulations of the Commission shall set forth the items of cost in which it may participate, and shall exclude any contribution to the acquisition of land or buildings. Payments under agreements entered into under this subsection may be made without regard to section 3324(a) and (b) of Title 31.

§2057 [§8] Banned hazardous products

Whenever the Commission finds that—

(1) a consumer product is being, or will be, distributed in commerce and such consumer product presents an unreasonable risk of injury; and

(2) no feasible consumer product safety standard under this Act would adequately protect the public from the unreasonable risk of injury associated with such product,

the Commission may, in accordance with section 9, promulgate a rule declaring such product a banned hazardous product.

§2057a Banning of butyl nitrite

(a) In general. Except as provided in subsection (b), butyl nitrite shall be considered a banned hazardous product under section 8 of the Consumer Product Safety Act (15 U.S.C. 2057).

(b) Lawful purposes. For the purposes of section 8 of the Consumer Product Safety Act, it shall not be unlawful for any person to manufacture for sale, offer for sale, distribute in commerce, or import into the United States butyl nitrite for any commercial purpose or any other purpose approved under the Federal Food, Drug, and Cosmetic Act.

(c) Definitions. For purposes of this section:

(1) The term "butyl nitrite" includes n-butyl nitrite, isobutyl nitrite, secondary butyl nitrite, tertiary butyl nitrite, and mixtures containing these chemicals.

(2) The term "commercial purpose" means any commercial purpose other than for the production of consumer products containing butyl nitrite that may be used for inhaling or otherwise introducing butyl nitrite into the human body for euphoric or physical effects.

(d) Effective date.   This section shall take effect 90 days after the date of the enactment of this subtitle [enacted Nov. 18, 1988]. . . .

§2060 [§11] Judicial review of consumer product safety rules

(a) Petition by persons adversely affected, consumers, or consumer organizations.   Not later than 60 days after a consumer product safety rule is promulgated by the Commission, any person adversely affected by such rule, or any consumer or consumer organization, may file a petition with the United States court of appeals for the District of Columbia or for the circuit in which such person, consumer, or organization resides or has his principal place of business for judicial review of such rule. Copies of the petition shall be forthwith transmitted by the clerk of the court to the Commission or other officer designated by it for that purpose and to the Attorney General. The record of the proceedings on which the Commission based its rule shall be filed in the court as provided for in section 2112 of title 28, United States Code. For purposes of this section, the term "record" means such consumer product safety rule; any notice or proposal published pursuant to section 7, 8, or 9; the transcript required by section 9(d)(2) of any oral presentation; any written submission of interested parties; and any other information which the Commission considers relevant to such rule.

(b) Additional data, views, or arguments.   If the petitioner applies to the court for leave to adduce additional data, views, or arguments and shows to the satisfaction of the court that such additional data, views, or arguments are material and that there were reasonable grounds for the petitioner's failure to adduce such data, views, or arguments in the proceeding before the Commission, the court may order the Commission to provide additional opportunity for the oral presentation of data, views, or arguments and for written submissions. The Commission may modify its findings, or make new findings by reason of the additional data, views, or arguments so taken and shall file such modified or new findings, and its recommendation, if any, for the modification or setting aside of its original rule, with the return of such additional data, views, or arguments.

(c) Jurisdiction; costs and attorney's fees; substantial evidence to support administrative findings.   Upon the filing of the petition under subsection (a) of this section the court shall have jurisdiction to review the consumer product safety rule in accordance with chapter 7 of title 5, United States Code, and to grant appropriate relief, including interim relief, as provided in such chapter. A court may in the interest of justice include in such relief an award of the costs of suit, including reasonable attorneys' fees (determined in accordance with section 10(e)(4)) and reasonable expert

witnesses' fees. Attorneys' fees may be awarded against the United States (or any agency or official of the United States) without regard to section 2412 of title 28, United States Code, or any other provision of law. The consumer product safety rule shall not be affirmed unless the Commission's findings under sections 9(f)(1) and 9(f)(3) are supported by substantial evidence on the record taken as a whole.

(d) Supreme Court review. The judgment of the court affirming or setting aside, in whole or in part, any consumer product safety rule shall be final, subject to review by the Supreme Court of the United States upon certiorari or certification, as provided in section 1254 of title 28 of the United States Code.

(e) Other remedies. The remedies provided for in this section shall be in addition to and not in lieu of any other remedies provided by law.

(f) Reasonable attorney's fee. For purposes of this section and sections 23(a) and 24, a reasonable attorney's fee is a fee (1) which is based upon (A) the actual time expended by an attorney in providing advice and other legal services in connection with representing a person in an action brought under this section, and (B) such reasonable expenses as may be incurred by the attorney in the provision of such services, and (2) which is computed at the rate prevailing for the provision of similar services with respect to actions brought in the court which is awarding such fee.

§2061 [§12] Imminent hazards

(a) Filing of action. The Commission may file in a United States district court an action (1) against an imminently hazardous consumer product for seizure of such product under subsection (b)(2) of this section, or (2) against any person who is a manufacturer, distributor, or retailer of such product, or (3) against both. Such an action may be filed notwithstanding the existence of a consumer product safety rule applicable to such product, or the pendency of any administrative or judicial proceedings under any other provision of this chapter. As used in this section, and hereinafter in this chapter, the term "imminently hazardous consumer product" means a consumer product which presents imminent and unreasonable risk of death, serious illness, or severe personal injury.

(b) Relief; product condemnation and seizure.

(1) The district court in which such action is filed shall have jurisdiction to declare such product an imminently hazardous consumer product, and (in the case of an action under subsection (a)(2) of this section) to grant (as ancillary to such declaration or in lieu thereof) such temporary or permanent relief as may be necessary to protect the public

from such risk. Such relief may include a mandatory order requiring the notification of such risk to purchasers of such product known to the defendant, public notice, the recall, the repair or the replacement of, or refund for, such product.

(2) In the case of an action under subsection (a)(1) of this section, the consumer product may be proceeded against by process of libel for the seizure and condemnation of such product in any United States district court within the jurisdiction of which such consumer product is found. Proceedings and cases instituted under the authority of the preceding sentence shall conform as nearly as possible to proceedings in rem in admiralty.

(c) Consumer product safety rule. Where appropriate, concurrently with the filing of such action or as soon thereafter as may be practicable, the Commission shall initiate a proceeding to promulgate a consumer product safety rule applicable to the consumer product with respect to which such action is filed.

(d) Jurisdiction and venue; process; subpoena.

(1) An action under subsection (a)(2) of this section may be brought in the United States district court for the District of Columbia or in any judicial district in which any of the defendants is found, is an inhabitant or transacts business; and process in such an action may be served on a defendant in any other district in which such defendant resides or may be found. Subpoenas requiring attendance of witnesses in such an action may run into any other district. In determining the judicial district in which an action may be brought under this section in instances in which such action may be brought in more than one judicial district the Commission shall take into account the convenience of the parties.

(2) Whenever proceedings under this section involving substantially similar consumer products are pending in courts in two or more judicial districts, they shall be consolidated for trial by order of any such court upon application reasonably made by any party in interest, upon notice to all other parties in interest.

(e) Employment of attorneys by Commission. Notwithstanding any other provision of law, in any action under this section, the Commission may direct attorneys employed by it to appear and represent it.

§2063 [§14] Product certification and labeling

(a) Certification accompanying product; products with more than one manufacturer.

(1) Every manufacturer of a product which is subject to a consumer product safety standard under this Act and which is distributed in

commerce (and the private labeler of such product if it bears a private label) shall issue a certificate which shall certify that such product conforms to all applicable consumer product safety standards, and shall specify any standard which is applicable. Such certificate shall accompany the product or shall otherwise be furnished to any distributor or retailer to whom the product is delivered. Any certificate under this subsection shall be based on a test of each product or upon a reasonable testing program; shall state the name of the manufacturer or private labeler issuing the certificate; and shall include the date and place of manufacture.

(2) In the case of a consumer product for which there is more than one manufacturer or more than one private labeler, the Commission may by rule designate one or more of such manufacturers or one or more of such private labelers (as the case may be) as the persons who shall issue the certificate required by paragraph (1) of this subsection, and may exempt all other manufacturers of such product or all other private labelers of the product (as the case may be) from the requirement under paragraph (1) to issue a certificate with respect to such product.

(b) Rules to establish reasonable testing programs. The Commission may by rule prescribe reasonable testing programs for consumer products which are subject to consumer product safety standards under this Act and for which a certificate is required under subsection (a). Any test or testing program on the basis of which a certificate is issued under subsection (a) may, at the option of the person required to certify the product, be conducted by an independent third party qualified to perform such tests or testing programs.

(c) Form and contents of labels. The Commission may by rule require the use and prescribe the form and content of labels which contain the following information (or that portion of its [sic] specified in the rule)—

(1) The date and place of manufacture of any consumer product.

(2) A suitable identification of the manufacturer of the consumer product, unless the product bears a private label in which case it shall identify the private labeler and shall also contain a code mark which will permit the seller of such product to identify the manufacturer thereof to the purchaser upon his request.

(3) In the case of a consumer product subject to a consumer product safety rule, a certification that the product meets all applicable consumer product safety standards and a specification of the standards which are applicable.

Such labels, where practicable, may be required by the Commission to be permanently marked on or affixed to any such consumer product. The Commission may, in appropriate cases, permit information required under paragraphs (1) and (2) of this subsection to be coded.

§2064[§15] Substantial product hazards

(a) "Substantial product hazard" defined.   For purposes of this section, the term "substantial product hazard" means—

(1) a failure to comply with an applicable consumer product safety rule which creates a substantial risk of injury to the public, or

(2) a product defect which (because of the pattern of defect, the number of defective products distributed in commerce, the severity of the risk, or otherwise) creates a substantial risk of injury to the public.

(b) Noncompliance with applicable consumer product safety rules; product defects; notice to Commission by manufacturer, distributor, or retailer.   Every manufacturer of a consumer product distributed in commerce, and every distributor and retailer of such product, who obtains information which reasonably supports the conclusion that such product—

(1) fails to comply with an applicable consumer product safety rule or with a voluntary consumer product safety standard upon which the Commission has relied under section 2058 of this title;

(2) contains a defect which could create a substantial product hazard described in subsection (a)(2) of this section; or

(3) creates an unreasonable risk of serious injury or death,

shall immediately inform the Commission of such failure to comply, of such defect, or of such risk, unless such manufacturer, distributor, or retailer has actual knowledge that the Commission has been adequately informed of such defect, failure to comply, or such risk.

(c) Public notice of defect or failure to comply; mail notice.   If the Commission determines (after affording interested persons, including consumers and consumer organizations, an opportunity for a hearing in accordance with subsection (f) of this section) that a product distributed in commerce presents a substantial product hazard and that notification is required in order to adequately protect the public from such substantial product hazard, the Commission may order the manufacturer or any distributor or retailer of the product to take any one or more of the following actions:

(1) To give public notice of the defect or failure to comply.

(2) To mail notice to each person who is a manufacturer, distributor, or retailer of such product.

(3) To mail notice to every person to whom the person required to give notice knows such product was delivered or sold.

Any such order shall specify the form and content of any notice required to be given under such order.

(d) Repair; replacement; refunds; action plan.   If the Commission determines (after affording interested parties, including consumers and

consumer organizations, an opportunity for a hearing in accordance with subsection (f) of this section) that a product distributed in commerce presents a substantial product hazard and that action under this subsection is in the public interest, it may order the manufacturer or any distributor or retailer of such product to take whichever of the following actions the person to whom the order is directed elects:

(1) To bring such product into conformity with the requirements of the applicable consumer product safety rule or to repair the defect in such product.

(2) To replace such product with a like or equivalent product which complies with the applicable consumer product safety rule or which does not contain the defect.

(3) To refund the purchase price of such product (less a reasonable allowance for use, if such product has been in the possession of a consumer for one year or more (A) at the time of public notice under subsection (c) of this section, or (B) at the time the consumer receives actual notice of the defect or noncompliance, whichever first occurs).

An order under this subsection may also require the person to whom it applies to submit a plan, satisfactory to the Commission, for taking action under whichever of the preceding paragraphs of this subsection under which such person has elected to act. The Commission shall specify in the order the persons to whom refunds must be made if the person to whom the order is directed elects to take the action described in paragraph (3). If an order under this subsection is directed to more than one person, the Commission shall specify which person has the election under this subsection. An order under this subsection may prohibit the person to whom it applies from manufacturing for sale, offering for sale, distributing in commerce, or importing into the customs territory of the United States (as defined in general note 2 of the Harmonized Tariff Schedule of the United States), or from doing any combination of such actions, the product with respect to which the order was issued.

(e) Reimbursement.

(1) No charge shall be made to any person (other than a manufacturer, distributor, or retailer) who avails himself of any remedy provided under an order issued under subsection (d) of this section, and the person subject to the order shall reimburse each person (other than a manufacturer, distributor, or retailer) who is entitled to such a remedy for any reasonable and foreseeable expenses incurred by such person in availing himself of such remedy.

(2) An order issued under subsection (c) or (d) of this section with respect to a product may require any person who is a manufacturer,

distributor, or retailer of the product to reimburse any other person who is a manufacturer, distributor, or retailer of such product for such other person's expenses in connection with carrying out the order, if the Commission determines such reimbursement to be in the public interest.

(f) Hearing. An order under subsection (c) or (d) of this section may be issued only after an opportunity for a hearing in accordance with section 554 of Title 5, except that, if the Commission determines that any person who wishes to participate in such hearing is a part of a class of participants who share an identity of interest, the Commission may limit such person's participation in such hearing to participation through a single representative designated by such class (or by the Commission if such class fails to designate such a representative). Any settlement offer which is submitted to the presiding officer at a hearing under this subsection shall be transmitted by the officer to the Commission for its consideration unless the settlement offer is clearly frivolous or duplicative of offers previously made.

(g) Preliminary injunction.

(1) If the Commission has initiated a proceeding under this section for the issuance of an order under subsection (d) of this section with respect to a product which the Commission has reason to believe presents a substantial product hazard, the Commission (without regard to section 2076(b)(7) of this title) or the Attorney General may, in accordance with section 2061(d)(1) of this title, apply to a district court of the United States for the issuance of a preliminary injunction to restrain the distribution in commerce of such product pending the completion of such proceeding. If such a preliminary injunction has been issued, the Commission (or the Attorney General if the preliminary injunction was issued upon an application of the Attorney General) may apply to the issuing court for extensions of such preliminary injunction.

(2) Any preliminary injunction, and any extension of a preliminary injunction, issued under this subsection with respect to a product shall be in effect for such period as the issuing court prescribes not to exceed a period which extends beyond the thirtieth day from the date of the issuance of the preliminary injunction (or, in the case of a preliminary injunction which has been extended, the date of its extension) or the date of the completion or termination of the proceeding under this section respecting such product, whichever date occurs first.

(3) The amount in controversy requirement of section 1331 of Title 28 does not apply with respect to the jurisdiction of a district court of the United States to issue or extend a preliminary injunction under this subsection.

(h) Cost-benefit analysis of notification or other action not required. Nothing in this section shall be construed to require the Commission, in

determining that a product distributed in commerce presents a substantial product hazard and that notification or other action under this section should be taken, to prepare a comparison of the costs that would be incurred in providing notification or taking other action under this section with the benefits from such notification or action.

§2065 [§16] Inspection and recordkeeping

(a) For purposes of implementing this Act, or rules or orders prescribed under this Act, officers or employees duly designated by the Commission, upon presenting appropriate credentials and a written notice from the Commission to the owner, operator, or agent in charge, are authorized—

(1) to enter, at reasonable times (A) any factory, warehouse, or establishment in which consumer products are manufactured or held, in connection with distribution in commerce, or (B) any conveyance being used to transport consumer products in connection with distribution in commerce; and

(2) to inspect, at reasonable times and in a reasonable manner such conveyance or those areas of such factory, warehouse, or establishment where such products are manufactured, held, or transported and which may relate to the safety of such products. Each such inspection shall be commenced and completed with reasonable promptness.

(b) Every person who is a manufacturer, private labeler, or distributor of a consumer product shall establish and maintain such records, make such reports, and provide such information as the Commission may, by rule, reasonably require for the purposes of implementing this Act, or to determine compliance with rules or orders prescribed under this Act. Upon request of an officer or employee duly designated by the Commission, every such manufacturer, private labeler, or distributor shall permit the inspection of appropriate books, records, and papers relevant to determining acting in compliance with this Act and rules under this Act.

§2066 [§17] Imported products

(a) Refusal of admission. Any consumer product offered for importation into the customs territory of the United States (as defined in general note 2 of the Harmonized Tariff Schedule of the United States) shall be refused admission into such customs territory if such product—

(1) fails to comply with an applicable consumer product safety rule;

(2) is not accompanied by a certificate required by section 2063 of this title, or is not labeled in accordance with regulations under section 2063(c) of this title;

(3) is or has been determined to be an imminently hazardous consumer product in a proceeding brought under section 2061 of this title;

(4) has a product defect which constitutes a substantial product hazard (within the meaning of section 2064(a)(2) of this title); or

(5) is a product which was manufactured by a person who the Commission has informed the Secretary of the Treasury is in violation of subsection (g) of this section.

(b) Samples. The Secretary of the Treasury shall obtain without charge and deliver to the Commission, upon the latter's request, a reasonable number of samples of consumer products being offered for import. Except for those owners or consignees who are or have been afforded an opportunity for a hearing in a proceeding under section 2061 of this title with respect to an imminently hazardous product, the owner or consignee of the product shall be afforded an opportunity by the Commission for a hearing in accordance with section 554 of Title 5 with respect to the importation of such products into the customs territory of the United States. If it appears from examination of such samples or otherwise that a product must be refused admission under the terms of subsection (a) of this section, such product shall be refused admission, unless subsection (c) of this section applies and is complied with.

(c) Modification. If it appears to the Commission that any consumer product which may be refused admission pursuant to subsection (a) of this section can be so modified that it need not (under the terms of paragraphs (1) through (4) of subsection (a) of this section) be refused admission, the Commission may defer final determination as to the admission of such product and, in accordance with such regulations as the Commission and the Secretary of the Treasury shall jointly agree to, permit such product to be delivered from customs custody under bond for the purpose of permitting the owner or consignee an opportunity to so modify such product.

(d) Supervision of modifications. All actions taken by an owner or consignee to modify such product under subsection (c) of this section shall be subject to the supervision of an officer or employee of the Commission and of the Department of the Treasury. If it appears to the Commission that the product cannot be so modified or that the owner or consignee is not proceeding satisfactorily to modify such product, it shall be refused admission into the customs territory of the United States, and the Commission may direct the Secretary to demand redelivery of the product into customs custody, and to seize the product in accordance with section 2071(b) of this title if it is not so redelivered.

(e) Product destruction. Products refused admission into the customs territory of the United States under this section must be exported,

except that upon application, the Secretary of the Treasury may permit the destruction of the product in lieu of exportation. If the owner or consignee does not export the product within a reasonable time, the Department of the Treasury may destroy the product.

(f) Payment of expenses occasioned by refusal of admission. All expenses (including travel, per diem or subsistence, and salaries of officers or employees of the United States) in connection with the destruction provided for in this section (the amount of such expenses to be determined in accordance with regulations of the Secretary of the Treasury) and all expenses in connection with the storage, cartage, or labor with respect to any consumer product refused admission under this section, shall be paid by the owner or consignee and, in default of such payment, shall constitute a lien against any future importations made by such owner or consignee.

(g) Importation conditioned upon manufacturer's compliance. The Commission may, by rule, condition the importation of a consumer product on the manufacturer's compliance with the inspection and recordkeeping requirements of this chapter and the Commission's rules with respect to such requirements.

(h) Product surveillance program.

(1) The Commission shall establish and maintain a permanent product surveillance program, in cooperation with other appropriate Federal agencies, for the purpose of carrying out the Commission's responsibilities under this chapter and the other Acts administered by the Commission and preventing the entry of unsafe consumer products into the commerce of the United States.

(2) The Commission may provide to the agencies with which it is cooperating under paragraph (1) such information, data, violator lists, test results, and other support, guidance, and documents as may be necessary or helpful for such agencies to cooperate with the Commission to carry out the product surveillance program under paragraph (1).

(3) The Commission shall periodically report to the Congress the results of the surveillance program under paragraph (1).

§2067 [§18] Exemption of exports

(a) Risk of injury to consumers within United States. This Act shall not apply to any consumer product if (1) it can be shown that such product is manufactured, sold, or held for sale for export from the United States (or that such product was imported for export), unless (A) such consumer product is in fact distributed in commerce for use in the United States, or (B) the Commission determines the exportation of such product presents an

unreasonable risk of injury to consumers within the United States, and (2) such consumer product when distributed in commerce, or any container in which it is enclosed when so distributed, bears a stamp or label stating that such consumer product is intended for export; except that this Act shall apply to any consumer product manufactured for sale, offered for sale, or sold for shipment to any installation of the United States located outside of the United States.

(b) Statement of exportation: filing period, information; notification of foreign country; petition for minimum filing period; good cause. Not less than thirty days before any person exports to a foreign country any product—

(1) which is not in conformity with an applicable consumer product safety standard in effect under this Act, or

(2) which is declared to be a banned hazardous substance by a rule promulgated under section 9 [15 U.S.C.S. §2058], such person shall file a statement with the Commission notifying the Commission of such exportation, and the Commission, upon receipt of such statement, shall promptly notify the government of such country of such exportation and the basis for such safety standard or rule. Any statement filed with the Commission under the preceding sentence shall specify the anticipated date of shipment of such product, the country and port of destination of such product, and the quantity of such product that will be exported, and shall contain such other information as the Commission may by regulation require. Upon petition filed with the Commission by any person required to file a statement under this subsection respecting an exportation, the Commission may, for good cause shown, exempt such person from the requirement of this subsection that such a statement be filed no less than thirty days before the date of the exportation, except that in no case shall the Commission permit such a statement to be filed later than the tenth day before such date.

§2068 [§19] Prohibited acts [omitted]

§2069 [§20] Civil penalties [omitted—provides for civil penalties up to $1,250,000]

§2070 [§21] Criminal penalties [omitted]

§2071 [§22] Injunctive enforcement and seizure [omitted]

§2072 [§23] Suits for damages

(a) Persons injured; costs; amount in controversy. Any person who shall sustain injury by reason of any knowing (including willful) violation of a consumer product safety rule, or any other rule or order issued by the Commission may sue any person who knowingly (including willfully) violated any such rule or order in any district court of the United States in the district in which the defendant resides or is found or has an agent, shall recover damages sustained, and may, if the court determines it to be in the interest of justice, recover the costs of suit, including reasonable attorneys' fees (determined in accordance with section 11(f)) and reasonable expert witnesses' fees; Provided, That the matter in controversy exceeds the sum or value of $10,000, exclusive of interest and costs, unless such action is brought against the United States, any agency thereof, or any officer or employee thereof in his official capacity.

(b) Denial and imposition of costs. Except when express provision is made in a statute of the United States, in any case in which the plaintiff is finally adjudged to be entitled to recover less than the sum or value of $10,000, computed without regard to any setoff or counterclaim to which the defendant may be adjudged to be entitled, and exclusive of interests and costs, the district court may deny costs to the plaintiff and, in addition, may impose costs on the plaintiff.

(c) Remedies available. The remedies provided for in this section shall be in addition to and not in lieu of any other remedies provided by common law or under Federal or State law.

§2073 [§24] Private enforcement

Any interested person (including any individual or nonprofit, business, or other entity) may bring an action in any United States district court for the district in which the defendant is found or transacts business to enforce a consumer product safety rule or an order under section 15, and to obtain appropriate injunctive relief. Not less than thirty days prior to the commencement of such action, such interested person shall give notice by registered mail to the Commission, to the Attorney General, and to the person against whom such action is directed. Such notice shall state the nature of the alleged violation of any such standard or order, the relief to be requested, and the court in which the action will be brought. No separate suit shall be brought under this section if at the time the suit is brought the same alleged violation is the subject of a pending civil or criminal action by the United States under this Act. In any action under this section the court may in the interest of justice award the costs of suit, including reasonable attorneys' fees (determined in accordance with section 11(f)) and reasonable expert witnesses' fees.

§2074 [§25] Private remedies

(a) Liability at common law or under State statute not relieved by compliance. Compliance with consumer product safety rules or other rules or orders under this Act shall not relieve any person from liability at common law or under state statutory law to any other person.

(b) Evidence of Commission's inaction inadmissible in actions relating to consumer products. The failure of the Commission to take any action or commence a proceeding with respect to the safety of a consumer product shall not be admissible in evidence in litigation at common law or under State statutory law relating to such consumer product.

(c) Public information. Subject to sections 6(a)(2) and 6(b) but notwithstanding section 6(a)(1), (1) any accident or investigation report made under this Act by an officer or employee of the Commission shall be made available to the public in a manner which will not identify any injured person or any person treating him, without the consent of the person so identified, and (2) all reports on research projects, demonstration projects, and other related activities shall be public information. . . .

§2079 [§30] Transfers of functions

(a) Hazardous substances and poisons. The functions of the Secretary of Health, Education, and Welfare under the Federal Hazardous Substances Act (15 U.S.C. 1261 et seq.) and the Poison Prevention Packaging Act of 1970 [15 U.S.C.S. §§1471 et seq.] are transferred to the Commission. The functions of the Secretary of Health, Education, and Welfare under the Federal Food, Drug, and Cosmetic Act (15 U.S.C. 301 et seq.), to the extent such functions relate to the administration and enforcement of the Poison Prevention Packaging Act of 1970 [15 U.S.C.S. §§1471 et seq.], are transferred to the Commission.

(b) Flammable fabrics. The functions of the Secretary of Health, Education, and Welfare, the Secretary of Commerce, and the Federal Trade Commission under the Flammable Fabrics Act (15 U.S.C. 1191 et seq.) are transferred to the Commission. The functions of the Federal Trade Commission under the Federal Trade Commission Act [15 U.S.C.S. §§41 et seq.], to the extent such functions relate to the administration and enforcement of the Flammable Fabrics Act are transferred to the Commission.

(c) Household refrigerators. The functions of the Secretary of Commerce and the Federal Trade Commission under the Act of August 2, 1956 (15 U.S.C. 1211) are transferred to the Commission. . . .

§2083 [§36] Congressional veto of consumer product safety rules

(a) The Commission shall transmit to the Secretary of the Senate and the Clerk of the House of Representatives a copy of any consumer product safety rule promulgated by the Commission under section 9 [15 U.S.C.S. §2058].

(b) Any rule specified in subsection (a) shall not take effect if—

(1) within the 90 calendar days of continuous session of the Congress which occur after the date of the promulgation of such rule, both Houses of the Congress adopt a concurrent resolution, the matter after the resolving clause of which is as follows (with the blank spaces appropriately filled): "That the Congress disapproves the consumer product safety rule which was promulgated by the Consumer Product Safety Commission with respect to and which was transmitted to the Congress on and disapproves the rule for the following reasons:"; or

(2) within the 60 calendar days of continuous session of the Congress which occur after the date of the promulgation of such rule, one House of the Congress adopts such concurrent resolution and transmits such resolution to the other House and such resolution is not disapproved by such other House within the 30 calendar days of continuous session of the Congress which occur after the date of such transmittal.

(c) Congressional inaction on, or rejection of, a concurrent resolution of disapproval under this section shall not be construed as an expression of approval of the rule involved, and shall not be construed to create any presumption of validity with respect to such rule.

(d) For purposes of this section—

(1) continuity of session is broken only by an adjournment of the Congress sine die; and

(2) the days on which either House is not in session because of an adjournment of more than 3 days to a day certain are excluded in the computation of the periods of continuous session of the Congress specified in subsection (b).

Pursuant to §7 of the Act, the Commission has promulgated numerous standards regulating the safety features of various consumer products. The complete regulations can be found in 16 C.F.R. §§1000 et seq., but here is a partial list of the products covered: matchbooks, cigarette lighters, power lawn mowers, swimming pool slides, hems, paint, containers using chloro-fluorocarbons, toys (including crayons), fireworks, cribs, pacifiers, bicycles, and, most controversially, gun safety locks. Attorneys whose clients manufacture products covered by these standards must take steps to ensure that the standards are carefully met. Conversely, attorneys whose clients are injured by defective consumer products should check to see whether the product violated a CPSA standard. The Consumer Product Safety Guide (CCH) contains an up-to-date compilation of all the relevant laws.

PROBLEM 33

The three-month-old child of Mr. and Mrs. Smith strangled when her head became wedged between the slats of a crib. The Smiths went to an attorney, who had them measure the distance between the slats. The result was 3 inches. According to 16 C.F.R. §1509.4, the maximum allowable distance between crib slats is $2\frac{3}{8}$ inches. What should the attorney do? See CPSA §§23, 24, 25. If the child had not died, but had been merely scared by the experience of being trapped between the slats, could §23 be used to recover the cost of buying a new crib and junking the old one (that is, does the "injury" mentioned in the statute include economic as opposed to personal harm)? See Annot., Monetary Remedies Under §23 of the Consumer Product Safety Act, 87 A.L.R. Fed. 587.[5]

PAYNE v. A. O. SMITH CORP.
United States District Court Southern District of Ohio, 1983
578 F. Supp. 733

RICE, District Judge.

Plaintiffs filed this diversity action on February 17, 1981, premised on a water heater explosion in Plaintiffs' home on August 14, 1979, from which they allegedly received personal and derivative injuries. Defendants, manufacturers of the water heater and gas control unit in question, were sued under four counts (negligence, warranty, strict liability, and "punitive damages"). In early February of 1983, Plaintiffs moved (doc. no. 162) to

---

5. One thing the Smiths might do is alert the Commission to the problem. In order to encourage consumer complaints, the Commission has created a hotline: (800) 638-2772.

file an amended complaint, which sought to (a) correct two minor errors in the original complaint, (b) increase the amount of damages prayed for, and (c) add a fifth cause of action, under the federal Consumer Products (sic) Safety Act (CPSA), 15 U.S.C. §2072. . . .

Defendants next argue that any CPSA cause of action would be barred by the applicable statute of limitations. As noted above, the accident in question occurred on August 14, 1979; the original complaint was filed some 18 months later, and the motion to file an amended complaint was filed about three and one-half years after the accident. Defendants argue that the two year limitations period in Ohio for personal injury torts, Ohio Rev. Code Ann. §2305.10 (Page 1982), should apply, barring the amendments. They also argue that, given the uniqueness of a CPSA cause of action, the amendment should *not* relate back under Rule 15(c). Plaintiffs originally joined battle on the issue of the uniqueness of a CPSA action; they have now abandoned that argument, concede the uniqueness of a CPSA cause of action, and contend that Ohio Rev. Code Ann. §2305.09 (Page 1982) (four year period for fraud and torts not otherwise listed) or Ohio Rev. Code Ann. §2305.07 (Page 1982) (six year period for liability based on a statute) governs, obviating the need to rely on the relation-back doctrine. See Plaintiffs' Supplemental Reply Memorandum, doc. no. 161. While the issues are close ones, the Court must agree with the Plaintiffs.

Section 23 of the CPSA, 15 U.S.C. §2072, enacted in 1972, sets out an express damage remedy for any "person who shall sustain injury by reason of any knowing (including willful) violation of a consumer product safety rule, or any other rule or order issued by" the Consumer Product Safety Commission (CPSC). Neither §2072, any other provision of the CPSA, nor the legislative history, see [1972] U.S. Code Cong. & Adm. News 4573 et seq., discusses any statute of limitations to apply to a §2072 action. In the absence of express Congressional directive, the Court must apply the most analogous state or federal statute of limitations. DelCostello v. International Brotherhood of Teamsters, [462] U.S. [151], 103 S. Ct. 2281, 2287-89, 76 L. Ed. 2d 476 (1983); Sutton v. Bloom, 710 F.2d 1188, 1190 (6th Cir. 1983), *petition for cert. filed*, 52 U.S.L.W. 3268 (U.S. Sept. 26, 1983) (No. 83-512). Cf. Stevens v. Tennessee Valley Authority, 712 F.2d 1047, 1053 (6th Cir. 1983) (an action under the Veterans Preference Act, 5 U.S.C. §3551, is of such uniqueness that "no state statute of limitation applies and that therefore the limitation upon the right of action in such actions as this is governed by the equitable doctrine of laches"); *DelCostello*, 103 S. Ct. at 2293 n.20.

The issue of what limitations period applies to a §2073 action appears to be one of first impression. Since the complaint as a whole is premised on the personal injuries allegedly arising from the water heater explosion,

Defendants contend that the most analogous state statute of limitations is the two-year statute for personal injuries, O.R.C. §2305.10. Applying a two-year period will time bar the amendment, *unless* the amendment relates back, under Rule 15(c), to the filing date of the original amendment. Rule 15(c) permits relation back "[w]henever the claim or defense asserted in the amended pleading arose out of the conduct, transaction, or occurrence set forth or attempted to be set forth in the original pleading. . . . " In applying this test, courts have typically asked if the facts alleged in the original complaint put the opposing party on notice that an additional claim could be raised. See Hageman v. Signal L.P. Gas, Inc., 486 F.2d 479, 484 (6th Cir. 1973); 6 C. Wright & A. Miller, Federal Practice and Procedure, §1497 at 497-98 (1971).

Plaintiffs candidly acknowledge that the relation back of the CPSA cause of action is problematic. As Defendants point out, a §2072 "claim involves activities relating to a defendant's understanding and compliance with a CPSC rule. These activities do not relate to the manufacture or sale of the product." Emerson Electric's Supplemental Memorandum, doc. no. 153, p.10. Moreover, causation and other issues may differ under a §2072 claim and a common law tort/product liability claim. Id. at 11-12. Accord, Kiser v. A. O. Smith Corp., No. 81-JM-979 (D. Colo. June 8, 1983) (transcript of oral ruling attached to doc. no. 153); Comment, The Consumer Product Safety Act & Private Causes of Action for Personal Injury: What Does a Consumer Gain?, 30 Baylor L. Rev. 115, 118-22 (1978). In short, it is doubtful that the facts alleged in the original complaint would have put Defendants "on notice" that they might also be sued under the CPSA. It is equally doubtful that the proposed CPSA claim could relate back to the date of the filing of the original complaint.

Plaintiffs, however, now eschew any reliance on the relation back doctrine, and contend that the CPSA claim is governed by either a four or six year statute of limitations (the claim being timely filed under either statute). If a CPSA action is so different from their original state law tort claim that relation back under Rule 15(c) is impossible, they also contend that the state limitations period for personal injury torts should not apply to the CPSA action. The Court finds this reasoning to be persuasive. The parties now agree that the CPSA claim is different from the causes of action in the balance of the complaint. For example, it appears that the *only* jury questions under a CPSA claim are whether an injury occurred, the amount of damages, and whether the Defendant "knowingly" violated certain safety rules. Jury issues in a typical tort suit are more numerous. See Comment, supra. Cf. Young v. Robertshaw Controls Co., 560 F. Supp. 288, 291 (N.D.N.Y. 1983). The differences between a CPSA action and a "garden variety" tort action contemplated by O.R.C. §2305.10 are sufficient to disclaim application of the latter statute. See Nickels v. Koehler Management Corp., 541 F.2d 611, 618 (6th Cir. 1976) (discussing differences and similarities of federal securities law and state common law fraud before applying state limitations period), *cert. denied*, 429 U.S. 1074, 97 S. Ct. 813, 50 L. Ed. 2d 792 (1977); Mason v. Owens-Illinois, Inc., 517 F.2d 520 (6th Cir. 1975) (discussing difference between federal civil rights law and Ohio Civil Rights Commission procedure; OCRC limitations period not applied). See generally, Sutton v. Bloom, supra.

As Plaintiffs suggest, the remaining, analogous Ohio limitations period would appear to be either O.R.C. §2305.09 (four years for fraud or for torts not specifically listed) or O.R.C. §2305.07 (six years for liability based on a statute). The latter provision has been construed to cover liability based on a *federal* statute, e.g., Mason v. Owens-Illinois, Inc., supra, and would seem to cover a CPSA claim, as well. However, the Court finds that §2305.09 provides an appropriate period, given that a CPSA action does partake of elements of a typical tort, even if it is not identical to same. Plaintiff's CPSA claim is not time barred when a four year statute is applied. The Court believes that in the interest of consistency and predictability, a uniform statute should, ideally, apply to the entirety of the proposed amended complaint. However, in this Circuit, when limitations periods must be borrowed, it is proper to "fragment" the complaint, if necessary, by applying different statutes of limitations to separate causes of action in a complaint. See Woods v. City of Dayton, 574 F. Supp. 689 at 695 (S.D. Ohio 1983), appeal docketed after final judgment entry, No. 83-3276 (6th Cir. April 2, 1983).

For these reasons, the CPSA claim in the proposed amended complaint is not barred by the applicable statute of limitations.

III

Finally, Defendants argue that even if an action under §23 of the CPSA is not time barred, Plaintiffs have failed to state a claim under same. They initially point out that the proposed amended complaint does not allege several of the elements listed in §23 (e.g., a "willful" violation), or the safety order or rule which the Defendant supposedly violated. Plaintiffs acknowledge these deficiencies, and suggest that a second, more detailed, proposed amended complaint be filed. The Court agrees, and orders that same be filed (see below).

Defendants also point out that Plaintiffs seek treble and punitive damages under their CPSA claim. Such damages are not provided for in the statute, and thus cannot be requested by Plaintiffs. See *Young*, supra, 560 F. Supp. at 294; Walba v. H & N Prescription Center, Inc., 539 F. Supp. 352, 354 (E.D.N.Y. 1982). Any such reference will be stricken by the Court.

Lastly, Defendants contend that Plaintiffs' entire CPSA claim must fail, since the CPSC rule which Defendants allegedly violated, 16 C.F.R. §1115 (1983), see Plaintiffs' Reply Memorandum, doc. no. 96, is only an "interpretative guideline," not a "substantive rule" meant to be enforced under §23 of the CPSA. Defendants have extensively briefed this issue, and their arguments are not without force. However, their specific contentions have been rejected by two previous district courts. Butcher [v. Robertshaw Controls Co., 550 Supp. 692, 696-698 (D. Md. 1981)]; *Young*, supra, 560 F. Supp. at 292-93 n.8. Even if Defendants' characterization of the cited regulation is correct, actions alleging violations of same are simply not foreclosed by the plain language of 15 U.S.C. §2072. Id. Accordingly, this Court rejects Defendants' position, as well. . . .

PROBLEM 34

Your client, Orient Toys, is a Japanese concern that makes toys in various cities in Asia and then ships them to foreign markets, with the United States being a primary target. On May 1 of this year, a company vice president called you with the bad news that the stuffed panda dolls the company has been selling in this country for the past six months have a major flaw: the dolls' eyes are rather easily pulled out, exposing the large hat pins that hold the eyes in place.

a. Are imported toys covered by the CPSA? See §17. Exported toys? See §18.

b. Now that your client has alerted you to the danger, what must you do and how quickly must you do it? See §15; the reporting requirements are explained in more detail in 16 C.F.R. §1115.

c. If there is no CPSC rule covering the panda doll eye problem, but you delay reporting the danger to the Commission for three months, can an injured consumer sue Orient Toys, using the violation of §15 as grounds for suit under §23? This issue is addressed in the case that follows.

ZEPIK v. TIDEWATER MIDWEST, INC.[6]
United States Court of Appeals, Seventh Circuit, 1988
856 F.2d 936

CUDAHY, Circuit Judge.

---

6. Footnotes in this case have been renumbered for clarity.

Ronald Zepik was injured while diving into an in-ground swimming pool at the home of some friends. He brought suit in federal court against four manufacturers of swimming pool components and a pool supply company raising claims based on the Consumer Products [sic] Safety Act ("CPSA") and on a variety of pendent state law theories, including strict liability, negligence, willful and wanton misconduct and breach of express and implied warranties. Zepik's complaint based subject matter jurisdiction solely on the federal question raised by the CPSA claim.

The district court dismissed the suit against the supplier and granted summary judgment on all counts in favor of the component manufacturers; Zepik appealed. We affirm the district court's rejection of the CPSA claim and remand the state claims for the district court to determine whether federal jurisdiction of the pendent claims exists under United Mine Workers v. Gibbs, 383 U.S. 715, 86 S. Ct. 1130, 16 L. Ed. 2d 218 (1966).

We summarize the relevant facts with all disputed issues resolved in Zepik's favor. On June 20, 1983, Ronald Zepik dove into a backyard swimming pool at the home of his friends, the Davises, and struck his head on the bottom. The accident left him a quadriplegic. In May 1985, Zepik brought suit against five companies that had manufactured or sold components incorporated in the Davises' pool. Claims against Ceeco Pool & Supply, Inc. (later known as Tide-water Midwest, Inc.) were dismissed with prejudice and that company plays no part in this appeal. Another company, Loren's Pool and Supply, Inc. ("Loren's"), sold materials used in constructing the pool, excavated the hole and provided technical assistance. The remaining three were identified by Zepik as component manufacturers: Frost Company ("Frost") manufactured the ladder; Pleasure Industries, Inc. ("Pleasure") manufactured the pipes and published a construction manual consulted during construction; Polynesian, Inc. ("Polynesian") made the wall panels and coping tile. The complaint alleged that defendants were liable, under various state law theories, for failing to warn of the danger of diving into shallow water, for failing to ensure that a safe way of entering the water would be available and for providing misleading assurances, express and implied, that diving into shallow water was safe. Count VII of the complaint, the basis for subject matter jurisdiction in the district court, invoked section 23(a) of the CPSA, 15 U.S.C. §2072(a) (1982), which provides a private right of action for "any person" injured "by reason of any knowing (including willful) violation of a consumer product safety rule, or any other rule or order issued by the Commission." Zepik claimed that the defendants had knowingly violated rules that require manufacturers, distributors and retailers to report product defects capable of creating "substantial product hazards." See 16 C.F.R. Part 1115 (1988).

The district court ruled in favor of the defendant-appellees in two separate decisions. On April 28, 1986, the district court granted summary judgment to Pleasure in Zepik v. Ceeco Pool & Supply, Inc., 637 F. Supp. 444 (N.D. Ind. 1986) ("*Zepik I*"). Although the district court rejected Pleasure's contention that the CPSA's private right of action does not extend to reporting violations, it ruled for Pleasure on this count on the ground that the reporting requirements do not require a manufacturer of pipes or a publisher of construction manuals to report defects in completed pools. Id. at 451. This disposition of the sole federal claim should have prompted the district court to consider whether dismissal of the state claims was required under the general principle that "if the federal claims are dismissed before trial, even though not insubstantial in a jurisdictional sense, the state claims should be dismissed as well." *Gibbs*, 383 U.S. at 726, 86 S. Ct. at 1139. Instead, the district court went on to consider the merits of the state law claims and to grant summary judgment to Pleasure across the board.

On November 12, 1987, the district court issued a memorandum and order disposing of Zepik's claims against the remaining three defendants. Zepik v. Ceeco Pool & Supply, Inc., 118 F.R.D. 455 (N.D. Ind. 1987) ("*Zepik II*"). The court granted a motion by Loren's to dismiss the CPSA count, having been persuaded by Drake v. Honeywell, Inc., 797 F.2d 603 (8th Cir. 1986), a decision handed down after *Zepik I* had been decided, that section 23(a) of the CPSA did not afford a private right of action for reporting violations. 118 F.R.D. at 458-59. The court further found that "no independent basis existed for this court's continued jurisdiction over the remaining pendent state claims" against Loren's and, citing two of this circuit's decisions under *Gibbs*, dismissed those claims as well. Id. at 459. This analysis, however, was not applied to Frost and Polynesian. These defendants, whose situations closely resembled Pleasure's, presumably saw a sure bet in moving for summary judgment on the strength of *Zepik I* and declined to raise arguments for dismissal based on *Drake* and *Gibbs*. The district court, "reluctant to dispose of the claims against those defendants on the basis of an argument they ha[d] not addressed," granted summary judgment for Frost and Polynesian on the CPSA and state law counts for reasons almost identical to those recited in *Zepik I*. See *Zepik II*, 118 F.R.D. at 459-65. As in the earlier order, the district court did not consider whether subject matter jurisdiction over the state law counts against Frost and Polynesian should survive the dismissal of the federal claim.

II

A

Zepik maintains that his private right of action against the defendants for their violations of reporting regulations issued under the CPSA derives from the plain meaning of the statute. Section 23(a) authorizes suits for damages, costs and legal fees in federal court by anyone injured "by reason of any knowing (including willful) violation of a consumer product safety rule, or any other rule or order issued by the Commission." Section 15(b) of the CPSA, 15 U.S.C. §2064(b) (1982), requires manufacturers, distributors and retailers of consumer products to inform the Commission immediately when they obtain any information suggesting that a product they make or distribute "contains a defect which could create a substantial product hazard." Part 1115 of the Commission's regulations, 16 C.F.R. Part 1115 (1988), sets forth the Commission's interpretation of the Act's reporting requirements. The complaint alleges that the defendants were aware that severe injuries had resulted from dives into shallow pools but failed to file the required reports, thereby violating the reporting regulations and incurring liability to victims of diving accidents, such as Zepik, injured "by reason of" the reporting violations.

Several district courts and a state Supreme Court have held that section 23(a) authorizes private actions based on violations of reporting requirements. See Hughes v. Segal Enters., Inc., 627 F. Supp. 1231 (W.D. Ark. 1986); Drake v. Lochinvar Water Heater, Inc., 618 F. Supp. 549 (D. Minn. 1985), *rev'd sub nom.* Drake v. Honeywell, Inc., 797 F.2d 603 (8th Cir. 1986); Wilson v. Robertshaw Controls Co., 600 F. Supp. 671 (N.D. Ind. 1985); Payne v. A. O. Smith Corp., 578 F. Supp. 733 (S.D. Ohio 1983); Young v. Robertshaw Controls Co., 560 F. Supp. 288 (N.D.N.Y. 1983); Butcher v. Robertshaw Controls Co., 550 F. Supp. 692 (D. Md. 1981); Swenson v. Emerson Elec. Co., 374 N.W.2d 690 (Minn. 1985), *cert. denied,* 476 U.S. 1130, 106 S. Ct. 1998, 90 L. Ed. 2d 678 (1986). *Butcher,* the first case in this line, set forth the basic "plain meaning" analysis on which the others have relied. *Butcher* focused on section 23(a)'s statement that knowing violation of "a consumer product safety rule or any other rule or order" gives rise to a private cause of action. In view of this broad language, *Butcher* rejected an argument that section 23(a) applies only to consumer product safety rules, 560 F. Supp. at 698-99, and subsequent cases rejected arguments that section 23(a) refers to legislative but not interpretive rules. *Wilson,* 600 F. Supp. at 674-75; *Young,* 560 F. Supp. at 292 n.8. *Butcher* also rejected the defendant's contention that failure to distinguish between legislative and interpretive rules under section 23(a) would produce an outcome that

Congress could not possibly have intended—admission to federal court for any product liability plaintiff able to raise a colorable claim that a defendant had knowingly violated interpretive rules implementing the CPSA's broad reporting obligation. *Butcher* did not dispute that this construction of section 23(a) could expand federal jurisdiction over product liability cases, but observed that this expansion might be "precisely the result intended by Congress." 550 F. Supp. at 700.

When the district court decided *Zepik I*, the *Butcher* line of cases was opposed only by Morris v. Coleco Industries, 587 F. Supp. 8 (E.D. Va. 1984), and Kahn v. Sears, Roebuck & Co., 607 F. Supp. 957 (N.D. Ga. 1985). *Morris* did not address whether 23(a)'s reference to "any other rule" included interpretive rules since the plaintiff in that case apparently alleged a violation of the statutory reporting requirement rather than the Part 1115 regulations interpreting that requirement. *Morris* held that the plaintiff's cause of action under the CPSA failed both because the alleged violation concerned the statute itself rather than a Commission rule or order and because the court found it "illogical . . . that Congress would have supposed that a failure to disclose a mishap to the Commission might proximately cause an injury." 587 F. Supp. at 9-10. *Kahn*, in which the plaintiff did allege a violation of the Part 1115 regulations, summarily determined that Part 1115 contained only interpretive rules, indistinguishable from the statute itself. This move placed *Kahn* on all fours with *Morris*, which the district court then adopted as more convincing than the cases in the *Butcher* line. 607 F. Supp. at 958. *Zepik I* followed the *Butcher* line of cases on the existence of a cause of action under section 23(a) without acknowledging this contrary authority. 637 F. Supp. at 451.

After the district court decided *Zepik I*, the Eighth Circuit issued the first circuit court decision addressing whether section 23(a) creates a private cause of action for violations of the Part 1115 reporting rules. Drake v. Honeywell, Inc., 797 F.2d 603 (8th Cir. 1986), *rev'g* Drake v. Lochinvar Water Heater, Inc., 618 F. Supp. 549 (D. Minn. 1985); accord Kukulka v. Holiday Cycle Sales, Inc., 680 F. Supp. 266 (E.D. Mich. 1988). Like *Butcher* and its progeny, *Drake* focused on the types of violations covered by section 23(a). The court observed that section 23(a) creates liability to private parties only for violations of Commission rules. Conspicuously omitted is a right to sue for violations of the statute itself. 797 F.2d at 604, 606.[7] The *Drake* court found

---

7. See also Note, Private Causes of Action Under the Reporting Rules of the Consumer Product Safety Act, 70 Minn. L. Rev. 955, 959-60 & n.23 (1986) (arguing that Congress' omission of statutory violations from list of acts giving rise to section 23(a) liability reflected preference for regulatory as opposed to statutory standard setting).

that this omission, which in its view distinguished section 23(a) from most other statutory provisions conferring private rights of action, demonstrated Congress' intent to prohibit private enforcement of the statute itself. This element of Congress' intent, according to *Drake,* must inform the construction of the phrase "any other rule or order."[8] Since interpretive rules amount to no more than restatements of statutory provisions, failure to distinguish between legislative rules and interpretive rules for purposes of section 23(a) "would seem to frustrate the congressional intent, expressed by the omission of [a right to sue for statutory violations in] section 23(a), to deny a private cause of action to those injured from a violation of the statute itself." Id. at 606. *Drake* also noted that the CPSA delegates legislative rulemaking authority to the Commission in small, section-specific parcels and that section 15(b), the principal source of authority for the Part 1115 reporting requirements, does not authorize legislative rulemaking. Furthermore, *Drake* observed that the Commission characterized the Part 1115 rules as interpretive when it issued them and that an agency's characterization is ordinarily accorded considerable deference. Id. at 607-08. Finding nothing in the legislative history to preclude the limitation of section 23(a) to legislative rules and persuasive practical reasons for federal courts to avoid the difficult issues of causation raised by plaintiffs' claims to have been injured "by reason of" reporting violations, the *Drake* court concluded that section 23(a) does not authorize private actions for reporting violations.

By the time the district court took up the motions for dismissal and summary judgment filed by Frost, Loren's and Polynesian in *Zepik II,*

---

8. The genesis of section 23(a)'s broad reference to "any other rule or order" is unclear. The bills enacted by the Senate and House contained identical, arguably narrower language. They stated:

Any person who shall sustain injury by reason of any knowing (including willful) violation of a *consumer product safety standard, regulation, or order* issued by the Commissioner may sue therefor. . . . S. 3419, 92d Cong., 2d Sess. 316(d)(2), 118 Cong. Rec. 21,844 (1972), *reprinted in* Bureau of National Affairs, The Consumer Product Safety Act: Text, Analysis, Legislative History App. at 208 (1973) (hereinafter "Legislative History"); H.R. 15003, 92d Cong., 2d Sess. 23(a), 118 Cong. Rec. 31,415 (1972), *reprinted in* Legislative History App. at 305 (emphasis supplied). The Conference Committee apparently viewed the insertion of "any other rule or order" in the final bill as inconsequential, since its report on the reconciliation of the two bills makes no reference to the section 23(a) private cause of action. H.R. Conf. Rep. No. 1593, 92d Cong., 2d Sess. (1972), *reprinted in* Legislative History App. at 311-42. The statement of the Senate Conferees refers to the private remedy provision briefly, referring to a cause of action against "a manufacturer who knows that the product does not meet an applicable product safety standard," but making no mention of remedies for other violations. 118 Cong. Rec. 36,198 (1972) (statement of Senator Moss), *reprinted in* Legislative History App. at 347.

Drake's analysis was available for consideration. Abandoning its position in *Zepik I*, the district court agreed with Loren's that Zepik's CPSA claim should be dismissed under *Drake*. See *Zepik II*, 118 F.R.D. at 458-59. However, in responding to the motions filed by Frost and Polynesian, the court assumed the existence of a private cause of action and granted summary judgment to Frost and Polynesian for the reasons given in *Zepik I*, that defendants had no duty to report possible defects in pools for which they provided only isolated components. Id. at 465. On appeal Zepik contends that *Zepik II*'s dismissal of the CPSA claim against Loren's incorrectly denied the existence of a private right of action for reporting violations and that both *Zepik I* and *Zepik II* erred in granting summary judgment on the CPSA claims that the district court treated as viable.

B

We agree with the result in *Drake* and with much of its reasoning. We hesitate, however, to rely exclusively on the distinction between interpretive and legislative rules as grounds for denying the existence of a private cause of action for violations of reporting requirements. *Drake* properly points out that private actions brought under the Commission's interpretive rules implicate a conflict between the omission of statutory violations and the broad reference to "any other rule" in section 23(a). This conflict may be resolved in one of two ways: the omission of authorization to bring an action directly under the statute may be given broad effect to limit the scope of the phrase "any other rule or order," or the phrase "any other rule or order" may be read expansively to limit the effect of the omission.

Placing greater weight on the omission, as *Drake* argues we should, has the possibly counterintuitive result of deputizing private Attorneys General to enforce rules formulated by the Commission while leaving the Commission alone to enforce congressional strictures restated in interpretive rules. The affront to intuition might be explained away easily if Congress could be seen to have forbidden legislative rulemaking in discrete areas, such as the reporting under section 15(b), where private actions were deemed inappropriate. But the possibility exists, as *Drake* concedes, that the Commission could have issued the Part 1115 regulations as legislative rules under authority of section 16(b), 15 U.S.C. §2065(b) (1982) (recordkeeping), or section 27(e), 15 U.S.C. §2076(e) (1982) (performance and technical data). See *Drake*, 797 F.2d at 608 n.8. If the Commission could, in fact, have issued the reporting requirements as legislative rules, a broad reading of the omission from section 23(a) must rely on a claim that Congress intended to allow the Commission to choose between issuing interpretive reporting rules, which would not give rise to a private cause of action, and issuing legislative reporting rules, which would. But if Congress had intended the omission from section 23(a) to be pregnant with such complex implications, one might expect some reference to these implications in the legislative history. If the drafters had no such purpose in mind, *Drake*'s argument for restricting the scope of the phrase "any other rule" in deference to the omission of a right to sue for statutory violations seems to lose much of its force.

We do not need to decide whether, despite these complications, *Drake*'s rationale would be sufficient in itself to defeat a private cause of action for reporting violations. We find additional reasons for barring this cause of action in the requirement that plaintiffs bringing suit under section 23(a) show that they incurred injury "by reason of" a violation of a Commission rule or order. The CPSA does not elaborate on the meaning of "by reason of," but in the absence of any indication that Congress intended to depart from conventional notions of causation we think the causal connection required here should be roughly equivalent to the causal connection required to establish common law tort liability. In Kelsey v. Muskin, Inc., 848 F.2d 39, 42-43 (2d Cir. 1988), the Second Circuit held that the doctrine of unforeseeable superseding cause defeated a diver's claim that he had been injured "by reason of" defendants' failures to report swimming pool hazards. See also Caraballo v. United States, 830 F.2d 19, 22-23 (2d Cir. 1987) (same doctrine defeats claim for diving injury under Federal Tort Claims Act). *Kelsey* appears to rely on New York tort law in affirming the district court's finding that the plaintiff failed to show that his injury occurred "by reason of" the alleged reporting violations. *Kelsey* suggests that causation under section 23(a) is defined by the tort law of the state where the injury occurred rather than by a uniform federal standard. The choice between these two sources of legal standards to fill gaps in the statute raises complexities that we need not address here. See Wahba v. H & N Prescription Center, Inc., 539 F. Supp. 352, 356-58 (E.D.N.Y. 1982) (while section 23 mandates a uniform federal standard of care, damage issues are to be resolved under state law standards). For our purposes, it is enough to observe that given the CPSA's structure and legislative history no plausible federal standard could deviate so radically from established concepts of causation in tort—including those prevailing under Indiana law—as to authorize suits under section 23 for reporting violations.

The causal connection between a defendant's reporting violation and a plaintiff's injury is too attenuated and speculative to satisfy generally applicable standards of causation in fact or proximate causation. To establish that an injury occurred "by reason of" a defendant's reporting violations, a plaintiff must show that: (1) by failing to report information that "reasonably support[ed] the conclusion that" a product was defective the defendant deprived the Commission of information not already known to it; (2) if the information had been reported, the Commission would have determined that a defect existed and undertaken to counteract the defect;[9] (3) the Commission's response would have been implemented in time to avert the injury to the plaintiff (and would have survived judicial and congressional scrutiny during the period between the Commission's response and the injury);[10] and (4) the Commission's response would have been effective in preventing the accident in question.

It is significant that not one of these propositions would require a plaintiff to distinguish between the seller of an article that was physically involved in an accident and sellers of similar articles that were not. Any competitor of Frost, Loren's, Pleasure or Polynesian who knowingly failed to inform the Commission of diving accidents in pools built with ladders, pipe or coping tile that lacked warnings against diving into shallow water could also have been named as defendants under Zepik's reading of the

---

9. The Commission's principal tools for responding to a dangerous product defect are "consumer product safety standards" specifying performance requirements or requiring warnings or instructions, 15 U.S.C. §§2056, 2058 (1982); bans on hazardous products, 15 U.S.C. §§2057-2058 (1982); recalls and injunctions against further distribution of products posing substantial hazards, 15 U.S.C. §§2064(c), (d), (g) (1982); and cajolery utilizing the threat of one of these formal actions to encourage private standard setting. For an overview, see Schwartz, The Consumer Product Safety Commission: A Flawed Product of the Consumer Decade, 51 Geo. Wash. L. Rev. 32 (1982). The sellers' obligation to report extends to all information that "reasonably supports" the existence of a substantial hazard, but the Commission may issue an order only after formally determining that a substantial hazard exists. Compare 15 U.S.C. §2064 (b) (1982) (reporting standard) with id. §§2058, 2064(c), (d) (1982) (prerequisites to Commission action). To determine which reporting violations represent "but for" causes of subsequent accidents, a judge or jury would have to consider both these standards. See Drake, 797 F.2d at 610 n.12 (quoting Note, supra note 7 at 977, n.144).

10. In investigating Commission delays in setting consumer product safety standards, one commentator found that under the pre-1981 procedures an average of 1042 days elapsed between the publication of a Notice of Proceeding and the issuance of a final rule. Schwartz, supra note 9 at 62-63. The 1981 amendments, Pub. L. No. 97-35, Title XII, §1202(b), 95 Stat. 703, 703-04 (1981) (codified at 15 U.S.C. §2056(b) (1982)), made it more difficult to issue a formal standard, adding steps that "seem well designed to discourage the Commission from developing mandatory standards." Schwartz, supra note 9 at 72. Banning a product involves the same procedures as issuing a standard, 15 U.S.C. §2057 (1982), although the recall procedure is somewhat more streamlined, 15 U.S.C. §2064 (1982). See generally Schwartz, supra note 9 at 68-71. To determine whether an injury occurred "by reason of" a reporting violation, it would be necessary to divine which of these options the Commission might have chosen and how long the option might have taken to implement in the particular case.

Speculation about the effects of a report would not end with predictions concerning the Commission's reaction. Further guesswork would be required as to the timing and result of judicial review. See, e.g., Aqua Slide 'N' Dive Corp. v. CPSC, 569 F.2d 831 (5th Cir. 1978) (setting aside Commission's safety standard for pool slides).

"by reason of" requirement of section 23(a). The theory under which the plaintiff's injury would be attributed to these defendants would be identical in all essential features to the theory asserted against the companies that manufactured or distributed the components that were actually incorporated in the pool in which Zepik was injured. Once liability to accident victims for reporting violations is established, nothing in section 23(a) suggests any basis for limiting liability to manufacturers, distributors or retailers of the articles actually involved in accidents.

Concededly, this relaxation of traditional notions of causation would not be entirely without precedent. A number of mostly recent products liability decisions have relaxed the traditional requirement that the plaintiff show by a preponderance of the evidence that the defendant manufactured the actual instrumentality of the plaintiff's injury. In some jurisdictions, plaintiffs who cannot tie their injuries to particular manufacturers have been permitted to sue a number of manufacturers of the same type of product under various formulations of the doctrine of enterprise liability. See, e.g., Hall v. E.I. Du Pont de Nemours & Co., 345 F. Supp. 353 (E.D.N.Y. 1972) (blasting cap manufacturers may be jointly liable to plaintiffs who cannot prove which manufacturer produced particular devices that caused their injuries where industry-wide safety standards indicate joint control over risk); Sindell v. Abbott Laboratories, 26 Cal. 3d 588, 163 Cal. Rptr. 132, 607 P.2d 924 (DES manufacturers subject to liability based on market share despite finding that they did not act in concert to impose risk), *cert. denied,* 449 U.S. 912, 101 S. Ct. 285, 66 L. Ed. 2d 140 (1980). But see, e.g., Thimpson v. Johns-Manville Sales Corp., 714 F.2d 581, 583 (5th Cir. 1983) (declining to effect "radical . . . expansion" of Louisiana tort liability by applying enterprise or market share theories), *cert. denied,* 465 U.S. 1102 (1984); Zafft v. Eli Lilly & Co., 676 S.W.2d 241 (Mo.1984) (DES plaintiff cannot, absent state legislation codifying relaxation of traditional causation requirement, recover on marker share of enterprise liability theories). However, all of the cases that have dispensed with the requirement that a defendant manufacturer be shown to have made the instrument of the plaintiff's injury were brought by plaintiffs unable to identify the manufacturer of the particular article or articles involved. See, e.g., *Hall,* 345 F. Supp. at 379-80; *Sindell,* 26 Cal. 3d at 610-11, 163 Cal. Rptr. at 144, 607 P.2d at 936.[11] Interpreting section 23(a) to encompass reporting violations

---

11. See generally Annotation, "Concert of Activity," "Alternative Liability," "Enterprise Liability," or Similar Theory as Basis for Imposing Liability upon One or More Manufacturers of Defective Uniform Product, in Absence of Identification of Manufacturer of Precise Unit or Batch Causing Injury, 22 A.L.R.4th 183 (1983 & Supp. 1987).

would create CPSA liability for manufacturers, distributors and retailers that could not be sued under the most expansive of state enterprise liability doctrines. If Congress had intended to bring about such a radical expansion of products liability—and of the federal courts' subject matter jurisdiction over these claims—it certainly could have done so. However, we see no indication in the legislative history or the structure of the CPSA that section 23(a)'s "by reason of" language was intended to be construed so broadly as to accomplish this result.[12]

It might be argued that Congress intended for the courts to construe "by reason of" broadly in order to ensure that reporting requirements were taken seriously. The Commission has come to rely heavily on reports from manufacturers and sellers and views underreporting as a serious problem. See *Drake*, 797 F.2d at 611. However, the Act authorizes civil fines of up to $2,000 for each reporting violation and criminal penalties of up to $50,000 and one year in prison if knowing violations continue once a notice of noncompliance has been issued. 15 U.S.C. §§2068-2070 (1982). Whatever added incentive to report might be gained by interpreting the phrase "by reason of" to permit private suits against violators of reporting requirements must be set against the consequences of this construction: a sharp departure from traditional standards of causation in tort and the expansion of federal subject matter jurisdiction to encompass a broad class of cases heretofore confined to state court except where the requirements of diversity jurisdiction are met. We are unwilling to adopt a reading of the phrase "by reason of" that would entail these consequences without solid support for this outcome in the legislative history or structure of the CPSA.

We therefore affirm the district court's orders dismissing the CPSA count against Loren's and granting summary judgment on this count to Frost, Pleasure and Polynesian. See Pfeil v. Rogers, 757 F.2d 850, 866 (7th

---

12. To the extent that Congress considered the effect of section 23(a) on the caseload of the federal courts, the prevailing concern appears to have been to restrain the increase. The bill reported by the House Commerce Committee, unlike the Senate bill, did not impose a threshold requirement on the amount in controversy in section 23(a) suits. An amendment to insert the Senate bill's $10,000 minimum into the House bill was enacted during the House debate. 118 Cong. Rec. 31,402-03 (1972), *reprinted in* Legislative History App. at 281-83. The amendment carried despite the argument of Representative Eckhardt that the increase in the federal courts' caseload was justified by the deterrent effect of a federal cause of action without a jurisdictional minimum. Even Representative Eckhardt, the House's strongest defender of an expansive private cause of action, does not appear to have contemplated that reporting violations would give rise to a private cause of action. See id. at 31,304, *reprinted in* Legislative History App. at 264 (arguing that section 23(a) would not cause hardship to retailers because injury must occur "by reason of a failure of a consumer product to comply with an applicable standard").

Cir. 1985) (summary judgment may be affirmed on grounds not relied upon by the district court), *cert. denied*, 475 U.S. 1107, 106 S. Ct. 1513, 89 L. Ed. 2d 912 (1986). . . .

NOTE

For a commentary on this case, see 75 Iowa L. Rev. 567 (1990). It is certainly beyond question that the federal government can sue and recover substantial penalties for failure to report dangerous products; see United States v. Mirama Enter., Inc., 387 F.3d 983 (9th Cir. 2004) (30,000 exploding juicers not reported—fine of $300,000).

PART 3
Credit

The word "credit" is from the Latin "credere" (to believe).

It is the rare consumer in this day and age who pays cash for all purchases. Instead, most of us make use of the widespread credit options available to consumers: debit and credit cards, credit purchase contracts, and outright loans. Much can go awry here, however. The records can become muddled so that the consumer is wrongly denied credit, discrimination can occur that prevents creditworthy individuals from qualifying for loans, the cost of credit can be hidden in outrageous ways, and creditors have centuries of experience in manipulating matters so that the credit-desiring consumer gets taken. This Part explores the ins and outs of credit transactions and the remedies the law grants to wronged consumers.

CHAPTER 5

Payment and Consumers

I. PROMISSORY NOTES

Under basic negotiable instruments law, a negotiable instrument, such as a promissory note, that gets into the hands of an innocent purchaser (called a *holder in due course*—see U.C.C. §3-302) can be enforced by such a purchaser *even though there are valid defenses*, such as fraud, that the maker could have asserted against the original payee to whom the maker gave the note, U.C.C. §§3-305, 3-306. The policy here is to promote the free alienability of such paper. Purchasers of the paper who qualify as holders in due course live in a less stressful commercial world.

Such a doctrine is fine as long as the parties involved are all merchants or experienced in the complexities of finance; whenever the maker of the promissory note is a consumer, however, the doctrine works much mischief.

PROBLEM 35

When Bill Gilbert needed a new car, he bought one on credit from Carte Car Company (CCC), signing a promissory note payable to the order of CCC and promising to make payments monthly over a four-year period. CCC sold ("discounted") the promissory note to the Carte Finance Company (CFC), a company with which it did a great deal of business. Two months later, due to an inherent defect, the car blew up, and Gilbert was injured. He refused to make further payments on the promissory note, and CFC sued him, contending that it was a holder in due course of the note and, as such, took free of his defense of breach of warranty. Who prevails here? See U.C.C. §§3-305(b) and 3-306.

Were the cited UCC sections all, CFC likely would have prevailed. But both the courts and the legislatures recognized the injustice of applying the holder in due course doctrine in a consumer setting, and they took action. The courts, faced with actual cases similar to the above, would struggle to find that the promissory note was not technically a "negotiable" instrument, and thus the holder in due course rules would not protect the transferee of the paper, see, e.g., Geiger Fin. Co. v. Graham, 123 Ga. App. 771, 182 S.E.2d 521 (1971). Or, as another favorite method of finding for the consumer, the courts would deny holder in due course status to finance companies that were "closely connected" with the original seller/payee. Thus, if the CCC and the CFC were just corporate shells for the same entity, or if the two did a great deal of business together so that the finance company was much involved in the original transaction, the courts would deny Article 3 protection to CFC. See, e.g., Jones v. Approved Bancredit Corp., 256 A.2d 739 (Del. 1969). Unhappy, the finance companies fought back with a "waiver of defenses" clause.

PROBLEM 36

When Bill Gilbert went into the Carte Car Company, the dealership did not make him sign a promissory note at all. Instead he simply signed a contract promising to make monthly payments for a four-year period. The contract contained this clause:

> Buyer acknowledges that this contract will be assigned to a finance company. The buyer hereby promises that any problems with the vehicle will be adjusted by negotiations with the seller of the vehicle, and will in no way affect the obligation of the buyer to make the agreed payments to the finance company. As against the finance company, buyer hereby waives any and all defenses buyer may have against the car company, and promises not to assert such defenses against the finance company.

Two months later, the car blew up, and Gilbert stopped making payments to the finance company, which sued. When Gilbert tries to respond by showing the defects in the car, the finance company pointed to the above "waiver of defenses" clause. Must Gilbert pay up?

The relevant UCC section is §9-206, which generally validates such clauses where the obligor is not a consumer. In consumer matters, §9-206 defers to any court decisions or legislation that may reach a different result. In some jurisdictions, "waiver of defenses" clauses in consumer contracts are declared illegal as a matter of public policy. See, e.g., Unico v. Owen, 50 N.J. 101, 232 A.2d 405 (1967). Some state legislatures have enacted statutes that expressly forbid such clauses in consumer sales. See, e.g., Ohio Rev. Code §1317.14.

QUOTES FOR THE ATTORNEY'S ARSENAL: "THE STANDARDS APPLICABLE TO CONSUMERS"

The attempt . . . to project the law merchant, designed and intended for dealing between merchants, into the field of what may be termed "household" law, has failed, as it was bound to fail, to meet the prevailing sense of justice.

Buffalo Indus. Bank v. DeMarzio, 162 Misc. 742, 743-744, 296 N.Y.S. 783, 785 (City Ct. 1937).

Much of this has been made moot by the promulgation of an FTC Regulation on point: the FTC Holder in Due Course Regulation, 16 C.F.R. §433 (effective November 14, 1977). Read it and use it to address the following Problem.

PROBLEM 37

Bill Gilbert bought a new car from Carte Car Company (CCC), which had him sign a promissory note, a consumer sales contract, and a number of other papers.

a. Advise CCC as its attorney. Does the FTC HIDC Regulation apply to this transaction? If so, what must the car dealership do to comply?

b. Instead of the above, CCC told Bill Gilbert that it did not finance car purchases, but that he instead must get a loan from a finance company. CCC recommended Carte Finance Company (CFC), with whom it did a lot of business. CFC's offices, as it happened, were right next door to the CCC lot.[1] Bill went over to CFC and signed a promissory note in return for the loan, which CFC then made to CCC. As attorney for CFC you must decide whether CFC need do anything to comply with the FTC Regulation.

c. As attorney for either entity, advise both clients what can happen to them if they ignore the FTC requirements and fail to include the mandatory legends.

---

1. When the retailer walks the consumer over to the finance company, this is sometimes known in the trade as "body-dragging."

d. If the mandatory legend is put on the contract and the promissory note that Bill Gilbert signs, does he have an affirmative cause of action against the finance company to recover damages caused him by the car dealership's breach of warranty? Compare Eachen v. Scott Hous. Sys., Inc., 630 F. Supp. 162 (M.D. Ala. 1986), with Cuchine v. H. O. Bell, Inc., 682 P.2d 723 (Mont. 1984).

If the required FTC legend is missing, the 1999 version of Article 9 of the Uniform Commercial Code puts it into effect anyway. Section 9-403:

(d) In a consumer transaction, if a record evidences the account debtor's obligation, law other than this article requires that the record provide a statement to the effect that the rights of an assignee are subject to claims or defenses that the account debtor could assert against the original obligee, and the record does not provide such a statement:

(1) the record has the same effect as if the record provided such a statement; and

(2) the account debtor may assert against an assignee those claims and defenses that would have been available if the record provided such a statement.

FORD MOTOR CREDIT CO. v. MORGAN[2]
Supreme Judicial Court of Massachusetts, 1989
404 Mass. 537, 536 N.E.2d 587, 8 U.C.C. Rep. Serv. 2d 524

O'CONNOR, J.

The defendants, Rose and William Morgan, appeal from a judgment denying them recovery on their counterclaims in an action brought by the plaintiff, Ford Motor Credit Company (Ford Credit), to recover amounts due on an automobile installment contract and to recover possession of the automobile covered thereby. We affirm the judgment.

The trial judge's findings of fact made in conjunction with Ford Credit's complaint and two counts of the counterclaim may be summarized as follows. On June 27, 1978, the Morgans purchased a new 1978 Mercury Zephyr automobile from Neponset Lincoln Mercury, Inc. (dealer). The Morgans had made several visits to the dealer, who assured them that the automobile was reliable and economical. In order to finance their purchase through Ford Credit, the Morgans signed a "Massachusetts Automobile Retail Installment Contract," a standard printed form contract prepared by

---

2. Footnotes in this case have been renumbered for clarity.

Ford Credit. Printed in capital letters at the bottom of the first page of the form was the following statement: "NOTICE[:] ANY HOLDER OF THIS CONSUMER CREDIT CONTRACT IS SUBJECT TO ALL CLAIMS AND DEFENSES WHICH THE DEBTOR COULD ASSERT AGAINST THE SELLER OF GOODS OR SERVICES OBTAINED PURSUANT HERETO OR WITH THE PROCEEDS HEREOF. RECOVERY HEREUNDER BY THE DEBTOR SHALL NOT EXCEED AMOUNTS PAID BY THE DEBTOR HEREUNDER." Section 19 of the contract requires purchasers to procure and maintain insurance on the vehicle at their own expense, "for so long as any amount remains unpaid" under the contract.

Ford Credit financed the automobile for $3,833. Payment was to be in thirty-six consecutive monthly installments of $137.13 each. On July 11, 1978, a certificate of title was issued to Rose Morgan listing Ford Credit as first lienholder. The Morgans drove the automobile for approximately eighteen months, for a distance of over 11,500 miles. During this time, they experienced several problems with the automobile, such as water leaking into the trunk, a faulty head gasket, rust, hood misalignment, and loss of shine. Their greatest complaint was that, when left unattended, the transmission would shift from "park" to "reverse," and would have to be shifted back to "park" before the vehicle could be started.

During the fall of 1979, the Morgans began having financial difficulty, and missed their monthly automobile payments for November and December. Before January 1, 1980, William Morgan rented a garage in which he concealed the automobile. He removed the battery and removed or deflated the tires. He also failed to renew his insurance for 1980. In January, Ford Credit notified the Morgans that they were in default on the credit contract and requested that the default be cured by February 6, 1980. The Morgans made no further payments. To that time, they had made fifteen of their monthly payments totalling $2,056.95. The Morgans continued to hide their automobile for approximately two months after the court issued a surrender order. As a result, William Morgan received what the trial judge termed a "well earned" contempt judgment, which Morgan subsequently purged by surrendering the vehicle. The court later authorized Ford Credit to sell the vehicle. William Morgan successfully moved to delay the sale of the vehicle pending inspection, examination, and testing. By the time it was inspected, it had been extensively vandalized and was a total loss. The loss was not recoverable due to the Morgans' failure to obtain insurance for 1980.

Ford Credit sought recovery of $2,628.87 plus costs and attorney's fees. The Morgans counterclaimed in three counts, each of which is predicated on the theory, which we reject, that as assignee of the contract, Ford Credit stands fully in the same position as the assignor-dealer, and thus, any wrongful acts of the dealer are fully attributable to, and may provide the basis of affirmative recovery from, Ford Credit. The first count alleged the dealer's fraud and deceit in making false representations to the Morgans on which they relied. The second count alleged a G.L. c.93A, §2 (1986 ed.), violation for unfair and deceptive practices. The third count was for the dealer's breach of express and implied warranties of merchantability and fitness for a particular purpose. The Morgans sought $7,061.68 in damages on each of the counts, and damages treble that amount under counts I and II.

Count I, except for damages, was submitted to a jury on special questions. The jury found that the dealer knowingly made false representations to the Morgans, on which the Morgans relied. Thereafter, the judge heard the complaint and counts II and III of the counterclaim without jury. The judge determined that the jury's special verdict provided the Morgans with a valid defense against Ford Credit's collection claim, but that the Morgans were not entitled to damages on any count of their counterclaim. The judge entered judgment for the Morgans on Ford Credit's complaint, and for Ford Credit on each of the counterclaims. The Morgans appealed to the Appeals Court, claiming that the judge erred in allowing their counterclaims to be used only defensively to extinguish Ford Credit's claim for the balance due on the credit contract. They also contend that the jury should have been permitted to assess damages as to counts I and III. We transferred the case to this court on our own initiative.

The Morgans' first contention is that the explicit language of the notice provision contained in the contract, which subjects holders to all "claims and defenses which the debtor could assert against the seller" permits them to recover affirmatively from Ford Credit for the dealer's wrongdoing. As the Morgans acknowledge, that notice provision is mandated by a Federal Trade Commission (FTC) rule which provides that it is an unfair or deceptive act or practice to take or receive a consumer credit contract which fails to include that provision. 16 C.F.R. §433.2 (1978). Therefore, we look to the FTC's purpose in enacting the rule as a guide to our interpretation of the contract provision.

The rule was designed to preserve the consumer's claims and defenses by cutting off the creditor's rights as a holder in due course.[3] Federal Trade

---

3. The FTC rule operates as follows. The required language that the assignee takes the contract "subject to" the consumer's claims and defenses against the seller places an express condition on the consumer's promise to pay a sum certain, thus destroying the negotiability precedent to an assignee's having holder in due course status. J. J. White & R. S. Summers, Uniform Commercial Code §14-8, at 722 (3d ed. 1988). *Thomas,* supra at 622. "It is as though the note said the following: 'The promise to pay embodied by this note is conditioned upon the absence of any valid defense in the hands of the maker.'" White & Summers, supra at 723. The

Commission, Preservation of Consumers' Claims and Defenses, Final Regulation, Proposed Amendment and Statement of Basis and Purpose, 40 Fed. Reg. 53505, 53524 (Nov. 18, 1975) (to be codified at 16 C.F.R. §433). See Thomas v. Ford Motor Credit Co., 48 Md. App. 617, 622 (1981). Under the holder in due course principle, which would apply were it not for the contract provision mandated by the FTC rule, the creditor could "assert his right to be paid by the consumer despite misrepresentation, breach of warranty or contract, or even fraud on the part of the seller, and despite the fact that the consumer's debt was generated by the sale." 40 Fed. Reg. at 53507. Thus, "[being] prevented from asserting the seller's breach of warranty or failure to perform against the assignee of the consumer's instrument, the consumer [would lose] his most effective weapon—nonpayment." Id. at 53509. Eliminating holder in due course status prevents the assignee from demanding further payment when there has been assignor wrongdoing, and rearms the consumer with the "weapon" of nonpayment.[4]

The FTC anticipated that in addition to nonpayment, affirmative recovery, that is, a judgment for damages against the assignee-creditor, would be available in limited circumstances. Thus, in its statement of policy and purpose, the FTC spelled out the avenues of relief under the rule as follows: "[A] consumer can (1) defend a creditor suit for payment of an obligation by raising a valid claim against a seller as a set-off, and (2) maintain an affirmative action against a creditor who has received payments for a return of monies paid on account." 40 Fed. Reg. at 53524. However, the FTC made clear that "[t]he latter alternative will only be available where a seller's breach is so substantial that a court is persuaded that rescission and restitution are justified. The most typical example of such a case would involve nondelivery, where delivery was scheduled after the date payments to a creditor commenced." Id. The FTC re-emphasized this point in stating, "[c]onsumers will not be in a position to obtain an affirmative recovery from a creditor, unless they have actually commenced payments and received little or nothing

---

language operates not due to any statute or regulation, but to the effect the notice has when it becomes part of the contract. *Thomas*, supra at 622. H. J. Alperin & R. F. Chase, Consumer Rights and Remedies 280 (1979 & Supp. 1988).

4. Merely raising a valid claim does not fully insulate the consumer from payments due if the value of the claim is less than payments outstanding. "Laymen, particularly automobile dealers, are wont to complain that under the rule any microscopic defect in the goods will give the buyer a right to quit paying, return the goods, and demand his money back. This is not an accurate statement of the law. . . . [M]ost defects in the underlying transaction do not give the buyer the right to stop paying entirely." White & Summers, supra at 729-730. However, in the present case, Ford Credit does not contest the judge's determination that the Morgans may raise their valid claim for fraud and deceit against the dealer as a complete defense to further payment.

of value from the seller. In a case of non-delivery, total failure of performance, or the like, we believe the consumer is entitled to a refund of monies paid on account." Id. at 53527. Finally, the FTC anticipated that the rule would enable the courts to weigh the equities in the underlying sale, and "remain the final arbiters of equities between a seller and a consumer." Id. at 53524. Thus, the function of the rule is to allow consumers to stop payments, and, in limited circumstances, not present here, where equity requires, to provide for a return of monies paid. The FTC did not intend that the rule would, as a matter of course, entitle a consumer to a full refund of monies paid on account.[5] It follows, of course, that there is no merit to the Morgans' assertions that the contractual language allows them affirmative recovery even beyond the amount they paid in. To expose a creditor to further affirmative liability would not only contravene the intention of the FTC, but would "place the creditor in the position of an absolute insurer or guarantor of the seller's performance." Home Sav. Ass'n v. Guerra, 733 S.W.2d 134, 136 (Tex. 1987). Michelin Tires (Canada) Ltd. v. First Natl. Bank, 666 F.2d 673, 679-680 (1st Cir. 1981). This we decline to do.

The Morgans do not quarrel with the judge's conclusion that, in the circumstances, they had no right to rescind the sale. Further, they do not argue that they received little or nothing of value from the dealer. We do not imply that such an argument would have been appropriate. However, absent such a showing, and absent any support for the argument that the language in the contract should receive any interpretation other than the one the FTC intended it to have, the Morgans' contention that the language mandated by 16 C.F.R. §433.2, affords them a right to affirmative recovery is without merit.[6]

---

5. The cases addressing affirmative recovery go no further than to hold that affirmative recovery is available up to the amounts paid in by the debtor. None has addressed the question whether a showing of rescission and restitution is a necessary precedent to such recovery. In each of these cases, it is arguable that the goods received were valueless. Home Sav. Ass'n v. Guerra, 733 S.W.2d 134 (Tex. 1987) (rock siding installed crumbled). Thomas v. Ford Motor Credit Co., 48 Md. App. 617 (1981) (car argued to be "valueless"). Hempstead Bank v. Babcock, 115 Misc. 2d 97 (N.Y. Sup. Ct. 1982) (solar heating system "never worked"). Tinker v. DeMaria Porsche Audi, Inc., 459 So. 2d 487 (Fla. App. 1984) (car "totally inoperable").

6. We do not hold that a consumer may only assert his rights defensively in response to a claim initiated by an assignee for balance due on the contract. This would be in clear contravention of the FTC's intention. 40 Fed. Reg. at 53526. Eachen v. Scott Hous. Sys., Inc., 630 F. Supp. 162, 164-165 (M.D. Ala. 1986). "Under such circumstances the financer may elect not to sue, in the hopes that the threat of an unfavorable credit report may move the consumer to pay." 40 Fed. Reg. at 53527. Therefore, it is clear that the account debtor may initiate suit to enforce his right, however limited it may be, to discontinue credit payments. See *Eachen*, supra at 164-165; Tinker v. DeMaria Porche Audi, Inc., supra at 492-493.

The Morgans also argue that Article 9 of the Uniform Commercial Code, G.L. c.106, §9-318(1) [now §9-404—ED.] (1986 ed.), lends statutory support to their claim for affirmative recovery. That section provides: "Unless an account debtor has made an enforceable agreement not to assert defenses or claims arising out of a sale as provided in section 9-206 the rights of an assignee are subject to (a) all the terms of the contract between the account debtor and assignor and any defense or claim arising therefrom; and (b) any other defense or claim of the account debtor against the assignor which accrues before the account debtor receives notification of the assignment." This court has never addressed the question whether the statute enables a consumer to recover affirmatively against an assignee-creditor.

There is nothing in §9-318 which suggests that such affirmative recovery is appropriate. As the First Circuit noted in *Michelin Tires (Canada) Ltd.*, supra at 677, "[t]he key statutory language is ambiguous. That 'the rights of an assignee are *subject to* . . . (a) all the terms of the contract' connotes only that the assignee's rights to recover are limited by the obligator's rights to assert contractual defenses as a set-off, implying that affirmative recovery against the assignee was not intended. . . . The words 'subject to,' used in their ordinary sense, mean 'subordinate to,' 'subservient to,' or 'limited by.' There is nothing in the use of the words 'subject to,' in their ordinary sense, which would even hint at the creation of affirmative rights." (Citations omitted.) While the First Circuit recognized that the use of the word "claim" appears to contemplate affirmative recovery, the court noted that the title of §9-318, "Defenses Against Assignee," and the Official Comment to this provision of the Uniform Commercial Code argue otherwise. Id. at 677-678. The Morgans attempt to distinguish *Michelin* on the ground that *Michelin* involved a suit against a creditor-bank which was a nonparticipating assignee, whereas here, as the judge found, the creditor knowingly participated in or was directly connected with the consumer sale. However, beyond making this factual distinction, the Morgans do not argue why the First Circuit's interpretation of the statute in *Michelin* should not extend to cases involving a participatory assignee, and no such reason is otherwise apparent. Moreover, G.L. c.255, 12F, suggests otherwise. That statute applies where the proceeds of a loan are used for a consumer purchase, and the creditor and seller are closely related. General Laws c.255, 12F, provides only that the creditor is "subject to all of the defenses of the borrower" arising from the sale or lease. Thus, to read §9-318 to allow affirmative recovery where a creditor and seller are closely connected would contradict the Legislature's later enactment, c.255, 12F.

The Morgans argue that in Graves Equip., Inc. v. M. DeMatteo Constr. Co., 397 Mass. 110 (1986), we "implicitly" recognized an account debtor's right to assert affirmative claims under §9-318. However, the decision in

Graves is inapposite here. In *Graves*, a contractor withheld retainages for materials delivered by a supplier. Id. at 111. The supplier assigned the right to the retainages, and subsequently breached the original contract. Id. The contractor claimed that it was entitled to offset the retainages as a consequence of the supplier's failure to perform despite the fact that the right to the retainages had been assigned. Id. We held that §9-318 "incorporates the common law rule that an assignee of contract rights stands in the shoes of the assignor and has no greater rights against the debtor than the assignor had." Id. at 112. Thus, under *Graves*, if the assignor would not be entitled to have collected retainages withheld due to its breach of contract, the assignee would not be so entitled. The common law principle that the assignee stands in the assignor's shoes means only that the debtor can raise the same defenses against the assignee as he could have raised against the assignor. See Quincy Trust Co. v. Pembroke, 346 Mass. 730, 732 (1964). Cf. Harrison Mfg. Co. v. Philip Rothman & Son, Inc., 336 Mass. 625, 628 (1958); Lewis v. Club Realty Co., 264 Mass. 588, 591 (1928). It has never been interpreted to mean that the assignee will be liable for all the assignor's wrongs.

The Morgans also argue that "to the extent that the appellee stands in the dealer's shoes," treble damages under G.L. c.93A should be assessed against the assignee. While the Morgans may well have a valid c. 93A claim against the dealer, we reject the claim that such liability should be extended to the dealer's assignee, in light of our determination that neither the contract provision required by the FTC rule nor G.L. c.106, §9-318, puts the assignee in the shoes of the assignor for purposes of being affirmatively liable for claims which could be brought against the assignor.

We conclude that in the circumstances of this case, the judge was correct in ruling that the Morgans were not entitled to affirmative recovery against Ford Credit. Thus, error, if any, that may have occurred in reference to counts II and III of the counterclaim was harmless. The Morgans were entitled to no more than a judgment in their favor on Ford Credit's original claim as ordered by the judge. Judgment affirmed.

While there are many cases agreeing with this decision, see Comer v. Person Auto Sales, Inc., 368 F. Supp. 2d 478 (M.D.N.C. 2005) (discussing cases), a number of courts addressing the issue have found that the clear language of the FTC legend creates an affirmative cause of action against the assignee without the necessity of proving a substantial ground for rescission of the underlying contract. See Beemus v. Interstate Natl. Dealer Serv., Inc., 823 A.2d 979 (Pa. Super. 2003) (discussing cases).

II. CREDIT CARDS

In the United States, there were 5 billion credit card solicitations mailed in 2004 alone—almost 17 for every American between the ages of 16 and 64 (181 million Americans have general usage credit cards in their pockets). The average person has a frightening number of credit cards at his or her disposal (an average of eight cards per household), and they cause no end of trouble.

A. Common Law

Credit card law is primarily statutory, coming from the Truth in Lending Act (and its concomitant Regulation Z). Some of the law in this area, however, arises purely as a matter of common law, with the following case being typical.

STIEGER v. CHEVY CHASE SAV. BANK, F.S.B.
District of Columbia, Court of Appeals, 1995
666 A.2d 479

Pryor, Senior Judge.

For the first time we are asked to determine whether a credit cardholder who permits use of the card by another for a specific purpose is liable for other uses not specifically authorized. The precise issue is whether, in such circumstances, the card user had "apparent authority" to use the card in the context of the provisions of the Truth-in-Lending Act, 15 U.S.C.A. §§1601 et seq. (1988). We agree with the Superior Court that for thirteen of the fifteen disputed charges the matching of the signature, combined with the cardholder's voluntary relinquishment of the card for a third party's use, constitutes such "apparent authority" under the Act, thereby making appellant liable for the full amount of the thirteen charges. We, therefore, affirm the decision of the Superior Court.

I.

On November 10, 1992, appellant brought suit against Chevy Chase Bank, F.S.B. ("Chevy Chase") claiming he should not be held liable for certain charges credited to his Chevy Chase Visa card. Appellant voluntarily gave his credit card to a Ms. Garrett for the limited purpose of renting a car and for hotel lodging during a business trip. Appellant contacted both the car rental agency and the hotel to determine what type of authorization would be needed for Ms. Garrett to use his Visa card. Both companies informed him that he must write a letter authorizing the charges. Appellant asserts that he wrote both companies, but was unable to produce a copy of the letter to the hotel, which he contends limited his liability to $350.00.

Shortly after the conclusion of Ms. Garrett's business trip, appellant learned that she had made several other charges he had not specifically authorized. His signature apparently had worn off the back of his credit card, and Ms. Garrett signed it as "P. Stieger" rather than Paul Stieger. On thirteen of the fifteen charges in dispute, Ms. Garrett had signed the charge slip "P. Stieger," and on the other two she signed her own name. Appellant has obtained a judgment against Ms. Garrett for $3200.00, but only $750.00 has been collected, and Ms. Garrett can no longer be located. Therefore, this action was brought to contest Chevy Chase's refusal to dismiss the charges as unauthorized.

Commissioner Diaz ruled in favor of Chevy Chase on all fifteen charges. Appellant appealed to the Superior Court asserting that the charges were unauthorized under the Truth-In-Lending Act. After review of the case, a judge of the Superior Court held that the Commissioner "had a factual and legal basis upon which she could properly decide that the voluntary relinquishment of the cardholder's credit card for one purpose gives the bearer apparent authority to make additional charges." (Citing Martin v. American Express, Inc., 361 So. 2d 597, 599-600 (Ala. Civ. App. 1978)).

The Superior Court judge also considered the Commissioner's reasonableness analysis. The Superior Court found that the merchants acted reasonably in accepting appellant's credit card in thirteen of the fifteen charges where the name signed ("P. Stieger") matched the signature on the card. However, the court reversed the two charges where Ms. Garrett had signed her own name. Appellant filed an application for allowance of appeal, and on April 29, 1994 we granted the application.

II.

In a broad sense, the resolution of this matter involves an economic consideration of whether the cardholder, card issuer, or merchant should bear the financial responsibility in the circumstances presented. The Truth-In-Lending Act was enacted "in large measure to protect credit cardholders from unauthorized use perpetrated by those able to obtain possession of a card from its original owner." Towers World Airways Inc. v. PHH Aviation Systems, Inc., 933 F.2d 174, 176 (2nd Cir.), *cert. denied,* 502 U.S. 823, 112 S. Ct. 87, 116 L. Ed. 2d 59 (1991). The Act specifically limits liability for the cardholder to a maximum of $50 for charges made by third parties that are "unauthorized." 15 U.S.C.A. §1643(a). However, the Act does not limit liability for the cardholder for third party charges made with "actual, implied or apparent authority." 15 U.S.C.A. §1602(o).

The essential question on appeal is whether the disputed charges were incurred by an "unauthorized user" under the Act. The statute specifically incorporates agency concepts by defining "unauthorized use" as "a use of a credit card by a person other than the cardholder who does not have actual, implied, or *apparent* authority for such use and from which the cardholder receives no benefit." 15 U.S.C.A. §1602(o) (emphasis added); see also 12 C.F.R. §226.12(b)(1) n. 22 (stating same). Thus, our inquiry focuses on whether the relinquishment of a credit card to another for a limited purpose, which is then expanded by the user to make additional charges not authorized by the cardholder, is an "unauthorized" use under 15 U.S.C.A. §1602(o), thereby limiting cardholder liability. Since actual or implied authority are [sic] not alleged in this case, the narrower issue is whether Ms. Garrett had apparent authority to use the card.

Our cases reveal that "[a]pparent authority arises when a principal places an agent 'in a position which causes a third person to reasonably believe the principal had consented to the exercise of authority the agent purports to hold. This falls short of an overt, affirmative representation by a principal. . . . '" Insurance Management of Washington, Inc. v. Eno & Howard Plumbing Corp., 348 A.2d 310, 312 (D.C. 1975) (quoting Drazin v. Jack Pry, Inc., 154 A.2d 553, 554 (D.C. 1959)); see also Feltman v. Sarbov, 366 A.2d 137, 139 (D.C. 1976) (stating same). Specifically, in this jurisdiction "apparent authority of an agent arises when the principal places the agent in such a position as to *mislead* third persons into believing that the agent is clothed with authority which in fact he does not possess." Jack Pry, Inc. v. Harry Drazin, 173 A.2d 222, 223 (D.C. 1961) (footnote omitted) (emphasis added).

"Though a cardholder's relinquishment of possession may create in another the appearance of authority to use the card, the statute clearly precludes a finding of apparent authority where the transfer of the card was without the cardholder's consent as in cases involving theft, loss, or fraud." *Towers*, supra, 933 F.2d at 177. As one court has stated: Where a credit cardholder, who was under no compulsion by fraud, duress, or otherwise, voluntarily permits the use of his or her credit card by another person, the cardholder has authorized the use of that card and is thereby responsible for any charges as a result of that use, even if he or she requested that the other person not charge over a certain amount or make charges on it for specified purposes. The user has apparent authority to use the card even after actual authority ceases; provided, however, that the cardholder is not liable for use of the card after the issuer has been notified that actual authority for others to use the card no longer exists. Standard Oil Co. v. Steele, 22 Ohio Misc. 2d 27, 489 N.E.2d 842, 844 (Ohio Mun. Ct. 1985).

Nearly every jurisdiction that has addressed a factual situation "where a cardholder voluntarily and knowingly allows another to use his card and that person subsequently misuses the card," *Martin*, supra, 361 So. 2d at 601, has determined that the agent had apparent authority, and therefore was not an "unauthorized" user under the Act limiting liability for the cardholder. See *Towers*, supra (concluding that Towers was liable for charges because Towers' consent and other conduct revealed the pilot's unrestricted access to the PHH card); *Martin*, supra (holding cardholder responsible for charges of business associate despite oral limitation of $500.00); American Express Travel Related Serv. Co., Inc. v. Web, Inc., 261 Ga. 480, 405 S.E.2d 652 (1991) (concluding that company is responsible for employee's misuse of the credit card resulting in charges of $27,000.00); Oclander v. First Nat'l Bank of Louisville, 700 S.W.2d 804 (Ky. Ct. App. 1985) (holding wife responsible for estranged husband's almost $12,000.00 in charges when wife mistakenly advised the bank that she had both cards in possession and the bank removed the "block" from the account); Cities Serv. Co. v. Pailet, 452 So. 2d 319 (La. Ct. App. 1984) (concluding that defendant liable for employees charges outside the scope of the limited business trip); *Standard Oil*, supra (holding company responsible for employee's charges); Walker Bank & Trust Co. v. Jones, 672 P.2d 73 (Utah 1983) (concluding that spouse was responsible for husband's charges despite notifying bank of intention not to be responsible for husband's charges when husband still maintained apparent authority to use the cards because cards had not been returned to the bank or the account closed), *cert. denied*, 466 U.S. 937, 104 S. Ct. 1911, 80 L. Ed. 2d 460 (1984); Mastercard, Consumer Credit Div. of First Wisconsin Nat'l Bank of Milwaukee v. Town of Newport, 133 Wis. 2d 328, 396 N.W.2d 345 (Ct. App. 1986) (holding town responsible for town clerk's personal charges); cf. Michigan Nat'l Bank v. Olson, 44 Wash. App. 898, 723 P.2d 438 (1986) (reversing summary judgment where factual dispute over whether husband's girlfriend had been given card to use or husband had used the card himself).

However, when a voluntary relinquishment of the card to a third party who returns it after its use is then followed by an involuntary surrender, i.e. stolen, of the card to the same third party, there is an "unauthorized" use under the Act. Blaisdell Lumber Co., Inc. v. Horton, 242 N.J. Super. 98, 575 A.2d 1386 (App. Div. 1990) (holding that plaintiff had not established card user as agent with express, implied or apparent authority to use credit card when lover stole card and used it without authorization); Vaughn v. United

States Nat'l Bank of Oregon, 79 Or. App. 172, 718 P.2d 769 (1986) (affirming jury verdict finding cardholder not liable to bank when, although previously giving his credit card and personal identification number to a third party for specific purchases, subsequent automatic teller withdrawal was the result of the third party stealing the card). No liability can attach to the cardholder when the card was not voluntarily relinquished, but rather was stolen. Thomas v. Central Charge Serv., Inc., 212 A.2d 533 (D.C. 1965); cf. Fifth Third Bank/Visa v. Gilbert, 17 Ohio Misc. 2d 14, 478 N.E.2d 1324 (Ohio Mun. Ct. 1984) (concluding that bank did not prove that unemancipated daughter was given access to credit card to make charges and therefore father not liable). In addition, if the cardholder notifies the card issuer that the card is being used in an unauthorized manner, the cardholder will not be liable for any charges made by the third party after the notice. See *Cities Serv.*, supra, *Standard Oil*, supra, but see *American Express*, supra (concluding that Act does not limit liability where notice is given to the issuer of the credit card).

We agree with these general principles because the voluntary relinquishment of the credit card, as distinguished from the stolen card situation, can often "mislead third persons into believing the agent is clothed with authority which in fact he does not possess." *Drazin*, supra, 173 A.2d at 223.

III.

Appellant argues that he had the right to expect Ms. Garrett to use the credit card only for the charges he authorized, and that he cannot be held liable for his agent acting beyond the scope of her authority. Appellant also asserts that Ms. Garrett could not reasonably present herself as Paul Stieger, and that a merchant should be required to give greater scrutiny to the person using the card.

Turning to the specific facts in this case, appellant gave Ms. Garrett his credit card to use. As the Superior Court noted, thirteen of the charges had the same signature as appeared on the back of the card. Appellant placed Ms. Garrett, by voluntarily giving her the card, "in such a position as to mislead third persons into believing that the agent is clothed with authority which in fact [s]he does not possess." *Jack Pry, Inc.,* supra, 173 A.2d at 223. To a merchant, voluntary relinquishment combined with the matching of a signature is generally a reasonable indication of apparent authority to utilize the credit card. See 15 U.S.C.A. §1643(a)(1)(F); 12 C.F.R. §226.12(b)(2)(iii) & Supp. I at 341 (requiring the card issuer to provide a means of verifying the authority of the card bearer such as a signature, photograph, fingerprint or electronic or mechanical confirmation).

We agree with the Superior Court that the Commissioner "could properly conclude that the third-party merchants' actions were reasonable," and that the "voluntary relinquishment of the cardholder's credit card for one purpose gives the bearer apparent authority to make additional charges." However, we agree with the Superior Court that the same cannot be said of the two charges where Ms. Garrett signed her own name rather than "P. Stieger." It is an unreasonable extension of the apparent authority provided to Ms. Garrett for a merchant to accept charges, where the signatures do not match, without any additional factors to mislead the merchant into believing that the person presenting the card is the agent of the cardholder.

Appellant attempted to limit his authorization exclusively to the hotel and car rental company, and to a specific dollar amount for each. He testified he did this by writing letters to the two companies limiting the amount Ms. Garrett could charge. These letters to the two companies would limit his liability to the amounts stated in the letters if they were in fact received by the companies when the credit card was offered as payment. Mr. Stieger was able to produce only a copy of the letter to the car company. The charge to the car company did not exceed the limit in the letter. However, Mr. Stieger was unable to produce a copy of the letter to the hotel that he asserts limited the amount Ms. Garrett could charge to $350. By testifying that he voluntarily gave his credit card to Ms. Garrett and wrote the hotel to authorize the charge, the bank has met its burden of showing apparent authority. Since Mr. Stieger has not submitted a copy of the letter limiting his exposure to $350, we agree with the Superior Court that the Commissioner did not err in concluding that Mr. Stieger is liable for the full amount of the hotel charge in excess of the $350.

In sum, Mr. Stieger was in the best position to control the uses of his credit card by not relinquishing it to a third party he could not trust, by notifying the card issuer that his credit limit should be lowered to a specific dollar amount, thereby limiting his exposure, or by notifying the card issuer upon becoming aware of certain unapproved purchases that any further purchases are unauthorized. As one court has noted "[i]n four-party arrangements of this sort [cardholder, issuer, third party and merchant], it is totally unrealistic to burden the card issuer with the obligation to convey to numerous merchants whatever limitation the cardholder has placed on the card user's authority." *Towers*, supra, 933 F.2d at 179 (footnote omitted). The Truth-In-Lending Act, although generally designed to protect credit cardholders, specifically reveals a congressional preference that where apparent authority exists, under the circumstances, the cardholder should bear the financial responsibility. Mr. Stieger voluntarily relinquished his credit card to an unreliable person, and thereby put Ms. Garrett in a position to mislead merchants to believe that she possessed apparent authority to utilize the card. Under the circumstances, Mr. Stieger should bear the financial responsibility for the unauthorized charges made by Ms. Garrett as determined by the trial court.

Affirmed.

RUIZ, Associate Judge, dissenting:

* * *

Stieger took care to find out how to authorize Garrett to make limited use of his charge card and followed the instructions given to him. The majority focuses primarily on Stieger's action in turning over the card to Garrett as if, instead of having provided the card so that she could use it only for such limited purposes, he had given her a master key that, without more, can open all doors. In this respect, however, it is important to remember that a credit card is not a bearer instrument. Were it otherwise, the result might be different. . . .

As the majority recognizes, however, because a credit card is not a bearer device, a third party is not reasonable in treating it as such by failing to check the identity of the user against the identity of the cardholder by at least matching the signature of the bearer with the signature on the card. Ante at 485. This point was reinforced by the evidence adduced by Stieger regarding the industry practice of requiring written authorization of the cardholder for use by an agent. The majority holds Stieger liable for those charges where Garrett signed Stieger's name, but not those for which she signed her own name. According to the majority, the merchants reasonably relied on her signature for the former because it matched the signature on the back of the card. However, there is no dispute that Stieger did not permit Garrett to sign his card; her signing of the card was an act of forgery, compounded each of the thirteen times that she signed the charge slips as "P. Stieger." Under the common law, the principal's liability for acts within the apparent authority of an agent is based on the merchants' reasonable reliance on an action of the principal. That was not the case here, where the merchants relied on Garrett's forgeries. Thus, Garrett did not have apparent authority, within the meaning of 15 U.S.C. §1643(a), to bind Stieger for the thirteen charges that she unlawfully signed "P. Stieger." . . .

PROBLEM 38

LeNore Larceny was the secretary for Howard Teeth, CEO of Luddite Technologies. American Express had issued a corporate credit card to Luddite with Howard as the cardholder, and he used it for many years for business expenses. American Express then sent him an offer for a platinum version of the card, which LeNore, reading his mail, accepted on his behalf, telling American Express that it should issue *two* corporate cards, one for Howard and one in her name. American Express did this. She gave Howard his card, telling him it was an upgraded version of the one he had been using. Over the next two years, LeNore charged more than $300,000 on the card imprinted with her name, paying the bills from the corporate account, and, since she was the only one reviewing the credit card bills, not mentioning her activity to anyone. Eventually an error in the bookkeeping department accidentally triggered an investigation that uncovered all of this, and Luddite Technologies demanded that American Express refund the missing $300,000, contending that this was unauthorized use of the card, for which Luddite was at most liable for $50 under the rules of the Truth in Lending Act. American Express replied that LeNore's use was *authorized* in that she had at least *apparent* authority to make these charges. How should this come out? See DBI Architects, P.C. v. American Express Travel-Related Serv., 388 F.3d 886 (D.C. Cir. 2004). Do the credit card rules apply to cards issued to businesses? See Reg. Z §226.2(a)(8).

DISCOVER BANK v. OWENS
Cleveland Municipal Court, 2004
129 Ohio Misc. 2d 71, 822 N.E.2d 869

ROBERT J. TRIOZZI, Judge.

This case concerns a complaint for breach of contract. Plaintiff, Discover Bank, a lender and issuer of credit cards, alleges that defendant used a Discover card provided by plaintiff to purchase goods or services, or to receive cash advances, and has breached the parties' agreement by failing to make minimum monthly payments required under the cardholder agreement. Discover claims that there is now a $5,564.28 balance due on the account, and because of defendant's failure to make payments, plaintiff contends that it is entitled to judgment against defendant for the entire amount due.

Representing herself, defendant Ruth M. Owens, in her answer to plaintiff's complaint, revealed that she had joined the growing number of Americans who perhaps due to reasons of disability, declining real wages, job displacement, and/or rising health-care costs, had found themselves overwhelmed by accumulated credit-card debt. As a result, Owens became one of several thousand Clevelanders annually who, as the result of ballooning credit-card debt, become the subject of a credit-card collection case in this court. In her handwritten answer to the plaintiff's complaint, Owens wrote:

> I would like to inform you that I have no money to make payments. I am on Social Security Disability. After paying my monthly utilities, there is no money left except little food money and sometimes it isn't enough. If my situation was different I would pay. I just don't have it. I'm sorry.

In seeking to establish the validity of its case against Owens, plaintiff provided the court with a copy of a "Cardmember Agreement," which sets forth the agreement terms for the Discover card issued to Owens. The agreement outlines, among other things, the minimum monthly payment requirement, the periodic finance charges, and the various fees that ultimately were applicable in this case: the late fee and the over-limit fee. In its complaint, plaintiff further provided a copy of the Discover Card Account Summary, which showed an unpaid balance for Owens's account of $5,564.28.

At the pretrial conference held by the court, Owens asserted that she had made her best effort to pay but that her financial circumstances prevented her from making any further payments on her account. Although she did not dispute the documentation showing the unpaid balance, Owens indicated that she had in fact made many payments over several years and wanted to make sure that they were properly credited. The matter was set for trial so that plaintiff could present copies of defendant's payment history to prove that the $5,564.28 balance was accurate.

At trial, plaintiff did present the entire history of defendant's monthly Discover card statements from January 1996 through May 2003, when defendant's account was sent for collection.

That evidence revealed that in January 1996 Owens received her Discover card statement, which showed a new balance of $1,460.73. The statement further reflected that her credit limit was set at $1,900. Owens had not used the credit card the previous month, but had incurred monthly finance charges. Additionally, her account was debited $10.34 for a Discover card product called CreditSafe Plus, which evidently would put her payments and finance charges on hold without affecting her credit rating should she become unemployed, hospitalized, or disabled. Presumably, since Owens was on Social Security Disability and already unemployed, the CreditSafe product pertained only to the eventuality of her becoming hospitalized. The January 1996 statement further reflected a timely payment on her account.

From January 1996 to March 1997, Owens did not make any purchases on her Discover card. She continued to incur monthly debits for the CreditSafe

Plus product and continued to incur monthly finance charges on the balance due on the account. During this time period, Owens did make payments on her account, but on several occasions (as set forth in the credit card agreement) she incurred additional fees for being late with her payments.

On March 27, 1997, Owens used her card for the last time, taking a $300 cash advance from Sears. With that transaction, her April 1997 statement showed that she now had a new balance of $1,895.53.

In May 1997 Owens made another payment; however, it was less than the minimum payment due. As a result she incurred another late-payment fee. Without making any purchases or taking any further cash advances, but with the accrual of monthly finances charges, Owens's balance now rose to $1,962.82. Because these additional charges had now put her over her credit limit, Owens incurred an additional $20 over-limit fee.

Over the next six years Owens continued to make payments on her account, but because of finance charges and fees her balance was never again to be under her credit limit of $1,900. Despite never using her credit card again, Owens was charged a monthly over-limit fee ranging from $20 to $29 per month. From May 1997 to May 2003, Owens was assessed a total of $1,518 in over-limit fees.

During this time period, despite the growing record of payment difficulties, Discover also continued to debit Owens's account for its CreditSafe Plus product. From May 1997 to May 1999, Owens was charged a total of $369.52 for a product which, despite her being on Social Security Disability, evidently did not apply to her credit predicament.

During this six-year period, Owens continued to attempt to meet her obligation and did make numerous payments. From May 1997 to May 2003 Owens paid Discover a total of $3,492. Since many of the payments were below the minimum monthly payment required and because other monthly payments were in fact not timely made, Owens further was assessed numerous late-payment fees, which over the six-year period totaled $1,160.

In short, despite never using the credit card again and having paid $3,492 on a $1,900 debt, with all the fees and accrued finance charges, Owens was nevertheless faced with a $5,564.28 balance still owing on the account.

How does something like this happen? Had Owens simply stopped paying on her account in May 1997, as perhaps some unscrupulous person might have considered, her account would have been closed and charged off at approximately $2,000, an amount that Discover would have sought to collect at the court seven years ago. If common practice at the court is any indicator at all, Discover might have readily agreed to negotiate a settlement at a small fraction of the amount due. Discover perhaps would have been surprised, but most likely content, to collect the entire amount, but most certainly it would never have anticipated collecting nearly 75 percent over what was owed in the first place.

But because Owens was not unscrupulous and evidently did her absolute best despite being on Social Security Disability, she found herself in debt so deeply that she ultimately came to the sad conclusion that it was a debt out from under which she could never climb. The court does not have before it the records prior to January 1996 to know just what Owens may have purchased for a few hundred dollars using her Discover card. Whatever it was it certainly cannot have been worth the thousands of dollars she actually paid, and most certainly was not worth the additional thousands of dollars still expected today by Discover.

No doubt some of the responsibility for this situation rests with Owens. It might have been unfair for a creditor to extend easy credit at stiff terms to someone who clearly was in a difficult financial predicament in the first place, but no one forced Owens to open the account and accept the card in the first place, and certainly no one forced her to use it, despite its allure for easy access to money in difficult financial times. Owens might have sought financial or legal counsel several years ago to work out some suitable arrangement with Discover, yet her instincts were always that she wanted to plug away at meeting her financial obligations. While clearly placing her on the moral high road, that same highway unfortunately was her road to financial ruin.

How is it that the person who wants to do right ends up so worse off? It is plain to the court that the creditor also bears some responsibility. Discover kept Owens's account open and active long after it was painfully obvious that she was never going to be able to make payments at the expected level. Under the law, an injured party has a duty to mitigate his damages and may not recover those damages that he could reasonably have avoided. S & D Mech. Contrs., Inc. v. Enting Water Conditioning Sys., Inc. (1991), 71 Ohio App. 3d 228, 593 N.E.2d 354; Geis v. Zylka (1995), 70 Ohio Misc. 2d 28, 650 N.E.2d 211. A contract may be held unenforceable when a creditor leaves a debtor with little disposable income and presses a demand for judgment despite being aware of the debtor's dire financial straits. City Fin. Services v. Smith (Jan. 4, 2000), Cleveland M.C. No. 97 CVF 00679, 2000 WL 288469. Even if plaintiff was technically within its rights in its handling of defendant's account, it was unreasonable and unjust for it to allow defendant's debt to continue to accumulate well after it had become clear that defendant would be unable to pay it. Unjust enrichment occurs when one retains money or benefits that, in justice and equity, belong to another. Hummel v. Hummel (1938), 133 Ohio St. 520, 528, 11 O.O. 221, 14 N.E.2d 923; Seward v. Mentrup (1993), 87 Ohio App. 3d

601, 603, 622 N.E.2d 756. Because of its failure to even minimally pay attention to Owens's circumstances, and for allowing the debt to accumulate unchecked, the court finds that Discover would be unjustly enriched if this court were now to grant judgment in its favor.

The court further finds the repeated six-year accumulation of over-limit fees to be manifestly unconscionable. A determination of unconscionability is to be made in light of a variety of factors, including "the sheer harshness of contractual terms together with unequal bargaining positions which renders certain consumer contracts suspect and worthy of judicial revision." Orlett v. Suburban Propane (1989), 54 Ohio App. 3d 127, 561 N.E.2d 1066. Unconscionability "has generally been recognized to include an absence of meaningful choice on the part of one of the parties, together with contract terms which are unreasonably favorable to the other party. Whether a meaningful choice is present in a particular case can only be determined by consideration of all the circumstances surrounding the transaction. In many cases the meaningfulness of the choice is negated by a gross inequality of bargaining power." Williams v. Walker-Thomas Furniture Co. (1965), 350 F.2d 445, 449. See, also, Cty. Asphalt, Inc. v. Lewis Welding & Eng. Corp. (1970), 323 F. Supp. 1300; Vanyo v. Clear Channel Worldwide, 156 Ohio App. 3d 706, 2004-Ohio-1793, 808 N.E.2d 482 ¶17; Evans v. Graham Ford, Inc. (1981), 2 Ohio App. 3d 435, 2 OBR 529, 442 N.E.2d 777.

After reviewing the cardmember agreement that plaintiff contends was applicable in this case, it is clear that the operation of its terms as it applied to Owens was unconscionable. This was not a case where Owens recklessly used her credit card to purchase items beyond the agreed-upon credit limit. After the fees and finance charges put her balance over the $1,900 credit limit, Owens never used the credit card again. Sixty months later, however, Discover continued to charge Owens a $29 monthly fee, despite the fact that she had made payments nearly twice the $1,900 she owed in the first place. The court further questions the CreditSafe fees consistently charged to Owens's account. At what point in the life of an unemployed, disabled, impoverished person was such a product ever designed to be used?

The Cleveland Municipal Court has authority in the cases before it "to hear and determine *all legal and equitable remedies* necessary or proper for a complete determination of the rights of the parties." (Emphasis added.) R.C. 1901.13(B) [citing cases]. The function of equity is to supplement the law where it is insufficient, moderating the unjust results that would follow from the unbending application of the law. Salem Iron Co. v. Hyland (1906), 74 Ohio St. 160, 77 N.E. 751. The chief characteristic of a court of equity is adequate power to afford full relief to the parties before it [citing cases]. A court of equity is a court of conscience that must apply rules of reason and righteousness, within the rules of equity applicable to the case before it. Id. The various revisions to Ohio's laws since statehood have not brought about any change in the scope of its courts' equity jurisdiction. 41 Ohio Jurisprudence 3d (1998), Equity, Section 3.

Equity may be invoked to prevent injustice or unfairness. Courts of equity will assist the wronged party on the ground of fraud, imposition, or unconscionable advantage if there has been great inequality in the bargain. Wagner v. Hummel (1937), 25 Ohio L. Abs. 400, 1937 WL 2359. To prevent a court of equity from exercising jurisdiction, it is not enough that there be a remedy at law; the remedy itself must be plain, adequate, and complete [citing cases]. An adequate remedy at law is one that affords relief with reference to the matter in controversy and is appropriate to the particular circumstances of the case [citing cases]. Defendant has no such remedy at law, so the exercise of this court's equitable jurisdiction is both necessary and proper.

Where equitable jurisdiction has once been asserted in a given field because of the absence or inadequacy of legal remedy, it will not be ousted by any subsequent change in the law that creates an adequate legal remedy or makes adequate an existing, but previously incomplete, legal remedy. Townsend v. Carpenter (1841), 11 Ohio 21, 1841 WL 42; Cram v. Green (1834), 6 Ohio 429, 1834 WL 31. Equity abhors penalties, such as an agreement to pay an arbitrarily fixed sum of money for failing to exactly perform some condition of a contract [citing cases]. The over-limit and late fees repeatedly piled on by plaintiff in this case over a seven-year period are just such penalties.

An equity court exercises a broad and flexible jurisdiction to grant remedial relief where justice or good conscience requires it. Bldg. Serv. & Maint. Union Local 47 v. St. Lukes Hosp. (1967), 11 Ohio Misc. 218, 40 O. O.2d 500, 227 N.E.2d 265. Equity courts are not bound by formula, or restrained by any limitation that tends to trammel the free and just exercise of judicial discretion. Keystone Driller Co. v. Gen. Excavator Co. (1933), 290 U.S. 240, 54 S. Ct. 146, 78 L. Ed. 293. Equity is able to adapt to new conditions and novel facts, allowing it to act in the role of a social reformer. Oliver v. Pray (1829), 4 Ohio 175, 1829 WL 26; Phillips v. Graves (1870), 20 Ohio St. 371, 1870 WL 46.

This court is all too aware of the widespread financial exploitation of the urban poor by overbearing credit-card companies. Defendant has clearly been the victim of plaintiff's unreasonable, unconscionable, and unjust business practices. Equity allows no wrong to be without a remedy. Columbus Packing Co. v. State (1919), 100 Ohio St. 285, 126 N.E. 291. This court has broad legal and equitable powers, and now brings them to bear for the debtor in this case. The appropriate remedy is clear:

Judgment for defendant.

B. *Regulation Z*

Title I of the Consumer Credit Protection Act of 1968 is the Truth in Lending Act. The statute was amended in 1970 to include substantive rules about credit cards. Pursuant to the Act's command, the Federal Reserve Board promulgated amendments to Regulation Z, the Act's regulatory counterpart, to address credit card issues. As we shall see in Chapter 7 infra, the TILA and Regulation Z are usually triggered by a credit arrangement in which a finance charge is imposed. When it comes to credit cards, however, there is no such requirement. Instead, the Act and Regulation encompass all kinds of credit cards, including those (such as American Express) that require the payment of the entire balance on receipt of the bill, as well as those (such as MasterCard or Visa) that permit deferred payment over a period of time.[7]

Use Regulation Z to answer the following Problems.

PROBLEM 39

Octopus National Bank decided to issue a credit card and was informed by other banks that had done so that the bank could make money out of this operation only if it could get its cards into the hands of a lot of consumers. If only a few of the cards were in use, the credit card division of the bank would be too expensive to justify itself. Consequently, ONB decided to mail out credit cards to each of its bank customers, along with an explanation that if the customers did not want the cards, they should mail them back to the bank in the envelope provided.

a. You are the attorney for the bank. Will you put your imprimatur on this scheme? See Reg. Z §226.12(a).

b. Could the bank get away with calling up the consumers, asking them if they would like to have one of the bank's credit cards, and then mailing them a card if they replied in the affirmative?

c. Assume that the bank advertises the cards not only by phone but in many other ways: in "TAKE ONE" displays at the bank, in

---

7. The definition of "credit card" in Regulation Z §226.2(a)(15) includes a subcategory called "charge card." The latter term refers to cards that require payment of the entire balance on receipt of the bill, while "credit card" refers to all kinds of cards consumers may use to obtain credit from a merchant. There are a few instances where the Regulation does draw distinctions that apply only to "charge cards"—see §226.5a, for example.

newspaper advertisements, and in applications mailed to customers along with their monthly bank statements. What disclosures must be made in such situations? Glance through Reg. Z §226.5a.

d. The bank's credit card includes a charge of $5 that the consumer must pay every quarter as an "activity fee." This fee is imposed regardless of whether the consumer has used the card during the quarter. Must this fee be disclosed, and, if so, would it suffice just to say "quarterly activity fee of $5"? See Reg. Z §226.5a(b)(2).

PROBLEM 40

Ebenezer Scrooge had always distrusted credit, so he was considerably annoyed one day to receive in the mail an unsolicited credit card from Dickens State Bank. He examined it critically and signed his name on the indicated blank, but then he decided he wanted to have nothing to do with it, so he threw the card away. His needy employee, Bob Cratchit, took the card from the trash can and used it to buy Christmas presents ($500 worth) for his large family. When Scrooge got the bill, he was very upset and called Dickens State Bank to protest. What amount, if any, does Scrooge owe the bank? See Reg. Z n.21a and §226.12(a) and (b). If Scrooge has a bank account with Dickens State, can the bank use its common law right of setoff to pay itself the credit card debt or any portion thereof? See Reg. Z §226.12(d).[8]

PROBLEM 41

Unlike Scrooge, Cindy Shopper loved credit cards. She had 17 in her purse when it was stolen from her at gunpoint one afternoon on the street. Cindy immediately got on the phone and called each of the

---

8. The Official Commentary to this section requires that the "consensual security interest" mentioned in subsection (2) be a *separately signed* writing stating that the account will be used as collateral for the credit card debt, and not merely be a clause in the credit card contract. Official Commentary .11 cmt. 12(d)(2). Further, this Commentary requires that the security interest in the consumer's account must be open (as a matter of state law) to other creditors or the card issuer cannot claim an interest therein either. Since this is not the case in most states (a consumer bank account can be collateral only for loans by the bank in which the account is maintained—Article 9 only allows bank accounts to be used as collateral for loans by others if the account is not a consumer account; §9-109(d)(13)), this is the chief stumbling block. The final thing to note is that the existence of the security agreement must be disclosed in the Truth in Lending statement itself.

card issuers, informing them of the theft of her cards. Two hours after she had made these calls, the thief charged more than $200 on each of the 17 cards. What amount does Cindy owe the card issuers?

Consumers usually get a better break than the law allows them. Most major credit card companies don't even hold consumers liable for any amount of unauthorized use of the card (and typically so provide in the credit card agreement and advertisements). This is about the only leeway that credit card companies grant. In most cases things get worse and worse for card users as time goes on. A popular new tactic is called "universal default." This is the practice of raising credit card interest rates whenever the consumer is known to have missed payments on *other* debts (such as a phone bill). The card issuers justify this by saying that the consumer's failure to pay any debt makes him/her a greater credit risk on all debts. The card issuers can generate income in other ways too: increased annual fees, extra charges for this and that (paying off balances by phone, for instance), hiking late fees (which have quadrupled since 1997), and many other ploys we will explore when we get to open-ended credit under the Truth in Lending Act. Bankers have all sorts of interesting names for their credit card customers. People who do not pay off their credit card balances every month are call "revolvers." People who pay them off are called "free loaders." In 2007, lenders collected over $18 billion in credit card fees and penalties.

PROBLEM 42

When she needed to buy a ceiling fan for her kitchen, Lorri Latek went to Adam's Fan Store, located in the mall near her home, and picked out the one she liked best. The fan's price was $80, and to pay for it Lorri used the Visa credit card sent her by Octopus National Bank. When she got the fan home and installed it, she was annoyed to discover that it made an awful racket when it was turned on. She called the store and was told that she probably had installed it wrong, but regardless whether that was true, the store never warranted its products, so she was stuck with the fan, racket and all. (Is this right? See U.C.C. §2-314.) The store refused to refund her money. When ONB sent Lorri her Visa bill, she wrote the bank a letter telling them that she refused to pay the $80 charged in favor of Adam's Fan Store, explaining what had happened.

a. Advise the bank. Should it look to Lorri or Adam's Fan Store for payment here? See Reg. Z §226.12(c).

b. Would you reach the same result if the fan had cost only $40?

c. Would you reach the same result if the fan had been purchased on a trip to Florida? (Lorri lives in Ohio.)

d. Would you reach the same result if the fan had cost $40 and had to be ordered from Florida, but its availability had been advertised in promotional material sent to Lorri by ONB along with the usual Visa bill?

e. What if the dispute were over a $30 defective muffler Lorri had bought using her Tiger Oil Company credit card at a Tiger Oil gas station? Could she refuse to pay the bill that Tiger Oil sent to her?

The last question raises the differences between a *bipartite* and a *tripartite* credit card. In the former case, the only entity that honors the credit card is the entity that issued the card. A large department store, for example, might issue a credit card good only at the department store. Such a card is called bipartite. On the other hand, when the card issuer—such as American Express, MasterCard, or Visa—authorizes many different entities to honor the card, a tripartite card is in use. Obviously our law will demand more of the issuer of a bipartite card because it has such control over the circumstances of its use.

HYLAND v. FIRST USA BANK
United States District Court, E.D. Pennsylvania, 1995
1995 WL 595861

GILES, District Judge.

Richard Hyland and Sharka Brod Hyland ("Plaintiffs") bring this action pursuant to the Truth in Lending Act, 15 U.S.C. §1601, et seq., and Regulation Z, 12 C.F.R. §226.12, for money damages for breach of warranty, promissory estoppel, and negligent misrepresentation. First USA Bank ("the Bank") moves pursuant to Federal Rule of Civil Procedure 12(b)(6) to dismiss this action for failure to state a claim upon which relief can be granted.

The court has jurisdiction over this matter pursuant to 15 U.S.C. §1640(e) and 28 U.S.C. §1331. For the reasons stated below, Defendant's motion is denied.

I. FACTUAL BACKGROUND

In February, 1994, First USA Bank issued a Gold Visa Card to the Plaintiffs. Complaint, PP 8-9. In May, 1994, Plaintiffs traveled to Greece for a vacation, where they purchased an oriental carpet ("the carpet") from Aris Evangelinos, the owner of an antique store in Nauplia, Greece. Complaint, PP 10, 12-13. Plaintiffs paid US $2,070.57 for the carpet with the Visa Card issued by the Bank.

Plaintiffs contend that in order to induce Plaintiffs to purchase the carpet, Evangelinos made express warranties that the carpet was an antique Kilim, circa 1930, that it was woven and embroidered with pure silk with a cotton warp, and that it had been colored with vegetable dyes. Complaint, P 17. Upon inspection by a United States carpet expert, Plaintiffs discovered that these express warranties were false. Complaint, PP 20-23. The Plaintiffs contacted the Bank and the merchant to obtain a credit. Complaint, PP 23-24, 28.

Plaintiffs allege that the Bank directed them to return the carpet to the merchant. Complaint, P 30. They did so via Federal Express. Complaint, P 34. However, the carpet was intercepted by Greek Customs, who informed Plaintiffs that a duty of approximately US $1,240 would have to be paid before the carpet could be released. Complaint, P 38. Plaintiffs refused to pay the duty, and notified the Bank that they would hold the Bank responsible for the loss of the carpet. Complaint, P 39. The carpet was ultimately confiscated by Greek Customs. Complaint, P 41.

Plaintiffs maintain that the Bank repeatedly assured them that it would assist the Plaintiffs in resolving the matter if Plaintiffs (1) returned the carpet to Evangelinos; and (2) provided a return receipt to the Bank. Complaint, P 30. Plaintiffs contend that they relied on the Bank's assurance of assistance, and ceased personal efforts to obtain a refund. Complaint, PP 28, 31. The Bank later informed Plaintiffs that consumer protection does not exist for purchases made outside of the United States. Complaint, P 37. Accordingly, the Bank refused to accept liability for the loss of the carpet. Complaint, PP 37, 40. . . .

III. DISCUSSION

A. BREACH OF WARRANTY CLAIM (COUNT I)

Plaintiffs allege that Evangelinos made certain express warranties regarding the authenticity of the carpet. The formation of an express warranty is governed by statute: Any affirmation of fact or promise made by the seller to the buyer which relates to the goods and becomes part of the basis of the bargain creates an express warranty that the goods shall conform to the affirmation or promise. 13 Pa. C.S.A. §2313(a)(1). Breach of warranty claims serve to protect buyers from loss where the goods purchased do not meet commercial standards or affirmations. Altronics of Bethlehem, Inc. v. Repco, Inc., 957 F.2d 1102, 1105 (3d Cir. 1992). In the present case,

Plaintiffs clearly allege that the carpet did not conform to the affirmations of authenticity made by Evangelinos. Complaint, PP 21-23, 45.

However, Plaintiffs have chosen not to sue Evangelinos directly. Instead, Plaintiffs allege that under §1666i of the Truth in Lending Act, and Regulation Z, 12 C.F.R. §226.12(c), Plaintiffs are permitted to assert against the Bank, as card issuer, the claim for breach of warranty that they are entitled to assert against Evangelinos. Complaint, P 49. Plaintiffs further allege that the Bank has waived and is estopped from asserting any limitations or defenses to liability on the Truth in Lending Act claim. Complaint, P 50. The Bank asserts that under §1666i(a)(3) of the Act, it cannot be held liable for the loss of the carpet because the transaction did not occur in the state of, or within 100 miles of, Plaintiffs' mailing address. Defendant's Motion to Dismiss, p.5. In addition, the Bank contends that it has not waived its right to assert the geographic limitation as a defense. Id. at 11.

As a general rule, the Truth in Lending Act provides that a card issuer who has issued a credit card to a cardholder pursuant to an open end consumer credit plan shall be subject to all claims (other than tort claims) and defenses arising out of any transaction in which the credit card is used as a method of payment or extension of credit. . . . 15 U.S.C. §1666i(a). However, a card issuer is liable for such claims only if "the place where the initial transaction occurred was in the same State as the mailing address previously provided by the cardholder or was within 100 miles from such address. . . . " 15 U.S.C. §1666i(a)(3). In the present case, Plaintiffs purchased the carpet in Greece, a foreign country that is neither in the same state nor within 100 miles of the Plaintiffs' mailing address. Therefore, the allegations in the Plaintiffs' complaint do not satisfy the geographical limitation provided by §1666i(a)(3). However, Plaintiffs also allege that the Bank waived the protection granted by this geographical limitation. Complaint, P 50; Plaintiff's Opposition to Defendant's Motion to Dismiss, p.8. Plaintiffs allege that by initially agreeing to assist Plaintiffs in an international dispute, the Bank knowingly waived its right to assert the geographical limitation as a defense. Complaint, PP 42 (incorporating PP 1-41), 50; Plaintiff's Opposition to Defendant's Motion to Dismiss, pp. 4, 8-9.

A waiver is a "voluntary and intentional relinquishment or abandonment of a known right." Helco, Inc. v. First National City Bank, 470 F.2d 883, 885 (3d Cir. 1972). In the present case, Plaintiffs allege that they "specifically asked the BANK whether the BANK could assist them in obtaining reimbursement from a seller who was located not merely out of state but, in fact, abroad, in Greece." Complaint, P 28. Plaintiffs contend that the Bank responded by assuring them that the Bank "could be of assistance." Id. The complaint further alleges that Plaintiffs spoke frequently with the Bank by telephone, and referred the Bank's customer service representative to the charge statement which showed that the purchase had been made in Greece. Complaint, P 30. According to Plaintiffs, the Bank repeatedly agreed to assist them. Id.

Reading the complaint liberally, and viewing the allegations in the complaint in a light most favorable to Plaintiffs, Haines v. Kerner, 404 U.S. 519, 520-21 (1972), we conclude that Plaintiffs have adequately alleged waiver of the geographic limitation by the Bank sufficient to survive a motion to dismiss.

B. PROMISSORY ESTOPPEL CLAIM (COUNT II)

Plaintiffs' second cause of action is brought under a promissory estoppel theory. The doctrine of promissory estoppel provides: A promise which the promisor should reasonably expect to induce action or forbearance on the part of the promisee or a third person and which does induce such action or forbearance is binding if injustice can be avoided only by enforcement of the promise. . . . Restatement (Second) of Contracts §90(1). For the promise to be binding and actionable, four elements must be satisfied: (1) there must have been a promise; (2) the promisor should reasonably have expected the promise to induce action or forbearance on the part of the promisee or a third person; (3) the promise does induce such action or forbearance; and (4) enforcement of the promise must be the only way of avoiding injustice. Pennsylvania has adopted the doctrine of promissory estoppel as provided by §90. Thatcher's Drug Store, Inc. v. Consolidated Supermarkets, Inc., 636 A.2d 156, 160 (Pa. 1994).

In the present case, Plaintiffs allege that the Bank promised that it would assist them in resolving their dispute with the Greek merchant. Complaint, PP 28, 30. Plaintiffs also allege that the Bank reasonably should have expected that its promise would induce action and forbearance on the part of the Plaintiffs. Complaint, P 53. Specifically, Plaintiffs allegedly told the Bank that if the Bank "could not assist them, they would continue to negotiate directly with the merchant." Complaint, P 28. Further, Plaintiffs contend that they were induced by the Bank's promise of assistance, and ceased independent efforts to settle with Evangelinos. Complaint, P 28, 31, 54. Finally, Plaintiffs allege in their complaint that they have suffered damage and that injustice can be avoided only by enforcement of the promise. Complaint, PP 55-56. Thus, Plaintiffs have pled all the requisite elements to support a claim for promissory estoppel. Accordingly, the Bank's motion to dismiss on this claim is also denied.

C. NEGLIGENT MISREPRESENTATION CLAIM (COUNT III)

Plaintiff's third cause of action is for negligent misrepresentation. The requisite elements for a negligent misrepresentation cause of action are: (1) a misrepresentation of a material fact; (2) the representor must either know of the misrepresentation, must make the misrepresentation without knowledge as to its truth or falsity, or must make the representation under circumstances in which he ought to have known of its falsity; (3) the representor must intend the representation to induce another to act upon it; and (4) the party acting in justifiable reliance on the misrepresentation must sustain injury. Gibbs v. Ernst, 647 A.2d 882, 890 (Pa. 1994).

Although the requisite elements for a negligent misrepresentation claim are not specifically pled in Count III of Plaintiffs' complaint, that Count incorporates by reference Paragraphs 1 through 41 of the complaint. See Complaint, P 57. Paragraphs 1 through 41 allege facts sufficient to support a negligent misrepresentation claim.

Plaintiffs contend that the Bank "negligently and carelessly" informed them that the Bank could assist them in resolving their dispute with Evangelinos. Complaint, PP 59-60. This fact, if proven, may constitute a material misrepresentation. Further, by assuring Plaintiffs that it could assist them, the Bank's representation may have been made under circumstances where the Bank "ought to have known of its falsity." *Gibbs*, 647 A.2d at 890. According to Plaintiffs' complaint, the Bank offered to assist Plaintiffs if they returned the carpet to Evangelinos and sent a return receipt to the Bank. Complaint, PP 29-30, 35. If true, this allegation may prove that the Bank intended this representation to induce Plaintiffs to act. Finally, Plaintiffs allege that they suffered injury as a result of the Bank's alleged misrepresentation. Complaint, P 61. Thus, Plaintiffs have pled the requisite elements to support a claim for negligent misrepresentation. Accordingly, the Bank's motion to dismiss this claim is denied.

An appropriate order follows. . . .

PROBLEM 43

When Marco Palmieri, who lived in New Jersey, made his reservation with Eager Air Lines to fly to Venice, Italy, on vacation, he was very happy even though the price was $1,050 round-trip and his Visa bill (with a credit limit of $2,000) was thereby charged to the maximum. He made the reservation in March, planning to take the trip the following July. The plane tickets first appeared on his April bill ($1,950 owed—previous charges plus the new plane ticket charge). In April, he paid Visa $300. He made no other charges on his credit card. In May, he paid Visa $300 more. Marco's plans fell through, however, when Eager Air Lines filed for bankruptcy in early June. Reading of the bankruptcy in the newspaper, he called the Eager Air Lines ticket office and was told that he ought to file a claim in the bankruptcy proceeding. When Marco got his June Visa bill ($1,390), he wrote the card issuer and explained what had happened. You are the attorney for the card issuer. Must it take all or part of the plane ticket charge off the Visa bill? See Reg. Z §226.12(c); look carefully at footnote 25. If the card issuer fails to credit the account, does Marco have any rights in the bankruptcy proceeding? See §507(a)(6) of the Bankruptcy Code (which should also be in your statute book).

Exporting Interest Rates. Each state has a usury statute specifying the interest rate card issuers may charge and regulating other terms of the agreement. Section 30 of the National Bank Act of 1864, Rev. Stat. §5197, as amended, 12 U.S.C. §85, provides that a national bank may charge its loan customers "interest at the rate allowed by the laws of the State . . . where the bank is located." In Marquette National Bank of Minneapolis v. First of Omaha Service Corp., 439 U.S. 299 (1978), the United States Supreme Court held that this provision authorizes a national bank to charge out-of-state credit-card customers an interest rate allowed by the bank's home state, even when that rate is higher than what is permitted by the states in which the cardholders reside. Subsequent to this decision a number of large credit card companies moved their headquarters to states allowing high rates of interest and exported that rate all over the country. In Smiley v. Citibank (South Dakota), N.A., 517 U.S. 73 (1996), the Supreme Court extended the rule of *Marquette* when it held that late payment fees were part of the interest rate, and hence could also be exported from the home state, thus trumping local state rules regulating such fees.

III. BILLING DISPUTES

Thousands of people using thousands of machines to process thousands of accounts are going to make mistakes. Customers who believe that they have detected such errors are naturally worried about straightening out these problems before they run into difficulties with their credit ratings. Congress became concerned by the troubles consumers had in getting the creditors to pay attention to consumer complaints, so it enacted the Fair Credit Billing

Act. The general scheme of the Act is to make the creditor respond to complaints: first with an acknowledgment of the complaint and then with a reasonable investigation to see whether it is justified. Before we explore the statute in greater detail, a few words are in order about other relief.

A. The Common Law

If you, the consumer, receive a bill from a credit card issuer and it contains an entry you believe to be an error, what remedy do you have? Prior to 1975, and the Fair Credit Billing Act (which became Chapter 4 of the Truth in Lending Act, §§161 to 171), the common law offered little help, though consumers could sometimes make much of "payment in full" checks and the idea of an accord and satisfaction. See also Annot., State Causes of Action for Credit Card Billing Errors, 53 A.L.R.4th 231.

A little reminder on the law of Contracts: an "accord" is the offer of something that is *different* from that which was originally due under the terms of the contract; a "satisfaction" is the agreement to take it. Thus if you and I are in a contract by which I have agreed to perform a magic act at your child's party for which you will pay me $100, and I call you up and tell you that in place of the magic act I will do a juggling act, I have made an offer of an *accord*; your agreement would be the *satisfaction*, and by this process we would work a modification of the contract.

Section 3-311 of the Uniform Commercial Code now regulates payment in full checks as they relate to an accord and satisfaction. Use that section to resolve the following Problems.

PROBLEM 44

Hazel Flagg was disgusted when the new sofa she had purchased was delivered dirty. She had it professionally cleaned, which cost her $50, so she deducted this amount from the amount she was billed for the sofa ($1,000) and sent the seller, Furniture of Tomorrow, a check for $950, along with a letter explaining the reason for the deduction and stating, "This check is sent as full payment for the sofa."

a. If the check had been conspicuously marked "Payment in Full," would the payee avoid the accord and satisfaction by scratching this language off of the check before cashing it? See Wolfe v. Eagle Ridge Holding Co., 869 N.E.2d 521, 63 U.C.C. Rep. Serv. 2d 382 (Ind. App. 2007).

b. Furniture of Tomorrow cashed the check on May 1. Two days later someone in the Consumer Complaint Department read Hazel's letter. Has an accord and satisfaction occurred? Is there any way to undo it and preserve the dispute over the $50? See §3-311(c)(2).

PROBLEM 45

The head of the Consumer Complaint Department at Furniture of Tomorrow calls you, the company's attorney, with the following dilemma. Buyers often have complaints and send in "payment in full" checks, but the corporate setup is such that the checks are routinely cashed before any investigation occurs. Refunding the money is time consuming (and sometimes the company does not realize the necessity for doing so for four or more months), and you are asked to set up a system whereby the company can avoid cashing the checks. What can it do? See §3-311(c)(1).

PROBLEM 46

The bill that came with Hazel's sofa stated, "Send disputed payments to Consumer Complaint Department (address)." Is it all right to bury this information in the fine print?

Assume that this language is prominently printed on the bill. Hazel did send the disputed check to that department, which immediately cashed it by accident. The head of Consumer Complaint calls you, the company attorney. Can the company still refund the money per §3-311(c)(2) and revive the dispute?

PROBLEM 47

When Hazel got the dirty sofa, she was so furious that she phoned the company and said that she was not going to pay a cent. The company sent her numerous bills, but she ignored them. Finally the company turned the matter over to Trash Collection Agency, which contacted Hazel directly and made threats about her credit rating. To get them out of her life, Hazel sent Trash Collection Agency a check for $950, marking it "payment in full." She did this in spite of the fact that all of the bills the company had sent her required disputed payments to be sent to the company's Consumer Complaint Department, giving an address for same. Trash Collection turned the check over to the collection department of Furniture of Tomorrow, which cashed it. A few days later, the head of Consumer Complaint finds all this out, and calls you, the company's attorney. Has an accord and satisfaction occurred? Can the company still refund the money per §3-311(c)(2) and revive the dispute?

PROBLEM 48

Assume instead that when Hazel became upset by the dirty sofa she sat down and wrote a letter to Albert Furniture, the President of Furniture of Tomorrow, explaining that the $950 check enclosed was tendered in full settlement of the dispute. She ignored the instruction to send complaints to the Consumer Complaint Department and mailed the check and accompanying letter directly to Albert Furniture at the main office of the company. Albert's secretary sent the check off to the collections department and the letter to Consumer Complaint. Two weeks later, at the bidding of the latter, the company refunded Hazel's $950 and demanded payment in full. Has an accord and satisfaction occurred?

Does it help in answering these Problems if the company can prove that the reason the sofa was dirty was not because it was delivered in that condition, but that Hazel's large dogs had climbed all over it while wet from a romp outdoors?

B. *The Fair Credit Billing Act*

GRAY v. AMERICAN EXPRESS CO.
United States Court of Appeals, District of Columbia Circuit, 1984
743 F.2d 10

MIKVA, Circuit Judge.

We are called upon to determine what rights, if any, appellant Oscar Gray[9] has against American Express arising from the circumstances under

---

9. [Editor's Note: At the time of this case, the plaintiff was a professor of law at the University of Maryland, a leading expert on the law of torts, and one of the authors of the law review articles on fraud cited in Chapter 1, at page 12.]

which it cancelled his American Express credit card. The District Court granted summary judgment to American Express; we vacate that judgment and remand for further proceedings.

I. BACKGROUND

Gray had been a cardholder since 1964. In 1981, following some complicated billings arising out of deferred travel charges incurred by Gray, disputes arose about the amount due American Express. After considerable correspondence, the pertinence and timeliness of which we will detail below, American Express decided to cancel Gray's card. No notification of this cancellation was communicated to Gray until the night of April 8, 1982, when he offered his American Express card to pay for a wedding anniversary dinner he and his wife already had consumed in a Washington restaurant. The restaurant informed Gray that American Express had refused to accept the charges for the meal and had instructed the restaurant to confiscate and destroy his card. Gray spoke to the American Express employee on the telephone at the restaurant who informed him, "Your account is cancelled as of now."

The cancellation prompted Gray to file a lengthy complaint in District Court, stating claims under both diversity and federal question jurisdiction. See 28 U.S.C. §§1331, 1332; see also 15 U.S.C. §1640. He alleged that the actions of American Express violated the contract between them, known as the "Cardmember Agreement," as well as the Fair Credit Billing Act (the "Act"), 15 U.S.C. §§1666-1666j, Pub. L. 93-495, Tit. III, 88 Stat. 1511 (1974). The District Court granted summary judgment for American Express and dismissed the complaint.

The surge in the use of credit cards, the "plastic money" of our society, has been so quick that the law has had difficulty keeping pace. It was not until 1974 that Congress passed the Act, first making a serious effort to regulate the relationship between a credit cardholder and the issuing company. We hold that the District Court was too swift to conclude that the Act offers no protection to Gray and further hold that longstanding principles of contract law afford Gray substantial rights. We thus vacate the District Court's judgment and remand.

II. DISCUSSION

A. THE STATUTORY CLAIM

Fair Credit Billing Act seeks to prescribe an orderly procedure for identifying and resolving disputes between a cardholder and a card issuer as to the amount due at any given time. The Supreme Court, in American Express

Co. v. Koerner, 452 U.S. 233, 235-37, 101 S. Ct. 2281, 2283-84, 68 L. Ed. 2d 803 (1981), succinctly described the mechanics of the Act as follows:

> If the [cardholder] believes that the statement contains a billing error [as defined in 15 U.S.C. §1666(b)], he then may send the creditor a written notice setting forth that belief, indicating the amount of the error and the reasons supporting his belief that it is an error. If the creditor receives this notice within 60 days of transmitting the statement of account, [§1666(a)] imposes two separate obligations upon the creditor. Within 30 days, it must send a written acknowledgment that it has received the notice. And, within 90 days or two complete billing cycles, whichever is shorter, the creditor must investigate the matter and either make appropriate corrections in the [cardholder's] account or send a written explanation of its belief that the original statement sent to the [cardholder] was correct. The creditor must send its explanation before making any attempt to collect the disputed amount. A creditor that fails to comply with [§1666(a)] forfeits its right to collect the first $50 of the disputed amount including finance charges. [15 U.S.C. §1666(e)]. In addition, [§1666(d)] provides that, pursuant to regulations of the Federal Reserve Board, a creditor operating an "open end consumer credit plan" may not restrict or close an account due to a [cardholder's] failure to pay a disputed amount until the creditor has sent the written explanation required by [§1666(a)] (footnote omitted).

Other obligations also attach. First, if "appropriate corrections" are made, the card issuer also must credit any finance charge on accounts erroneously billed. 15 U.S.C. §1666(a)(B)(i). Second, the card issuer must notify the cardholder on subsequent statements of account that he need not pay the amount in dispute until the card issuer has complied with §1666. 15 U.S.C. §1666(c)(2). Third, the card issuer may not report, or threaten to report, adversely on the cardholder's credit before the card issuer had discharged its obligations under §1666, 15 U.S.C. §1666a(a), and, if the cardholder continues to dispute the bill in timely fashion, the card issuer may report the delinquency only if it also reports that the amount is in dispute and tells the cardholder to whom it has released this information. 15 U.S.C. §1666a(b). The card issuer is further obligated to report any eventual resolution of the delinquency to the same third parties with whom it earlier had communicated. 15 U.S.C. §1666a(c). Finally, a card issuer that fails to comply with any requirements of the Act is liable to the cardholder for actual damages, twice the amount of any finance charge, and costs of the action and attorney's fees. 15 U.S.C. §1640(a).

American Express is, of course, a creditor for purposes of the Act. *Koerner*, supra, 452 U.S. at 241 n.8, 101 S. Ct. at 2286 n.8.

1.   The Billing Error

The billing dispute in issue arose after Gray used his credit card to purchase airline tickets costing $9312. American Express agreed that Gray could pay for the tickets in 12 equal installments over 12 months. In January and February of 1981, Gray made substantial prepayments of $3500 and $1156 respectively. He so advised American Express by letter of February 8, 1981. There is no dispute about these payments, nor about Gray's handling of them. At this point the numbers become confusing because American Express, apparently in error, converted the deferred payment plan to a current charge on the March bill. American Express thereafter began to show Gray as delinquent, due at least in part to the dispute as to how and why the deferred billing had been converted to a current charge.

The District Court held that Gray failed to trigger the protection of the Act because he neglected to notify American Express in writing within 60 days after he first received an erroneous billing. Gray insists that his first letter to American Express on April 22, 1981, well within the 60-day period set forth in the statute, identified the dispute as it first appeared in the March, 1981 billing. According to Gray's complaint, the dispute continued to simmer for over a year because American Express never fulfilled its investigative and other obligations under the Act.

The District Court made no mention of the April 22, 1981 letter, deeming instead a September, 1981 letter as the first notification from Gray as to the existence of a dispute. We conclude that the District Court erred in overlooking the April letter.

Gray's April 22, 1981 letter complained specifically about the March bill and the miscrediting of the prepayments. Whatever the import and impact of other correspondence and actions of the parties, we hold that, through this earlier letter, Gray triggered the procedural protections of the Act. The letter enabled the card issuer to identify the name and account number, indicated that the cardholder believed that an error existed in a particular amount and set forth the cardholder's reasons why he believed an error had been made. 15 U.S.C. §1666(a); see Lincoln First Bank, N.A. v. Carlson, 103 Misc. 2d 467, 426 N.Y.S.2d 433 (1980) (returned credit slip, with nothing more, could suffice as notice under the Act). The later correspondence and activities may be treated as evidentiary in nature—sufficient perhaps to show that American Express fulfilled all of its obligations under the Act, but not pertinent to the question of whether the Act was triggered in the first place. See Byers v. Burleson, 713 F.2d 856, 859 (D.C. Cir. 1983) (appellate court reviewing summary judgment determines whether there is genuine issue of material fact and, if not, whether the law was correctly applied).

2. Reporting and Collection Efforts

Gray alleged in count III that, notwithstanding his having given notice of dispute under §1666 through his letters, American Express nevertheless turned over his account for collection to a bill collection agency. The District Judge dismissed this count (misdesignating it as count IV) by concluding that it failed to state a claim for relief. The District Court erred. See 15 U.S.C. §§1640(a), 1666a. We think that count III states an independent cause of action under §1666a because Gray's April 22, 1981 correspondence brought the dispute within the Act's coverage. The question of American Express' compliance with the reporting and collection requirements of the Act also warrants consideration on remand.

3. The Act and the Cardmember Agreement

As we have indicated above, the District Court summarily resolved Gray's statutory claims by wrongly concluding that the Act did not apply. On appeal, American Express also urges that, even if the Act is otherwise pertinent, Gray was bound by the terms of the Cardmember Agreement which empowered American Express to cancel the credit card without notice and without cause. The contract between Gray and American Express provides:

> [W]e can revoke your right to use [the card] at any time. We can do this with or without cause and without giving you notice.

American Express concludes from this language that the cancellation was not of the kind prohibited by the Act, even though the Act regulates other aspects of the relationship between the cardholder and the card issuer.

Section 1666(d) of the Act states that, during the pendency of a disputed billing, the card issuer, until it fulfills its other obligations under §1666(a)(B)(ii), shall not cause the cardholder's account to be restricted or closed because of the failure of the obligator to pay the amount in dispute. See also 12 C.F.R. §266.14(d). American Express seems to argue that, despite that provision, it can exercise its right to cancellation for cause unrelated to the disputed amount, or for *no* cause, thus bringing itself out from under the statute. At the very least, the argument is audacious. American Express would restrict the efficacy of the statute to those situations where the parties had not agreed to a "without cause, without notice" cancellation clause, or to those cases where the cardholder can prove that the sole reason for cancellation was the amount in dispute. We doubt that Congress painted with such a faint brush.

The effect of American Express's argument is to allow the equivalent of a "waiver" of coverage of the Act simply by allowing the parties to contract it away. Congress usually is not so tepid in its approach to consumer problems. See 118 Cong. Rec. 14,835 (1972) (remarks by Sen. Proxmire, principal proponent of the Act, concerning a technical amendment to a predecessor bill later carried over into the Act; its purpose was to prevent "possible evasion" by precluding the creditor from including a predispute waiver provision in the card agreement); 119 Cong. Rec. 25,400 (1973) (remarks by Sen. Proxmire on S. 2101, another predecessor: "The legislation seeks to establish a system for *insuring* that billing disputes or inquiries are resolved in a fair and timely manner.") (emphasis added); see also Mourning v. Family Publications Service, Inc., 411 U.S. 356, 375-77, 93 S. Ct. 1652, 1663-64, 36 L. Ed. 2d 318 (1973) (Truth-in-Lending Act should not be narrowly construed); Koerner v. American Express Co., 444 F. Supp. 334, 341 (E.D. La. 1977) (*Koerner* trial court's recitation of Act's legislative history reflecting congressional concern about card issuers' "high-handed tactics" in handling of consumer billing disputes).

Moreover, the consumer-oriented statutes that Congress has enacted in recent years belie the unrestrained reading that American Express gives to the Act in light of its contract. Waiver of statutory rights, particularly by a contract of adhesion, is hardly consistent with the legislature's purpose. The rationale of consumer protection legislation is to even out the inequalities that consumers normally bring to the bargain. To allow such protection to be waived by boiler plate language of the contract puts the legislative process to a foolish and unproductive task. A court ought not impute such nonsense to a Congress intent on correcting abuses in the market place.

Finally, American Express also contends that, even if the Act is not waived totally, its cancellation was proper because it was for reasons other than those prohibited by the statute. A showing of whatever limited grounds for cancellation remain available under §1666(d) while a dispute is pending calls for substantial evidentiary proceedings, however. If American Express seeks to avail itself of these grounds, a more substantial factual predicate than that established through summary judgment is necessary. See Harlow v. Fitzgerald, 457 U.S. 800, 816, 102 S. Ct. 2727, 2737, 73 L. Ed. 2d 396 (1982).

Thus we hold that the Act's notice provision was met by Gray's April 22, 1981 letter and remand the case to the District Court for trial of Gray's statutory cause of action. American Express will be obliged to justify its conduct in this case as fully satisfying its obligations under the Act.

B.   THE CONTRACT CLAIM

Gray stated a second cause of action in diversity, a contract claim, in which he alleged that American Express violated the Cardmember Agreement by wrongfully cancelling it. Notably, in *Koerner*, supra, the Supreme Court on very similar facts observed that a cardholder could state, in addition to, and separate from, his federal claim under the Act, a claim under state law for cancellation arising out of a credit card billing dispute. 452 U.S. at 239-40 & n.6, 101 S. Ct. at 2285, & n.6. See also Hill v. American Express Co., 257 S.C. 86, 184 S.E.2d 115 (1971). Although a state law claim was raised, and addressed, in this case, neither the parties nor the District Court considered the preliminary question of choice of law. The parties failed again to address it on appeal. As a court sitting in diversity, we are obliged, however, to examine that issue. . . .

2.   Notice

We are asked to interpret the "without notice" provision in the Cardmember Agreement. Gray challenges the card issuer's extreme and, in our view, unreasonable interpretation of this language. The District Court concluded that the notice provision was enforceable. We disagree.

It is certainly true that, from the common law immemorial, parties have been free to include whatever conditions and limitations that they may desire in a contract. See Restatement (Second) of Contracts, Introductory Note, ch. 8, at p.2 (1981); see also id. §72 comment b (contract provides opportunity for freedom of action and exercise of judgment). Absent a statutory prohibition or some public policy impediment, id. §178, the very essence of freedom of contract is the right of the parties to strike good bargains and bad bargains. See id. §79 comment c (exchange of unequal values); see also Dorman v. Cohen, 66 A.D.2d 411, 413 N.Y.S.2d 377 (1st Dept. 1979) ("mutuality of obligation" does not mean equality). However traditional "cancellation for cause" and "with notice" provisions are to a contract, parties sometimes agree to give them up. See, e.g., A. S. Rampell, Inc. v. Hyster Co., 3 N.Y.2d 369, 165 N.Y.S.2d 475, 144 N.E.2d 371 (1957) (merchant-to-merchant context). Appellant thus would not be the first nor the last cardholder to have surrendered substantial rights. Nor does the fact that Gray paid $35.00 per year for his cardholding privileges automatically entitle him to receive notice or to insist on some showing of cause before his card is cancelled. Indeed, American Express generously provides for a pro-rata refund of the annual charge in the event of cancellation.

The problem, then, is not, as Gray would suggest, the unconscionable nature per se of this clause. Nor is it that this clause contradicts in any actionable way the advertising and puffing that he claims American Express used to entice him into the relationship. (E.g., "When you're out of cash, you're not out of luck."; "flexibility to travel and entertain when and where you want, virtually without interruption.") The problem stems from the card issuer's attempt to interpret the "without notice" provision so as to give the creditor's internal cancellation decision effect as against irreversible transactions that already have been completed.

Commonly understood, the function of notice is to provide forewarning of an event. Similarly, in the context of contractual relations, notice allows the party notified to contemplate, and to prepare for, an action that will occur. See 1 M. Merrill on Notice 1, 526 (1952). By contrast, and reasonably interpreted, a contract that is cancellable without notice implies that it can be terminated without forewarning. Such a contract provision ordinarily does not suggest, however, that the cancellation is effective retrospectively to events that transpired prior to notification of the decision to cancel. Cf. Fifty States Management Corp. v. Public Service Mut. Ins. Co., 67 Misc. 2d 778, 324 N.Y.S.2d 345 (1971) (after loss occurs, rights of parties become fixed; cancellation may not be effected retroactively) (citing Duncan v. N.Y. Mut. Ins. Co., 138 N.Y. 88, 33 N.E. 730 (1983)); Marjean, Inc. v. Ammann, 6 A.D.2d 878, 177 N.Y.S.2d 882 (2d Dept. 1958) ("[N]otice given pursuant to the 'escape clause' in the contract did not terminate liability as to obligations already accrued, but only as to liabilities thereafter accruing."). Indeed, counsel for American Express made this point for us indirectly at oral argument. When he was asked whether, based on his client's interpretation of the "without notice" clause, American Express was empowered to cancel the agreement "retroactively," he answered "yes," but was quick to add that his client would never take such action against a cardholder. We see little, if any, principled distinction, however, between admittedly "retroactive" cancellation and cancellation effective against irreversible obligations incurred after cancellation but before the cardholder learns his card has been cancelled.

The importance of effective notice of contract termination has not escaped the attention of the New York courts and legislature, particularly where an individual could suffer substantial harm if a contract to which he is a party is cancelled without his ever knowing. The most obvious examples come from the field of insurance law where New York, by statute, requires an insurer to give notice of its decision to cancel a policy. See, e.g., N.Y. Ins. Law §168 (McKinney's 1983) (fire insurance). The obvious, and salutary, purpose behind this policy is not to allow the insured to contest the decision, but to enable him to take steps to avoid a lapse in protection—a risk not wholly unlike that which a cardholder who intends to use his card to pay for a completed and irreversible transaction expects to avoid.

The parallel between New York insurance law and credit card law carries into contract interpretation, too. The New York case law instructs us to interpret credit card agreements by using the "rules for construction of insurance contracts." Uni-Serv Corp. v. Frede, 50 Misc. 2d 823, 271 N.Y.S.2d 478, 483 (1966), *aff'd* 53 Misc. 2d 644, 279 N.Y.S.2d 510 (1967). Like the insurance contract, the Cardmember Agreement was not negotiated, but was prepared exclusively by the card issuer; consequently, it should be construed narrowly against the creditor. Id.; see Miller v. Continental Ins. Co., 40 N.Y.2d 675, 389 N.Y.S.2d 565, 358 N.E.2d 258 (1976); Restatement (Second) of Contracts §206 (in choosing among interpretations, meaning which operates against drafters is preferred). This rule blends two independent canons of construction: first, that a contract is interpreted against its drafter and second, that a contract of adhesion should be strictly construed. See Surrey Strathmore Corp. v. Dollar Savings Bank, 36 N.Y.2d 173, 179, 366 N.Y.S.2d 107, 112, 325 N.E.2d 527, 531 (1975) (Wachtler, J., dissenting) (canons distinguished); see also Miner v. Walden, 101 Misc. 2d 814, 422 N.Y.S.2d 335, 337 (1979) ("adhesion contract" is a "standard contract form" offered without realistic opportunity to bargain and in which consumer must acquiesce to obtain desired product or service).

These authorities confirm our conclusion, as a court sitting in diversity, that the interpretation American Express proffers would not find favor in the New York courts. There can be no dispute that American Express drew the language for a broad application. But if American Express were correct in its interpretation, it even could refuse to honor past charges long since incurred—an outcome that must be rejected even in application of *strictum jus*. The right to cancel "without giving you notice" means that the decision to cancel can be entirely unilateral and instantaneous. It cannot, however, be an internalized decision which is never communicated to the cardholder. Such a reading defies any reasonable expectation that the parties could have had about their contractual relationship. See *Uni-Serv*, supra, 271 N.Y.S.2d at 483 ("It is not to be assumed that people act unreasonably to their own disadvantage, and an interpretation which assumes that they so acted is not favored.") (quoting Brown v. McGraw-Hill Book Co., Inc., 25 A.D.2d 317, 269 N.Y.S.2d 35, 38 (1st Dept. 1966), *aff'd*, 20 N.Y.S.2d 826, 285 N.Y.S.2d 72, 231 N.E.2d 768 (1967)); see also 1 Williston on Contracts §105 at 418 (3d ed. 1957) (interpret contract so as not to favor arbitrary cancellation clause); cf. Tymshare, Inc. v. Covell, 727 F.2d 1145, 1154 (D.C. Cir. 1984) (applying Virginia law; "[I]t is simply not likely that the parties had in mind a power quite as absolute as appellant suggests. . . . [A]greeing to such a provision [retroactive compensation reduction] would require a degree of folly . . . we are not inclined to posit where another plausible interpretation of the language is available."). Thus, we think that the "without notice" provision is given full weight by allowing the cancellation to be unilateral and to be given contemporaneous effect upon communication. To say that "without notice" also means that it never need be communicated to the cardholder extends the clause, and the waiver it contains, "to circumstances not covered." 2 M. Merrill, supra, 899 at p.427 (waiver of notice construed narrowly).

Indeed, the interpretation of the language urged by American Express would subsume the entire contract and make the underlying contractual relationship illusory. See Niagara Mohawk Power Corp. v. Graver Tank & Mfg. Co., 470 F. Supp. 1308, 1316 (N.D.N.Y. 1979) (applying New York law; presence of notice requirement in otherwise broad termination provision prevents promise from being illusory); Restatement (Second) of Contracts §77 comment a (illusory promises); 1A Corbin on Contracts §163 at p.76 (1963) ("If a promisor reserves the power to cancel at any time without notice, his promise seems to be unenforceable, . . . "); 1 Williston, supra, §105 at p.418 ("An agreement wherein one party reserves the right to cancel at his pleasure cannot create a contract.") (footnote omitted). We therefore hold that, even as a contract of adhesion, the language quoted above has limitations. The card can be revoked without cause and without any waiting period, but it cannot be revoked for transactions that already have occurred.

American Express suggests that if the clauses are not upheld in the manner it urges, there will be a great risk thrown on the credit card business. We think they protest too much. Within the limits of state and federal statutes, credit cards can still be cancelled without cause and without notice. But the cancellations can affect only transactions which have not occurred before the cancellation is communicated to the cardholder. In practical terms American Express will have to make an effort to communicate its cancellation decision to the cardholder. The effort may be as informal as a phone call or a telegram. We leave to future cases the question of what constitutes a good faith effort to communicate the cancellation decision to the cardholder.

Nor need we decide what fact situations would allow the communication of the cancellation to take place through the merchant involved in the transaction. If a cardholder seeks to use his American Express card to buy a car, for example, we think that a communication, through the car dealer, that the card has been cancelled prior to title passing to the cardholder may effect notice in reasonable fashion. But where the meal has been consumed, or the hotel room has been slept in, or the service rendered, the communication through the merchant comes too late to void the credit for that transaction.

Even contracts of adhesion are contracts. To allow cancellation without any communication of the decision is to turn the contract into a snare and deceit. It may well be that an *offeree* has less expectation of performance and that the terms and conditions or withdrawal of the offer can be, as American Express argues, much more absolute and *ex parte*. See Restatement (Second) of Contracts §42 comment a. But contracts, as opposed to offers, are made of sterner doctrine; to interpret this contract so as to sanction the conduct of American Express in this case would empty the agreement of all meaning. . . .

We therefore hold that the cancellation without notice provision, as interpreted by American Express, is unenforceable. We remand the case to the District Court to resolve Gray's claims under the contract.

C. DISCOVERY

Because the case is to be remanded for further proceedings, we think it appropriate to comment on the appellee's extraordinary use of interrogatories below. It appears to be of some significance to this case that Gray is a lawyer, because only a lawyer, tenacious even beyond the professional custom, would have been able to withstand the expenses and excesses of this litigation. Perhaps the presence of a lawyer-plaintiff caused American Express particular concern that occasioned their plethora of interrogatories; perhaps it was the shorter, but nonetheless substantial, set of interrogatories that plaintiff served on defendant. Whoever was the instigator and whatever the reason, the various sets of interrogatories and their answers are in the hundreds of pages. They run as far afield as inquiring the name of every law firm that plaintiff had been affiliated with since 1951 to asking all of the "professional credentials" that he had acquired in his lifetime; from psychiatrists consulted since 1978 to meals eaten at the fated restaurant since the suit was filed. The length, scope and detail of the interrogatories propounded by American Express suggest a strategy of attrition rather than a legitimate discovery of the facts needed to resolve a dispute over the account.

We cannot expect the District Judge to police the quantity or equality of interrogatories when discovery is abused in the way it appears to have been in this case. Gray did object to some of the interrogatories, as did American Express. But when the parties do not raise the question of general abuse of discovery, it is difficult for a trial judge, viewing the process segmentally, to realize how burdensome it has become. On remand, we think the trial court should take the quantity and relevance of the discovery into account in setting the case for trial and in determining what, if any, further discovery should be allowed, and in deciding whether sanctions for abusive litigation practices are appropriate. See Roadway Express, Inc. v. Piper, 447 U.S. 752, 764-67,

100 S. Ct. 2455, 2463-64, 65 L. Ed. 2d 488 (1980) (inherent power to impose sanctions); Fed. R. Civ. P. 26(b), (g) and Notes of Advisory Committee, 1983 Amendment (amended rule "contemplates greater judicial involvement in the discovery process").

The size of the record and the vigor with which the defenses have been pursued make it apparent that only a stubborn professional could seek to avail himself of the protection guaranteed by statute and the common law. The courts must exercise control so that access to justice is not foreclosed by such tactics at the preliminary stages of suit. Deep pockets and stubbornness ought not be prerequisites to bringing a case like this one to issue.

III. CONCLUSION

The District Court's order of summary judgment and dismissal is hereby vacated. The case is remanded for further proceedings consistent with this opinion.

So Ordered.

Dealing with a credit card issuer's computer can be maddening. Say this sentence to any group of Americans and get ready to hear their horror stories. To alleviate the difficulties, the Fair Credit Billing Act creates certain duties on the part of the card issuer whenever the consumer complains of an alleged billing error. Look at Reg. Z §226.13 (the regulation implementing the FCBA's dispute resolution rules) to answer the following Problem.

PROBLEM 49

Mary Bush opened her monthly bill from Big Department Store and was puzzled to find a charge for $63 that she did not remember incurring. The charge was described as "MERCH." There was also a numerical symbol showing that the department in which she charged the merch was the draperies department. She could not remember buying any draperies. She received the bill on March 5, and two days later she wrote a letter to Big Department Store asking for clarification of the charge.

a. Does this request qualify as a "billing error" under Regulation Z?

b. Would it have been a "billing error" if she had been complaining about the *quality* of the goods purchased with her credit card?

c. If the bill that the store sent her had demanded that she write complaints on a separate slip of paper, and not on the bill itself, could the store safely ignore any complaints she wrote on the bill? See Reg. Z n.29. Why would the creditor care where the consumer wrote the complaint?

d. What must the department store do now, and how quickly must the store do it?

e. If the credit manager for Big Department Store gets on the phone to Mary and works everything out in one call, need the store comply with the procedures created by the Fair Credit Billing Act? See Reg. Z n.28.

f. If the store sends Mary another monthly bill during the investigatory period, can it include the $63 as part of the amount due? See Reg. Z n.30. If a credit reporting agency requests credit information about Mary's account during this period, can it report the $63 as delinquent?

g. Three weeks after Mary complained, the investigation by the credit manager turned up a charge slip with Mary's name signed to it reflecting a purchase by her of a throw rug priced at $63. The store mailed this information to Mary, along with a copy of the charge slip. It did not normally give its customers any grace period in which to pay without incurring finance charges, so it told Mary that she had to pay the $63 plus interest since March 1. Is this the law?

h. Mary, still sure that she had not purchased a rug at Big Department Store, wrote immediately, continuing to protest the charge. Big Department Store ignored her letter and reported her as delinquent to a credit reporting agency (though it also reported that she still disputed the debt). Mary calls you, her cousin the attorney, for advice. What, if anything, can she do now?

PROBLEM 50

Two months later, Mary Bush opened her periodic statement from Octopus National Bank, which had issued her a Visa card the previous year. It contained a charge for an item she had returned to the merchant the day after she bought it, and for which the merchant had said he would reverse the charge.

a. How quickly must the merchant fulfill this promise? See Reg. Z §226.12(e).

b. Is Mary's written complaint a "billing error" as those words are used in §226.13(a)?

c. The bank failed to respond to Mary's letter in any way, but continued to send her monthly bills reflecting the purchase. Mary took the bill to the merchant, who apologized and said he had forgotten to send through the credit to her account. The merchant promptly gave her a refund in cash. Now Mary calls you, her cousin who handled the last Problem so well, and asks if she has any rights against Octopus National Bank? See the Truth in Lending Act §130(a) (and remember that the Fair Credit Billing Act is technically called "Chapter 4" of the TILA) and then look at TILA §161 (particularly (e) of that section).

DILLARD DEPARTMENT STORES, INC. v. OWENS
Court of Appeals of Texas, Corpus Christi, 1997
951 S.W.2d 915

SEERDEN, Chief Justice.

Dillard Department Stores appeals from a judgment denying its claim against Richard Owens for payment of a charge card debt and awarding Owens attorney's fees. Dillard raises ten points of error complaining of the award of attorney's fees and, alternately, of the admission of improper evidence at trial. We affirm in part, and reverse and suggest remittitur in part.

Owens opened an account with Dillard in 1970 and received a charge card in his own name. Owens then married Davis on November 1, 1990. However, shortly thereafter, the couple separated, Davis moved to Kansas, and Owens filed for divorce in Nueces County, Texas, at the beginning of December 1990. While in Wichita, Kansas, Davis obtained from Dillard a temporary charge card on Owens' account on December 22, 1990. Between December 23, 1990, and December 28, 1990, Davis purchased some $5,000 worth of goods from Dillard on the charge card.

When Owens received the bill for Davis' purchases in January 1991, he protested by sending a letter of dispute to Dillard complaining that the charges were unauthorized. Dillard acknowledged the dispute and requested that Owens come into its Corpus Christi store, examine the receipts and sign an affidavit declaring that the purchases were fraudulently made. Owens did so. Dillard then contacted Davis, who informed Dillard of the marriage and said that the purchases had been authorized. Dillard then sent a letter to Owens on April 1, 1991, denying his assertions of fraud.

Dillard sued Owens and Davis to recover payment for Davis' purchases under theories of breach of contract, quantum meruit, implied contract, unjust enrichment, and community debt. Owens generally denied Dillard's petition and counterclaimed for a declaratory judgment that no contract exists with Dillard whereby he authorized Davis to charge purchases to his account, and that he is not liable for such charges. Owens alleged that he made a good faith attempt to resolve his disagreement with Dillard under the Federal Truth-in-Lending Act, 15 U.S.C. §1666i. Finally, Owens requested attorney's fees from Dillard.

The case was tried to a jury on the uncontroverted facts set forth above. The jury rejected Dillard's theory that Owens authorized Davis to make purchases on his Dillard's charge card, or that Davis' purchases were for necessaries. The jury found that Owens made a good faith attempt to obtain satisfactory resolution of the disputed charges with Dillard, that Dillard did not send a written explanation or clarification to Owens after having conducted an investigation setting forth the reasons Dillard believes the account was correctly shown in the statement, and that Dillard should have deleted all of the disputed charges from Owens' account. The jury further found that reasonable and necessary attorney's fees for Owens' attorney were $10,000 for trial, $7,500 for appeal to the Court of Appeals, $3,500 for application for writ of error to the Texas Supreme Court, and $3,500 if the writ of error is granted.

The trial court rendered judgment that Dillard take nothing from Owens, and that Owens recover attorney's fees from Dillard in the amounts found by the jury. However, the trial court's judgment did not grant any declaratory relief in favor of Owens.

Dillard generally has not challenged the take-nothing judgment on its claims against Owens. However, by nine points of error, Dillard complains of the trial court's award of attorney's fees to Owens.

By its first and second points of error, Dillard complains that, because declaratory relief was inappropriate and ultimately not awarded to Owens, the trial court erred in granting attorney's fees under the authority of the Uniform Declaratory Judgments Act. Owens concedes that the trial court granted no additional declaratory relief to him and that he has no claim for attorney's fees under the Uniform Declaratory Judgments Act. . . .

By its third through seventh points of error, Dillard complains that TILA likewise does not support an award of attorney's fees to Owens, because he asserted no affirmative claim for relief under the Act, nor was he awarded damages for a violation thereof.

The Truth-in-Lending Act generally regulates specified aspects of consumer credit and billing practices. Its overall purpose is "to protect the consumer against inaccurate and unfair credit billing and credit card practices." 15 U.S.C. §1601(a); see Fairley v. Turan-Foley Imports, Inc., 65 F.3d

475, 477 (5th Cir. 1995). Accordingly, TILA is enforced strictly against creditors and construed liberally in favor of the consumer. *Fairley,* 65 F.3d at 482; Thomas v. Myers-Dickson Furniture Co., 479 F.2d 740, 748 (5th Cir. 1973).

The provision of TILA dealing with civil liability states generally that "any creditor who fails to comply with any requirement imposed under [specified parts of the Act] with respect to any person is liable to such person in an amount equal to the sum of—(1) any actual damage sustained by such person as a result of the failure; (2) [statutory penalties]; (3) in the case of any successful action to enforce the foregoing liability or in any action in which a person is determined to have a right of rescission under section 1635 of this title, the costs of the action, together with a reasonable attorney's fee as determined by the court. . . . " 15 U.S. C. §1640(a).

In the present case, if Dillard, as creditor, failed to comply with a provision of TILA in its attempt to collect the asserted credit card debt against Owens, and if Owens was successful in an action to enforce liability against Dillard for such noncompliance, then Owens also has a right to reasonable attorney's fees. Our first question is whether Dillard breached any duty to Owens under TILA for which Owens could hold it liable.

The responsibilities of creditor and debtor under the TILA with regard to billing disputes are generally set forth in section 1666, which requires the debtor to initiate written notice of any billing error. The creditor must then acknowledge the disputed charge and either correct it or "send a written explanation or clarification to the obligor, after having conducted an investigation, setting forth to the extent applicable the reasons why the creditor believes the account of the obligor was correctly shown in the statement and, upon request of the obligor, provide copies of documentary evidence of the obligor's indebtedness. . . . " 15 U.S.C. §1666(a)(B)(ii). The creditor's failure to comply with these requirements causes him to forfeit the right to collect the disputed amounts up to $50.00. 15 U.S.C. §1666(e). Section 1666i generally preserves the claims and defenses of the debtor against the creditor arising out of a credit card transaction, if the debtor has, among other things, "made a good faith attempt to obtain satisfactory resolution of a disagreement or problem relative to the transaction from the person honoring the credit card." 15 U.S.C. §1666i(a).

The jury findings in the present case show that, while Owens complied with section 1666i by making a good faith attempt to obtain a satisfactory resolution of the billing error, Dillard did not comply with the requirement of section 1666(a)(B)(ii) concerning a written explanation or clarification setting forth the reasons the account was correctly shown.

By its sixth point or [sic] error, Dillard challenges the legal and factual sufficiency of the evidence to support the jury's finding that it violated this requirement. . . .

It is undisputed that Dillard sent its April 1, 1991, letter to Owens asserting his liability for the debt in the following terms:

> We are in receipt of a fraud affidavit in [sic] which you completed. However, after research and investigation, we find that you and Dianna McKay Owens were legally married at the time the purchases in question were made. For this reason, we are unable to process your request as fraud. We feel this should be handled as a civil matter.

We conclude that the letter itself demonstrates Dillard's failure to comply with the requirements of TILA concerning a satisfactory explanation for why it continued to hold Owens liable for Davis' purchases. Although Dillard did mention Owens' marriage to Davis as an impediment to "processing" his fraud claim, this ambiguous and conclusory statement offers no justification as to the basis on which Dillard asserted that Owens remained liable for such purchases. Dillard's theory at trial, that the purchases were for "necessaries" which one spouse is obliged to provide to the other, was never mentioned in the letter or investigated beyond merely a cursory review of the items purchased. Accordingly, the letter and surrounding circumstances offered legally and factually sufficient evidence that Dillard violated this provision of TILA. We overrule Dillard's sixth point of error.

However, in order for Owens to be entitled to attorney's fees, we must further find under section 1640(a)(3) that Owens was successful in an action to enforce liability against Dillard for its noncompliance with TILA.

Although Owens recovered no actual damage award against Dillard, he did successfully defeat Dillard's claim against him for Davis' unauthorized use of the charge card. Moreover, Dillard's violation of TILA played a substantial part in its attempt to recover the improper charges against Owens. Had Dillard attempted to comply with TILA by stating its full theory of liability in a proper written explanation to Owens, it is likely that the futility of its attempt to enforce the debt against him would have become obvious at that time, and both parties could have avoided the time and expense of the present proceedings.

The purpose of the protections afforded a consumer under section 1666 is not, after all, to change the substantive law with regard to his liability for the underlying debt, but to protect him from the intimidating process of bargaining over a disputed debt with a creditor in a superior bargaining position. Without such protections, the creditor may use that bargaining power to encourage payment of even an illegitimate debt by threatening to force the consumer to expend substantial time and money to protect his rights. The fact that the creditor ultimately loses his claim in court does not diminish the expense to the consumer of protecting his rights, unless that consumer either brings an affirmative claim for the statutory penalties and/or collects attorney's fees and costs for his defense.

In another context, the Fifth Circuit has recognized the dilemma that a consumer faces in trying to enforce the provisions of TILA, under which Congress had intended to create "a system of 'private attorney generals' who will be able to aid the effective enforcement of the Act." Sosa v. Fite, 498 F.2d 114, 121 (5th Cir. 1974) (quoting *Thomas,* 479 F.2d at 748). Accordingly, the *Sosa* court allowed attorney's fees to a debtor who successfully sued to rescind a consumer credit transaction under section 1635 of the Act, even though the debtor's action did not fall within the literal application of section 1640 at that time. So long as the action "vindicates congressional policy," the *Sosa* court concluded that it was within the trial court's discretion to award attorney's fees to the successful debtor. *Sosa,* 498 F.2d at 121; see also Purtle v. Eldridge Auto Sales, Inc., 91 F.3d 797, 800 (6th Cir. 1996) (plaintiff in a TILA case need not prove that he or she suffered actual monetary damages in order to recover the statutory damages and attorney's fees); but see Rachbach v. Cogswell, 547 F.2d 502, 506 (10th Cir. 1976) (criticizing *Sosa* for failing to follow the "American Rule" that attorney's fees are not ordinarily recoverable in the absence of statutory authorization).

The same policy considerations expressed by the *Sosa* court justify allowing attorney's fees to the consumer who successfully defends an action by a creditor who has violated TILA by its improper attempts to collect the underlying debt. Had Dillard complied with TILA and properly handled the present dispute, it likely would have been resolved much earlier in Owens' favor and he would not have had to spend a significant amount of money defending his rights before the trial court and now this Court. One obvious purpose of TILA is to simplify the resolution of disputes and to place the consumer on a more equal footing in the resolution of such disputes. When the creditor fails to follow TILA procedures, he encourages misunderstandings, a lack of communication, and ultimately litigation. The costs of such litigation should not fall on the innocent consumer, but on the creditor who has failed to comply with TILA.

We conclude that the trial court had authority to award attorney's fees to Owens under TILA. Accordingly, we overrule Dillard's first seven points of error.

By its eighth and ninth points of error, Dillard complains that the amount of attorney's fees awarded to Owens was excessive and unsupported by legally or factually sufficient evidence.

Generally, when substantive federal claims, defenses or rights are raised in state court, state law and rules still govern the manner in which the federal questions are tried and proved. See Jack B. Anglin Co. v. Tipps, 842 S.W.2d 266, 268 (Tex. 1992). Accordingly, although Owens' claim for attorney's fees may arise under federal substantive law, the process of proving and awarding such damages is controlled by Texas procedure and rules of proof generally with regard to attorney's fees.

Texas law generally requires an award for attorney's fees to be based on sufficient evidence presented at trial to support the amount awarded. Valley Coca-Cola Bottling Co. v. Molina, 818 S.W.2d 146, 149 (Tex. App–Corpus Christi 1991, writ denied); cf. Tex. Civ. Prac. & Rem. Code Ann. §38.004 (Vernon 1997) (providing for judicial notice of reasonable and customary attorney's fees awarded under that statute in certain limited circumstances).

In the present case, attorney John Warren testified as an expert witness for Owens to usual hourly rates of between $100 and $175 for consumer law cases in Nueces County, Texas. He also testified to a reasonable and necessary number of hours between 100 and 130 to represent Owens on the entire case at trial. However, Warren testified that $7,500 (50 hours at $150 per hour) would be a reasonable and necessary fee for prosecution of the counterclaim alone through trial. Finally, Warren testified that a fee of between $4,000 and $5,000 would be reasonable for appeal to the court of appeals, between $2,500 and $3,000 for application for writ of error to the Supreme Court of Texas, and an additional $2,500 to $3,000 to argue the case before the Supreme Court of Texas.

The jury assessed reasonable and necessary attorney's fees for Owens at $10,000 for trial, $7,500 for appeal to the Court of Appeals, $3,500 for application for writ of error to the Texas Supreme Court, and $3,500 if the writ of error is granted, and the trial court granted judgment for those amounts.

Dillard initially complains that the award of attorney's fees for trial of the case should have been limited to the $7,500 that Warren estimated with regard to prosecuting the counterclaim. However, Warren's testimony supports higher attorney's fees of $10,000 for both prosecution of the counterclaim and defense against Dillard's claim. As our analysis of Owens' substantive right to attorney's fees under section 1640 of the Truth-in-Lending Act shows, he is entitled to such fees not only in relation to the counterclaim, but also to compensate him for the costs of defending against Dillard's illegitimate claim for payment.

However, with regard to appellate attorney's fees, we agree with Dillard that the amounts awarded to Owens clearly exceed the upper amounts to which Warren testified. Accordingly, we will suggest a remittitur of the excess amounts awarded. See *Valley Coca-Cola*, 818 S.W.2d at 149. We overrule in part, and sustain in part, Dillard's eighth and ninth points of error.

By its tenth point of error, Dillard complains that the trial court erred in admitting evidence of Federal Trade Commission charges made against Dillard.

Owens offered at trial a September 21, 1994, press release published in the "FTC News" alleging that:

> Dillard Department Stores, Inc. has been charged by the Federal Trade Commission with violating federal law by making it unreasonably difficult for consumers to remove unauthorized charges from their Dillard's charge-card bills. For example, the FTC alleged, Dillard's has forced customers who claim unauthorized charges to file notarized affidavits and agree to testify against the purported unauthorized user in court. Dillard's also allegedly treats payment for questioned charges as a waiver of a cardholder's claim that the charges were unauthorized, and holds cardholders liable for charges by their spouses, even when the charges were unauthorized and applicable state law does not impose liability, the FTC charged.

Dillard made numerous objections to the press release, based among other things on hearsay, relevance, prejudice, improper attack on character, and failure to authenticate. The trial court overruled Dillard's objections and allowed the press release into evidence.

Whether or not this press release was properly entered into evidence, we do not believe that its erroneous admission would require a new trial. Dillard generally admitted at trial to the course of conduct outlined in the press release as it applied to Dillard's dealings with Owens. Moreover, the questions presented to the jury required them to determine whether that conduct, and particularly Dillard's handling of Owens' billing dispute, satisfied the requirements of TILA §1666 with regard to the investigation and explanation of charges, matters which the FTC press release did not address.

We conclude that the admission of the press release was not reasonably calculated to cause, nor did it probably cause, the rendition of an improper judgment. *See* Tex. R. App. P. 81(b)(1). We overrule Dillard's tenth point of error.

With regard to the award of attorney's fees generally, we AFFIRM the judgment of the trial court. However, with regard to appellate attorney's fees, we suggest that, within thirty days of this opinion, Owens file a REMITTITUR in this Court decreasing his award of appellate attorney's fees to $5,000 for his appeal to this Court, and $3,000 each for an application for writ and argument before the Texas Supreme Court. If Owens files such a remittitur, we will reform the judgment and AFFIRM. Otherwise, we will REVERSE and REMAND this cause for a redetermination of appellate attorney's fees.

PROBLEM 51

Joseph Armstrong bought a sofa at Plush Furnishings, Inc. using the MasterCard issued him by Bank of the Midwest. Plush Furnishings promised to deliver the sofa the following week, but troubles with its own supplier kept delaying the delivery. Two weeks later Joseph got the MasterCard bill from the bank, but he still hadn't received his sofa. When he sat down to pay his bills three weeks later, he got worried about the unwarranted charge, so he phoned the bank and told them the problem. The person who took his call (whose name he failed to get) was very sympathetic. Five weeks later he got a second bill from the bank, and, when he paid his bills two weeks after that, this time he wrote them a letter explaining that he had not received the sofa in spite of repeated calls to Plush Furnishings. The bank's credit department wrote Mr. Armstrong a reply stating that since he, Armstrong, had not made a written complaint within 60 days of the mailing of the first periodic statement, the bank had no further responsibilities in the matter. He was advised to settle the dispute with the merchant. Is the bank right? See Reg. Z §226.12(c).

BELL v. MAY DEPT. STORES CO.[10]
Supreme Court of Missouri, 1999
6 S.W.3d 871

RONNIE L. WHITE, Judge.

John E. Bell appeals from summary judgment entered against him and in favor of Respondent, the May Department Stores Company, d/b/a Famous Barr Company ("Famous Barr") on April 14, 1997. The trial court entered summary judgment on Count I of Bell's petition, which claims Famous Barr violated the Truth in Lending Act, 15 U.S.C. section 1666, *et seq.,* and Regulation Z, specifically 12 C.F.R. section 226.13. The trial court also entered summary judgment on Count II of Bell's petition, which

---

10. Footnotes in this case have been renumbered for clarity.

claims Famous Barr tortiously interfered with Bell's credit expectancy. We reverse and remand.

I.   FACTUAL BACKGROUND

* * *

A review of the record yields the following facts and reasonable inferences therefrom in the light most favorable to Bell. Bell purchased a ceiling fan on August 2, 1992, at Famous Barr and charged the purchase price of $132.16 to his Famous Barr credit card account. After installing it a few weeks later, Bell determined the fan was defective because it made an unacceptable level of noise at all speeds and he was unable to fix it. Famous Barr never inspected the fan to dispute Bell's determination.

Famous Barr billed Bell for the cost of the fan on September 1, 1992, with payment due on September 25. On or about September 23, 1992, Bell told a Famous Barr representative his fan was defective and he did not intend to pay for it. Bell also sent Famous Barr a letter memorializing this conversation, dated October 27, 1992, following the directives on the back of his Famous Barr billing statement[11] and making a general reference to "Regulation Z." Famous Barr wrote Bell acknowledging its receipt of his letter.

Famous Barr later contacted Bell in November and agreed to locate a replacement fan and reimburse Bell for the installation cost. They never discussed the details, nor did they agree when Bell should ultimately pay for the fan. Bell waited for Famous Barr to locate a replacement fan and notify him, but he was never notified.

Bell again notified Famous Barr when his November 1992 statement contained a past due notice for the unpaid fan. Famous Barr assured Bell it had simply made a mistake. From May through October 1993, however, Bell's monthly statement showed past due notices, late fees, and finance

---

11. The reverse side of the billing statement provides, in pertinent part:

If you think your bill is wrong . . . , write us on a separate sheet of paper and mail it to the address below as soon as possible. We must hear from you no later than 60 days after we sent you the first bill on which the error or problem appeared. . . .

You do not have to pay any amount in question which we are investigating, but you are still obligated to pay the parts of your bill that are not in question. While we investigate your questions, we cannot report you are delinquent or take any action to collect the amount in question. . . .

If you have a problem with the quality of goods . . . that you purchased with a credit card, and you have tried in good faith to correct the problem with the merchant, you may not have to pay the remaining amount due on the goods. . . .

charges. Except for the disputed price of the fan, Bell *always* paid his balance in full each month. On May 4, 1993, Famous Barr informed Bell it was sending his account to three credit reporting agencies, including TRW.[12] It made similar written threats to Bell and reports throughout the summer and threatened to report the most derogatory rating of "R9." Bell contacted Famous Barr to explain the dispute numerous times. He was assured no further action would be taken to collect the disputed amount and that the matter would not affect his credit rating.

Famous Barr used a computer billing system that automatically generated billing statements, dunning notices, and derogatory reports to credit agencies. If Famous Barr determined there was a legitimate dispute regarding the quality of a product, then it would not suppress the reporting of information to a credit agency. If negative information were reported erroneously, then Famous Barr would have to contact the credit agencies directly to delete it.

In August 1993, the parties reached a provisional settlement agreement. Famous Barr agreed to credit Bell's account with all finance and late fee charges and reinstate his credit line. Bell agreed to pay for the fan if Famous Barr sent a letter permitting the imminent buyer of Bell's house to exchange the fan. Nevertheless, on September 1, 1993, Famous Barr assessed late fees and finance charges for nonpayment, closed Bell's account, and reported derogatory information to the credit reporting agencies.

After memorializing this settlement agreement and sending a copy to Famous Barr on September 13, 1993, Bell received written confirmation that Famous Barr would "delete all derogatory information." On October 4, 1993, Bell re-dated his September 1993 letter and mailed it with a check for the price of the fan. Later that month, however, Bell found his Famous Barr account closed due to "poor prior payment history." Bell wrote a letter to Famous Barr quoting the pertinent sections of Regulation Z and demanding

---

12. This letter stated in pertinent part:

THE PAYMENT PERFORMANCE OF YOUR FAMOUS-BARR ACCOUNT IS BEING REPORTED TO THE FOLLOWING CREDIT BUREAUS[:]

CBI/EQUIFAX

TRANSUNION CORPORATION

TRW INFORMATION SERVICES

THIS MAY WELL AFFECT YOUR ABILITY TO OBTAIN OR RETAIN CREDIT ELSEWHERE.

IT IS URGENT THAT YOU FORWARD PAYMENT AT ONCE OR CONTACT [FAMOUS BARR] IMMEDIATELY.

the deletion of adverse or derogatory credit history from his file. Famous Barr reinstated Bell's account, faxed letters to the credit reporting agencies to that effect, and sent Bell a copy. The parties later discovered the corrective letters that Famous Barr sent to the credit reporting agencies contained the wrong account number.

In early summer 1994, Bell applied to the European American Bank ("EAB") for a TWA credit card, hoping to earn frequent flyer miles with his purchases. EAB refused to extend credit based upon derogatory Famous Barr information contained in a credit report from TRW. TRW's report did not reflect Famous Barr's request to delete all derogatory credit information. Bell also discovered Famous Barr had requested other credit reporting agencies to delete his entire twenty-two year credit history with Famous Barr, the large majority of which was positive. Bell sued.

II. *COUNT I—REGULATION Z OF THE TRUTH IN LENDING ACT*

* * *

Count I in Bell's petition claims Famous Barr violated 15 U.S.C. sections 1666(b)(3) & 1666a (1994) by reporting him delinquent to various credit reporting agencies after receiving notice of a "billing error" and prior to resolving that error. Count I also claims Famous Barr violated 15 U.S.C. sections 1666(b)(3) & (d) by restricting and closing his Famous Barr account after receiving notice of a "billing error" and prior to resolving that error.[13]

12 C.F.R. section 226.13(a)(3) defines a "billing error" as a "reflection on or with a periodic statement of an extension of credit for property or services *not accepted* by the consumer or the consumer's designee, or not delivered to the consumer or the consumer's designee as agreed." Famous Barr argues the "billing error" alleged by Bell and essential to his claim did not occur because Bell accepted the fan. We apply state law to resolve whether Bell accepted it.

In Missouri, Article 2 of the Uniform Commercial Code governs the acceptance of goods. Acceptance occurs when the buyer: 1) after an opportunity to inspect the goods, informs the seller that the goods are conforming or that he will keep them despite their nonconformity; 2) fails to make an effective rejection; or 3) does any act inconsistent with the seller's

---

13. If Famous Barr committed these violations, then it may be liable to Bell for actual damages, twice the amount of any finance charge, and the cost of the action and attorney's fees. 15 U.S.C. section 1640(a).

ownership. [Uniform Commercial Code §2-606] Famous Barr argues Bell accepted the fan because he did not reject it.

For an effective rejection, the buyer must notify the seller in accordance with the contract or within a reasonable time if the contract is silent. [Uniform Commercial Code §2-602] The statute does not require written notice. What constitutes a reasonable time for rejecting defective goods is a jury question when fair-minded persons could disagree. Actions of the parties, such as assurances from the seller, also may affect what constitutes a reasonable time. "If the buyer does not use the goods as his own, but rescinds the contract and holds the merchandise as bailee for the seller, the buyer is not liable for the sale price (assuming the rejection was justified)."[14]

A reasonable jury could find Bell did not accept the fan. He properly notified Famous Barr and Famous Barr duly received notice of the defective fan. Bell's rejection of the fan within three months of purchase was reasonable, especially since Bell did not install it until some weeks after he bought it and tried to fix it. Bell also notified Famous Barr of his rejection within the sixty-day period prescribed by both 12 C.F.R. section 226.13(b)(1) and Famous Barr's own billing statement. In addition, Bell did not commit acts inconsistent with Famous Barr's ownership of the rejected fan. Bell neither used the fan, nor prevented Famous Barr from removing it. Famous Barr even encouraged Bell to retain it pending replacement.

Also contrary to the decision of the trial court, summary judgment is improper because a reasonable jury could find Bell attempted to resolve his dispute with Famous Barr in good faith. Bell claimed he long awaited the availability of a replacement fan and the parties dispute when they first agreed Bell would pay for it.

If a reasonable jury finds Bell did not accept the fan, and acted in good faith, then it can find a "billing error" existed. If a "billing error existed," Famous Barr violated the Federal Truth in Lending Act by closing Bell's account and reporting him to credit agencies. The decision of the trial court granting Famous Barr's motion for summary judgment on Count I is reversed.

III. COUNT II—INTENTIONAL INTERFERENCE WITH CREDIT EXPECTANCY

Count II of Bell's petition claims Famous Barr intentionally interfered with Bell's credit expectancy by reporting false and negative information to credit agencies. This tort is one sort of intentional interference with a business expectancy and is comprised of the following elements: (1) a valid

---

14. Paramount Sales Co., Inc. v. Stark, 690 S.W.2d 500, 504 (Mo. App. 1985) (finding buyer properly rejected goods).

credit expectancy; (2) defendant's knowledge of the expectancy; (3) a denial of credit induced or caused by defendant's intentional interference; (4) absence of justification; and (5) damages. We find Bell presented genuinely disputed facts to meet each of these five elements so that a jury could find that Famous Barr intentionally interfered with his valid credit expectancy.

A. CREDIT EXPECTANCY

An expectancy is "that which is expected or hoped for." To have valid credit expectancy one need not have a formal contract. There must be, however, a reasonable expectation of obtaining credit. This expectancy cannot be too indefinite or remote. The dispute in this case centers on whether Bell could have had valid credit expectancy at the time derogatory information was reported without having had a credit application pending with any creditor. . . .

Bell presented undisputed evidence that he had a perfect credit history until Famous Barr reported derogatory information. He made $15,000.00 in credit card purchases per year on average, had financing for his home, and no creditor had ever reported him delinquent. He also had a credit account with Famous Barr for twenty-two years, which he paid in full every month. In addition, Bell never was denied credit until denied by EAB. Finally, Bell showed he repeatedly asked Famous Barr to remove derogatory information from his credit report. Although Bell had no credit application pending at the time Famous Barr reported derogatory information, a reasonable jury could find he had valid credit expectancy based on his longstanding clean credit history, and his efforts to keep it clean. This holding is consistent with the rule that no formal contract is required for valid credit expectancy.

We stress that only a *valid* or *reasonable* expectancy of credit satisfies the test. Not only must plaintiff *expect* to apply for credit, but also plaintiff must have a *reasonable chance* of obtaining credit. What constitutes a reasonable chance of obtaining credit is usually a question of fact for the jury to decide where fair-minded persons could disagree. In this case, a reasonable jury could find Bell's chance of obtaining credit was reasonable by his credit report being devoid of any delinquency. We hold a reasonable jury could find Bell had valid credit expectancy.

Famous Barr argues we should follow Haas v. Town and Country Mortgage Company[15] to conclude Bell had no valid expectancy of credit because he had no credit application pending with EAB when Famous Barr reported derogatory information. In *Haas*, plaintiffs sought to buy a

---

15. 886 S.W.2d 225.

piece of property that was being foreclosed and assumed the mortgage from the owner. Plaintiffs were negligent by not inquiring about the eligibility requirements of the mortgage loan they assumed, and one week after closing defendant mortgagee informed them they were ineligible because the loan was reserved for first time buyers. Defendant gave plaintiffs certain options, none of which plaintiffs exercised. Despite being advised by their own title company to make loan payments until the problem was resolved, plaintiffs missed payments. Consequently, defendant reported that plaintiffs were delinquent. Plaintiffs thereafter were denied credit and charged higher-than-normal interest rates on a car loan. The court of appeals reversed the judgment the trial court entered in favor of plaintiffs' claim for tortious interference with a business expectancy. It found "no evidence in the record that at the time [defendant] issued the credit reports that plaintiffs had established a business relationship either with any of the credit card companies which denied them credit or with the lender of the car loan."[16]

Despite similarities between *Haas* and the instant case, *Haas* does not control because of important factual differences. Unlike the instant case, in *Haas* there was no evidence defendant wrongfully reported derogatory information to credit card companies. Plaintiffs neglected to learn the eligibility requirements of their loan and they were advised to continue re-paying the loan. It is reasonable to conclude the court rejected plaintiffs' claim of intentional interference with a business expectancy claim because defendant was justified in reporting the derogatory information—the fourth element of this tort claim.

Also unlike the instant case, in *Haas* there was no evidence of the strength of plaintiffs' credit history. It found plaintiff's "mere hope" of establishing a credit relationship "tenuous" and not "evinc[ing] the existence of a valid business relationship or expectancy." The court may have found that while plaintiffs had credit expectancy, they lacked a *valid* or *reasonable* expectancy. This language also suggests the court rejected plaintiff's claim because insufficient evidence showed defendant's actions caused plaintiffs' creditors to deny them credit—the third element of this tort claim.

Notwithstanding these factual differences, the court in *Haas* may have under-appreciated the claim of tortious interference with credit expectancy. It ruled against plaintiffs because they had no "established" business relationship with a creditor. It considered the "mere hope" of establishing a credit relationship "tenuous" and not "evinc[ing] the existence of a valid business relationship or expectancy." The court incorrectly focused exclusively on an

---

16. *Id.* at 228.

established business relationship. As explained above, a formal credit contract is not necessary for valid credit expectancy. Expectancy is just that: hope. If that hope is reasonable, then plaintiff has valid credit expectancy. In neither its factual background nor its analysis did the court in *Haas* cite any evidence of plaintiffs' credit history. Nor did it consider the reasonableness or validity of plaintiff's hope of obtaining credit.

To the extent *Haas* and [other cases] require a pending credit application in order to find valid credit expectancy, they are overruled.

B. KNOWLEDGE OF CREDIT EXPECTANCY

The tort of intentional interference with credit expectancy "presupposes [defendant's] knowledge of the plaintiff's [expectancy], or at least facts which would lead a reasonable person to believe that such [expectancy] exists. Without such knowledge, there can be no intent and no liability."[17]

The evidence Bell presented shows a genuine dispute whether Famous Barr knew or should have known of his credit expectancy. In July 1993, Famous Barr wrote Bell one of a series of dunning letters threatening, "[Y]our credit bureau report will show a derogatory rating of R9 for the next seven years. This may result in denial when trying to obtain car loans, charge cards, apartment rental, home mortgage, and even employment." These letters permit an inference that Famous Barr believed Bell cared about the effect a derogatory rating would have on his ability to obtain credit and likely were attempts to encourage Bell to pay to avoid a derogatory report. In addition, Bell repeatedly notified Famous Barr of his receipt of these letters and asked it not to make derogatory reports. Finally, although plaintiff need not show defendant knew or should have known plaintiff's credit expectancy was *valid* or *reasonable,* it may be fairly inferred that Famous Barr knew or reasonably should have known of Bell's valid credit expectancy because his credit history with Famous Barr was perfect.

It is also irrelevant that Famous Barr could not have known Bell would apply specifically to EAB for credit. As noted above, there is evidence Famous Barr knew or reasonably should have known of Bell's more general credit expectancy.

C. INTENT AND CAUSATION

"The person claiming tortious interference has the burden of proving that the other party actively and affirmatively took steps to induce the

---

17. W. Page Keeton et al., *Prosser and Keeton on the Law of Torts,* section 129, at 982 (5th ed. 1987) (using "contract or interest" instead of "[expectancy]").

breach and that the expectancy would have come to fruition but for the actor's improper conduct."[18] Bell must show both intent and causation.

Famous Barr had the requisite intent if it knew interference was certain or substantially certain to occur as a result of its actions, even if its express purpose was not to interfere. The evidence Bell presented shows a genuine dispute whether Famous Barr had this intent or knowledge. Bell showed he disputed the bill for the fan, and that Famous Barr recognized and conceded this dispute. He repeatedly notified Famous Barr that, in light of the billing error, derogatory reports were wrongful. Famous Barr threatened to file and actually filed the reports anyway. Bell also presented evidence that derogatory information filed by Famous Barr remained on his credit report even after Bell paid for the fan. Finally, its dunning letters show Famous Barr knew these derogatory reports were detrimental to Bell's credit rating. Famous Barr claims its intent was negated by its attempts to correct the derogatory reports, by its automated reporting system, by its claim not to know how credit providers use credit reports, or by the cooperation of its employees. This evidence, however, merely shows a dispute of fact. A reasonable jury could find Famous Barr intended to interfere with Bell's credit expectancy, even if only by knowing the report was substantially certain to interfere.

The evidence Bell presented also shows a genuine dispute whether Famous Barr's derogatory report caused EAB to deny credit to Bell. Bell presented evidence EAB denied credit to Bell because of derogatory information on Bell's TRW-credit report. The only such derogatory information on that report was supplied by Famous Barr. Bell also presented evidence Famous Barr continued, for a time, to report derogatory information even after promising to desist. Famous Barr does present evidence showing how it unsuccessfully tried to remove all derogatory information from Bell's credit reports. It is also undisputed Famous Barr never contacted EAB directly. This evidence, however, merely shows causation is disputed. In a light most favorable to Bell, a reasonable jury could find that but for Famous Barr's improper conduct, EAB would not have denied credit to Bell.

D. JUSTIFICATION

"One may act in a manner that interferes with another's business expectancy if by so doing one is acting to protect one's own economic interests."[19] The evidence Bell presented shows a genuine dispute whether Famous Barr was justified in reporting derogatory information to protect its

---

18. American Bank of Princeton v. Stiles, 731 S.W.2d 332, 344 (Mo. App. 1987).

19. Tri-County Retreading, Inc. v. Bandag, Inc., 851 S.W.2d 780, 785 (Mo. App. 1993) (holding plaintiff's claim of intentional interference with a business expectancy failed because

economic interests. Bell presented evidence he properly rejected the fan, Famous Barr promised to replace it but never did, and Famous Barr reported derogatory information while assuring Bell it did not expect payment. As explained in Part II above, a reasonable jury could find Famous Barr reported derogatory information while a billing error existed in violation of the Federal Truth in Lending Act. As such, the actions of Famous Barr may not have been justified.

E.   DAMAGES

Famous Barr does not dispute that Bell was damaged when EAB denied him credit and the chance to earn TWA frequent flyer miles. We do not decide whether summary judgment is proper on Bell's claim for punitive damages in Count II because it was never reached by the trial court.

IV.   CONCLUSION

For the foregoing reasons, we reverse the judgment of the trial court and remand for further proceedings in accordance with this opinion.

IV. ELECTRONIC FUND TRANSFERS

The Electronic Fund Transfers Act (EFTA), 15 U.S.C. §§1693 to 1693r, was passed by Congress in 1978 and became fully effective in 1980; it is Title IX of the Consumer Credit Protection Act. Its purpose is to regulate the debit cards given by banks to consumers to allow them to tap their checking accounts at bank machines ("automated teller machines" or "ATMs" in banking lingo), at point-of-sale ("POS"), or by automatic payment from the account ("preauthorized electronic fund transfers").[20] Prior to the enactment of the statute, these matters were regulated, if at all, by contract between the bank and its customers. Because the banks did not always play fair with the consumers, Congress acted to create significant consumer protection in the statute (it does not apply to business checking accounts). The Act authorizes the Federal Reserve Board to issue a regulation supplementing the statute, and this Regulation, called "Regulation E," has the force of law, as does the Federal Reserve Board's Official Commentary on the statute and Regulation.

---

defendant's interference was justified to protect its economic interests) (quoting O'Connor v. Shelman, 769 S.W.2d 458, 461 (Mo. App. 1989)).

20. Everything in the statute seems to be covered by a mandatory three initials: the consumer can work an EFT by using his/her PIN at an ATM or a POS.

A. *Documentation*

The statute requires the bank that issues the debit card to provide the consumer with various documents containing explanations of the transactions that follow. The Federal Reserve Board has promulgated model forms for these disclosures, and §915(d)(2) states that reliance on these forms will insulate the bank from liability for disclosure problems. Hence the better part of wisdom is not to devise one's own forms, but to use the FRB's model ones without change. These forms can be acquired by writing the FRB or by consulting the Federal Banking Law Reporter (CCH).

At the time of the creation of the contract by which the customer agrees to accept a debit card, the Act requires disclosure of the terms of the contract, including a statement of the consumer's possible liability for unauthorized transfers. See EFTA §906; Reg. E §205.7. Thereafter at least once a year the consumer must be sent a notice explaining the procedure to be followed in the event the consumer wants to complain of an error on the monthly statement. See Reg. E §205.8.

Every use by the consumer of an automated teller machine (ATM) must be accompanied by a receipt showing the details of the transaction, unless the consumer waives this right at the time the machine is used. EFTA §906(a); Reg. E §205.9(a).

Each month the bank must mail to the consumer a periodic statement showing the EFT activity in the account during the period. See EFTA §906(c), Reg. E §205.9(b).

B. *Issuing the Card*

Section 911 of the statute forbids a bank issuing debit cards from mailing them out on an unsolicited basis (except as a renewal of an existing card). The same section, however, does permit the bank to send out cards if they are in an unvalidated condition. Here "validated" means that the card can be used immediately to tap the consumer's account. If the consumer must take some action in order to validate the card (apply for a personal identification number (PIN), for example), then it is all right to mail unsolicited cards.

PROBLEM 52

Football University wanted to pay all its employees by preauthorized EFT credits to their accounts. Some of the employees protested, saying they would rather have checks. You are the attorney for the university. Look carefully at §913 of the statute (it is trickier than it at first seems) and decide whether your client can force the employees to accept payment by electronic transfer; see Reg. E §205.2(b)(2).

Football University discovered that many of its employees had no bank account at all (bankers refer to such individuals as the "unbanked"). It therefore issued payroll cards to such employees, allowing them to draw down their wages at ATMs or point-of-sale transactions (like the grocery store). Does the EFTA apply to these payroll cards?

C. Preauthorized EFTs

PROBLEM 53

Polly Travis signed an agreement with Octopus National Bank, which had issued her a credit card, by which the bank could pay itself $100 on the first of each month out of her checking account in reduction of her credit card bill. Does this agreement violate the Truth in Lending Act? See Reg. Z §226.12(d). In April of one year, Polly was having particular trouble with her bills, so she phoned ONB on April 26 and told the bank employee who answered the phone to stop the May 1 payment. Polly was considerably annoyed to learn that the bank made the payment anyway. The bank says that it has no record of her call, and that it is bank policy to require all stop-payment orders to be in writing. Polly calls you, the attorney who drew up her will. Does she have any rights against the bank? See EFTA §§907, 910, and 914.

One battleground in Congress was the notification requirement to be imposed on banks whenever a preauthorized EFT is made. The consumer groups wanted notice sent out each time; the banks wanted no notice at all. The compromise is reflected in Reg. E §205.10(a), which states that the bank shall provide notice by one of the following means:

> (i) The institution shall transmit oral or written notice to the consumer, within 2 business days after the transfer, that the transfer occurred;
> (ii) The institution shall transmit oral or written notice to the consumer, within 2 business days after the date on which the transfer was scheduled to occur, that the transfer did not occur; or
> (iii) The institution shall provide a readily available telephone line that the consumer may call to ascertain whether or not the transfer occurred, and shall

disclose the telephone number on the initial disclosures required by §205.7 on each periodic statement.

QUESTION

Which of these, do you suppose, is the solution adopted by almost every EFT institution?

D. *Error Resolution*

It is estimated that fraud losses to financial institutions from ATMs amount to more than $40 million annually. Experts believe that 90 percent of this comes from bank employee misbehavior and the rest from consumer fraud. On top of this criminal problem, the complexity of the system leads to perfectly innocent errors in the reporting and recordation of EFT activity. In 2007, it was estimated that 360,659 ATMs were handling more than 1 billion transactions yearly, and in 2009 debit card use passed credit card use for the first time. Debit cards were used to make 67.6 percent of purchases, meaning that there were more than 26.2 billion point-of-sale transactions. Mistakes will come of this.

If the consumer believes that the periodic statement contains an error, the consumer may complain, and the legal rules that follow are based in large part on the similar rules from the Fair Credit Billing Act that we have just studied. Use EFTA §908 and Reg. E §205.11 to resolve the following Problem.

PROBLEM 54

Sally Philips received her monthly bank statement and was puzzled to see thereon a supposed $200 withdrawal from her account made at an ATM. Since Sally was suspicious of these banking machines, she had never used one, so she was sure this was a mistake. On Monday, September 1, she phoned the bank that had issued her the debit card and told the bank official who answered all that she knew about the problem. The bank official took her call and promised to look into the matter.

a. She asked the bank to put the money back into her account immediately. The bank told her it didn't have to do that. Is the bank right? See Reg. E §205.11(c).

b. Assume that on Friday, September 12, the bank puts the $200 back in Sally's account, and tells her that this is being done provisionally while the bank investigates the matter. Is she allowed to withdraw it? See Reg. E §205.11(c). If the bank investigates the matter and resolves it by October 15, has the bank fulfilled its legal responsibilities?

c. The bank's investigation turned up the following information. Sally had loaned her debit card to her Aunt LeRoy, who had made the $200 withdrawal and given the money to Sally, who had forgotten the transaction. The bank determined this on October 1, and immediately removed the $200 from the account. That same day four of Sally's checks bounced as a result, causing her $3,000 in damages on a deal that fell through because of the dishonored checks. Sally calls you, her favorite attorney, and asks you if the bank is allowed to do this. Is it? See EFTA §§915(a) and 908(e), Reg. E §205.11(d)(2), and U.C.C §4-402.

E. Unauthorized Transfers

The basic rule, copied from credit card law, is that the consumer is liable for no more than $50 of any unauthorized EFT (and even less if the consumer manages to notify the bank of the problem before $50 is transferred). The consumer is not responsible for any amount, however, unless the consumer has *accepted* the debit card. An "unauthorized" EFT is defined in Reg. E §205.2 as follows:

(*m*) "Unauthorized electronic fund transfer" means an electronic fund transfer from a consumer's account initiated by a person other than the consumer without actual authority to initiate the transfer and from which the consumer receives no benefit. The term does not include any electronic fund transfer (1) initiated by a person who was furnished with the access device to the consumer's account by the consumer, unless the consumer has notified the financial institution involved that transfers by the person are no longer authorized, (2) initiated with fraudulent intent by the consumer or any person acting in concert with the consumer, or (3) that is initiated by the financial institution or its employee.

PROBLEM 55

When Arthur Beer walked up to the ATM, someone stepped into line behind him. While Beer was taking his debit card from his wallet, the person behind him stuck a gun in his back and ordered him to withdraw the maximum amount. Is this an "unauthorized" EFT, so that his liability is limited to $50? See the Federal Reserve Board's Official Staff Commentary on Regulation E, 12 C.F.R. §205, EFT-2 Q2-28.

PROBLEM 56

When his sister was sorely in need of money, Carl Consumer loaned her his bank card and told her the personal identification number, making her promise to withdraw no more than $200. Before he knew it, she had withdrawn $1,000. Carl phoned the bank and demanded that she be allowed to take out no more. Subsequent to his phone call she withdrew another $300. What is Carl's liability?

PROBLEM 57

The bank's computer malfunctioned one day and mysteriously debited $100 from all the accounts in the bank, transferring the money to an account marked "Computer Maintenance." Is this an "unauthorized EFT" under the above definition?

As §205.6 of Regulation E makes clear, the usual liability for unauthorized EFTs is $50 (and not even that if the consumer manages to notify the financial institution before the unauthorized EFT is incurred). There are, however, two situations in which the consumer faces the possibility of greater liability than the usual risk of $50.

The first occurs where the consumer learns of the loss or theft of the access device but does not notify the bank within two business days after so learning. This carelessness exposes the consumer to up to $500 worth of liability for the unauthorized EFTs that subsequently occur. The policy justification for this result is obvious: a consumer who knows that the card is gone is hardly playing fair in not reporting the loss and should bear greater liability. The typical reason the consumer does not report the problem is that he/she knows who took the card (a friend or relative) and doesn't want to blow the whistle without first trying to get the card back. That reaction may be understandable, but it increases the consumer's exposure.

The second situation for enhanced consumer liability involves the monthly statement's return. If the statement reflects an unauthorized EFT and the consumer does not complain about it within the usual 60-day period (see above), the consumer has *unlimited* liability for unauthorized EFTs first occurring after the close of the 60-day period if the bank can establish that these EFTs never would have happened if the consumer had notified the bank of the problem. This is a "last clear chance" sort of rule, and puts the liability on the person in the best position to detect the problem.

PROBLEM 58

While Carl Consumer was asleep one day, his sister Nancy sneaked into his bedroom and stole his bank card. She knew his PIN because he had once loaned her the card and authorized her to make a small series of withdrawals, but this time it was an outright theft.[21] She took the card on April 30, and used it to take $500 from his account with Octopus National Bank on that same day. He missed the card when he woke up, and he rightly guessed that Nancy had taken it. Rather than notify the bank, he tried to track her down and retrieve the card. On May 5, she used the card to remove $800 from his bank account, and then she left the state. Heartsick at her perfidy, Carl slumped into a depression so severe that he could not leave his bed. On May 31, the bank sent Carl the usual bank statement; it reflected all these transactions. On June 10, Nancy returned to the state and used the card to take $3,000 from Carl's account.

    a. What is his liability?

    b. Would his liability change if the $3,000 had been taken from his account not on June 10 but on September 25?

    c. Can Carl escape from liability by contending that he was sick? See Reg. E §205.6(b)(4).

OGNIBENE v. CITIBANK, N.A.
Civil Court of the City of New York, Small Claims, 1981
112 Misc. 2d 219, 446 N.Y.S.2d 845

MARA T. THORPE, Judge.

Plaintiff seeks to recover $400.00 withdrawn from his account at the defendant bank by an unauthorized person using an automated teller machine. The court has concluded that plaintiff was the victim of a scam which defendant has been aware of for some time.

Defendant's witness, an assistant manager of one of its branches, described how the scam works: A customer enters the automated teller ma-

---

21. At one of the seminars I have conducted on this topic, a banker in California told me that at her bank the EFT agreement contains a clause whereby disclosure of the PIN to any party makes that person thereafter an authorized user of the debit card, and that this clause had withstood a court challenge. Its utility in situations like the one in the Problem is obvious. For a case saying that disclosure of the PIN for one authorized use does not make subsequent uses authorized as well, see Vaughan v. United States National Bank, 79 Or. App. 172, 718 P.2d 769 (1986).

chine (ATM) area for the purpose of using a machine for the transaction of business with the bank. At the time that he enters, a person is using the customer service telephone located between the two automated teller machines and appears to be telling customer service that one of the machines is malfunctioning. This person is the perpetrator of the scam and his conversation with customer service is only simulated. He observes the customer press his personal identification code into one of the two machines. Having learned the code, the perpetrator then tells the customer that customer service has advised him to ask the customer to insert his Citicard into the allegedly malfunctioning machine to check whether it will work with a card other than the perpetrator's. When a good [S]amaritan customer accedes to the request, the other machine is activated. The perpetrator then presses a code into the machine, which the customer does not realize is his own code which the perpetrator has just observed. After continuing the simulated conversation on the telephone, the perpetrator advises the customer that customer service has asked if he would try his Citicard in the allegedly malfunctioning machine once more. A second insertion of the card permits cash to be released by the machine, and if the customer does as requested, the thief has effectuated a cash withdrawal from the unwary customer's account.

Plaintiff testified that on August 16, 1981, he went to the ATM area at one of defendant's branches and activated one of the machines with his Citibank card, pressed in his personal identification code and withdrew $20.00. While he did this a person who was using the telephone between plaintiff's machine and the adjoining machine said into the telephone, "I'll see if his card works in my machine." Thereupon he asked plaintiff if he could use his card to see if the other machine was working. Plaintiff handed it to him and saw him insert it into the adjoining machine at least two times while stating into the telephone, "Yes, it seems to be working."

Defendant's computer records in evidence show that two withdrawals of $200.00 each from plaintiff's account were made on August 16, 1981, on the machine adjoining the one plaintiff used for his $20.00 withdrawal. The two $200.00 withdrawals were made at 5:42 p.m. and 5:43 p.m. respectively; plaintiff's own $20.00 withdrawal was made at 5:41 p.m. At the time, plaintiff was unaware that any withdrawals from his account were being made on the adjoining machine.

The only fair and reasonable inferences to be drawn from all of the evidence are that the person who appeared to be conversing on the telephone observed the plaintiff enter his personal identification code into the machine from which he withdrew $20.00 and that he entered it into the adjoining machine while simulating a conversation with customer service about that machine's malfunctioning. It is conceded in the testimony of defendant's assistant branch manager that it would have been possible for a person who was positioned so as to appear to be speaking on the telephone physically to observe the code being entered into the machine by plaintiff. Although plaintiff is not certain that his card was inserted in the adjoining machine more than twice, the circumstances indicate that it was inserted four times. No issue of fraud by plaintiff or anyone acting in concert with him has been raised by defendant. Having observed plaintiff's demeanor, the court found him to be a credible witness and is of the opinion that no such issues exist in this case.

The basic rights, liabilities and responsibilities of the banks which offer electronic money transfer services and the consumers who use them have been established by the federal legislation contained in 15 U.S.C.A. §§1693 et seq., commonly called the Electronic Fund Transfers Act (EFT). Although the EFT Act preempts state law only to the extent of any inconsistency (15 U.S.C.A. §1693q), to date New York State has not enacted legislation which governs the resolution of the issues herein. Therefore, the EFT Act is applicable.

The EFT Act places various limits on a consumer's liability for electronic fund transfers from his account if they are "unauthorized." Insofar as is relevant here, a transfer is "unauthorized" if 1) it is initiated by a person other than the consumer and without actual authority to initiate such transfer, 2) the consumer receives no benefit from it, and 3) the consumer did not furnish such person "with the card, code or other means of access" to his account. 15 U.S.C.A. §1693a(11).

In an action involving a consumer's liability for an electronic fund transfer, such as the one at bar, the burden of going forward to show an "unauthorized" transfer from his account is on the consumer. The EFT Act places upon the bank, however, the burden of proof of any consumer liability for the transfer. 15 U.S.C.A. §1693g(b). To establish full liability on the part of the consumer, the bank must prove that certain conditions of consumer liability, set forth in 15 U.S.C.A. §1693g(a), have been met and that certain disclosures mandated by 15 U.S.C.A. §1693c(a)(1) and (2) have been made. Id.

Plaintiff herein met his burden of going forward. He did not initiate the withdrawals in question, did not authorize the person in the ATM area to make them, and did not benefit from them.

However, defendant's position is, in essence, that although plaintiff was duped, the bank's burden of proof on the issue of authorization has been met by plaintiff's testimony that he permitted his card to be used in the adjoining machine by the other person. The court does not agree.

The EFT Act requires that the consumer have furnished to a person initiating the transfer the "card, code, or other means of access" to his account to be ineligible for the limitations on liability afforded by the Act when transfers are "unauthorized." The evidence establishes that in order to obtain access to an account via an automated teller machine, both the card and the personal identification code must be used. Thus, by merely giving his card to the person initiating the transfer, a consumer does not furnish the "means of access" to his account. To do so, he would have to furnish the personal identification code as well. See 12 C.F.R. 205.2(a)(1), the regulation promulgated under the EFT Act which defines "access device" as "a card, code or other means of access to [an] . . . account *or any combination thereof*" (emphasis added).

The court finds that plaintiff did not furnish his personal identification code to the person initiating the $400.00 transfer within the meaning of the EFT Act. There is no evidence that he deliberately or even negligently did so. On the contrary, the unauthorized person was able to obtain the code because of defendant's own negligence. Since the bank had knowledge of the scam and its operational details (including the central role of the customer service telephone), it was negligent in failing to provide plaintiff-customer with information sufficient to alert him to the danger when he found himself in the position of a potential victim. Although in June, 1981, after the scam came to defendant's attention, it posted signs in its ATM areas containing a red circle approximately 2½ inches in diameter in which is written "Do Not Let Your Citicard Be Used For Any Transaction But Your Own," the court finds that this printed admonition is not a sufficient security measure since it fails to state the reason why one should not do so. Since a customer of defendant's electronic fund transfer service must employ both the card and the personal identification code in order to withdraw money from his account, the danger of loaning his card briefly for the purpose of checking the functioning of an adjoining automated teller machine would not be immediately apparent to one who has not divulged his personal identification number and who is unaware that it has been revealed merely by virtue of his own transaction with the machine.

Since the bank established the electronic fund transfer service and has the ability to tighten its security characteristics, the responsibility for the fact that plaintiff's code, one of the two necessary components of the "access device" or "means of access" to his account, was observed and utilized as it was must rest with the bank.

For the foregoing reasons and in view of the fact that the primary purpose of the EFT Act and the regulation promulgated thereunder is the protection of individual consumers (12 C.F.R. 205.1(b)), the court concludes that plaintiff did not furnish his code to anyone within the meaning of the Act. Accordingly, since the person who obtained it did not have actual authority to initiate the transfer, the transfer qualifies as an "unauthorized" one under 15 U.S.C.A. §1693a(11) and the bank cannot hold plaintiff fully liable for the $400.00 withdrawal.

To avail itself of the limited liability imposed by the Act upon a consumer in the event of an "unauthorized" transfer, the bank must demonstrate (1) that the means of access utilized for the transfer was "accepted" and (2) that the bank has provided a way [in] which the user of the means of access can be identified as the person authorized to use it. 15 U.S.C.A. §1693g(a) and (b). One definition of "accepted" under the Act is that the consumer has used the means of access. 15 U.S.C.A. §1693a(1). Both of the foregoing conditions of liability have been met here since plaintiff used the means of access to his account to withdraw the $20.00 and had been given a personal identification code.

Additionally, the bank must prove that it disclosed to the consumer his liability for unauthorized electronic fund transfers and certain information pertaining to notification of the bank in the event the consumer believes that an unauthorized transfer has been or may be effected. 15 U.S.C.A. §§1693c (a)(1) and (2) and 1693g(b). Defendant did not establish that it made such disclosures to plaintiff. Accordingly, it is not entitled to avail itself of the benefit of the limited liability for unauthorized transfers imposed upon consumers by the Act.

For the foregoing reasons, judgment shall be for plaintiff in the sum of $400.00.

PROBLEM 59

When Arthur Beer received his PIN he was worried he would forget it, so he wrote the number right on his debit card. His wallet was stolen with the card in it, and Arthur reported the loss to the bank immediately. Two hours after his phone call to the bank, someone used the card to withdraw $200 from an ATM. Is Arthur liable for any of this amount? See the Official Staff Commentary to Regulation E at Q6-6.5.

F. The Bank's Civil Liability

The statute creates three different civil liability sections, as follows.

1. Complaints

If the consumer complains of an error on the periodic statement, as mentioned above, the bank must conduct a good faith investigation of the problem. The bank can face liability over and above that in §915 (described below) for failing to do so. EFTA §908(e):

(e) If in any action under 915, the court finds that—

(1) the financial institution did not provisionally recredit a consumer's account within the ten-day period specified in subsection (c) of this section, and the financial institution (A) did not make a good faith investigation of the alleged error, or (B) did not have a reasonable basis for believing that the consumer's account was not in error; or

(2) the financial institution knowingly and willfully concluded that the consumer's account was not in error when such conclusion could not have been drawn from the evidence available to the financial institution at the time of its investigation, then the consumer shall be entitled to treble damages determined under §915(a)(1).

2. Failure to Make or Stop Payment

According to §910 of the Act, the failure of a bank to make an EFT as agreed or the failure of a bank to stop payment on a preauthorized EFT whenever the consumer has given a proper notice makes the bank liable for all damages proximately caused by the bank's carelessness. It is a defense to the bank that there was insufficient money in the account or in the bank machine, or that the account was frozen by legal process. Subsection (b) of the section gives the bank further defenses based on acts of God or technical malfunctions known to the consumer at the time the consumer attempted to use the ATM.

3. General Liability

The basic section controlling civil liability is §915 of the statute. Use it to resolve the following Problem.

PROBLEM 60

Attorney Sam Ambulance used his debit card at the Octopus National Bank ATM located just outside the bank's main entrance.

When he examined the slip the machine gave him, he noticed that it failed to identify in any way which ATM had been used.

a. Is this a violation of the statute? See Reg. E §205.9(a).

b. Sam immediately filed a class action against the bank for this alleged violation. What recovery can Sam hope for?

c. If Sam was using the card for business purposes only, does the EFTA apply at all?

d. The bank's response to Sam's lawsuit was to send him a letter saying that it had made a legal error and failed to program its machines to state which one was being used, but that it was correcting the error. The letter then informed Sam that the machine he had used should have been designated "ATM, Main Entrance of Bank." Does this letter avoid bank liability? See §915(e).

e. If the lawsuit is resolved in favor of the bank, can it get its attorney's fees and costs from Sam? See §915(f).

G. Checks and Electronic Banking

PROBLEM 61

When Mary Colpitts reached the checkout counter at Big Department Store, she gave the clerk a check for the amount of her purchases. The clerk promptly scanned the check and returned it to her, telling Mary that the check would be collected electronically. The check cleared through her checking account that same afternoon, surprising Mary, who had counted on the usual "float" period before the check was presented to her bank. Is this transaction subject to the check collections rules in Article 4 of the Uniform Commercial Code or some other statute?

In this Problem the consumer has had her check turned into an electronic image that will be used to debit her bank account. Commonly this is called *electronic check conversion* (and mysteriously given the initials "ECK"). It is governed by the same rules we explored above for debit card use, since this is considered an EFT. The relevant regulations for this situation require the merchant who has scanned the check at the point of sale ("POS") to return the original paper check to the consumer (or, if the merchant has received the check through the mail—an "accounts receivable conversion" or "ARC"—to destroy it); see proposed Electronic Fund

Transfer Regulation E, 12 C.F.R. §205.3(b)(2),[22] and the rules of the National Automated Clearinghouse Association.[23]

After the tragedy of September 11, 2001, the grounding of airplanes for days meant that check collection (which is done by plane) came to a standstill. It became obvious that in the new millennium the daily movement of tons of paper was a poor way to collect checks. Effective in 2004, Congress enacted the "Check Clearing for the 21st Century Act" or "Check 21,"[24] which allows banks to photograph checks and then destroy them. The photographed image is passed along from bank to bank and then to the customer. If anyone balks at taking the imaged version, the banks are authorized to print out the image, which is now called a "substitute check." The statute provides that no one may refuse to take a substitute check, which is legally equivalent to the original check for all purposes, state and federal. The statute further permits consumers who protest that an imaged check has been improperly posted against an account to demand an expedited recrediting for the amount involved. The rules from the statute as to how quickly the bank must respond are adapted word for word from the same rules we have just explored under the EFTA for allegations of improper EFT debits; see Check 21 Act §7.

---

22. See also Regulation E Official Staff Interpretation §205.3(b)—3.

23. The most relevant NACHA rules are 3.7.3, 2.1.2, 3.7.1, 2.9.3.3, and 2.9.3.4, in that order.

24. 12 U.S.C. §§5001-5018. The text of the statute is at http://www.bankersonline.com/check21/check21act.pdf.

CHAPTER 6
Qualifying for Credit

I. THE FAIR CREDIT REPORTING ACT

It is said that there is undoubtedly a credit report extant on every United States citizen unless he/she is either under 18 or dead. The largest credit bureaus send out more than 16 million consumer credit reports every year. If those credit reports contain derogatory information (true or not) about a consumer's creditworthiness, the possibility of that person getting more credit is lessened. Even someone with a good credit history can find that history erased instantly by computer error or human evil and then must try to cope with the nightmare of a bad credit file. Worse, the consumer may know nothing of this adverse information, and, even if it is discovered and corrected in one file, chances are that the "bum info" has already been shared with other computers and is still out there growing exponentially to haunt future transactions (a process called "repollution").

QUOTES FOR THE ATTORNEY'S ARSENAL: "DESTRUCTION OF REPUTATION BY COMPUTER"

. . . [W]ith the trend toward computerization of billings and the establishment of all sorts of computerized data banks, the individual is in great danger of having his life and character reduced to impersonal "blips" and keypunch holes in a stolid and unthinking machine which can literally ruin his reputation without cause, and make him unemployable or uninsurable, as well as deny him the opportunity to obtain a mortgage to buy a home. We are not nearly as much concerned over the possible mistaken turndown of a consumer for a luxury item as we are over the possible destruction of his good name without his knowledge and without reason.

House debate over FCRA, 116 Cong. Rec. at 36,570 (1970).

The credit bureaus argue that they are doing the best they can with a complicated endeavor. Consider the numbers involved. Millions of consumers and their multitudes of transactions must be organized into a retrievable format and then disseminated to customers requesting the files.

The data is gathered every month[1] from 2 billion elements (public records, payment histories, insurance claims, employment records, personal interviews, etc.) and entered into 1.5 billion credit files. Of course mistakes will come of this. What to do about it—and how much society will tolerate—is the task of lawmakers and jurists.

A. The Common Law

If you learn that a consumer reporting agency is passing around false information about you, what are your rights? The common law response is grounded in various tort theories, with defamation being the primary one.

Defamation (libel or slander) occurs in connection with credit problems when false information concerning the defamee is circulated. Credit reporting agencies were often sued for defamation of credit by angry consumers, but the agencies typically could defend by using the *doctrine of qualified privilege*. This doctrine created an exemption for liability in defamation for anyone who passed on false information as long as (1) the person transmitting the information did not know it was false (i.e., was not *malicious*), and (2) the person receiving the information had a legitimate need to know the information. See Restatement of Torts (Second) §§593-604. Getting around this doctrine proved impossible in many a lawsuit. The doctrine of qualified privilege, in truncated form, lives on in §610(e) of the Fair Credit Reporting Act (discussed below).

Defamation has one further drawback, and it is a major one: truth is a defense.

PROBLEM 62

Mrs. Shoe once had a lot of money, but she became ill and lost her job, and for the first time in her life she has had to struggle with bills. She failed to pay her doctor's bill for three months, figuring that her doctor would wait. Her doctor, however, was annoyed at the number of clients who had stiffed him, and, since he was an amateur pilot, he decided to get even with them one by one. Mrs. Shoe was startled

---

1. Furnishers of credit information to the largest credit bureaus use a "Metro 2" software program to standardize the data and report it to the bureaus. Similarly, consumer complaints are handled through an online consumer dispute resolution system called E-OSCAR (Online Solution for Complete and Accurate Reporting). See the web site of the Consumer Data Industry Association: www.cdiaonline.org.

one morning to look up in the sky over her house and see "MRS. SHOE DOESN'T PAY HER BILLS" written in smoke. She called an attorney and asked whether she could do anything about this.

Since truth is a defense, Mrs. Shoe has not been defamed. Her best theory is *invasion of privacy*, a tort action (where truth of the publication is not a defense) we will explore along with overzealous collection attempts in Chapter 11. For now it is enough to note that the theory provides relief whenever, as in the Problem, there is an unwarranted publication of financial difficulties to those (such as Mrs. Shoe's neighbors) who have no need to hear this information. If a credit bureau had been poking into her affairs trying to determine her worthiness for credit, insurance, or employment, certainly the common law tort of invasion of privacy would furnish her no relief whatever.

B. Scope of the Fair Credit Reporting Act

Until 1970 the credit reporting industry was not subject to any comprehensive regulation. As an apparent response to both the potential injury to consumers through errors and the concern for privacy, on October 26, 1970, Congress enacted the Fair Credit Reporting Act (FCRA), making it Title VI of the Consumer Credit Protection Act. The law both regulates the consumer reporting industry and places disclosure obligations on users of consumer reports. For a major commentary on the Act, see National Consumer Law Center, Fair Credit Reporting Act (5th ed. 2002, with supplement each year). In 2003 the Fair and Accurate Credit Transactions Act (FACTA or the "FACT Act") made major amendments to FCRA, solving problems with the original version and addressing new issues such as identity theft. FACTA requires many notices to consumers alerting them to various rights (such as getting free annual reports, what to do if victimized by identity theft, etc.), and the Federal Trade Commission has promulgated model forms for these purposes and created both an Official Commentary to the statute (see 16 C.F.R. Part 600) and Regulations supplementing many sections of the Act (16 C.F.R. 603, et seq.).

In examining the Fair Credit Reporting Act, it is essential to make a distinction between two kinds of credit reporting. First, there are reports that include information on a consumer's character, general reputation, personal characteristics, or mode of living. These reports generally are obtained by personal interviews with neighbors, business associates, and friends; are frequently used for insurance- or employment-related purposes; and are described in the Act as "investigative consumer reports." Read §606.

PROBLEM 63

When Business Corporation's senior management heard rumors that one of its key employees was heavily involved in drug use, it hired Sherlock Holmes, a private investigator, to look into this. Holmes did a lot of snooping around, talked to the employee's neighbors and associates, and eventually submitted a report to Business Corporation stating that the charges were true. The company decided to fire the employee. Does this trigger the FCRA? If so, has the company already violated the statute? See §§604(b)(2) and (3), and 603(x).

The second kind of ordinary credit reports are issued by credit bureaus (called "consumer reporting agencies" in FCRA). These reports focus on credit information obtained from creditors, which are, generally, part of a network that both supplies information and consumes the services supplied by the consumer reporting agency. The leading three consumer reporting agencies in the United States (along with ways to contact them to learn what the credit reports show) are TransUnion, at (1-800) 888-4213 (www.tuc.com); Experian, at (1-888) 397-3742 (www.experian. com); and Equifax, at (1-800) 685-111 (www.equifax.com). Under §612(a) of FCRA, consumers are entitled to get one free copy of their credit report each year; contact www.annualcreditreport.com or (877) 322-8228.

Most lending decisions are based on a *credit score* reported by these agencies, which is computed based on various factors in the credit history. The most widely used of these scores is the FICO rating, created by Fair, Isaac and Co. (hence the initials), of San Rafael, California. This score runs from 300 to 850, with a really good score being above 700. The score is determined by the consumer's payment record (35 percent), total amount of outstanding debt (30 percent), how long the consumer has had existing accounts—old is better than new (15 percent), frequency of applications for new credit (10 percent), and how much credit and the types of credit the consumer has incurred (10 percent). Consumers are not entitled to a free FICO score; there is a charge for obtaining it. See www.myfico.com. Consumers are, however, entitled to an explanation of their credit score without charge; see §609(f). The three major credit reporting agencies mentioned in the last paragraph have also developed their own new credit scoring methodology to compete with FICO; it is called VantageScore (with the score ranging from 501 to 990, along with letter grades of A through F).

MILLSTONE v. O'HANLON REPORTS

United States District Court, Eastern District of Missouri, 1974
383 F. Supp. 269, *aff'd*, 528 F.2d 829 (8th Cir. 1976)

WANGELIN, District Judge.

This action is before the Court for decision on the merits following the trial to the Court sitting without a jury.

Plaintiff, James C. Millstone (herein Millstone) brought this action alleging violation of 15 U.S.C. §§1681 et seq., commonly known as the "Fair Credit Reporting Act," against the defendant, O'Hanlon Reports, Inc. (herein O'Hanlon). The Court being fully apprised of the premises hereby makes the following findings of fact and conclusions of law.

FINDINGS OF FACT

1. This Court has jurisdiction over the subject matter of this suit and the parties hereto pursuant to 15 U.S.C. §1681p.

2. The plaintiff, James C. Millstone, is an Assistant Managing Editor of the St. Louis Post-Dispatch, a local daily newspaper. He has worked for the Post-Dispatch in various positions since 1958. Prior to his return to the St. Louis area in 1971, he worked in Washington, D.C. as a correspondent for approximately seven years covering various federal agencies, including the White House, and had an FBI clearance to travel with Presidents Johnson and Nixon.

3. The defendant, O'Hanlon Reports, Inc., is a corporation, formerly known as the National Inspection Bureau, Inc., d/b/a O'Hanlon Reports, Inc., operating under the laws of the State of New York and licensed to do business in the State of Missouri as well as most of the States of the Union. It has as its purpose the investigation and collection of information concerning consumers of predominantly real property insurance and automobile insurance.

4. In August of 1971, Millstone and his family moved to St. Louis, Missouri, so that he might take up his duties as news editor for the St. Louis Post-Dispatch. He thereafter contacted his insurance agent, Norman Kastner, and asked Kastner to place auto insurance for him. Kastner placed the policy with Firemen's Fund Insurance Company. The policy took effect on November 15, 1971, and several days later Millstone, in accordance with 15 U.S.C. §1681d received a notice that a personal investigation would be made in connection with the new policy.

5. On December 20, 1971, Walter McPherson from the Firemen's Fund Insurance Company informed Kastner (and Kastner informed Millstone) that the policy would be cancelled. After assurances from Kastner of Millstone's character and reputation, the insurance company reversed its decision the following day. Millstone voluntarily cancelled the policy.

6. Millstone discovered from McPherson that the cancellation had been brought about because of a consumer credit report which had been made by the defendant, O'Hanlon Reports, Inc.

7. On December 22, 1971, Millstone went to the office of O'Hanlon Reports where he spoke to William O'Connell, the Office Manager. Millstone was told that he was entitled to know what was in his report but that O'Hanlon was entitled to reasonable notice of ten (10) days before giving the information. When Millstone protested, O'Connell called the New York Home Office of O'Hanlon and allowed Millstone to speak to a Kenneth Mitchell. Mitchell told Millstone that the information would be available as soon as possible but that he could not give disclosure immediately because the Millstone file was en route from St. Louis to New York through the mails. After Millstone left the office, O'Connell then mailed the file to New York.

8. On December 28, 1971, Millstone received the disclosure of the information in its file from O'Connell at the O'Hanlon offices. O'Connell read the disclosure from a single sheet of paper which had been prepared by David Slayback, the Vice President of O'Hanlon. The disclosure sheet stated in part that:

> The file shows that you are very much disliked by your neighbors at that location [Millstone's Washington residence], and were considered to be a "hippy type." The file indicates that you participated in many demonstrations in Washington, D.C., and that you also housed out-of-town demonstrators during demonstrations. The file indicates that these demonstrators slept on floors, in the basement and wherever else there was room on your property. The file shows that you were strongly suspected of being a drug user by neighbors but they could not positively substantiate these suspicions. You are shown to have had shoulder length hair and a beard on one occasion while living in Washington, D.C. The file indicates that there were rumors in the neighborhood that you had been evicted by neighbors from three previous residences in Washington, D.C. prior to living at the 48th Street, N.W. location.

This disclosure sheet which Millstone was not allowed to examine was the only item that Millstone was informed of by O'Connell.

9. After protesting virtually all the information contained in the disclosure, Millstone asked O'Connell to explain certain facts contained therein. O'Connell told Millstone that he had no further information and could not answer the questions. He told Millstone that his instructions from the Home Office were only to read the disclosure sheet prepared in New York and to take careful note of any dispute from the customer. At no time was Millstone allowed to look at the actual consumer report file maintained by O'Hanlon upon him, nor were any actual portions of that file read to Millstone at any time by Mr. O'Connell.

10. O'Connell once again called New York and allowed Millstone to speak. David Slayback defended the method and propriety of disclosure to Millstone and neither would nor could explain such matters as the basis and meaning of the statement that Millstone was strongly suspected of being a "drug user."

11. Slayback ordered the Manager of his Silver Springs office, the office which had conducted the original investigation of Millstone, to re-investigate the information. Raymond T. Jonas, the Branch Manager, took approximately three days to complete the re-investigation and then sent his report to the New York office. This re-investigation report contained statements that the Millstone children had "torn up" part of a neighbor's garden and that Mrs. Millstone had used terms such as "pig," and "old hag" to a neighbor and his wife and that she was considered by the neighbors to be a "paranoid," and that Mr. Millstone was considered to be a "hippy type" because he allowed peace demonstrators to stay in his house. Mrs. Millstone was also alleged to have stated that she would allow her children to use drugs.

12. On or about January 12, 1972, O'Connell notified Millstone that the re-investigation was completed and at a meeting between the two read to Millstone both the first and second disclosure sheets along with a cover letter written by Mr. Slayback to the Firemen's Fund Insurance Company. The thrust of these documents was to correct the previous allegations that Millstone was a: "drug user," "hippy type" and the statements about the "peace demonstrators staying at the Millstone residence."

13. On or about January 15, 1972, the Federal Trade Commission, which had received a complaint and request for investigation from Millstone, contacted O'Hanlon, and informed Millstone that the investigation had commenced.

14. In a registered letter dated January 20, 1972, David Slayback informed Millstone of further information contained in the defendant's files, including previously undisclosed criticism of the Millstone children and a statement that Millstone was "utterly lacking in reason and judgment." After Millstone disputed this information in a telephone conversation he received a letter dated February 17, 1972, in which Slayback informed Millstone that the disputed points were not in the new report and thus would not be re-investigated.

15. In each conversation and meeting with O'Hanlon's agents, Millstone requested to see his file but was flatly denied access to it. After O'Connell mailed the file to the New York office of the defendant it remained there.

16. At no time prior to the filing of this lawsuit was Millstone informed of certain critical comments about his wife contained in his file. Millstone

first learned of such criticism upon receipt of the answers to plaintiff's interrogatories.

17. From the period of time beginning December 20, 1971 and continuing until the end of February, 1972, the evidence adduced at trial shows that Millstone suffered significant amounts of worry, anxiety and concern over the information which was contained in O'Hanlon's file about him and to whom that information was being disseminated. The evidence also shows that his family life was disrupted to the extent of lack of sleep and a general upsetting of the household in work routine.

18. O'Hanlon's procedures for making disclosure to Millstone were in conformity with previously planned procedural processes explained to managers of the defendant's branch offices several months prior to the effective date of the Fair Credit Reporting Act. These procedures were contained in a handbook which each manager received and which was introduced into evidence at the trial as plaintiff's exhibit 13 (herein referred to as Manual). The procedures called for in the Manual state in pertinent part:

> The important thing is to NEVER check the files in the presence of the consumer . . . (Manual, 609-610-611, p.1.).
>
> Prior to the time of your appointment with the consumer, you will have received the Statement of Disclosure from the Home Office. At the time of your appointment, ANY and ALL information you may have relating to the consumer, such as copies of files, copy of your statement, index cards, etc. are to be in your desk drawer, OUT OF SIGHT, of the consumer. You are not to show anything, or acknowledge that you have anything, other than the Statement of Disclosure.
>
> Actual disclosure will be accomplished by reading the Statement of Disclosure to the consumer. The statement is to be read word for word, at your normal reading speed. It is not to be read slowly enough for anyone to copy down word for word, nor is it to be read so fast that the Consumer will not understand what you are saying. Part or all of the Statement of Disclosure may be re-read if the Consumer indicates that he did not understand what you are telling him. The Consumer and/or the person with him may not have a copy of the Statement, nor may they be allowed to read the Statement, or touch it. (emphasis added by capitalization is that contained in the Manual) (Manual, p.1-2).

19. The original report on Millstone was prepared by Alexander Mayes, an employee of defendant in defendant's Silver Springs office. Mayes contacted four neighbors of the Millstones on the block where they last lived while residing in Washington, D.C.

20. Of the four persons contacted, one refused to speak to Mayes, two others told him that they knew of trouble in the neighborhood but knew nothing first hand and wished not to become involved. All the data recovered in Mayes' report was gleaned from a discussion with one neighbor identified as one McMillan, now deceased. Mayes gathered the data in a

period of less than one-half hour. Mayes worked on a commission basis and received approximately one-third of the fee charged by the defendant, which amounted approximately to $1.85 in the Millstone investigation.

21. The time spent by defendant's agents on gathering information for automobile insurance reports is anywhere from ten minutes to one-half hour. The data gathered for real estate insurance transactions may take slightly longer.

22. An investigator for O'Hanlon such as Mayes would average 140 to 160 reports every two weeks.

23. O'Hanlon's Manual concerning the maximum possible accuracy required of such a business organization dealing in consumer reports states that O'Hanlon must: "Adopt procedures to assure maximum possible accuracy of our information on consumers. We must continue to report our facts as we see them be they favorable or adverse, but we must make an additional effort to be sure of those facts." Concerning adverse information, the Manual goes on to state: "When adverse information is developed, it should be verified by at least one other source to avoid the reporting of any prejudice or inaccurate information." (Manual, 607, p.2). There was no evidence produced which showed any attempt to verify the adverse information in Millstone's file.

24. O'Hanlon continues to maintain the procedures described hereinabove and David Slayback described them as reasonable.

25. Procedures for disclosure have been changed by O'Hanlon since December, 1971; a consumer will now have his file read to him on request after the file has been examined by the Home Office. Defendant continues to reserve the option of not disclosing information about others relevant to the consumer and contained in his file. For example, Slayback testified that if a report contained adverse information of a serious nature about a consumer's wife, the Company would not disclose that information to the consumer. The defendant would only disclose such information to its client.

26. Branch managers of defendant were not prepared by O'Hanlon to conduct disclosures and to answer questions concerning files by the consumers.

27. Concerning the disclosure procedures followed in the instant case, Slayback testified that the first disclosure was incomplete, and the reason therefor was his rush to satisfy Millstone's demand for disclosure; in his letter of January 20, 1972, he informed Millstone that the reason for the exclusion was that he had not received the information from his Silver Springs office at the time that he prepared the first disclosure. He stated that Millstone's "utter lack of reasoning and judgment" could be implied from the contents of the first consumer report.

28. The reason that adverse information about Millstone's wife was contained in the consumer report and not disclosed was not explained in any way.

29. Millstone's character, reputation in the community, working and personal habits, and the character of his reputation and family [were] dealt with extensively by character witnesses of national and public reputation at the trial. These character witnesses were unstinting in their praise of Mr. Millstone.

CONCLUSIONS OF LAW

These conclusions will be broken into three parts. Counsel for defendant has placed great emphasis in both his pretrial memoranda and his post-trial briefs on the constitutional problems arising out of such a lawsuit concerning infringement of First Amendment freedoms. Accordingly, the constitutional problem will be dealt with first, and the general law provisions relating to 15 U.S.C. §§1681 et seq., along with damages, will be dealt with separately. . . .

II

The remainder of this action revolves around the questions of whether or not defendant O'Hanlon is liable under Section 1681n and Section 1681o of this aforecited title. Section 1681n allows the recovery of actual damages, costs and reasonable attorneys fees along with punitive damages for willful non-compliance with the Act in question, and Section 1681o allows actual damages along with costs and attorneys fees for negligent non-compliance with this Act. The standard of care imposed by the aforecited statutory sections is that:

> Whenever a consumer reporting agency prepares a consumer report it shall follow reasonable procedures to assure maximum possible accuracy of the information concerning the individual about whom the report relates. 15 U.S.C. §1681e(b).

It is clear to this Court as the trier of fact that the defendant was in violation of §1681e(b), in that its procedures of gathering personal information about consumers, such as Millstone, was only from neighbors from the consumer's residence and that these items were not verified. The evidence also shows that defendant's agent Mayes knowingly included false information in the report which defendant compiled concerning Millstone. In his report agent Mayes refers to a pool of four neighbors, with full knowledge that he spoke only to three neighbors. Also, the report repeatedly asserts that all of the sources were in agreement when Mayes in fact received information from only one source, Mr. McMillan. Considering the prior unblemished record of Millstone and the fact that defendant's own operations Manual concerning such derogatory information states: "When adverse information is developed, it should be verified by at least one other source to avoid the reporting of any prejudicial or inaccurate information," the actions of O'Hanlon's agent Mayes are so wanton as to be certainly a willful non-compliance with the standard of care imposed by the Act. These actions by defendant's agent Mayes are so heinous and reprehensible as to justify the harsh damages imposed by Section 1681n. Defendant's methods of reporting on consumer's credit backgrounds as shown at trial were so slipshod and slovenly as to not even approach the realm of reasonable standards of care as imposed by the statute. Defendant's reporting methods were so wanton as to be clearly willful non-compliance with the Fair Credit Reporting Act in the eyes of this Court.

Independent of the previously discussed willful violation of the statute is the defendant's violation of §1681g(a)(1) in that it failed to disclose, and continued until pre-trial discovery forced such disclosure, the nature and substance of all the information contained in its files concerning Millstone. To say that O'Hanlon was parsimonious in its disclosures in this case would be an exercise in understatement. Defendant has stated to the Court that its policy remains not to disclose certain information to consumers which O'Hanlon itself deems appropriate. The previously quoted sections of defendant's operation Manual are ample evidence of plaintiff's attitudes and actions concerning this matter. Millstone was forced to return to defendant's offices on several occasions and each time was able to elicit a little more information from the defendant which concerned him. At no time until his lawsuit was joined and discovery was undertaken did O'Hanlon inform Millstone of the entire amount of information concerning him in O'Hanlon's files. Concerning disclosure to consumers, the legislative history of the statutory sections states:

> The House offered the amendment to delete the words "the nature and substance of" in section 609(1). The intent was to permit the consumer to examine all the information in this file except for sources of investigative information, while not giving the consumer the right to physically handle his file. The Senate conferees did not agree to this amendment, contending that the existing language already accomplished this result. The conferees of both Houses intend that this important provision be so interpreted. United States Code, Congressional and Administrative News, p.4415 (91st Congress, Second Session, 1970).

O'Hanlon was made aware of this intent by Regulations of the Federal Trade Commission prior to the effective date of this Act. The actions of

O'Hanlon in having the file mailed to its New York office, and instructing its employee in St. Louis to tell Millstone that the file was en route to New York and that he could not tell Millstone what was in it when the file was actually in St. Louis are further indications of the willful non-compliance of defendant with this Act. The whole thrust of defendant O'Hanlon's actions was an attempt to withhold from Millstone the information that was rightfully due him under the law. The evidence in the case at bar as a whole is so overwhelming and persuasive as to leave no other conclusion but that O'Hanlon was in willful violation of various previously discussed portions of the Fair Credit Reporting Act and should therefore be subject to the liabilities enumerated in Section 1681n.

III

In regards to damages, the Court further finds that although plaintiff suffered no lost wages nor incurred medical expenses on the account of the injuries therein, he suffered by reason of his mental anguish and had symptoms of sleeplessness and nervousness which were amply testified to, and because of the repeated and numerous times in which plaintiff had to contact O'Hanlon, in many cases having to leave his employment for meetings on account of the defendant's actions as stated above, the plaintiff is entitled to actual damages in the amount of $2,500.00.

Considering the willful non-compliance of O'Hanlon with the requirements of the statute, this Court will assess the sum of $25,000 against defendant O'Hanlon as punitive damages in this action. This Court also finds that the sum of $12,500 will be awarded to plaintiff from defendant for attorneys fees, and the Court will further order that defendant pay costs in this matter. In consequence, judgment for the plaintiff as stated above will be entered.

In 1996, Congress passed major amendments to the Fair Credit Reporting Act (effective September 30, 1997), including §606(d)(4), which would have aided Mr. Millstone had it been in effect at the time. Read it.

PROBLEM 64

George Gladhand was a lobbyist registered with the state legislature. One of his political adversaries was Paula Pushy, also a lobbyist. George decided to see if he could dig up some political dirt on

Paula, so he asked the Big Eye Credit Reporting Agency to do an investigative report on her private life, telling the agency why he wanted it. Big Eye did so, and Paula found out about it. She sued both George and Big Eye under FCRA, and they defended by arguing that, technically, the Act did not apply since the report was not a "consumer report" under the definitions found in §§603(d) and 604. What should result? Compare Henry v. Forbes, 433 F. Supp. 5 (D. Minn. 1976), with Rice v. Montgomery Ward, 450 F. Supp. 668 (M.D.N.C. 1978).

BAKER V. McKINNON
United States Court of Appeals, Eighth Circuit, 1998
52 F.3d 1007

McMILLIAN, Circuit Judge.

Laura J. McKinnon, an attorney, appeals from a final judgment entered in the United States District Court for the Western District of Arkansas, following a bench trial, finding that she had intentionally and willfully violated the Fair Credit Reporting Act (FCRA or the Act), 15 U.S.C. §§1681 et seq. Bakker v. McKinnon, Civil No. 96-5112 (W.D. Ark. July 21, 1997) (mem. op.). The district court awarded to each appellee, Dr. Johnny L. Bakker and his two daughters, Teresa Bakker and Carrie Ann Bakker, $500 in compensatory damages and $5,000 in punitive damages. For reversal, appellant contends that the district court erred in finding that she violated the FCRA and in awarding an unreasonable amount for punitive damages. . . .

I

In September 1996 appellees Dr. Johnny L. Bakker, who is a dentist, and his adult daughters, Teresa Bakker and Carrie Ann Bakker, filed this lawsuit alleging that appellant had requested several consumer credit reports about them from a local credit bureau in violation of the FCRA. Appellant represents several women patients of Dr. Bakker who claimed that Dr. Bakker had committed dental malpractice by improperly touching them during the course of dental treatments. Appellant filed lawsuits in state court on behalf of these women against Dr. Bakker.

The district court found that appellant and her associates had engaged in numerous acts which, in the district court's view, "grossly crossed the line in respect to what is proper in conducting litigation." Mem. op. at 2 (footnote omitted). Basically, the district court concluded that appellant and her associates had requested the credit reports as part of the litigation process to force a settlement. Id. at 3-9. The district court noted that a speaker at a meeting of the Arkansas Trial Lawyer's Association (of which appellant was a member of the board of governors and a former president) had recommended that consumer credit reports be routinely obtained against defendants or prospective defendants. Id. at 7.

Appellant admitted that she (or, more precisely, someone in her office) obtained the credit reports, but she argued that (1) she obtained them for a commercial or a professional purpose and, thus, the credit reports were not consumer credit reports within the meaning of the FCRA, 15 U.S.C. §§1681a(d), 1681b, or (2) in the alternative, assuming the credit reports were consumer reports within the meaning of the FCRA, she had a legitimate business need for requesting them, id. §1681b(3)(E). Dr. Bakker's attorney had informed appellant that CNA Insurance Co. was defending Dr. Bakker under reservation of rights letters. Appellant testified that she obtained the credit reports about Dr. Bakker and his daughters in order to determine whether he was judgment proof and whether he was transferring his assets to his daughters. Appellant filed a motion for summary judgment, alleging that the credit reports were not consumer reports or, in the alternative, they were obtained for a legitimate business need. The district court denied the motion for summary judgment, holding that the credit reports were consumer reports within the meaning of the FCRA. Order at 5-7 (Apr. 25, 1997) (order denying defendant's motion for summary judgment). The district court decided that the key is the purpose for which the information was collected, not the use to which the information contained therein is put. Id. at 6, citing St. Paul Guardian Ins. Co. v. Johnson, 884 F.2d 881, 883 (5th Cir. 1989) (St. Paul Guardian). Here, the credit reports apparently consisted primarily of a listing of outstanding credit card and similar debts. Mem. op. at 9. The district court also rejected appellant's legitimate business need argument because she and appellees were not involved in a business transaction within the meaning of the FCRA. Order at 7. The district court rejected the "broad" interpretation of "business transaction" and instead limited "business transaction" to consumer credit, insurance or employment transactions. Id.; see Ippolito v. WNS, Inc., 864 F.2d 440, 451 (7th Cir. 1988), *cert. dismissed,* 490 U.S. 1061 (1989). The district court also noted that appellant's reason for obtaining the credit reports was not a "business need" within the meaning of the FCRA because "determining whether an adverse party in litigation will be able to satisfy a judgment is plainly a purpose unrelated to 'an individual's eligibility for credit, insurance or employment.'" Order at 8, citing Mone v. Dranow, 945 F.2d 306, 308 (9th Cir. 1991) (per curiam) (citing cases).

Before trial, the district court had advised the attorneys that, in light of its previous rulings, the only issue left for trial was damages. Mem. op. at 12. Appellees testified about how appellant's wrongful requests for their credit reports had violated their privacy. The district court found that appellant and her associates had willfully violated the FCRA, 15 U.S.C. §1681q, by requesting consumer reports on appellees in "a blatant attempt to extract a settlement from the insurance carrier for Dr. Bakker by whatever means were at hand." Id. at 14. The district court characterized the multiple requests for credit reports as part of a "vendetta" pursued by appellant and her associates against Dr. Bakker and his family to harass and coerce them into settling the litigation. The district court awarded each appellee actual damages in the amount of $500 and punitive damages in the amount of $5,000. Id. at 16-17. Subsequently, the district court awarded appellees attorney's fees and costs. Order at 1-2 (Aug. 12, 1997) (order granting plaintiffs' motion for attorney's fees and costs). This appeal followed. . . .

III

Appellant argues the district court erred in finding that she violated the FCRA. Appellant argues she requested the credit reports in the course of a commercial or professional transaction, that is, in her capacity as an attorney representing clients in litigation, and not in connection with any type of consumer transaction involving appellees' credit, insurance or employment. Appellant argues that credit reports obtained in connection with commercial or professional transactions are not covered by the FCRA. Appellant also argues that there was no evidence that she obtained the credit reports under false pretenses. In the alternative, appellant argues that, assuming for purposes of analysis that the credit reports are consumer reports within the meaning of the FCRA, she did not violate the FCRA because she had a legitimate "business need" for obtaining them within the meaning of 15 U.S.C. §1681b(3)(E). We do not agree.

The underlying facts are not substantially disputed. Whether the credit reports were consumer reports and, if so, whether the business need exception applies are questions of statutory interpretation of the FCRA. The district court found that appellant had engaged in numerous acts, which in its view, grossly crossed the line in respect to what is proper in conducting litigation; during the litigation against Dr. Bakker, appellant had attempted to "dig up as much dirt" as possible about appellees without regard to its relevance; appellant had threatened to destroy and ruin Dr. Bakker's dental practice through litigation and publicity; and appellant had improperly accused Dr. Bakker of being a child molester. Mem. op. at 2-8 (citing letters dated January 23, 1992, and February 14, 1992). The district court found that appellant's reason for obtaining the credit reports was a blatant attempt to coerce a settlement from Dr. Bakker's insurance carrier.

[The court quoted FCRA §604(a).] . . .

Appellant testified that she obtained the credit report on Dr. Bakker seeking information concerning his ability to satisfy a judgment if the parties settled the underlying litigation. She admitted that the first credit report did not contain any such information. Yet, she subsequently obtained a second credit report on Dr. Bakker and his two daughters. Her explanation for obtaining credit reports on Dr. Bakker's daughters was to see if Dr. Bakker was transferring assets to his daughters. Appellant gave no explanation why she thought the later reports might provide helpful information even though the earlier report had not done so. Mem. op. at 9-10.

Appellant argues that, because she obtained the credit reports in connection with the underlying litigation against Dr. Bakker, they were obtained for a commercial or professional use and not in connection with a consumer transaction. Thus, she contends that the credit reports are not consumer reports covered by the FCRA. The district court rejected this argument, holding that appellant's alleged purpose did not alter the fact that the credit reports in question were consumer reports within the meaning of the Act. Order at 5. The definition of "consumer reports" under the Act is "limited to information that is 'used or expected to be used or collected' in connection with a 'business transaction' involving one of the 'consumer purposes' set out in the statute, that is, eligibility for personal credit or insurance, employment purposes, and licensing." Ippolito v. WNS, Inc., 864 F.2d at 451.

We hold that, regardless of appellant's intended use of the credit reports, these reports are consumer reports within the meaning of the FCRA because the information contained therein was collected for a consumer purpose. Under the FCRA whether a credit report is a consumer report does not depend solely upon the ultimate use to which the information contained therein is put, but instead, it is governed by the purpose for which the information was originally collected in whole or in part by the consumer reporting agency. St. Paul Guardian, 884 F.2d at 883-84.

> In other words, even if a report is used or expected to be used for a non-consumer purpose, it may still fall within the definition of a consumer report if it contains information that was originally collected by a consumer reporting agency with the expectation that it would be used for a consumer purpose.

Ippolito v. WNS, Inc., 864 F.2d at 453. Furthermore, appellant's contract with the Credit Bureau of Fayetteville/Springdale indicated that the reports were subject to the Act and that she agreed that she would only request the information when she intended to use the information in relation to consumer purposes identical to those set out in the Act, i.e., eligibility for personal credit or insurance, employment purposes and licensing or a business transaction involving the consumer.

Next, appellant contends pursuant to §1681b(3)(E) that she had a legitimate business need for the credit reports. Appellees, of course, argue that appellant failed to articulate a legitimate business need within the Act's exception. We hold that appellant cannot be said to have a legitimate business need within the meaning of the Act unless and until she can prove or establish that she and appellees were involved in a business transaction involving a consumer. In order to be entitled to the business need exception found in §1681b(3)(E), the business transaction must relate to "a consumer relationship between the party requesting the report and the subject of the report" regarding credit, insurance eligibility, employment, or licensing. Houghton v. New Jersey Mfrs. Ins. Co, 795 F.2d 1144, 1149 (3d Cir. 1986). Appellant admits that she and appellees were not involved in any consumer transaction involving the extension of credit, insurance, employment, or licensing. Thus, no consumer relationship existed between appellant, the party requesting the reports, and appellees, the subjects of the reports, and the business need exception did not apply. We also reject appellant's argument that, as an attorney representing clients in litigation, she had a business need to obtain credit reports on the opposing parties. See Duncan v. Handmaker, 149 F.3d 424, 1998 WL 292256, at *2-3; cf. Mone v. Dranow, 945 F.2d at 308 (employer's obtaining credit report for purpose of determining whether employee would be able to satisfy judgment was not for lawful purpose).

Finally, we consider appellant's argument that the punitive damages award was unreasonable. Title 15 U.S.C. §1681q provides criminal penalties for knowingly and willfully obtaining a credit report under false pretenses. A violation of this criminal statute is a violation of any requirement imposed under the subchapter within the meaning of §§1681n and 1681o. Hansen v. Morgan, 582 F.2d 1214, 1218 (9th Cir. 1978) (violation of §1681q forms a basis of civil liability under §§1681n and 1681o). Therefore, obtaining a credit report under false pretenses creates civil liability under the FCRA. Where civil liability exists because of a willful failure to comply with the requirements of the Act, the consumer may recover (1) any actual damages sustained by the consumer as a result of the failure; (2) such punitive damages as the court may allow; and (3) in the case of any successful action to enforce liability under this section, the costs of the action together with reasonable attorney's fees as determined by the court. 15 U.S.C. §1681n(a).

Therefore, the question becomes whether the evidence showed that appellant's and her associates' conduct in obtaining the reports was willfully done. "To show willful noncompliance with the FCRA, [the plaintiff] must show that [the defendant] 'knowingly and intentionally committed an act in conscious disregard for the rights of others,' but need not show 'malice or evil motive.'" [Citations omitted.] In Millstone v. O'Hanlon Reports, Inc., 528 F.2d 829 (8th Cir. 1976) (O'Hanlon), an opinion written by Associate Justice Tom C. Clark, sitting by designation, the credit reporting agency had produced a report on the plaintiff which was filled with inaccuracies. There was evidence that the defendant's agent did a sloppy job because he had only devoted, at most, 30 minutes to prepare the report. Justice Clark concluded that the defendant had willfully violated both the spirit and the letter of the FCRA by "trampling recklessly" upon the plaintiff's rights thereunder, upheld the recovery of damages for "mere mental pain and anxiety," and also held that the trial court was acting within its discretion when it awarded punitive damages. Id. at 834-35. "Actual damages are not a statutory prerequisite to an award of punitive damages under the [FCRA]." Yohay v. City of Alexandria Employees Credit Union, Inc., 827 F.2d 967, 972 (4th Cir. 1987) (noting an award of punitive damages in the absence of any actual damages, in an appropriate case, comports with the underlying deterrent purpose of FCRA).

Here, the district court found that at the very early stages of the underlying litigation, appellant and her associates set out upon a course of conduct, which in the words of O'Hanlon, 528 F.2d at 835, "willfully violated both the spirit and the letter of the Fair Credit Reporting Act . . . by trampling recklessly upon [appellees'] rights thereunder." That conduct was obviously a blatant attempt to extract a settlement from Dr. Bakker's insurance carrier, without regard to whether such conduct was fair or a clear violation of Rule 4.4 of the Arkansas Rules of Professional Conduct.

The district court further found that appellant intentionally and egregiously threatened Dr. Bakker with loss of his profession, both by the destruction of his name and by forfeiture or suspension of his dental license. Appellant's conduct included allegations that Dr. Bakker and his wife had been involved in child molestation matters, allegations that could have had a devastating effect upon their lives even if false. Finally, the district court found that appellant's multiple requests for credit reports on Dr. Bakker and his daughters were designed and intended to carry on the "vendetta" that appellant's law firm pursued against appellees.

While it is true that appellees were not able to produce any actual out-of-pocket expenses or costs incurred as a result of appellant's willful conduct, appellees testified about how they felt when appellant obtained their credit reports and violated their privacy, thereby causing them some emotional distress. We hold that the district court did not abuse its discretion in awarding appellees actual and punitive damages.

Accordingly, the judgment of the district court is affirmed.

PROBLEM 65

Decide whether the following matters are covered by the Fair Credit Reporting Act:

a. Professor Chalk was sitting in his office one day when the phone rang. It was Judge Able, who needed a new law clerk and was considering hiring Portia Moot, who had just graduated from law school and had been one of Professor Chalk's students. The judge asked Chalk what he thought of Moot's work while she had been Chalk's research assistant. When Chalk gives his opinion, is this a "consumer report" under §603(d)?

b. Richard Dauntless went to Murgatroyd Motors and picked out the car of his dreams. The salesman told Dauntless that his credit would have to be approved by Oakapple Finance Company, since the car dealership did not itself extend credit. Dauntless filled out a credit application, which Murgatroyd Motors faxed to Oakapple Finance Company, which promptly faxed back to the dealership the statement "CREDIT REFUSED." Is this decision not to extend credit a "consumer report"? Who must do what? See §§603(d) and 615.

PROBLEM 66

After she had been an associate at the firm of Factory, Factory & Money for six years, Portia Moot came under consideration for a partnership. At the same time, by coincidence, she decided to get married. Ever mindful of the firm's image, the firm's Partnership Committee contacted the Big Eye Credit Bureau and asked for a credit report on the man Portia was about to wed. A senior partner from the firm told the credit bureau that Portia's husband was under consideration for a job with the firm. The credit report showed that Portia's fiancé paid his bills on time, but when he found out what had happened, he sued the firm. Has it violated the Act? See §§616(b) and 619; Zamora v. Valley Fed. Sav. & Loan Assn., 811 F.2d 1368 (10th Cir. 1987).

"Prescreening" is the name given to the process used by credit card issuers and insurance companies in which consumer reporting agencies are asked by these users to produce a list of creditworthy individuals to whom offers of credit cards/insurance are then made. In 2000 3.5 billion prescreened offers were extended to consumers. Since the users here cannot reasonably expect to enter into contracts with all the people whose credit reports they examine, there was quite an argument in the early days of the statute as to whether these reports were requested for legitimate business purposes. In the end the matter was settled by amendments to FCRA allowing the use of credit reports for prescreening if "firm offers" of credit/insurance are then extended to those deemed to be good risks.

PROBLEM 67

Because she had a flawless credit record, Portia Moot weekly received two or three offers of new credit cards. Weary of dealing with this sort of mail, she mentions the issue to you, an attorney she met at a cocktail party. Do you have any advice for her? See FCRA §§615(d) and 604(e).[2] If Portia receives an offer of credit that is so qualified that it is illusory, can she argue that the credit card issuer has violated the Act by obtaining her credit report without really intending to make a "firm offer"? See Murray v. New Cingular Wireless Services, Inc., 523 F.3d 719 (7th Cir. 2008).

Resellers.   There are entities that purchase credit reports from consumer reporting agencies and then sell these reports to others. FCRA calls such entities "resellers" and imposes certain duties upon them, primarily that of making sure the end users are obtaining the reports for permissible purposes; see §607(e). In Lewis v. Ohio Professional Electronic Network LLC, 248 F. Supp. 2d 693 (S.D. Ohio 2003), an organization formed by various police entities to share arrest records was held liable for failure to do this in a situation where a consumer's social security number was mistakenly confused with that of a criminal, and the individual lost his job as a result.

Trans Union Corp. v. Federal Trade Commission
United States Court of Appeals, District of Columbia Circuit, 2001
245 F.3d 809

TATEL, Circuit Judge:

Petitioner, a consumer reporting agency, sells lists of names and addresses to target marketers—companies and organizations that contact consumers with offers of products and services. The Federal Trade Commission

---

2. The phone number for the opt-out is (888) 567-8688.

determined that these lists were "consumer reports" under the Fair Credit Reporting Act and thus could no longer be sold for target marketing purposes. Challenging this determination, petitioner argues that the Commission's decision is unsupported by substantial evidence and that the Act itself is unconstitutional. Because we find both arguments without merit, we deny the petition for review.

I

Petitioner Trans Union sells two types of products. First, as a credit reporting agency, it compiles credit reports about individual consumers from credit information it collects from banks, credit card companies, and other lenders. It then sells these credit reports to lenders, employers, and insurance companies. Trans Union receives credit information from lenders in the form of "tradelines." A tradeline typically includes a customer's name, address, date of birth, telephone number, Social Security number, account type, opening date of account, credit limit, account status, and payment history. Trans Union receives 1.4 to 1.6 billion records per month. The company's credit database contains information on 190 million adults.

Trans Union's second set of products—those at issue in this case—are known as target marketing products. These consist of lists of names and addresses of individuals who meet specific criteria such as possession of an auto loan, a department store credit card, or two or more mortgages. Marketers purchase these lists, then contact the individuals by mail or telephone to offer them goods and services. To create its target marketing lists, Trans Union maintains a database known as MasterFile, a subset of its consumer credit database. MasterFile consists of information about every consumer in the company's credit database who has (A) at least two tradelines with activity during the previous six months, or (B) one tradeline with activity during the previous six months plus an address confirmed by an outside source. The company compiles target marketing lists by extracting from MasterFile the names and addresses of individuals with characteristics chosen by list purchasers. For example, a department store might buy a list of all individuals in a particular area code who have both a mortgage and a credit card with a $10,000 limit. Although target marketing lists contain only names and addresses, purchasers know that every person on a list has the characteristics they requested because Trans Union uses those characteristics as criteria for culling individual files from its database. Purchasers also know that every individual on a target marketing list satisfies the criteria for inclusion in MasterFile.

The Fair Credit Reporting Act of 1970 ("FCRA"), 15 U.S.C. §§1681, 1681a-1681u, regulates consumer reporting agencies like Trans Union, imposing various obligations to protect the privacy and accuracy of credit information. The Federal Trade Commission, acting pursuant to its authority to enforce the FCRA, see 15 U.S.C. §1681s(a), determined that Trans Union's target marketing lists were "consumer reports" subject to the Act's limitations. The FCRA defines "consumer report" as:

> Any written, oral, or other communication of any information by a consumer reporting agency bearing on a consumer's credit worthiness, credit standing, credit capacity, character, general reputation, personal characteristics, or mode of living which is used or expected to be used or collected in whole or in part for the purpose of serving as a factor in establishing the consumer's eligibility for—
>   (A) credit or insurance to be used primarily for personal, family, or household purposes;
>   (B) employment purposes; or
>   (C) any other purpose authorized under section 1681b of this title.

15 U.S.C. §1681a(d)(1). Finding that the information Trans Union sold was "collected in whole or in part by [Trans Union] with the expectation that it would be used by credit grantors for the purpose of serving as a factor in establishing the consumer's eligibility for one of the transactions set forth in the FCRA," and concluding that target marketing is not an authorized use of consumer reports under section 1681b, In re Trans Union Corp., 118 F.T.C. 821, 891 (1994), the Commission ordered Trans Union to stop selling target marketing lists, id. at 895.

Trans Union petitioned for review. In Trans Union Corp. v. FTC, 317 U.S. App. D.C. 133, 81 F.3d 228 (D.C. Cir. 1996) (*"Trans Union I"*), we agreed with the Commission that selling consumer reports for target marketing violates the Act. 81 F.3d at 233-34. We nevertheless set aside the Commission's determination that Trans Union's target marketing lists amounted to consumer reports. Id. at 231-33. The Commission, we held, failed to justify its finding that Trans Union's lists, by conveying the mere fact that consumers had a tradeline, were communicating information collected for the purpose of determining credit eligibility. We found that the Commission had failed to provide evidence to support the proposition that "the mere existence of a tradeline, as distinguished from payment history organized thereunder," was used for credit-granting decisions or was intended or expected to be used for such decisions. Id. at 233. . . .

On remand, following extensive discovery, more than a month of trial proceedings, and an initial decision by an Administrative Law Judge, the Commission found that Trans Union's target marketing lists contain information that credit grantors use as factors in granting credit. Accordingly, the Commission concluded, the lists are "consumer reports" that Trans

Union may not sell for target marketing purposes. FTC Opinion at 33. The Commission also rejected Trans Union's argument that such a restriction would violate its First Amendment rights. Applying intermediate scrutiny, the Commission found that the government has a substantial interest in protecting private credit information, that the FCRA directly advances that interest, and that the Act's restrictions on speech are narrowly tailored. Id. at 37-52. The Commission thus ordered Trans Union to "cease and desist from distributing or selling consumer reports, including those in the form of target marketing lists, to any person unless [the company] has reason to believe that such person intends to use the consumer report for purposes authorized under Section [1681b] of the Fair Credit Reporting Act." In re Trans Union Corp., Final Order, No. 9255 (Feb. 10, 2000). Trans Union again petitions for review.

II

As we pointed out in *Trans Union I*, the first element of the FCRA's definition of consumer report—"bearing on a consumer's credit worthiness, credit standing, credit capacity, character, general reputation, personal characteristics, or mode of living," 15 U.S.C. §1681a(d)(1)—"does not seem very demanding," for almost any information about consumers arguably bears on their personal characteristics or mode of living. See 81 F.3d at 231. Indeed, Trans Union does not challenge the Commission's conclusion that the information contained in its lists meets this prong of the definition of consumer report.

Whether the company's target marketing lists qualify as consumer reports thus turns on whether information they contain "is used or expected to be used or collected in whole or in part for the purpose of serving as a factor in establishing the consumer's eligibility for [credit]." 15 U.S.C. §1681a(d)(1). According to the Commission, "a factor in establishing the consumer's eligibility for [credit]," id., includes any type of information credit grantors use in their criteria for "prescreening" or in "credit scoring models." See FTC Opinion at 16-17. "Prescreening" involves selecting individuals for guaranteed offers of credit or insurance. See id. at 18; see also *Trans Union I*, 81 F.3d at 234 (defining "prescreening" as "the sale of a list of people preselected for credit worthiness by some specified criteria, where the buyer of the list agrees in advance to make a firm offer of credit to each listed person"). "Credit scoring models" are statistical models for predicting credit performance that are developed by observing the historical credit performance of a number of consumers and identifying the consumer characteristics that correlate with good and bad credit performance. See

FTC Opinion at 17. Applying its prescreening/credit scoring model standard, the Commission found that Trans Union's lists contain the type of information "'used' and/or 'expected to be used' . . . as a factor in establishing a consumer's eligibility for credit." Id. at 15; see also id. n.19.

Trans Union urges us to reject the Commission's interpretation of the Act in order to avoid what the company calls "serious constitutional questions." Pet'r Opening Br. at 9. In support, it cites DeBartolo Corp. v. Florida Gulf Coast Building & Construction Trades Council, where the Supreme Court refused to defer to the NLRB's interpretation of a provision of the NLRA because the Court believed it raised serious First Amendment problems. 485 U.S. 568, 574-77, 108 S. Ct. 1392, 99 L. Ed. 2d 645 (1988). But as we demonstrate in Section III, infra, Trans Union's constitutional arguments are without merit, so we have no basis for rejecting the Commission's statutory interpretation on that ground. . . .

We have the same reaction to the brief's occasional suggestions that the Commission's decision was arbitrary and capricious. Not only do these suggestions appear in a section entitled "The Commission's Interpretation Of FCRA Raises Serious Constitutional Questions," see, e.g., Pet'r Opening Br. at 19 (referring to "illogical contradictions"), but the list of issues presented for review neither mentions the arbitrary and capricious standard nor otherwise questions the reasonableness of the Commission's decision.

We thus turn to the one non-constitutional argument that Trans Union clearly mounts: that the Commission's decision is unsupported by substantial evidence. A footnote to the title of this portion of its brief states:

> The Order is replete with statements unsupported by the evidence. . . . The word limitation of [Federal Rule of Appellate Procedure] 32(a)(7) makes it impossible to address each such misstatement here. It is the responsibility of the Commission's counsel, however, to ensure that the Court is not misled by the statements in the Order not supported by the evidence.

Id. at 21 n.7. To bring a substantial evidence challenge, however, Trans Union must do more than assert generally that the decision is unsupported by substantial evidence. It must identify the specific findings it challenges and demonstrate that each finding is either unsupported by evidence or, because the Commission unreasonably discounted contrary evidence, unsupported by "the record in its entirety." See Universal Camera Corp. v. NLRB, 340 U.S. 474, 488, 95 L. Ed. 456, 71 S. Ct. 456 (1951). The 14,000 words permitted by Rule 32(a)(7) are more than enough to accomplish this task.

Instead of challenging the Commission's findings regarding specific target marketing products, Trans Union points to evidence relating to the general question of whether the information in its target marketing lists is used to determine credit worthiness. This is not the question before us. As we indicate above, the Commission interprets "factor in establishing the consumer's eligibility for credit," 15 U.S.C. §1681a(d)(1), to include any information considered by lenders in prescreening, which, as two witnesses testified, can involve consideration of criteria other than credit worthiness, e.g., whether a given consumer is likely to respond to an offer of credit. Because Trans Union has not challenged the Commission's interpretation of the statute, its argument that the information the company sells is not actually used to determine credit worthiness is beside the point. Moreover, Trans Union cites no testimony refuting the Commission's finding that the information in its target marketing lists is used in prescreening.

Not only has Trans Union thus failed to mount a proper substantial evidence challenge to the Commission's finding that lenders take list information into account in credit models and prescreening, but we have no doubt that the decision does find support in the record. Consider, for example, Trans Union's "Master File/Selects" product line, which allows marketers to request lists based on any of five categories of information: (1) credit limits (e.g., consumers with credit cards with credit limits over $10,000), (2) open dates of loans (e.g., consumers who took out loans in the last six months), (3) number of tradelines, (4) type of tradeline (e.g., auto loan or mortgage), and (5) existence of a tradeline. The Commission cites testimony and other record evidence that support its finding that lenders consider each of these five categories of information in prescreening or credit scoring models. Beginning with credit limits, the Commission cites the testimony of a statistician who builds credit scoring models. FTC Opinion at 19. That witness explained that scoring models rely in part on consumer utilization of credit, calculated by dividing a consumer's current outstanding balance by the consumer's credit limit. To support its finding regarding open dates of loans, the Commission relied on the testimony of a vice president of a company that builds credit scoring models. Id. According to that witness, some scoring models use the open date of the oldest tradeline in a consumer's credit file as a predictive characteristic. The witness also testified that some credit scoring models use the date of the most recently opened tradeline to determine credit risk. To support its finding that information about the number of tradelines in a consumer's credit file is a consumer report, the Commission cites the testimony of a vice president in charge of direct mail processing for a bank's credit card department who explained that, in its credit making decisions, her bank considers the number of tradelines consumers possess. Id. at 20 n.30. The Commission also points to record evidence demonstrating that Trans Union itself uses the number of tradelines as a predictive characteristic in its credit scoring models. Id. at 20. As to the type of tradeline, the Commission cites the testimony of representatives of companies that design credit models who explained that some credit scoring models, including two used by Trans Union, take into account possession of a bank card. FTC Opinion at 21-22. One witness testified that Trans Union scoring models also consider possession of a finance company loan to be a predictive characteristic. Another witness, this one representing a credit card company, testified that his company's scoring models assign points for possession of a mortgage, retail tradeline, or bank card. Id. at 21.

The record also contains sufficient evidence to support the Commission's resolution of the issue remanded by *Trans Union I*: whether mere existence of a tradeline is "a factor in credit-granting decisions." 81 F.3d at 233. An employee of a bank that issues credit cards testified that to be eligible for credit, an individual must have at least one tradeline. FTC Opinion at 25. The vice president of credit scoring at another credit card issuer testified that the very first question her company asks in prescreening is whether the consumer has a tradeline that has been open for at least a year. Challenging the implications of this testimony, Trans Union argues that banks ask whether consumers have tradelines not because the existence of a tradeline is itself a factor in determining credit eligibility, but because banks want to determine whether there is enough information in consumer files to make credit eligibility determinations. This may be true. But as we explain above, our task is limited to determining whether substantial record evidence supports the Commission's finding that banks consider the existence of a tradeline as a factor in prescreening or credit models. Because the record contains such evidence, we have no basis for questioning the Commission's decision.

Trans Union has identified one potentially troubling inconsistency in the Commission's decision. As the company points out, record evidence demonstrates that lenders consider names and addresses when prescreening consumers for guaranteed offers of credit, yet the Commission does not prohibit the sale of names and addresses for target marketing purposes. Regarding addresses, the Commission's opinion says, "although some lenders will not extend credit to consumers with a P.O. Box address, we do not find that the P.O. Box feature bears on 'credit worthiness, credit standing, credit capacity, character, general reputation, personal characteristics or mode of living.'" Id. at 31 n.50. It is not clear, however, why receiving mail at a post office should not be considered an aspect of an individual's "mode of living." We need not resolve this issue, however, because Trans Union presents neither an arbitrary and capricious nor a statutory interpretation challenge to the Commission's failure to prohibit the sale of names and addresses. See supra at 6-7.

Nor must we resolve any inconsistency between the Commission's decision in this case and a 1993 consent agreement between the Commission and a Trans Union competitor, TRW (now Experian). In contrast to the Commission's decision here, that agreement allowed TRW to sell information about consumers' ages to target marketers. Again, although this might suggest that the Commission has acted arbitrarily and capriciously in treating similarly situated entities differently, Trans Union has not made such a challenge. The Commission thus seems correct that "the TRW Consent is not before us in this matter and it is without precedential effect on this opinion." FTC Opinion at 16 n.22.

[The court then rejected the constitutional challenges to the FTC Opinion.]

Having considered and rejected Trans Union's other arguments, we deny the petition for review.

So Ordered.

PROBLEM 68

Martindale-Hubbell, Inc. is a publisher that yearly undertakes the Herculean task of compiling a directory of every attorney in the United States and rating him or her according to general reputation and other criteria. This directory is then sold nationwide to law libraries, firms, agencies, and others. If a lawyer receives a rating that the lawyer thinks is too low, can the lawyer discover the contents of Martindale-Hubbell's file on him or her? Is this matter covered by the Fair Credit Reporting Act? See Bergen v. Martindale-Hubbell, Inc., 176 Ga. App. 745, 337 S.E.2d 770 (1985).

C. Identity Theft

The statistics on identity theft are startling and getting worse. Over 8.3 million American adults (which is 3.7 percent of the entire population of such adults) were victims of identity theft in 2005 (causing a significant amount of out-of-pocket expenses and wasted time). Those so targeted feel the brunt of the assault not only in destruction of their credit rating but also psychologically as their very personhood is sullied. Businesses, too, are much harmed by this criminal activity, losing more than a billion dollars every year to identity theft. Some of the rules we have studied thus far give partial relief to consumers who are dealing with the problem. As we have learned, credit card customers have limited liability for unauthorized use of both their credit and debit cards (see Chapter 5), and false information in the credit records of consumer reporting agencies can be dealt with in part by the dispute resolution rules of FCRA, to be studied in the next section of this chapter. The 2003 rewrite of FCRA added even more detailed provisions addressing the nightmare that follows in the wake of identity theft. The federal government has created a web site giving guidance to victims of identity theft, www.consumer.gov/idtheft.

PROBLEM 69

A hacker broke into the computer files of Ponzi, Inc. and stole the credit records of all of its consumer customers. One of these was Alice Bluegown, who was astounded when she began receiving numerous bills for purchases she had never made, frequent calls from very impolite debt collectors, and even an embarrassing visit from the police bunko squad. You are her next-door neighbor, so naturally she frantically calls you for legal advice. What can she do to prevent future trouble and clean up her much-damaged credit rating? See §§605A and 605B.

In addition to those mentioned in the sections you have just read, the 2003 amendments created a number of other duties in connection with identity theft. Section 615(e) commands the federal agencies to develop "red flag" guidelines for consumer reporting agencies and creditors so that suspicious circumstances will not go unremarked. The Federal Trade Commission has released compliance information on its web site: http://www.ftc.gov/bcp/edu/pubs/business/alerts/alt050.shtm. Per §605(h), if a consumer reporting agency gets a request for a report from a user and that request has a different *address* for the consumer than the one the agency has on file, the agency must notify the user of the discrepancy, thus triggering an investigation. Merchants and others who electronically print out receipts showing credit card transactions are forbidden to display on the receipt either the expiration date of the card or more than the last five digits of the card number; §605(g). Victims of identity theft have a right to get copies of all records of business transactions between the thief and creditors; §609(e). To prevent the spreading of false information, §623(a)(6) forbids furnishers of credit information who have been notified of identity theft to report the disputed debts as still outstanding to new consumer reporting agencies, and §615(f) forbids them from selling such a debt to others for collection. Any debt collector who has been notified by the supposed debtor that the involved debt springs from an identity theft must notify the original creditor that this claim has been made; §615(g) (we will discuss other rights that involve debt collectors in Chapter 11).

Finally, it should be mentioned that over half of the states have enacted "credit freeze" laws, which allow consumers to block access to their files in the event of suspected identity theft, thus providing a quick way to preserve the status quo until the difficulty can be straightened out.

D. Fair Credit Reporting Act Procedures

There are four major players in FCRA disputes: the consumer, the consumer reporting agency, the furnishers of the information in the files, and the user of the credit report. Each of these parties has duties triggered by the various provisions of the Act, as explored below.

All the studies show that credit reports are rife with errors, the statistics being truly alarming. One would think it was in the best interests of the credit bureaus to work hard to make sure the files were absolutely correct, and they do put some time into this, but they are consoled by the thought that the number of errors against the consumer and in favor of the consumer by and large balance out, leaving the reports more or less reliable overall. The individual consumers hurt by misinformation in their files are of course less sanguine about the destruction of their credit rating. The leading credit bureaus receive tens of thousands of complaints from angry consumers every *week* (and spend very little time processing them—think of the enormous expense involved).

PROBLEM 70

Out of work, Bruce Wayne applied for a job with the Gotham City Detective Agency. The agency, without telling Wayne, secretly ordered the Big Eye Credit Bureau to conduct an in-depth investigation of Wayne by interviewing his friends and neighbors. One of them, John Joker, lied to the credit bureau and told them Wayne was a swinger. The agency then refused to hire Wayne and wouldn't tell him why. He investigated on his own and found out about the Big Eye report. When he went to the Big Eye office, they refused even to talk to him. He went home and put on a disguise and then went back to Big Eye, pretending to be a microchiropterist intent on hiring Bruce Wayne. For a fee they gave him Wayne's credit report. Answer these questions:

a. Did the agency or the bureau, or both, violate §606 of the Act?
b. May Wayne sue Joker? See §610(e).

c. Did the detective agency violate the Act when it refused to tell him why he was not hired? See §615. What is it required to tell him? If it does not do so, can he sue them? See §615(h)(8).

d. May the credit bureau charge Wayne a fee for the credit report on himself? See §612.

e. What damages may he recover against the credit bureau? The detective agency? See §§616, 617.

f. Did Wayne himself violate the Act? See §§616(b) and 619.

PROBLEM 71

When Clark Kent applied for a credit card from Metropolis State Bank, it obtained a credit report on him from a consumer reporting agency, and, based on it, decided that he was a subprime risk and thus not entitled to the 15 percent interest rate that it gave to most of its credit card customers. MSB instead notified Kent that he was being granted a credit card with an interest rate of 25 percent. Is this risk-based pricing decision an "adverse action," thus triggering a requirement that the bank notify him that he is being charged a higher rate based on a bad credit report? See §615(h), a section added in 2003, agreeing with the conclusions of Reynolds v. Hartford Financial Services Group, Inc., 416 F.3d 1097 (9th Cir. 2005).

Privacy.   Concerned that consumers were in danger of losing all privacy in their very personal financial matters in this computer age, Congress enacted the Gramm-Leach-Bliley Act (15 U.S.C. §6801, et seq.), sometimes called the Financial Services Modernization Act, which President Clinton signed into law in 1999. The statute mandates clear disclosure by all financial institutions of their privacy policies on financial information shared with others. The disclosure must be made when accounts are opened and annually thereafter, giving consumers the right to opt out and thereby forbid the distribution of nonpublic financial information. Thus many consumers were sent opt-out forms, sometimes buried in other disclosures, and little understood by most. Since so few consumers exercised the right to opt out when common sense indicates that most would if they understood the issue, some members of Congress have urged that the statute be amended so that the reverse occurs: the financial information cannot be shared with others unless the consumer affirmatively *opts in*; however, as of this writing (the spring of 2009), no changes in the statute had been made. The statute does not allow private civil actions, leaving enforcement of the

Act to various administrative agencies. In 2003, the FTC promulgated the Standards For Safeguarding Customer Information Rule (the so-called "Safeguards Rule") at 16 C.F.R. Part 314.

PROBLEM 72

John Smith has always appeared healthy and hearty, but he is HIV-positive, a fact he has taken great care to conceal from everyone except his doctor. He is now taking drugs that keep him in good health, but he has recently applied for a new job and is worried that a credit report might disclose his HIV status. How realistic is this worry? See FCRA §604(g).

PROBLEM 73

Early in 2014, when Portia Moot applied for a $100,000 life in-surance policy with the Norisk Insurance Company, the application contained a statement that an investigation would be made into the applicant's character, general reputation, personal characteristics, and mode of living, and that applicants had a right to a written ex-planation as to the nature and scope of the investigation. Portia filled out the application, writing in the margin, "Please send me this written explanation" and drawing an arrow to the clause promising one. Norisk immediately ordered a complete report on Portia from the Big Eye Credit Bureau.

a. Does either Norisk or Big Eye have duties under §606 that have not been met?

b. Big Eye's investigation was made easier by the fact that it had done a personal investigation on Portia Moot the year before. May it use that information? See §614.

c. Big Eye's prior investigation had turned up the fact that Portia didn't pay her taxes and had a tax lien filed against her in 2005, filed a bankruptcy petition in late 2003, and was given a bankruptcy dis-charge from her debts in May 2004. May it reveal these matters to Norisk? See §605.

d. Norisk turned Portia down. What must it tell her? See §615.

e. Portia knew a mistake had to have been made, since she had always paid her taxes and had never been through bankruptcy. What are her rights? See §§609, 610, 611.

f. After Portia straightened all this out, Norisk granted her life insurance coverage. The policy had a provision that obviated the need for the payment of premiums if the policyholder became incapacitated. Portia became ill two years later and gave notice to Norisk of her intention to take advantage of this provision. Norisk hired Big Eye Credit Bureau to conduct an investigation to determine if Portia was indeed incapacitated, but Norisk did not tell Portia that it was having this investigation done. Has Norisk violated FCRA? See Hovater v. Equifax, Inc., 823 F.2d 413 (11th Cir. 1987).

The original version of FCRA contained little regulation of the furnishers of information to consumer reporting agencies, but §623 now addresses their responsibilities in detail. One thing it requires is that when a creditor reports a bad debt to the consumer reporting agency, the creditor must specify *when the account became delinquent*; §623(a)(5). This is important because under §605 accounts more than seven years old may no longer be routinely reported as overdue.

The major thrust of §623 is to keep furnishers of information from misreporting credit transactions and to make them investigate and correct those the consumer disputes. Read §623 and use it to resolve the following Problem.

PROBLEM 74

When Portia Moot was turned down for a job because a credit report disclosed that she had an overdue account with Big Department Store, she contacted the store itself and told the credit manager that he had better check the records: Portia had always paid the bills the store sent her on time, and three months ago she had closed this account when the balance was zero. The credit manager of the store calls you, the store's attorney, and asks for advice. Because of a computer crash some months ago, the store's records are in chaos. Assuming it can find Portia's records, how much of an investigation must Big Department Store conduct? Can it simply check its own records or must it look into the truth behind those records (an expensive proposition)? See Johnson v. MBNA Am. Bank, NA, 357 F.3d 426 (7th Cir. 2004). Instead of incurring the expense of reinvestigating, can Big Department Store simply delete the account from its records and stop making any reports at all to consumer reporting agencies about her? See McKeown v. Sears, Roebuck & Co., 335 F. Supp. 2d 917 (W.D. Wis. 2004). Suppose that Big Department

Store, in response to Portia's letter, informed her that it would correct its records and stop reporting her as delinquent to the consumer reporting agencies, but then, due to a bureaucratic snafu, continued to send out the erroneous report on her and did not give her the notice of negative information required by §623(a)(7). Can she sue Big Department Store? See §623(c). What can she do? See §623(b).

GORMAN v. WOLPOFF & ABRAMSON, LLP[3]
United States Court of Appeals, Ninth Circuit (2009)
552 F.3d 1008

BERZON, Circuit Judge:

John Gorman tried to buy a satellite television system using his credit card, issued by MBNA America Bank. He was unsatisfied with the system purchased, and lodged a challenge with MBNA to dispute the charge. Unhappy with MBNA's response, Gorman instituted this lawsuit against MBNA, alleging violations of the Fair Credit Reporting Act, 15 U.S.C. §§1681-1681x, libel, and violations of Cal. Civ. Code section 1785.25(a). The district court dismissed his California statutory claim and granted MBNA summary judgment on the other causes of action. . . . We affirm in part and reverse in part.

I. BACKGROUND

In December 2002, John Gorman paid for the delivery and installation of a new satellite TV system on a Visa credit card issued by MBNA America Bank ("MBNA"). The charge, $759.70, was posted on his January 2003 credit card statement. According to Gorman, the merchant, Four Peaks Home Entertainment ("Four Peaks"), delivered a used and defective TV system and botched the installation, damaging his house in the process. Gorman told Four Peaks he was refusing delivery of the goods and asked for a refund, but Four Peaks refused to refund the charges unless Gorman arranged to return the TV system. The defective equipment is still in Gorman's possession.[4]

---

3. Footnotes in this case have been renumbered for clarity.

4. MBNA claims that Four Peaks shipped Gorman new, replacement equipment and that Gorman retains both the defective and replacement equipment. Gorman disputes having received any replacement system. Gorman also claims that he made the merchandise available to Four Peaks for pickup, and that doing so was sufficient to require a refund under Cal. Com. Code section 2602(2)(b) ("If the buyer has before rejection taken physical possession of goods in which he does not have a security interest under the provisions of this division (subdivision (3) of Section 2711), he is under a duty after rejection to hold them with reasonable care at the

In February 2003, Gorman notified MBNA that he was disputing the charges and submitted copies of emails between himself and Four Peaks. The attached emails showed that Gorman had informed a Four Peaks representative that the delivered goods were "unacceptable and [were] rejected." He also noted damage from the installation and notified Four Peaks that he "plan[ned] to dispute the credit card charges in their entirety, as the damage exceeds the amount of the charges."

MBNA responded to the dispute notice with a request for additional information from Gorman about the dispute, including proof that the merchandise had been returned. A month passed, and MBNA wrote Gorman again, stating that as he had not responded, it assumed the charge was no longer disputed. Gorman answered that he continued to dispute the charge, and referred MBNA to his original notice of dispute. He did not claim to have returned the equipment, but stated that the merchandise "has been available for the merchant to pick up." MBNA again requested proof that the goods had been returned; Gorman did not reply.

In April 2003, MBNA informed Gorman that it was "unable to assist [him] because the merchandise has not been returned to the merchant." Gorman called an MBNA representative saying, again, that all relevant information was in his original letter. MBNA then contacted Four Peaks, which told MBNA that it had shipped replacement equipment to Gorman but that he had not sent the old equipment back to them.

In July 2003, MBNA again informed Gorman that it could not obtain a credit on his behalf without further information from him. Gorman, who is a lawyer, responded in writing on his law firm's letterhead, stating that MBNA had all the information it needed, that he had left several unanswered messages with MBNA asking to speak with someone about the dispute, and that he would "never" pay the disputed charge. He further stated that MBNA had violated the Fair Credit Billing Act, that he was "entitled to recover attorneys' fees for MBNA's violation," and that he was offsetting his legal fees against his current account balance and so would make no more payments on the card, for the TV system or anything else. The balance at that time was more than $6,000.

Gorman's letter to MBNA worked, at least temporarily. In August 2003, MBNA removed the Four Peaks charge and related finance charges and late fees from Gorman's credit card bill. Over the next two months, MBNA

---

seller's disposition for a time sufficient to permit the seller to remove them."). He also testified in his deposition that Four Peaks never sent him pre-paid shipping labels. It is not clear whether he would have shipped the merchandise back had he received such labels.

again contacted Four Peaks, which once more informed MBNA that it would not issue a credit for Gorman's charge until he returned the refused equipment. When MBNA called Gorman, he informed them he had the merchandise and "ha[d] no intention of ever [returning] it." In October, MBNA reposted the charge to Gorman's account.

After he stopped making payments on his card, Gorman claims, he received numerous harassing phone calls. During one of these calls, Gorman alleges, an MBNA representative told him, "We're a big bank. You either pay us or we'll destroy your credit."

In January 2004, MBNA reported Gorman's account to the credit reporting agencies ("CRAs") as "charged-off." Between May 2004 and November 2005, Gorman informed the three major credit reporting agencies (Equifax, TransUnion, and Experian) that their credit reports included inaccurate information.

As required by federal law, the CRAs sent MBNA notices of dispute containing descriptions of Gorman's complaints (as understood by the CRAs) and asking the bank to verify the accuracy of his account records. MBNA responded by reviewing the account records and notes. After ascertaining that its prior investigation did not support Gorman's claimed dispute, MBNA notified the CRAs that the delinquency was not an error. According to Gorman, MBNA did not notify the CRAs that the charges remained in dispute, and the CRAs did not list the charges as disputed.

Since his credit reports began listing his MBNA account as delinquent, Gorman has been denied credit altogether or offered only high interest rates on at least three occasions. He contends that the MBNA account is the only negative entry on his credit report.

In September 2004, Gorman sued MBNA. The complaint alleges violations of the federal Fair Credit Reporting Act ("FCRA"), 15 U.S.C. §§1681-1681x and a California credit reporting law, Cal. Civ. Code section 1785.25(a), and also alleges a claim for libel. Gorman seeks injunctive relief, damages resulting from MBNA's reporting of his account, and damages from lost wages for the time he spent dealing with his credit that he would have otherwise spent billing clients. The district court dismissed Gorman's California statutory claim as preempted and granted MBNA summary judgment on all other claims. Gorman timely appeals.

For the reasons stated below, we affirm in part and reverse in part the district court's grant of summary judgment on the FCRA claims; we affirm the district court's grant of summary judgment on Gorman's libel claim; and we reverse the district court's dismissal of Gorman's California statutory claim.

II. ANALYSIS

A. FAIR CREDIT REPORTING ACT CLAIMS

1. Statutory Background

Congress enacted the Fair Credit Reporting Act ("FCRA"), 15 U.S.C. §§1681-1681x, in 1970 "to ensure fair and accurate credit reporting, promote efficiency in the banking system, and protect consumer privacy." Safeco Ins. Co. of Am. v. Burr, 551 U.S. 47, 127 S. Ct. 2201, 2205, 167 L. Ed. 2d 1045 (2007). As an important means to this end, the Act sought to make "consumer reporting agencies exercise their grave responsibilities [in assembling and evaluating consumers' credit, and disseminating information about consumers' credit] with fairness, impartiality, and a respect for the consumer's right to privacy." 15 U.S.C. §1681(a)(4). In addition, to ensure that credit reports are accurate, the FCRA imposes some duties on the sources that provide credit information to CRAs, called "furnishers" in the statute.[5] Section 1681s-2 sets forth "[r]esponsibilities of furnishers of information to consumer reporting agencies," delineating two categories of responsibilities. Subsection (a) details the duty "to provide accurate information," and includes the following duty:

> (3) Duty to provide notice of dispute. If the completeness or accuracy of any information furnished by any person to any consumer reporting agency is disputed to such person by a consumer, the person may not furnish the information to any consumer reporting agency without notice that such information is disputed by the consumer.

§1681s-2(a)(3).

Section 1681s-2(b) imposes a second category of duties on furnishers of information. These obligations are triggered "upon notice of dispute"— that is, when a person who furnished information to a CRA receives notice from the CRA that the consumer disputes the information. See §1681i(a)(2) (requiring CRAs promptly to provide such notification containing all relevant information about the consumer's dispute). Subsection 1681s-2(b) provides that, after receiving a notice of dispute, the furnisher shall:

> (A) conduct an investigation with respect to the disputed information;
> (B) review all relevant information provided by the [CRA] pursuant to section 1681i(a)(2) . . . ;

---

5. "The most common . . . furnishers of information are credit card issuers, auto dealers, department and grocery stores, lenders, utilities, insurers, collection agencies, and government agencies." H.R. Rep. No. 108-263, at 24 (2003).

(C) report the results of the investigation to the [CRA];

(D) if the investigation finds that the information is incomplete or inaccurate, report those results to all other [CRAs] to which the person furnished the information . . . ; and

(E) if an item of information disputed by a consumer is found to be inaccurate or incomplete or cannot be verified after any reinvestigation under paragraph (1) . . . (i) modify . . . (ii) delete [or] (iii) permanently block the reporting of that item of information [to the CRAs].

§1681s-2(b)(1). These duties arise only after the furnisher receives notice of dispute from a CRA; notice of a dispute received directly from the consumer does not trigger furnishers' duties under subsection (b). See id.; *Nelson v. Chase Manhattan Mortgage Corp.*, 282 F.3d 1057, 1059-60 (9th Cir. 2002).

The FCRA expressly creates a private right of action for willful or negligent noncompliance with its requirements. §§1681n & *o*; see also *Nelson*, 282 F.3d at 1059. However, §1681s-2 limits this private right of action to claims arising under subsection (b), the duties triggered upon notice of a dispute from a CRA. §1681s-2(c) ("Except [for circumstances not relevant here], sections 1681n and 1681*o* of this title do not apply to any violation of . . . subsection (a) of this section, including any regulations issued thereunder."). Duties imposed on furnishers under subsection (a) are enforceable only by federal or state agencies.[6] See §1681s-2(d).

Gorman alleges that MBNA violated several of the FCRA "furnisher" obligations. We hold that some of the alleged violations survive summary judgment and some do not.

2. MBNA's "Investigation" upon Notice of Dispute

Gorman's first allegation is that MBNA did not conduct a sufficient investigation after receiving notice from the CRAs that he disputed the

---

6. *Nelson* explained the likely reason for allowing private enforcement of subsection (b) but not subsection (a) as follows:

Congress did not want furnishers of credit information exposed to suit by any and every consumer dissatisfied with the credit information furnished. Hence, Congress limited the enforcement of the duties imposed by §1681s-2(a) to governmental bodies. But Congress did provide a filtering mechanism in §1681s-2(b) by making the disputatious consumer notify a CRA and setting up the CRA to receive notice of the investigation by the furnisher. See 15 U.S.C. §1681i(a)(3) (allowing CRA to terminate reinvestigation of disputed item if CRA "reasonably determines that the dispute by the consumer is frivolous or irrelevant"). With this filter in place and opportunity for the furnisher to save itself from liability by taking the steps required by §1681s-2(b), Congress put no limit on private enforcement under §§1681n & *o*. . . .

charges, as required by §1681s-2(b)(1)(A). As Gorman's claim arises under subsection (b), it can be the basis for a private lawsuit. See *Nelson,* 282 F.3d at 1059-60. We must decide (1) whether §1681s-2(b)(1)(A) requires a furnisher to conduct a "reasonable" investigation, and if so, (2) whether a disputed issue of material fact exists as to the reasonableness of MBNA's investigation.

a. Must an Investigation Be Reasonable?

The text of the FCRA states only that the creditor shall conduct "an investigation with respect to the disputed information." §1681s-2(b)(1)(A). MBNA urges that because there is no "reasonableness" requirement expressly enunciated in the text, the FCRA does not require an investigation of any particular quality; *any* investigation into a consumer's dispute—even an entirely unreasonable one—satisfies the statute.

This court has not addressed MBNA's contention about the FCRA's investigation requirement. But, MBNA made—and lost—the same argument before the Fourth Circuit. Johnson v. MBNA Am. Bank, NA, 357 F.3d 426, 429-31 (4th Cir. 2004). Concluding that the statute includes a requirement that a furnisher's investigation not be unreasonable, the Fourth Circuit first noted that the plain meaning of the term "investigation" is a "'detailed inquiry or systematic examination,'" which necessarily "requires some degree of careful inquiry." Id. at 430 (quoting Am. Heritage Dictionary 920 (4th ed. 2000)). Second, the Fourth Circuit reasoned that because the purpose of the provision is "to give consumers a means to dispute—and, ultimately, correct—inaccurate information on their credit reports," id. at 430-31, a "superficial, *un*reasonable inquir[y]" would hardly satisfy Congress' objective. Id. at 431. The Seventh Circuit, without discussing the issue, has also found an implicit reasonableness requirement. See Westra v. Credit Control of Pinellas, 409 F.3d 825, 827 (7th Cir. 2005) ("Whether a defendant's investigation [pursuant to §1681s-2(b)(1)(A)] is reasonable is a factual question normally reserved for trial."); see also *Johnson,* 357 F.3d at 430 n. 2 ("[D]istrict courts that have considered the issue have consistently recognized that the creditor's investigation must be a reasonable one." (citing cases)).

The Fourth Circuit's reasoning in *Johnson* is entirely persuasive. By its ordinary meaning, an "investigation" requires an inquiry likely to turn up information about the underlying facts and positions of the parties, not a cursory or sloppy review of the dispute. Moreover, like the Fourth Circuit, we have observed that "a primary purpose for the FCRA [is] to protect consumers against inaccurate and incomplete credit reporting." *Nelson,* 282 F.3d at 1060. A provision that required only a cursory investigation would not provide such protection; instead, it would allow furnishers to escape their obligations by merely rubber stamping their earlier submissions, even where circumstances demanded a more thorough inquiry.

MBNA counters by pointing to §1681i(a)(1)(A), which provides, in relevant part (with emphasis added):

> [I]f the completeness or accuracy of any item of information contained in a consumer's file at a consumer reporting agency is disputed by the consumer and the consumer notifies the agency directly, or indirectly through a reseller, of such dispute, the agency shall, free of charge, conduct a *reasonable reinvestigation* to determine whether the disputed information is inaccurate. . . .

Thus, MBNA argues, Congress specified a "reasonable" investigation in another part of the statute, and purposely chose not to do so for furnishers of information.

It is most often the case that "[w]here Congress includes particular language in one section of a statute but omits it in another section of the same Act, it is generally presumed that Congress acts intentionally and purposely in the disparate inclusion or exclusion." *Russello v. United States,* 464 U.S. 16, 23, 104 S. Ct. 296, 78 L. Ed. 2d 17 (1983) (internal quotation and citation omitted). But we should be careful not to read too much into the apparent disparity in language upon which MBNA relies. Where, as here, there are convincing alternative explanations for a difference in statutory language, the presumption applies with much less force. See Field v. Mans, 516 U.S. 59, 67-69, 116 S. Ct. 437, 133 L. Ed. 2d 351 (1995) ("Without more, the [negative] inference might be a helpful one. But [where] there is more . . . the negative pregnant argument should not be elevated to the level of interpretive trump card.").

As we have noted, the term "investigation" on its own force implies a fairly searching inquiry. It is thus likely that, if anything, the "reasonable" qualifier with regard to *re*investigations by CRAs signals a *limitation* on the CRAs' duty, not an expansion of it beyond what "investigation" itself would signal. And, indeed, the statute goes on to spell out the CRA's investigative duty in some detail, requiring, inter alia, that the CRA provide notification of the dispute within five business days of receipt of notice of a dispute. The furnisher's investigation obligation under §1681 is triggered by receiving the CRA notification, required as a central aspect of the CRA's own investigation, and includes the obligation to "report the results of [its] investigation to the [CRA]." §1681s2-(b)(1)(C). In other words, the CRA's "reasonable reinvestigation" consists largely of triggering the investigation by the furnisher. It would make little sense to deem the CRA's investigation "reasonable" if it consisted primarily of requesting a superficial, unreasonable investigation by the furnisher of the information.

Nevertheless, MBNA urges that "Congress intended to impose a more rigorous duty of investigation on CRAs than on furnishers of information." But MBNA does not tell us why Congress would mandate shoddy or superficial furnisher investigations, not calculated to resolve or to explain the actual disagreement or to aid in the CRA's "reasonable reinvestigation." Indeed, as the statute recognizes, the furnisher of credit information stands in a far better position to make a thorough investigation of a disputed debt than the CRA does on reinvestigation. With respect to the accuracy of disputed information, the CRA is a third party, lacking any direct relationship with the consumer, and its responsibility is to "*re*investigate" a matter once already investigated in the first place. §1681i(a)(1) (emphasis added). It would therefore make little sense to impose a more rigorous requirement on the CRAs than the furnishers. Instead, the more sensible conclusion is that, if anything, the "reasonable" qualifier attached to a CRA's duty to reinvestigate limits its obligations on account of its third-party status and the fact that it is repeating a task already completed once. Requiring furnishers, on inquiry by a CRA, to conduct at least a reasonable, non-cursory investigation comports with the aim of the statute to "protect consumers from the transmission of inaccurate information about them." Kates v. Crocker Nat'l Bank, 776 F.2d 1396, 1397 (9th Cir. 1985).

We thus follow the Fourth and Seventh Circuits and hold that the furnisher's investigation pursuant to §1681s-2(b)(1)(A) may not be unreasonable.

b. MBNA's Investigation Was Reasonable

As discussed, a furnisher's obligation to conduct a reasonable investigation under §1681s-2(b)(1)(A) arises when it receives a notice of dispute from a CRA. Such notice must include "all relevant information regarding the dispute that the [CRA] has received from the consumer." §1681i(a)(2)(A). It is from this notice that the furnisher learns the nature of the consumer's challenge to the reported debt, and it is the receipt of this notice that gives rise to the furnisher's obligation to conduct a reasonable investigation. Accordingly, the reasonableness of the furnisher's investigation is measured by its response to the specific information provided by the CRA in the notice of dispute. The pertinent question is thus whether the furnisher's procedures were reasonable in light of what it learned about the dispute from the description in the CRA's notice of dispute. See *Westra,* 409 F.3d at 827 ("[The furnisher's] investigation in this case was reasonable given the scant information it received regarding the nature of [the consumer's] dispute.").

MBNA received four notices of dispute regarding Gorman's account. Gorman argues that the district court erred in granting summary judgment as to the reasonableness of MBNA's investigation in response to these notices because triable issues of fact remain. We have held that "summary judgment is generally an inappropriate way to decide questions of reasonableness because 'the jury's unique competence in applying the "reasonable man" standard is thought ordinarily to preclude summary judgment.'" In re Software Toolworks Inc., 50 F.3d 615, 621 (9th Cir. 1994) (quoting TSC Indus. v. Northway, Inc., 426 U.S. 438, 450 n. 12, 96 S. Ct. 2126, 48 L. Ed. 2d 757 (1976)). However, summary judgment is not precluded altogether on questions of reasonableness. It is appropriate "when only one conclusion about the conduct's reasonableness is possible." Id. at 622; see also *Westra,* 409 F.3d at 827. We thus consider the sufficiency of MBNA's investigation with respect to each of the notices.

i. "Claims Company Will Change"

In a notice of dispute received May 13, 2004, TransUnion provided the following information concerning Gorman's MBNA account: "Claims company will change. Verify all account information." The notice provided no further information about the nature of the dispute. In response to this notice, MBNA "review[ed] the account notes to determine whether MBNA had agreed to delete any charges or to modify the account information in any way." It concluded that "[n]o such commitment had been made." MBNA's review of the account information provided by TransUnion did reveal "some minor differences." As a result, MBNA submitted updated address, date of birth, and account delinquency information to TransUnion.

The cursory notation, "[c]laims company will change," provided no suggestion of the nature of Gorman's dispute with Four Peaks. We conclude therefore that a jury could not find MBNA's response unreasonable. MBNA reasonably read the vague notice as indicating that MBNA had previously agreed to change certain account information. MBNA's review of its internal account files to determine whether any such agreement had been reached was all that was required to respond reasonably to this notice of dispute. The account notes reveal that MBNA had communicated with Four Peaks several times and do not reveal any agreement by MBNA to credit those charges, or any others. MBNA could not have reasonably been expected to undertake a more thorough investigation of the Four Peaks incident based on the scant information contained in this notice.

ii.   "Fraudulent Charges"

MBNA received two notices disputing "fraudulent charges" on Gorman's account. A notice of dispute from Experian, dated May 18, 2004, stated: "Consumer claims account take-over fraudulent charges made on account. Verify Signature provide complete ID." In response to this notice, MBNA "verif[ied] that the name, address, date of birth and social security number reported by Experian matched the information that was contained in MBNA's records concerning the account." It also "review[ed] the account notes and check[ed] with the fraud department to determine whether there had ever been a fraud claim submitted with respect to the account." Because the identification information matched and no fraud claim had been submitted, MBNA reported to Experian that the information it previously reported was accurate and requested that Experian tell Gorman to contact MBNA if he suspected fraud.

MBNA received another dispute notice from TransUnion, dated November 29, 2005, that listed two disputes: (1) "Disputes present/previous Account Status History. Verify accordingly"; (2) "Consumer claims account take-over fraudulent charges made on account. Verify Signature provide or confirm complete ID." MBNA conducted the following inquiry:

> [V]erif[ied] that the account history that was being reported matched the account history data in MBNA's records, including the balance, the amount past due, the high credit and credit limit for the account. . . . [V]erif[ied] that the name, address, date of birth and social security number reported by TransUnion matched the information that was contained in MBNA's records concerning the account. . . . [R]eview[ed] the account notes and check[ed] with the fraud department to determine whether there had ever been a fraud claim submitted with respect to the account.

Because this investigation did not reveal that any information was inaccurate, MBNA verified the information previously submitted to TransUnion.

Neither notice identified the nature of Gorman's dispute as centering on the Four Peaks charge or indicated that the dispute concerned rejection of the goods charged for. Indeed, the notices did not describe the fraudulent transactions in any detail; they were silent as to the approximate date of the charges, their amount, and the identity of the merchant. Moreover, Gorman has never contended that the disputed charges were initially unauthorized or were the result of identity theft, as the dispute notices indicated. Not surprisingly, MBNA's review of its internal account notes showed no evidence of fraudulent activity, and all previous account data reported by the CRAs matched MBNA's records. We conclude that, as in the case of the first notice of dispute, MBNA could not reasonably have been expected to investigate

Gorman's challenge to the Four Peaks charge based on the vague and in-accurate information it received from the CRAs in these notices.

iii. *"Promised Goods/Services Not Delivered"*

One notice of dispute did provide more accurate and specific information relating to Gorman's dispute with MBNA. A December 2004 notice from Experian stated: "Claims inaccurate information. Did not provide specific dispute. Provide complete ID and verify account information." The notice further provided, in a section for "FCRA Relevant Information": "PROMISED GOODS/SERVICES NOT DELIVERED. I TIMELY DISPUTED THE CHARGES UNDER THE TIL ACT." In response to this notice, MBNA

> review[ed] its records to confirm that all of the account information that was being reported by Experian matched MBNA's records. MBNA also reviewed the account notes to determine if any dispute submitted by Gorman concerning the account had been resolved in his favor. Since the reported information matched the information in MBNA's records, and because the prior investigation of the charge with Four Peaks Entertainment had not been resolved in favor of Gorman, MBNA verified all the information that it had reported about the account as accurate.

Unlike the other three notices of dispute, the December 2004 notice contained enough information to alert MBNA to the specific nature of Gorman's actual claim: the reported debt was not owed because he had not received the goods he was promised. Simply verifying that the basic reported account data matched MBNA's internal records may not have been a reasonably sufficient investigation of this particular dispute.

But MBNA's investigation was more thorough than simply a review of bare account data. The review of internal records revealed that MBNA had previously investigated the Four Peaks charge and that the dispute had not been resolved in Gorman's favor.

Nevertheless, Gorman claims that a jury could still find MBNA's efforts unreasonable, because it failed to *re*investigate the dispute. As an initial matter, there is no evidence that MBNA's original investigation of the Four Peaks incident was deficient or unreliable. MBNA contacted both Gorman and Four Peaks several times as part of the investigation. Its requests that Gorman provide more information were met with refusals to supply additional information or no response at all. MBNA's correspondence with Four Peaks also evidences a diligent attempt to ascertain the validity of the charges. For example, MBNA asked about Gorman's opportunity to return the merchandise and was told that Gorman received shipping labels to return the merchandise.

Importantly, the CRA notice of dispute that triggered MBNAs duty to investigate did not identify any reason to doubt the veracity of the initial investigation. Furthermore, the notice of dispute did not provide any new information that would have prompted MBNA to supplement the initial investigation with any additional procedures or inquiries.

We agree that "[w]hether a reinvestigation conducted by a furnisher in response to a consumer's notice of dispute is reasonable . . . depends in large part on . . . the allegations provided to the furnisher by the credit reporting agency." Krajewski v. Am. Honda Fin. Corp., 557 F. Supp. 2d 596, 610 (E.D. Pa. 2008). Without any indication in the allegations that the initial investigation lacked reliability or that new information was available to discover, MBNA's decision not to repeat a previously-conducted investigation cannot have been unreasonable. Congress could not have intended to place a burden on furnishers continually to reinvestigate a particular transaction, without any new information or other reason to doubt the result of the earlier investigation, every time the consumer disputes again the transaction with a CRA because the investigation was not resolved in his favor. Thus, although reliance on a prior investigation *can* be unreasonable, cf. Bruce v. First U.S.A. Bank, Nat'l Ass'n, 103 F. Supp. 2d 1135, 1143-44 (E.D. Mo. 2000) (concluding that a furnisher's investigation was not necessarily reasonable when an initial investigation was deficient for, among other reasons, failing to contact the consumer), that was not the case here.

Gorman disputes this conclusion, insisting that under the Fourth Circuit's opinion in *Johnson,* it is per se unreasonable for a furnisher to rely solely on internal account records when investigating a consumer dispute. Gorman misreads *Johnson,* which recognized that the reasonableness of an investigation depends on the facts of the particular case, most importantly the CRA's description of the dispute in its notice. See *Johnson,* 357 F.3d at 431 (noting that confining the investigation to internal computer notes was not necessarily reasonable *in light of* the specificity of the description of the dispute in the notice).

In *Johnson,* the CRA's notice to MBNA read: "CONSUMER STATES BELONGS TO HUSBAND ONLY"; "WAS NEVER A SIGNER ON ACCOUNT. WAS AN AUTHORIZED USER." Id. at 429. The underlying facts were that Johnson's future husband opened an MBNA credit card account. Some years later, after they were married, Johnson's husband filed for bankruptcy, and MBNA told Johnson she was responsible for the balance, maintaining that she was a co-applicant, and therefore a co-obligor, on the account. *Johnson,* 357 F.3d at 428-29. Johnson argued that she was merely an authorized user. Id.

In response to the notice to the CRAs, MBNA only confirmed Johnson's identifying information and confirmed that its internal computer system indicated she was the sole responsible party on the account. Id. at 431. At no time did MBNA try to ascertain whether Johnson's information—that she had not signed the application form—was correct. The Fourth Circuit held this investigation unreasonable:

The MBNA agents also testified that, in investigating consumer disputes generally, they do not look beyond the information contained in the CIS [MBNA's internal computer system] and never consult underlying documents such as account applications. Based on this evidence, a jury could reasonably conclude that MBNA acted unreasonably in failing to verify the accuracy of the information contained in the CIS. Id.

In contrast to *Johnson,* in Gorman's case MBNA did review all the pertinent records in its possession, which revealed that an *initial* investigation had taken place in which MBNA contacted both Gorman and the merchant. Thus, unlike in *Johnson,* MBNA had—albeit earlier—gone outside its own records to investigate the allegations contained in the CRA notice, and on reading the notice, did consult the relevant information in its possession. *Johnson* does not indicate that a furnisher has an obligation to repeat an earlier investigation, the record of which is in the furnisher's records.

We emphasize that the requirement that furnishers investigate consumer disputes is procedural. An investigation is not necessarily unreasonable because it results in a substantive conclusion unfavorable to the consumer, even if that conclusion turns out to be inaccurate.

In short, although "reasonableness" is generally a question for a finder of fact, summary judgment in this case was appropriate.

3. *MBNA's Failure to Provide Notice of Dispute*

Gorman next argues that MBNA failed to notify the CRAs that he continued to dispute the delinquent charges on his account. He contends that in reporting the delinquency without also reporting his ongoing dispute, MBNA violated its obligations under 12 C.F.R. §226.13, and thus furnished "incomplete or inaccurate" credit information in violation of the FCRA. MBNA neither concedes nor disputes that it was so obligated, but argues on summary judgment that the statute does not permit Gorman to raise this claim. Also, in the alternative, MBNA contends that Gorman did not submit enough evidence to show whether his credit reports included a notice that the delinquency was disputed or whether MBNA did not so notify the CRAs. We must decide (1) whether the failure to notify the CRAs that the delinquent debt was disputed is actionable under §1681s-2(b), and if so, (2) whether Gorman introduced sufficient evidence on summary judgment to show that MBNA so notified the CRAs.

a.   Gorman's Claim Is Actionable

If a consumer disputes the accuracy of credit information, the FCRA requires furnishers to report that fact when reporting the disputed information. Section 1681s-2(a)(3) provides: "If the completeness or accuracy of any information furnished by any person to any consumer reporting agency is disputed to such person by a consumer, the person may not furnish the information to any consumer reporting agency without notice that such information is disputed by the consumer." As noted, however, the statute expressly provides that a claim for violation of this requirement can be pursued only by federal or state officials, and not by a private party. §1681s-2(c)(1) ("Except [for circumstances not relevant here], sections 1681n and 1681*o* of this title [providing private right of action for willful and negligent violations] do not apply to any violation of . . . subsection (a) of this section, including any regulations issued thereunder."); see also *Nelson,* 282 F.3d at 1059. Thus, Gorman has no private right of action under §1681s-2(a)(3) to proceed against MBNA for its initial failure to notify the CRAs that he disputed the Four Peaks charges.

Gorman does have a private right of action, however, to challenge MBNA's subsequent failure to so notify the CRAs after receiving notice of Gorman's dispute under §1681s-2(b). In addition to requiring that a furnisher conduct a reasonable investigation of a consumer dispute, §1681s-2(b) also requires a creditor, upon receiving notice of such dispute, to both report the results of the investigation *and,* "if the investigation finds that the information is incomplete or inaccurate, report those results" to the CRAs. §1681s-2(b)(1)(C), (D). Gorman argues that MBNA's reporting of the Four Peaks charge and delinquency, without a notation that the debt was disputed, was an "incomplete or inaccurate" entry on his credit file that MBNA failed to correct after its investigation. As this claim alleges that obligations imposed under §1681s-2(b) were violated, it is available to private individuals.

The Fourth Circuit has recently held that after receiving notice of dispute, a furnisher's decision to continue reporting a disputed debt without any notation of the dispute presents a cognizable claim under §1681s-2(b). See Saunders v. Branch Banking & Trust Co. of Va., 526 F.3d 142, 150 (4th Cir. 2008). In *Saunders,* a consumer alleged that he incurred late fees and penalties as a result of a creditor's own admitted accounting errors; the creditor, Branch Banking & Trust (BB & T), refused to waive the fees, and the consumer responded by withholding payments on the loan. Id. at 145-46. BB & T reported the loan to the CRAs as "in repossession status," and, after suffering adverse credit decisions, the consumer contacted the CRAs to report the dispute. Id. at 146. The CRAs sent a notice of dispute to BB & T, triggering its obligations to investigate and verify the accuracy of the reported information under §1681s-2(b)(1). BB & T responded by updating the consumer record to reflect that it had written off the debt as uncollectible, but failed to indicate that the consumer still disputed the validity of the obligation. Id. The consumer brought suit under §1681s-2(b) and a jury found that BB & T had violated its obligations.

The Fourth Circuit affirmed. The court reasoned that in enacting §1681s-2(b)(1)(D), "Congress clearly intended furnishers to review reports not only for inaccuracies in the information reported but also for omissions that render the reported information misleading." Id. at 148. Although the report may have been "technically accurate" in the sense that it reflected the consumer's failure to make any payments on the loan, the court noted that it had previously held that "a consumer report that contains technically accurate information may be deemed 'inaccurate' if the statement is presented in such a way that it creates a misleading impression." Id. (citing Dalton v. Capital Associated Indus., Inc., 257 F.3d 409, 415-16 (4th Cir. 2001)). The Fourth Circuit went on to note that a consumer's failure to pay a debt that is not really due "does not reflect financial irresponsibility," and thus the omission of the disputed nature of a debt could render the information sufficiently misleading so as to be "incomplete or inaccurate" within the meaning of the statute. Id. at 150. *Saunders* went on to reject the contention that Congress meant to exempt furnishers of information from private liability by placing the initial obligation to report disputes in subsection (a), stating that "[n]o court has ever suggested that a furnisher can excuse its failure to identify an inaccuracy when reporting pursuant to §1681s-2(b) by arguing that it should have *already* reported the information accurately under §1681s-2(a)." Id. at 149-50.

This reasoning is persuasive. Like *Saunders,* several other courts have held that a credit entry can be "incomplete or inaccurate" within the meaning of the FCRA "because it is patently incorrect, or because it is misleading in such a way and to such an extent that it can be expected to adversely affect credit decisions." Sepulvado v. CSC Credit Servs., Inc., 158 F.3d 890, 895 (5th Cir. 1998); see also Koropoulos v. Credit Bureau, Inc., 734 F.2d 37, 40 (D.C. Cir. 1984) ("Certainly reports containing factually correct information that nonetheless mislead their readers are neither maximally accurate nor fair to the consumer. . . ."). As the Fourth Circuit observed, holding otherwise would create a rule that, as a matter of law, an omission of the disputed nature of a debt never renders a report incomplete or inaccurate. See *Saunders,* 526 F.3d at 150. Not only might such a rule intimidate consumers into giving up bona fide disputes by paying debts not actually due to avoid damage to their credit ratings, but it also contravenes the purpose of the FCRA, to protect against "unfair credit reporting methods." See 15 U.S.C. §1681(a)(1).

Holding that there is a private cause of action under §1681s-2(b) does not mean that a furnisher could be held liable on the merits simply for a failure to report that a debt is disputed. The consumer must still convince the finder of fact that the omission of the dispute was "misleading in such a way and to such an extent that [it] can be expected to have an adverse effect." *Saunders,* 526 F.3d at 150 (quotation omitted). In other words, a furnisher does not report "incomplete or inaccurate" information within the meaning of §1681s-2(b) simply by failing to report a meritless dispute, because reporting an actual debt without noting that it is disputed is unlikely to be materially misleading. It is the failure to report a bona fide dispute, a dispute that could materially alter how the reported debt is understood, that gives rise to a furnisher's liability under §1681s-2(b). Cf. id. at 151 ("[W]e assume, without deciding that a furnisher incurs liability under §1681s-2(b) only if it fails to report a meritorious dispute.").

It is true, as we have said, that a furnisher's initial failure to comply with this requirement is not privately enforceable. But as the Fourth Circuit noted, this does not excuse the furnisher's failure to correct the omission after investigating pursuant to §1681s-2(b). See *Saunders*, 526 F.3d at 150. The purpose of §1681s-2(b) is to require furnishers to investigate and verify that they are in fact reporting complete and accurate information to the CRAs after a consumer has objected to the information in his file. See *Johnson,* 357 F.3d at 431 ("[Congress] create[d] a system intended to give consumers a means to dispute—and, ultimately, correct—inaccurate information on their credit reports."). A disputed credit file that lacks a notation of dispute may well be "incomplete or inaccurate" within the meaning of the FCRA, and the furnisher has a privately enforceable obligation to correct the information after notice. §1681s-2(b)(1)(D). We thus conclude that the statute permits Gorman to bring his claim regarding MBNA's failure to report the charge still disputed. . . .

III. CONCLUSION

For the foregoing reasons, we AFFIRM in part and REVERSE in part the district court's order.

E. Credit Repair Organizations

In today's society someone with a poor credit history faces major roadblocks to getting anything accomplished that requires financing. This fact gave rise to a new industry: credit repair organizations that claimed, for a fee, to be able to help consumers re-establish a good credit record. In fact, there is no easy way to do this; people with bad credit need to work at building a new credit history that will attract the attention of lenders. All that these credit repair organizations did to earn their fee was to advise the consumer of his/her rights under the Fair Credit Reporting Act, hardly the sort of relief the consumer was looking for. Some of these organizations did help their customers out but only by advising them how to commit fraud on consumer reporting agencies. When the Federal Trade Commission looked into credit repair organizations in the early 1990s, it could not find a single legitimate operation. In 2008 the FTC and 24 state agencies engaged in "Operation Clean Sweep," a nationwide effort to shut down the most serious offenders; see http://www.ftc.gov/opa/2008/10/opcleansweep.shtm.

Finally, Congress acted to address the problem. In 1996, it enacted a statute dealing with these matters, the Credit Repair Organizations Act, 15 U.S.C. §§1679 et seq., Title IV of the Consumer Credit Protection Act (which should be in your statute book). The statute forbids lies by the credit repair organization, requires the organization to give the consumer a free description of his/her rights under the Fair Credit Reporting Act, does not allow prepayment of any fees by the consumer, provides the consumer with a three-day cooling-off period in which to cancel any contract signed with the credit repair organization, and allows for a private right of action that gives the consumer actual damages, punitive damages, and attorney's fees. The hope is that the statute will effectively put these organizations out of business forever. The Federal Trade Commission also has jurisdiction under the CROA to prosecute offenders, and has been vigorous in doing so. In one case where the defendant organizations were caught teaching consumers how to swindle lenders by using taxpayer identification numbers instead of social security numbers, the FTC ordered them to stop these practices and pay a civil penalty of $11,000. See FTC File Nos. X99 0035 and X99 0062 (2000). See also FTC v. Gill, 265 F.3d 944 (9th Cir. 2001) ($1,335,912.14 judgment against credit repair organization *and its attorney* for outrageous conduct including advising customers to file phony disputes with credit bureaus so as to remove damaging credit history).

PARKER v. 1-800 BAR NONE, A FINANCIAL CORP., INC.

United States District Court, Northern District of Illinois, 2002
2002 WL 215530

MANNING, J.

Plaintiff Keva Parker brings this action against Defendants 1-800 Bar None, a Financial Corporation, Inc. ("Bar None") and Gateway Chevrolet, Oldsmobile, Inc. ("Gateway"), pursuant to the Credit Repair Organizations Act ("CROA"), 15 U.S.C. §1679 et seq., alleging that Bar None and Gateway engaged in fraudulent practices to entice consumers with "subprime" credit to borrow money to buy cars. This matter comes before this Court on Defendants' Motions to Dismiss, pursuant to Federal Rule of Civil Procedure 12(b)(6). For the following reasons, Defendants' Motions to Dismiss are DENIED.

BACKGROUND

Bar None contracts with automobile dealers, such as Gateway, to generate subprime financing leads. To generate leads, Bar None advertises in the local news media that it can obtain or provide auto financing for anyone, no matter how bad his or her credit, and that it can "restore your credit." Consumers who call in response to the advertisement are referred to local dealers, such as Gateway, who pay Bar None for the referrals.

In late April 2001, Parker saw a Bar None television commercial that represented that no matter how bad the viewer's credit, that he or she could "get the car you need and deserve that day," and that Bar None could help "restore credit." Parker called the number in the ad, was asked various questions, and was told to visit Donald Hund at Gateway. She was further instructed to bring a check stub, two phone bills, and her checkbook.

On May 2, 2001, Parker met with Hund at Gateway, and was shown a car which she wished to purchase but was told that she did not qualify for ordinary financing. Instead, Hund told her to write a check for $6000.00, representing the purchase price of the car, even though she did not and would not have that much money in her account. She was also told to sign a "hold check" agreement with NDC Check Services. Parker was told that the check would be held for thirty days, after which NDC would make payment arrangements with her. Parker did as she was instructed, and left with the car. Thereafter, she had approximately $200.00 worth of work performed on the car.

Soon after, however, Parker had second thoughts, and wondered if something might be wrong with the deal she had entered into with Gateway and NDC. She consulted the manager of the bank where she had her checking account, who told her that she had been asked to write a bad check to a check guaranty company, and that this could ruin her credit rather than restore it. Parker then stopped payment on the check and returned the car to Gateway.

Parker subsequently filed this action against Bar None and Gateway alleging that they had engaged in misrepresentation of credit repair services in violation of the CROA. In response, Defendants Bar None and Gateway have filed Motions to Dismiss pursuant to Rule 12(b)(6). . . .

ANALYSIS

The CROA was enacted in 1994 as part of an amendment to the Consumer Credit Protection Act ("CCPA"), 15 U.S.C. §1601 et seq. Consumer Credit Reporting Reform Act, Sen. Rpt. 103-209 (Dec. 9, 1993). The Senate Committee found that:

> consumers have a vital interest in establishing and maintaining their credit worthiness and credit standing. As a result, consumers who experience problems may seek assistance from credit repair organizations offering to improve the credit standing of such consumers. The Committee further finds that certain advertising and business practices of these organizations have harmed consumers, particularly consumers of limited economic means and who are inexperienced in credit matters.
>
> The purpose of [the CROA] is to ensure that consumers who utilize the services of credit repair organizations have the necessary information to make informed decisions regarding the purchase of those services and to protect the public from unfair and deceptive business practices by credit repair organizations.

Id. at §402. The Report cites testimony from the Federal Trade Commission stating that

> [f]raudulent companies that lead consumers to believe that the companies can "repair" bad credit histories have bilked consumers of millions of dollars in the past several years, have caused consumer reporting agencies to waste time and money reinvestigating spurious disputes, and have been the focus of numerous enforcement actions by the FTC.

Id. at §K. Congress itself found that

> economic stabilization would be enhanced and the competition among the various financial institutions and other firms engaged in the extension of consumer credit would be strengthened by the informed use of credit. The informed use of credit results from an awareness of the cost thereof by consumers. It is the purpose of this title to assure a meaningful disclosure of credit terms so that the consumer will be able to compare more readily the various credit terms available to him and avoid the uninformed use of credit, and to protect the consumer against unfair and inaccurate credit billing and credit card practices.

15 U.S.C. §1601(a).

In enacting the CCPA, of which the CROA is part of [sic], Congress intended for courts to broadly construe its provisions in accordance with its remedial purpose. Brothers v. First Leasing, 724 F.2d 789, 793 (9th Cir.1984). Moreover, courts should construe consumer protection statutes "liberally [ ] in favor of" consumers. Bizier v. Globe Fin. Serv., Inc., 654 F.2d 1, 3 (1st Cir. 1981). It is in this context which this Court must rule on Defendants' Motions to Dismiss and the questions of law raised therein.

Defendants contend that Parker's Complaint should be dismissed because she has failed to allege that: (I) Defendants are credit repair organizations under the CROA; (II) Defendants engaged in fraudulent practices as defined by the CROA; and (III) she suffered any damages. The Court will consider each of these arguments in turn.

I.   CREDIT REPAIR ORGANIZATIONS UNDER THE CROA

Defendants contend that Parker failed to plead sufficient facts to show that either Defendant is a "credit repair organization" under the CROA.

The CROA defines a "credit repair organization" as:

> (A) . . . any person who uses any instrumentality of interstate commerce or the mails to sell, provide, or perform (or represent that such person can or will sell, provide, or perform) any service, in return for the payment of money or other valuable consideration, for the express or implied purpose of—
>> (i) improving any consumer's credit record, credit history, or credit rating; or
>> (ii) providing advice or assistance to any consumer with regard to any activity or service described in clause (i). . . .

15 U.S.C. §1679a(3)(A). Thus, to establish that a defendant is a credit repair organization under the CROA, a plaintiff must allege that the defendant: (1) used an instrumentality of interstate commerce or the mails; (2) to provide or sell, or represent that such person will provide or sell; (3) in return for valuable consideration; (4) for the types of services listed in clauses (i) and (ii).

Here, Parker alleges that Bar None "regularly advertises in local news media that it can obtain or provide auto financing for anyone, no matter how bad their credit, and that it can 'restore your credit.'" (Cmplt. at ¶12.) Therefore, the Court finds that Parker has alleged facts sufficient to satisfy elements 1 and 4. Bar None, however, contends that Parker has failed to plead sufficient facts to show that Bar None sold or represented it would sell services in return for valuable consideration.

Bar None argues because it only referred Parker to Gateway, who in turn referred her to NDC, that it did not provide any services to Parker as required under section 1679a(3)(A). The plain language of section 1679a(3)(A), however, does not require an entity to actually "provide" the services listed to qualify as a credit repair organization. Instead, the entity need only "represent" that it can or will provide such services. 15 U.S.C. §1679a(3)(A); Sannes v. Jeff Wyler Chevrolet, Inc., 1999 WL 33313134, at *2 (S.D. Ohio, March 31, 1999). Here, Parker alleges that Bar None's advertisement stated that it could "restore your credit" (Cmplt. at ¶12), a representation that Bar None did or could provide services such as those described in clauses (i) and (ii) of section 1679a(3)(A). Consequently, this Court holds that Parker has alleged sufficient facts to meet the "services" requirement of section 1679a(3)(A).

Bar None also contends that Parker has failed to sufficiently allege that Bar None received payment or other valuable consideration, as required by section 1679a(3)(A), because Parker cannot allege that she paid Bar None for the referral to Gateway. In support of this argument, Bar None relies on *Sannes*, 1999 WL 33313134. In *Sannes*, the plaintiff, who leased an automobile from the defendant car dealership, filed an action against the defendant alleging that an advertisement promising to "[r]e-establish your credit through one of the largest banks in Ohio" violated the CROA. Id. at *1. After responding to the ad, the plaintiff leased the vehicle from the defendant, who arranged financing through a bank (not named as a defendant). Id. The defendant moved to dismiss on the grounds that it was not a credit repair organization under the CROA because it "does not charge or accept the payment of money or other valuable consideration in return for the service." Id. at *2. When the consumer purchases a car from the defendant, the defendant only charges for the cost of the car, which is the same whether or not the plaintiff finances the car or not. Id. at *3. Based on the court's finding that the defendant did not charge an additional cost if the car was financed and its finding that Congress did not intend to include "auto dealerships, who arrange for purchase financing ancillary to their primary business of selling and leasing motor vehicles," the court concluded that the dealership was not a credit repair organization under the CROA. Id. at *4.

Here, however, unlike the defendant in *Sannes*, Bar None did not engage in offering financing assistance ancillary to some other, primary purpose. Bar None's advertisement purports to provide financing and credit repair services. (Cmplt. at ¶12.) Moreover, the situation here is distinct from that in *Sannes* where there were only two parties, the consumer and the dealership. Here, in contrast, we have a consumer, a dealership, and Bar None. While it is true that, like the plaintiff in *Sannes*, Parker did not pay directly for Bar None's credit services, unlike the dealership in *Sannes*, Bar None was paid for its services by Gateway, which paid Bar None for the referral of customers. Thus, the Court finds that this is sufficient to constitute payment required by section 1679a(3)(A).

The finding that Parker's Complaint sufficiently alleges payment of consideration is further supported by the plain language of section 1679a(3)(A) which only requires that a "credit repair organization" receive "the payment of money or other valuable consideration." This section does not specifically require that the credit repair organization receive the consideration directly from the consumer, only that the credit repair organization receive consideration. Therefore, given the plain language of the statute and the broad remedial purpose in enacting the CROA, this Court finds that Bar None did not need to receive consideration directly from Parker to fall under section 1679a(3)(A). . . .

II. DECEPTIVE AND FRAUDULENT PRACTICES UNDER THE CROA

Even if this Court held that Bar None is not a "credit repair organization" under section 1679a(3)(A), Parker can nevertheless state a claim against Bar None and Gateway under section 1679b of the CROA. Under section 1679b(a), it is a violation of the CROA for any "person" to:

> (3) make or use any untrue or misleading representation of the services of the credit repair organization; or
> (4) engage, directly or indirectly, in any act, practice, or course of business that constitutes or results in the commission of, or an attempt to commit, a fraud or deception on any person in connection with the offer or sale of the services of the credit repair organization.

15 U.S.C. §1679b(a)(3)-(4). Unlike section 1679a, section 1679b(a) applies to "persons" which encompasses a broader group than credit repair organizations. *Bigalke*, 162 F. Supp. 2d at 999; Vance v. National Benefit Assn., 1999 WL 731764, at *4 (N.D. Ill. Aug 30, 1999). In *Bigalke*, this court explained that:

> even if this Court held that Creditrust was not a credit repair organization within the meaning of the act, section 1679b(a), which Bigalke alleges Creditrust violated, still applies to Creditrust. The plaintiff in Vance alleged that the defendant violated section 1679b(a)(3) and (4). The court held that the defendant, a bank, was not a credit repair organization because section 1679a(B)(iii) specifically excludes banks. Nevertheless, the court denied the defendant's motion to dismiss because it found that section 1679b(a) applies to "person[s]" which is a broader definition than that of a credit repair organization.

162 F. Supp. 2d at 999 (internal citations omitted). Thus, even had this Court concluded that Bar None is not a credit repair organization under the act, that finding would not be sufficient to dispose of Parker's claim against it. Likewise, regardless of whether Gateway is a credit repair organization under the act, section 1679b(a) applies to it as well. . . .

III. ACTUAL AND PUNITIVE DAMAGES

Finally, Bar None and Gateway contend that Parker's Complaint should be dismissed because she: (1) has not alleged actual damages as a result of Defendants alleged wrongdoing; and (2) is not eligible for punitive damages without actual damages.

Under section 1679g(a)(1), the court may award actual damages for violations of the CROA in "(A) the amount of any actual damage sustained by such person *as a result of such failure;* or (B) any amount paid by the person to the credit repair organization." 15 U.S.C. §1679g(a) (emphasis added). Therefore, under the plain language of section 1679g(a)(1), Parker need not establish that she incurred damages as a result of payments to Bar None or Gateway. Instead, she need only establish that she incurred damages "as a result of" their violations of the CROA. 15 U.S.C. §1679g(a)(1)(A).

Here, Parker has alleged that she spent approximately $200 for repairs on the car prior to returning it to Gateway. Therefore, without purchasing the car, which occurred as a result of Defendants' actions, Parker would not have spent the $200 on the car which she later returned after learning that Defendants' actions put her credit in further jeopardy. Thus, construing the complaint liberally and viewing the allegations in the light most favorable to the non-moving party, as this Court is required to do, *Craigs, Inc.*, 12 F.3d at 688, this Court holds that Parker has alleged actual damages "as a result of" the Defendants' violations of the CROA.

Parker further contends that even if she failed to plead actual damages, she is still entitled to punitive damages. The CROA provides for the award of punitive damages in the following situations:

> (A) Individual actions. In the case of any action by an individual, such additional amount as the court may allow.
> (B) Class actions. In the case of a class action, the sum of—
>   (i) the aggregate of the amount which the court may allow for each named plaintiff; and
>   (ii) the aggregate of the amount which the court may allow for each other class member, without regard to any minimum individual recovery.

15 U.S.C. §1679g(a)(2). Defendants contend that the term "additional" implies that punitive damages may be awarded only where actual damages are awarded.

Although courts have not yet addressed this exact issue, statutes with similar provisions which were enacted as part of the Consumer Credit Protection Act ("CCPA"), 15 U.S.C. §1601, et seq., suggest punitive damages may be awarded under the CROA without the award of actual damages. Moreover, in enacting the CCPA Congress intended for courts to broadly construe its provisions in accordance with its remedial purpose. Brothers v. First Leasing, 724 F.2d 789, 793 (9th Cir. 1984). . . .

Accordingly, based on the case law construing other provisions of CCPA and the legislative purpose of CROA, this Court holds that punitive damages under section 1679g(a)(2) are not merely ancillary to actual damages, but are instead an independent basis for relief. Consequently, Parker's Complaint cannot be dismissed for failure to state a claim for damages.

CONCLUSION

For the foregoing reasons, Defendant Bar None's and Defendant Gateway's Motions to Dismiss [12-1, 23-1] are DENIED. It is so ordered.

PROBLEM 75

After her 1995 car died on the interstate one day, Portia Moot needed an automobile to get to work and elsewhere. She went down to Smiles Motors and looked at several vehicles before agreeing to buy one of them. Checking her credit information, the salesman at Smiles told her that it was unlikely that she would qualify for a loan unless "certain adjustments" were made in her credit history. He then helped her fill out the application, but increased her monthly paycheck amount by $800 and told her to say that was the correct amount if a financing entity were to contact her. He also added her mother's name as co-signer and told Portia to sign her mother's name on the relevant application. Is Smiles Motors a "credit repair organization"? Is it in violation of the Credit Repair Organizations Act? See 15 U.S.C. §1679(b) (§404 of the Act itself); Lacey v. William Chrysler Plymouth Inc., 2004 WL 415972 (N.D. Ill. 2004); Costa v. Mauro Chevrolet, Inc., 390 F. Supp. 2d 720 (N.D. Ill. 2005).

There certainly are legitimate (mostly nonprofit) organizations that help distressed debtors consolidate their debts and arrange payment schedules with creditors, while counseling their clients about better financial habits. In 2005 Congress amended the Bankruptcy Code and required credit counseling as a condition precedent to the filing of a bankruptcy petition (this is often done perfunctorily over the Internet). That same year the National Conference of Commissioners on Uniform State Laws completed work on the Uniform Debt-Management Services Act to help regulate such entities, and proposed it to the states for consideration. As of early 2009 only Colorado, Delaware, Rhode Island, and Vermont had adopted it. The text of the statute can be found at www.law.upenn.edu/bll/archives/ulc/ucdc/2005Final.htm.

II. THE EQUAL CREDIT OPPORTUNITY ACT

In 1974 Congress passed the Equal Credit Opportunity Act, making it Title VII of the Consumer Credit Protection Act. The statute was enacted largely as a result of the women's movement in the late 1960s and early 1970s, which demonstrated convincingly that when it came to the granting of credit in those days, women were routinely treated very differently from men. The statute has also proved useful in racial discrimination cases. In 2005, a highly publicized class action in the federal district court in Nashville, alleging that African-American car buyers were charged higher interest rates than comparable white customers, was settled after more than two years of maneuvers, with the credit-granting banks agreeing to offer car loans with no dealer markups to 2.4 million minority customers. In Gallegos v. Rizza Chevrolet, Inc., 2003 WL 22326523 (N.D. Ill. 2003), the consumer successfully argued that the statute was violated when a car purchase transaction was negotiated in Spanish, but the paperwork (which turned out to be, to his surprise and dismay, actually a lease agreement) was written in English, a language which he did not speak fluently.

As originally worded, the Act prohibited discrimination in the granting of credit only on the basis of sex, race, or marital status, but in 1977 the Act was amended to expand the list of protected categories to include all those listed in §701(a) of the statute. Read it to resolve the following Problem.

PROBLEM 76

Remember Cindy Shopper (from Problem 41), who lost 17 of her credit cards when they were stolen from her, but who managed to escape liability for their unauthorized use because she notified the card issuers of the theft before any amount had been charged? One of the card issuers, Octopus National Bank, sent Cindy a letter and told her that unless she paid the $200 the thief charged after her phone call, the bank was going to cancel her card. She calls you—her cousin, the attorney. Can they do this to her? The ONB card is her favorite because the bank charges the lowest interest rate she can find. See Truth in Lending Act §§133 and 130. Has the bank also violated the Equal Credit Opportunity Act?

MARKHAM v. COLONIAL MORTGAGE SERVICE CO. ASSOCIATES[7]

United States Court of Appeals, District of Columbia Circuit, 1979
605 F.2d 566

SWYGERT, Circuit Judge.

The Equal Credit Opportunity Act, 15 U.S.C. §§1691, et seq., prohibits creditors from discriminating against applicants on the basis of sex or marital status. We are asked to decide whether this prohibition prevents creditors from refusing to aggregate the incomes of two unmarried joint mortgage applicants when determining their creditworthiness in a situation where the incomes of two similarly situated married joint applicants would have been aggregated. The plaintiffs in this action, Jerry and Marcia Markham, appeal the judgment of the district court granting defendant Illinois Federal Service Savings and Loan Association's motion for summary judgment. We reverse. The plaintiffs also appeal the judgment of the district court granting a motion for summary judgment on behalf of defendants Colonial Mortgage Service Co. Associates, Inc., Al Shoemaker, and B.W. Real Estate, Inc. As to this matter, we affirm.

I

In November 1976, plaintiffs Marcia J. Harris[8] and Jerry Markham announced their engagement and began looking for a residence in the Capitol Hill section of Washington, D.C. One of the real estate firms which they contacted, defendant B.W. Real Estate, Inc., found suitable property for them, and in December 1976, Markham and Harris signed a contract of sale for the property.

Upon the recommendation of B.W. Real Estate, plaintiffs agreed to have defendant Colonial Mortgage Service Co. Associates, Inc. (Colonial Mortgage) conduct a credit check. Plaintiffs subsequently submitted a joint mortgage application to Colonial Mortgage, who in turn submitted it to Colonial Mortgage Service Company (Colonial-Philadelphia), a business entity located in Philadelphia and not a party to this action.

---

7. Footnotes in this case have been renumbered for clarity.

8. Plaintiffs were married on April 9, 1977, and the complaint was amended to reflect the name change of Marcia Harris.

In March 1976, Colonial-Philadelphia had entered into an agreement with defendant Illinois Federal Service Savings and Loan Association (Illinois Federal), whereby Illinois Federal agreed to purchase certain mortgages and trust deeds offered it by Colonial-Philadelphia. Pursuant to this agreement, Colonial-Philadelphia offered plaintiffs' mortgage application to Illinois Federal.

Plaintiffs and B.W. Real Estate had decided that February 4, 1977 would be an appropriate closing date for the purchase of the Capitol Hill residence. Accordingly, plaintiffs arranged to terminate their current leases, change mailing addresses, and begin utility service at the new property. On February 1, the loan committee of Illinois Federal rejected the plaintiffs' application. On February 3, the eve of the settlement date, plaintiffs were informed through a B.W. Real Estate agent that their loan application had been denied because they were not married. They were advised that their application would be resubmitted to the "investor"—who was not identified—on February 8, but that approval would be contingent upon the submission of a marriage certificate.

On February 8, the Illinois Federal loan committee reconsidered the plaintiffs' application, but again denied it. A letter was sent that date from Illinois Federal to Colonial-Philadelphia, which letter stated that the application had been rejected with the statement: "Separate income not sufficient for loan and job tenure."

On February 9, 1977 plaintiffs filed this suit, alleging violation of the Equal Credit Opportunity Act. After the district court separately granted the motions of Illinois Federal and the other defendants for summary judgment on May 25, 1978, plaintiffs brought this appeal.

II

A

We address first the appeal from the district court's summary judgment entered in favor of Illinois Federal. The district court concluded as a matter of law that plaintiffs could not state a claim under the Equal Credit Opportunity Act even if they showed that Illinois Federal's refusal to aggregate their incomes resulted, in whole or in part, in the denial of their loan application. This conclusion was based on the premise that creditors need not ignore the "special legal ties created between two people by the marital bond." It was the court's conclusion that under Illinois law the mere fact of marriage provides creditors with greater rights and remedies against married applicants than are available against unmarried applicants. Presumably the district court believed that this excused Illinois Federal under

15 U.S.C. §1691d(b), which allows a creditor to take "[s]tate property laws directly or indirectly affecting creditworthiness" into consideration in making credit decisions.

We fail to see the relevance of any special legal ties created by marriage with respect to the legal obligations of joint debtors. This was not an instance where a single person is applying for credit individually and claiming income from a third party for purposes of determining creditworthiness. In such an instance, the absence of a legal obligation requiring continuance of the income claimed by the applicant from the third party would reflect on the credit applicant's creditworthiness. Inasmuch as the Markhams applied for their mortgage jointly, they would have been jointly and severally liable on the debt. Each joint debtor would be bound to pay the full amount of the debt; he would then have a right to contribution from his joint debtor. See 4 A. Corbin, Contracts §§924, 928 (1951). See also Clayman v. Goodman Properties, Inc., 171 U.S. App. D.C. 88, 518 F.2d 1026 (1973); Welch v. Sherwin, 112 U.S. App. D.C. 124, 300 F.2d 716 (1962); Ill. Ann. Stat. ch. 76, 3 (Smith-Hurd). While it may be true that judicially enforceable rights such as support and maintenance are legal consequences of married status, they are irrelevancies as far as the creditworthiness of joint applicants is concerned. Illinois Federal would have had no greater rights against the Markhams had they been married, nor would the Markhams have had greater rights against each other on this particular obligation. Thus, inasmuch as the state laws attaching in the event of marriage would not affect the creditworthiness of these joint applicants, section 1691d(b) may not be used to justify the refusal to aggregate the plaintiffs' incomes on the basis of marital status.

B

We turn to a consideration of whether the Equal Credit Opportunity Act's prohibition of discrimination on the basis of sex or marital status makes illegal Illinois Federal's refusal to aggregate plaintiffs' income when determining their creditworthiness. Illinois Federal contends that neither the purpose nor the language of the Act requires it to combine the incomes of unmarried joint applicants when making that determination.

We start, as we must, with the language of the statute itself. March v. United States, 165 U.S. App. D.C. 267, 274, 506 F.2d 1306, 1313 (1974). 15 U.S.C. §1691(a) provides:

> It shall be unlawful for any creditor to discriminate against any applicant, with respect to any aspect of a credit transaction—
>   (1) on the basis of . . . sex or marital status. . . .

This language is simple, and its meaning is not difficult to comprehend. Illinois Federal itself has correctly phrased the standard in its brief: The Act forbids discrimination "on the basis of a person's marital status, that is to treat persons differently, all other facts being the same, because of their marital status. . . ." Brief for Defendant Illinois Federal at 18. Illinois Federal does not contend that they would not have aggregated plaintiffs' income had they been married at the time. Indeed, Illinois Federal concedes that the law would have required it to do so.[9] Thus, it is plain that Illinois Federal treated plaintiffs differently—that is, refused to aggregate their incomes—solely because of their marital status, which is precisely the sort of discrimination prohibited by section 1691(a)(1) on its face.

Despite the section's clarity of language, Illinois Federal seeks to avoid a finding of prohibited discrimination by arguing that it was not the Congressional purpose to require such an aggregation of the incomes of non-married applicants. It can be assumed, *arguendo*, that one, perhaps even the main, purpose of the Act was to eradicate credit discrimination waged against women, especially married women whom creditors traditionally refused to consider apart from their husbands as individually worthy of credit. But granting such an assumption does not negate the clear language of the Act itself that discrimination against *any* applicant, with respect to *any* aspect of a credit transaction, which is based on marital status is outlawed. When the plain meaning of a statute appears on its face, we need not concern ourselves with legislative history, see Caminetti v. United States, 242 U.S. 470, 485, 37 S. Ct. 192, 61 L. Ed. 442 (1917), especially when evidence of the legislation's history as has been presented to us does not argue persuasively for a narrower meaning than that which is apparent from the statutory language.[10] See Boston Sand & Gravel Co. v. United States,

---

9. 12 U.S.C. 1735f-5 requires that "every person engaged in making mortgage loans secured by residential real property consider without prejudice the combined income of both husband and wife for the purpose of extending mortgage credit . . . to a married couple or either member thereof." See also Brief for Defendant Illinois Federal at 14.

10. For example, defendant Illinois Federal makes much of certain statements of Representative Leonora Sullivan, to whom it refers as a sponsor of the Act, in its attempt to define the Act's purpose and scope in narrow terms. See Brief for Defendant Illinois Federal at 10-11. While not purporting to engage in an extensive review of the relevant history, we do note in passing the following remarks of Representative Sullivan offered in connection with the 1976 Amendment to the Act which she called "[o]stensibly a 'women's' law":

> The Equal Credit Opportunity Act . . . will undoubtedly help many women, and men too, who are creditworthy and who happen to be single, divorced, separated or widowed, in overcoming traditional and often irrational discriminations in the credit market. . . .

121 Cong. Rec. 27136 (1975).

278 U.S. 41, 48, 49 S. Ct. 52, 73 L. Ed. 170 (1928). We believe that the meaning of the words chosen by Congress is readily apparent.

Illinois Federal expresses the fear that a holding such as we reach today will require it to aggregate the incomes of all persons who apply for credit as a group. Lest it be misinterpreted, we note that our holding is not itself that far-reaching. It does no more than require Illinois Federal to treat plaintiffs—a couple jointly applying for credit—the same as they would be treated if married. We have not been asked to decide what the effect of the Act would have been had plaintiffs not applied for credit jointly. Nor do we have before us a question of whether the Act's marital status provision in any way applies to a situation where more than two people jointly request credit. We hold only that, under the Act Illinois Federal should have treated plaintiffs—an unmarried couple applying for credit jointly—the same as it would have treated them had they been married at the time.

Illinois Federal also contends that, regardless of this court's decision on the issue of income aggregation, the judgment of the district court should be affirmed. The premise of this contention is that, even had the incomes of plaintiffs been combined, Illinois Federal would still not have extended the loan because of lack of sufficient job tenure or credit history. Due to the district court's basis for decision and the state of the record, we are not in position to pass on the validity of this separate issue.

The district court entered summary judgment for Illinois Federal on the ground that the failure to aggregate incomes was not a violation of the Act. Thus, having no need to do so, it never reached the question of whether plaintiffs were otherwise eligible for the loan. Whether Illinois Federal would have otherwise extended the loan is a question of fact that is material, given our disposition of the aggregation issue. Accordingly, if there is a genuine dispute over that issue, summary judgment is inappropriate. Fed. R. Civ. P. 56. On the record, there appears to be such a dispute. Although Illinois Federal contends that plaintiffs would remain ineligible regardless of aggregation, plaintiffs assert that they were told the loan would be forthcoming if they produced a marriage certificate. Because we remand the case to the district court, we deem it sufficient to note the appearance of a genuine issue of material fact on this state of the record. Following remand, further discovery and additional affidavits may either confirm or dispel this appearance.

III

Plaintiffs also appeal from the district court's entry of summary judgment in favor of the other defendants: Colonial Mortgage, Al Shoemaker, and B.W. Real Estate. The district court based its judgment on alternative grounds, holding first that these defendants had done nothing which could be construed as a discriminatory act, and second, that regardless of their actions they were not "creditors" as that term is used in the Act. We affirm on the first ground, thus we do not reach the second.

There is no indication that these three defendants participated in Illinois Federal's decision to discriminate or in any way benefited therefrom. At most, plaintiffs' allegations describe a course of conduct whereby these defendants acted as conduits, transferring information from plaintiffs to Illinois Federal and relaying decisions back. Inasmuch as we are unable to find on the record an instance where one of these three defendants participated in a decision to discriminate against plaintiffs on the basis of marital status, we affirm the order of the district court granting summary judgment in favor of defendants Colonial Mortgage, Al Shoemaker, and B.W. Real Estate.

IV

There remain two issues requiring our attention. Plaintiffs have appealed from the district court's order denying their motion for an interim award of attorney fees. We note simply that the Act provides:

> In the case of any successful action . . . the costs of the action, together with a reasonable attorney's fee as determined by the court, shall be added to any damages awarded by the court. . . .

15 U.S.C. §1691e(d). Because this case has not yet come to a conclusion, not even a preliminary one,[11] and is not yet a "successful action," we hold the district court did not abuse its discretion in denying plaintiffs an interim fee award. . . .

QUESTIONS

Is this decision right? The legislative history shows that the purpose of the statute was to protect women from discrimination in the granting of credit, and that marital status was included in the statute because women were being denied credit on the basis that they either were or were not

---

11. Cf. Howard v. Phelps, 443 F. Supp. 374 (E.D. La. 1978), relied on by plaintiffs, where the court allowed an interim award of attorney fees under the Civil Rights Attorney Fees Awards Act, 42 U.S.C. §1988, after preliminary injunctive relief had been obtained.

married. Do you believe that the drafters would have intended a result that promotes and protects an unmarried relationship?

In the briefs, the creditors argued that a finding for the plaintiffs in this case would open the floodgates, leading to a requirement that creditors extend credit to homosexual couples or to a group of people applying for credit as a commune. The court ducked those issues as not properly presented. Think it over and be prepared to make the arguments on either side of these two issues.

PROBLEM 77

Lucas Rosa applied for a loan while dressed in traditionally feminine attire. The bank officer told him to come back when he was wearing gender-appropriate clothing and looked more like his driver's license photo. He sued the bank, alleging a violation of ECOA. How should this come out? See Rosa v. Park West Bank & Trust Co., 214 F.3d 213 (1st Cir. 2000).

Section 703 of the statute commands the Federal Reserve Board to promulgate a regulation (having the force of law) to implement the Act, and the Board has responded with Regulation B, 16 C.F.R. §202. Section 202.4 contains the basic commandment of the entire regulation: "A creditor shall not discriminate against an applicant on a prohibited basis regarding any aspect of a credit transaction." The Federal Reserve Board also has adopted an Official Staff Commentary which has the force of law. For up-to-date versions of the statute, Regulation B, and the Commentary, see the Consumer Credit Guide (CCH). For commentary on the same, see National Consumer Law Center, Credit Discrimination (4th ed. 2005, with 2008 supplement). Various governmental agencies also have administrative enforcement powers under the statute, which can include significant penalties (in one case, $800,000!—see www.ftc.gov/os/1999/franklinconsent.htm).

PROBLEM 78

During one of the low periods in the relationship between the United States and Iran, Octopus National Bank announced that it would not issue credit cards to anyone who was an Iranian foreign national living in the USA. The bank was promptly sued by an Iranian, who alleged a violation of ECOA. Is the bank allowed to discriminate

against Iranians? Against aliens in general? See Bhandari v. First
Natl. Bank of Commerce, 808 F.2d 1082 (5th Cir. 1987); cf. Reg. B
§202.6(b)(7).

A. *Scope*

Most of the statutes we study in this course are limited in their application to consumer transactions. The Equal Credit Opportunity Act, however, is broader than that. The Women's Business Ownership Act of 1988,
Pub. L. No. 100-533, 102 Stat. 2689, amended the ECOA effective April 1,
1990, to extend its protection to business credit as well as consumer credit,
although sometimes the provisions of the law specifically extend to only
one or the other. Furthermore, as Reg. B §202.3 explains, portions of the
statute and regulation apply to all kinds of credit, even those extended
to government borrowers, §202.3(d), credit granted by public utilities,
§202.3(a), and the purchase of securities on credit, §202.3(b). The Act also
subjects "incidental credit" to partial compliance. "Incidental credit" is
defined in §202.3(c) as that extended with no finance charge, in four or
fewer installments, not pursuant to a credit card. An example would be a
doctor who permits patients to repay in four installments and does not
charge interest thereon.

In any given case where credit is being extended and the lender is
arguably in violation of ECOA, Reg. B's §202.3 and its Official Commentary should be consulted with care to see whether the Regulation
applies to the transaction.

B. *Applications*

As we shall see, the rejection of an applicant for credit triggers various
compliance steps, the most important of which is written notification of the
reasons for the adverse action (§202.9). That in turn makes it particularly
important that all involved understand exactly what an "application" is.

PROBLEM 79

Joe Armstrong phoned Nightflyer Loan Company and asked the
loan officer whether Nightflyer would lend him $10,000. The officer
replied that Nightflyer never lent consumers more than $5,000. Joe

thanked him, and when he was not furnished with the §202.9 notice of reasons for adverse action within 30 days, as therein required, he sued, contending this was a violation of ECOA. Look at the definitions of "application" and "adverse action" in Reg. B §202.2 and decide whether he has a case.

PROBLEM 80

Hilda Howard was a professor of mathematics at Football University. She went to Octopus National Bank to apply for a loan to finance a new porch for her home. At the time of the application she was eight months pregnant. The loan officer, Michael Misogynist, asked her the following questions. Decide which, if any, violate Reg. B §202.5 or §202.6.

a. "Why have you come here? We'll take your application, because the law says we must, but it's a useless gesture since we never loan money to pregnant women." See also Reg. B §202.4(b).

b. "Are you pregnant?" See §§202.5(d)(4) and 202.6(b)(3).

c. "Do you plan to quit your job when the baby is born?" Cf. §202.6(b)(5).

d. "Are you married?" See §202.5(d)(1).

e. "What is your husband's income? Will your husband be willing to lend his name as a co-signer?" As to this last question, see §§202.5(c) and 202.7(d).

f. "Do you own a telephone? In whose name is the phone listed?" Cf. §202.6(b)(4).

PROBLEM 81

You are the new attorney for Solid Savings & Loan. The company fired its last attorney when the policies he had approved caused Solid to be sued under ECOA and to pay $15,000 in damages. The president of Solid tells you to review everything the company is doing and make very sure the company is not exposed to liability. You notice that the company's loan application begins this way:

Mr. [ ], Mrs. [ ], Miss [ ], Ms. [ ] (check one) _____ (fill in name). The company requires each applicant to file a $10 application fee with his application. The fee is refundable if the loan is approved.

Is this part of the application form in compliance with the Regulation? See Reg. B §202.5(d)(3).

PROBLEM 82

When wealthy businesswoman Carol Ledger applied for a loan with Nightflyer Loan Company, the loan officer told her that it was their policy to require all applicants to have their spouses co-sign the loan. Ledger protested that her husband was not involved in this transaction, but the officer still insisted that he sign. Does this violate Reg. B §202.7(d)? Would it matter if the applicants lived in California? What would be the result if Nightflyer told her that it was their policy that all loans had to have a co-signer, but that it need not be the spouse?

EURE v. JEFFERSON NATIONAL BANK[12]
Supreme Court of Virginia, 1994
248 Va. 245, 448 S.E.2d 417

Opinion by Chief Justice HARRY L. CARRICO.

This case involves the Equal Credit Opportunity Act, 15 U.S.C. §§1691 through 1691f (1988 & Supp. IV 1992) (ECOA or the Act). In pertinent part, the Act provides that "it shall be unlawful for any creditor to discriminate against any applicant, with respect to any aspect of a credit transaction . . . on the basis of . . . marital status." 15 U.S.C. §1691(a)(1). Any creditor who fails to comply with the requirements of the Act shall be liable to an aggrieved applicant for actual damages, 15 U.S.C. §1691e(a), and for punitive damages not to exceed $10,000, 15 U.S.C. §1691e(b). Pursuant to §1691b(a)(1), the Federal Reserve Board has prescribed regulations to carry out the purposes of the Act. One such regulation provides that "a creditor shall not require the signature of an applicant's spouse . . . , other than a joint applicant, on any credit instrument if the applicant qualifies under the creditor's standards of creditworthiness for the amount and terms of the credit requested." 12 C.F.R. §202.7(d)(1) (1993).

In the present case, the record shows that on July 17, 1987, Chesapeake Bay Builders, Inc. (Bay Builders) executed a promissory note in the sum of $100,000, payable to the order of Chesapeake Bank and Trust (Chesapeake Bank), the predecessor in interest to the appellee, Jefferson National Bank (Jefferson National). On the same date, Charles H. Eure, Jr., who was a

---

12. Footnotes in this case have been renumbered for clarity.

principal in Bay Builders, and his spouse, Louise R. Eure, executed an "Unconditional Guaranty" in which they agreed to guarantee payment of "all liabilities" of Bay Builders to Chesapeake Bank.

Bay Builders defaulted in payment of the note, and Jefferson National made demand upon the guarantors to pay the balance due. When the demand was not met, Jefferson National brought this action against Bay Builders and the guarantors seeking to recover the sum of $72,714.10, plus interest, attorney's fees, and costs.

In her responsive pleadings, Louise R. Eure asserted the defense that she was required to sign the guaranty "solely on the basis of her marital status as the wife of Charles H. Eure, Jr.," that the transaction violated the Act, and, therefore, that the guaranty was void as applied to her. In a pretrial hearing, the trial court struck Mrs. Eure's defense and later entered judgment against her for the balance due on the promissory note executed by Bay Builders.

We awarded Mrs. Eure an appeal limited to the question whether the trial court erred in ruling that the Act does not provide a defense to a person whose signature has been required on a credit instrument solely because of his or her status as a spouse of an applicant for credit. Finding that the court erred in its ruling, we will reverse.

At the outset of our discussion, we note that Mrs. Eure had no interest in Bay Builders, that she was not a joint applicant for credit, and that Chesapeake Bank made no inquiry concerning Mrs. Eure's credit standing. Further, Jefferson National does not question Mr. Eure's creditworthiness; indeed, a financial statement submitted to Chesapeake Bank at the time it extended credit to Bay Builders showed that Mr. Eure earned more than $200,000 per year as president of Norfolk Shipbuilding and Drydock Corp. and that he had a net worth in excess of $2 million.

Nor can it seriously be questioned that Mrs. Eure's signature was required on the guaranty. While Chesapeake Bank's loan officer testified that "there was no banking regulation, rule or policy which required" Mrs. Eure's signature, he admitted it was "a fairly common practice" to "ask the wife [of a stockholder in a closely held corporation, such as Bay Builders,] to sign on board a guaranty." Furthermore, one of the "terms and conditions" upon which Chesapeake Bank committed itself to make the $100,000 loan in question was that Mrs. Eure would be a guarantor, along with her spouse, of the promissory note covering the loan.

This reduces Jefferson National's argument to the proposition that the Act may not be used defensively to avoid liability on a credit instrument.[13]

---

13. Jefferson National does argue that any right Mrs. Eure may have had to rely on the ECOA violation either for the recovery of damages or for defensive use was barred by the

Jefferson National maintains that the Act specifically provides only for the recovery of damages, which may be sought by way of counterclaim, and that, had Congress intended to provide additional relief in the form of a defense, "it would have included such a provision" in the Act.

Jefferson National opines that Congress's intent to not provide a defense in the Act is evident from a comparison of its provisions with those of the Truth in Lending Act, 15 U.S.C. §§1601 through 1667e (1988 & Supp. IV 1992). Jefferson National points out that, originally, the Truth in Lending Act contained no provision allowing it to serve as a defense; later, however, it was amended to provide that it did not bar a consumer from "asserting a violation [of its provisions] as an original action, or as a defense or counterclaim to an action to collect amounts owed by the consumer." 15 U.S.C. §1640(h). The legislation under consideration here has not been similarly amended, Jefferson National says, and, hence, ECOA "simply does not contemplate the extraordinary relief of debt avoidance."

On the other hand, Mrs. Eure argues that she does not seek "invalidation of the debt" covered by the promissory note but only to have the guaranty she executed declared unenforceable as to her. She concedes the correctness of decisions cited by Jefferson National wherein use of the Act as a defensive measure was denied. See, e.g., Riggs Nat'l Bank v. Linch, 829 F. Supp. 163 (E.D. Va. 1993); CMF Virginia Land, L.P. v. Brinson, 806 F. Supp. 90 (E.D. Va. 1992). However, she distinguishes those decisions on the ground that, in each instance, both the borrower and the borrower's spouse sought to invalidate a credit instrument on the basis of a violation of the Act. To permit use of the Act as a defense in such circumstances, Mrs. Eure says, "would allow the primary debtor to escape liability on a debt instrument executed independently of any ECOA violation."

Here, Mrs. Eure maintains, she was not a primary debtor on the loan made by Chesapeake Bank; she merely guaranteed a loan made to her spouse's corporation, a transaction from which she derived no benefit. She says that "allowing only her to escape liability on an instrument executed solely as a result of an ECOA violation would further the goals of ECOA to deter discrimination in credit transactions while reinforcing the necessary expectations that primary debtors, debtors who have received the benefits of the loan, will remain liable for repayment of the debt."

---

two-year statute of limitations contained in the Act. 15 U.S.C. §1691e(f) (1988). Mrs. Eure concedes that had she sought to recover damages for the ECOA violation, rather than to assert it as a defense, her claim would have been barred. But she says the two-year statute does not bar defensive use of the violation, and we agree. United States v. Western Pac. R.R. Co., 352 U.S. 59, 72, 1 L. Ed. 2d 126, 77 S. Ct. 161 (1956) (using statute of limitations to cut off defense is contrary to statute's purpose of keeping stale litigation out of the courts).

Continuing, Mrs. Eure asserts that Jefferson National is incorrect in saying that Congress intended the provision for the award of actual and punitive damages to be the exclusive remedy for ECOA violations. Mrs. Eure points out that Congress "did more" than provide a remedy by way of damages; it granted both state and federal courts broad equitable jurisdiction in enforcing the Act. In 15 U.S.C. §1691e(c), "the appropriate United States district court or any other court of competent jurisdiction" is given the authority to "grant such equitable and declaratory relief as is necessary to enforce the requirements imposed under [ECOA]." And this grant of equitable jurisdiction, Mrs. Eure maintains, distinguishes ECOA from the Truth in Lending Act, which contains no similar grant.

Furthermore, Mrs. Eure argues, "it is a fundamental principle of contract law that contracts executed in violation of law cannot be enforced." The guaranty agreement she signed, Mrs. Eure maintains, is "a contract growing out of an illegal act and a contract contrary to public policy" under both ECOA and a similar Virginia statute.[14] She says that both federal and Virginia decisions provide "the authority to set aside the obligations of an instrument executed in violation of ECOA." Hence, she concludes, a decision by this Court "not to enforce a Guaranty Agreement procured in violation of ECOA will be supported by clear precedent."

We agree that "clear precedent" will support such a decision. Indeed, the clearest federal precedent on the subject is found in a decision of the Supreme Court of the United States. Kaiser Steel Corp. v. Mullins, 455 U.S. 72, 70 L. Ed. 2d 833, 102 S. Ct. 851 (1982), is directly on point on the question whether the specific remedies provided for the violation of an act of Congress must be deemed exclusive or whether the violation may also be used defensively to avoid the obligation of a contract.

Mullins involved a contract requiring the steel company to make contributions to employee health and retirement funds based on the hours worked by the company's miners and on the coal it produced and purchased from others. The company made the contributions based on the hours its miners worked and on the coal it produced. However, the company failed to report the coal it purchased from others and to make contributions based on the purchased coal. The company defended its failure on the ground that the requirement to make contributions based on purchased coal was void and unenforceable as violative of sections 1 and 2 of the Sherman Act, 15 U.S.C. §§1 and 2, and section 8(e) of the National Labor Relations Act, 29 U.S.C. §158(e).

---

14. Va. Code §§59.1-21.19 through 59.1-21.28 comprise Virginia's Equal Credit Opportunity Act. The provisions of the Virginia act generally parallel those of the federal act.

The Court noted that "sections 1 and 2 of the Sherman Act prohibit contracts, combinations, and conspiracies in restraint of trade, as well as monopolization and attempts to monopolize." 455 U.S. at 78. The Court also noted that "section 8(e) of the NLRA forbids contracts between a union and an employer whereby the employer agrees to cease doing business with or to cease handling the products of another employer." Id.

The respondent espoused two propositions which, he said, were established by the Court's earlier opinion in Kelly v. Kosuga, 358 U.S. 516, 3 L. Ed. 2d 475, 79 S. Ct. 429 (1959), first, "that when a contract is wholly performed on one side, the defense of illegality to enforcing performance on the other side will not be entertained," and, second, "that the express remedies provided by the Sherman Act are not to be added to by including the avoidance of contracts as a sanction." *Mullins*, 455 U.S. at 81. In response, the Court stated it was apparent from the opinion in *Kosuga* that "both propositions were subject to the limitation that the illegality defense should be entertained in those circumstances where its rejection would be to enforce conduct that the antitrust laws forbid." *Mullins*, 455 U.S. at 81-82.

The Court held that while "employer contributions to union welfare funds may be quite legal more often than not, . . . an agreement linking contributions to purchased coal, if illegal, is subject to the defense of illegality." Id. at 82. And the Court allowed the defense notwithstanding the fact that both the Sherman Act and the NLRA provided specific remedies for their violation. Criminal penalties as well as civil relief by way of treble damages and injunction are provided for violations of the Sherman Act's provisions. 15 U.S.C. §§1, 2, 15, and 26. For violations of the NLRA, the National Labor Relations Board is empowered "to prevent any person from engaging in any unfair labor practice (listed in section 158 of this title) affecting commerce." 29 U.S.C. §160(a). Neither act contains any provision permitting defensive use of a violation to avoid liability under a contract. In allowing such defensive use in *Mullins*, the Court stated:

> Refusing to enforce a promise that is illegal under the antitrust or labor laws is not providing an additional remedy contrary to the will of Congress. A defendant proffering the defense seeks only to be relieved of an illegal obligation and does not ask any affirmative remedy based on the antitrust or labor laws. "Any one sued upon a contract may set up as a defence that it is a violation of [an] act of Congress, and if found to be so, that fact will constitute a good defence to the action."

Id. at 81 n.7 (quoting Bement v. National Harrow Co., 186 U.S. 70, 88, 46 L. Ed. 1058, 22 S. Ct. 747 (1902)).

These views apply with equal force here. To deny Mrs. Eure the right to use the ECOA violation defensively would be to enforce conduct that is forbidden by the Act. Such use, therefore, would not be contrary to the will of Congress or in any manner inconsistent with or derogatory of the remedies specifically provided by the Act. Indeed, to permit such use would give effect to the clear legislative intent to deter discrimination in the particular area of endeavor regulated by ECOA.

Virginia law is in accord. In Blick v. Marks, Stokes and Harrison, 234 Va. 60, 360 S.E.2d 345 (1987), we stated that "generally, a contract based on an act forbidden by a statute is void and no action will lie to enforce the contract." Id. at 64, 360 S.E.2d at 348. While *Blick* was decided under an exception to the general rule, applicable if it is manifest the General Assembly did not intend to render contracts made in contravention of the statute void, id., we cautioned that the line of cases applying the exception should be "compared, not confused, with . . . a different set of decisions," id. at 66, 360 S.E.2d at 349. These "different" decisions, we said, stand for the proposition that a contract made in violation of a statute enacted to protect the public against fraud or imposition or to safeguard the public health or morals " 'is illegal and unenforceable by the guilty party.' " Id. (quoting Lasting Products Co. v. Genovese, 197 Va. 1, 8, 87 S.E.2d 811, 816 (1955)).

Listed as an example of the "different" decisions was Bowen Electric Co. v. Foley, 194 Va. 92, 72 S.E.2d 388 (1952), where we held that the plaintiff-appellant's failure to register as a contractor as required by statute barred its recovery of the balance due on a contract for the erection of an outdoor theater. Also listed was Colbert v. Ashland Construction Co., 176 Va. 500, 11 S.E.2d 612 (1940), where we held that the plaintiff-appellant's failure to register under the fictitious name statute barred his recovery of the balance due on a construction contract.

We think that ECOA, like the statutes involved in *Foley* and *Colbert*, is a statute enacted to protect the public against fraud or imposition or to safeguard the public health or morals. In both *Foley* and *Colbert*, we allowed defensive use of a statutory violation to avoid liability under a contract. We hold that Mrs. Eure was entitled to make similar use of the ECOA violation involved in this case to avoid liability, but only her liability, under the guaranty agreement she executed in favor of Chesapeake Bank.

Accordingly, we will reverse the judgment of the trial court and enter final judgment here in favor of Mrs. Eure.

Reversed and final judgment.

PROBLEM 83

When Alice Stein found the house of her dreams, she decided to buy it in spite of the steep price ($175,000). She applied for a mortgage on the house by way of a loan from Octopus National Bank, but the bank denied her the loan, saying that the appraisal report it had had done on the house valued the property at no more than $90,000. This sounds wrong to her—there must be a mistake. The bank has refused to show her the appraisal it received. What should she do? See Reg. B §202.5a(a); ECOA §706.

C. Evaluation

1. Evaluation Systems

There are two methods for the evaluation of creditworthiness: a judgmental system and a credit scoring system. In a judgmental system, the decision to extend credit is made on a subjective basis. The loan officer uses his or her years of experience to determine whether a certain loan is a good one. In a credit scoring system, only objective criteria are used. Key attributes of the consumer (such as length of employment, current income level, make of automobile) are given numerical values and then totaled. If the applicant's score is high enough, the loan is approved. Read Reg. B §202.2(p) and (t).

The Federal Reserve Board itself has struggled to make the regulatory tests intelligible. As the following press release demonstrates, the Board has depended on the credit-granting industry to provide the data needed to develop the regulation.

FEDERAL RESERVE BOARD PRESS RELEASE
July 17, 1979

> *Issues on which the Federal Reserve Board*
> *seeks comment on its April 19 request for*
> *suggestions on how Regulation B can be made*
> *to apply more effectively to credit scoring*

A number of commenters have asked for a non-technical explanation of issues involved in the Board's April 19 request for comment on how the specific rules of Regulation B should apply to four practices of creditors using credit scoring systems. This memorandum was prepared by Board staff in order to help commenters who do not have a technical background address some of the principal issues of the request for comment published on April 19. While it would be appreciated if any comment on those proposals could be received by August 20, any comment received while staff is analyzing the response to the proposals will be fully considered. Comments should be addressed to the Secretary, Board of Governors of the Federal Reserve System, Washington, D.C. 20551. All comments should refer to docket number R-203.

BACKGROUND

The need to focus the regulation more specifically on credit scoring. It must be emphasized that the purpose of the Board's request for comment was to strengthen the regulation and not to remove any existing protections against discrimination in credit transactions. When Regulation B was adopted, the Board focussed primarily on discriminatory practices under the judgmental systems used by the vast majority of creditors—that is to say, systems which grant or deny credit on the basis of the remembered experience and subjective intuitions of individual credit-grantors. At that time, the Board had general knowledge about the way in which credit scoring systems operated, but little information about specific scoring practices. Except for some rules relating to age, the regulation was not designed to accommodate the special problems posed by credit scoring.

Since that time, the Board and its staff have learned a great deal more about credit scoring. It has become increasingly apparent that the specific rules contained in the regulation to prevent discrimination under judgmental systems have an uncertain effect on credit scoring systems. To achieve the objectives of the Equal Credit Opportunity Act and regulation, the Board may need to establish additional specific rules for scoring systems.

What is a credit scoring system? All credit analysis, whether performed judgmentally by loan officers or by credit scoring systems, is based on the principle that past credit experience predicts future credit performance. Thus it is expected that the characteristics of future creditworthy applicants will resemble recent creditworthy borrowers. Judgmental systems rely upon the experience of credit officers to identify the characteristics of past creditworthy customers that are reliable indicators of creditworthiness. A credit scoring system uses statistical methods to evaluate and compare past creditworthy and noncreditworthy applicants. This is done in order to identify those characteristics that predict creditworthiness and to assign numerical values to those characteristics. The numbers are then used to construct a combined score for individual applications to determine whether credit should be extended.

As distinct from most judgmental systems which involve a subjective appraisal of all the material in an applicant's file before credit is extended, credit scoring systems only value those characteristics that previous statistical analysis indicates are predictive of creditworthiness.

To build a statistically reliable scoring system, it is necessary to have a fairly large number of accounts—at least several thousand—with which a particular creditor has had actual experience. It is important to note that the experience of one creditor can be very different from that of another, and that accounts of even different branches of the same creditor can differ widely, so that ordinarily each one must build its own system in order to get acceptable results.

The accounts are divided into "goods" and "bads," i.e., into accounts that have paid satisfactorily and those that have defaulted. Then all the information is taken that was known about each applicant *at the time of application*. This usually includes information on the application itself and information from a credit report if the creditor obtained a report. Each item of information is recorded, for example, number of years on job, whether the applicant has a telephone in the home, age of applicant, amount of income, whether the applicant owns or rents, and so forth.

A point to emphasize is that the particular items of information that are on the applications and hence available to build the system may differ from creditor to creditor. There is no uniform set of items that all creditors do in fact take into account when making a credit decision. Also, there is no uniformity as to which items of information will turn out to predict, for any particular creditor or applicant population, whether or not an applicant will pay back the credit on time.

In order to find out which items will best predict customer behavior each item of information is also tabulated to show how often it occurs on "good" and on "bad" accounts, either alone or in combination with other items. Then the tabulations are analyzed statistically to see how much more often each item or combination occurs in one group or the other. If, for example, "telephone in home," turns up much more frequently in "good" than in "bad" accounts, then that item becomes a candidate to be included in a scoring system.

When all the items have been evaluated to identify those which are most useful in identifying accounts that are likely to pay on time each one that is selected is given a numerical value reflecting how useful it is for that purpose. No fixed number of items is used, but ten or a dozen items might be typical. When the numbers are added up it becomes possible to determine how likely it is that an application with a given "score" will result in an account that will pay on time.

The creditor using a credit scoring system has a business incentive to lend as much as possible, so long as losses from default do not reduce profits below an acceptable level. By setting the score higher or lower, the creditor can affect the amount that will be lent and also affect the amount of losses. The higher the required score, the less the risk of loss, but the less credit will be extended. Many creditors set a minimum score below which credit will not be granted and a higher number above which credit will be granted automatically. Then they do further checking on applications whose scores fall into the medium range and make a judgmental decision based on the further checking.

ISSUES

How to make certain that applicants have all their reliable income considered? Regulation B forbids the discounting of income that is reliable simply because the income is part-time, or derived from some source of which creditors may have traditionally been suspicious, such as pensions, child support, or alimony. Applicants need not declare alimony, child support, or separate maintenance, but if they choose to do so the creditor can ask if it is paid regularly but cannot discount it because of its source.

There are certain difficulties, however, in implementing this principle in credit scoring systems. Some of the factors that the Board must consider in deciding if the regulation should be amended are as follows.

First, there are a number of credit scoring systems which do not take income into account at all. In these systems, other items of information have been found to be more predictive or data on income were not collected in the first place.

Another factor is that some creditors, in building credit scoring systems, have found that taking "secondary" income into account does not improve the predictive value of the system. This could perhaps result from the way in which the systems are built. For example, if a creditor did not evaluate the likelihood that alimony, when it appeared on an application would be paid regularly, but simply tabulated the presence of alimony as a factor to be used in building a system, it might be that—because it is often not reliable—alimony would turn out not to have predictive value. The Board hopes to obtain more factual information about how such systems have actually been built. It also hopes to receive comment on what sort of rules would be most likely to result in all reliable income being considered, in systems that do use income as a predictive item.

Are the protected classes more likely, or not, to have two or more jobs? Some creditors have found that holding more than one job is a factor that is more likely to be associated with non-payment of credit. Persons who have borrowed on the assumption that they will be able to continue to work on two or more jobs may find themselves less able to repay if they must give up one. Are minorities, women, the elderly, or persons belonging to particular religious groups, more likely than the general population to hold more than one job? Is this a factor which creditors should not be permitted to take into consideration in building a credit scoring system? Or is it neutral, so that if holding more than one job turns out to be a predictive for a particular creditor, it could be used?

What kind of explanation is specific enough to satisfy the regulation for applicants who have been denied credit because their score is not high enough? The Act requires that applicants be given the specific reasons when they are denied credit. There are several reasons for this requirement. One is so that the applicant can correct any mistakes that may have been made in evaluating the application. For example, the credit history may be incomplete, or contain a mistake, or may even belong to a different person with a similar name. Another reason is to help applicants learn what they can do to make themselves more creditworthy. Also, it is believed that disclosure tends to prevent arbitrary credit decisions.

The first purpose is not difficult to achieve. Applicants provide the information on applications. The Fair Credit Reporting Act already requires that applicants who are denied credit must be told if a credit bureau report was obtained by the creditor and how to contact the credit bureau in order to verify the information on the history.

The second purpose is more difficult to achieve. The specific details of credit scoring systems have been kept secret partly because the systems are expensive to build and creditors do not want to share them with their competitors. More important, creditors fear that if the complete system were public information, it would be too easy for people who were poor credit risks or who actually wanted to defraud the creditor to falsify their applications in order to reach a passing score. The question is, how can anything less than a full outline of the system help applicants improve their credit rating?

A number of alternative suggestions have been made. The Federal Trade Commission has obtained agreements from some creditors to disclose the four items on which the applicant fell further below the maximum or median number of points that could be awarded. Other variations have been suggested for selecting what seem the most significant items. Another suggestion is that creditors explain that the total score is not sufficient, which is closest to a scientifically correct answer, but not very helpful, and illegal under the statute and regulation. Another suggestion that has been made is to forbid the use of credit scoring. But while it is very important to eliminate bias and prejudice from the way in which scoring systems are built (for example, using the Zip code in an applicant's address, where Zip code correlates with race), properly built scoring systems can help get away from the subjective prejudices of individual credit grantors. This is because the system exists in black and white and can be checked; the criteria used by individual credit grantors are much harder to pin down and verify.

CONCLUSION

The Board has asked for comment on all the issues discussed above, with a view to finding out how Regulation B can be made most effective as a tool for eliminating discrimination in the credit granting process, where credit scoring is used. All comments received will be carefully considered.

2. Effects Test

Footnote 2 to §202.6 of Regulation B explains that Congress intended an "effects test" in determining whether a creditor's practices discriminate on a prohibited basis. The effects test, developed for similar issues in civil rights cases, looks at circumstantial evidence (a disparate impact, for example) to determine whether the creditor is discriminating in an impermissible manner and ignores the subjective intent of the creditor. The rationale behind the test is this: creditors are not likely to take the stand and confess to an evil purpose in doing what they did, so the plaintiff does not have the burden of showing intended villainy to prove a violation of the statute. Instead the injured consumer establishes merely that the creditor's practices, whether intended to or not, have the *effect* of discriminating on a prohibited basis, and then the burden shifts to the creditor to justify the practice as necessary to meet legitimate business needs. If the creditor does this, the burden shifts back to the plaintiff to prove that there are other ways of accomplishing the creditor's objectives that do not discriminate on a prohibited basis. See Coleman v. General Motors Acceptance Corp., 196 F.R.D. 315 (M.D. Tenn., 2000) (class action certified contending African-Americans charged 2.5 percent finance charge markup over whites buying cars—"disparate impact" theory utilized as part of effects test).

CHERRY v. AMOCO OIL CO.

United States District Court, Northern District of Georgia, 1979
481 F. Supp. 727

EVANS, District Judge.

This is an action brought under the Equal Credit Opportunity Act, 15 U.S.C. §§1691 et seq., and Regulation B of the Board of Governors of the Federal Reserve System, 12 C.F.R. 202, in which Plaintiff Cherry seeks damages for alleged violations of the Act arising from Defendant Amoco's rejection of Plaintiff's application for a gasoline credit card. This action is presently before the Court on Defendant's Motion to Dismiss and Motion for Summary Judgment. Both parties have submitted briefs on these motions and have also complied with Local Court Rule 91.72 by filing separate statements of material facts as to which there is no genuine issue to be tried. The United States of America has been allowed to file as Amicus Curiae with a brief opposing the present motions to dismiss and for summary judgment.

Plaintiff Cherry filed this complaint on April 26, 1978. Based on the original complaint and later submissions by the Plaintiff in this case, Cherry's basic allegation is two-fold: she claims that the Defendant denied her credit on the basis of a racially discriminatory factor which is in violation of 15 U.S.C. §1691(a)(1), and also that she was denied credit for reasons which were false, misleading, or not stated with the specificity required by 12 C.F.R. 202.9(b)(2). Cherry's claim of racial discrimination is based on Amoco's "credit experience in the [Plaintiff's] immediate geographical area" which was given by Defendant as one of three factors determining the rejection of Cherry's application. The "immediate geographical area" is determined by the applicant's zip code and Cherry, a white woman, argues that such a factor is the equivalent of racial discrimination due to the segregated pattern of housing in the Atlanta area. As to her other claim, Cherry argues that the other two factors given by Amoco in rejecting her application, "level of income" and "type of bank references," are false, misleading, or not stated with specificity as required by law.

Defendant Amoco's Motion to Dismiss is based on Amoco's argument that Plaintiff Cherry lacks standing to litigate this claim and that the complaint itself fails to state a claim upon which relief can be granted. In order to properly evaluate these contentions by the Defendant, the relevant provisions of the Equal Credit Opportunity Act, 15 U.S.C. §§1691 et seq., must be discussed. Section 1691(a)(1) reads as follows:

> (a) It shall be unlawful for any creditor to discriminate against *any* applicant, with respect to *any* aspect of a credit transaction—

(1) on the basis of race, color, religion, national origin, sex or marital status, or age (provided the applicant has the capacity to contract). (Emphasis added.)

Section 1691(d)(2) reads as follows:

(2) Each applicant against whom adverse action is taken shall be entitled to a statement of reasons for such action from the creditor. A creditor satisfies this obligation by—
    (A) providing statements of reasons in writing as a matter of course to applicants against whom adverse action is taken; or
    (B) giving written notification of adverse action which discloses (i) the applicant's right to a statement of reasons within thirty days after receipt by the creditor of a request made within sixty days after such notification, and (ii) the identity of the person or office from which such statement may be obtained. . . .

Section 1691(d)(3) then says "A statement of reasons meets the requirements of this section only if it contains the specific reasons for the adverse action taken." The Act gives no further explanation of what is required as to specificity, but Regulation B of the Board of Governors of the Federal Reserve System makes mention of it in 12 C.F.R. 202.9(b)(2), which says:

A statement of reasons for adverse action shall be sufficient if it is specific and indicates the principal reason(s) for the adverse action. A creditor may formulate its own statement of reasons in checklist or letter form or may use all or a portion of the sample form printed below, which, if properly completed, satisfies the requirements of paragraph (a)(2)(i) of this section.

The sample form mentioned above contains a checklist of nineteen "principal reasons for adverse action concerning credit" as well as a blank space for "other specify." One of the reasons on the checklist is "insufficient income," which is similar to but not the same as "level of income" given as one of Amoco's principal reasons in rejecting Cherry's application. Amoco's other two reasons, "type of bank references" and "our credit experience in your immediate geographical area," are not included among the nineteen reasons on the sample form. However, 12 C.F.R. 202.9(b)(2) does not indicate that the sample form is meant to include all valid reasons but merely serves as examples of "specific" valid reasons.

Having reviewed the record in this case, the Court finds that the two primary claims arising from Plaintiff Cherry's complaint do state claims upon which relief may be granted under the provisions of the Equal Credit Opportunity Act as stated above. §§1691(a)(1) prohibits racial discrimination in any aspect of a credit transaction. Cherry alleges that Amoco's rejection factor of "our credit experience in your immediate geographical

area" involves racial discrimination when it is applied to an area with a
racially segregated housing pattern and therefore such a rejection factor is
in violation of §1691(a)(1). Section 1691(d)(3) requires that a creditor give
specific reasons for rejecting a credit application and Cherry alleges that
the factors of "level of income" and "type of bank references" are
false, misleading, and lack specificity in violation of §1691(d)(3). Under
§1691e(a), civil liability arises as follows:

> Any creditor who fails to comply with any requirement imposed under this title
> [15 U.S.C. §§1691 et seq.] shall be liable to the aggrieved applicant for any actual
> damages sustained by such applicant acting either in an individual capacity or as a
> member of a class.

Cherry's claims that the rejection factors used by Amoco in this case are
in violation of §1691(a)(1) and 1691(d)(3) do state a claim for which relief
may be granted under §1691e(a) and therefore no dismissal will be granted
on the basis of failure to state a claim.

Defendant Amoco's Motion to Dismiss is really based on its argument
that Plaintiff Cherry lacks standing to litigate a claim of racial discrimination because Cherry is not a member of the race which she alleges is
discriminated against by Amoco's use of "our credit experience in your
immediate geographical area" as a determinative factor in rejecting credit
applications. The Court recognizes that the issue of Cherry's standing to
claim racial discrimination in violation of the Equal Credit Opportunity Act
presents a question of first impression. Although cases involving issues of
standing under other circumstances may offer assistance in determining this
matter, the Court must ultimately look to the Act itself and any relevant
legislative history to decide whether the Plaintiff in this case has standing.
In order to best analyze this standing question the Court will start with a
general view and then move to an investigation of the Act itself.

The most recent Supreme Court case to deal with a question of standing
was Davis v. Passman, 442 U.S. 228, 99 S. Ct. 2264, 60 L. Ed. 2d 846
(1979). In footnote 18, the Court said:

> [S]tanding is a question of whether a plaintiff is sufficient adversary to a defendant to
> create an Article III case or controversy, or at least to overcome prudential limita-
> tions on federal court jurisdictions, see Warth v. Seldin, 422 U.S. 490, 498, 95 S. Ct.
> 2197, 2204, 45 L. Ed. 2d 2197 (1975). . . . And under the criteria we have set out,
> petitioner clearly has standing to bring this suit. If the allegations of her complaint
> are taken to be true, she has shown that she "personally has suffered some actual or
> threatened injury as a result of a putatively illegal conduct of the defendant."
> Gladstone, Realtors v. Village of Bellwood, 441 U.S. 91, 99, 99 S. Ct. 1601, 1608, 60
> L. Ed. 2d 66 (1979) (at 107, n.18, 99 S. Ct. at 2274, n.18, 60 L. Ed. 2d at 859, n.18).

The Court dealt with standing in a more direct manner in Gladstone, Realtors v. Village of Bellwood, 441 U.S. 91, 99 S. Ct. 1601, 60 L. Ed. 2d 66 (1979). Under *Gladstone*, standing is first viewed under the test of Article III of the Constitution:

> The constitutional limits on standing eliminate claims in which the plaintiff has failed to make out a case or controversy between himself and the defendant. (441 U.S. at 99, 99 S. Ct. at 1608, 60 L. Ed. 2d at 76)

If Article III is satisfied, then the "prudential limitations" test is applied, as described in *Gladstone* as follows:

> Even when a case falls within these constitutional boundaries, a plaintiff may still lack standing under the prudential principles by which the judiciary seeks to avoid deciding questions of broad social import where no individual rights would be vindicated and to limit access to the federal courts to those litigants best suited to assert a particular claim. . . . He also must assert his own legal interests rather than those of third parties (cites omitted). (441 U.S. 99-100, 99 S. Ct. 1608, 60 L. Ed. 2d 77)

However, the Court in *Gladstone* indicated that Congress can provide for broad standing if still within the Article III limitations:

> Congress may, by legislation, expand standing to the full extent permitted by Art. III, thus permitting litigation by one who otherwise would be barred by the prudential standing rules (cite omitted). In no event, however, may Congress abrogate the Art. III minima: A plaintiff must always have suffered a distinct and palpable injury to himself (cite omitted). (441 U.S. 100, 99 S. Ct. 1608, 60 L. Ed. 2d 77)

In *Gladstone*, the Court held that §812 of the Fair Housing Act, 42 U.S.C. §3612, allowed standing to sue as broad as is permitted by Article III, and therefore individual residents of the "target" area, many of them white, could challenge the sales practices of defendant brokerage firms involving "steering" blacks toward and whites away from the "target" area on the basis of allegations that such a practice destroyed the integrated character of the "target" area.

In considering the standing of Cherry to sue under the Equal Credit Opportunity Act in light of the general requirements outlined in *Gladstone*, this Court must accept as true all material allegations of the complaint and construe the complaint in favor of the complaining party. See Warth v. Seldin, 422 U.S. 490, 501, 95 S. Ct. 2197, 45 L. Ed. 2d 2197 (1975). Accepting the truth of Cherry's allegation that the rejection factor of "our credit experience in your immediate geographical area" used by Amoco is racially discriminatory, the question before this Court is whether Cherry has standing to sue in this case based on such a claim. Under §1691(a)(1), it is unlawful for a creditor to discriminate against "any" applicant "on the basis of race." The statutory language does not say on the basis of "that applicant's" race or "his or her" race. Where a creditor fails to comply with the prohibition against racial discrimination, the creditor is liable to the "aggrieved" applicant in a private action under §1691e(a). Therefore the language of the statute itself suggests that the Act is meant to prevent racially discriminatory behavior on the part of creditors in their credit transactions and that when such behavior exists the statute will protect anyone affected or aggrieved by that discriminatory behavior.

The focus of the statutory language on creditors' liability for the effects of racial discrimination is also reflected in the legislative history of the 1976 amendments to the Act which expanded coverage from discrimination based on sex or marital status to discrimination based on race, religion, national origin, and age as well. The report of the Senate Committee on Banking, Housing and Urban Affairs dealing with these amendments, Senate Report No. 94-589, said in part:

> In determining the existence of discrimination on these grounds, as well as on the other grounds discussed below, courts or agencies are free to look at the effects of a creditor's practices as well as the creditor's motives or conduct in individual transactions. (1976 U.S. Code Cong. & Admin. News, pp. 403, 406)

Under this analysis of the statute, whenever discrimination exists in violation of §1691(a)(1), then the creditor guilty of such violation is liable to *anyone* adversely affected by such unlawful discrimination. In theory one might suppose that those "adversely affected" will always be members of the group having the particular characteristic upon which the discrimination is based, but in practical terms that is not necessarily so.

Plaintiff Cherry's allegations present a good example of the real or practical application of the Act's prohibition of racial discrimination in credit transactions. Cherry is a resident of a predominantly black zip code area of Atlanta, which purportedly has a racially segregated housing pattern in a relative sense (not complete or full segregation). The plaintiff alleges that the use of the rejection factor "our credit experience in your immediate geographical area" by Amoco allows the defendant to discriminate against blacks by rejecting credit applications from predominantly black neighborhoods in Atlanta. However, by discriminating against blacks in those neighborhoods the rejection factor in question may also have the effect of causing the rejection of credit applications from non-blacks who happen to live in those neighborhoods. This is exactly what Cherry claims happened to her. Her zip code area is predominantly black and scores low on the rejection factor being discussed, and according to Amoco this factor has been weighed in conjunction with two other factors in an inseparable manner that results in the rejection of Cherry's application.

Assuming that there exists racial discrimination as alleged by the plaintiff, then she has been directly affected by such discrimination in that it resulted in the rejection of her credit application and she is therefore an "aggrieved applicant" under §1691e(a) and has standing to sue under the Act itself. By alleging that she has been personally injured by the rejection of her credit application on the basis of an allegedly discriminatory factor used by the defendant, Cherry has made out a case and controversy against Amoco and therefore has standing to sue under Article III of the Constitution. "Prudential limitations" do not prevent Cherry from having standing to sue in this case because she is asserting her own legal interests and the court is not being asked to decide "questions of broad social import where no individual rights would be vindicated." Even if prudential principles suggested a lack of standing in the present case, the use of "any applicant" and "the aggrieved applicant" as the language in the Equal Credit Opportunity Act would allow Cherry to pursue this litigation under the broad standing analysis used in *Gladstone*, supra.

In light of the foregoing discussion, the Court finds that Plaintiff Cherry has stated a claim upon which relief may be granted and that she has standing to litigate such a claim in this case. Therefore, Defendant Amoco's Motion to Dismiss is hereby denied. The Court also finds that there are disputed material facts in this case, especially as to the discriminatory nature of "our credit experience in your immediate geographical area," and therefore Defendant Amoco's Motion for Summary Judgment is hereby denied.

PROBLEM 84

As the new attorney for Solid Savings & Loan, you have a meeting with the vice president in charge of loans. He tells you that he wants to ask applicants detailed questions about their income. It is his experience that people (particularly women) with part-time jobs rarely keep those jobs very long (so he wants to exclude consideration of that salary as reliable income), that people on welfare never have enough money to repay debts (so welfare income is ignored in the evaluation of their income), and that ex-husbands often fail to pay alimony or child support (so if the applicant is a woman relying on such payments, they too can be discounted). Assume that the vice president can produce statistics showing that these suppositions are correct. Do you have any advice for the company? See Reg. B §202.6(b)(5).

3. Age

Testimony before Congress established that older Americans pay their debts with more regularity than younger Americans. When you think about this, it is almost bound to be true. A 22-year-old just starting out in life is much more likely to have problems paying the bills than a 65-year-old, who has had plenty of time to get his or her financial affairs in order. Available statistics show that of those older than 65 only 12 percent are living below the poverty line, while 65 percent of those with homes have paid off their mortgages and have significant other assets. For this reason, Regulation B provides that discrimination on the basis of age is allowed. First, the applicant must have the legal capacity to enter into a contract (thus the creditor can discriminate against an applicant because he or she is only 11). Second, older applicants (62 or older, see §202.2(o)) may always be given *favorable* treatment. Whether an applicant's age may be used against him or her also depends on the type of evaluation system used. Read Reg. B §202.6(b)(2) carefully.

PROBLEM 85

First Savings and Loan had a credit scoring system that used age as a predictive variable. Applicants were asked their age and their response was given a number (with higher numbers being more likely to be granted credit): ages 18-21, 0; ages 22-29, 1; ages 30-39, 2; ages 40-62, 3;and ages 63 and above, 4. Is this legal?

PROBLEM 86

Second Savings and Loan uses a judgmental system to evaluate credit applications. Loan officer Nancy Keen tells you that the only time she discriminates against older applicants is when she does not believe they will outlive the loan term. For example, last week she turned down a 67-year-old for a 20-year mortgage loan. Is Second Savings and Loan violating Regulation B? See §202.2(y); the Official Staff Commentary to §202.6(b) addresses this issue.

4. Credit History

Before the adoption of ECOA, many married women had trouble establishing a good credit rating because they were lumped in with whatever credit history their husbands had. One of the key aims of the new statute was to deal with this problem.

PROBLEM 87

When Alice Thenardier finally divorced the miserable wretch she had been married to, she discovered that the two credit cards they had both used during marriage were listed in his name. In reality, he had used one of the credit cards and she had used the other. He never paid his bills, so the credit history on that card is very bad; she always paid her bills, so that card has a good credit history. Can she make a lender divorce her from the bad credit card's record, but keep her wedded to the favorable history of the card she actually used? See §202.6(b)(6).

D. Extension of Credit

PROBLEM 88

Unhappily, John and Mary's marriage did not work out and they filed for a divorce. They had had a joint account with Big Department Store. When Mary, who had been the primary user of the charge account, wrote Big Department Store and informed them of the divorce, asking that the account hereafter be carried in her name, the store responded by canceling her right to use the account, though they sent a letter to John stating that he could continue to make charges on the account. The store justified this by saying that the account had been opened on the basis of John's income alone, so that Mary would have to reapply. Upset, Mary calls you, the attorney who handled her divorce. Does she have a cause of action? See Reg. B §202.7(c). See also Miller v. American Express, 688 F.2d 1240 (9th Cir. 1982) (automatic cancellation of credit card on death of husband not permitted by ECOA).

E. Special-Purpose Credit Programs

PROBLEM 89

Football University is a co-ed school. In 1911, Alice Money left $1 million to a special trust fund to be used to lend money to needy college women attending the university. May the trustees of the fund refuse to lend money to male applicants? See Reg. B §202.8.

F. Notifications

One of the major ECOA battlegrounds in Congress was the issue of creditor notifications. The women's groups wanted the creditor to give written notification of the reasons why credit was denied whenever that occurred. They argued that without a written notification, proving that discrimination was taking place would be very difficult. The lobbyists for the credit associations did not want to have to justify their credit decisions, particularly not in writing. For the result, see Reg. B §202.9.

PIERCE V. CITIBANK (SOUTH DAKOTA)
United States District Court, Oregon, 1994
843 F. Supp. 646

FRYE, Judge:
The matter before the court is the motion of the plaintiff, Linda J. Pierce, for partial summary judgment (#22).

UNDISPUTED FACTS

Linda J. Pierce obtained Citibank Chase VISA Account No. 5424 1800 2276 3277 with defendant Citibank (South Dakota), N.A. based on her own creditworthiness. Her husband, Michael Pierce, maintained several accounts with defendant Citicorp Credit Services, Inc. (Citicorp). Citicorp is a corporate affiliate of Citibank. When Michael Pierce became delinquent on his Citibank bankcard account, Citicorp closed all of his accounts. When Citicorp notified Michael Pierce by letter on January 11, 1991 that it had closed all of his accounts, Citicorp included the account number of Linda Pierce among the numbers of the accounts closed. Linda Pierce, who lived with her husband, did not receive notice of the closing of her account, and her name was not included on the notice sent to Michael Pierce.

Linda Pierce continued to receive regular statements on Account No. 5424 1800 2276 3277 and continued to make payments on that account until she learned that the account had been closed when she talked by telephone to a customer service representative of Citibank on or about May 15, 1991. In that telephone conversation, the customer service representative informed Linda Pierce that she could not use her card until the accounts of Michael Pierce were brought current because her account was linked with those of her husband.

On July 18, 1991, Linda Pierce sent a registered letter to Citibank requesting a written response within ten days as to why her account had not been renewed. On September 11, 1991, Citibank renewed her account and reinstated her credit privileges. In a letter dated September 11, 1991, Citibank informed Linda Pierce: "I want you to know that we sincerely appreciate the effort you've made to return your account to good standing." Exhibit 4 to Plaintiff's Motion for Partial Summary Judgment. Linda Pierce used the account until she filed a petition in bankruptcy on May 18, 1992. . . .

CONTENTIONS OF THE PARTIES

Linda Pierce contends that Citicorp, and Citibank acting as an agent for Citicorp, have violated 15 U.S.C. §1691(d)(2) by failing to provide her written notice of the closure or suspension of her charge account. The defendants contend that even though there is no record of any written notification being sent to Linda Pierce, she is not entitled to relief under 15 U.S.C. §1691(d)(2) because (1) her claim is barred by the statute of limitations; (2) she waived her right to written notice by receiving actual notice of the cancellation; and (3) Citibank's failure to notify her in writing was an inadvertent error permissible under 12 C.F.R. §202.2(s). Linda Pierce contends that these defenses are affirmative defenses which have never been pled by the defendants, and therefore cannot be raised at this time.

ANALYSIS AND RULING

15 U.S.C. §1691(d)(2) states:

> A creditor satisfies this obligation by—
> (A) providing statements of reasons in writing as a matter of course to applicants against whom adverse action is taken.

15 U.S.C. §1691(d)(3) states that "[a] statement of reasons meets the requirements of this section only if it contains the specific reasons for the adverse action taken."

The defendants argue that there is a dispute of material fact as to whether the cancellation of Linda Pierce's credit privileges was an "adverse action." The defendants argue that where action is taken on an account which is overdue, it is not an adverse action. However, Steve Beranek, an assistant vice president of Citicorp, stated in his affidavit that "at least one reason for the revocation of plaintiff's account could have been Michael Pierce's delinquency on his accounts," defeating the assertion of Citibank that the only reason the account was closed was because payments were overdue. Id. at p. 2, para. 5.

Beranek admits that the defendants have no record of generating or producing an adverse action notice stating the reasons for the closure of Linda Pierce's account. Id. at p. 3, para. 9. Beranek further admits that no document was found in Linda Pierce's records during the discovery process. Id.

Citibank directs the court to the letter it sent on September 11, 1991 to Linda Pierce advising her of the reinstatement of her privileges. In that letter, Citibank congratulates Linda Pierce for returning her account to good standing. Citibank suggests in the letter of September 11, 1991 that the account of Linda Pierce was closed based on her delinquency. The letter states, in part: "It is a great pleasure to tell you we have decided to renew your Citibank Classic MasterCard card account. I want you to know that we sincerely appreciate the effort you've made to return your account to good credit standing." Exhibit 4 to Plaintiff's Motion for Partial Summary Judgment. The court finds that this letter does not establish a genuine issue of material fact because it is not adequate as a matter of law as a notification of the specific reasons for adverse action as required by 15 U.S.C. §1691(d)(2) and (3).

Furthermore, Beranek admitted that he did not know the reason why Linda Pierce's account was closed, stating, in part, that "it is impossible for me to say that the account was closed because of the delinquency of Michael Pierce or because a collections unit had made a decision that plaintiff was 'high risk' as a result of her own account." Affidavit of Steve Beranek, p. 2, para. 6. Therefore, Beranek's attestations with regard to the adequacy of the notification of adverse action are insufficient to establish a material fact. Citibank has presented no other evidence as to its failure to provide notification with specific reasons for adverse action as required by 15 U.S.C. §1691(d)(2) and (3).

Defendants argue that the letter of January 11, 1991 to Michael Pierce informing him of the closure of his accounts, which included the account number of Linda Pierce, raises an issue of fact as to whether the failure to notify was due to inadvertent error excusable under Section 202.14(c) of Regulation B to the Equal Credit Opportunity Act. Section 202.14(c) provides that "[a] creditor's failure to comply with Sections ... 202.9, 202.10 ... is not a violation if it results from an inadvertent error. On discovering an error under Sections 202.9 and 202.10, the creditor shall correct it as soon as possible. Section 202.2(s) of Regulation B provides that "inadvertent error means a mechanical, electronic or clerical error that a creditor demonstrates was not intentional and occurred notwithstanding the maintenance of procedures reasonably adopted to avoid such errors."

Linda Pierce contends that there is no issue of material fact as to the defense of inadvertent error because Citibank did not satisfy the requirement of Section 202.14(c) that it corrected the error as soon as possible upon discovery. In his affidavit, Beranek states that he does not know the reasons for the suspension of the credit privileges of Linda Pierce. The defendants have not provided evidence that Linda Pierce received an explanation for Citicorp's decision to close her account.

Although there is an issue of fact as to whether Citicorp inadvertently failed to send a letter to Linda Pierce at the same time as it sent the letter to Michael Pierce, this fact is not material to the claim of Linda Pierce. Linda Pierce contends that even after she requested specific reasons for the defendants' acts by telephone and by certified letter, Citibank did not provide those reasons. The court concludes that the defendants have presented no evidence from which the trier of fact could find that its failure to provide specific reasons after the written request of Linda Pierce constituted inadvertent error under Section 202.14(c). Without the defense of inadvertent error, the fact of the reinstatement of Linda Pierce's account is not sufficient to satisfy the requirements of 15 U.S.C. §1691(d)(3).

The defendants argue that even if they violated 15 U.S.C. §1691(d)(2) and (3), Linda Pierce waived her right to notice by receiving actual notice of the closure and by reinstating and using her account after reinstatement. The defendants cite Freeman v. Koerner Ford of Scranton, 370 Pa. Super. 150, 536 A.2d 340 (Pa. Super. 1987). In *Freeman*, the plaintiff did not waive his right to notice by seeking to reinstate his application. He waived his right to notice by exhibiting behavior which amounted to a withdrawal of his credit application. Id. at 231. Linda Pierce did not waive her right to notification. When she discovered that she had not been informed, she attempted to correct the problem and determine the reasons for the suspension of her privileges.

Finally, the defendants argue that the claim of Linda Pierce is barred by the statute of limitations. 15 U.S.C. §1691e(f) provides that "no such action shall be brought later than two years from the date of the occurrence of the violation." Linda Pierce alleges that she discovered that her Citibank account had been closed on May 15, 1991 when she telephoned Citibank for an explanation. Linda Pierce has presented evidence that she continued to receive statements and to make payments between February, 1991 and May, 1991. The statements that she received do not indicate that the account had been closed or that credit privileges had been suspended. Defendants have not presented any facts which establish that Linda Pierce knew that her account was closed in February, 1991 when Michael Pierce received a letter informing him of the closure of his accounts.

The crux of the claim of Linda Pierce is (1) she was not notified of the closure of her account; and, therefore (2) her claim did not arise until she knew of the failure of Citibank to notify her, which occurred on May 15,

1991. The two-year bar of 15 U.S.C. §1691e(f) runs from the date of discovery with respect to 15 U.S.C. §1691(d)(2) and (3). To interpret the two-year bar to run from the date of the actual account closure, before Linda Pierce's claim was discovered, would be illogical and defeat the purpose of 15 U.S.C. §1691(d)(2) and (3).

CONCLUSION

The motion of Linda Pierce for partial summary judgment on the fifth claim for relief (#22) is GRANTED.

PROBLEM 90

After Bruce Wayne (from Problem 70) failed to get a job, he applied for a loan from the Nightflyer Loan Company. NLC received a bad credit report on Wayne from Big Eye Credit Bureau and turned Wayne down. He phoned them and asked why, but was told nothing. Assuming this action violates §615 of the Fair Credit Reporting Act, does it also violate the Equal Credit Opportunity Act? How much can Wayne recover? See ECOA §706.

PROBLEM 91

When Big Department Store turned down Lynn Brown for credit, it sent her a written explanation stating merely, "You did not impress the loan officer as a good credit risk." In a judgmental system of credit evaluation is this sufficient? If the store had used a credit scoring system, would it satisfy the Regulation to inform her "You did not score high enough on our system to be creditworthy"?

G. Credit Reports

PROBLEM 92

Big Department Store always kept accounts of married applicants in the name of the husband and did not keep track of whether the husband or the wife had made the charges to the account. When a credit bureau requested information on the credit history of a wife, the store would send out the account information on the whole account. Is this practice wrong? See Reg. B §202.10.

H. Monitoring

It occurred to Congress that once creditors said they were not discriminating on prohibited grounds in the granting of credit, there would be no records to test whether this was true. For purposes of monitoring compliance with ECOA, Congress has reversed itself and now requires creditors considering first mortgage lending to keep records on the race, sex, marital status, and age of all applicants and report this to the federal government. Applicants are to be told that this information will be used for no other purpose than federal policing of the creditors' compliance with the statute. If the applicant balks at giving the information, the creditor is supposed to guess at the answers and report the guess. Read Reg. B §202.13. It should also be noted that the Regulation encourages creditors to engage in "self-tests" to determine compliance with the Act and protects them from liability if they do so; see Reg. B §202.15.

I. Attorney's Fees

The civil remedy for violation of the statute and Regulation is found in §706 of the statute. We shall explore the meaning of many of its provisions when we get to the similar language of Truth in Lending Act §130 in Chapter 8. For now, it is important to note the election of remedy mandated by §706(i). If the conduct of the creditor allegedly violates both ECOA and the Civil Rights Act, the injured consumer can sue under one or the other, but not both.

ECOA and virtually all of the consumer protection statutes permit the prevailing consumer to recover attorney's fees. How are these fees measured? In federal cases, the courts look to the factors listed in Johnson v. Georgia Highway Express, Inc., 488 F.2d 714, 717-719 (5th Cir. 1974): (1) the time and labor required; (2) the novelty and difficulty of the questions presented; (3) the skill requisite to perform the legal service properly; (4) the preclusion of other employment by the attorney due to acceptance of the case; (5) the customary fee; (6) whether the fee is fixed or contingent; (7) time limitations imposed by the client or the circumstances; (8) the amount involved and the results obtained; (9) the experience, reputation, and ability of the attorneys; (10) the "undesirability" of the case; (11) the nature and length of the professional relationship with the client; and (12) awards in similar cases. The courts typically award the so-called "lodestar" amount, determined by multiplying the number of hours reasonably expended on the litigation by a reasonable hourly rate, see Hensley v. Eckerhart, 461 U.S. 424, 433 (1983); though in cases where the consumer alleges a technical violation of whatever statute is involved and recovers only a small amount, some courts will not award the lodestar figure, see Carroll v. Wolpoff & Abramson, 53 F.3d 626 (4th Cir. 1995).

The attorney who expects to recover attorney's fees had better keep accurate records of the time expended and introduce them into evidence prior to the rendition of judgment. For more on the recovery of attorney's fees in consumer law cases, see the discussion of this issue at length in "Introduction to the Practice of Consumer Law," which begins this book.

CHAPTER 7
Truth in Lending: Disclosure

I. USURY

A. A History Lesson

> If you lend money to my people, to the poor among you, you shall not deal with them as a creditor, you shall not exact interest from them.

Exodus 22:25

> [He] hath given forth upon usury, and hath taken increase: shall he then live? He shall not live: he hath done these abominations; he shall surely die; his blood shall be upon him.

Ezekiel 18:13

> Those who charge usury are in the same position as those controlled by the devil's influence. This is because they claim that usury is the same as commerce. However, GOD permits commerce, and prohibits usury. Thus, whoever heeds this commandment from his Lord, and refrains from usury, he may keep his past earnings, and his judgment rests with GOD. As for those who persist in usury, they incur Hell, wherein they abide forever.

Koran 2:275

> [A]ll the saints and all the angels of paradise cry then against [the usurer], saying, "To hell, to hell, to hell." Also the heavens with their stars cry out, saying "To the fire, to the fire, to the fire." The planets also clamor, "To the depths, to the depths, to the depths."

St. Bernardine (1380-1444), *De Evangelio Aeterno*, sermon 45, art. 3, cl. 3 in 2 Opera Omnia (de la Haye ed. 1745)

Lenders earn money by having their debts repaid, on time, with enough interest that the lender recaptures expenses and then makes a reasonable (or sometimes not so reasonable) profit. To one reared in a capitalist system, there is nothing remarkable about this. Who could quarrel with it?

It therefore comes as something of a shock to realize how sinful many religions have made it for a lender to take any interest at all. Both the Koran and the Bible (see above) condemn the practice, with everlasting damnation being its rather extreme punishment. See Paul B. Rasor, Biblical Roots of Modern Consumer Credit Law, 10 J.L. & Religion 157 (1994) Through many civilizations there has been a battle between lenders' insistence on their due and the clergy's demand that no (or little) interest be allowed. In 1571, usurers were condemned because they sold "time which belonged only to God"; Marion Hamilton, The Ancient Maxim of Caveat Emptor, 40 Yale L.J. 1133, 1140 (1931). Granted, there had been abuses. History is replete with examples of people or kingdoms in dire circumstances and willing to agree to any rate demanded. In ancient Greece lenders asked and received 48 percent a month (576 percent a year). In subsequent centuries, rates of 100 percent and better were routinely charged. If the desperate will sign anything (and they will), they will agree to interest rates that make the eyes pop.[1] Nonetheless there is a certain paternalism to usury statutes, and as we go through the materials that follow, you might ask yourself exactly who we are trying to protect and ponder the wisdom of doing so through caps on the economic incentives to lend money.

Gradually the Catholic Church, through its ecclesiastical courts, approved an interest rate of 6 percent per year as "just" (this was called the "just price" doctrine) and condemned any amount above that figure as usurious. Imbued with the imprimatur of the Church, the number "6" took on an aura of permissibility. It was enacted into law. Getting around the commercially suicidal figure of 6 percent proved a challenge.

B. The Calculations

A discussion of usury is complicated by the antipathy some people (including the author) feel toward mathematics. For those for whom this is

---

1. In the modern world it is not unusual for pawnshops to charge 40 percent a year (and loan sharks routinely go for a rate in excess of 250 percent). Payday lenders have rates that can be as high as 780 percent in some states! For a decision holding that a business which advanced consumers money against future tax refunds was subject to state usury statutes, see State v. Udis, 31 P.3d 161 (Colo. 2001).

true, relax. This isn't going to be difficult. For those who enjoy the math, see Marion Benfield, The Usury Headache, 19 Case W. Res. L. Rev. 823 (1968), for a more satisfying discussion. Another helpful work on point is the National Consumer Law Center's book The Cost of Credit (3d ed. 2005, with yearly supplements); it explores the rate regulations in each state and at the federal level.

Suppose that there is a general usury statute forbidding loans for more than 6 percent annually. Is the statute violated by the following transactions?

PROBLEM 93

When sailors in the United States Navy run low on funds, there is always a fellow shipmate willing to lend money (the author knows this from his service years). A typical loan is on the order of $5 this week and a repayment of $6 next week. Is this legal?

PROBLEM 94

Portia Moot borrowed $1,000 from her father and promised to repay it at the end of a year with 6 percent interest. At the end of the year she repaid him $1,060. Has the statute been violated?

PROBLEM 95

Portia Moot borrowed $1,000 from her father and promised to repay him $1,060, making a partial payment on the first of each month. Is this a 6 percent rate? Is the father guilty of usury? See Lucas v. Central Trust Co., 50 Ohio App. 2d 109, 361 N.E.2d 1080 (1976).

PROBLEM 96

Portia Moot asked her father for a $1,000 loan at the 6 percent rate. He agreed, but made her allow him to take the interest out first (a practice called "discounting"). Thus he lent her $940, and she repaid $1,000, making monthly payments on the first of each month. Is this usurious?

Consider for a moment what interest is. Interest is the gain that the lender makes from the repayment of the loan; it is the reward the lender receives for risking the transfer of the money. You should then be able to see that the lender is at greatest risk when the most amount of money is outstanding (early in the loan), and hence earns more of the interest at the beginning of the loan (when the risk is high) and less in the ending months (when the amount still due is less). In Problem 94, Portia was paying a true 6 percent interest rate because she had the full use of the money for the year's period. In Problem 95, however, she began paying back the money immediately, and so she did not have the full use of all of it for the loan period. This means that the lender's risk is not as high in Problem 95 as it was in Problem 94, but since he got the use of the repayment faster he was in reality earning more interest than in Problem 94. Where the debtor repays the loan in monthly installments, the quoted "6 percent" interest rate is a sham. Such a rate (called an "add-on" rate), measured from the lender's risk, is actuarially much higher, and works out to 10.9 percent.

Where, as in Problem 96, the monthly repayments are coupled with the loan of less money (the "discount"), the lender's risk is even lower. Correspondingly, the actuarial rate is higher: 11.58 percent.

How can you determine the actual interest rate? A rough formula (the "constant ratio" method) is as follows:

$$\frac{(2 \times \text{number of payment periods in year})(\text{finance charge})}{(\text{amount financed})(\text{total of payments plus one})}$$

This formula is not strictly accurate because it does not consider the effect of compounding, or the issue mentioned above that the finance charge is repaid faster than the principal because it is earned earlier. The true actuarial rate will be slightly lower than that produced by this formula, but charts or computer programs are required to figure it out.[2]

ANTONELLI v. NEUMANN
Court of Appeals, Florida, 1988
537 So. 2d 1027

Baskin, Judge.

Vincent and Mary Ann Antonelli appeal a final judgment entered in an action Ken Neumann brought to recover sums evidenced by two promissory

---

2. Further, this formula will not predict the discount rate. There is a complicated formula that will do so, but I will spare you the explanation and instead refer you to the relevant tables. Tables for computing Truth in Lending disclosures are discussed below.

notes executed in conjunction with a $100,000 loan from Neumann to the Antonellis. Following a non-jury trial, the trial court found that appellants failed to establish their usury defense by clear and convincing evidence and entered judgment in favor of Neumann. This appeal ensued. We reverse. . . .

The four prerequisites for proving a usurious transaction are: (1) an express or implied loan; (2) an understanding between the parties that the money must be repaid; (3) an agreement to pay a rate of interest in excess of the legal rate; and (4) a corrupt intent to take more than the legal rate for the use of the money loaned. Dixon v. Sharp, 276 So. 2d 817 (Fla. 1973); Rollins v. Odom, 519 So. 2d 652 (Fla. 1st DCA), *review denied*, 529 So. 2d 695 (Fla. 1988); Rebman v. Flagship First Natl. Bank, 472 So. 2d 1360 (Fla. 2d DCA 1985); Bermil Corp. v. Sawyer, 353 So. 2d 579 (Fla. 3d DCA 1977). On March 3, 1981, the parties executed two agreements: (1) an agreement in which Neumann consented to deposit $100,000 in the trust account of the Antonellis' attorney, to be held in trust until the parties executed two promissory notes for loans totaling $100,000, and (2) an agreement whereby Neumann would perform landscape consulting work on the Antonellis' condominium project. Neumann loaned appellants $100,000; the Antonellis executed two $50,000 notes at the statutory legal interest limit of 18% per annum. §687.03, Fla. Stat. (Supp. 1980). The Antonellis remitted timely interest payments in addition to payments equal to 2% of the loan amount. The Antonellis marked each 2% check "landscape consultant fee." Subsequently, the Antonellis ceased making payments. At issue is whether the parties agreed that Neumann would receive a higher rate of interest than the 18% stated on the notes. Where, as here, the notes appeared to require the legal rate of interest, the borrower has the burden of proving that the parties employed a corrupt device to conceal a usurious transaction and that it was in the full contemplation of the parties. See Davanzo v. Miami Natl. Bank, 301 So. 2d 797 (Fla. 3d DCA 1974), *cert. denied*, 315 So. 2d 185 (Fla. 1975). "The requisite corrupt or purposeful intent . . . is satisfactorily proved if the evidence establishes that the charging or receiving of excessive interest was done with the knowledge of the lender," *Dixon*, 276 So. 2d at 821, and "is determined by a consideration of all the circumstances surrounding the transaction." *Rollins*, 519 So. 2d at 657.

In determining whether an agreement is usurious, the court may disregard the form of the agreement and consider the substance of the transaction. Growth Leasing, Ltd. v. Gulfview Advertiser, Inc., 448 So. 2d 1224 (Fla. 2d DCA 1984); May v. U.S. Leasing Corp., 239 So. 2d 73 (Fla. 4th DCA 1970); Kay v. Amendola, 129 So. 2d 170 (Fla. 2d DCA 1961). Thus, notations on the checks describing the payments as consulting work are not dispositive of the issue. Cf. *American Acceptance Corp. v. Schoenthaler*, 391 F.2d 64 (5th Cir.) (although discount charged is not set forth in note, note was device to avoid usury and did not constitute actual transaction), *cert. denied*, 392 U.S. 928, 88 S. Ct. 2287, 20 L. Ed. 2d 1387 (1968). "Where . . . an illogical and spurious transaction is entered into for the purpose of making that which is usurious appear otherwise, the lenders will not be excused from the penalties of the usury statute by pleading ignorance of the law or that they did not intend usury." *Lee Constr. Corp. v. Newman*, 143 So. 2d 222, 225 (Fla. 3d DCA), *cert. denied*, 148 So. 2d 280 (Fla. 1962).

In the case before us, the record contains a letter dated October 4, 1981, from Neumann to the Antonellis. In that letter Neumann states:

> Please acknowledge the two photostatic documents herein as verification of the two promissory notes as well as the date of departure from Joliet. The dates appearing on the promissory notes will iniciate [sic] the point from which the interest will be accrued. Have you found a way around paying the 20% as agreed, or will you have to pay the 18% and the additional 2% under a different pretext? If my my [sic] calculations are accurate at a 20% rate, the *monthely* [sic] interest due is $833.00, and the monthly interest due for 18% is $750.00. Multiplied by 5 month intervals, the interest due would be $4165.00 and $3750.00 respectively. Of course the 20% rate sounds better, but if complications are a sure result, we can work out further details later. Please note that the note dated on April 20 is now due on September 20, 1981, and the note dated on May 19, 1981 will be due on October 19, 1981. Consequently, please remit the one check as quickly as possible and the other on the 19 of October. My financial obligations on this end to the bank definately [sic] require punctuality. Thank you for your cooperation on this matter, and don't foreget [sic] to send me a set of prints of the project.

The letter reflects Neumann's intention to require more than the legal rate of interest. The description of the Antonellis' payments of an additional 2% as landscape consulting fees for their condominium project was merely a contrivance to conceal a usurious transaction. The trial court inferred that the 2% payments were credits against the landscape agreement, but a review of the evidence fails to support that conclusion. Thus, we hold that the trial court's decision was clearly erroneous.

Additional indicia of usury appear in the record. First, the landscape consulting agreement, executed contemporaneously with the loan agreement, provided that Neumann would be paid $1,000 per unit and 5% of amounts exceeding $150,000 "upon the closing of the sale of each individual apartment." The 2% payments, purportedly for consulting fees, however, were made simultaneously with each interest payment. Thus, the payments were made in advance of the condominium sales, contrary to the

a recommendation that the states adopt special small-loan legislation. A Model Small Loan Law was promulgated and adopted in many states. The basic compromise reached in this small-loan legislation was that in consumer loan transactions higher interest rates should be permitted, but in order to charge these higher rates the lenders would have to submit to much regulation of the terms of the deal.

Where legislative relief was not forthcoming, lenders tried a host of devices to escape from the low rates imposed by the usury statutes. Many of these took advantage of the calculation possibilities described above (add-on rates, discount rates, etc.), or played some of the tricks described below. The courts, sympathetic to the lenders' dilemma, went along with some outrageous fictions in order to allow commercially reasonable rates to be imposed even though, according to actuarial calculations, the usury rate was being shattered.

If we define interest as the charge a lender makes for the use of the money, that charge must be high enough to not only cover the lender's expenses (including the lost interest the loaned amount would have brought if invested elsewhere) but produce a profit as well. If the usury rate is set artificially low, a lender might be tempted to play around with the components of the interest rate, as in the next Problem.

PROBLEM 97

Two days before their wedding, John and Mary decided to buy a new car. They called around town asking about financing and finally went to Facade Motors, which had quoted them a 10 percent interest rate. When they went to sign the contract, however, they discovered that in addition to a rate of 10 percent, the amount financed included charges for "credit investigation," "service charge," "legal examination," and "secretarial services." Is Facade Motors guilty of usury? See Henslee v. Madison Guar. Sav. & Loan Assn., 297 Ark. 183, 760 S.W.2d 842 (1989).

The Morris Plan, invented around 1910 by Arthur J. Morris, a Virginia attorney, makes use of the add-on method to avoid low interest ceilings for loans made by a financial institution. Under the Morris plan, weekly installment payments on the loan are placed in a non-interest-bearing "investment certificate" account at the lending institution. At the maturity of the loan, the financial institution pays itself by debiting the account. If the state statute would permit a maximum interest rate of 8 percent, and the bank makes a $100 loan using that base rate but requires this *weekly* investment, the actuarial rate is really 17.7 percent on an annual basis.

PROBLEM 98

State law put an 18 percent limit on loans to consumers, but allowed corporate borrowers to agree to any rate at all. Sandy and Dave Bunge decided to borrow $2,000 for their vacation in Europe. When they went down to Nightflyer Finance Company, the loan officer told them that the deal would go through only if they agreed to incorporate and then borrow the money at a 30 percent rate. They agreed to this, and all the necessary papers (including the promissory note of their corporation, which they personally guaranteed) were drawn up and signed. Later the Bunges consulted their lawyer about this, and she promptly filed suit on their behalf, contending that the loan was usurious. The corporate exemption from the usury statute is clear on its face: corporations can agree to any interest rate. Should the courts carve an exception here? See Havens v. Woodfill, 266 N.E.2d 221 (Ind. App. 1971).

IN RE VENTURE MORTGAGE FUND, L.P.[4]
United States Court of Appeals, Second Circuit, 2002
282 F.3d 185

JACOBS, Circuit Judge.

Appellants Theodore Brodie and ATASSCO appeal from an order entered in the United States District Court for the Southern District of New York (Berman, J.), affirming the order of the United States Bankruptcy Court for the Southern District of New York (Bernstein, C.J.), expunging under New York's usury laws unsecured claims filed by appellants against the bankrupt estate of Venture Mortgage Fund, L.P. ("Venture Mortgage"). Venture Mortgage was controlled and operated by David Schick, another debtor in this bankruptcy proceeding; in 1997, Schick pleaded guilty to bank and wire fraud in connection with a Ponzi scheme conducted at least in part through Venture Mortgage. ATASSCO is an entity used by Allen Sausen and Leonard Sausen for the purpose of investing with Venture

---

4. Footnotes in this case have been renumbered for clarity.

Mortgage and Schick. The record does not indicate what kind of entity ATASSCO may be.

On appeal, appellants emphasize that they were not loan-sharks victimizing Schick, but (to the contrary) were the victims of Schick's Ponzi scheme. They thus argue that the voiding of the loans does not comport with the purposes of New York's usury statutes. Specifically, appellants argue (i) that the usury statutes are designed to protect the poor from their desperation, not to protect Ponzi schemers; (ii) that they were lured into the transactions by a 27% interest rate proposed and dangled before them by the borrower and that they therefore lacked any intent to violate the usury statutes; and (iii) that because Schick drafted the loan documents and was a lawyer whom they had once consulted on an unrelated matter, and in whom they placed trust concerning the legality of the loans, a special relationship existed that estops the trustees (in Schick's shoes) from asserting the defense of usury to void the loans.

We agree with both the bankruptcy court and the district court that the loans at issue, bearing annual interest exceeding 25%, violate the plain language of New York's criminal usury statute. See N.Y. Penal Law §190.40 (McKinney 2001). It has not been contested—here, in the bankruptcy court, or in the district court—that a transaction that violates New York's criminal usury statute is void ab initio, either by virtue of §5-511 of New York's General Obligations Law or (as trustee's counsel argues) by reason of public policy. We affirm because the arguments interposed to defeat voiding lack merit. . . .

I

In the early 1990s, Schick confided to appellants a wonderful business opportunity: Schick needed to post "earnest money" in escrow in order to bid on distressed mortgage pools. The mortgage pools, once acquired cheaply at auction, could easily and immediately be resold at substantial profit (so-called "mortgage flip" transactions). To get this "earnest money," Schick solicited funds from appellants (and many others) and assured them that their investments would remain untouched in the escrow accounts, and would be returned to them "risk-free" with interest exceeding 20% per annum. On that basis, Brodie loaned $500,000 to Venture Mortgage in August 1992 and ATASSCO, along with several other investors, loaned $2.75 million in July 1995. Venture Mortgage punctiliously met all of its obligations on these loan transactions at the promised interest rates.

Pleased and enthusiastic, appellants were soon importuning Schick for new opportunities to make more such loans. After a while, Schick yielded to his victims and agreed to accept, on behalf of Venture Mortgage, three loans at an annual interest rate of 27%: in December 1995, Brodie "rolled over" $200,000 in principal from his earlier loan, and ATASSCO loaned $1.1 million in new funds; in February 1996, ATTASCO loaned an additional $850,000. These three loans are the transactions voided by the bankruptcy court.

In May 1996, several swindled creditors filed an involuntary Chapter 11 petition against Schick and the various entities controlled by Schick. Appellants filed timely claims against the respective bankruptcy estates to recover on their loans. The bankruptcy trustees filed motions to expunge appellants' claims on the grounds of usury. The bankruptcy court granted the motions to expunge, and the district court affirmed.

II

Appellants argue that the legislative purpose of New York's usury statutes is "'to protect desperately poor people from the consequences of their own desperation.'" Seidel v. 18 East 17th Street Owners, Inc., 79 N.Y.2d 735, 586 N.Y.S.2d 240, 598 N.E.2d 7, 9 (1992) (quoting Schneider v. Phelps, 41 N.Y.2d 238, 243, 391 N.Y.S.2d 568, 359 N.E.2d 1361 (1977)). Although Schick, enriched by large fraudulent loans, cannot be described as desperately poor, and although appellants cannot be described as loan-sharks (and are, if anything, the victims of the transactions), the New York usury laws do not recognize these distinctions. "It is axiomatic that the plain meaning of a statute controls its interpretation, and that judicial review must end at the statute's unambiguous terms. Legislative history and other tools of interpretation may be relied upon only if the terms of the statute are ambiguous." Lee v. Bankers Trust Co., 166 F.3d 540, 544 (2d Cir. 1999) (internal citations omitted). Therefore, the particular distinctions that the appellants draw furnish no ground for reversing the order of expungement.

Appellants also argue that, since they were lured by the borrower into entering loan transactions that (notwithstanding the usurious rate of interest) were in fact grossly disadvantageous to them because Schick planned to steal the principal, they lacked any intent to violate the usury statute. However, the application of New York's usury statutes does not depend upon a finding of intent. "A loan is usurious if the lender intends to take and receive a rate of interest in excess of that allowed by law even though the lender has no specific intent to violate the usury laws." Hammond v. Marrano, 88 A.D.2d 758, 451 N.Y.S.2d 484, 485 (App. Div. 4th Dep't 1982).

Finally, appellants argue that the trustees are estopped from asserting usury as a defense to these loans. The New York Court of Appeals has "recognized that a borrower may be estopped from interposing a usury defense when, through a special relationship with a lender, the borrower induces reliance on the legality of the transaction." Seidel, 586 N.Y.S.2d 240, 598 N.E.2d at 11. The basis for the estoppel claim is that Schick drafted the loan documents, was a lawyer whom Appellants had once consulted on an unrelated matter, and was a person Appellants trusted to assure the legal enforceability of the loans. We agree with the district court, however, that the bankruptcy court did not clearly err in finding that (i) the record discloses no special relationship of the kind contemplated in Seidel, 586 N.Y.S.2d 240, 598 N.E.2d at 10-12;[5] and (ii) even if there were such a special relationship, neither Brodie nor ATASSCO relied on Schick for any advice that the loan transactions conformed to law.[6]

We therefore affirm.

QUOTES FOR THE ATTORNEY'S ARSENAL:
"SNIFFING OUT USURY"

The form of the contract is not conclusive of the question. The desire of lenders to exact more than the law permits and the willingness of borrowers to concede whatever may be demanded to obtain temporary relief from financial embarrassment have resulted in a variety of shifts and cunning devices designed to evade the law. The character of a transaction is not to be judged by the mere verbal raiment in which the parties have clothed it, but by its true character as disclosed by the whole evidence. If, when so judged, it appears to be a loan or forbearance of money for a greater rate of interest than that allowed by law, the statute is violated and its penalties incurred, no matter what device the parties may have employed to conceal the real character of their dealings.

Springer v. Mack, 222 Ill. App. 72, 75 (1921).

PROBLEM 99

Because 365 (or, in a leap year, 366) is an awkward number to work with, Octopus National Bank decided to round it off and use 360 as the

---

5. The bankruptcy court found that "the only 'special relationship' they shared was the symbiotic one existing between an investor with a lot of cash and a deal maker who could apparently put it to good and very profitable uses." In re Venture Mortgage Fund, L.P., 245 B.R. 460, 477 (Bankr. S.D.N.Y. 2000).

6. The bankruptcy court found that "In truth, the overriding—indeed the only—impetus impelling [Appellants] to invest with Schick was the promise of future riches that seemed too good to be true." In re Venture Mortgage, 245 B.R. at 478.

number of days in a year for purposes of loan computations. If ONB is at the maximum legal rate of interest already, does this method of calculation cause it usury trouble? See American Timber v. First Natl. Bank, 511 F.2d 980 (9th Cir. 1975).

QUOTES FOR THE ATTORNEY'S ARSENAL: "DICKENS ON USURY"

In like manner, did young Ralph Nickleby [a budding usurer] avoid all those minute and intricate calculations of odd days, which nobody who has worked sums in simple-interest can fail to have found most embarrassing, by establishing the one general rule that all sums of principal and interest should be paid on pocket-money day, that is to say, on Saturday: and that whether a loan were contracted on the Monday, or on the Friday, the amount of interest should be, in both cases, the same. Indeed he argued, and with great show of reason, that it ought to be rather more for one day than for five, inasmuch as the borrower might in the former case be very fairly presumed to be in great extremity, otherwise he would not borrow at all with such odds against him.

Charles Dickens, Nicholas Nickleby, Chapter 1 (1839).

Today most states have a general interest statute setting the rate considered not usurious, varying widely in rate. In New York it is 16 percent, while in Illinois it is only 5 percent. The rates of some states were set so low (and, for the reasons mentioned above, were difficult for the legislature to change), the national economy was thought to be affected. Congress passed the Depository Institutions Deregulation and Monetary Control Act of 1980, part of which, 12 U.S.C. §1735f-7, preempts state usury statutes in certain situations,[7] substituting a fluctuating federal rate. The loans affected are first mortgage loans secured by residential real estate and loans made by institutions insured by the Federal Deposit Insurance Corporation. Of particular interest to consumers is that mobile homes are called "residential manufactured homes" and their financing is exempt from state usury laws only if the lender complies with consumer protection regulations promulgated by the Federal Home Loan Bank Board.[8]

---

7. Section 501(b)(2) permits the states to opt out of the federal preemption if they enacted a statute doing so before April 1, 1983. A number of states did opt out, though some have subsequently opted back in, leaving (as I understand it) only Iowa and Wisconsin and the Commonwealth of Puerto Rico out of the federal scheme (and Wisconsin has liberalized its usury laws so that this hardly matters). Maine engaged in a partial preemption. See Consumer Cred. Guide (CCH) para. 510.

8. The regulations can be found at 12 C.F.R. §590.4.

PROBLEM 100

The State of Georgia's interest rate for consumer mobile home financing was 10 percent. The penalty for willful violations was double the amount of the finance charge. This statute, however, was over-ridden for a period by the federal statute mentioned above. Using the federal rate, the mobile home lender charged more than 20 percent interest. The contract for the repayment of the debt, which was se-cured by the mobile home, included a clause providing that in the event of default the lender could repossess the mobile home without warning. Assume that such a clause is forbidden by the federal reg-ulations mentioned above. If so, what remedy is there to the injured borrower? See Quiller v. Barclays American/Credit, Inc., 727 F.2d 1067 (11th Cir. 1984), *aff'd en banc,* 764 F.2d 1400 (11th Cir. 1985).

In addition to this confusion, the legislative landscape is a mess. All states have a basic usury statute, but also have enacted special statutes permitting some lenders (banks, small-loan companies, retail sellers, the governor's brother, etc.) to charge higher rates. For a collection of all the state statutes on point (state by state), see the Consumer Credit Guide (CCH).

D. *Time-Price Differential*

PROBLEM 101

When Marmaduke Pointdextre decided to sell the family home, the only buyer he could find was a tradesman named John Wells. Wells agreed to buy the home for $80,000, but when Pointdextre heard that Wells could not finance a mortgage with a financial insti-tution and Pointdextre would have to take a mortgage for the pur-chase price, he upped the home's price to $130,000. Wells agreed to pay it, and the paperwork was signed. Wells's business had a bad spell and he was unable to make payments on the debt. When Pointdextre threatened foreclosure, Wells filed suit against him, ar-guing that the transaction was usurious. Pointdextre replied that the difference between the price of the home if cash were paid and the price where the seller was willing to wait and chance nonpayment was not the taking of interest and thus could not be usurious. Is this cash-price/time-price differential the exaction of interest?

In the English case of Beete v. Bidgood, 108 Eng. Rep. 792 (K.B. 1827), the court agreed with the Pointdextre argument and established the rule that in the sale of property the time-price differential was neither a loan nor a forbearance of money and hence was never usurious. The doctrine, avoiding the artificially low ceilings set by 6 percent usury statutes, proved popular in the courts. In Hogg v. Ruffner, 66 U.S. 115, 118 (1861), the United States Supreme Court explained it all:

> But it is manifest that if A propose[s] to sell to B a tract of land for $10,000 in cash, or for $20,000 payable in ten annual installments, and if B prefers to pay the larger sum to gain time, the contract cannot be called usurious. A vendor may prefer $100 in hand to double the sum in expectancy, and a purchaser may prefer the greater price with the longer credit, and one who will not distinguish between things that differ may say, with apparent truth, that B pays a hundred per cent for forbearance, and may assert that such a contract is usurious but whatever truth there may be in the premises, the conclusion is manifestly erroneous. Such a contract has none of the characteristics of usury; it is not for the loan of money, or forbearance of a debt.

The time-price differential effectively shields credit sales from the usury statutes, a result so desirable that it was reached by all state supreme courts considering the question except for those of Arkansas[9] and Nebraska, where the confusion this judicial honesty caused was eventually resolved by legislative means. The doctrinal freedom represented by the time-price differential exemption, however, was abused, so that most states enacted retail installment sales acts that specified the maximum amount that credit sellers could charge as a time-price differential (that is, interest). We will consider these statutes in Chapter 10 infra. For now it is enough to note that the fiction that the time-price differential was not interest no longer matters. Both federal and state law now treat it as if it were interest, and the free ride suggested by cases such as Hogg v. Ruffner is now over. See Cornist v. B.J.T. Auto Sales, Inc., 272 F.3d 322 (6th Cir. 2001) (charging credit buyers of automobiles more than cash buyers triggers the Truth in Lending Act).

Against all this background many credit laws were enacted, and eventually the federal government stepped into the picture with its own attempt to organize rate disclosure. For an interesting historical exploration of rate regulation, see Christopher L. Peterson, Truth, Understanding, and High-Cost Consumer Credit: The Historical Context of the Truth in Lending Act, 55 Fla. L. Rev. 807 (2003).

---

9. Arkansas's constitution forbids charging more than 17 percent interest, and the Arkansas Supreme Court has vigorously enforced that prohibition, causing some financial distress. For the most recent battle, one involving payday lending, see McGhee v. Arkansas State Bd. of Collection Agencies, 375 Ark. 52, 2008 WL 4823540 (2008).

II. TRUTH IN LENDING: THE FEDERAL RESPONSE

A. Introduction

By the middle of the 20th century, usury law was chaotic, with the courts and legislatures conspiring to permit avoidance of the statutes on point. From the consumer's point of view, this chaos meant that it was impossible to shop for credit because a quotation of any given rate meant nothing at all. Was it a true actuarial rate? Add-on? Discount? Were there special extra fees that had to be paid in addition to the quoted rate?

The solution to all this was a federal statute that regulated the computation and disclosure of the terms of consumer credit transactions. The statute is the Truth in Lending Act, 15 U.S.C. §§1601 et seq. (Title I of the Consumer Credit Protection Act of 1968).[10] It is important to realize that the statute is *not* a usury statute; nowhere in the statute are rates set. Instead TILA is a *disclosure* statute. It mandates uniform methods of computation and explanation of the terms of the deal, so that the informed consumer can rely on the rates disclosed when comparing them with those disclosed by other possible lenders.

The Act requires the Federal Reserve Board to promulgate a regulation implementing the Act; the Board responded with Regulation Z, 12 C.F.R. §226. It is every bit as much fun to read as it sounds (the kind of thing Mark Twain once described as "chloroform in print"), but remember this: knowledge is power. A mastery of the minutiae of TILA and Regulation Z puts you in charge of any situation in which the statute comes up. No one can learn all these consumer statutes (and their interrelationship) overnight. If you already have a grounding in the area, everyone will listen to what you say. Of course, some attorneys have no choice. If you become counsel for a financial institution or a large retailer, Regulation Z will become the object of your constant study. For expert commentaries on TIL, see R. Clontz, J. Douglas, Truth in Lending Manual (6th ed. 1991); Ralph J. Rohner, Fred H. Miller, Truth in Lending (2000); National Consumer Law Center, Truth in Lending (5th ed. 2003, with yearly supplements).

You should also know that Regulation Z is further explained by the Federal Reserve Board's Official Staff Commentary, which is the sole interpretive vehicle of the Regulation and as such has the force of law. The Commentary is updated at least annually, when the Board publishes

---

10. Actually, the technical name of Title I of the Consumer Credit Protection Act is "Consumer Credit Cost Disclosure," but no one calls it that, instead preferring to accept the invitation in §101: "This title may be cited as the Truth in Lending Act."

proposed amendments for comment by the public. The Board also has promulgated model forms for use in compliance with Regulation Z. If the creditor uses these forms without significant change, the creditor is completely insulated from liability for disclosure violations (even if, for example, a court should hold that the model form does not comply with the statute or Regulation Z), TILA §130(f). The forms are found at the end of the Regulation as appendices.

B. Scope

The original version of TILA applied to agricultural loans as well as consumer loans, but the major 1980 revision of the statute, called the Truth in Lending Simplification Act, limited TIL to credit extensions made primarily for personal, family, or household purposes. It is particularly crucial that attorneys be able to tell what transactions are covered by TILA, so the next few Problems explore that issue.

PROBLEM 102

Portia Moot's law practice revolved around the following areas: bankruptcy, domestic problems, and criminal defense. Many of her clients were strapped for cash, so she permitted them to pay their bills over a year's period, having them sign a written agreement to make monthly payments. She charged them no interest. Should she be giving them TIL statements when she works out this payment arrangement? See Reg. Z §226.2(a)'s definition of "creditor"; see also §226.3. The footnote to that definition of "creditor" is also important here. How authoritative is the footnote? See Reg. Z §226.2(b)(4). What would you do if you were Portia to avoid TILA's clutches?

Why would TILA cover transactions in which no finance charge is being imposed? Even before the statutory language addressed the issue (as it now does), the Federal Reserve Board promulgated its "more than four installments" rule as part of the original version of Regulation Z. The rule requires TIL statements in consumer credit transactions payable in more than four installments even though no interest is being charged. This rule was promptly challenged as an abuse of the Board's authority and the issue went right to the Supreme Court.

MOURNING v. FAMILY PUBLICATIONS SERVICE
United States Supreme Court, 1973
411 U.S. 356

Mr. Chief Justice BURGER delivered the opinion of the Court.

We granted the writ of certiorari in this case to resolve whether the Federal Reserve Board exceeded its authority under §105 of the Truth in Lending Act in promulgating that portion of Regulation Z commonly referred to as the "Four Installment Rule."

Respondent is a Delaware corporation which solicits subscriptions to several well-known periodicals. In 1969, one of respondent's door-to-door salesmen called on the petitioner, a 73-year-old widow residing in Florida, and sold her a five-year subscription to four magazines. Petitioner agreed to pay $3.95 immediately and to remit a similar amount monthly for 30 months. The contract form she signed contained a clause stating that the subscriptions could not be canceled and an acceleration provision similar to that found in many installment undertakings, providing that any default in installment payments would render the entire balance due. The contract did not recite the total purchase price of the subscriptions or the amount which remained unpaid after the initial remittance, and made no reference to service or finance charges. The total debt assumed by the petitioner was $122.45; the balance due after the initial payment was $118.50.

Petitioner made the initial payment, began to receive the magazines for which she had contracted, and then defaulted. Respondent declared the entire balance of $118.50 due and threatened legal action. Petitioner brought this suit in United States District Court, alleging that respondent had failed to comply with the disclosure provisions of the Truth in Lending Act. She sought recovery of the statutory penalty and reimbursement for the costs of the litigation, including reasonable attorney's fees.

In support of her claim, petitioner submitted to the District Court a series of "dunning" letters which she had received from respondent. One letter, dated December 16, 1969, stated:

> After making the terms of our contract clear to you, we went ahead in good faith and had your subscriptions entered for the entire periods you had agreed to take. The contract you signed is: Not subject to cancellation after acceptance or verification.
>
> Knowing, therefore, the obligations we have incurred in your name, we feel confident that you will continue your magazine subscriptions and make the convenient monthly payments regularly and promptly.

A second letter, received a week later from respondent's agent, declared:

> After an account is three months delinquent it is brought to my attention. I feel that you should realize that you are receiving our merchandise which we have paid for.

Had you dealt directly with the publishers yourself, you would have had to pay them in advance for the magazines.

Again, let me remind you that we have ordered these magazines in advance and that you have incurred an obligation to repay us. <u>This is a credit account, and as such must be repaid by you on a monthly basis</u>, much the same as if you had purchased any other type of merchandise on a monthly budget plan. [Emphasis supplied; underlined words are emphasized in the original letter.]

Respondent admitted sending each of the above letters to petitioner. In addition, respondent submitted one affidavit to the District Court, describing the nature of the contracts which it offered to its clients. The affidavit stated that a customer who ordered magazine subscriptions from respondent was required to pay for all magazines during the first half of the contract term. Thus, according to the affidavit, at all times during the course of contract, a purchaser who has complied with the terms of the contract has paid for more magazines than he has received. Respondent did not, however, submit any affidavit to the court contesting any of the facts stated in its "dunning" letters. On this record, both parties moved for summary judgment, declaring explicitly that no factual question remained undecided.

Section 121 of the Truth in Lending Act requires merchants who regularly extend credit, with attendant finance charges, to disclose certain contract information "to each person to whom consumer credit is extended and upon whom a finance charge is or may be imposed. . . ." Among other relevant facts, the merchant must, where applicable, list the cash price of the merchandise or service sold, the amount of finance and other charges, and the rate of the charges. Failure to disclose renders the seller liable to the consumer for a penalty of twice the amount of the finance charge, but in no event less than $100 or more than $1,000. The creditor may also be assessed for the costs of the litigation, including reasonable attorney's fees and, in certain circumstances not relevant here, may be the subject of criminal charges.

Section 105 of the Act provides:

The [Federal Reserve] Board shall prescribe regulations to carry out the purposes of [the Act]. These regulations may contain such classifications, differentiations, or other provisions, and may provide for such adjustments and exceptions for any class of transactions, as in the judgment of the Board are necessary or proper to effectuate the purposes of [the Act], to prevent circumvention or evasion thereof, or to facilitate compliance therewith.

Accordingly, the Board has promulgated Regulation Z, which defines the circumstances in which a seller who regularly extends credit must make the disclosures outlined in §128. The regulation provides that disclosure is necessary whenever credit is offered to a consumer "for which either a finance charge is or may be imposed or which pursuant to an agreement, is or may be payable in more than four installments."

Relying on the rule governing credit transactions of more than four installments, the District Court granted summary judgment for petitioner. The court found that respondent had extended credit to petitioner, which by agreement was payable in more than four installments, but had failed to comply with the disclosure provisions of the Act.

The Court of Appeals reversed, holding that the Board had exceeded its statutory authority in promulgating the regulation upon which the District Court relied. The regulation was found to conflict with §121 of the Act since it required that disclosure be made in regard to some credit transactions in which a finance charge had not been imposed. As an alternative ground for its decision, the Court of Appeals held that the regulation created a conclusive presumption that credit payments made in more than four installments included a finance charge. Relying on Schlesinger v. State of Wisconsin, 270 U.S. 230, 46 S. Ct. 260, 70 L. Ed. 557 (1926), and Heiner v. Donnan, 285 U.S. 312, 52 S. Ct. 358, 76 L. Ed. 772 (1932), the court concluded that such an irrebuttable presumption of fact violated the Due Process Clause of the Fifth Amendment.

I

Passage of the Truth in Lending Act in 1968 culminated several years of congressional study and debate as to the propriety and usefulness of imposing mandatory disclosure requirements on those who extend credit to consumers in the American market. By the time of passage, it had become abundantly clear that the use of consumer credit was expanding at an extremely rapid rate. From the end of World War II through 1967, the amount of such credit outstanding had increased from $5.6 billion to $95.9 billion, a rate of growth more than 4½ times as great as that of the economy. Yet, as the congressional hearings revealed, consumers remained remarkably ignorant of the nature of their credit obligations and of the costs of deferring payment. Because of the divergent, and at times fraudulent, practices by which consumers were informed of the terms of the credit extended to them, many consumers were prevented from shopping for the best terms available and, at times, were prompted to assume liabilities they could not meet. Joseph Barr, then Under Secretary of the Treasury, noted in testifying before a Senate subcommittee that such blind economic activity is inconsistent with the efficient functioning of a free economic system such as ours, whose ability to provide desired material at the lowest cost is dependent on the asserted preferences and informed choices of *consumers*.

The Truth in Lending Act was designed to remedy the problems which had developed. The House Committee on Banking and Currency reported, in regard to the then proposed legislation:

> [B]y requiring all creditors to disclose credit information in a uniform manner, and by requiring all additional mandatory charges imposed by the creditor as an incident to credit be included in the computation of the applicable percentage rate, the American consumer will be given the information he needs to compare the cost of credit and to make the best informed decision on the use of credit.

This purpose was stated explicitly in §102 of the legislation enacted:

> The Congress finds that economic stabilization would be enhanced and the competition among the various financial institutions and other firms engaged in the extension of consumer credit would be strengthened by the informed use of credit. The informed use of credit results from an awareness of the cost thereof by consumers. It is the purpose of this subchapter to assure a meaningful disclosure of credit terms so that the consumer will be able to compare more readily the various credit terms available to him and avoid the uninformed use of credit.

The hearings held by Congress reflect the difficulty of the task it sought to accomplish. Whatever legislation was passed had to deal not only with the myriad forms in which credit transactions then occurred, but also with those which would be devised in the future. To accomplish its desired objective, Congress determined to lay the structure of the Act broadly and to entrust its construction to an agency with the necessary experience and resources to monitor its operation. Section 105 delegated to the Federal Reserve Board broad authority to promulgate regulations necessary to render the Act effective. The language employed evinces the awareness of Congress that some creditors would attempt to characterize their transactions so as to fall one step outside whatever boundary Congress attempted to establish. It indicates as well the clear desire of Congress to insure that the Board had adequate power to deal with such attempted evasion. In addition to granting to the Board the authority normally given to administrative agencies to promulgate regulations designed to "carry out the purposes" of the Act, Congress specifically provided, as noted earlier, that the regulations may define classifications and exceptions to insure compliance with the Act. . . . The Board was thereby empowered to define such classifications as were reasonably necessary to insure that the objectives of the Act were fulfilled, no matter what adroit or unscrupulous practices were employed by those extending credit to consumers.

One means of circumventing the objectives of the Truth in Lending Act, as passed by Congress, was that of "burying" the cost of credit in the price of goods sold. Thus in many credit transactions in which creditors claimed that no finance charge had been imposed, the creditor merely assumed the cost of extending credit as an expense of doing business, to be recouped as part of the price charged in the transaction.[11] Congress was well aware, from its extensive studies, of the possibility that merchants could use such devices to evade the disclosure requirements of the Act. The Committee hearings are replete with suggestions that such manipulation would render the Act a futile gesture in the case of goods normally sold by installment contract. Opponents of the bill contended that the reporting provisions would actually encourage merchants who had formerly segregated their credit costs not to do so. They predicted that the effect of the Act would thus be to reduce the amount of information available to the consumer, a result directly contrary to that which was intended. Proponents of the legislation claimed that the Act would enhance the consumer's ability to make an informed choice even if finance charges were hidden. In response to a claim that credit costs would be incorporated in the price of goods, Senator Douglas, who first proposed the Truth in Lending Act, stated:

> I would like to call to your attention, Senator, for purposes of the record, that this bill does not provide for judgment solely on the basis of the . . . annual interest rate or the total finance charges. It also provides that there shall be a statement of the cash price or delivery price of the property or service to be acquired. Both things are to be stated, price and finance charges, and the judgment of the consumer can be on the basis of both of these factors, not merely on one alone; and if a merchant tries to have a low finance charge and bury it in a high cash price or delivered price, then the purchaser can shop on price just as much as on the finance charges.

---

11. For example, two merchants might buy watches at wholesale for $20 which normally sell at retail for $40. Both might sell immediately to a consumer who agreed to pay $1 per week for 52 weeks. In one case, the merchant might claim that the price of the watch was $40 and that the remaining $12 constituted a charge for extending credit to the consumer. From the consumer's point of view, the credit charge represents the cost which he must pay for the privilege of deferring payment of the debt he has incurred. From the creditor's point of view, much simplified, the charge may represent the return which he might have earned had be been able to invest the proceeds from the sale of the watch from the date of the sale until the date of payment. The second merchant might claim that the price of the watch was $52 and that credit was free. The second merchant, like the first, has forgone the profits which he might have achieved by investing the sale proceeds from the day of the sale on. The second merchant may be said to have "buried" this cost in the price of the item sold. By whatever name, the $12 differential between the total payments and the price at which the merchandise could have been acquired is the cost of deferring payment.

It was against this legislative background that the Federal Reserve Board promulgated regulations governing enforcement of the Truth in Lending Act. In September, 1968, with the aid of an advisory board composed of representatives of diverse retail, lending, and consumer groups, the Board compiled and released a draft of proposed regulations. Comments and criticisms from interested parties were invited. After more than 1,800 responses were received and considered by the Board, the regulations were reviewed and published in the Federal Register.

The Four Installment Rule was included in the original published draft of the regulations and was not amended prior to its final adoption. The Board's objective in promulgating the rule was to prevent the Act from fulfilling the prophecy which its opponents had forecast. As J. L. Robertson, vice chairman of the Board of Governors, stated in an advisory letter issued a year later:

> The Board felt that it was imperative to include transactions involving more than four installments under the Regulation since without this provision the practice of burying the finance charge in the cash price, a practice which already exists in many cases, would have been encouraged by Truth in Lending. Obviously this would have been directly contrary to Congressional intent.

Furthermore, even as to sales in which it was impossible to determine what, if any, portion of the price recompensed the creditor for deferring payment, the regulation at least required that the consumer be provided with some information which would enable him to make an informed economic choice.

II

The standard to be applied in determining whether the Board exceeded the authority delegated to it under the Truth in Lending Act is well established under our prior cases. Where the empowering provision of a statute states simply that the agency may "make . . . such rules and regulations as may be necessary to carry out the provisions of this Act," we have held that the validity of a regulation promulgated thereunder will be sustained so long as it is "reasonably related to the purposes of the enabling legislation." Thorpe v. Housing Authority of City of Durham, 393 U.S. 268, 280-281, 89 S. Ct. 518, 525, 21 L. Ed. 2d 474 (1969). See also American Trucking Assns. v. United States, 344 U.S. 298, 73 S. Ct. 307, 97 L. Ed. 337 (1953). . . .

In light of our prior holdings and the legislative history of the Truth in Lending Act, we cannot agree with the conclusion of the Court of Appeals that the Board exceeded its statutory authority in promulgating the Four

Installment Rule. Congress was clearly aware that merchants could evade the reporting requirements of the Act by concealing credit charges. In delegating rulemaking authority to the Board, Congress emphasized the Board's authority to prevent such evasion. To hold that Congress did not intend the Board to take action against this type of manipulation would require us to believe that, despite this emphasis, Congress intended the obligations established by the Act to be open to evasion by subterfuges of which it was fully aware. . . . [T]he language of the enabling provision precludes us from accepting so narrow an interpretation of the Board's power.

Given that some remedial measure was authorized, the question remaining is whether the measure chosen is reasonably related to its objectives. We see no reason to doubt the Board's conclusion that the rule will deter creditors from engaging in the conduct which the Board sought to eliminate. The burdens imposed on creditors are not severe, when measured against the evils which are avoided. Furthermore, were it possible or financially feasible to delve into the intricacies of every credit transaction, it is clear that many creditors to whom the rule applies would be found to have charged for deferring payment, while claiming they had not. That some other remedial provision might be preferable is irrelevant. We have consistently held that where reasonable minds may differ as to which of several remedial measures should be chosen, courts should defer to the informed experience and judgment of the agency to whom Congress delegated appropriate authority.

Respondent contends, however, that the Four Installment Rule must be abrogated since it is "inconsistent" with portions of the enabling statute. The purported conflict arises because the statute specifically mentions disclosure only in regard to transactions in which a finance charge is in fact imposed, although the rule requires disclosure in some cases in which no such charge exists. Respondent argues that, in requiring disclosure as to some transactions, Congress intended to preclude the Board from imposing similar requirements as to any other transactions.

To accept respondent's argument would undermine the flexibility sought in vesting broad rulemaking authority in an administrative agency. In American Trucking Assns. v. United States, supra, we noted that it was not:

> a reasonable canon of interpretation that the draftsmen of acts delegating agency powers, as a practical and realistic matter, can or do include specific consideration of every evil sought to be corrected. . . . [N]o great acquaintance with practical affairs is required to know that such prescience, either in fact or in the minds of Congress, does not exist. Its very absence, moreover, is precisely one of the reasons why regulatory agencies such as the Commission are created, for it is the fond hope of their authors that they bring to their work the expert's familiarity with industry conditions which members of the delegating legislatures cannot be expected to possess. 344 U.S., at 309-310, 73 S. Ct., at 314 (citations omitted).

Neither the sections of the Truth in Lending Act which refer specifically to transactions involving finance charges nor any other sections of the Act indicate that Congress attempted to list comprehensively all types of transactions to which the Board's regulations might apply. To the contrary, §105's broad grant of rulemaking authority reflects an intention to rely on those attributes of agency administration recognized in *American Trucking*. We cannot then infer that references in the Act to transactions involving credit charges were intended to limit the deterrent measures which the Board might choose. . . .

Since the deterrent effect of the challenged rule clearly implements the objectives of the Act, respondent's contention is reduced to a claim that the rule is void because it requires disclosure by some creditors who do not charge for credit and thus need not be deterred. The fact that the regulation may affect such individuals does not impair its otherwise valid purpose. . . .

Where, as here, the transactions or conduct which Congress seeks to administer occur in myriad and changing forms, a requirement that a line be drawn which insures that not one blameless individual will be subject to the provisions of an act would unreasonably encumber effective administration and permit many clear violators to escape regulation entirely. . . . [T]his rationale applies to administrative agencies as well as to legislatures. . . .

We are also unable to accept respondent's argument that §130 does not allow imposition of a civil penalty in cases where no finance charge is involved but where a regulation requiring disclosure has been violated. Section 130 provides that the penalty assessed shall be twice the amount of the finance charge imposed, but not less than $100. Since the civil penalty prescribed is modest and the prohibited conduct clearly set out in the regulation, we need not construe this section as narrowly as a criminal statute providing graver penalties, such as prison terms. We have noted above that the objective sought in delegating rule making authority to an agency is to relieve Congress of the impossible burden of drafting a code explicitly covering every conceivable future problem. Congress cannot then be required to tailor civil penalty provisions so as to deal precisely with each step which the agency thereafter finds necessary. In light of the emphasis Congress placed on agency rule making and on private and administrative enforcement of the Act, we cannot conclude that Congress intended those who failed to comply with regulations to be subject to no penalty or to criminal penalties alone. As the District Court concluded, imposition of the minimum sanction is proper in cases such as this, where the finance charge is nonexistent or undetermined.

Finally, the Four Installment Rule does not conflict with the Fifth Amendment under our holdings in Schlesinger v. State of Wisconsin, 270

U.S. 230, 46 S. Ct. 260, 70 L. Ed. 557 (1926), and Heiner v. Donnan, 285 U.S. 312, 52 S. Ct. 358, 76 L. Ed. 772 (1932). In *Schlesinger* and *Heiner*, we held that certain taxing provisions violated the Due Process Clauses of the Fifth and Fourteenth Amendments because they conclusively presumed the existence of determinative facts. The challenged rule contains no comparable presumption. The rule was intended as a prophylactic measure; it does not presume that all creditors who are within its ambit assess finance charges, but, rather, imposes a disclosure requirement on all members of a defined class in order to discourage evasion by a substantial portion of that class.

The Truth in Lending Act reflects a transition in congressional policy from a philosophy of "Let the buyer beware" to one of "Let the seller disclose." By erecting a barrier between the seller and the prospective purchaser in the form of hard facts, Congress expressly sought "to . . . avoid the uninformed use of credit." 15 U.S.C. §1601. Some may claim that it is a relatively easy matter to calculate the total payments to which petitioner was committed by her contract with respondent; but at the time of sale, such computations are often not encouraged by the solicitor or performed by the purchaser. Congress has determined that such purchasers are in need of protection; the Four Installment Rule serves to insure that the protective disclosure mechanism chosen by Congress will not be circumvented.

That the approach taken may reflect what respondent views as an undue paternalistic concern for the consumer is beside the point. The statutory scheme is within the power granted to Congress under the Commerce Clause. It is not a function of the courts to speculate as to whether the statute is unwise or whether the evils sought to be remedied could better have been regulated in some other manner.

Reversed and remanded.

[The dissenting opinions of Justice DOUGLAS (joined by Justices STEWART and REHNQUIST) and Justice POWELL are omitted.]

NOTES AND QUESTIONS

1. This case made it clear that the United States Supreme Court will give great deference to the opinions of the Federal Reserve Board when TIL issues arise. Subsequent cases have expanded on this theme. In Ford Motor Credit Co. v. Milhollin, 44 U.S. 555, 565 (1980), the Court stated that Federal Reserve Board interpretations of TILA are binding on courts unless they are "demonstrably irrational." The Court rarely takes TILA cases (apparently detesting them), and the

few cases it has taken have all been resolved in favor of the Board's position. Creditors should take warning from this: what the Board says is highly likely to be what the courts will say too.

2. Following the case, subsequent amendments to the statute itself mandated that the "more than four installments" rule continue, so the authority of the Board to promulgate the rule is moot.

3. In the Problem prior to the case, could Portia have avoided the necessity of giving TIL statements if her repayment agreements were completely oral? See Reg. Z §226.2(a)(17).

4. If Portia required payment in exactly four installments but made her clients pay 10 percent interest, would she have to give TIL statements?

5. If Portia's clients are buying a business, does she have to give TIL statements? See Reg. Z §226.3.

QUOTES FOR THE ATTORNEY'S ARSENAL: "EXPERTISE OF THE BOARD"

[W]holly apart from jurisprudential considerations or congressional intent, deference to the Federal Reserve is compelled by necessity; a court that tries to chart a true course to the Act's purpose embarks upon a voyage without a compass when it disregards the agency's views. The concept of "meaningful disclosure" that animates TILA . . . cannot be applied in the abstract. Meaningful disclosure does not mean more disclosure. Rather, it describes a balance between "competing considerations of complete disclosure . . . and the need to avoid . . . [information overload]." And striking the appropriate balance is an empirical process that entails investigation into consumer psychology and that presupposes broad experience with credit practices. Administrative agencies are simply better suited than courts to engage in such a process.

Ford Motor Credit Co. v. Milhollin, 444 U.S. 555, 568-569 (1980).

PROBLEM 103

A spa assigns all its contracts with customers to a finance company that investigates the consumers before allowing them to join, prepares the paperwork, and is the corporate parent of the spa with which it is closely connected. If the spa goes bankrupt, can the consumers argue that the spa was only a front for the real "creditor," the finance company, which is therefore liable for the TIL mistakes of the spa? See Reg. Z §226.2(a)(17); TILA §131.

PROBLEM 104

When Portia Moot entered law school, she took out a substantial loan to finance her education. Must the lender give her a TIL statement? See Reg. Z §226.3(f).

PROBLEM 105

The Ugly Utility Company agreed to let its customers pay their heating bills on a credit plan for which they were charged interest. Must Ugly Utility give TIL statements? See §226.3(c).

PROBLEM 106

Tom and Nancy Yuppie settled on the car of their dreams: a $30,000 sports car. The car dealership gave them no TIL statement at all. Tom, a classmate of yours who dropped out of law school after the first year, was puzzled by this and gave you a call. Do the Yuppies have a lawsuit here? See Reg. Z §226.3(b).

PROBLEM 107

Use the same section for this one: Mr. and Mrs. Consumer bought a mobile home for $50,000. Must there be a TIL statement? What if they use it only on vacations and normally live in a condominium? See §226.2's definition of "dwelling."

ADIEL v. CHASE FEDERAL SAVINGS & LOAN ASSN.[12]
United States Court of Appeals, Eleventh Circuit, 1987
810 F.2d 1051

HATCHETT, Circuit Judge.

In this appeal, the appellant urges that we reverse the district court's ruling that the Truth In Lending Act applies to a transaction in which a creditor makes a loan to a commercial entity with the knowledge that the

---

12. Footnotes in this case have been renumbered for clarity.

loan will be assumed by a non-commercial entity with no changes in the terms of the loan. Finding no error, we affirm.

FACTS

Rehavam and Eleanor Adiel, the class representatives in this class action, entered into a contract with Lakeridge Associated, Ltd. (Lakeridge), to purchase a townhouse to be built by Lakeridge.[13] Shortly thereafter, Lakeridge executed and delivered to Chase Federal Savings & Loan Association (Chase) an application for a mortgage loan. Chase approved the loan. Lakeridge executed a promissory note payable to Chase and a mortgage securing the loan. Lakeridge used the funds from the loan to construct the townhouse.

As provided for in the purchase agreement, the Adiels submitted a mortgage loan application directly to Chase for the same amount as Lakeridge's loan. The purchase agreement between Lakeridge and the Adiels provided that the Adiels would reimburse Lakeridge for loan costs, including loan points, paid to Chase. The agreement further provided that should the Adiels secure financing with a lending institution other than Chase, the Adiels would pay Lakeridge "an additional 2% of the purchase price for [Lakeridge's] closing the transaction with [the Adiels'] lender."

The Adiels' application for a loan with Chase was for a multi-purpose residential loan. Upon receipt of the application, Chase unilaterally inserted a clause indicating that the application was for the assumption of an existing mortgage on the lot the Adiels had agreed to purchase. The mortgage to be assumed was the mortgage Lakeridge executed in favor of Chase, which obligated Lakeridge to make regular payments of principal and interest. The parties are in disagreement as to the amount of mortgage payments actually made by Lakeridge, but they agree that at some time Chase voluntarily waived its right to full payments on the note and mortgage.

Chase evaluated the Adiels' application, and notified them that they had been approved for assumption of the Lakeridge mortgage. At or about the time of closing, the Adiels executed a standard change of ownership form and an assumption of mortgage form. They also reimbursed Lakeridge the loan points which Lakeridge had paid Chase. The Adiels at this point became primary obligors under the note and mortgage.

---

13. The district court certified the class as: "Those purchasers of homes at the Lakeridge complex whose purchases were financed by the Defendant and which purchasers purchased said homes for his, hers, or their family dwelling and utilized it for said purpose."

Other class members' transactions were similar to the Adiels'; therefore, we use the Adiels' transaction as an example.

The Adiels brought this class action seeking damages for Chase's failure to present them with truth-in-lending documents. Chase contended, based upon various staff opinions of the Federal Reserve Board, and based on the implementing regulations, that truth-in-lending disclosures were not required.

The district court held that the transactions were subject to the provisions of the Truth In Lending Act and found that Chase did not comply with the provisions set forth in Regulation Z.[14] 15 U.S.C. §§1601-1693. Adiel v. Chase Fed. Sav. & Loan Assn., 586 F. Supp. 866 (S.D. Fla. 1984). The district court awarded the class statutory damages of $287,375.99. 630 F. Supp. 131.

Chase, the appellant, contends that the loans made to Lakeridge were for a business purpose; therefore, the loans are exempt from the Act. Additionally, Chase contends that the assumptions of the notes and mortgages were not "new transactions" within the meaning of 12 C.F.R. §226.8(j) and not refinancing.

Chase and the class urge that we find error in the damage award. Chase argues that the district court erred in awarding almost the maximum amount of statutory damages allowable under the Act. By cross-appeal, the class urges a finding of error in the district court's ruling that to recover actual damages, each class member must show that but for the violation, better credit on more favorable terms would have been obtained.

DISCUSSION

Title 12 C.F.R. §226.8(a) states the general rule that "[a]ny creditor when extending credit other than open end credit shall, . . . make the disclosures required by this section with respect to any transaction consummated on or after July 1, 1969."

Section 226.3(a) of Regulation Z provides that the Truth In Lending Act does not apply to "[e]xtensions of credit to organizations, including governments, or for business or commercial purposes. . . ."

We must look to the purpose of the loan to determine whether the Truth [I]n Lending Act applies. Poe v. First National Bank of DeKalb County, 597

---

14. Regulation Z, the truth-in-lending regulation, can be found in the form in which it existed at the time of these events in Title 15 U.S.C.A. following section 1700. The provisions of Part 226 of Title 12 of the Code of Federal Regulations were subsequently replaced by a new set of regulations. All references in this opinion are to the sections in effect at the time of these events.

F.2d 895 (5th Cir. 1979). Although the funds in this case were originally loaned to Lakeridge to construct townhouses, and were thus used for commercial purposes, to find that no consumer credit transaction occurred between Chase and the Adiels (the class) is to ignore the commercial reality of the situation. Chase would have us adopt a rule that in situations such as this, in which a loan is sought by a party with the express intention of transferring responsibility shortly thereafter to a third party, that the proper focus is only upon the original transaction. Chase thus argues that because the funds in this case were initially loaned to a commercial entity for a business purpose, the loan arrangement cannot be considered a consumer transaction. This theory is without merit.

It was clearly contemplated at the outset that the ultimate obligation would run from the Adiels to Chase. This is partly shown by the fact that Chase did not hold Lakeridge to strict compliance with the terms of the mortgage. Additionally, by imposing upon the Adiels a 2-percent "penalty" should they obtain financing elsewhere, the Adiels were left with no other reasonable choice than to apply to Chase for a mortgage. We agree with the district court: the ultimate purpose of the loan was to extend consumer credit to the Adiels.

Title 12 C.F.R. §226.8(j) provides: "[i]f any existing extension of credit is refinanced, or two or more extensions of credit are consolidated or an existing obligation increased, such transaction shall be considered a new transaction subject to the disclosure requirements of this Part." Chase argues that no "refinancing" occurred in this case because no existing extension of consumer credit was assumed and no change was made in the terms of the Lakeridge loan when the Adiels "assumed" it.[15] Chase further argues that it has found no cases in which a court found a "refinancing" which involved a situation other than a change in the terms of an existing consumer loan to the same person. Chase notes that none of the terms in this case were changed; the monthly payments, maturity dates, and interest rate remained the same. Consequently, the transactions were originally commercial loans and were assumed as commercial loans.

---

15. Title 12 C.F.R. §226.8(k) provides, in pertinent part:

(k) Assumption of an obligation. Any creditor who accepts a subsequent customer as an obligor under an existing obligation shall make the disclosures required by this part to that customer before he becomes so obligated.

The district court concluded that because Lakeridge was not a "customer" under the Act, the Adiels did not meet the definition of a "subsequent customer," and thus no "assumption" occurred under the Act. This issue was not directly raised on appeal.

Chase argues that in order for section 226.8(j) to apply, an existing extension of consumer credit must be in effect. Chase also cites 12 C.F.R. §226.2(jj) which provides, "[u]nless the context indicates otherwise, 'credit' shall be construed to mean 'consumer credit,' 'loan' to mean 'consumer loan,' 'transaction' to mean 'consumer credit transaction' and 'lease' to mean 'consumer lease.'" Chase's position is that a "new transaction" under section 226.8(j) really means an existing extension of "consumer" credit. We hold that in this case, the context indicates otherwise.

The intent of the Truth In Lending Act is to promote the informed use of consumer credit. 15 U.S.C. §1601(a). The Adiels and the other class members were consumers who desired credit for consumer purposes. Chase was fully aware of their identities and of the purposes for which they intended to use the funds. Chase required the Adiels and the other class members to submit applications for loans and reserved the right to disapprove their applications. The change of ownership forms showed them to be new borrowers. We thus hold that the transactions constituted "refinancing."

DAMAGES

Chase also contends that the district court abused its discretion in its award of statutory damages under the Truth In Lending Act. After review of the district court's memorandum opinion and order on damages, we conclude that its award of $287,375.99 to the class fell within the statutory maximum in 15 U.S.C. §1640(a)(2)(B), and we conclude that the district court properly considered the factors set forth in the statute.

The Adiels, for the class, cross-appeal the damage recovery contending that the district court erred in failing to also award them actual damages. The class contends that the loan points paid to Lakeridge as reimbursement constituted an illegal finance charge and should be considered damage actually incurred. The Class members may have been led to believe they were paying the loan points directly to Chase and not as reimbursement to Lakeridge. Yet, it does not follow that the charge was illegal. They contracted to "pay the lending institution's closing costs" which included "loan points and all other costs directly related to the Mortgage." Since they were the ultimate recipients of the loans, this is not unreasonable.

The district court stated that it was awarding statutory damages in lieu of actual damages due, in part, to the fact that actual damages in cases such as these are difficult to prove. The statute sets forth as one of the factors to be considered in determining statutory damages the amount of actual damages incurred. In determining the amount of damages, the district court took into consideration the dollar amount of loan points the class paid and imposed an amount of $750 for each of the 149 members of the class. Thus, the amount which the class seeks to characterize as actual damages was awarded as part of the statutory damages. We note that the class seeks to have this amount characterized as actual damages in an attempt to recover prejudgment interest. The district court did not abuse its discretion in awarding statutory damages rather than actual damages.

Accordingly, the district court is affirmed.

Affirmed.

QUESTION

This case was decided under the original version of TILA. The enactment of the Truth in Lending Simplification Act in 1980 resulted in a rewrite of both the statute and Regulation Z. Do we get the same result as the court reached under the current wording of Reg. Z §226.20?

Insurance Financing and TILA.   There is some confusion as to the application of TILA to insurance company creditors. The McCarran Act, 15 U.S.C. §1012(b), mandates that no act of Congress shall be construed to invalidate, impair, or supersede any law enacted by any state for the purpose of regulating the business of insurance, unless the federal act specifically relates to the business of insurance. Does this mean that a loan by an insurance company would not require TIL disclosures? Some courts think so, but the bulk have required TIL disclosures. See discussion in Cody v. Community Loan Corp., 606 F.2d 499 (5th Cir. 1979), and Autry v. Northwest Premium Serv. 144 F.3d 1037 (7th Cir. 1998).

III. DISCLOSURE: FINANCE CHARGE AND ANNUAL PERCENTAGE RATE

A. Introduction

The two most important terms in a TIL disclosure statement are the finance charge, defined in Reg. Z §226.4(a), and the annual percentage rate, defined in §§226.14(a) and 226.22(a). They are different ways of expressing the same thing: the true amount of interest (and related charges) being exacted in the credit transaction. The finance charge is the interest imposed over the life of the loan *expressed as a dollar amount*. The annual percentage rate (APR) is the actuarially correct yearly interest *expressed as a percentage*.

Why do consumers need both? Because either, standing alone, does not give an indication as to the desirability of the transaction. Consider a credit extension advertised as 5 percent. Is that a great rate? Not when you learn that the loan will go on for 50 years and that the dollar total (the "finance charge") you will pay will be a very hefty sum. You would have been better off paying 18 percent for one year with a finance charge that would be a lot less.

HERMAN

"Each hour."

Herman. Copyright © 1989 by Jim Unger. HERMAN is reprinted with permission from Laughingstock Licensing Inc., Ottawa, Canada.

Because the finance charge and the APR are so important, Regulation Z provides that their disclosure must be more conspicuous than any other disclosures, §§226.5(a)(2) and 226.17(a)(2). The failure to do this is a frequent (and obvious) violation of the Act.[16]

B. Elements of the Finance Charge

The Battle Joined.   The Federal Reserve Board wants the creditor to identify as part of the finance charge all charges (with certain exceptions)

---

16. Since the finance charge and the APR must be more conspicuous than other disclosed terms, does this mean that in radio advertising the announcer must shout when mentioning these items? See Reg. Z §226.5(a)(2) n.9.

that the consumer pays in a credit transaction that he or she does *not* pay in a cash transaction; read Reg. Z §226.4(a). Creditors, on the other hand, want to keep the finance charge (and therefore the APR also) as low as possible. If you are a creditor so minded, one way to do this is to convince yourself that the charge at issue doesn't meet the definition of "finance charge." That way you may not ever have to disclose it, or, at worst, you can disclose it separately and not include it in the computation of the finance charge.

With this tension in mind, read §226.4(a) through (f) carefully (omitting subsection (d) on credit insurance, which we will cover later in this chapter).

FIRST ACADIANA BANK v. FEDERAL DEPOSIT INSURANCE CORP.[17]
United States Court of Appeals, Fifth Circuit, 1987
833 F.2d 548

PATRICK E. HIGGINBOTHAM, Circuit Judge.

First Acadiana Bank seeks review of a final administrative order by the Federal Deposit Insurance Corporation. The FDIC found the Bank in violation of the Truth-in-Lending Act and FDIC regulations and ordered the Bank to reimburse certain customers. We affirm.

I

In 1984, the FDIC notified First Acadiana Bank of Eunice, Louisiana, that it was in violation of the Truth-in-Lending Act and FDIC regulations. Since October 1, 1982, the Bank's policy has been to require each car-loan borrower to employ a bank-approved attorney to prepare a valid chattel mortgage on the car. For two-thirds of such customers, these legal fees were included in the amount financed by the Bank. The amount of the fee was always determined by the attorney and ranged from $55 to $151 per loan.

When the Bank financed such a fee, it did not add it to the "finance charge" listed on the disclosure form presented to the borrower. Nor was the fee included in the computation of the annual percentage rate (APR) listed on the same form. Had these fees been included in the finance charge, the APR in any given loan would have been from half a point to ten points higher than that quoted by the Bank. However, the fees were included in the category "amount financed" and separately disclosed to the borrower.

After the Bank refused to alter its policy pursuant to the compliance examiner's report, the FDIC Board of Review issued a Notice of Charges

---

17. Footnotes in this case have been renumbered for clarity.

and of Hearing. An administrative law judge entered an initial decision against the Bank that the FDIC's Board of Directors adopted in whole.

The FDIC order commands the Bank to cease and desist from failing to include the attorneys' fees as part of the finance charge on its disclosure form. The Board also ordered the Bank to identify all consumer automobile loans it made since October 1, 1982, in which the finance charge and annual percentage rate were understated. The Bank must then reimburse each borrower to the extent of the understatement.

II

The Truth-in-Lending Act requires the Bank to disclose to the borrower, among other things, three components of a credit transaction: the "amount financed," the "finance charge," and the "annual percentage rate." 15 U.S.C. §1638 (1982). The APR is a function of the loan's duration, payment terms, and the finance charge. See id. §1606 (1982).

The statute's definition of "finance charge" is:

> the sum of all charges, payable directly or indirectly by the person to whom the credit is extended, and imposed directly or indirectly by the creditor as an incident to the extension of credit. The finance charge does not include charges of a type payable in a comparable cash transaction. . . .

Id. §1605.[18]

The statute also provides examples of finance charges. These include, among others, a "[s]ervice or carrying charge," a "[l]oan fee" or "finder's fee," a "[f]ee for an investigation or credit report," and a premium for "any guarantee or insurance protecting the creditor against the obligor's default." Id.

Under the Act's definition, the attorneys' fees obviously constitute part of the finance charge. Payment of the fees was "incident to the extension of credit," because the Bank would not extend credit otherwise. See Berryhill v. Rich Plan, 578 F.2d 1092, 1099 (5th Cir. 1978) ("The important question is whether the seller refuses to extend credit until the customer agrees to another charge."); see also Jonathan M. Landers, Determining the Finance

---

18. Regulation Z, issued by the FDIC, includes a similar definition of "finance charge":

> The finance charge is the cost of consumer credit as a dollar amount. It includes any charge payable directly or indirectly by the consumer and imposed directly or indirectly by the creditor as an incident to or a condition of the extension of credit. It does not include any charge of a type payable in a comparable cash transaction.

12 C.F.R. §226.4(a) (1987).

Charge Under the Truth In Lending Act, 1977 Am. B. Found. Res. J. 45, 57-58. Likewise, the attorneys' fee to perfect a mortgage is not "of a type payable in a comparable cash transaction," because a cash sale would involve no security interest.

In addition, the fees were "imposed directly or indirectly by the creditor," and thus within the Act's definition. The Bank contends that the fee was imposed not by the Bank but by the attorney perfecting the mortgage insofar as the attorney set the amount of the fee and kept the proceeds. According to the Bank, its policy was simply the practical consequence of Louisiana's strict requirements for a valid chattel mortgage.

We reject the Bank's approach. The Bank has required its borrowers, as a condition to the extension of credit, to pay an avoidable economic cost. Louisiana law does not require the Bank to take a mortgage on a car loan, or to have an attorney complete the mortgage documents. The fact that the precise amount of the fee was set by a third party makes no difference.

We also do not agree that the disputed fees could be finance charges only if the Bank had retained them. Cf. Abbey v. Columbus Dodge, Inc., 607 F.2d 85, 86 (5th Cir. 1979) (finance charge includes filing fee only partly retained by lender). Although the Bank retained no fee, it retained a substantial benefit from the attorneys' services: a perfected security interest.

It would be difficult to reconcile any other interpretation with the Act's explicit examples of finance charges, several of which involve payments to third parties. "Finders fees," a "fee for an investigation or credit report," or an insurance premium against the borrower's default all may be set and retained by a party other than the lender.

We also do not believe, as the Bank contends, that separate disclosure of the attorneys' fee eliminated the need to comply with the Act's particular requirements. Congress unambiguously set forth the procedures necessary to ensure informed borrowing. Accurate disclosure of the finance charge and APR is essential to the "informed use of credit" Congress sought to achieve. See 15 U.S.C. §1601 (1982). Exclusion of these fees from the finance charge had the effect of understating the annual percentage rate by as much as ten percentage points. The Bank's non-compliance thus was more serious than the technical violations excused by some courts. See Redhouse v. Quality Ford Sales, Inc., 511 F.2d 230, 237 (10th Cir. 1975).

III

The Bank also challenges the FDIC's order that the Bank reimburse the disputed fee to each borrower who did not receive statutorily adequate disclosure. We conclude that the FDIC's remedy is consistent with the congressional mandate.

The Truth-in-Lending Act allows the FDIC to

> require the creditor to make an adjustment to the account of the person to whom credit was extended, to assure that such person will not be required to pay a finance charge in excess of the finance charge actually disclosed or the dollar equivalent of the annual percentage rate actually disclosed, whichever is lower.

15 U.S.C. §1607(e)(1). And under the Act, the FDIC

> *shall require such an adjustment* when it determines that such disclosure error resulted from (A) *a clear and consistent pattern or practice of violations*, (B) gross negligence, or (C) a willful violation which was intended to mislead the person to whom the credit was extended.

Id. §1607(e)(2) (emphasis added). Because the Bank has stipulated that it engaged in a "pattern or practice" of excluding the disputed fees from the "finance charge," the Bank's policy was the kind of behavior for which restitution was statutorily mandated.

Even if we believed the Bank's extenuation of "good faith"—a plea belied by the Bank's refusal, to this date, to comply with the FDIC's order—the statutory remedy still would be appropriate. The enforcement section of the statute makes no good faith exception. Indeed, because the Act mandates reimbursement where there has been either a "pattern or practice" or a willful violation, it is implied that the "pattern or practice" need not be intentional or in bad faith.

The Bank's final complaint is that it would be unfair to make the Bank pay back fees it never received. Congress made no such exception to the reimbursement remedy, even though the examples of finance charges listed in the Act included fees paid to third parties. It is not our job to decide whether the legislative directive is just.

Affirmed.

JERRE S. WILLIAMS, Circuit Judge, specially concurring:

The opinion for the Court omits a highly significant fact in this case, and as a result reaches a conclusion which extends the definition of "finance charges" under the law beyond reasonable statutory limits. The critical fact is that the Bank recommended two attorneys regularly who were closely associated with the Bank to draft the chattel mortgages which the Bank required. The inclusion of those fees in the "amounts financed" portion of the disclosure form was automatic, and the bank collected the fees and paid the attorneys. Under these circumstances I agree that these fees were finance charges.

At least some of the chattel mortgages were drafted by other attorneys in the community who were not recommended by and had no connection with the Bank. The FDIC takes the position that the fees charged by those attorneys also are finance charges of the Bank but then specifically eschews any attempt to take action against the Bank for failure to include those fees on the ground of pragmatic difficulty.

Since the opinion for the Court does not properly distinguish between a wholly independent action by a lawyer which is necessary and properly required by the Bank before it will issue a loan from the "in house" actions of the Bank in this case, I find it important to dispute this broad interpretation of the statute by the FDIC and by the panel opinion.

I start with the proposition that it is reasonable and sound for a Bank to require that before it gives an automobile loan it will demand a chattel mortgage. It is also reasonable for the Bank to require that the chattel mortgage be drafted by a lawyer. These are simply qualifications which a Bank has a right to make before it will engage in the voluntary act of granting a loan on an automobile. We are not here testing the right of the Bank to demand professional qualifications. Under the reasoning of the panel opinion, if the chattel mortgage had been drafted by the applicant on a standard form sold in the stores or anyone else, the cost of purchasing the form would, under the reasoning of the majority, constitute a "finance charge." If the Bank required that such loan applications be typed, the cost of typing the applications would be a finance charge. If the automobile in question had been purchased at a foreclosure sale, the cost of obtaining the requisite documents to establish clear title from the court clerk would also be a finance charge. I suppose even the ink or pencil used by an individual applicant to fill out an application would be a finance charge.

I recognize that the regulation and the statute provide that all charges payable directly or "indirectly" by the person to whom the credit is extended and imposed directly or "indirectly" by the creditor are covered. But "indirectly" must have reasonable and sensible limits.

The net effect of the position of the panel majority is the implication that the Bank does not have the right to demand the chattel mortgage in connection with the automobile loan because the law does not "require" that it obtain a chattel mortgage. Thus, while it is free to do so, it must include the cost of this completely reasonable requirement in its competitive interest rate. I venture that it would be remarkable indeed if the State of Louisiana would be willing to hold in a case in which the Bank charged the maximum interest rate that the fact that to qualify for the loan a wholly independent hiring of an attorney by the consumer to help prepare the loan application papers would result in a finding that the Bank was charging usurious interest. Yet this is the implication of the majority opinion. I cannot read the statute that broadly. . . .

This sweeping vagueness of the word "indirect" simply requires an analysis of the use of the word in context. I for one cannot conceive that a wholly independent fee paid directly to an attorney or someone else to help in an application for a loan to a Bank must be considered a "finance charge" of the Bank and could result in a claim of usury against the Bank. These are not finance charges by the Bank at all. . . .

QUESTION

Since this case was decided, Regulation Z was amended to add §226.4(a)(1). How would that section apply to the "parade of horribles" (use of standard forms, typing applications, clearing auto titles, pen and ink to fill out the forms) Judge Williams lists in his special concurrence?

PROBLEM 108

Your client is a corporate lender that makes a wide number of different types of credit extensions. It is your job to advise this client whether the following items are part of the finance charge in its dealings with consumers.

a. Sales taxes.

b. Fees for preparing the TIL statement.

c. The fee charged by the Secretary of State's office for filing a financing statement so that the creditor perfects its security interest in whatever the collateral happens to be.

d. The fee paid by prospective borrowers when they submit an application asking to be considered for a loan.

e. Credit report fees for investigating these people. Does it matter whether the borrowers are buying a home or a car?

GIBSON v. BOB WATSON CHEVROLET-GEO, INC.
United States Court of Appeals, Seventh Circuit, 1997
112 F.3d 283

POSNER, Chief Judge.

We have consolidated the appeals from the decisions dismissing on the pleadings three class-action suits against Chicago-area automobile dealers for violation of the Truth in Lending Act, 15 U.S.C. §§1601 et seq. These suits are among some fifteen almost identical class actions filed by the same law firm against such dealers. For unexplained reasons the cases, having initially been randomly assigned to different district judges in the Northern District of Illinois, were *not* reassigned to a single judge, as authorized by N.D. Ill. R. 2.31, but remained with the original judges, eleven of whom have ruled on motions to dismiss the complaint or to grant summary judgment for the defendant. Six have denied such motions and five, including the three whose rulings are brought to us by these consolidated appeals, have granted them.

The facts are very simple, and can be illustrated by Gibson's case. She bought a used car from Bob Watson Chevrolet on credit. The dealer gave her a statement captioned "Itemization of Amount Financed." The statement contains a category referred to as "Amounts Paid to Others on Your Behalf," under which appears an entry that reads: "To North American for Extended Warranty $800.00." The dealer admits that a substantial though at present unknown amount of the $800 was retained by him rather than paid over to the company that issued the warranty (North American). The question is whether the failure to disclose this retention violates the Truth in Lending Act.

There are two possible violations. First, when the dealer sells cars for cash rather than on credit, it marks up the warranty less (according to the plaintiffs), and hence retains a smaller amount of the warranty charge. Because the charge by the issuer of the warranty is presumably unaffected by the amount of the dealer's mark-up, the dealer is levying an additional charge on its credit customers that plaintiffs call a "finance charge," which must be disclosed to the customer. 15 U.S.C. §§1605(a), 1638(a)(3); 12 C.F.R. §226.18(d) and Pt. 226, Supp. I §4(a); Cowen v. Bank United of Texas, FSB, 70 F.3d 937, 940 (7th Cir. 1995).

Second, the Act requires the lender or creditor to provide "a written itemization of the amount financed," including "each amount that is or will be paid to third persons by the creditor [the dealer here] on the consumer's behalf, together with an identification of or reference to the third person." 15 U.S.C. §1638(a)(2)(B)(iii). The argument that Bob Watson Chevrolet (as before, we're using Gibson's case as typical of all three cases) violated this provision is straightforward, and let us start with it. The amount to be paid to North American on Gibson's behalf is not stated correctly in the written itemization of the amount financed that Gibson received. It is true that the consumer is not entitled to the statement unless he makes a written request for it, §1638(a)(2)(B); 12 C.F.R. §226.18(c)(2), and there is no indication that Gibson did. But the creditor is allowed to skip this stage and simply provide the itemization of the amount financed without being asked for it. 12 C.F.R. Pt. 226, Supp. I §18(c)(1). That appears to be what Bob Watson Chevrolet did. In any event, it furnished the itemization, and the itemization contains a false representation.

The defendants emphasize quite properly that the Act is not a general prohibition of fraud in consumer transactions or even in consumer credit transactions. Its limited office is to protect consumers from being misled about the cost of credit. If the dealer retains the same amount of the warranty charge on credit purchases as he does on cash purchases, he is not misleading the consumer about the cost of buying on credit. But it is a contested issue whether the retention (mark-up) is the same; and even if it is, this is not a defense to the claim of inaccurate itemization. Section 1638(a)(2)(B)(iii) is free-standing. It requires disclosure—meaning, we do not understand the defendants to deny, accurate disclosure, Fairley v. Turan-Foley Imports, Inc., 65 F.3d 475, 479 (5th Cir. 1995)—of amounts paid to third persons by the creditor on the consumer's behalf, whether or not cash customers pay less. Bob Watson Chevrolet did not accurately disclose the amount that it paid North American for the extended warranty on the car that Gibson purchased. It said it paid $800; in fact it paid less.

The defendants argue that the Federal Reserve Board, the oracle of the Truth in Lending Act, 15 U.S.C. §1604(a); Anderson Bros. Ford v. Valencia, 452 U.S. 205, 219, 101 S. Ct. 2266, 2273-74, 68 L. Ed. 2d 783 (1981); Ford Motor Credit Co. v. Milhollin, 444 U.S. 555, 565-69, 100 S. Ct. 790, 796-99, 63 L. Ed. 2d 22 (1980); McGee v. Kerr-Hickman Chrysler Plymouth, Inc., 93 F.3d 380, 383 (7th Cir. 1996); Cowen v. Bank United of Texas, FSB, supra, 70 F.3d at 943, has issued an Official Staff Commentary that authorizes the dealers to do what they did here. The commentary (a part of the Federal Reserve Board's Regulation Z) addresses the situation in which the creditor retains a portion of the fee charged to a customer for a service provided by a third party, such as an extended warranty. It provides that "the creditor in such cases may reflect that the creditor has retained a portion of the amount paid to others. For example, the creditor could add to the category 'amount paid to others' language such as '(we may be retaining a portion of this amount).'" 12 C.F.R. Pt. 226, Supp. I §18(c)(1)(iii)(2). The commentary, being limited to the case in which the fee "is payable in the same amount in comparable cash and credit transactions," id., has no bearing on the claim that the dealers in these cases are hiding a finance charge. But as to the other possible violation, the failure to itemize accurately, the defendants contend that the words "may" and "could" show that they can if they want disclose that they are retaining some of the fee, but that they are not required to do so. In other words, they read the commentary to say: "You may conceal the fact that you are pocketing part of the fee that is ostensibly for a third party, but if you are a commercial saint and would *prefer* to tell the truth, you may do that too." So interpreted, however, the commentary not only would be preposterous; it would contradict the statute. The only sensible reading of the commentary is as authorizing the dealer to disclose only the fact that he is retaining a portion of the charge, rather than the exact amount of the retention. Even this is a considerable stretch of the statute; and it is as far as, if not farther than, the statute will stretch.

The defendants' only other argument is that they have a safe harbor in form H-3 (another part of Regulation Z), 12 C.F.R. Pt. 226, App. H-3. A disclosure that complies with the form is not actionable. 15 U.S.C. §§1604(b), 1640(f); 12 C.F.R. Pt. 226, Supp. I Introduction para. 1. Captioned "Amount Financed Itemization Model Form," the form contains a line for "Amounts paid to others on your behalf," and underneath it a line which reads "$___ to (other)." Compliance with the form in Gibson's case would have required Bob Watson Chevrolet to list next to North American's name the actual amount paid to North American for the extended warranty. So the H-3 defense fails too—and for the further and independent reason that the safe harbor is unavailable to disclosures required to be given numerically, such as disclosure of the *amount* financed. 15 U.S.C. §1604(b).

Two observations, one procedural, the other substantive, remain to be made about the issue of the undisclosed markup as a finance charge, the first alleged violation. In only one of our three cases (Hernandez's) was it actually pressed as a separate violation. In the others it was folded in with the failure-to-itemize claim, perhaps because the latter is a stronger claim but doesn't permit as large an award of damages. 15 U.S.C. §1640(a). But since we must reverse all three cases with respect to the second violation, so that further proceedings in the district court are necessary in any event, and since the other two cases were dismissed on the pleadings, we do not think that the claim of a hidden finance charge can be deemed waived in those cases by not having been made more perspicuously in the complaints. But, coming to our substantive observation, we emphasize that the claim has merit only if the dealer's markup on third-party charges is *systematically* higher on sales to credit customers than on sales to cash customers. If a dealer merely charges what the traffic will bear, the fact that a *particular* credit customer may be paying a higher mark-up than a *particular* cash customer would not transform the difference in mark-ups into a finance charge; it would have in fact no causal relation to the extension of credit. We cannot find a case that holds this, but it seems clear as a matter of principle; and it may very well describe this case—but the plaintiffs are entitled to an opportunity to show that it does not.

It wouldn't surprise us if the district judges in these three cases, and the judges in the similar cases that have been dismissed, thought that the plaintiffs' law firm is harassing Chicago-area automobile dealers with complaints about purely technical violations of a highly technical and much-criticized statute. Yet it is far from clear that the alleged violations should be regarded as entirely technical, even the violation of the requirement of accurate itemization of third-party charges. The consumer would have a greater incentive to shop around for an extended warranty, rather than take the one offered by the dealer, if he realized that the dealer was charging what the defendants' lawyer described as a "commission," and apparently a very sizable one, for its efforts in procuring the warranty from a third party. Or the consumer might be more prone to haggle than if he thought that the entire fee had been levied by a third party and so was outside the dealer's direct control. Or he might go to another dealer in search of lower mark-ups on third-party charges.

It is true that exposing this little fraud is a benefit only tenuously related to the objectives of the Truth in Lending Act, on which see 15 U.S.C. §1601 (declaration of purpose). It is almost as great a fraud on cash purchasers as on credit purchasers; yet its exposure will benefit only the latter. (The relation that we are describing as tenuous lies in the fact that the size of the dealer's "commission" may be a clue to the presence of a hidden finance charge.) But statutes often outrun their rationales. We do not know why the drafters wanted third-party transactions listed separately, and by both amount and payee. There may have been a concern that nominal third-party payees might turn out to be affiliates of the creditor, or a desire to help consumers separate credit charges from other charges; the latter goal in particular would tie the requirement a little more securely to the underlying purposes of the statute. But we are just guessing.

The claim that what the dealers were doing here is concealing a finance charge has a closer connection to the Act's purposes. If the amount retained of the fee for an extended warranty or other third-party service is greater in credit transactions than in cash transactions, then in deciding whether to pay cash or buy on credit the consumer will assume that if he pays cash he will have to pay the same additional fee to get the extended warranty; if the facts are as the plaintiffs claim, he would not. The purchaser thinks he'll have to pay $800 for an extended warranty whether he pays cash or buys on credit, whereas if the retention really is smaller on cash purchases than on credit purchases and the third party's fee net of the retention is the same, the customer will not have to pay $800 if he pays cash for the car. This is a type of fraud that goes to the heart of the concerns that actuate the Truth in Lending Act. Cf. Mourning v. Family Publications Service, Inc., 411 U.S. 356, 366-68, 93 S. Ct. 1652, 1659-60, 36 L. Ed. 2d 318 (1973).

Anyway the issue is not whether these violations are technical, or whether technical violations should be actionable, or whether consumer class actions should be discouraged, but whether the complaints in these cases state a claim. And since they do, the dismissal of the plaintiffs' state-law fraud claims on the ground that disclosures that comply with the Truth in Lending Act do not violate the Illinois consumer protection laws, 815 ILCS 375/5(4), 505/2, which confer immunity for acts "specifically authorized" by a federal or state agency, 815 ILCS 505/10b(1); Lanier v. Associates Finance, Inc., 114 Ill. 2d 1, 101 Ill. Dec. 852, 859, 499 N.E.2d 440, 447 (1986), was erroneous too. The judgments are therefore reversed with instructions to reinstate the lawsuits. We hope it's not too late for the district court to reassign all the identical Truth in Lending auto dealer class actions to one judge.

Reversed and remanded.

PROBLEM 109

Donna DeGeorge somehow overdrew her checking account. The bank, pursuant to its written deposit agreement with her, paid one of the checks (for $12) that was drawn against the overdrawn account, but it returned another one (written for $50). For the $12 check it paid, the bank imposed a $10 service charge against her account. For the $50 check that it sent bouncing back to the merchant (who charged Donna a $15 returned check fee), the bank took $10 from her account as an NSF ("Not Sufficient Funds") charge. Since the account was only slightly overdrawn ($1.22) when these two checks were first presented, and since all these charges mount up, Donna became annoyed. At a cocktail party she learns you are a lawyer and she asks you if the bank can do this to her. Sensing a class action, you whip out your pocket copy of Regulation Z. What do you tell her? Compare §226.4(b)(2) and (c)(3).

There has been a fierce argument about whether TILA covers overdraft fees (and the so-called "bounce protection" plans offered by many banks). Banks have tried to duck giving TIL statements by arguing that paying an overdraft is never *required* by written agreement but is always an *option* to the bank. But advertising to consumers about bounce protection plans typically makes it sound as if the bank *will* pay the overdrafts, and this argument therefore is suspicious. Banks earn an eye-popping amount of money from paying overdrafts and assessing fees—more than $53.1 billion in 2006 (!)—doing this with 30 percent of their customers and therefore making such fees a major source of income. For a detailed discussion of this issue, see Bounce Protection: Payday Lending in Sheep's Clothing?, 8 N.C. Banking Inst. 349 (2004).

PROBLEM 110

All the while he was in law school, Gilbert Smith lived in a tiny apartment above a small neighborhood grocery store owned by an elderly couple named Mom and Pop. Mom let Gilbert charge purchases to a running tab, and monthly she sent him a bill. The bill has printed on it "Five Percent Late Charge for Payments Made After Tenth of the Month." Since Gilbert, ever struggling to pay his bills, never made a payment in the first 10 days of the month, Mom charged him the late charge each month. He paid it too, but the day he was sworn in to the Bar, he filed suit in federal court against Mom and Pop's Grocery, charging that they had failed to give TIL statements. Is he going to win this one? See Reg. Z §226.4(c)(2).

BRIGHT v. BALL MEMORIAL HOSPITAL ASSN.[19]
United States Court of Appeals, Seventh Circuit, 1980
616 F.2d 328

WILL, Senior District Judge.

Appellants Kathy Bright and Susan Barber seek reversal of the district court's determination that appellee Ball Memorial Hospital Association, Inc. ("Ball Memorial" or "Hospital") was not a "creditor" within the meaning of the Truth in Lending Act ("Act"), 15 U.S.C. §§1601, et seq., and seek a further determination that Ball Memorial violated the provisions of the Act as to them. For the reasons stated, we affirm the district court's judgment on grounds other than those relied upon by the district court.

BACKGROUND

Ball Memorial is a not-for-profit hospital incorporated under the laws of the State of Indiana. Located in Delaware County, Indiana, Ball Memorial

---

19. Footnotes in this case have been renumbered for clarity.

serves its own and four surrounding counties and operates as the primary referral hospital for East Central Indiana. It is a general public hospital, admitting all persons without regard to ability to pay.

Upon admission to the hospital, inpatients are shown and asked to sign an "Initial Credit Disclosure Statement and Consent to Treatment" form. The Initial Credit Disclosure Statement initially states: "You are requested to remit the balance due on your account with the hospital at the time of discharge." This Statement further sets forth, however, conditions under which an inpatient may pay the account balance in installments "IF IT IS NECESSARY" for the patient to use such a procedure. The conditions include the imposition of a "FINANCE CHARGE OF ¾% per month on any unpaid balance, unpaid for more than thirty (30) days." Similarly, one of the pamphlets contained in the "Hospital Patient Guide" given to each inpatient informs the patient that the account is "payable at the time of your discharge," but also informs the patient that, if unable to pay the entire bill,

> you or your relative must be prepared to talk with the credit manager . . . to make satisfactory credit arrangements. Our credit department will discuss with you financial arrangements and will set up the payment of your account according to your ability to pay.

This pamphlet also makes "FINANCIAL DISCLOSURE" of a "FINANCE CHARGE" which "will be added to all uncollected or past due accounts."

Pursuant to these written directives and additional oral instructions, Ball Memorial will make arrangements, prior to discharge, with inpatients without insurance or other third-party coverage who are unable to pay the bill in full upon discharge such that an installment payment schedule is established. These schedules sometimes call for payment in more than four installments. Regardless of whether the agreements contemplate more than four installments, a ¾% monthly charge is assessed on the outstanding account balance each month while the installments are paid. Patients making these arrangements subsequently receive from the Hospital an initial bill and a coupon book embodying the installment plan arranged, and subsequently receive monthly statements of their balances as the installments are paid. They do not receive the billing statements which are described in Ball Memorial's general billing cycle, infra.

Inpatients not making such installment payment arrangements at the time of discharge receive an initial bill from Ball Memorial on the fourth day after discharge which delineates the specific charges assessed to their accounts. On the reverse side of this initial bill is a schedule of information headed *"FINANCE CHARGE,"* which advises the patient that a "FINANCE CHARGE" of ¾% per month or a 50¢ "HANDLING CHARGE," whichever is greater, will be added to any unpaid balance of 30 days or more, but that no such charge would be imposed if the bill were paid in full within 30 days. The schedule concludes by stating that "All charges are in compliance with the Truth and [sic] Lending Act and Uniform Consumer Credit Code."

If an inpatient has not made payment arrangements with the Hospital, on the eighteenth day after discharge the patient is mailed the first billing statement which indicates the total amount due. On its face, the statement states: "Your account is now due and payable. Please remit today." This statement, as do all subsequent statements, also bears the language: "Payment is due in full when service is rendered." On its reverse side, the statement contains a schedule of information headed "FINANCE CHARGE" which is identical to the schedule of information contained on the reverse side of the initial bill, except for the addition of the following:

9) The chart below demonstrates the minimum monthly payment required under Ball Memorial Hospital's credit policy.

IF YOUR ORIGINAL BALANCE IS	10-200	201-300	301-400	401-500	501-600	601-700	701-800	OVER 800
YOUR MINIMUM MONTHLY PMT IS	10	15	20	25	30	35	40	5%

10) You may pay a larger part or all of the balance of your account at any time.

Where no payment arrangements have been made, on the forty-eighth day after discharge the patient is mailed a second billing statement identical to the first in all respects except that the face now bears the language: "No doubt you have overlooked payment of your account, please make your remittance now." It is at the forty-eighth day that Ball Memorial considers an account to be delinquent. If payment in full is received before this time, the monthly charge which would have been assessed on the first month is waived. At this point, the monthly charge of ¾% of the unpaid balance or 50¢ is first assessed.

If no payment arrangements are made, Ball Memorial mails a third statement on the sixty-second day after discharge. This statement is identical to the first two, except it bears the language: "We are surprised that you continue to ignore your past due account. We must insist on immediate payment." Along with this statement, inpatients automatically receive a coupon book, dividing the patient's obligation into monthly installment payments along lines consistent with the table set forth above. If at this point the patient begins making payments pursuant to the coupon book, the patient does not receive the fourth or fifth statements discussed below. Rather, the patient will receive a monthly statement showing the payments received, the monthly charges imposed, and the balance due. These bills are on forms identical to those used for inpatients who arranged installment payment schedules prior to their discharge from the Hospital, and continue until the bill is paid in full.

On the seventy-sixth day after discharge, a patient who has not arranged to pay his bill or begun making installment payments is mailed the fourth statement. This statement is identical to the first three, except it now bears the language: "It is apparent that you have ignored all our previous notices. If there is any reason for delay of your payment contact this office now." A fifth and final statement is mailed on the ninetieth day after discharge. This statement is identical to the first four, except it is stamped "Final Notice" in red, and contains the legend: "Final Notice. Unless this account is paid in full, by it will be turned over to an outside collection agency."

In addition to these written statements, Ball Memorial attempts to make contact with patients by telephone during the same time period in an effort to secure payment. The Hospital's decision finally to turn inpatient accounts over to an outside collection agency is apparently made on a case-by-case basis after the fifth and final statement is sent. Accounts are not assigned out for collection where patients are making installment payments.

Ball Memorial's billing procedures with respect to outpatients are similar to those used for inpatients, but differ in several respects. Outpatients apparently receive neither the Initial Credit Disclosure Statement nor the Hospital Patient Guide at the time of service. The Hospital generally treats these patients on a cash basis, and only in rare circumstances where the outpatient's bill is large will it initially attempt to arrange an installment payment plan. The initial bill received by outpatients on the fourth day after discharge is not identical to that received by inpatients. Rather, an out-patient's initial bill is mailed on the statement form used generally by Ball Memorial. Outpatients subsequently receive the same series of first through fifth statements, except that the periodic charge disclosed on the reverse side of the statement form is labeled a "HANDLING CHARGE." Coupon books are not mailed to outpatients routinely with the third statement, but are apparently sent only to those whose bill exceeds $40. Outpatient accounts are automatically turned over to a collection agency fourteen days after the fifth statement is sent.

Appellant Bright was an inpatient at Ball Memorial July 6-10, 1977. While in the Hospital, Bright was apparently shown a copy of the Initial Credit Disclosure Statement, but did not sign it. Presumably, she was also given a copy of the Hospital Patient Guide. At the time of her discharge, she made no arrangements with the Hospital to repay her bill. Bright subsequently received her initial bill, and the first, second, and third statements from the Hospital. She also received a coupon book with the third statement, containing more than four coupons.

Bright never utilized the coupon book to make a payment to the Hospital. Yet, even after the bill remained unpaid for more than 104 days, Bright's debt was not referred to an outside collection agency because she and the Hospital were working together to secure payment of the obligation. When efforts to secure public financial assistance for Bright were unsuccessful, Bright and Ball Memorial, on November 1, 1977, orally agreed to a payment plan whereby Bright would repay her bill in $15 monthly installments. Several days later, Bright and Ball Memorial orally modified the agreement to payments of $20 per month. Bright made no payments pursuant to either of these agreements. On March 1, 1978, Bright paid $30 to the Hospital, which was credited to her July 10, 1977 account and a previous account owing to the Hospital. Further contacts and negotiations followed, and on March 23, 1978, Ball Memorial and Bright agreed that her entire obligation (originally $933.35) would be satisfied if Bright would pay $15 per month for 24 months. Since March 23, 1978, Bright has made no payments to Ball Memorial.

Appellant Barber received outpatient care at Ball Memorial on numerous occasions, some of which entailed the provision of services charged at more than $40. Presumably, she received an initial bill and the first through fifth statements from the Hospital with respect to each outpatient visit. Along with the third [sic] statements she has received, Barber received at least one coupon book containing more than four coupons and presumably has received others for those bills which exceeded $40. Barber has never reached any agreement with the Hospital on repayment nor has she paid anything for any of the services. Handling charges were added to her accounts and her accounts were turned over to a collection agency.

Appellants filed suit as a class action against the Hospital, alleging that its billing and credit procedures were in violation of the Truth in Lending Act, 15 U.S.C. §§1601, et seq. Before reaching the issue of class certification, the district court granted Ball Memorial's motion to dismiss for lack of subject matter jurisdiction. Treating the motion to dismiss as one for summary judgment, the district court apparently held that Ball Memorial was not a "creditor" within the meaning of 15 U.S.C. §1602(f) under any circumstances involving its billing practices. Specifically, the district court found that Ball Memorial neither extended "credit" "in the ordinary course of business" nor imposed a "finance charge" within the meaning of the Act, and that the purposes of the Act would not be served by extending its coverage to "institutions such as Ball Memorial."

Without approving the broad ruling of the district court that Ball Memorial is not a "creditor" under the Act, we affirm that court's judgment on the ground that Ball Memorial did not consummate credit transactions with either Bright or Barber.

CONSUMMATION OF CREDIT TRANSACTIONS WITH APPELLANTS

Regulation Z, 12 C.F.R. §226.8(a) provides that all disclosures required for a "creditor" by the Act must be made prior to the time that the "transaction is consummated." Regulation Z, 12 C.F.R. §226.2(kk) further specifies that:

> A transaction shall be considered consummated at the time a contractual relationship is created between a creditor and a customer or a lessor and lessee irrespective of the time of performance of either party.

In regard to a factual situation involving a hospital similar to this case, the Federal Reserve Board staff has stated:

> If services are performed for patients under the general assumption that the bill will be paid upon discharge and if subsequently it is necessary for the hospital to finance that bill, the "transaction" for purposes of Section 226.8 is the credit transaction and not the physical act of performing the hospital services. Accordingly, in meeting the requirements of Section 226.8(a) that disclosures must be made "before the transaction is consummated" the hospital need only make disclosures prior to consummation of the financing arrangements.

Federal Reserve Board (FRB) Unofficial Staff Interpretation No. 170 (October 24, 1969), Cons. Cred. Guide (CCH) ¶30,498.[20] For appellants to

---

20. While the Federal Reserve Board interpretive regulations and staff opinion letters are not binding upon the courts, these constructions of the statute and the Board regulations are entitled to substantial deference "because of the important interpretive powers granted to the agency in this very complex field." Croysdale v. Franklin Savings Association, 601 F.2d 1340,

be able to claim that the Hospital violated the Truth in Lending Act as to them, they must have consummated credit transactions with the Hospital.

Appellant Bright argues that credit transactions between Ball Memorial and her were consummated on a number of occasions. First, Bright apparently contends that her payment of $30 to Ball Memorial on March 1, 1978 evidences her acceptance of installment payment terms offered by the Hospital. The facts do not support this contention. Bright's $30 payment some four months after she had reached the $15 per month and $20 per month work-out agreements with the Hospital in November 1977 was clearly not responsive to either of those work-out agreements nor to the terms of the coupon book which Bright had even earlier received along with the third statement from the Hospital. Under these circumstances, Bright's March 1 payment was merely a one-time partial payment of her account, the acceptance of which by the Hospital does not constitute an agreement to a credit transaction. See, e.g., FRB Unofficial Staff Interpretation No. 170, supra.

Second, Bright contends that the two agreements which she reached with the Hospital in early November 1977, $15 and $20 per month respectively, satisfy the "consummation" requirement. As an initial matter, there is no indication in the record whether, in either of these agreements with the Hospital, the agreement embodied a commitment by Bright to pay the Hospital the ¾% monthly charges on the outstanding balance in addition to repayment of the original balance of over $900. We do not, however, find that either agreement was one involving the extension of "credit" so as to require disclosures under the Act.

The Federal Reserve Board staff has consistently indicated that "informal workout arrangements" reached between a vendor and a customer do not require disclosures under the Act even though the workout involves more than four installments or payment in full of the underlying obligation. In FRB Official Staff Interpretation FC-0101 (July 19, 1977), Cons. Cred. Guide (CCH) ¶31,637, the Federal Reserve Board staff reviewed a bank's plan which allowed its delinquent customers to repay their debts on terms different from those originally agreed upon. Specifically, the bank established a "deficiency balance" in each delinquent account and then made contact by telephone with the debtor, giving the debtor an opportunity to pay the deficiency balance in full or in installments.

If the debtor elected to pay in installments, a monthly payment commensurate with the debtor's ability to pay was established and the customer

---

1344 n.4 (7th Cir. 1979). See also Smith v. No. 2 Galesburg Crown Finance Corp., No. 78-2155, et al., 615 F.2d 407 at 417-418 (7th Cir. 1980).

was mailed a form letter and coupon book reflecting the agreement. The staff concluded:

> your bank's plan, as outlined above, is an informal workout arrangement requiring no new Truth in Lending disclosures. In staff's view, a formal written workout arrangement would involve some new evidence of indebtedness executed by the customer, such as a new note, contract or other form of written agreement. We do not believe that a unilateral written communication by either the creditor or the customer (such as a letter confirming matters previously discussed either orally or in writing) renders a workout arrangement formal and subject to the disclosure requirements of Regulation Z even though the plan might, like yours, involve repayment in more than four installments on terms differing from the original installment credit transaction.

Similarly, in FRB Unofficial Staff Interpretation No. 1230 (August 9, 1977), Cons. Cred. Guide (CCH) ¶31,669, the staff stated that where a bank offered its delinquent customer the opportunity to pay the obligation in monthly installments smaller than the agreements previously agreed upon, and the customer then wrote or telephoned to agree to these or other monthly payment arrangements, it would not regard the situation as a "formal written prejudgment workout agreement" because no new evidence of indebtedness was executed. The distinctions drawn between informal and formal workout agreements clearly apply to entities other than banks. See FRB Unofficial Staff Interpretation No. 1221 (July 19, 1977), Cons. Cred. Guide (CCH) ¶31,660.

Bright's early November 1977 oral agreements with Ball Memorial were reached more than 110 days after Bright's discharge as an inpatient on July 10, 1977. Given the computerized billing system utilized by the Hospital, by November 1, Bright had been mailed all five statements sent during the Hospital's billing cycle, including the coupon book sent along with the third statement. At this point on the billing cycle, the usual next step taken by the Hospital was to refer the account to a collection agency. At no time prior to November 1 did Bright ever make any explicit agreement with the Hospital to pay her bill nor did she take any action, such as making a partial payment, indicating implicit acceptance of the Hospital's installment payment option.

Given these circumstances, it is clear that the Hospital regarded Bright's account as delinquent and was seeking at the time of these notices and discussions to make some arrangement short of referring Bright's account to a collection agency. The terms of the agreements reached between Bright and the Hospital were substantially different from the terms for installment payments set forth generally on the billing statements previously sent by the Hospital. These statements indicate that for a bill the size of Bright's

($933.35), the minimum monthly payment was 5% of the outstanding balance: Bright's agreements were for the substantially smaller sums of $15 and $20 per month. Moreover, these agreements were reached without a new written evidence of Bright's indebtedness in a manner consistent with the Federal Reserve Board interpretations. Bright's November 1977 agreements were thus "informal workout agreements" not requiring the disclosures provided by the Act *even* though these agreements contemplated payment in more than four installments and may have entailed payment of monthly ¾% charges on the outstanding balance.

Finally, Bright and Barber contend that consummation occurred when they, having failed to make any payments on their accounts, had monthly charges assessed against them beginning on the forty-eighth day after discharge. Specifically, appellants argue that, since the Hospital's self-described "finance charges" were in fact levied against their accounts and since the Hospital, when it seeks judgments in cases filed to collect the accounts, includes the "finance charges," the Hospital itself considers them to have agreed to the charges. Appellants further contend that the charges assessed were "finance charges" within the meaning of the Act.

Ball Memorial conceded at oral argument that it assessed these charges on appellants' accounts (and others like them), but did so on the basis that these charges were "late payment" charges, and not "finance charges." Regulation Z, 12 C.F.R. §226.4(c). The question before us is thus whether the charges assessed by the Hospital against Bright and Barber's accounts subsequent to the forty-eighth day after discharge were bona fide charges made for late payment or were "finance charges," such that Ball Memorial consummated a credit transaction with them. We conclude that these charges were "late payment" charges. . . .

Regulation Z, 12 C.F.R. §226.4(c) distinguishes between "late payment" and "finance" charges:

> A late payment, delinquency, default, reinstatement, or other such charge is not a finance charge if imposed for actual unanticipated late payment, delinquency, default, or other such occurrence.

Appellants argue initially that the monthly charges imposed on their accounts were "anticipated" within the meaning of §226.4(c) because the Hospital obtained approximately $78,000 in revenue from such charges during the period from July 1, 1977 through September 1978, and because it budgets for this revenue in the annual budget. This argument, however, misconstrues the meaning of "unanticipated" in §226.4(c). The fact that a business may expect to have delinquent accounts and anticipate the possible receipt of some revenues from the charges imposed on such accounts does not automatically render such charges "finance charges." Rather, "unanticipated" within §226.4(c) means that the failure of any customer to pay his bill on time is not anticipated in any particular case. See FRB Unofficial Staff Interpretation No. 1301 (May 23, 1978), Cons. Cred. Guide (CCH) ¶31,792.

In an effort to clarify the difference between a "late payment charge" and a "finance charge," the Federal Reserve Board has issued an interpretive rule. 12 C.F.R. §226.401. In this rule, which has been held valid, Kroll v. Cities Service Oil Co., 352 F. Supp. 357, 363 (N.D. Ill. 1972), the Board considered a vendor which billed its customers so that the full bill was due within a stipulated period after billing, with no installment payment option. If the bill was not paid in full by the end of the period, the vendor imposed a periodic charge on the unpaid balance until fully paid. The Board stated:

> When in the ordinary course of business a vendor's billings are not paid in full within that stipulated period of time, and under such circumstances the vendor does not, in fact, regard such accounts in default, but continues or will continue to extend credit and imposes charges periodically for delaying payment of such accounts from time to time until paid, the charge so imposed comes within the definition of a "finance charge." . . .

This rule indicates that whether a charge ostensibly imposed for late payment is a "finance charge" depends on whether the vendor regards accounts not paid within the required period to be in default and whether the vendor continues to extend credit to the customer in default. See Continental Oil Co. v. Burns, 317 F. Supp. 194, 196 (D. Del. 1970).

Whether or not the vendor considers its customers' accounts delinquent must be judged by its actions taken as a whole. See FRB Official Staff Interpretation FC-0060 (April 4, 1977), Cons. Cred. Guide (CCH) ¶31,570; FRB Unofficial Staff Interpretation No. 1171 (March 31, 1977), Cons. Cred. Guide (CCH) ¶31,568; FRB Unofficial Staff Interpretation (July 9, 1969), Cons. Cred. Guide (CCH) ¶30,088. Particularly relevant is whether the vendor continues to extend credit to its customers after the time of default, though the continued extension of credit under exigent circumstances should not defeat a finding that the charges are in fact "late payment" charges. See FRB Unofficial Staff Interpretation No. 912 (August 13, 1975), Cons. Cred. Guide (CCH) ¶31,246 (hospital furnishing services to delinquent patients only where "certified medical necessity" exists); FRB Unofficial Staff Interpretation (July 9, 1969), supra (occasional extension by hospital of credit to delinquent patients in emergency situations).

Also particularly relevant is whether the vendor takes "commercially reasonable" efforts to correct the delinquency situation both through clear notification to its customer that the customer is delinquent, see FRB Unofficial Staff Interpretation No. 797 (May 16, 1974), Cons. Cred. Guide (CCH) ¶31,119; FRB Unofficial Staff Interpretation No. 414 (October 23, 1970), Cons. Cred. Guide (CCH) ¶30,600, and through efforts to collect the delinquent account. See, e.g., FRB Official Staff Interpretation FC-0060, supra; FRB Unofficial Staff Interpretation No. 1171, supra.

Applying these general principles to the facts of this case, we conclude that the ¾% monthly charge imposed upon Bright's inpatient bill and the 50¢ handling charge imposed upon Barber's outpatient bills commencing with the forty-eighth day after discharge were bona fide late payment charges. Most importantly, Ball Memorial considers its patient accounts not paid within the forty-eight day period to be delinquent and takes "commercially reasonable" efforts to collect those accounts once they are determined to be delinquent. Subsequent to the forty-eighth day, Ball Memorial sends statements on the sixty-second, seventy-sixth and ninetieth days—each clearly advising the patient that the account is considered overdue and insisting upon payment. Ball Memorial additionally attempts to make contact by telephone with its patients during this period in an effort to collect on the accounts. Accounts on which no payment agreement is reached and where no payments have been made are generally referred to an outside collection agency less than two months after the Hospital considers them delinquent.

Appellants argue particularly that the facts that (1) Ball Memorial mails the coupon book with the third statement, and does not continue to send dunning notices to or refer to a collection agency those patients who begin to pay through the coupon book and (2) Ball Memorial does not refer its accounts to a collection agency until after the 104th billing day demonstrates that the Hospital does not treat these accounts as delinquent. We disagree.

That Ball Memorial does not immediately refer its delinquent accounts to a collection agency hardly indicates commercially unreasonable efforts to collect these accounts. See Vega v. First Federal Savings & Loan Association of Detroit, 433 F. Supp. 624, 628 (E.D. Mich. 1977). See also FRB Unofficial Staff Interpretation No. 1301, supra. Rather, the Hospital's combined use of telephonic and mail communications over the less than two months following the forty-eighth day prior to its referral to a collection agency appears well designed to attempt a repayment of the debt. This practice is hardly designed to amass large monthly charges while the account lies dormant and unpaid.

Nor does Ball Memorial's mailing of the coupon book with the third statement, nor its failure to send dunning notices to those patients who commence installment payments pursuant to the coupon book, indicate that the charges assessed to these appellants' accounts are "finance charges." We need not decide on this appeal whether patients who commence installment payments based on the coupon book consummate "credit" transactions with the Hospital since neither appellant did so. Insofar as appellants' accounts are concerned, the generalized mailing of such coupon books to delinquent inpatients and outpatients with balances over $40 indicates nothing more than a sincere effort on the Hospital's part to seek some repayment. The Hospital's practice not to mail dunning statements to or to assign the accounts of those delinquent patients who have commenced installment payments merely demonstrates the Hospital's good common sense.

Finally, appellants argue that the Hospital's use of the label "finance charge" on its printed materials indicates that the charges are, in fact, "finance charges" under the Act. While we agree with appellants that this terminology is relevant to our determination, see FRB Unofficial Staff Interpretation No. 1172, supra, it is by no means determinative. See FRB Unofficial Staff Interpretation No. 414, supra. In this regard, we agree with the district court that "the substance of the billing system controls, not its labels." We conclude, therefore, that the monthly charges assessed against Bright's and Barber's accounts were bona fide "late payment" charges under Regulation Z, 12 C.F.R. §226.4(c).

Since the charges assessed against appellants' accounts were bona fide "late payment" charges, their imposition did not constitute the consummation of a credit transaction by the Hospital with either appellant. Thus, even though the Hospital may have been a potential "creditor" under the Act in its offering the extension of credit to the appellants, the disclosure obligations imposed by the Act did not arise as to them. Regulation Z, 12 C.F.R. §226.8(a).

Accordingly, we need not address the question of whether Ball Memorial's credit and billing procedures violated the Act, and we affirm the judgment of the district court on the grounds stated.

PROBLEM 111

In real estate mortgages, the lender frequently requires the up-front payment of "points." Each point is 1 percent of the mortgage amount and is used as an inducement to the lender to make the loan.

When Scarlet was selling her home, Tara, she learned that the lenders in the area were all demanding that the buyer pay two points as a closing cost, and this fact was losing her potential buyers. To counter the problem, Scarlet raised her asking price for Tara by an amount sufficient to cover the points, and then agreed with the lender that she would pay the points at the closing. Are the points part of the finance charge? Compare Reg. Z §§226.4(b)(3) and 226.4(c)(5).

C. The Annual Percentage Rate

The annual percentage rate is determined by formulas explained in §226.14(c) and, for closed-end transactions, in Appendix J to the Regulation; see §226.22(a). Reliance on the tables produced by the Board (even if they prove to be in error) insulates the creditor from liability, see §226.22 n.45d. Nowadays the APR is most commonly ascertained by the use of computer programs designed to make sure the disclosure is accurate.

IV. DISCLOSURE: OPEN-END TRANSACTIONS

All TIL disclosures must be given to the consumer in a copy the consumer can keep. Traditionally this has meant that the consumer was handed or mailed a physical piece of paper, but in recent years the trend is toward electronic disclosure. Both the federal government, in the Electronic Signatures in Global and National Commerce Act, 15 U.S.C. §7001 (commonly known as "E-Sign"), and the states, with the adoption of the Uniform Electronic Transactions Act (UETA), have given us legislation designed to change laws requiring the use of paper in legal matters to permit electronic substitutes. As a consequence, the various federal and state agencies responsible for disclosures to consumers in all the statutes and regulations discussed in this book, including TILA, are busy adopting regulations permitting creditors to make their disclosures over the Internet. Whether this will lead to more or less actual disclosure of the relevant information to the consumer is still up in the air. This issue will be discussed further in the final chapter, Consumers in Cyberspace.

The Truth in Lending Act draws a distinction between open-end credit and closed-end credit. The former occurs when the parties intend the creditor to make repeated extensions of credit: MasterCard, Visa, revolving charge accounts at department stores, or your own running tab at the neighborhood grocery store. In closed-end credit situations, the parties contemplate only one transaction: a loan so that the consumer can go on vacation, the sale of an automobile on credit, the purchase of a house. Read Reg. Z §226.2(a)(10) and (20). The disclosures for each are quite different. Subpart B of Regulation Z deals with open-end credit and Subpart C with closed-end credit.

The open-end credit rules apply to *all* consumer credit card issuers, even if the creditor does not impose a finance charge and requires payment of the bill as a whole (with no installments), Reg. Z §226.2(a)(17)(iii). Thus American Express is required to comply with Subpart B of Regulation Z, even though it does not collect a finance charge and use of its traditional credit card requires the cardholder to pay the bills as submitted.

HOUSEHOLD CREDIT SERVICES, INC. v. PFENNIG
United States Supreme Court, 2004
541 U.S. 232

Justice THOMAS delivered the opinion of the Court.

Congress enacted the Truth in Lending Act (TILA), 82 Stat. 146, in order to promote the "informed use of credit" by consumers. 15 U.S.C. §1601(a). To that end, TILA's disclosure provisions seek to ensure "meaningful disclosure of credit terms." Ibid. Further, Congress delegated expansive authority to the Federal Reserve Board (Board) to enact appropriate regulations to advance this purpose. §1604(a). We granted certiorari, 539 U.S. 957, 123 S. Ct. 2639, 156 L. Ed. 2d 654 (2003), to decide whether the Board's Regulation Z, which specifically excludes fees imposed for exceeding a credit limit (over-limit fees) from the definition of "finance charge," is an unreasonable interpretation of §1605. We conclude that it is not, and, accordingly, we reverse the judgment of the Court of Appeals for the Sixth Circuit.

I

Respondent, Sharon Pfennig, holds a credit card initially issued by petitioner Household Credit Services, Inc. (Household), but in which petitioner MBNA America Bank, N.A. (MBNA), now holds an interest through the acquisition of Household's credit card portfolio. Although the terms of respondent's credit card agreement set respondent's credit limit at $2,000, respondent was able to make charges exceeding that limit, subject to a $29 "over-limit fee" for each month in which her balance exceeded $2,000.

TILA regulates, inter alia, the substance and form of disclosures that creditors offering "open end consumer credit plans" (a term that includes credit card accounts) must make to consumers, §1637(a), and provides a civil remedy for consumers who suffer damages as a result of a creditor's failure to comply with TILA's provisions, §1640. When a creditor and a consumer enter into an open-end consumer credit plan, the creditor is required to provide to the consumer a statement for each billing cycle for which there is an outstanding balance due. §1637(b). The statement must include the account's outstanding balance at the end of the billing period, §1637(b)(8), and "[t]he amount of any finance charge added to the account during the period, itemized to show the amounts, if any, due to the application of percentage rates and the amount, if any, imposed as a minimum or fixed charge," §1637(b)(4). A "finance charge" is an amount "payable directly or indirectly by the person to whom the credit is extended, and imposed directly or indirectly by the creditor as an incident to the extension of credit." §1605(a). The Board has interpreted this definition to exclude "[c]harges . . . for exceeding a credit limit." See 12 CFR §226.4(c)(2) (2004) (Regulation Z). Thus, although respondent's billing statement disclosed the imposition of an over-limit fee when she exceeded her $2,000 credit limit, consistent with Regulation Z, the amount was not included as part of the "finance charge."

On August 24, 1999, respondent filed a complaint in the United States District Court for the Southern District of Ohio on behalf of a purported nationwide class of all consumers who were charged or assessed over-limit fees by petitioners. Respondent alleged in her complaint that petitioners allowed her and each of the other putative class members to exceed their credit limits, thereby subjecting them to over-limit fees. Petitioners violated TILA, respondent alleged, by failing to classify the over-limit fees as "finance charges" and thereby "misrepresented the true cost of credit" to respondent and the other class members. Class Action Complaint in No. C2-99 815 ¶¶34-39, App. to Pet. for Cert. A39-A40. Petitioners moved to dismiss the complaint pursuant to Federal Rule of Civil Procedure 12(b)(6) on the ground that Regulation Z specifically excludes over-limit fees from the definition of "finance charge." 12 CFR §226.4(c)(2) (2004). The District Court agreed and granted petitioners' motion to dismiss.

On appeal, respondent argued, and the Court of Appeals agreed, that Regulation Z's explicit exclusion of over-limit fees from the definition of "finance charge" conflicts with the plain language of 15 U.S.C. §1605(a). The Court of Appeals first noted that, as a remedial statute, TILA must be liberally interpreted in favor of consumers. 295 F.3d 522, 528 (CA6 2002). The Court of Appeals then concluded that the over-limit fees in this case were imposed "incident to the extension of credit" and therefore fell squarely within §1605's definition of "finance charge." Id., at 528-529. The Court of Appeals' conclusion turned on the distinction between unilateral acts of default and acts of default resulting from consumers' requests for additional credit, exceeding a predetermined credit limit, that creditors grant. Under the Court of Appeals' reasoning, a penalty imposed due to a unilateral act of default would not constitute a "finance charge." Id., at 530-531. Respondent alleged in her complaint, however, that petitioners "allowed [her] to make charges and/or assessed [her] charges that allowed her balance to exceed her credit limit of two thousand dollars," App. to Pet. for Cert. A39, ¶34, putting her actions under the category of acts of default resulting from consumers requests for additional credit, exceeding a pre-determined credit limit, that creditors grant. The Court of Appeals held that because petitioners "made an additional extension of credit to [respondent] over and above the alleged 'credit limit,'" id., ¶35, and charged the over-limit fee as a condition of this additional extension of credit, the over-limit fee clearly and unmistakably fell under the definition of a "finance charge." 295 F.3d, at 530. Based on its reading of respondent's allegations, the Court of Appeals limited its holding to "those instances in which the creditor knowingly permits the credit card holder to exceed his or her credit limit and then imposes a fee incident to the extension of that credit." Id., at 532, n. 5.

II

Congress has expressly delegated to the Board the authority to prescribe regulations containing "such classifications, differentiations, or other provisions" as, in the judgment of the Board, "are necessary or proper to effectuate the purposes of [TILA], to prevent circumvention or evasion thereof, or to facilitate compliance therewith." §1604(a). Thus, the Court has previously recognized that "the [Board] has played a pivotal role in 'setting [TILA] in motion. . . . '" Ford Motor Credit Co. v. Milhollin, 444 U.S. 555, 566, 100 S. Ct. 790, 63 L. Ed. 2d 22 (1980) (quoting Norwegian Nitrogen Products Co. v. United States, 288 U.S. 294, 315, 53 S. Ct. 350, 77 L. Ed. 796 (1933)). Indeed, "Congress has specifically designated the [Board] and staff as the primary source for interpretation and application of truth-in-lending law." 444 U.S., at 566, 100 S. Ct. 790. As the Court recognized in *Ford Motor Credit Co.*, twice since the passage of TILA, Congress has made this intention clear: first by providing a good-faith defense to creditors who comply with the Board's rules and regulations, 88 Stat. 1518, codified at 15 U.S.C. §1640(f), and, second, by expanding this good-faith defense to creditors who conform to "any interpretation or approval by an official or employee of the Federal Reserve System duly authorized by the Board to issue such interpretations or approvals," 90 Stat. 197, codified as amended, at §1640(f). 444 U.S., at 566-567, 100 S. Ct. 790.

Respondent does not challenge the Board's authority to issue binding regulations. Thus, in determining whether Regulation Z's interpretation of TILA's text is binding on the courts, we are faced with only two questions. We first ask whether "Congress has directly spoken to the precise question at issue." Chevron U.S.A. Inc. v. Natural Resources Defense Council, Inc., 467 U.S. 837, 842, 104 S. Ct. 2778, 81 L. Ed. 2d 694 (1984). If so, courts, as well as the agency, "must give effect to the unambiguously expressed intent of Congress." Id., at 842-843, 104 S. Ct. 2778. However, whenever Congress has "explicitly left a gap for the agency to fill," the agency's regulation is "given controlling weight unless [it is] arbitrary, capricious, or manifestly contrary to the statute." Id., at 843-844, 104 S. Ct. 2778.

A

TILA itself does not explicitly address whether over-limit fees are included within the definition of "finance charge." Congress defined "finance charge" as "all charges, payable directly or indirectly by the person to whom the credit is extended, and imposed directly or indirectly by the creditor as an incident to the extension of credit." §1605(a). The Court of Appeals, however, made no attempt to clarify the scope of the critical term "incident to the extension of credit." The Court of Appeals recognized that, "'[i]n ascertaining the plain meaning of the statute, the court must look to the particular statutory language at issue, as well as the language and design of the statute as a whole.'" Id., at 529-530 (quoting K mart Corp. v. Cartier, Inc., 486 U.S. 281, 291, 108 S. Ct. 1811, 100 L. Ed. 2d 313 (1988)). However, the Court of Appeals failed to examine TILA's other provisions, or even the surrounding language in §1605, before reaching its conclusion. Because petitioners would not have imposed the over-limit fee had they not "granted [respondent's] request for additional credit, which resulted in her exceeding her credit limit," the Court of Appeals held that the over-limit fee in this case fell squarely within §1605(a)'s definition of "finance charge." 295 F.3d, at 528-529. Thus, the Court of Appeals rested its holding primarily on its particular characterization of the transaction that led to the over-limit charge in this case.

The Court of Appeals' characterization of the transaction in this case, however, is not supported even by the facts as set forth in respondent's complaint. Respondent alleged in her complaint that the over-limit fee is imposed for each month in which her balance exceeds the original credit limit. App. to Pet. for Cert. A39, ¶35. If this were true, however, the over-limit fee would be imposed not as a direct result of an extension of credit for a purchase that caused respondent to exceed her $2,000 limit, but rather as a result of the fact that her charges exceeded her $2,000 limit at the time respondent's monthly charges were officially calculated. Because over-limit fees, regardless of a creditor's particular billing practices, are imposed only when a consumer exceeds his credit limit, it is perfectly reasonable to characterize an over-limit fee not as a charge imposed for obtaining an extension of credit over a consumer's credit limit, but rather as a penalty for violating the credit agreement.

The Court of Appeals thus erred in resting its conclusion solely on this particular characterization of the details of credit card transactions, a characterization that is not clearly compelled by the terms and definitions of TILA, and one with which others could reasonably disagree. Certainly, regardless of how the fee is characterized, there is at least some connection between the over-limit fee and an extension of credit. But, this Court has recognized that the phrase "incident to or in conjunction with" implies some necessary connection between the antecedent and its object, although it "does not place beyond rational debate the nature or extent of the re-quired connection." Holly Farms Corp. v. NLRB, 517 U.S. 392, 403, n. 9, 116 S. Ct. 1396, 134 L. Ed. 2d 593 (1996) (internal quotation marks omitted). In other words, the phrase "incident to" does not make clear whether a substantial (as opposed to a remote) connection is required. Thus, unlike the Court of Appeals, we cannot conclude that the term "finance charge" unambiguously includes over-limit fees. That term, standing alone, is ambiguous.

Moreover, an examination of TILA's related provisions, as well as the full text of §1605 itself, casts doubt on the Court of Appeals' interpretation of the statute. A consumer holding an open-end credit plan may incur two types of charges—finance charges and "other charges which may be im-posed as part of the plan." §§1637(a)(1)-(5). TILA does not make clear which charges fall into each category. But TILA's recognition of at least two categories of charges does make clear that Congress did not contem-plate that all charges made in connection with an open-end credit plan would be considered "finance charges." And where TILA does explicitly address over-limit fees, it defines them as fees imposed "in connection with an extension of credit," §1637(c)(1)(B)(iii), rather than "incident to the extension of credit," §1605(a). Furthermore, none of §1605's specific examples of charges that fall within the definition of "finance charge" includes over-limit or comparable fees. See, e.g., §1605(a)(2) ("[s]ervice or carrying charge"); §1605(a)(3) (loan fee or similar charge); §1605(a)(6) (mortgage broker fees).

As our prior discussion indicates, the best interpretation of the term "finance charge" may exclude over-limit fees. But §1605(a) is, at best, ambiguous, because neither §1605(a) nor its surrounding provisions provides a clear answer. While we acknowledge that there may be some fees not explicitly addressed by §1605(a)'s definition of "finance charge" but which are unambiguously included in or excluded by that definition, over-limit fees are not such fees.

B

Because §1605 is ambiguous, the Board's regulation implementing §1605 "is binding in the courts unless procedurally defective, arbitrary or capricious in substance, or manifestly contrary to the statute." United States v. Mead Corp., 533 U.S. 218, 227, 121 S. Ct. 2164, 150 L. Ed. 2d 292 (2001).

Regulation Z's exclusion of over-limit fees from the term "finance charge" is in no way manifestly contrary to §1605. Regulation Z defines the term "finance charge" as "the cost of consumer credit." 12 CFR §226.4 (2004). It specifically excludes from the definition of "finance charge" the following:

(1) Application fees charged to all applicants for credit, whether or not credit is actually extended.
(2) Charges for actual unanticipated late payment, *for exceeding a credit limit*, or for delinquency, default, or a similar occurrence.
(3) Charges imposed by a financial institution for paying items that overdraw an account, unless the payment of such items and the imposition of the charge were previously agreed upon in writing.
(4) Fees charged for participation in a credit plan, whether assessed on an annual or other periodic basis.
(5) Seller's points.
(6) Interest forfeited as a result of an interest reduction required by law on a time deposit used as security for an extension of credit.
(7) [Certain fees related to real estate.]
(8) Discounts offered to induce payment for a purchase by cash, check, or other means, as provided in section 167(b) of the Act. §226.4(c) (emphasis added).

The Board adopted the regulation to emphasize "disclosures that are relevant to credit decisions, as opposed to disclosures related to events occurring after the initial credit choice," because "the primary goals of [TILA] are not particularly enhanced by regulatory provisions relating to changes in terms on outstanding obligations and on the effects of the failure to comply with the terms of the obligation." 45 Fed. Reg. 80649 (1980). The

Board's decision to emphasize disclosures that are most relevant to a consumer's initial credit decisions reflects an understanding that "[m]eaningful disclosure does not mean more disclosure," but instead "describes a balance between 'competing considerations of complete disclosure . . . and the need to avoid . . . [informational overload].'" *Ford Motor Credit Co.*, 444 U.S., at 568, 100 S. Ct. 790 (quoting S. Rep. No. 96-73, p. 3 (1979)). Although the fees excluded from the term "finance charge" in Regulation Z (e.g., application charges, late payment charges, and over-limit fees) might be relevant to a consumer's credit decision, the Board rationally concluded that these fees—which are not automatically recurring or are imposed only when a consumer defaults on a credit agreement—are less relevant to determining the true cost of credit. Because over-limit fees, which are imposed only when a consumer breaches the terms of his credit agreement, can reasonably be characterized as a penalty for defaulting on the credit agreement, the Board's decision to exclude them from the term "finance charge" is surely reasonable.

In holding that Regulation Z conflicts with §1605's definition of the term "finance charge," the Court of Appeals ignored our warning that "judges ought to refrain from substituting their own interstitial lawmaking for that of the [Board]." *Ford Motor Credit Co.*, supra, at 568, 100 S. Ct. 790. Despite the Board's rational decision to adopt a uniform rule excluding from the term "finance charge" all penalties imposed for exceeding the credit limit, the Court of Appeals adopted a case-by-case approach contingent on whether an act of default was "unilateral." Putting aside the lack of textual support for this approach, the Court of Appeals' approach would prove unworkable to creditors and, more importantly, lead to significant confusion for consumers. Under the Court of Appeals' rule, a consumer would be able to decipher if a charge is considered a "finance charge" or an "other charge" each month only by recalling the details of the particular transaction that caused the consumer to exceed his credit limit. In most cases, the consumer would not even know the relevant facts, which are contingent on the nature of the authorization given by the creditor to the merchant. Moreover, the distinction between "unilateral" acts of default and acts of default where a consumer exceeds his credit limit (but has not thereby renegotiated his credit limit and is still subject to the over-limit fee) is based on a fundamental misunderstanding of the workings of the credit card industry. As the Board explained below, a creditor's "authorization" of a particular point-of-sale transaction does not represent a final determination that a particular transaction is within a consumer's credit limit because the authorization system is not suited to identify instantaneously and accurately over-limit transactions. Brief for Board of Governors of Federal Reserve System as Amicus Curiae in No. 00-4213(CA6), pp. 7-9.

Congress has authorized the Board to make "such classifications, differentiations, or other provisions, and [to] provide for such adjustments and exceptions for any class of transactions, as in the judgment of the Board are necessary or proper to effectuate the purposes of [TILA], to prevent circumvention or evasion thereof, or to facilitate compliance therewith." §1604(a). Here, the Board has accomplished all of these objectives by setting forth a clear, easy to apply (and easy to enforce) rule that highlights the charges the Board determined to be most relevant to a consumer's credit decisions. The judgment of the Court of Appeals is therefore reversed.

Open-end transactions require some disclosures of the credit terms at three different times: when the account is opened (Reg. Z §226.6), on each periodic statement (i.e., the monthly bill) (Reg. Z §226.7), and annually, when the creditor must send the consumer a summary of the consumer's rights under the Fair Credit Billing Act (Reg. Z §226.9(a)). And, as we have seen, the advertisement of the availability of a credit card requires the disclosures mandated by Reg. Z §226.5a.

PROBLEM 112

Big Department Store hires you to advise it on the details of the credit card plan it is considering instituting. Answer the following questions for the company vice president in charge of consumer matters.

a. Does the company have to send out monthly bills? See Reg. Z §226.5(b)(2)(i).

b. Does the company have to give its customers a grace period in which to pay without incurring finance charges? Reg. Z §226.7(j). If it does give a grace period, can it structure its mailing of the bills so as to keep the period very short? See §226.5(b)(2)(ii); Reg. AA §227.22 (effective July 1, 2010).

c. If the company does business in many states, all of which have different APR limits, can it disclose them all on the initial statement and periodic statements, or must it give different statements for each jurisdiction?

d. Reg. Z §§226.6(a)(3) and 226.7(e) both require the creditor to identify the method used to determine the balance. What does this mean?

CONSUMER CREDIT POLICY STATEMENT NO. 4
Federal Trade Commission, May 7, 1970

THE PREVIOUS BALANCE METHOD

Since the Truth in Lending Act was passed on July 1, 1969, many consumers have discovered an important but previously unnoticed fact about most of their revolving charge accounts. This fact is that when the bill is not paid in full each month, the resulting finance charges are computed upon the *previous* (or opening) balance in the account, without any regard to the payment made by the customer.

Revolving charge accounts, referred to as "open end credit" by the Truth in Lending Act, are all characterized by a plan that has three aspects.

First, the creditor may permit the customer to make purchases (or loans) from time to time, usually by means of a credit card.

Second, the customer has the privilege of paying the balance in full or in installments; and

Third, the finance charge may be computed by the creditor from time to time on an *outstanding* unpaid balance. It is this third aspect of open end credit that has confused many consumers.

A major portion of the Congressional hearings dealing with Truth in Lending over several years was devoted to open end credit.

The primary controversy centered around the problems of adapting the Act's point-of-sale disclosure and annual percentage rate calculation requirements to open end credit. After much debate, it was decided that the annual percentage rate of finance charges could be calculated by simply multiplying the periodic rate (usually 1½ percent per month) by the number of periods in a year to arrive at what is more a nominal (18 percent) than an effective rate.

It is important to remember that this nominal method of calculating the annual percentage rate applies *irrespective* of which of the several methods of calculating finance charges is used by the open end creditor. . . .

The most common and the least beneficial means of computing finance charges is the "previous balance" method. This is employed by well over half of all open end creditors in America. By this method, if there is any balance remaining unpaid in the account at the end of the current billing cycle, the periodic rate of finance charge is imposed upon the amount of the "previous balance" (that is the outstanding balance in the account at the beginning of the billing cycle). It does not take into account any payments, returns or purchases during the billing cycle.

For example, if you receive a bill for $100 and pay part of that amount ($50), your next month's bill (assuming no other purchases) will show finance charges of 1½% computed upon the "previous balance" of $100 ($1.50). This will be added to your balance remaining unpaid ($50.00) for a "new balance" of $51.50. This is clearly permissible according to the Truth in Lending Act.

While Congress did not forbid this "previous balance" method, it chose to regulate this practice by expressly requiring full disclosure when the account is opened and on every periodic bill. When the account is opened all creditors are required to disclose, among other things:

> [t]he conditions under which a finance charge may be imposed, including an explanation of the time period, if any, within which any credit extended may be paid without incurring a finance charge . . . [and] the method of determining the balance upon which a finance charge may be imposed.
>   Further, on each periodic billing statement all creditors are required to disclose, among other things:
>   [t]he balance on which the finance charge was computed and a statement of how the balance was determined. If the balance is determined without first deducting all credits during the billing cycle, that fact and the amount of such credits shall also be disclosed.

Therefore, although the "previous balance" method is permitted under the Truth in Lending Act—and taken advantage of by most creditors—the law requires that the customer be clearly told about it both when he opens his account and on each periodic bill.

While the "previous balance" method is the most popular one with today's creditors, there are many other methods of computing finance charges on open end credit accounts. Virtually all of them are more advantageous to customers. There are three other methods worthy of mention that are quite common and all will be preferred by consumers over the "previous balance" method.

AVERAGE DAILY BALANCE METHOD

The "average daily balance" method is used by some creditors. It relates the finance charge only to an amount which is the sum of the actual amounts outstanding each day during the billing period, divided by the number of days in the billing period. Payments are credited on the exact date of receipt. By this method, early payments of your account or a payment larger than the "minimum payment due" will result in a smaller finance charge.

ADJUSTED BALANCE METHOD

Some creditors calculate finance charges by using a method that is even more advantageous to their customers than the "average daily balance." Commonly called the "adjusted balance" method, it relates the rate of finance charge to the balance remaining in the account *after* deducting payments and credits.

Under this system, the customer gets maximum benefit from his payment without the necessity of paying early during the billing cycle. To use our earlier illustration, a $50 payment on an account with a "previous balance" of $100 will result in a finance charge of $.75 instead of the $1.50 yielded to a "previous balance" creditor. While these amounts may seem insignificant, the nation's larger open end creditors would lose millions of dollars annually merely by employing the "adjusted balance" as distinguished from the "previous balance" method.

PAST DUE BALANCE METHOD

Still other creditors use a method whereby they impose no finance charges even in the event of receiving no payment during the billing cycle, so long as full payment is received within 55 days from the original cycle's closing date. Known as the "Past Due Balance" method, it permits a customer to pay his bill in full every other month and still avoid all finance charges. Counting from the date of actual purchase, this method allows up to 90 days of free use of merchandise without charge for the credit.

One of the primary purposes of the Truth in Lending Act is to promote the informed use of credit. The choice of credit plans and rates remains the individual creditor's own business decision. While most open end creditors continued to employ the same credit plans after the effective date of the Act, now for the first time consumers are furnished information about their credit accounts in language that is both meaningful and uniform.

Therefore, the Commission not only urges consumers to read the information that the Truth in Lending Act requires creditors to furnish, but to use that information where possible to shop for advantageous credit terms.

The Commission further urges consumers to be aware that the careful timing of purchases and payments under various credit plans available can result in significant savings in finance charges.

MARS v. SPARTANBURG CHRYSLER PLYMOUTH[21]
United States Circuit Court, Fourth Circuit, 1983
713 F.2d 65

K. K. HALL, Circuit Judge.

Carrie Mars appeals from a district court order granting summary judgment in favor of the First National Bank of South Carolina and Spartanburg Chrysler Plymouth, Inc., appellees. On appeal, Mars contends that the appellees' disclosure statement contained certain violations of the Federal Truth in Lending Act (Act), 15 U.S.C. §1601 et seq. and the original Federal Reserve Regulation Z, 12 C.F.R. §226.[22] The district court held that these violations were only technical and because Mars sustained no actual injury as a result of them, no liability on the part of the creditors arose. We disagree and reverse the judgment of the lower court.

I

Both in the district court and on appeal, Mars argues that the appellees' disclosure form specifically violated §226.8(c)(5) of Regulation Z. This section required that the term "unpaid balance" be used on a consumer credit sale disclosure form when referring to the "unpaid balance of cash price," plus, all other charges included in the amount financed, but which are not part of the finance charge.[23] In the present case, appellees used the term "amount financed" on their disclosure statement as opposed to the

---

21. Footnotes in this case have been renumbered for clarity.

22. The Truth in Lending Act and Regulation Z were amended on March 31, 1980 and April 7, 1981, respectively. Compliance with those amendments was optional with the creditors until October 1, 1982. During the transition period, as a general rule, all disclosures were to be made either in accordance with the previous regulation or in accordance with the revised regulation, but a creditor could not mix the regulatory requirements. 46 Fed. Reg. 50290.

Because the creditors, appellees, in the instant case elected not to exercise their option to operate under the new amendments and revisions on the date of the contract, this case must be decided under the statute and regulation which existed before the 1980-81 amendment.

23. The term "unpaid balance" was defined by several subsections of 12 C.F.R. §226.8(c) which stated:

(1) The cash price of the property or service purchased, using the term "cash price."

(2) The amount of the downpayment itemized, as applicable, as downpayment in money, using the term "cash downpayment," downpayment in property, using the term "trade-in," and the sum, using the term "total downpayment."

(3) The difference between the amounts described in subparagraphs (1) and (2) of this paragraph, using the term "unpaid balance of cash price."

(4) All other charges, individually itemized, which are included in the amount financed but which are not part of the finance charge.

(5) The sum of the amounts determined under subparagraphs (3) and (4) of this paragraph, using the term "unpaid balance."

term "unpaid balance." Further, Mars asserts that appellees' disclosure statement violated §226.6(a) of original Regulation Z[24] because certain numerical amounts in the paragraphs labelled "Late Payment" and "Prepayment" were disclosed in eight point type rather than the required ten point type.

Appellees concede that the disclosure in question contains technical variations from Regulation Z. However, they contend that the minor variation in language and type size should not give rise to liability because Mars was given sufficient disclosure of information to make a meaningful comparison of credit terms, thereby meeting the objective of the Act.

The district court agreed with the appellees, and held that the technical violations asserted by Mars could not have influenced her choice of credit. Hence, the district court concluded that the purpose of the Act was achieved through the disclosure form utilized and that Mars sustained no actual injury. Therefore, the district court found that Mars' complaint was meritless and entered summary judgment in favor of appellees. From this order Mars appeals.

II

We disagree with the district court's analysis that a technical violation of the Act without actual harm imposes no liability. Congress declared that the purpose of the Act was:

> to assure a meaningful disclosure of credit terms so that the consumer will be able to compare more readily the various credit terms available to him and avoid the uninformed use of credit, and to protect the consumer against inaccurate and unfair credit billing. . . .

15 U.S.C. §1601(a). To insure that the consumer is protected, as Congress envisioned, requires that the provisions of the Act and the regulations implementing it be absolutely complied with and strictly enforced. As we noted in Barber v. Kimberell's Inc., 577 F.2d 216, 220 (1978), where the term "total time balance" was used in a truth and [sic] lending disclosure

---

24. The Federal Reserve Board set forth in Regulation Z, 12 C.F.R. §§226.6-226.8 disclosure requirements imposed upon creditors in consumer credit transactions. Section 226.6 (a), in pertinent part, stated:

> Disclosures; General rule . . . all numerical amounts and percentages shall be stated in figures and shall be printed in not less than the equivalent of 10 point type, .075 inch computer type or elite size typewritten numerals, or shall be legibly handwritten.

form as opposed to the term "total of payments" as required by Regulation Z, "a technical violation of the Act [is] sufficient to subject [the creditor] to civil liability under §1640." We conclude, therefore, that appellees are liable to Mars for the technical violations found in their disclosure form.

Although we agree with the district court that Mars sustained no actual injuries, §1640(a)(2)(A)(i) permits statutory damages twice the amount of any finance charge in connection with the transaction. The damages awarded shall not be less than $100 nor greater than $1,000. As the record reveals that Mars' finance charge was $1,174.35, she is entitled to statutory damages in the amount of $1,000.

Further, §1640(a)(3) permits a successful plaintiff to recover the costs of the action, together with a reasonable attorney's fee as determined by the court. Because in the instant case, the district court did not consider the amount of costs and attorney's fee to which Mars is entitled, we remand the case for such a determination.

Reversed and remanded.

The Fair Credit Billing Act (covered in Chapter 5, supra) gives the consumer a mechanism for disputing billing errors. Note that Regulation Z requires the creditor to give the consumer a summary of Fair Credit Billing Act rights and procedures when the account is opened, §226.6(d) (Appendix G to Regulation Z has a model form), and thereafter once a year, §226.9(a). In order that the consumer know *where* to send complaints, each periodic statement must provide an address for notice of billing errors, §226.7(k).

PROBLEM 113

When Gerald Czech received his monthly statement from Master-Card, it did not identify the transactions in any way other than giving the merchant's name and address, plus the date and amount of the transactions. Does Czech have a class action here? See §226.8(a)(3).

Credit cards are of two types: bipartite (two parties involved) and tripartite (three parties involved). In the bipartite card, the only entities are the consumer and the card issuer, and the card is honored only by the card issuer (Big Department Store, for example), or subsidiaries of the card issuer (Texaco and its gas stations, for example). With tripartite cards there are three parties: the consumer, the merchants who honor the card, and the card issuer (MasterCard, Visa, American Express, etc.). In the initial version of Regulation Z, the Federal Reserve Board treated both kinds of cards alike and required the card issuer to identify the transactions clearly. This caused major problems for tripartite card issuers because the merchants were often very sloppy in passing this information back to the card issuer in a manner such that the transaction could be identified at all. Eventually the Board yielded to the pleas of the tripartite card issuers, and now Reg. Z §226.8 has different transaction identification rules for the two types of cards. Only bipartite card issuers are now required to identify the transaction (and, having control at the card use level, such card issuers should be in a good position to do so).[25]

PROBLEM 114

His financial records in chaos one month, Czech overpaid his account at Big Department Store, sending in $20 too much. Does the store have to send it back to him, or can it simply reflect it as a credit on future bills? See Reg. Z §226.11.

PROBLEM 115

Big Bank decided to dramatically up the interest rate it charged its credit card accounts one year after it had solicited a number of new customers by promising them a very attractive rate. Can it do this unilaterally or must it give the customers warning? See Reg. Z §226.9(b) and (c). If the bank had originally solicited the customers by promising them a "fixed 10% interest rate for life!" could it later raise the rate to 14 percent? See Reg. AA §227.24, the case reprinted below, and DeMando v. Morris, 206 F.3d 1300 (9th Cir. 2000). Reg. Z §226.5(c) mandates that the required disclosures must "reflect the legal obligation between the parties." Is that language relevant to this dispute?

---

25. If the bipartite card issuer's system of identifying the transaction fails, there may be hope in §226.8 n.16.

ROBERTS v. FLEET BANK (R.I.)[26]
United States Court of Appeals, Third Circuit, 2003
342 F.3d 260

FUENTES, Circuit Judge.

This Truth in Lending Act case concerns a credit card solicitation that Fleet Bank (R.I.), N.A. and Fleet Credit Card Services, L.P. (collectively "Fleet") sent to Appellant, Denise Roberts, encouraging her to open an account with Fleet based on a promise of a "7.99% Fixed" annual percentage rate ("APR"). The solicitation stated that the interest rate was "NOT an introductory rate" and that "[i]t won't go up in just a few short months." The solicitation also stated that "[w]ith an extraordinary 7.99% Fixed APR . . . the Fleet Titanium MasterCard goes beyond all expectations." Sometime after Roberts opened her Fleet account, the bank sent her a letter stating that it was increasing the 7.99% fixed APR to 10.5%. Roberts brought this class action claiming that Fleet violated the federal Truth in Lending Act ("TILA"), 15 U.S.C. §1601 et seq., when it failed to clearly and conspicuously disclose that the fixed-rate APR that it was offering was limited in duration and subject to its asserted contractual right to change the interest rate at any time. The District Court granted summary judgment to Fleet, concluding that the materials Fleet sent to Roberts allowed it to change the rate.

We agree with Roberts that Fleet's solicitation materials could cause a reasonable consumer to be confused about the temporal quality of the offer. We therefore believe that a material question of fact exists as to whether the bank made any misleading statements in the mailings to Roberts and failed to disclose information required under the TILA "clearly and conspicuously." Accordingly, we reverse the entry of summary judgment and remand for further proceedings.

I. BACKGROUND

A. FACTUAL

In May 1999, Roberts received a packet of solicitation materials from Fleet urging her to apply for its new "Titanium MasterCard." The packet included an introductory flyer, a solicitation letter, a "Pre-Qualified . . . Invitation," and an Initial Disclosure Statement ("IDS"). The introductory flyer indicated that the card would have a "7.99% Fixed APR" on both

---

26. Footnotes in this case have been renumbered for clarity.

purchases and balance transfers. Under the heading "FINANCIAL ADVANTAGES," the flyer again stated that the fixed APR was 7.99%.

In addition to the flyer, the solicitation letter emphasized that the card would carry a "7.99% Fixed APR." The letter further stated that the "exceptionally low 7.99%" would apply not only to any purchases made with the card but also to any balance transfers from existing credit card accounts to the Titanium account. The letter twice claimed that the 7.99% fixed APR was "NOT an introductory rate," and promised that "[i]t won't go up in just a few short months."

In order to obtain the "Titanium MasterCard," the recipient was required to complete the "Pre-Qualified . . . Invitation" form. The front side of the invitation indicated that the credit card carried a "7.99% Fixed APR on purchases and balance transfers." On the back of the invitation Fleet listed the "TERMS OF PRE-QUALIFIED OFFER" and the "CONSUMER INFORMATION" sections. The first two sentences of the "TERMS OF PRE-QUALIFIED OFFER" stated the following:

> I request a Fleet Titanium MasterCard account upon acceptance of my request by Fleet Bank (RI), National Association in Rhode Island. I agree to the terms of the Cardholder Agreement mailed with my Card, including those which provide that the Cardholder Agreement and my account will be governed by Rhode Island and Federal law and that my Agreement terms (including rates) are subject to change.

The "CONSUMER INFORMATION" section contained the "Schumer Box," the table of basic credit card information required under the TILA, 15 U.S.C. §1601 et seq., as amended by the Fair Credit and Charge Card Disclosure Act of 1988.[27] The Schumer Box contained a column with the heading "Annual Percentage Rate (APR) for Purchases and Balance Transfers." The box beneath that heading indicated "7.99% APR" was the applicable rate. Inside the Schumer Box, Fleet listed two specific circumstances under which that rate could change: (1) if the prospective cardholder failed to meet any repayment requirements; or (2) upon closure of the account. Fleet listed no other circumstances under which the 7.99% APR could be changed.

---

27. Although the statute contains no reference to a "Schumer Box," the tabular chart required under the TILA has become popularly referred to as the "Schumer Box" in honor of the principal sponsor of the House bill, Congressman, now Senator, Charles Schumer. See Joseph W. Gelb & Peter N. Cubita, Credit Card Application and Solicitation Disclosure Legislation: An Alternative to the Rate Ceiling Approach, 43 Bus. Law. 1557, 1561 (1988); Cara Schwarzkopf, Credit-Ability, Newsday, Mar. 23, 2001.

The IDS instructed the pre-approved applicant to "[p]lease read this together with the TERMS OF PRE-QUALIFIED OFFER and the CONSUMER INFORMATION enclosed." Under the heading "Rate Information," the IDS indicated that the APR for the Fleet Titanium Card would be 7.99% for any purchases or balance transfers. Like the Schumer Box, the IDS noted two specific circumstances under which Fleet could change the fixed rate: (1) failure of the prospective cardholder to meet any repayment requirements; or (2) closure of the account. Fleet included no other circumstances in the IDS under which it could change the 7.99% APR.

Roberts completed and returned the invitation to Fleet. In June 1999, she received her Fleet Titanium MasterCard, along with the Cardholder Agreement. Section 10 of the Agreement, titled "Annual Percentage Rate," indicated that the APR would be 7.99%. In this section Fleet also reiterated that it reserved the right to change the rate under the circumstances described above. However, in Section 24 of the Cardholder Agreement, titled "Change in Terms," Fleet stated that:

> We have the right to change any of the terms of this Agreement at any time. You will be given notice of a change as required by applicable law. Any change in terms governs your Account as of the effective date, and will, as permitted by law and at our option, apply both to transactions made on or after such date and to any outstanding Account balance.

Fleet later sent Roberts a letter notifying her that Fleet would be increasing the fixed-rate APR on the Titanium MasterCard. In July 2000, thirteen months after Roberts had received her card, Fleet increased the fixed rate APR to 10.5%.

B. PROCEDURAL

On December 5, 2000, Roberts filed this class action, asserting a claim pursuant to the TILA and claims under Rhode Island law for violation of the Unfair Trade Practices and Consumer Protection Act, R.I. Gen. Laws §6-13.1-1 et seq., breach of contract, and unjust enrichment. Fleet moved to dismiss the TILA claim on February 12, 2001, submitting as exhibits to the motion documents that Fleet asserted the District Court could consider as incorporated into the Complaint. On June 5, 2001, the District Court, stating that "[s]ince all parties rely on matters outside the pleadings, the motion will be treated as a motion for partial summary judgment under Fed. R. Civ. P. 56," granted Fleet's motion based on its conclusion that Fleet had not violated the disclosure requirements of the TILA. Roberts v. Fleet Bank (R.I.), 2001 WL 892846, at *1 (E.D. Pa. June 5, 2001). The

District Court added that Roberts was "at liberty to pursue the remaining counts of her complaint." Id.

On July 3, 2001, Fleet moved for summary judgment on the pendent state law claims. On August 22, 2001, Roberts responded to the motion and moved for relief from the June 5, 2001 Order pursuant to Fed. R. Civ. P. 60(b). In a Memorandum and Opinion dated November 20, 2001, the District Court treated Roberts' motion under Rule 60(b) as a motion for reconsideration, and declined to change its decision on the TILA claim. The District Court also entered summary judgment against Roberts on her state law claims. Roberts appealed. . . .

III. DISCUSSION

A. THE TRUTH IN LENDING ACT

Congress enacted the TILA in 1969. The stated purpose of the TILA is "to assure a meaningful disclosure of credit terms so that the consumer will be able to compare more readily the various credit terms available to him and avoid the uninformed use of credit, and to protect the consumer against inaccurate and unfair credit billing and credit card practices." 15 U.S.C. §1601(a). In 1988, concerned that consumers were still not receiving accurate information about the potential costs of credit cards, Congress strengthened the TILA's protections for credit card consumers through enactment of the Fair Credit and Charge Card Disclosure Act, "a bill to provide for more detailed and uniform disclosure by credit and charge card issuers, at the time of application or solicitation, of information relating to interest rates and other costs which may be incurred by consumers through the use of any credit or charge card." S. Rep. No. 100-259, at 1 (1988), reprinted in 1998 U.S.C.C.A.N. 3936, 3937.

In particular, Congress determined that consumers were being inundated with credit card solicitations that failed to disclose basic cost information about the cards being promoted. Prior to the passage of the Fair Credit and Charge Card Disclosure Act, the TILA did not require issuers to provide such information until the consumer actually received the card. Congress decided that demanding early disclosure of relevant cost information from credit card companies would enable consumers to shop around for the best cards. See S. Rep. No. 100-259, at 2-3 (1988), reprinted in 1988 U.S.C.C.A.N. 3936, 3937-38.

Congress delegated the responsibility of "prescrib[ing] regulations to carry out the purposes of" the TILA to the Federal Reserve Board. 15 U.S.C. §1604(a). In response to this mandate, the Board promulgated "Regulation Z," 12 C.F.R. §226, and it also published a comprehensive "Official Staff

Interpretation," 12 C.F.R. Pt. 226 Supp. 1. Both of these measures were published in accordance with "the broad powers that Congress delegated to the Board to fill gaps in the statute." Ortiz v. Rental Management, Inc., 65 F.3d 335, 339 (3d Cir. 1995). In light of Congress' explicit delegation of authority, we defer quite broadly to the Board's interpretation. See Ford Motor Credit Co. v. Milhollin, 444 U.S. 555, 565, 100 S. Ct. 790, 63 L. Ed. 2d 22 (1980) (noting that because TILA is a complicated act, such deference is necessary). See generally Chevron, U.S.A., Inc. v. Natural Res. Def. Council, et al., 467 U.S. 837, 844-45, 104 S. Ct. 2778, 81 L. Ed. 2d 694 (1984).

The TILA requires a credit card provider to disclose certain information in "direct mail applications and solicitations," including "annual percentage rates." 15 U.S.C. §1637(c)(1)(A)(i). The Board's regulations also require "[a] credit card issuer" to disclose the applicable "annual percentage rate." 12 C.F.R. §226.5a(b)(1) (requiring disclosure of "[e]ach periodic rate that may be used to compute the finance charge on an outstanding balance for purchases . . . expressed as an annual percentage rate"). The TILA requires that information described in 15 U.S.C. §1637(c)(1)(A), such as "annual percentage rates," must be "clearly and conspicuously disclosed" in a "tabular format." 15 U.S.C. §1632(a) and (c). Likewise, the Board's regulations mandate that disclosures required under 12 C.F.R. §226.5a(b)(1) through (7) "be provided in a prominent location on or with an application or a solicitation, or other applicable document, and in the form of a table with headings, content, and format substantially similar to any of the applicable tables found in Appendix G." 12 C.F.R. §226.5a(a)(2). The Board's regulations also dictate that a "creditor shall make the disclosures required by this subpart clearly and conspicuously in writing." 12 C.F.R. §226.5(a)(1). Hence, both the TILA and Board-promulgated regulations require a credit card issuer to disclose the applicable annual percentage rate clearly and conspicuously in a table, commonly referred to as the Schumer Box.

I. Schumer Box

Roberts asserts that Fleet failed to clearly and conspicuously inform consumers that the 7.99% APR was subject to change at any time. The IDS and the Schumer Box included in Fleet's solicitation materials stated only two conditions under which Fleet could raise Roberts' APR: (1) failure of the cardholder to meet any repayment requirement; or (2) upon closure of the account. Roberts argues that, because a reasonable consumer could read this list as exhaustive and conclude that the 7.99% APR could be raised only under those two described circumstances, this disclosure was neither clear nor conspicuous.

Because the purpose of the TILA is to assure meaningful disclosures, "the issuer must not only disclose the required terms, it must do so accurately." Rossman v. Fleet Bank (R.I.) Nat'l Ass'n, 280 F.3d 384, 390-91 (3d Cir. 2002)." The accuracy demanded excludes not only literal falsities, but also misleading statements." Id. (citing Gennuso v. Commercial Bank & Trust Co., 566 F.2d 437, 443 (3d Cir. 1977)). As "the TILA is a remedial consumer protection statute, we have held it 'should be construed liberally in favor of the consumer.'" *Rossman*, 280 F.3d at 390 (quoting Ramadan v. Chase Manhattan Corp., 156 F.3d 499, 502 (3d Cir. 1998)). See also Begala v. PNC Bank, Ohio, N.A., 163 F.3d 948, 950 (6th Cir. 1998) ("We have repeatedly stated that TILA is a remedial statute and, therefore, should be given a broad, liberal construction in favor of the consumer."); Fairley v. Turan-Foley Imps., Inc., 65 F.3d 475, 482 (5th Cir. 1995) ("The TILA is to be enforced strictly against creditors and construed liberally in favor of consumers. . . .").

Construing the TILA strictly against the creditor and liberally in favor of the consumer, as we must, we believe that the TILA disclosures in this case, read in conjunction with the solicitation materials, present a material issue of fact as to whether Fleet clearly and conspicuously disclosed its right to change the APR. We therefore conclude that the District Court erred in granting summary judgment to Fleet on Roberts' TILA claim.

In the Schumer Box, Fleet stated that the 7.99% APR could change in the event of nonpayment or closure of the account. Fleet listed no other conditions under which the 7.99% APR could change. We believe that it would be just as reasonable, if not more reasonable, for a consumer to conclude from the information contained in the Schumer Box that the 7.99% APR could be changed only under the two listed circumstances as it would be for a consumer to conclude that Fleet could change the APR at any time. Roberts has raised a genuine issue of material fact as to the adequacy of Fleet's disclosures and should have been permitted to proceed to trial on the matter.

Fleet argues that it adequately disclosed the necessary information in the Schumer Box and that the Board's regulations prevent it from including a "change in terms" provision in the Schumer Box. We rejected a similar argument in *Rossman*. The dispute in *Rossman* arose from solicitation materials Fleet sent to potential customers indicating that its Platinum MasterCard carried no annual fee. 280 F.3d at 387. Despite the fact that Fleet indicated in the Schumer Box that it would not charge an annual fee, Fleet instituted an annual fee within the first year of Rossman's receipt of the credit card. See id. at 388-89. Fleet argued to the Court that a clear and conspicuous statement of its authority to change the annual fee at any time was unnecessary because the change-in-terms provision of the agreement is not among the terms that must be disclosed in tabular format under the TILA. See id. at 394. In rejecting this argument, the Court stated that the issue was "not Fleet's obligation to disclose the change-in-terms provision, but its obligation to disclose annual fees." Id.

Similarly, in this case, the issue is not Fleet's obligation to disclose the change-in-terms provision, but its obligation to disclose the APR. Our inquiry focuses on whether Fleet's disclosures in the Schumer Box provided "an accurate representation of the legal obligation of the parties . . . when the relevant solicitation was mailed." Id. at 391. As we explained above, we believe Roberts raised a question of material fact as to whether Fleet clearly and conspicuously provided an accurate representation of the APR.

2. Solicitation Materials

Roberts claims that Fleet's representations in the solicitation letter that the APR would be an "extraordinary," "low" fixed APR of 7.99% and that the rate was neither "introductory," nor would it rise "in just a few short months" further support her position that Fleet failed to comply with the TILA. Before addressing this argument, we must first decide whether the TILA permits a Court to analyze the solicitation materials, in addition to the information contained in the Schumer Box, in determining whether a reasonable consumer would comprehend the required disclosures.

Fleet does not specifically argue that we are not permitted to consider information outside of the Schumer Box in determining whether a credit card company has complied with the requirements of TILA. Fleet does argue, however, that the "clear and conspicuous" standard only applies to required disclosures in the Initial Disclosure Statement and the Schumer Box. While we agree with the premise of this argument, we reject its broader implications.[28] When Congress decided to require credit card issuers to disclose required terms in a clear and conspicuous manner, we doubt that it intended for us to ignore other statements made by those issuers in their credit card solicitation materials. Because "[t]he purpose of the TILA is to assure 'meaningful' disclosures," we have recognized that "[t]he accuracy demanded excludes not only literal falsities, but also misleading statements." *Rossman*, 280 F.3d at 390 (citations omitted). As detailed above, Congress amended TILA with the Fair Credit and Charge

---

28. When questioned at oral argument about whether the phrase "rates are subject to change" would more clearly and conspicuously disclose the contractual terms than the phrase "won't go up in just a few short months," which appeared in the solicitation letter, counsel for Fleet responded that the solicitation letter is not the TILA disclosure.

Card Disclosure Act in order to grant consumers better access to information and to allow consumers to more easily compare the terms of various credit cards. Congress created the Schumer Box to assist consumers in accessing such information, not to shield credit card companies from liability for information placed outside of the Schumer Box. As a result, while we recognize that the TILA only applies the "clear and conspicuous" standard to required disclosures, we conclude that the TILA permits us to consider materials outside of the Schumer Box in determining whether the credit issuer disclosed the required information clearly and conspicuously.

With that background established, we agree with Roberts that the claims in the introductory letter that the "fixed 7.99% APR"[29] is "NOT an introductory offer" and "won't go up in just a few short months" could cause a reasonable consumer to be confused about the temporal quality of the offer. Fleet argues that the phrase "my Agreement terms (including rates) are subject to change," which is included in the Terms of Pre-Qualified Offer section of the Invitation, makes clear that the 7.99% APR is not permanent. However, read in conjunction with information contained in the Schumer Box right below it, that statement could lead a consumer to conclude that the rates are subject to change only for the two reasons outlined in the Schumer Box.

In its defense, Fleet relies on Paragraph 24 of the Cardholder Agreement that states "[w]e have the right to change any of the terms of this Agreement at any time." This provision, however, fails to cure any of the TILA defects in the initial mailing. To begin with, Fleet only mails the Cardholder Agreement after a consumer has accepted the invitation. Thus, a consumer will not learn, until after the acceptance of the invitation, that the APR can be changed by Fleet at any time. Indeed, Fleet's practice of mailing the Cardholder Agreement containing important rate change information, after the consumer accepts the card, is contrary to the TILA mandate that credit card solicitations disclose all required information. See S. Rep. No. 100-259, at 1 (1988), reprinted in 1988 U.S.C.C.A.N. 3936, 3937. Nonetheless, Fleet argues that it is prohibited from including "change in terms" information in the Schumer Box. However, as we previously stated, this argument avoids

---

29. We recognize that a fixed rate is not necessarily permanent. See "Shop—The Credit Card You Pick Can Save You Money," http:// www.federalreserve.gov/pubs/shop at "Glossary of Credit Terms." ("The interest rate on fixed-rate credit card plans, though not explicitly tied to changes in other interest rates, can also change over time. The card issuer must notify you before the 'fixed' interest rate is changed."). The potential problem in this case is not that Roberts could have concluded that the rate was permanent solely based on the use of the word "fixed." Rather, the concern is that Fleet may have misled potential consumers by indicating that the rate could only change in the instances it specified in the solicitation materials.

the central issue in this case, which is whether the APR was adequately disclosed. Additionally, we note that the "right to change" language in Paragraph 24 contradicts the statement in the introductory letter that this APR "won't go up in just a few short months."[30]

In sum, after reading the materials together as a whole, we believe that a question of fact exists as to whether Fleet made any misleading statements in the mailing and failed to disclose information required under the TILA "clearly and conspicuously." . . .

IV. CONCLUSION

Accordingly, for the reasons stated above, we reverse the judgment of the District Court on the TILA claim and affirm the grant of judgment on the state law issues.

PROBLEM 116

After law student Portia Moot had taken the course in Consumer Law, she decided to play around with the rules. She went to Computer City and told the store manager that she wanted to buy a computer. The one she eventually selected cost $800. She asked the manager if she could pay for this purchase with her Visa card, and he assured her that she could. She asked him what Visa was currently charging merchants as a fee for paying the credit card slips when they were presented to Visa, and the manager said that the current discount rate was 5 percent of the amount of the slips. "Do you mean that Visa will give you only $760 when you send in my charge slip?" she asked. "That's right," the manager replied. Portia whipped out her checkbook. "How about I write you a check for $765, and we skip the credit card?" Portia suggested. The manager readily agreed to this. "Wait a minute," Portia said, "I just realized that I don't have that much in my checking account. I guess I'll have to use the Visa card after all." The manager shrugged and took her credit card. Two days later, Portia brought suit against both Computer City and the bank that had issued her the Visa card. Her suit noted that the bank was already charging her the maximum interest rate allowed by law. Her suit had two

---

30. When questioned about this contradictory language at oral argument, counsel for Fleet admitted that "arguably there is an inconsistency." By acknowledging this "arguable" inconsistency in language, Fleet essentially conceded that a reasonable consumer could find the materials to be confusing and misleading.

counts: violation of the state usury statutes, and disclosure violations under TILA. Her theory was this: the willingness of the manager to accept an amount less than the sticker price if she paid cash showed that the sticker price for the computer was inflated to conceal a hidden interest charge in the amount of the credit card discount rate, and that rate (on top of the interest rate being charged her by the bank) was both usurious and not disclosed to her. Is she going to win this one? See Reg. Z §§226.9(d), 226.2(a)(17)(ii), 226.4(b)(9), and 226.4(c)(8), and TILA §167(b). As to the usury argument, see TILA §171(c).

V. DISCLOSURE: CLOSED-END TRANSACTIONS

Even under the original version of TILA, compliance with the disclosure rules was always easier for open-end creditors than for closed-end ones. The latter disclosures, varying as they do from transaction to transaction, were a great deal more complicated and, as construed by the courts, impossible of compliance. An example: during the 1970s, a Legal Services lawyer in Cincinnati won case after case against creditors who committed TIL violations in closed-end sales and loans. Finally sick of losing, the creditors hired the Legal Services attorney to draft TIL forms for them that would comply with the law. For a fee, he did so, only to have his forms immediately and successfully attacked by consumers in Kentucky for being out of compliance with the technicalities of the statutory scheme.

This sort of thing could not go on. In effect, consumers involved in lawsuits with their creditors were spotted at least $100 and their attorney's fees, per TILA §130. For a thoughtful article on the situation (and still relevant in major part to the issues raised by TILA), see Landers, Some Reflections on Truth in Lending, 1977 Ill. L.F. 660. Congress came to the rescue with the 1980 passage of the current version of the statute, the Truth in Lending Simplification Act. As rewritten, TILA is now (believe it or not) less complex and easier to follow. Particularly for closed-end creditors, the disclosures became both simpler and fewer.

First scan casually the rules of Reg. Z §§226.17 and 226.18, and then use the following Problems and cases to focus on details.

PROBLEM 117

When your high school friend Norma Smith called you about the problems she had been having with the new car she bought last month, you told her to bring in all her paperwork connected with the automobile. While she is sitting in your office complaining about the rudeness of the service department manager, you are glancing at the TIL statement. You notice several interesting things.

a. You can't read it because the computer printout she received is too faint to decipher.

b. The TILA disclosures are mixed with different disclosures required by state law.

c. The statement reflects an APR that is higher than allowed by the state retail installment sales statute. As to this, see TILA §111(b).

d. Norma tells you that she signed the contract to buy the car on a Sunday. The next day she went in to get financing and fill out all the paperwork, and the sales manager had the clerk backdate the TIL statement to Sunday. See Polk v. Crown Auto, Inc., 221 F.3d 691 (4th Cir. 2000).

SMITH v. THE CASH STORE MANAGEMENT, INC.
United States Court of Appeals, Seventh Circuit, 1999
195 F.3d 325

FLAUM, Circuit Judge.

Valerie Smith sued The Cash Store, Ltd.; The Cash Store Management, Inc.; and The Cash Store Management, Inc.'s officers and directors (collectively "Cash Store") on behalf of a putative class for violations of the Truth in Lending Act ("TILA"), 15 U.S.C. §1601 et seq., and Illinois state contract law and consumer fraud statutes. This is an appeal from the district court's dismissal of Smith's suit for failure to state a claim under TILA. For the reasons set forth below, we affirm in part and reverse in part.

BACKGROUND

Cash Store operates at least sixteen loan establishments in Illinois. These establishments specialize in making short-term, high interest "payday loans," typically two weeks in duration and carrying annual percentage rates greater than 500%. When a Cash Store customer is granted a loan, the customer writes out a check, post-dated to the end of the loan period, for the full amount that he is obligated to pay. At the end of the two week period, the customer has the option of continuing the loan for an additional two week period by paying the interest.

Between June 13, 1998 and September 19, 1998, Smith obtained eight such loans from Cash Store. On each occasion she signed a standard

"Consumer Loan Agreement" form. Each loan agreement stated an annual interest rate of 521%. Each loan agreement also contained the statement: "Security. Your post-dated check is security for this loan." Upon entering into or renewing each loan, Cash Store stapled to the top of the loan agreement a receipt which labeled the finance charge in red ink as either a "deferred deposit extension fee" or a "deferred deposit check fee," depending on whether the transaction was a renewal or an original loan.

The details of the loan agreement are important because the content and presentation of such agreements are regulated under TILA, 15 U.S.C. §1601 et seq., and implementing Federal Reserve Board Regulation Z ("Regulation Z"), 12 C.F.R. §226. Congress enacted TILA to ensure that consumers receive accurate information from creditors in a precise, uniform manner that allows consumers to compare the cost of credit from various lenders. 15 U.S.C. §1601; Anderson Bros. Ford v. Valencia, 452 U.S. 205, 220, 68 L. Ed. 2d 783, 101 S. Ct. 2266 (1981). Regulation Z mandates that: "The creditor shall make the disclosures required by this subpart clearly and conspicuously in writing, in a form that the consumer may keep. The disclosures shall be grouped together, shall be segregated from everything else, and shall not contain any information not directly related to the [required] disclosures. . . ." 12 C.F.R. §226.17(a)(1). The mandatory disclosures, which must be grouped in a federal disclosure section of a written loan agreement, include, among other things, the finance charge, the annual percentage rate, and any security interests that the lender takes. 12 C.F.R. §226.18.

On March 16, 1999, Smith filed a class action complaint, amended on April 6, 1999, against Cash Store in the United States District Court for the Northern District of Illinois. She sued on behalf of a putative class for violations of TILA, for relief from an unconscionable loan contract, and for violations of the Illinois Consumer Fraud Act. The district court dismissed with prejudice the TILA claims for failure to state a claim upon which relief can be granted, Fed. R. Civ. P. 12(b)(6), and then exercised its discretion to dismiss without prejudice the remaining supplemental state claims, as permitted by 28 U.S.C. §1367(c)(3).

DISCUSSION

Smith argues on appeal that two of Cash Store's practices violate TILA, and that the district court's dismissal of the claims was therefore erroneous. The first practice relates to the receipts that Cash Store routinely stapled to the top of Smith's loan agreements. Smith contends that the receipts physically obscured the required federal disclosures and that they characterized the finance charges in a misleading way. The second practice relates to the security interest disclosures, which Smith contends were inaccurate. We address each of these allegations in turn.

THE RECEIPT CLAIM

TILA requires that a creditor make the required disclosures "clearly and conspicuously in writing. . . . " 12 C.F.R. §226.17. Smith alleges that the cash register receipt that Cash Store stapled to the upper left-hand corner of the loan agreements physically covered up some of the required disclosures. Furthermore, on her receipts were printed, in red, the terms "deferred deposit extension fee" or "deferred deposit check fee," whereas the term "finance charge" is used in the federal disclosure box. Smith argues that both of these practices render the required disclosures on the loan agreement neither "clear" nor "conspicuous."

The district court dismissed the claim relating to the Cash Store receipt on the ground that the allegations did not state a cause of action. It held that neither Cash Store's stapling of a receipt to the loan documents nor the printed contents of the receipt violated TILA, having found that "Cash Store's practice of stapling a small receipt to its TILA disclosures could not reasonably confuse or mislead Smith as to the terms of the loan." Smith v. Cash Store Mgmt., Inc., 1999 U.S. Dist. LEXIS 9040, No. 99 C 1726, 1999 WL 412447, at *3 (N.D. Ill. June 8, 1999).

A complaint should not be dismissed for failure to state a claim unless it appears beyond doubt that the plaintiff can prove no set of facts to support his claim which would entitle him to relief. Conley v. Gibson, 355 U.S. 41, 45-46, 2 L. Ed. 2d 80, 78 S. Ct. 99 (1957); Caremark, Inc. v. Coram Healthcare Corp., 113 F.3d 645, 648 (7th Cir. 1997). "The issue is not whether a plaintiff will ultimately prevail but whether the claimant is entitled to offer evidence to support the claims." *Caremark*, 113 F.3d at 648 (quoting Scheuer v. Rhodes, 416 U.S. 232, 236, 40 L. Ed. 2d 90, 94 S. Ct. 1683 (1974)). As we recently stated, "Rule 12(b)(6) should be employed only when the complaint does not present a legal claim." Johnson v. Revenue Mgmt. Corp., 169 F.3d 1057, 1059 (7th Cir. 1999). Because the district court may not dismiss the complaint under Rule 12(b)(6) unless it is legally insufficient, we review that decision de novo. *Caremark*, 113 F.3d at 648.

As noted above, Regulation Z requires that "the creditor shall make the disclosures required by this subpart clearly and conspicuously." 12 C.F.R §226.17. The "sufficiency of TILA-mandated disclosures is to be viewed from the standpoint of an ordinary consumer, not the perspective of a Federal Reserve Board member, federal judge, or English professor." Cemail v. Viking Dodge, 982 F. Supp. 1296, 1302 (N.D. Ill. 1997).

Whether or not Cash Store's practices run afoul of Regulation Z is a factual issue, and the district court therefore erred in dismissing the receipt claims under Rule 12(b)(6). In her amended complaint, Smith contends that the stapled receipt contradicted and obfuscated the required disclosures. Am. Compl., P 19. Her claim may fail on the facts, "but assessing factual support for a suit is not the office of Rule 12(b)(6)." *Johnson*, 169 F.3d at 1059. Although our holding does not preclude Cash Store from arguing, at the summary judgment stage, that Smith cannot prove her claims, Smith's complaint alleging that the stapled receipt obscured the disclosures and that the printed contents of the receipt were confusing or misleading states a valid legal claim under TILA, and that is sufficient to pass Rule 12(b)(6) scrutiny.

THE SECURITY INTEREST CLAIM

Smith also contends that the district court erred in holding that Cash Store's statement, "Your post-dated check is security for this loan," was a lawful disclosure under TILA. TILA requires creditors to disclose accurately any security interest taken by the lender and to describe accurately the property in which the interest is taken. 15 U.S.C. §1638; 12 C.F.R. §226.18. Regulation Z defines "security interest" as "an interest in property that secures performance of a consumer credit obligation and that is recognized by state or federal law." 12 C.F.R. §226.2(a)(25). Smith contends that Cash Store's statement in the loan agreement violates TILA because, under Illinois law, the check does not serve as security.

Subject to narrow exceptions, "hypertechnicality reigns" in the application of TILA. Cowen v. Bank United of Texas, FSB, 70 F.3d 937, 941 (7th Cir. 1995). Regulation Z specifies that certain federal disclosures must be grouped together in the loan agreement and also directs that the agreement "not contain any information not directly related to the [required] disclosures." 12 C.F.R. §226.17(a)(1). In Bizier v. Globe Financial Services Inc., the First Circuit explained that overinclusive security interest disclosures "cannot be dismissed as de minimis or hypertechnical." Overinclusive disclosures might deter a borrower's "future borrowing or property acquisition out of an exaggerated belief in the security interest to which they would be subject, or [give] a lender an apparent right which, even if ultimately unenforceable, could serve as a significant bargaining lever in any future negotiations concerning rights or obligations under the loan." 654 F.2d 1, 3 (1st Cir. 1981); see also Tinsman v. Moline Beneficial Fin. Co., 531 F.2d 815, 818-19 (7th Cir. 1976) (holding that an overbroad disclosure of security interests violated TILA). All TILA disclosures must be accurate, Gibson v. Bob Watson Chevrolet-Geo, Inc., 112 F.3d 283, 285 (7th Cir. 1997), and lenders are generally strictly liable under TILA for inaccuracies, even absent a showing that the inaccuracies are misleading, Brown v. Marquette Savings and Loan Assoc., 686 F.2d 608, 614 (7th Cir. 1982). Smith contends that if the check that Smith handed over upon agreeing to the loan does not give Cash Store a security interest, then its statement to that effect violates TILA.

Cash Store first responds that the check acts as "security" because it gives Cash Store alternate routes to collect its debt. The check might facilitate payment because the loan agreement provides that Cash Store may deposit it on the loan due date if another form of payment is not made. If the check were to bounce, Cash Store could sue Smith under Illinois "bad check" statutes. According to Cash Store, the check then "secures" the loan by making repayment easier or by placing Cash Store in a stronger litigating position under Illinois law if Smith does not pay back the loan. Hence, the statement "Security: Your post-dated check is security for this loan" is accurate, and perhaps even required under TILA.

This argument, standing alone, is incomplete because it confuses "security" with "security interest." True, Cash Store may be in a better position with the check than without it, and in that sense it may regard its loan as more "secure." But this is a broader sense of "security" than that contemplated by Regulation Z. The regulations define "security interest"—which is a term of art referring to a specific class of transactions—as "an interest in property that secures performance of a consumer credit obligation and that is recognized by state or federal law." 12 C.F.R. §226.2(a)(25). Illinois commercial law, in turn, defines it as "an interest in personal property . . . which secures payment or performance of an obligation." 810 ILCS 5/1-201(37). By creating a security interest through a security agreement, a debtor provides that a creditor may, upon default, take or sell the property—or collateral—to satisfy the obligation for which the security interest is given. 810 ILCS 5/9-105(1)(c) ("'Collateral' means the property subject to a security interest, and includes accounts and chattel paper which have been sold."). Because TILA restricts what information a lender can include in its federal disclosures, the question before us is not simply whether the post-dated check makes repayment more likely ("security") but whether it can meet the statutory requirements of "collateral" ("security *interest*").

Cash Store also maintains that Article 9 of the Illinois Uniform Commercial Code ("Illinois U.C.C."), which governs secured transactions, applies "to any transaction (regardless of its form) which is intended to create a security interest in personal property . . . including . . . instruments."

810 ILCS 5/9-102(1)(a). Because the check is an instrument, it can be used to create a security interest by the terms of the Illinois U.C.C. See In re Brigance, 234 B.R. 401, 404-05 (W.D. Tenn. 1999) (holding that, under Tennessee's U.C.C., a borrower's personal check can serve as collateral in which a security interest can be obtained).

We again believe that this argument is incomplete. While Article 9 of the Illinois U.C.C. generally authorizes the use of instruments as collateral to secure a loan, it is not immediately clear whether this provision applies to a post-dated check issued by the *borrower*.

Neither the ease of recovery in the event of default nor the simple fact that a check is an instrument [is] sufficient to create a security interest. It is the economic substance of the transaction that determines whether the check serves as collateral. Cf. Cobb v. Monarch Finance Corp., 913 F. Supp. 1164, 1177-78 (N.D. Ill. 1995) (distinguishing between a mechanism set up to facilitate repayment of a loan and an interest that secures a loan in the event of default). Therefore, in turning to our resolution of whether Cash Store took a security interest, our analysis must focus on the economic substance of Smith's pledged check.

We begin with the premise that collateral must be of some value to secure a loan; it cannot simply be additional evidence of indebtedness. Prior to the U.C.C., courts had "uniformly" answered in the negative the question of whether "the pledge of an independent promise of the debtor to pay a sum of money can be made valid security for a debt." New York Trust Co. v. Palmer, 101 F.2d 1, 4 (2d Cir. 1939); see also Union Nat'l Bank v. People's Savings & Trust Co., 28 F.2d 326, 328 (3d Cir. 1928) ("The term 'collateral security' implies the transfer to a creditor of an interest in or a lien on property, or an obligation which furnishes a security in addition to the responsibility of the debtor. The execution and delivery by the debtor of additional unsecured evidence of his indebtedness does not constitute collateral security."). Although we recognize that the U.C.C. has liberalized the scope of secured transactions, see 810 ILCS 5/9-101, U.C.C. cmt., we will assume that, even after Illinois' adoption of the U.C.C., collateral must have some value beyond the promise to pay contained in a loan agreement itself. Cf. City of Chicago v. Michigan Beach Housing Coop., 242 Ill. App. 3d 636, 609 N.E.2d 877, 886, 182 Ill. Dec. 343 (Ill. App. Ct. 1993) (holding that certain tax credits could not serve as collateral because they had "no independent value in and of themselves").

Smith argues that, having already promised contractually through the loan agreement to pay the amount printed on the check, the pledged check gives Cash Store no interest that it did not already have. The Illinois U.C.C. expressly provides that a check does not operate as an assignment of the bank account on which it is drawn. 810 ILCS 5/3-408. And the check itself has no intrinsic value beyond the minuscule value of a scrap of paper. According to Smith, then, the post-dated check does not secure the loan because it merely restates the promise to pay already contained in the loan agreement. Hitner v. Diamond State Steel Co., 176 F. 384, 391-92 (C.C.D. Del. 1910) ("It hardly admits of discussion that the mere duplication or multiplication of a promise to pay or of an acknowledgment of liability to pay a certain sum representing the total real indebtedness to a creditor, whatever may be its effect in furnishing in certain exigencies alternative or cumulative evidence of the real demand, cannot constitute collateral security.").

Smith may be correct that a second promise to pay, identical to the first, would not serve as collateral to secure a loan, because the second promise is of no economic significance: in the event that the borrower defaults on the first promise, the second promise to pay provides nothing of economic value that the creditor could seize and apply towards repayment of the loan. In this case, however, the post-dated check is not merely a second, identical promise. It is, indeed, a promise to pay the same amount as the first, but it has value to the creditor in the event of default beyond the value of the first promise. That is because a holder of both the loan and the check has remedies available to him that a holder of only the loan agreement does not. For example, the holder of the check has available remedies created by the Illinois bad check statute, 810 ILCS 5/3-806, which mandates that if a check is not honored, the drawer shall be liable for interest and costs and expenses incurred in the collection of the amount of the check.

Smith's own statement that the check is of no intrinsic value is instructive: it is its extrinsic legal status and the legal rights and remedies granted the holder of the check, like the holder of a loan agreement, that give rise to its value. Upon default on the loan agreement, Cash Store would get use of the check, along with the rights that go with it. Cash Store could simply negotiate it to someone else. Cash Store could take it to the bank and present it for payment. If denied, Cash Store could pursue bad check litigation. Additional value is created through these rights because Cash Store need not renegotiate or litigate the loan agreement as its only avenue of recourse.

It is not important that, as Smith argues, by the time Cash Store gets use of the check it might be clear that Smith would not or could not make good on a promise for that amount. Cash Store's likelihood of, for example, successfully pursuing bad check litigation goes to the issue of valuation of the check (one might roughly calculate it as its face value plus supplementary awards created by the bad check statute, discounted by the probability of successfully pressing the claim) not the issue of whether the check has any value beyond the promise contained in the original loan agreement. In the same way, there is the chance that Smith would call her bank and cancel the post-dated check before the loan's due date, but this potentiality, depending on how the loan agreement might affect her legal right to do so, goes to how much holding the check is worth, not whether it has any value at all. Some additional value is created by the bad check statute and other legal provisions governing instruments.

This is not to say that by putting up a check as collateral, a lender like Cash Store necessarily takes a security interest in the amount printed on the face of the instrument. Rather, the rights created by state commercial law can, and in this case do, create some value in the instrument. We are therefore satisfied that Cash Store could lawfully assert under TILA that Smith's post-dated check was security for the loan.

Conclusion

For the reasons stated above, we AFFIRM the district court's dismissal of the security interest claim, and we REVERSE and REMAND the district court's dismissal of the receipt claim for further proceedings consistent with this opinion.

[The opinion of Circuit Judge Manion, concurring and dissenting in part, is omitted.]

NOTE ON PAYDAY LENDING

In recent years quite a large of amount of so-called payday lending is going on, whereby an employee borrows against his/her future paychecks with such lenders and agrees to pay an interest rate that is outrageously high. There have been major arguments about whether these loans are usurious, but most states now regulate them (poorly) by a special statute. See Creola Johnson, Payday Loans: Shrewd Business or Predatory Lending?, 87 Minn. L. Rev. 1 (2002); Ronald J. Mann and Jim Hawkins, Just Until Payday, 54 UCLA L. Rev. 855 (2007); Christopher L. Peterson, Usury Law, Payday Loans, and Statutory Slight of Hand: Salience Distortion in American Credit Pricing Limits, 92 Minn. L. Rev. 1110 (2008). As the case that follows demonstrates, payday lenders have been creative in working around statutory prohibitions on their activities. In the state of Ohio, the legislature passed a statute capping payday loans at 28 percent, with a maximum 31-day term. Payday lenders responded with outrage—6,000 jobs would be lost, they warned, as 1,600 stores closed, and loans would be unavailable to the poorest segment of society. They promptly spent $19 million on a 2008 attempt to amend the Ohio constitution and overturn the new statute. When that failed, the lenders switched over to a different Small Loan Statute, manipulated its provisions, and kept right on making loans at breathtaking interest rates.

Military servicemembers and their dependents are given special rights in connection with payday loans pursuant to the 2007 Military Lending Act, 10 U.S.C. §987, and the Department of Defense regulations implementing the Act; see 32 C.F.R. pt. 232. Among other things, the new rules cap interest rates at 36 percent, ban mandatory arbitration clauses, forbid rolling the debt over into a new loan with less favorable terms, strike prepayment penalties, and bar any waiver of legal rights. The same rules also protect service-members in credit extensions using their car titles as collateral for loans, as well as tax-refund anticipation loans. Finally, the Servicemembers Civil Relief Act, 50 App. U.S.C. §501 et seq., has broad rules covering all loans to servicemembers, protecting them, for example, from default judgments, evictions, and termination of various benefits such as life insurance without adequate notice.

CLAY v. OXENDINE[31]
Court of Appeals of Georgia, 2007
285 Ga. App. 50, 645 S.E.2d 553

BERNES, Judge.

The appellants in this case include numerous individuals and corpora-tions who operate consumer cash advance and finance businesses in the State of Georgia. Appellees John Oxendine, the Industrial Loan Commis-sioner for the State of Georgia, and Thurbert E. Baker, the Attorney General for the State of Georgia (collectively, the "state"), commenced this civil action alleging that appellants' use of a consumer "sale/leaseback" trans-action violates the anti-payday lending statute, OCGA §16-17-1 et seq., and the Georgia Industrial Loan Act, OCGA §7-3-1 et seq. ("GILA"). The state thereafter moved for partial summary judgment as to appellants' liability and moved to strike appellants' jury demand. The trial court granted the motions. On appeal, appellants contend that the trial court erred (1) by ruling that their "sale/leaseback" transactions constituted illegal payday loans as a matter of law; (2) by denying their right to a jury trial; and (3) by

---

31. Footnote in this case has been renumbered for clarity.

holding the appellant corporate officers individually liable. For the reasons that follow, we affirm. . . .

[T]he evidence shows that appellants operate numerous consumer cash advance and finance businesses serving citizens throughout the State of Georgia. In 2002, the state investigated appellants' businesses in response to consumer complaints that appellants charged excessive interest and engaged in abusive collection tactics. Appellants argued that their practice of making cash advances did not amount to loans. Following that investigation and an administrative hearing, the Industrial Loan Commissioner issued a finding that appellants were engaging in illegal payday lending and ordered them to cease and desist in those business practices. See USA Payday Cash Advance Centers v. Oxendine, 262 Ga. App. 632, 632-633, 585 S.E.2d 924 (2003).

In November 2002, appellants changed their business practices to engage in a "rent a bank" arrangement, whereby they served as the agent of an out-of-state bank that made payday loans. The Commissioner's investigation of this payday loan arrangement was addressed in BankWest v. Oxendine, 266 Ga. App. 771, 598 S.E.2d 343 (2004). Thereafter, the provisions of OCGA §§16-17-1(c), 16-17-2(b)(4), and 16-17-2(d) were enacted, effective May 1, 2004, to statutorily declare "rent a bank" arrangements to be violations of GILA and the Georgia usury statutes for which civil and criminal liability would be imposed.

Appellants then began to engage in the "sale/leaseback" transactions at issue here, whereby their consumer customers purportedly sold personal property items to appellants, then immediately leased the items back from appellants. Following an investigation, the state concluded that the "sale/leaseback" transactions were nothing more than disguised, illegal payday loans. Consequently, the state commenced the instant action.

1. In granting partial summary judgment to the state on the issue of liability, the trial court concluded that appellants' "sale/leaseback" transactions were payday loans in violation of the anti-payday lending statute (OCGA §16-17-1 et seq.), GILA (OCGA §7-3-1 et seq.), and the Commissioner's previously issued cease and desist order. On appeal, appellants argue that the trial court failed to apply proper summary judgment standards requiring that the evidence be construed in their favor as the nonmovants, and that the trial court's ruling was precluded by evidence that their customers had no obligation to repay the debt. We discern no error.

A payday loan is a loan of short duration, typically two weeks, at an astronomical annual interest rate. Payday loans are the current version of salary buying or wage buying. The fees, charges, and interest on a payday loan are between 15 percent and 30 percent of the principal for a two-week loan, constituting a pretext for usury.

(Citations and punctuation omitted.) *USA Payday Cash Advance Centers,* 262 Ga. App. at 633-634, 585 S.E.2d 924. "Because the maturity date of these loans is usually set to coincide with the borrower's next payday, the loans are often called 'payday loans.'" *BankWest,* 266 Ga. App. at 771, 598 S.E.2d 343.

The Georgia General Assembly enacted OCGA §16-17-1 et seq. to declare payday loans illegal and to impose "substantial criminal and civil penalties over and above those currently existing under state law . . . in order to prohibit this activity in the State of Georgia and to cause the cessation of this activity once and for all." OCGA §16-17-1(c). Payday lending under this statutory scheme "encompasses all transactions in which funds are advanced to be repaid at a later date, notwithstanding the fact that the transaction contains one or more other elements." OCGA §16-17-1(a). A payday loan is illegal "notwithstanding the fact that the transaction also involves . . . [t]he selling or providing of an item, service, or commodity incidental to the advance of funds." OCGA §16-17-2(b)(2).

To determine whether there has been a violation of OCGA §16-17-2,

> the trial court shall be authorized to review the terms of the transaction in their entirety . . . [and] shall not be bound in making such determination by the parol evidence rule or by any written contract but shall be authorized to determine exactly whether the loan transaction includes the use of a scheme, device, or contrivance and whether in reality the loan is in violation of the provisions of subsection (a) of Code Section 16-17-2 based upon the facts and evidence relating to that transaction and similar transactions being made in the State of Georgia.

OCGA §16-17-6.

Payday loans under $3,000 are further regulated by GILA, OCGA §7-3-1 et seq.

> Since [GILA] was enacted to define and prevent usury and to provide a source of regulated funds for those who had been borrowing at usurious rates from loan sharks, street shylocks and wage-buyers, then [payday loans] come within the jurisdiction of the Act. . . . If the maximum interest rate is over the limit set by OCGA §7-3-14 of ten percent or the lender fails to hold an industrial license issued by the Commissioner, then "payday loans" violate [GILA]. See 2002 Op. Atty. Gen. No. 2002-3.

USA Payday Cash Advance Centers, 262 Ga. App. at 634, 585 S.E.2d 924. The Industrial Loan Commissioner is vested with authority to investigate, conduct hearings, and issue a cease and desist order if he has cause to believe that any person is in violation of GILA. OCGA §7-3-23. A violation of the cease and desist order constitutes a public nuisance for which the

Commissioner is entitled to an injunction to be granted by the superior courts. OCGA §7-3-23.

With this statutory framework in mind, we turn to the contentions in the present case. Appellants contend that their "sale/leaseback" transactions cannot be construed as loans coming within the provisions of OCGA §16-17-1 et seq. and GILA because a loan entails the advancement of funds that must be repaid at a later date. See OCGA §§7-3-3(4); 16-17-1(a). Appellants emphasize that the transactions at issue were reflected by a written bill of sale identifying the property sold and the sales price and by a lease agreement disclosing the lease terms, the initial lease payment due, and three options that can be exercised at the end of the lease term. The leases purportedly allowed the customer to either (1) renew the lease for another lease period; (2) repurchase the property for the sales price, without credit for any rental payments made; or (3) return the property and owe nothing more. Appellants contend that the third option to return the property without rendering payment under the lease agreement precludes the transaction from being considered a loan, since there is no obligation to repay the money received by the consumer for the sale of his or her items.

Notwithstanding appellants' suggestion, however, the terms of their written lease with customers are not talismanic in this context.

> [W]hether a given transaction is a purchase . . . or a loan of money . . . depends, not upon the form of words used in contracting, but upon the real intent and understanding of the parties. No disguise of language can avail for covering up usury, or glossing over an usurious contract. The theory that a contract will be usurious or not, according to the kind of paper bag it is put up in, or according to the more or less ingenious phrases made use of in negotiating it, is altogether erroneous. The law intends that a search for usury shall penetrate to the substance.

Pope v. Marshall, 78 Ga. 635, 640(2), 4 S.E. 116 (1887). See also *BankWest*, 266 Ga. App. at 776(1), 598 S.E.2d 343.[32] As such, we do not consider

---

32. Payday lenders have often been accused of using sham transactions in efforts to disguise the fact that they engage in illegal payday loan transactions and in efforts to evade usury laws. See Watson v. State, 235 Ga. App. 381, 509 S.E.2d 87 (1998) (sham storage fees). See also Upshaw v. Ga. Catalog Sales, 206 F.R.D. 694 (M.D. Ga. 2002) (sham catalog gift certificates); Henry v. Cash Today, 199 F.R.D. 566 (S.D. Tex. 2000) (sham advertising sales); Cashback Catalog Sales v. Price, 102 F. Supp. 2d 1375 (S.D. Ga. 2000) (sham gift certificates and catalog coupons). Also see Alabama Catalog Sales v. Harris, 794 So. 2d 312, 317, n. 4 (Ala. 2000) (sham catalog gift certificates); Short On Cash.Net of New Castle v. Dept. of Financial Institutions, 811 N.E.2d 819 (Ind. Ct. App. 2004) (sham internet service contracts); Greenberg v. Com. ex rel. Atty. Gen. of Va., 255 Va. 594, 499 S.E.2d 266 (1998) (sham checks at a discount). Likewise, payday lenders have used lease-purchase transactions in efforts to disguise usurious loans. See Pope, 78 Ga. 635, 4 S.E. 116. See also Moran v. Kenai Towing & Salvage,

appellants' claims in a vacuum, but rather must look at the totality of the circumstances in analyzing whether appellants' "sale/leaseback" arrangement was a sham transaction to disguise an illegal payday loan scheme.

Regardless of the written provisions of the sale/leaseback contracts, the state presented evidence establishing that appellants' sale/leaseback arrangements contained the same salient features of a payday loan transaction that violate OCGA §16-17-1 et seq. and GILA. An audit supervisor from the Commissioner's Office explained the practice and economic structure of payday lending, and three of appellants' customers provided affidavits describing the transactions that they engaged in with the appellants' businesses.

Consistent with the practice of payday lending, the customers were required to apply for an advancement of funds by providing the name of their employers and length of employment, their salary and pay dates, checking account information, a recent pay stub, and bank statements. The customers also provided a check or electronic debit authorization in the amount of the principal amount advanced to them plus interest.

Following the advancement of funds, the customers' first payment was due within two weeks. The customers could be released from the agreement by paying the principal amount advanced to them plus a 25% to 27% fee, amounting to an APR of 650% to 702%. If the customers were unable to do so, then they were required to renew the transaction term for another two-week period by paying another 25% to 27% fee. None of these payments was applied to the principal amount owed. If the customers failed to make a required payment, their checks were cashed or an electronic debit from their bank account was made immediately thereafter.

At the same time, the state presented evidence that the component of the transaction involving the sale and lease of personal property was nothing more than a sham. In this respect, the state pointed to appellants' records which reflect that the same cell phone and power pack were "sold" and listed on the "sale/leaseback" documents submitted by numerous different customers during the same time period, and these same items were assigned different values to correspond with the "sale" or loan amount. Other "sale/leaseback" documents of record also show that the value assigned to the personal property leased back to the customer was not based on an actual appraised market value, but rather was made to directly correspond to the

---

523 P.2d 1237, 1242-1243 (Alaska 1974); SAL Leasing v. State ex rel. Napolitano, 198 Ariz. 434, 10 P.3d 1221 (App. 2000); Reitze v. Humphreys, 53 Colo. 177, 125 P. 518 (1912); Browner v. Dist. of Columbia, 549 A.2d 1107 (D.C. 1988); Kuykendall v. Malernee, 516 P.2d 558 (Okla. Ct. App. 1973).

loan amount approved for the customer. For example, in one of its transactions, appellants assigned an astronomical value of $450 to a can opener
and coffee maker to correspond with the amount the customer was loaned.
Finally, several of appellants' customers explained that the bill of sale
stated something other than the transaction that they actually agreed to, and
that they only signed the "sale/leaseback" documents because they needed
the money.

Based on this combined evidence, the state met its burden of proving
that appellants were engaged in illegal payday lending. After the state
discharged its burden by referencing affidavits, depositions, and other
documents in the record establishing that appellants were so engaged,
appellants could not rest on their pleadings, but rather were required to
point to specific evidence giving rise to a triable issue. Smith v. Lewis, 259
Ga. App. 548, 578 S.E.2d 220 (2003). This, the appellants failed to do.

First, appellants came forward with no evidence to refute that the "sale/
leaseback" arrangements contained the same salient features as an illegal
payday loan. Although appellants pointed to the deposition testimony of
one of the customers to allege that he had memory problems, the customer's
recollection of the nature of his transaction with appellants was clear and
consistent.

Second, appellants failed to offer any evidence refuting the state's
evidence showing that the sale and lease of personal property was a sham
component of the transactions. In this respect, there is no evidence in the
record indicating that appellants ever inspected any of the personal property
to determine its condition at the time the lease was made or sought to acquire
possession of the property listed by the customers after a default. Moreover,
appellants failed to offer any specific evidence to explain the discrepancy in
the records reflecting that the same two items were purportedly "sold" and
"leased" by numerous different customers during the same time period and
that these items were assigned different values to correspond with the
"sale" amount to be paid under the "lease." While appellants speculated
that there may have been an entry error by its employees or a computer
glitch to explain this information in their corporate documents, "mere
speculation, conjecture, or possibility [are] insufficient to preclude summary
judgment." Rosales v. Davis, 260 Ga. App. 709, 712(2), 580 S.E.2d 662
(2003). See also Medders v. Kroger Co., 257 Ga. App. 876, 878, 572 S.E.2d
386 (2002).

In light of this evidentiary record, we conclude that the trial court did
not err in granting the state's motion for partial summary judgment. The
evidence set forth above conclusively demonstrates that appellants' "sale/

leaseback" transactions constituted payday loans in violation of OCGA §16-17-1 et seq. and GILA. . . .

3. Lastly, appellants claim that the trial court erred by holding the appellant corporate officers individually liable for the corporate transactions.

"The concept of piercing the corporate veil is applied in Georgia to remedy injustices which arise where a party has over extended his privilege in the use of a corporate entity in order to defeat justice, perpetuate fraud or to evade contractual or tort responsibility." (Citation and punctuation omitted.) Amason v. Whitehead, 186 Ga. App. 320, 321-322, 367 S.E.2d 107 (1988).

> A corporation possesses a legal existence separate and apart from that of its officers and shareholders so that the operation of a corporate business does not render officers and shareholders personally liable for corporate acts. A corporate officer who takes part in the commission of a tort by the corporation is personally liable therefor, but an officer of a corporation who takes no part in the commission of a tort committed by the corporation is not personally liable unless he specifically directed the particular act to be done or participated or cooperated therein (or if he disregarded the corporate form so as to authorize piercing of the corporate veil).

(Citation and punctuation omitted.) Lawton v. Temple-Warren Ford, Inc., 203 Ga. App. 222, 223(b), 416 S.E.2d 527 (1992). See also Kilsheimer v. State, 250 Ga. 549, 299 S.E.2d 733 (1983). "An officer of a corporation cannot assert that criminal acts, in the form of corporate acts, were not his acts merely because carried out by him through the instrumentality of the corporation which he controlled and dominated in all respects and which he employed for that purpose." Parish v. State, 178 Ga. App. 177, 178(1), 342 S.E.2d 360 (1986).

The evidence conclusively established that appellants took part in, specifically directed, participated or cooperated in the payday lending activities upon which their individual liability could be imposed.

Judgment affirmed.

In any event, the Federal Reserve has amended its Official Commentary to Regulation Z to make it clear that such lenders must give TIL disclosures:

> 2. Payday loans; deferred presentment. Credit includes a transaction in which a cash advance is made to a consumer in exchange for the consumer's personal check, or in exchange for the consumer's authorization to debit the consumer's deposit account,

and where the parties agree either that the check will not be cashed or deposited, or that the consumer's deposit account will not be debited, until a designated future date. This type of transaction is often referred to as a "payday loan" or "payday advance" or "deferred presentment loan." A fee charged in connection with such a transaction may be a finance charge for purposes of Sec. 226.4, regardless of how the fee is characterized under state law. Where the fee charged constitutes a finance charge under Sec. 226.4 and the person advancing funds regularly extends consumer credit, that person is a creditor and is required to provide disclosures consistent with the requirements of Regulation Z. See Sec. 226.2(a)(17).

GONZALEZ v. SCHMERLER FORD
United States District Court, Northern District of Illinois, 1975
397 F. Supp. 323

MAROVITZ, District Judge.

Plaintiff Roger Gonzalez brings suit against Schmerler Ford, an automobile dealership engaged in selling new and used automobiles at retail to consumers, and charges defendant with violation of the Truth in Lending Act, 15 U.S.C.A. §1601 et seq., and Federal Reserve Regulation Z, 12 C.F.R. §226, by failing timely to disclose credit information in the sale of a used 1972 Pinto.

The Truth in Lending Act provides that "in connection with each consumer credit sale . . . , the creditor shall disclose" divers items enumerated within the Act relating to the true cost of money or credit so that a consumer may compare rates between lenders or sellers. 15 U.S.C.A. §1638(a). Bissette v. Colonial Mortgage Corp. of D.C., 340 F. Supp. 1191 (D.D.C. 1972), *rev'd on other grounds*, 155 U.S. App. D.C. 360, 477 F.2d 1245 (1973). Subsection (b) of 15 U.S.C.A. §1638 provides that, "the disclosures required . . . shall be made before the credit is extended, and may be made by disclosing the information in the contract or other evidence of indebtedness to be signed by the purchaser." Regulation Z elaborates upon this requirement, stating that "such disclosures shall be made before the transaction is consummated," 12 C.F.R. §226.8(a), and further, that "a transaction shall be considered consummated at the time a contractual relationship is created between a creditor and a customer irrespective of the time of performance of either party." 12 C.F.R. §226.2(cc).

The auto purchase at suit herein involves primarily two documents, one executed October 1, 1973, and one executed October 3, 1973. The October 1 document indicates that the Pinto was to be purchased for the sum of $2255.00, ten dollars of which was to be paid on October 1, and the remaining $2245.00 of which was to be paid on October 3. The October 3 document reflects an installment sales contract detailing a cash down payment, a trade-in on plaintiff's old car, and full disclosure of the credit information required by law. Plaintiff contends that the October 3 document is based upon an oral agreement of October 1 wherein plaintiff agreed to buy the used 1972 Pinto upon the expectation that Schmerler could arrange financing.

The central problem of the suit hinges on the dispute as to whether the document executed by the parties on October 1, 1973, accurately reflects the intention of plaintiff to purchase his car in one cash payment due on October 3, 1973, or whether that document only reflects plaintiff's commitment to buy the car subject to being able to arrange financing, with both parties knowing that a credit sale is contemplated from the outset of the transaction; the former situation would not require credit disclosures on October 1 since the Act has excluded from its coverage transactions in which finance charges are payable in four or fewer installments, 12 C.F.R. §226.2(k), whereas the latter situation arguably would necessitate an October 1 disclosure on the theory that a credit sale was consummated on that date, even though the written installment contract was not executed until October 3. . . .

First, the parties have stipulated that on October 1, 1973, prior to the execution of any document, the plaintiff stated to an employee of defendant that he desired that the sale be made with the lowest monthly payments possible. Defendant argues that plaintiff's "desire" in this respect is not tantamount to plaintiff's conditioning his purchase on receiving those credit terms. Nonetheless, after negotiating a price on the 1972 Pinto with James Saxon, the salesman in this case, Roger Gonzalez was escorted into the office of the finance manager, Mr. Victor Duski. Duski proceeded to prepare a worksheet which was sent by teletype to Ford Motor Credit Corporation wherein was noted, *inter alia*, the price of the vehicle, the net trade-in, the cash down payment, and the desired time for extension of credit. Defendant claims that a credit check is run on all purchasers, including those paying on a cash basis, and explains the $300.00 down payment as indicating not that plaintiff was to return with that sum, but merely that that figure is the sum which plaintiff offered to pay *if* his credit was approved. Duski does state, though, in the course of his deposition:

> *Q:* But your understanding on October 1st was that Mr. Gonzalez would bring in an additional $300.00 for cash payment?
> *A:* It must have been, yes. (Duski deposition, p.36.)

We believe both parties knew that Gonzalez was not entering into a cash transaction on October 1, and that that document was not intended to reflect the agreement of the parties as to how plaintiff would pay for the car.

Having so concluded, we find the most difficult issue still before us, to wit: was the credit sale consummated on October 1, or on October 3 when the written installment contract was executed?

Plaintiff contends that disclosures may be necessary at the time of sale even though there is no written installment contract in force at the time of sale. He relies for this proposition on the following excerpt from a Federal Reserve Board letter discussing a situation much like the one herein:

> [Y]ou indicate that when a sale is made, the dealer and buyer enter into a buyer's agreement whereby the buyer agrees to buy for the cash price set forth therein and the seller agrees to sell at that price. If the buyer wishes for the dealer to arrange financing, then the dealer attempts to do so, and if able to do so, the dealer and buyer enter into a retail installment contract wherein the required disclosures are set forth. If the dealer is unable to arrange financing or the financing arranged is unacceptable to the buyer, then there is no sale. You question whether this procedure complies with the requirements regarding the timing of disclosures under Regulation Z.
>
> Regulation Z specifies that disclosures must be made prior to consummation of the credit transaction (see §226.2(cc) [¶3511]). Exactly when consummation occurs is determined by when a contractual relationship as to the financing arises between the parties under State law.
>
> In the case you describe, there may thus be two "consummations," one of the sale and one of the financing, which occur at different times. On the other hand, in some cases the sale and financing may be so interrelated that they occur simultaneously. In those circumstances the disclosure would need to be made prior to the execution of the sale documents. Staff believes that where the sale is conditioned on the seller arranging specific financing whose terms are known to the seller, so that the financing is an integral part of the sale to the extent that a contractual relationship has been created between the creditor and a customer with regard to that financing, "consummation" of the credit transaction may have occurred at the time of execution of the sale documents and disclosures should be made at that point.

Griffith Garwood, Chief, Truth in Lending Section, FRB Letter, August 9, 1972, No. 623, CCH Consumer Credit Reporter ¶30,872.

Professor Johnson, a consultant on the Truth in Lending Regulations for the Federal Reserve Board, in commenting on a similar fact situation, stated that the expectation of the parties would force one to conclude that there are not

> actually two separate transactions in this case, one for a sale of goods and one for credit. The purpose of the purchase order procedure is only to allow a salesman to get a floor commitment from the buyer that can be used to counteract the buyer's remorse while he awaits clearance in the credit office. Since most of the seller's sales are on credit, the salesman knows when he gets the buyer's signature on the purchase order that the likelihood of a credit transaction is great. Disclosure is of little help to a buyer who is told in the credit office that he has a choice either of signing the creditor's conditional sales contract form or of having collection procedures instituted against him because he is unable to come up with the cash.

Johnson, Jordon, and Warren, Attorney's Guide to Truth in Lending, p.111 (California Continuing Education of the Bar, 1969).

In the case at bar buyer has not only signed the "one-note" of October 1, but has also signed a Used Car Buyers Order, and taken his Pinto home. Hence, while we have concluded that the "one-note" of October 1 is not a binding and valid contract, in reality the only way a consumer remains free to negotiate and to reject defendant's credit offer under defendant's present procedures is for the consumer to subject himself to a lawsuit.

Schmerler Ford would have the court sidestep this insurmountable problem and hold that the financing discussions of October 1 are not an integral part of the sale to such a significant extent that a contractual relationship was created between the creditor and customer with regard to that financing. Defendant stresses that the sale could not possibly have been conditioned on its arranging specific financing whose terms were known to it, inasmuch as Schmerler Ford did not know for certain that Ford Motor Credit Corporation would approve Gonzalez's credit and inasmuch as defendant did not even negotiate an interest rate with plaintiff until October 3.

This argument asks us to overlook defendant's close relationship and intimacy with Ford Motor Credit Corporation and Duski's experience as a credit manager. Defendant must have been able to predict with some degree of accuracy which customers would receive credit and upon what type of terms. To the extent that defendant could not give sufficiently explicit details, it was protected by 12 C.F.R. §226.6(f), which provides:

> If at the time disclosures must be made, an amount or other item of information required to be disclosed, or needed to determine a required disclosure, is unknown or not available to the creditor, and the creditor has made a reasonable effort to ascertain it, the creditor may use an estimated amount or an approximation of the information, provided the estimate or approximation is clearly identified as such, is reasonable, is based on the best information available to the creditor, and is not used for the purpose of circumventing or evading the disclosure requirements of this part.

Further, the term "specific financing" as used in Federal Reserve Board letter, No. 623, supra, cannot be construed in an overly narrow manner when the result of such a construction is to render sterile the disclosure requirements of the Truth in Lending Act in transactions like the one at bar. By having buyers sign a one-note when, in fact, a credit sale is contemplated, defendant has provided itself with "the best of both worlds" and effectively circumvented the Act. If no external financing can be arranged, defendant can threaten suit for cash based upon the October 1 document; if financing is arranged, buyer must negotiate his terms without benefit of prior disclosures for comparative credit shopping purposes, or else attempt backing out of the purchase at the risk of being sued on the October 1 document. Finally, we note that defendant always had the option on October 1, if it felt unable to disclose credit requirements or estimates thereof, to avoid signing plaintiff to a colorably binding contract, in which case it would be clear there was no sale on that date.

In sum, we find that financing was an integral part of the sale of the 1972 Pinto to plaintiff on October 1, and that defendant's procedures compelled credit disclosures on that date.

The parties have stipulated that the finance charge assessed in the transaction is $712.94. Pursuant to 15 U.S.C.A. §1640, plaintiff is entitled to twice that amount, not to exceed $1,000.00, in addition to the costs of the action together with a reasonable attorney's fee, which we determine to be the sum of $300.00. An order shall enter conforming to this decision.

PROBLEM 118

How many things wrong can you find in the TIL statement on next page?

LAWSON v. REEVES

Supreme Court of Alabama, 1988
537 So. 2d 15

SHORES, Justice.

The plaintiffs brought a claim for statutory damages under the federal Truth-in-Lending Act, 15 U.S.C. §1601 et seq. The complaint alleged violation of that Act and Regulation Z, promulgated by the Board of Governors of the Federal Reserve System pursuant to §105 of the Act, 15 U.S.C. §1604. The Act provides for damages of twice the amount of finance charges not disclosed as required by the Act, plus attorney fees.

The trial court dismissed the complaint, and the plaintiffs appealed. We reverse and remand.

The facts are as follows: The plaintiffs, Ruby Lawson and her son, Carl Brumlow (hereinafter "consumers"), purchased two used automobiles from the defendants, Scott Reeves and Roy Limbaugh, d/b/a Rocket City Auto Sales (hereinafter "creditor").

The consumers signed a sales contract and a security agreement, reflecting a sale price for one of the cars at $1511.83 plus $63.33 sales tax, payable $500 down and the balance in two payments of $50 each and thereafter 47 weekly payments of $30 each, and a final payment of $1.83.

TRUTH IN LENDING STATEMENT

ANNUAL PERCENTAGE RATE	FINANCE CHARGE	AMOUNT FINANCED	TOTAL OF PAYMENTS	TOTAL SALE PRICE
The cost of your credit as a yearly rate.	The dollar amount the credit will cost you.	The amount of credit provided to you or on your behalf.	The amount you will have paid after you have made all payments as scheduled.	The total cost of your purchase on credit, including your down-payment.
$_____	$_____	$_____	$_____	$_____

ITEMIZATION OF AMOUNT FINANCED:

Amount of unpaid sales price: _____

Amount paid to you directly: _____

Amount paid to others on your behalf: _____

Filing fees paid to public officials: _____

Credit Life Insurance: _____

Credit Health Insurance: _____

A Security Interest will be taken in:

_____ The item purchased

_____ Other (describe: _____)

Prepayment: If you pay the debt early you:

_____ will not have to pay a penalty.

_____ will have to pay a penalty.

_____ will receive a rebate of part of the finance charge.

_____ will not receive a rebate of part of the finance charge.

Late charge: See contract for late charges.

PROMISE TO PAY:

The undersigned hereby agrees to pay $_____ to the order of the Octopus National Bank, and waives all rights to presentment, notice of dishonor, and protest.

_____
(Signature of consumer)

See your purchase contract for other rights and duties.

I received a copy of this statement before signing the contract of purchase.

Date: _____   _____
(Signature of consumer)

The contract states that the finance charge is "0" and the annual percentage rate is "0%." The contract on the second car is similar.

The issue presented here is whether a cause of action has been stated under the federal Truth-in-Lending Act by allegations that finance charges were not disclosed but were included in the sale price of an item, payable over a period of time under an installment contract. The federal courts have answered this issue in the affirmative. "Finance charge" is defined by the Act:

> [With certain exceptions,] the amount of the finance charge . . . shall be determined as the sum of all charges, payable directly or indirectly by the person to whom the credit is extended, and imposed directly or indirectly by the creditor as an incident to the extension of credit. . . . Examples of charges which are included in the finance charge include any of the following types of charges which are applicable:
>
> (1) Interest, time price differential, and any amount payable under a point, discount, or other system of additional charges.
>
> (2) Service or carrying charge.
>
> (3) Loan fee, finder's fee, or similar charge.
>
> (4) Fee for an investigation or credit report.
>
> (5) Premium or other charge for any guarantee or insurance protecting the creditor against the obligor's default or other credit loss.

15 U.S.C. §1605(a).

Before the consummation of the transaction, a creditor (who meets the requirements of 15 U.S.C. §1602) is required to disclose, among other things, the financing fee charged a consumer (who meets the requirements of 15 U.S.C. §1602) in a sales contract. 15 U.S.C. §1638; 12 C.F.R. §§226.17 and 226.18 (part of "Regulation Z"); see also Myrick v. Finance America Credit Corp., 404 So. 2d 700 (Ala. Civ. App. 1981).

The legislative history of the Truth-in-Lending Act reflects that Congress believes that economic stabilization will be enhanced, and competition among firms engaged in the extension of consumer credit will be strengthened, by the informed use of consumer credit. The informed use of credit results from consumer awareness of its cost. The purposes of the Truth-in-Lending Act are to ensure disclosure of credit terms so that the consumer will more readily be able to compare the various credit terms available, to avoid the uninformed use of credit, and to protect the consumer against unfair credit practices. 15 U.S.C. §1601. The Truth-in-Lending Act is to be liberally construed in favor of the consumer and strictly enforced by the courts. Sellers v. Wollman, 510 F.2d 119 (5th Cir. 1975), Steib v. St. James Bank & Trust Co., 642 F. Supp. 910 (E.D. La. 1986).

In a case dealing with Congress's power to authorize the promulgation of Regulation Z by the Federal Reserve Board, which encompassed the "four installment rule," the United States Supreme Court, in affirming Regulation Z and the authority under which it was promulgated, acknowledged the problem of circumventing the Truth-in-Lending Act by including finance charges in the sale price of the item. The Court stated:

> One means of circumventing the objectives of the Truth in Lending Act, as passed by Congress, was that of "burying" the cost of credit in the price of goods sold. Thus in many credit transactions in which creditors claimed that no finance charge had been imposed, the creditor merely assumed the cost of extending credit as an expense of doing business, to be recouped as part of the price charged in the transaction. Congress was well aware, from its extensive studies, of the possibility that merchants could use such devices to evade the disclosure requirements of the Act. . . .
>
> It was against this legislative background that the Federal Reserve Board promulgated regulations governing enforcement of the Truth in Lending Act. . . .
>
> . . . The Board's objective in promulgating the [four-installment] rule was to prevent the Act from fulfilling the prophecy which its opponents had forecast.

Mourning v. Family Publications Service, 411 U.S. 356, 93 S. Ct. 1652, 36 L. Ed. 2d 318 (1972).

We are, of course, bound by decisions of the Supreme Court of the United States construing federal statutes, and we defer to the United States Courts of Appeals' decisions which do so, particularly the decisions of the old 5th Circuit, now the 11th Circuit, into whose jurisdiction Alabama falls. Therefore, we are particularly impressed with the decision of the 5th Circuit in Killings v. Jeff's Motors, Inc., 490 F.2d 865 (5th Cir. 1974). In that case, as here, the plaintiff bought a used car from the defendant. She made a down payment and signed an installment sales contract, under which she agreed to pay a certain amount each month until the balance was paid. There, as here, the contract form contained a vendor's disclosure as required by the Act, 15 U.S.C. §1601 et seq. It reflected "none" under "finance charge." Here, the contract shows "0" under "finance charge." There, the district court found, and the court of appeals affirmed, that the transaction did contain an undisclosed finance charge in violation of §1638. There, the parties stipulated that there was a difference of $325.28 between the "highest figure customarily charged in Alabama for similar merchandise during the relevant period." The court held that, under those circumstances, $325.28 was an undisclosed finance charge, and that the buyer was entitled to recover twice that amount plus attorney fees under §1640(a)(2)(A)(i) and (a)(3).

The appellees argue that *Killings* is distinguishable because there was no stipulation in this case as to the difference between the price charged for the used cars and their actual value. That argument misses the exact point made on appeal, viz., that the trial court erred in refusing to permit the buyer to introduce evidence on that very point. Alternatively, the appellees argue that the appellant failed to preserve the issue for review. We disagree. The record shows the installment contract, whereby the price of $1511.83, after a down payment of $500, is payable in two payments of $50 each and 47 weekly payments of $30 each and a final payment of $1.83.

The record shows:

> *Mr. Rowe:* Judge, could we make an offer of evidence on the issue of the value of the car for the record? What we would like to show and establish through this witness [the plaintiff] and some experts is that the value was significantly less than the stated purchase price, and that price was to include—
> *The Court:* But my question is, did somebody make her buy it for that? Did they have any discussions about that?
> *Mr. Rowe:* No, sir, but I think when you are talking about consumers—they are buying a package of financing and a car and they are not—
> *The Court*: I don't accept that argument.

At that point, the Court granted the appellees' motion to dismiss.

We hold that a claim for relief exists under the federal Truth-in-Lending Act, 15 U.S.C. §§1601 et seq., for non-disclosure of hidden finance charges, when the installment sales contract does not disclose an annual percentage rate, but the stated price exceeds the actual value of the item sold. The buyer is required to prove by competent evidence the difference between the actual value of the item sold and the stated sale price.

Because the trial court erred in disallowing evidence of the actual value of the items involved in this case, its judgment is reversed and the cause is remanded.

Reversed and Remanded.

QUESTION

Is the case right? Many automobiles are sold through a promotion promising either no interest rate or an impossibly low one.[33] Does this automatically create TIL problems for the seller/creditor?

---

33. Zero percent financing has been described as a form of "bait and switch." Only buyers with excellent credit rating typically qualify for the loan; others are steered to higher rates with the seller's own financing arm or a closely connected lender. Even for buyers who qualify, often the inflated cost of the vehicle absorbs any imagined savings, and frequently the fine print clauses ("If you fail to make a payment on time, the interest rate becomes 25%") can dramatically up the interest rate should the consumer make the slightest misstep.

Adjustable-Rate Loans. In recent decades, credit extensions have frequently included an interest rate that is not *fixed* at the outset, but instead fluctuates according to a rate set by some outside source (called the "index"). Typically, the borrower agrees to pay a rate that is a certain amount *over* the index rate (the difference is called the "margin"). To keep such a transaction from getting out of hand, the contract will sometimes provide a "cap" on either the amount by which the index can rise or the amount of the payments. If the cap is on the payment amount, the payments may not service the debt, meaning that they are not large enough to satisfy the interest being charged (much less the principal), and the unpaid interest is added to the debt. This process (called "negative amortization") can result in more being owed at the end of the loan period than was borrowed, and requires the debtor to pay a large, lump-sum amount to retire the debt (a so-called "balloon payment"). If the consumer cannot afford the balloon payment, the debt must either be refinanced (a process sometimes called "flipping"—because the borrower is "flipped" from one loan to another), or default occurs. If the consumer's house is on the line as collateral for the loan, the consequences can be catastrophic.[34] For the disclosures required in a closed-end transaction secured by the consumer's home, see Reg. Z §226.19(b). In the next chapter, we will consider similar disclosures as part of a discussion of home equity loans.

PROBLEM 119

Connie White had wanted a fur coat all her life, but her salary as a nurse made the purchase of a good one a luxury she could not afford. She did, however, become curious about a credit plan for fur coats that other nurses told her about. She asked one of her friends to put her in contact with the seller, and the next evening a salesman from Furs of the World explained the company's credit plan. He told her that she should select the fur coat of her dreams from his catalog and he would sell it to her on a time payment plan. Enthused, Connie selected her favorite coat and signed the contract. The coat was delivered the following week, and Connie loves it. Her problem is that

---

34. Some states do not permit adjustable rate mortgages secured by the consumer's home. The Alternative Mortgage Transaction Act of 1982, 12 U.S.C. §§3801 et seq., superseded these state law prohibitions unless the states opted out of the federal preemption. States doing so are Maine, Massachusetts, New York, South Carolina, and Wisconsin (Arizona has elected a partial exemption for loans made under its Consumer Loans Law).

a nursing strike at the hospital has curtailed Connie's income, and she can't afford the payments. Furs of the World is threatening to repossess, and so many other creditors are hounding her that Connie is considering filing a bankruptcy petition. She has come to you, a bankruptcy attorney, and told you this tale. She shows you the paperwork, and you are surprised to find that the TIL statement is one for an open-end credit plan, stating that the parties contemplate the consumer will place orders for many fur coats. The APR is 25 percent, which is the highest rate permitted by state law for both closed-end and open-end consumer credit sales. Connie tells you that she never led the salesman to believe that she would ever in the future buy another fur coat. Why would the creditor have done this? Is there any advantage in this situation to the open-end disclosures over the closed-end ones? See Benion v. Bank One, Dayton, N.A., 144 F.3d 1056 (7th Cir. 1998).

PROBLEM 120

After Professor Chalk had lived in the same house for 15 years, he suddenly was hired by a law school in another part of the country. The woman that Chalk's current law school hired to replace him wants to take over his current mortgage (which has a low interest rate) rather than get a new mortgage and pay off the old one. The two professors went down to Octopus National Bank, the mortgagee, and explained what was going on. Is this a *refinancing* or an *assumption* as those words are defined in Reg. Z §226.20? Is ONB required to give a new TIL statement in this situation?[35]

VI. CREDIT ADVERTISING

The driving idea behind Truth in Lending is that early, proper disclosure of credit terms permits the consumer to shop around for credit and make the best credit buy. Whether this actually goes on can be questioned, but for a moment let us assume that consumers really do compare credit terms before

---

35. In one of the few consumer protection provisions created by the Truth in Lending Simplification Act (which was very creditor oriented), Reg. Z §226.18(q) now requires that the initial TIL disclosure statement in residential mortgage transactions reveal whether the mortgage is assumable by subsequent purchasers of the dwelling.

signing a contract. In such a world, the advertising of credit terms would have to be watched carefully to make sure that it didn't mislead the consumer at the moment of first contact.

The problem, as with usury and fraud, is that it is very easy for the creditor to state things in such a way as to be literally true, but substantively quite misleading. The common law of fraud and Regulation Z both prohibit out-and-out lies in credit advertising (as would a raft of state deceptive practices statutes). The Regulation Z condemnations can be found in §§226.16(a) (open-end credit) and 226.24(a) (closed-end credit).[36]

Beyond that, Regulation Z adopts what has been called the "trigger terms" approach to credit advertising. In the two Regulation Z sections just cited, the law permits certain terms to be advertised without the federal government's taking an interest. But certain credit terms, as listed in these sections, *trigger* a requirement of the disclosure of other material terms of the contract. This rule tends to divide credit advertising into two camps: all or nothing.

PROBLEM 121

The advertising vice president of Big Department Store calls your law office. The VP wants to know if newspaper advertisements of the following terms will trigger the necessity of further disclosures.

a. "ANNUAL PERCENTAGE RATE 18 PERCENT!" Does it matter whether this is for open- or closed-end credit? Is it allowable to abbreviate it to "APR 18%!"?

b. In a refrigerator sale: "NO DOWN PAYMENT!"

c. "NO PAYMENTS UNTIL FEBRUARY!"

The advertising sections of the Truth in Lending Act are in Part C of the statute. This is important because the civil liability section (§130) permits the injured consumer to sue only for violations of Part B (TIL Disclosures), Part D (Fair Credit Billing), or Part E (Consumer Leasing). Thus, there is no private right of action in favor of consumers injured by the violation of TIL advertising rules. Instead, the enforcement is administrative, with the Federal Trade Commission being the watchdog. But the amount of credit advertising is large and the resources of the FTC are meager; the upshot is that you can open the morning newspaper, glance at billboards, and turn on the radio or TV and hear violation after violation of the advertising rules.

---

36. It should be noted that the Federal Trade Commission publishes a "How To Advertise Consumer Credit" manual.

PROBLEM 122

Though they were both recently graduated from college, newly-weds Ralph and Josephine Rakestraw decided they had to have a new car even if they had to scrimp to afford one. Josephine called around to various car dealers in town and asked about financing. The sales manager at Facade Motors offered her the best deal, telling her that his interest rate was only 9 percent. Since that beat the 10 per-cent two other dealerships were offering, Ralph and Josephine went down to Facade Motors, picked out the car of their dreams, and signed the paperwork. Later, in the quiet of their home, Josephine got to looking through the paperwork and was disturbed to see that the TIL statement listed the APR as 17.5 percent. When she called the Facade Motors sales manager and complained, he told her that the 9 percent rate he had quoted her had been the "add-on" rate. Not understanding, but still plenty mad, Josephine calls you for advice. Can Facade Motors get away with this? See TILA §146. Is there relief at common law or under other statutes?

VII. CREDIT INSURANCE

With rare exceptions, credit insurance is sold at rates that are outra-geous. Most consumers could get the required coverage much cheaper through their existing insurance policies or through an independent insur-ance agent. They do not do so because the credit insurance seems (to the consumer) a small part of the deal, not worth the bother of shopping around. But to the creditor, particularly large national creditors, the amount earned on credit insurance is a good hefty sum, and they resent attempts to regulate it. Many states have statutes doing just that, typically requiring the state department of insurance to monitor credit insurance policies and forbidding the worst abuses (such as issuing a policy greater than the term of the loan, or failing to rebate unearned insurance premiums if the loan is paid early).[37]

Credit insurance falls into two broad types: (1) credit life, health, or accident insurance (hereafter, for convenience sake, simply called "credit

---

37. Creditors report a "penetration rate" (the number of borrowers electing to take the credit insurance) of between 95 percent and 100 percent. Landers, Determining the Finance Charge Under Truth in Lending, 1977 Am. B. Found. Res. J. 45, 121 n.169. For a history of credit insurance and the problems it has caused, see Comment, Credit Insurance: Abuse and Reform, 10 B.C. Indus. & Com. L. Rev. 439 (1969).

life insurance"), which pays the debt if the consumer gets ill or dies, and (2) credit property insurance, which pays the debt if the collateral is destroyed.[38]

Creditors would like to bury the charges for these matters if possible, but Regulation Z has some discrete rules on point. Credit *property* insurance helps the creditor protect its interest in the collateral, and is generally therefore allowed to be disclosed separately apart from the finance charge. Credit *health/life* insurance protects the risk of lending to the wrong person, and is therefore more obviously placed in the finance charge. However, for both of these, if the credit insurance is disclosed in the ways described in §226.4(d), the premiums therefor may be separately disclosed and need not be added into the finance charge. If the creditor is unwilling (or fails to take the right steps) to disclose the credit insurance in the manner required, then the premiums are part of the finance charge and will have to be added in. §226.4(b).

PROBLEM 123

The following credit insurance clauses appear in four different TIL statements. Decide which ones violate the separate disclosure provisions and therefore require that the amount involved be included in the finance charge.

a. Credit property insurance is required, but may be purchased from any reputable source. (No separate signature blank next to this statement.)

b. Credit life insurance is required; it costs $12. Consumer agreeing to this charge must sign this statement. (Signature blank provided.)

---

38. Credit property insurance is sold in a number of formats. "Vendor's single interest" [VSI] insurance, for example, insures only the debt owed to the creditor and not the debtor's equity in the property (and thus coverage decreases as the loan is paid down). With VSI the creditor is also paid repossession costs. Should the property be destroyed, the creditor would be paid the amount of the debt that is still due, but the debtor would get nothing from this insurer. "Dual interest" insurance protects both parties. TIL mandates that VSI policies include a waiver of the insurer's subrogation rights against the borrower. Reg. Z §226.4(d) n.5. Another type of insurance is called "gap" insurance. Say that the credit property insurance only covers the *current value* of the car that is the subject of the transaction, and at the time when the car is totaled in an accident it is only worth half of the outstanding debt owed the financing creditor; "gap" insurance makes up the difference so that the debtor does not have to pay the remaining half (the "gap" between the value of the collateral and the amount due).

c. Credit life insurance may be purchased from the entity of your choice, but is required as part of this transaction. If you desire us to furnish it, the cost is $12. In such case, sign this statement. (Signature blank provided.)

d. Credit property insurance is required; it costs $6 and must be purchased from us. (Signature blank provided.)

ADAMS v. PLAZA FINANCE CO.
United States Court of Appeals, Seventh Circuit, 1999
168 F.3d 932

POSNER, Chief Judge.

This class suit against Plaza Finance Company seeks statutory (not compensatory) damages for violation of the Truth in Lending Act, 15 U.S.C. §§1601 et seq.; see §1640(a). The district court granted summary judgment for the defendant largely on the basis of a district court decision, since reversed by the Fifth Circuit in Edwards v. Your Credit, Inc., 148 F.3d 427 (5th Cir. 1998), in a case virtually identical to this one. A number of similar cases are pending elsewhere. Alvin C. Harrell, "Consumer Credit," 52 Consumer Finance L.Q. Rep. 104, 106 (1998).

In view of the procedural posture of our case, we construe the facts as favorably to the plaintiff as the record will permit. The defendant specializes in making small, short-term loans to individuals who have bad credit (the default rate on its loans is 25 percent). It lent the named plaintiff $307 for ten months, of which $7 went to pay for a premium for "nonfiling insurance," that is, insurance against losses to the finance company resulting from its failure to file (record) its security interest. The Truth in Lending disclosure form that the plaintiff was given listed, besides $307 as the "amount financed" (see Federal Reserve Board Regulation Z, 12 C.F.R. §226.18(b)), a "finance charge" (basically the amount of interest charged for the loan, but including certain service charges as well, see 15 U.S.C. §1605(a)) of $128 and an annual interest rate of 83 percent. In computing the interest rate for Truth in Lending purposes, the finance company uses the finance charge as the interest and the amount financed as the principal. Hence, other things being equal, the disclosed interest rate is higher the higher the finance charge and lower the higher the amount financed. This creates an incentive for lenders, who want the interest rate to look as low as possible, to shift items from the finance charge (interest) to the amount financed (principal).

The loan to the plaintiff was secured by a wage assignment plus a security interest in various items of the borrower's personal property, such as a television set. Unless such an interest is recorded in the local UCC registry of security interests in personal property, the holder of the interest will not be able to enforce it against a subsequent secured creditor who records his own security interest. UCC §9-312(5)(a), 810 ILCS 5/9-312(5)(a); Midwest Decks, Inc. v. Butler & Baretz Acquisitions, Inc., 272 Ill. App. 3d 370, 649 N.E.2d 511, 516, 208 Ill. Dec. 455 (Ill. App. 1995). (Filing generally is unnecessary to perfect a purchase-money security interest, UCC §§9-302(1)(d), 307(2), 810 ILCS 5/9-302(1)(d), 307(2), but that type of security interest is not involved in this case.) Because the rules in Article 9 of the Uniform Commercial Code regulating filing are complex and demanding, see, e.g., UCC §§9-103, 9-401, 9-403(2), it is easy for a lender to make a mistake, such as filing in the wrong place or failing to renew the filing statement after its expiration; and lenders sometimes insure themselves against the consequences of such a mistake by buying nonfiling insurance. The Truth in Lending Act permits a lender to include as a service fee a premium for such insurance. 15 U.S.C. §1605(d)(2). The $7 that Plaza charged the plaintiff was the per-loan premium it pays to Voyager Property and Casualty Insurance Company for the insurance. This is the same insurance company that was involved in the Fifth Circuit's *Edwards* decision. Although Voyager is licensed to sell nonfiling insurance in Illinois, where the loan to the plaintiff was made, there is no suggestion that Illinois has determined that Voyager's contract with Plaza and its performance of that contract are consistent with the terms of the license or the insurance law of Illinois. Indeed, we can find nothing in the record or in the law of Illinois to indicate what Illinois understands by "nonfiling insurance."

The plaintiff argues that the "insurance" which Voyager has sold Plaza either is not insurance at all, or is not nonfiling insurance but instead default insurance—and a premium for default insurance, unlike a premium for nonfiling insurance, must be included in the finance charge. 12 C.F.R. §226.4(b)(5). Interest is compensation not only for the time value of money but also for the risk of default, and so a charge to the borrower that is intended to compensate the lender for that risk is functionally part of the borrower's interest expense. A premium for default insurance is such a charge, and so it belongs in the "finance charge" (interest) column of the disclosure form.

The usual purpose of insurance is to shift risk from an individual or other entity that is risk averse, and so would prefer to substitute a cost certain (a fixed insurance premium) for the risk of incurring a larger cost, to an entity that by pooling independent risks can minimize the overall risk to itself. [Citations omitted.] The simplest example is life insurance. A person who does not want to bear the financial risk of dying young can buy life insurance, for which he pays a fixed premium. The financial risk of his early death is shifted to the insurance company, which by pooling that risk with the risk of its policy holders who die old can eliminate the risk of incurring an unexpectedly steep loss from a premature death. By pooling, the insurance company shields itself from that risk; by joining the pool, the insured eliminates the risk to himself.

No risk-shifting purpose is discernible in the arrangement between Plaza and Voyager. Their original contract expressly capped Voyager's potential liability to Plaza at 90 percent of the premiums paid by Plaza. This meant that no risk was shifted to Voyager. If Plaza paid Voyager premiums of $50,000, and had insured losses of $100,000, for a total loss-related cost of $150,000, it would receive $45,000 in insurance proceeds from Voyager, leaving it with a net cost of $105,000 ($150,000 − $45,000)—a net cost greater than the premiums, greater even than the incurred loss, that is, the loss against which Plaza nominally insured. Plaza was in effect a self-insurer, and the cost of self-insurance is not within the dispensation to exclude premiums for nonfiling insurance from the finance charge. 12 C.F.R. Part 226, Supp. I, §226.4(e)(4) (Official Staff Commentary on Regulation Z).

Of course insurance policies always have limits; but when the limit is at or below the premium, the insured is not shifting risk by buying the policy. This cannot be the end of the analysis, however. Insurance has other functions besides risk-shifting, including smoothing costs over time, providing assistance in defending against claims (liability insurers typically provide a defense if their insured is sued for conduct covered or even just arguably covered by the policy), and exploiting various tax opportunities. Wisconsin Power & Light Co. v. Century Indemnity Co., 130 F.3d 787, 791 (7th Cir. 1997); Sears, Roebuck & Co., supra. But at argument Plaza's lawyer was able to identify only one possible function of Voyager's insurance, and that is to avoid having to include $7 in the finance charge. By its lawyer's own acknowledgment, Plaza is getting nothing in the way of a service from its so-called insurer, whether for bearing risk or for anything else, in exchange for the $7 that it pays Voyager—or rather for the 70 cents it pays Voyager, for it gets the rest of the $7 back. If the only function of the insurance policy is to monkey with the disclosed interest rate, it is not a bona fide policy; it is a fraud.

And that is, so far as the record indicates, the only function of the "nonfiling insurance" that Plaza bought from Voyager: to enable the lender (Plaza) to shift $7 of what otherwise would be an interest charge from the finance-charge column on the Truth in Lending disclosure form to the amount-financed column. See 12 C.F.R. §226.18(b)(2). The expense to the borrower is the same, but the disclosed annual interest rate is lower. Remember that items added to the finance charge count as interest in computing the disclosed annual interest rate, and so increase that rate, while items added to the amount financed increase the denominator in the interest-rate calculation and so reduce the disclosed rate. In this case, the disclosed interest rate would have risen to 89 percent if $7 had been subtracted from the amount financed and added to the finance charge. The smaller the loan, the bigger the difference that the shift of $7 makes. Consider a very simple example: a one-year loan (amount financed) of $50 (and Plaza makes loans that small), and a finance charge of $40 payable at the end of the year, and hence an annual interest rate of 80 percent. (Simple rather than compound interest is assumed, to keep the example simple.) If $7 is shifted from the amount financed to the finance charge, the annual interest rate skyrockets to 109 percent ($47/$43). That's a scary figure; it might frighten off even the necessitous borrowers who are Plaza's principal customers.

During the period covered by the complaint, the insurance contract with Voyager was altered to drop the 90-percent-of-premiums cap. This change eliminated the most illusory feature of the contract. But the plaintiff, who received her loan from Plaza after the change, contends that Voyager and Plaza have an informal understanding that Plaza will not submit claims in excess of 90 percent of the premiums that it has paid during a given period; hence the change in the policy was merely cosmetic. If so, the inference that the arrangement between these two companies is not an insurance policy of any sort, but a sham that has no purpose other than to facilitate an evasion of the Truth in Lending Act's requirements, would be compelling in the absence of contrary evidence not yet presented by Plaza. . . .

The plaintiff's alternative ground for contending that Plaza has violated the Act . . . is that if there is real insurance here, and not a complete sham, it is insurance against default rather than insurance against the consequences of not filing a security interest. A lender files a security interest only if it thinks it might want to seize the collateral in the event of default. The plaintiff has presented evidence from which it can be inferred, with enough confidence to defeat summary judgment, that Plaza does not want to seize the collateral for its loans, because they are tiny loans to people who own no valuable property. The taking of the security interest is intended merely to frighten the borrower. [Citations omitted.] Had the named plaintiff defaulted on her $307 loan, it would not have been worth Plaza's while to institute legal process to obtain and sell her personal property. Rather than wanting to file and occasionally through neglect failing to do so and wanting insurance against that eventuality, Plaza doesn't want to bother to file, has no desire for insurance against the consequences of not filing (there are no consequences, so there is nothing to insure against), and never has submitted a nonfiling claim to Voyager.

Most of the claims that it submits to Voyager are for losses caused by a default by a borrower who cannot be located (a "skip"). In these cases, the borrower's property can't be located either. Failure to have recorded a security interest in the property can have no consequence for Plaza in such a case; Plaza can't enforce a security interest in property that it can't find. Some of the claims involve borrowers who have defaulted because they died, and a few involve borrowers who have entered Chapter 7 bankruptcy. But in neither of these classes of case is there any indication that property in which Plaza had a security interest was ever snatched away from it by a creditor who had a superior interest by reason of having recorded his interest.

Insurance companies sometimes pay claims that don't actually come within the scope of the insurance policy. They do so because of their own inadvertence, fraud by the insured, ambiguity in the policy, or a desire to maintain good relation with valued customers. We want to emphasize, lest lenders find themselves obliged by innocent mistake to pay potentially very large statutory damages in class actions, that nonfiling insurance doesn't cease to be so merely because the insurance company sometimes pays on claims that don't fit within the strict terms of the policy. But so far as the record discloses, Voyager has *never* paid a claim by Plaza for a loss due to nonfiling. Not rarely; never. So far as the record discloses, the insurance contract is in fact a contract for default insurance, not nonfiling insurance, and the law treats the two types of insurance differently.

If an insurance company issues an automobile liability policy to a person who does not own or drive an automobile, and then pays the claims that the person submits for accidents caused by his bicycle, the policy would not be an automobile liability policy but a bicycle liability policy. Cf. Nolker v. Wallace, 317 So. 2d 4 (La. App. 1975). And so it is here: penetrating form to substance is the right approach in a Truth in Lending Act case in which an insurance policy says "nonfiling" but all the claims submitted and paid under it are for defaults the costs of which to the insured have nothing to do with the insured's having failed to record a security interest. This is not just our idea, or that of the Supreme Court, Ford Motor Credit Co. v. Cenance, 452 U.S. 155, 158, 68 L. Ed. 2d 744, 101 S. Ct. 2239 (1981) (per curiam); the Federal Reserve Board, in its regulation interpreting and applying the Act, has made clear that it is the actual character of a policy of insurance—what it really insures—rather than the name, that controls its classification for purposes of the Act. See 12 C.F.R. Pt. 226, Supp. I, §226.4(d)(10), p. 314 (1998) (Official Staff Commentary).

We emphasize that in speaking of penetrating the outer form to find the inner substance, we (and the Supreme Court, and the Federal Reserve Board) are not referring to the "substance" of the credit transaction. The Act is not a usury law; it does not limit interest rates; all it requires is truthful and (it is hoped) informative disclosure of the interest rate and the other terms of credit. The relevant substance is truth; and its protection is inconsistent with allowing a lender to call something "nonfiling insurance" that is not insurance against nonfiling losses and indeed may not be insurance at all. Since the Truth in Lending Act permits premiums for nonfiling insurance to be included in the amount financed but requires default insurance premiums to be included in the interest charge, a lender cannot be permitted to designate a premium as being for nonfiling insurance if it is really, clearly, and always for default insurance. . . .

At argument Plaza's lawyer reminded us that his client did not conceal the $7 charge from the plaintiff; she knew she was paying it. What she didn't know was what interest rate she was paying. Maybe she didn't care. But the provision of the Truth in Lending Act that requires disclosure of the annual interest rate assumes that borrowers, or some appreciable number of them at any rate, do care; and we are not at liberty to question the premises of a valid statute. Id. at 287.

We do worry about opening a can of worms in which class action lawyers can rummage for discrepancies between the terms and actual performance of contracts relating to the various service charges that the Act permits to be included in the amount financed. But to forbid inquiry into performance would open a big loophole, as a host of cases (besides Edwards, a virtual clone of this case) attest. [Citations omitted.] Nothing in the language or history of the Act, or the cases interpreting it, authorize courts to forbid plaintiffs to prove if they can that a finance charge has been mislabeled as part of the amount financed in circumstances that negate an inference of that the mislabeling is due to a mistake by a third party, such as a nonfiling insurer who occasionally pays what is really a loss due to default rather than nonfiling. We need not consider the outer bounds of "occasionally," since the plaintiff's submission is that the parties to the so-called insurance contract never intended for any nonfiling claim to be submitted and paid and that no such claim ever was submitted or paid.

We emphasize that the facts recited in this opinion are merely those adduced in the summary judgment proceedings and viewed in a light favorable to the plaintiff. The trial may cast the facts in a different light. But the grant of summary judgment was error.

Reversed.

EASTERBROOK, Circuit Judge, dissenting. . . .

The idea that borrowers can collect penalties because an insurance company paid out too much to their lender—a practice that increases the lender's total collections and thus drives down the rate of interest to risky customers—makes sense only under a statute that elevates form over substance, as the TILA does. Lenders must follow prescribed forms of disclosure; it is essential not only to disclose how much the borrower pays for credit (as Plaza did) but also to disclose each element on the right line of the right form. 15 U.S.C. §1638. Borrowers can collect statutory penalties if the forms are disregarded, even if they do not suffer injury, indeed even if the practice benefits them. 15 U.S.C. §1640(a)(2). Plaza's practice was better for borrowers than paying the $7 filing fee, though perhaps worse than another option. Plaza paid $7 per customer to Voyager and recovered approximately $6.30 (less its administrative costs of making claims); it could have saved another 70 cents by omitting both filing and insurance. But under the TILA we assess not the difference among $7 for filing, $7 for nonfiling insurance, and $6.30 added to interest, but the difference between $7 in the "amount financed" and $7 in the "finance charge." What my colleagues hold, and what the majority of the fifth circuit held in *Edwards*, is that plaintiffs may prevail by piercing the form of Voyager's policy to get at the substance of the parties' practice, and thus to conclude that the $7 belonged in the "finance charge."

A substance-over-form approach is fundamentally incompatible with the TILA's penalty provisions, which exalt form over substance. It just won't do to have a system in which the propriety of classification can be known only after the fact. If my colleagues are correct, then a lender that tried to play it safe by putting the cost of nonfiling insurance into the "finance charge" could be challenged, and required to pay penalties, if a court later decided that the transaction really *was* nonfiling insurance that had to go into the "amount financed." But the TILA assumes that the classifications are knowable ex ante and fixed at the time of the loan; an ex ante approach to classification and disclosure is discordant with an ex post inquiry to determine the "substance" of the transaction. No wonder the TILA includes a rule against using hindsight to assess the adequacy of disclosure. 15 U.S.C. §1634. . . .

PROBLEM 124

When you asked your client, Connie Consumer, about the credit life insurance that she had agreed to buy (her signature is next to the requisite clause on the TIL statement), she tells you that the sales agent told her that credit life insurance was required and she had to initial the insurance clause if she wanted the deal to go through. The TIL statement clearly states that credit life insurance is not required. When Connie pointed this out to the sales agent, he said that the law made them say that, but the insurance was nonetheless mandatory. Is there a TIL violation here? Will the parol evidence rule cause trouble? Compare Anthony v. Community Loan & Inv. Corp., 559 F.2d 1363 (5th Cir. 1977), and Mims v. Dixie Fin. Corp., 426 F. Supp. 627 (N.D. Ga. 1976), with Marine Midland Bank v. Burley, 73 A.D.2d 1041 (N.Y. Sup. Ct. 1980).

In the Homeowners Protection Act of 1998, 12 U.S.C. §§4901 et seq., Congress recognized that mortgagors were paying for home mortgage insurance for much longer than the mortgagee really needed its protection. Thus, the Act requires the mortgagee to cancel mortgage insurance whenever the payments on the mortgage reach 80 percent of the value of the property, so that a substantial equity cushion has been built up to protect the original loan in the case of default. The statute requires disclosures as to this, and contains a civil action section providing that violations lead to actual damages, statutory damages of up to $2,000 in an individual action, costs, and attorney's fees.

STONE v. DAVIS[39]
Supreme Court of Ohio, 1981
66 Ohio St. 2d 74, 419 N.E.2d 1094

This cause originated as a foreclosure action filed in the Court of Common Pleas of Ashtabula County by George and Clara Stone, sellers and mortgagees of a dairy farm located in Austinburg Township, Ashtabula County, against appellee Judy V. Davis, one of the purchasers and mortgagors of the farm, and other individuals and entities holding alleged lien interests in the farm, including appellant Ashtabula County Savings & Loan Company (hereinafter "Ashtabula S & L").

In 1972, Danny I. Davis and his wife, Judy Davis, 21 and 19 years old respectively, negotiated with the Stones for the purchase of their dairy farm in Ashtabula County. In order to finance the major part of this purchase, the

---

39. Footnote in this case has been renumbered for clarity. [Editor's note: At the time of the transaction described in this case, the Truth in Lending Act applied to agricultural loans—a category eliminated by the adoption of the Truth in Lending Simplification Act in 1980.]

Davises applied to Ashtabula S & L (since merged with Cardinal Federal Savings & Loan) for a $60,000 mortgage loan.

By letter dated October 26, 1972, Ashtabula S & L notified the Davises that it had approved their mortgage loan application.[40] On the day following the making of its loan commitment to the Davises, Ashtabula S & L presented them with a document entitled "Notice to Customers Required by Federal Law, Federal Reserve Regulation Z," which contained an itemization of the costs of their loan. The Davises acknowledged receipt of this disclosure form on October 27, 1972, by dating and affixing their signatures to it.

Relevant to the instant controversy, the following language appeared within the disclosure form concerning the subject of "Other Insurance":

> Credit life, accident, health or loss of income insurance is not required to obtain this loan. No charge is made for such insurance and no such insurance is provided unless the borrower signs the appropriate statement. (type of insurance) is available at a cost of $ _____ , for the _____ year term of the initial policy.

Below this language appeared the following juxtapositional statements: "I desire _____ insurance coverage," and "I DO NOT desire such insurance coverage." Underneath each of these statements were two blank lines for a date and a signature.

In the disclosure form presented to the Davises, the word "mortgage" had been typed onto the blank space of the first statement. On the lines under this statement, Danny Davis signed his name and entered the date "10/27/72."

What transpired next in connection with Danny Davis' expressed desire for mortgage insurance was disputed by the parties to this controversy. The trial court, however, found that Ashtabula S & L thereafter neither took any steps to procure mortgage insurance for Danny Davis nor advised Davis that he was to procure the insurance himself. In any event, no mortgage insurance was ever obtained for Davis.

Thereafter, the sale of the Stones' property to the Davises was completed, and they began operation of the dairy farm. In the Spring of 1975, the Davises encountered business difficulties when their herd of dairy cows contracted a reproductive disease which required that it be sold. As a result of this problem, the Davises fell behind on their mortgage payments to both their sellers, the Stones, who had financed part of the purchase price of the

---

40. The Davises subsequently agreed to the terms of the loan proposed by Ashtabula S & L, and the latter agreed to act as escrow agent in the sale of the farm. The sale was apparently consummated on November 30, 1972, when a deed conveying the farm to the Davises was filed with the Ashtabula County Recorder.

farm, and Ashtabula S & L. The Davises were three months in default on these mortgages when, on July 18, 1975, Danny Davis died as a result of injuries he sustained in a motorcycle accident.

Following her husband's death, Judy Davis made some 30 additional monthly mortgage payments to Ashtabula S & L, but her loan nevertheless remained in default. The Stones thereupon instituted this foreclosure action in the Court of Common Pleas on June 20, 1977.

After filing answers to the Stones' complaint, appellant Ashtabula S & L and appellee Davis cross-claimed against each other. In its cross-claim, Ashtabula S & L alleged that Judy Davis was indebted to it on the remaining balance of a $60,000 mortgage loan it had made to her and her deceased husband Danny Davis to finance part of the purchase price of the Stones' farm.

In her cross-claim, Judy Davis alleged that Ashtabula S & L, either negligently or in breach of a promise to do so, had failed to procure mortgage insurance for her husband Danny; that, as a proximate result, when Danny Davis died in an accident in 1975, he was not covered by any mortgage insurance; and that Ashtabula S & L was therefore liable to her for the amount of the lost mortgage insurance proceeds.

Appellant's and appellee's cross-claims were severed from the other claims in the Stones' foreclosure action and tried without a jury to the common pleas court. At the time of the trial of the parties' cross-claims in October 1978, Judy Davis' account with Ashtabula S & L showed a principal balance of $58,572.08 and accrued interest of $2,780.55 on the original $60,000 loan she and her husband had taken out in October 1972.

The trial court rendered a judgment for Judy Davis, holding that Ashtabula S & L had breached a duty to inform the Davises that they had to procure mortgage insurance themselves if they so desired it, and was therefore liable to Judy Davis for her loss of mortgage insurance proceeds.

On appeal, the Court of Appeals affirmed the trial court's judgment. . . .

JOHN V. CORRIGAN, Justice.

In this appeal, Ashtabula S & L advances six propositions of law which are considered infra.

I

Propositions of law Nos. 1 through 3, which may be treated together, read as follows:

[1.] A federal truth-in-lending Regulation Z disclosure form promulgated by the Federal Reserve Board does not render a creditor using such form liable under Ohio law in either contract or tort for the nonexistence of insurance for which a debtor has indicated his "desire" on the disclosure form.

[2.] A lending institution dealing at arm's length with a prospective borrower prior to the creation of any debtor-creditor or other contractual relationship has no tort law duty to affirmatively advise and counsel the prospective debtor as to the legal mechanics or the legal consequences of either the prospective lending transaction or collateral matters.

[3.] The Federal Truth-in-Lending Act contains and creates its own exclusive remedies and liabilities, and an Ohio court's application of the Act and of forms promulgated thereunder by a federal agency in disregard of the Act's express limitations upon liability is violative of both the federal and the Ohio Constitutions.

The major thrust of the argument underlying these propositions of law is that a lending institution, which complies with the disclosure requirements of federal truth-in-lending law (Sections 1601 et seq., Title 15, U.S. Code) and, in so doing, notifies its loan customer that procurement of mortgage insurance is not a condition for the loan and need be purchased only if the customer so desired, does not, upon eliciting from the customer an expressed desire for mortgage insurance, assume a further duty to disclose to the customer how such insurance may be procured. We do not accept appellant's argument as a correct statement of Ohio law, and, for the reasons which follow, we hold instead that a lending institution does assume this further duty of disclosure and, in negligently failing to observe this duty, may become liable for any injury to the customer proximately caused.

In Umbaugh Pole Bldg. Co. v. Scott (1979), 58 Ohio St. 2d 282, 390 N. E.2d 320, we recognized that, in most instances, the relationship of a creditor to his debtor, governed by the principles of freedom of contract, was not a fiduciary relationship. There, we held that evidence which revealed that the creditor had given advice to the debtor concerning the operation of the debtor's business was insufficient to transform what was otherwise a business relationship into a fiduciary relationship. In so holding, we conclude that, in the matter upon which the advice there was rendered, the parties were operating at arm's length, each seeking to protect his own legitimate business interests. Id., at page 287, 390 N.E.2d 320.

The facts are different in the case *sub judice* and more compelling of a conclusion that, in broaching the subject of mortgage insurance, Ashtabula S & L was acting as a fiduciary to Danny and Judy Davis, its loan customers.

"A 'fiduciary relationship' is one in which special confidence and trust is reposed in the integrity and fidelity of another and there is a resulting position of superiority or influence, acquired by virtue of this special trust." In re Termination of Employment (1974), 40 Ohio St. 2d 107, 115,

321 N.E.2d 603. A fiduciary relationship need not be created by contract; it may arise out of an informal relationship where both parties understand that a special trust or confidence has been reposed. *Umbaugh*, supra.

The facts surrounding and the setting in which a bank gives advice to a loan customer on the subject of mortgage insurance warrant a conclusion that, in this aspect of the mortgage loan process, the bank acts as its customer's fiduciary and is under a duty to fairly disclose to the customer the mechanics of procuring such insurance.

We observe that, while a bank and its customer may be said to stand at arm's length in negotiating the terms and conditions of a mortgage loan, it is unrealistic to believe that this equality of position carries over into the area of loan processing, which customarily includes advising the customer as to the benefits of procuring mortgage insurance on the property which secures the bank's loan.

In the case before us, Judy Davis and her husband Danny came to Ashtabula S & L as a young married couple, apparently encountering the complex mortgage loan process for the first time in their lives. Undoubtedly, their every action in assisting the expeditious processing of their loan was guided by officers of Ashtabula S & L, upon whom they justifiably relied as experts in the field of loan processing. When Ashtabula S & L broached the subject of mortgage insurance and elicited an expressed desire for it by Danny Davis, both sides to the loan transaction must have understood that a special trust or confidence had been reposed in Ashtabula S & L to advise and assist the Davises in procuring the insurance. When Ashtabula S & L negligently failed to adhere to its customary policy of informing the Davises that they must procure the mortgage insurance themselves, it breached the fiduciary duty of fair disclosure which it owed to them.

We find, contrary to appellant's arguments, that our holding is supported by the existence of federal truth-in-lending law. In the enactment of this legislation on loan disclosure aimed at promoting the informed use of credit, Congress implicitly recognized that, in matters integrally related to the complex loan processing procedure utilized in the modern banking system, the principle of freedom of contract must be aided, the arm's length bargaining assisted, by imposing certain duties of disclosure upon banks. Moreover, Congress expressly provided that its disclosure scheme was not intended to preclude the States from formulating their own disclosurer [sic] requirements, so long as they were not inconsistent with the federal scheme. Section 1610, Title 15, U.S. Code. Therefore, we find the cases from other jurisdictions cited by appellant, in support of the proposition that use of a Regulation Z disclosure form, approved by the Federal Reserve Board as sufficient to satisfy the requirement of truth-in-lending law, cannot give rise to a cause of action under State law in tort or contract, to be inapposite or, at best, unpersuasive. See Burgess v. Charlottesville S. & L. Assn. (D.C.W.D. Va. 1972), 349 F. Supp. 133, remanded at 477 F.2d 40 (C.A. 4, 1973); Peer v. First Federal S & L Assn. of Cumberland (1975), 273 Md. 610, 331 A.2d 299; and In re Estate of Johnson (1975), 195 Neb. 131, 236 N.W.2d 838. But, see, Bass v. Home Federal S. & L. Assn. (1979), 266 Ark. 770, 587 S.W.2d 48.

We further find support for our holding in the recognition that banks do not act as disinterested experts in advising loan customers of the availability of mortgage insurance, but instead have a direct pecuniary interest in inducing the customer to procure it. Mortgage insurance serves to protect the bank's investment in a loan by providing a ready source of funds for the loan's repayment should the debtor subsequently suffer an untimely death. Furthermore, as was brought out in testimony presented at the trial of the case now before us, banks often act as collection agents for mortgage insurance, adjusting their debtor's payment schedule to include payment of the insurance premiums and then remitting the collected premiums to the insurance company, receiving in return a percentage commission for this service.

In light of all the foregoing considerations, we hold that, in broaching the subject of mortgage insurance to a loan customer, a lending institution has a duty to advise the customer as to how this insurance may be procured. Where, as in the instant case, a bank uses a Regulation Z disclosure form to elicit from a customer his desire for mortgage insurance and thereafter negligently fails to further advise the customer that he must procure it himself, the bank breaches its duty of disclosure, and may be held liable for any proximately caused injury to the customer resulting from such negligence. . . .

Judgment affirmed.

There have been a number of cases dealing with the issue of the TIL statement as a "contract" or as creating some sort of duty by the creditor to fulfill all of the terms disclosed. Not surprisingly, this most often surfaces as involving the need to procure credit insurance. See Mark Budnitz, The Sale of Credit Life Insurance: The Bank as Fiduciary, 62 N.C. L. Rev. 295 (1984).

CHAPTER 8
Truth in Lending: Remedies

I. DAMAGES

A. Administrative Enforcement

Section 108 of the Truth in Lending Act lists the various federal agencies responsible for monitoring compliance with the statute. If these agencies discover that a creditor is in violation, they can take a number of steps. Section 108(e) permits the agency to order creditors in serious violation to adjust accounts of consumers so that they do not have to pay a greater finance charge (or APR) than was disclosed to them. If the adjustment is less than $1 per account, the agency may order the amount paid to the United States Treasury (but only after a year has passed, so that the statute of limitations will have run on the possible civil actions). TILA §108(e)(3).

You might also take note of §113 of the statute. It exempts the government (as creditor) from all criminal or civil penalties. Thus, while the offending governmental lender has to pay actual damages, costs, and attorney's fees under §130, it never is responsible for the punitive damages that are automatically imposed against private defendants.

B. Civil Actions

QUOTES FOR THE ATTORNEY'S ARSENAL: "SECTION 130 EXPLAINED"

It is a source of some irony that creditors partially supported the private remedy in the congressional deliberations. Thus, when Congress considered the desirability of private versus administrative enforcement, creditors discovered that their fear of federal bureaucrats was greater than of plaintiffs' lawyers.

Landers, Some Reflections on Truth in Lending, 1977 Ill. L.F. 669, 686 n.41 (also quoting testimony of creditor lobbyists).

Section 130 of the Truth in Lending Act has been construed in a lot of cases. Because TILA was the first major consumer protection statute on a national level, its provisions, especially its bona fide error defense, have been widely copied by later statutes, both federal and state. Therefore, much of what we will study here can be exported as persuasive authority for the construction of other consumer statutes.

PROBLEM 125

Fresh out of law school, you have been hired by the firm of Factory, Factory & Money. The firm has recently begun representing Big Department Store, a nationwide retailer; one of the reasons you were hired was your supposed expertise in consumer law (which means only that you took and passed this course). The firm dumps a copy of all the store's TIL documents on your desk and you begin examining them. The first thing you notice is that the TIL statement used in closed-end transactions (the store sells major appliances) does not list the finance charge at all. When you ask the vice president in charge of credit purchases for the store, she tells you that the last lawyers who handled this told her it was enough just to disclose the APR; there was no need to do the computations necessary to disclose the finance charge also.

Look carefully at TILA §130(a).

a. Is the failure to make this disclosure one of the material disclosure requirements or not?

b. The typical finance charge on one of these sales (the company made 84,000 of them last year) is between $200 and $300. What is the potential liability in an individual action? In a class action?

c. Can the store avoid liability by sending out corrected TIL statements? See §130(b).

d. As a tactical matter, would that be wise? See §130(e).

e. Big Department Store sold all these consumer accounts to First Mortgage Company. Is First Mortgage also subject to §130 liability? See TILA §131.

PROBLEM 126

Bankruptcy attorney Angelina Barth was astounded at the number of TIL violations on the statement that Nightflyer Finance Company gave to her clients, Mr. and Mrs. Suburb. Assuming that the Suburbs' bankruptcy trustee can be talked into abandoning the TIL claim so that the Suburbs can bring it, advise Ms. Barth, who went to law school with you and knows you took the Consumer Law course, about a few things.

a. Can the Suburbs get the punitive damages of double the amount of the finance charge (with the $100 minimum and the $1,000 cap[1]) for each violation? See TILA §130(g).

b. Can the Suburbs sue individually and each get the punitives? See §130(d).

c. If it has been more than a year since the TIL statement was first given to the Suburbs, can they (or their trustee in bankruptcy) still use the TIL claim as a setoff from the creditor's claim on the debt? Compare §§130(e) and 130(h), and the case that follows.

d. If the Suburbs sue Nightflyer and prevail, will the court's award of attorney's fees to Ms. Barth be subject to setoff to pay the creditor's counterclaim for the amount of the debt? See Plant v. Blazer Fin. Serv., Inc., 598 F.2d 1357 (5th Cir. 1979).

HAMILTON v. OHIO SAVINGS BANK
Supreme Court of Ohio, 1994
70 Ohio St. 3d 137, 637 N.E.2d 887

Plaintiffs-appellants, Frances E. Hamilton, Barbara A. Seidel and George L. Seidel, obtained residential mortgages from defendant-appellee, Ohio Savings Bank, formerly known as Ohio Savings Association ("Ohio Savings"). Hamilton's mortgage was for the principal sum of $44,000 and was to be payable in consecutive monthly installments of $364.79 with the "remaining balance, of principal and interest, if any," payable at the end of the twenty-nine-year mortgage term. The stated interest rate was 9.25 percent. The Seidel mortgage secured a principal amount of

---

1. A technical reading of §130(a)(2)(A) might lead to the conclusion that the $100/$1,000 caps are limited only to lease transactions under subparagraph (ii), and some courts so held. This had the extraordinary effect of allowing consumers to recover twice the amount of the finance charge in all other cases, and that was more liability than Congress ever intended, as the legislative history clearly shows. The original version of §130(a) applied these caps in all cases, and subsequent amendments to the section by Congress created a drafting snafu that moved the caps into the lease subparagraph only. In Koons Buick Pontiac GMC, Inc. v. Nigh, 543 U.S. 50 (2004), the Court instructed the lower courts to ignore the drafting error and apply the caps in all TIL cases, which drew a stern dissent from Justice Scalia, who is in favor of rigidly reading all statutes exactly as drafted, so that drafting errors get enforced until changed by Congress itself.

$32,400 with monthly payments of $262.76 over a period of twenty-nine years. Its stated interest rate was nine percent per annum. The Hamilton mortgage was executed in September 1976 and the Seidel mortgage was signed in August 1977.

Both mortgages contained the following language regarding interest calculation:

> Such interest shall be computed monthly by (i) obtaining a daily interest factor based upon a 360-day year, (ii) multiplying such factor by the actual number of days in each calendar month, and (iii) applying the result against the unpaid balance of this note outstanding on the last day of each month.

"Regulation Z" consumer disclosure notices, pursuant to Section 226.1 et seq., Title 12, C.F.R., were provided to both mortgagors. The record contains two different Hamilton Regulation Z forms. One is attached to the appellee's motion for summary judgment and is entitled "Joint Appendix Exhibit 'E.'" On this form a typewritten notation was included that stated "THE CONTRACT INTEREST RATE IS 9.25% (365/360 method)." The second Regulation Z form is attached as plaintiff's Exhibit 4 to the deposition of Judy Ledin. The same typewritten language is included but it would appear that the "365/360" language was altered to read "360/360." Given the state of these documents, it is difficult to ascertain exactly what was done. The Seidel Regulation Z form does not indicate how interest will be calculated.

Ultimately, another Ohio Savings mortgagor, John P. Clark, who holds degrees in both mathematics and economics, discovered that when the 360/360 method of interest calculation is used, the stated interest rate was less than that actually charged and paid to the bank. Based on this theory, the appellants claim that the actual rate of interest on the Hamilton note became 9.37 percent rather than 9.25 percent, and on the Seidel note, 9.12 percent rather than nine percent. Additionally, because the bank had based the monthly payment on a 365/360 calculation, both notes carried monthly payments that were insufficient to fully amortize the principal over the term of the loan. According to appellants, this will result in outstanding balances at the end of the twenty-nine year term on both notes, necessitating final payments of $6,493 on the Hamilton note and $4,702.34 on the Seidel note.

Hamilton and the Seidels filed suit on their own behalf and all others similarly situated, claiming violations of the federal Truth in Lending Act, Section 1601 et seq., Title 15, U.S. Code, as well as common-law claims of fraud, unjust enrichment, conversion and breach of contract. After protracted litigation, appellee moved for summary judgment. The bank argued that the 365/360 method of interest calculation was legal and fully disclosed; the understated monthly payment was a mistake by the bank that actually inured to the benefit of appellants by understating their monthly payments by roughly $3 to $4; and the appellants' actions were time-barred. The trial court granted summary judgment for the bank and the court of appeals affirmed, holding, *inter alia*, that appellants' Truth in Lending claims were barred by the one-year statute of limitations found in Section 1640(e), Title 15, U.S. Code

MOYER, Chief Justice.

The threshold issue is whether appellants' claims are time-barred, thereby divesting the trial court of subject matter jurisdiction. Section 1640(e), Title 15, U.S. Code provides: "Any action under this section may be brought in any United States district court, or in any other court of competent jurisdiction, within one year from the date of the occurrence of the violation. . . ."

The determinative question is what is meant by "occurrence of the violation." There is a divergence of views among the federal courts regarding the application of that phrase. At least three approaches have been used to determine when the statutory period commences. The first maintains that Congress clearly intended that the statute of limitations begins to run at the execution of the contract and should be strictly enforced. Stevens v. Rock Springs Natl. Bank (C.A. 10, 1974), 497 F.2d 307. The second view is based on the notion that nondisclosure of the actual interest rates represents a continuing violation of the contract and the limitations period should be fluid and liberally applied. See Postow v. OBA Fed. S. & L. Assn. (C.A.D.C. 1980), 627 F.2d 1370 (adopting "continuing violation" theory in limited situations). The final theory is that offered by the Sixth Circuit in Jones v. TransOhio Savings Assn. (C.A. 6, 1984), 747 F.2d 1037. The *Jones* court reasoned that to strictly enforce the one-year statute of limitations would run counter to the expressed purpose of the Act and its remedial nature. Therefore, the court held that under certain circumstances the statute might equitably be tolled. See, also, King v. California (C.A. 9, 1986), 784 F.2d 910 (expressly adopting the Sixth Circuit's reasoning).

We adopt the third application of the statute because under the appropriate circumstances, tolling the statute of limitations will effectuate the purpose of Congress in adopting the Truth in Lending Act. Section 1601(a), Title 15, U.S. Code provides:

> . . . It is the purpose of this subchapter to assure a meaningful disclosure of credit terms so that the consumer will be able to compare more readily the various credit terms available to him and avoid the uninformed use of credit, and to protect the consumer against inaccurate and unfair credit billing and credit card practices.

The Act was designed as a consumer protection statute aimed at permitting informed choices and guarding against divergent and possibly fraudulent practices. *King*, supra, 784 F.2d at 915. Its provisions are remedial in nature and should be liberally construed. *Jones*, supra, 747 F.2d at 1040. As stated by the Sixth Circuit: ". . . Only if Congress clearly manifests its intent to limit the federal court's jurisdiction will it be precluded from addressing allegations of fraudulent concealment which by their very nature, and if true, serve to make compliance with the limitations period imposed by Congress an impossibility." Id. at 1041.

Therefore, we conclude that in the case before us, the statute of limitations began to run at the time the mortgages were executed. However, the time within which appellants are required to bring an action against the bank may be tolled until they discovered or had reasonable opportunity to discover the alleged fraud or nondisclosures that formed the basis for their Truth in Lending action. This determination necessarily involves questions of fact that preclude summary judgment. On remand, the trial court should determine when the appellants could reasonably have discovered the divergent terms of the mortgage, note and disclosure forms, and whether they filed this action within one year from that date.

As to appellants' common-law claims, we are likewise persuaded that summary judgment was inappropriate. The record is contradictory as to what was disclosed to whom. On one document, the 365/360 method is disclosed; on another it is not. Summary judgment may not be granted when reasonable minds could come to differing conclusions. Civ. R. 56(C). Whether the method of interest calculation and the incomplete amortization of the loan within the stated term were disclosed is a question of fact. Whether these items amounted to misrepresentations, fraudulent conduct, or merely harmless mistakes, is also an issue best left to the finder of fact, thereby precluding summary judgment.

For the foregoing reasons, the judgment of the court of appeals is reversed, and this matter is remanded to the trial court for further proceedings consistent with this opinion.

Judgment reversed and cause remanded.

For an Annotation on the TIL statute of limitations and counterclaims, see Annot., 36 A.L.R. Fed. 657; see also Note, Restrictions on Defenses and Counterclaims Based on Truth In Lending Violations, 13 Wake Forest L. Rev. 189 (1977).

QUOTES FOR THE ATTORNEY'S ARSENAL:
"SECTION 130 EXPLAINED FURTHER"

A reading of the foregoing provision, which is bolstered by the overwhelming majority of case decisions which have construed it, clearly reveals that, once a creditor violation of Truth-in-Lending requirements is proven, liability follows absolutely and the debtor must be awarded damages according to the scheme established by Congress. Under [§130], a debtor who suffers no actual damages as a result of his creditor's violation of the Act is nevertheless entitled to recover, in an individual action, twice the amount of the finance charge involved in their transaction, not less than $100 nor more than $1,000. Congress' probable intent in allowing recovery in instances where no damage has been done to the debtor may have been to more fully insure creditor compliance with Truth-in-Lending requirements in all consumer loan transactions, despite the possible unattractiveness of debtors' claims in individual instances. However much we may disapprove of this aspect of the scheme adopted by Congress, because of its often times effect of working what we, as judges, perceive to be unjust results in individual cases, we nonetheless are compelled to apply the law as it has been written or as it may reasonably be construed.

SunAmerica Fin. Co. v. Williams, 2 Ohio App. 3d 272, 274-275, 442 N.E.2d 83, 86 (1981).

QUOTES FOR THE ATTORNEY'S ARSENAL: "LEGAL TECHNICALITIES"

A "technicality" is a rule of law upon which you lose. Should you win, it then becomes a cornerstone of American justice!

Judge J. Wilson Parker, quoted in the concurring opinion of Circuit Judge James C. Hill in Shroder v. Suburban Coastal Corp., 729 F.2d 1371, 1384 n.2 (11th Cir. 1984).

The statute clearly provides for the recovery of attorney's fees, and their award is mandatory, not discretionary (as it is in some statutes, such as Magnuson-Moss). For a discussion of the case law on TILA attorney's fees, see Annot., 29 A.L.R. Fed. 906. Some judges are more receptive than others to this award, and when they decide to dig in their heels, they can make the TILA attorney's life miserable.

MIRABAL v. GENERAL MOTORS ACCEPTANCE CORP.[2]
United States Court of Appeals, Seventh Circuit, 1978
576 F.2d 729

Before SWYGERT, SPRECHER and WOOD, Circuit Judges.
Per curiam.

---

2. Footnotes in this case have been renumbered for clarity.

The issue presented in this appeal is whether the district court abused its discretion in determining that petitioner, attorney for plaintiffs, was entitled to $2,000 in attorney's fees and $690.10 in costs.

I

Plaintiffs purchased a new car in 1971 from Ed Murphy Buick-Opel for which the cash price was $4,497.65. This purchase was financed in the amount of $2,460 through General Motors Acceptance Corporation (GMAC) on a 36-month installment contract. Defendants understated the annual percentage rate applicable to the transaction in the installment contract and GMAC sent a letter to plaintiffs informing them of this error, which letter plaintiffs denied receiving.

Plaintiffs filed an action charging violations of the Truth in Lending Act, 15 U.S.C. §§1601 et seq., and two Illinois statutes. The district court found seven violations of the Truth in Lending Act and awarded $1,000 to plaintiffs for each violation. The district court also found violations of both Illinois statutes and awarded damages in excess of $1,000, bringing the total to over $8,000. On appeal, this court held that multiple recovery for multiple errors in a single disclosure statement was impermissible and that defendants had not violated the two Illinois statutes. Mirabal v. General Motors Corp., 537 F.2d 871 (7th Cir. 1976). The judgment was reduced to a total of $2,000 "plus costs and attorney's fees. . . ." 537 F.2d at 885.

On remand petitioner alleged that he had expended 350 hours on the case, 120 at the trial level and 230 on the appeal. He also alleged that GMAC's attorneys were paid over $30,000 for handling the case. The district court awarded petitioner the total costs requested and attorney's fees in the amount of $2,000. Petitioner appeals from the attorney's fee award.

II

The district court has broad discretion in making an award of attorney's fees because of the advantage of close observation of the work product of an attorney and an understanding of the skill and time required in the suit. Lea v. Cone Mills Corporation, 467 F.2d 277, 279 (4th Cir. 1972). Our review is limited to the determination of whether the district court abused this discretion. Waters v. Wisconsin Steel Works, 502 F.2d 1309, 1322 (7th Cir. 1974).

The instant case involves a car costing less than $5,000 and a loan of less than $2,500. Plaintiffs ultimately prevailed to the extent of $2,000 after getting somewhat over $8,000 at the original trial. Petitioner has thus received in attorney's fees an amount equal to that which his clients recovered in total.

Although the determination of hours necessary to effectively handle a case is not subject to exact determination, the amount which petitioner claims to have spent on the present case seems clearly out of proportion with the amount in controversy. Moreover, Congress has limited the liability of Truth in Lending Act violators to $1,000 per violation. 15 U.S.C. §1640(a). To grant attorney's fees greatly in excess of a client's recovery requires strong support from the circumstances of the particular case. The instant case involved a one-time individual claim based mainly on a bona fide arithmetical error. As this court declared in Sprogis v. United Air Lines, Inc., 517 F.2d 387, 391 (7th Cir. 1975), when it balked at the fee request presented there:

> First, this case does not represent the typical . . . claim envisioned by Congress and in the past sponsored by various public interest organizations. Second, the claim for attorneys' fees is not proportionate to the recovery of damages by plaintiff. Third, the precedential value of this decision is not controlling in light of [its reliance on an admitted arithmetical error].

Additionally, to grant large attorney's fee awards on the basis of relatively small injury would encourage suits which do not further the client's interest or the public's interest. The costs of these suits already force many claims to settlement. See Landers, Some Reflections on Truth in Lending, 1977 Ill. L.F. 660, 680-81. Indeed, petitioner himself has inadvertently provided this court with an example of the questionable results in such suits. See Plaintiffs' Reply Memorandum (Document 16), page 4, and the letter attached to it. There petitioner made a settlement in a Truth in Lending case in which his client received $400 while petitioner was paid $12,000 as attorney's fees for the settlement. While such disproportionate sums may be exacted in settlement agreements, we should be loathe to automatically provide judicial approval for such results when these cases reach the courts.

Petitioner also claims that the attorneys for GMAC were paid over $30,000 and that this amount is indicative of what he should be paid (Petitioner's Brief, page 20). This contention was repeated at oral argument. This circuit has held that it is an abuse of discretion to determine attorney's fees solely on the basis of hours spent times billing rate. *Waters*, supra, at 1322. Petitioner wants us to go a step further and award him a fee based on what the *opposing side* spent in time and money. This ignores the fact that a given case may have greater precedential value for one side than the other. Also, a plaintiff's attorney, by pressing questionable claims and refusing to settle except on outrageous terms, could force a defendant to incur substantial fees which he later uses as a basis for his own fee claim. Moreover, the amount of fees which one side is paid by its client is a matter involving various motivations in an on-going attorney-client relationship and may, therefore, have little relevance to the value which petitioner has provided to his clients in a given case.

Therefore, for the reasons discussed above, we conclude that the district court properly acted within its discretion in setting the award of attorney's fees at $2,000.

Affirmed.

SWYGERT, Circuit Judge, dissenting.

Despite the thoughtful analysis of the majority's opinion, I am unable to agree with the conclusion it reaches. The enormous disparity between the amount of money received by defendants' attorneys and plaintiffs' attorney disturbs my sense of fairness. Plaintiffs won their lawsuit (though losing part of it on appeal), and yet their counsel received only one-fifteenth of what defendants' counsel was paid for defending the suit. This, together with the summary manner in which the fee proceeding was handled, compels me to dissent. . . .

In awarding plaintiffs' attorney $2,000 for 350 hours of work, the district court said that the expenditure of this many hours on this case was "utterly unnecessary." In the judge's view, most of these hours were spent in advancing "excessive legal theories." Which theories were excessive and what hours were unnecessary were not specified in the order.

I find it anomalous that the district court, after finding seven different Truth in Lending violations and two state disclosure violations and awarding plaintiffs over $8,000, is now able to say that plaintiffs' counsel advanced excessive legal theories. Moreover, was it "utterly unnecessary" for plaintiffs' counsel to defend the judgment once defendants chose to appeal? And, was it "utterly unnecessary" for plaintiffs to cross-appeal? I believe that plaintiffs not only had the right, but under Canon Seven of the Code of Professional Responsibility,[3] plaintiffs' attorney had the duty to protect the judgment he obtained for his clients. Furthermore, had plaintiffs not cross-appealed, they would have recovered only $1,000 instead of the $2,000 ultimately awarded by this court.

If the district court had held a hearing as plaintiffs requested, we might now know what theories it believed were excessive and what hours were therefore unnecessary. In short, we would be informed how the court arrived at the $2,000 figure. But in the absence of such reasons, the only reasonable

---

3. Canon Seven provides: "A lawyer should represent a client zealously within the bounds of the law."

inference is that the fee award was matched to the judgment which plaintiffs ultimately obtained. But if it is an abuse of discretion to set fees solely on the basis of a formula applying hours spent times billing rate, Waters v. Wisconsin Steel Works, 502 F.2d 1309, 1322 (7th Cir. 1976), I believe it is equally abusive to award fees solely by the amount of recovery obtained.[4]

The conclusion reached by the majority seems to be based primarily on the belief that the granting of large attorney fee awards (regardless of the validity of such an award in a particular case) will encourage the filing of questionable claims which defendant-creditors will be forced to settle because the costs of litigation will become too prohibitive. I share this concern and believe it is an important consideration in making a fee award. My difficulty, however, is that it does not fit the facts of this case.

The record here is barren of any evidence that plaintiffs pressed questionable claims or refused to settle except on outrageous terms. If anything, the record proves the contrary. The district court found that defendants had violated two state laws and had violated the Truth in Lending Act in seven different ways. This court affirmed the violation concerning understating the annual percentage rate; it did not have to consider the merits of the other Truth in Lending violations because of the interpretation given the 1974 amendment.

Nor is this a case where the defendants were at the mercy of the plaintiffs, who typically set the perimeters of a lawsuit. At trial it was the defendants who had the burden of establishing their affirmative defense of a bona fide mistake. Furthermore, after losing on all issues, it was defendants who chose to appeal and challenge the findings of the trial court. The point is this: All the aces were not in plaintiffs' hands as the defendants would suggest. Unlike the typical case, the defendants here held some of the aces. The defendants were legally justified in electing to make a militant defense; they also had the right to appeal an adverse judgment. But in deliberately choosing such a course of action, they cannot now be heard to complain that it would be unfair to require them to pay a reasonable fee to plaintiffs' attorney.

---

4. I too agree that petitioner is not entitled to an award of $30,000 just because defense counsel received such a sum. But I do not agree that such evidence is irrelevant. One of the factors which district courts are to consider in setting a reasonable fee is "[t]he fee customarily charged in the locality for similar legal services." *Waters,* supra, 502 F.2d at 1322. What better evidence is there of this information than the fee which defendants paid their attorneys? I fully concur with the Second Circuit when it said in Taylor v. Scarborough, 66 F.2d 589, 591 (2d Cir. 1933):

> While the fee paid counsel by the other side is by no means conclusive of what is a reasonable fee for the plaintiffs' services, we do think that it is quite persuasive in the circumstances here disclosed.

Defendants are not without weapons to curtail, if not stop entirely, the possibility of "forced settlements." If a plaintiff's settlement demands are unreasonable, a defendant may make an offer of judgment pursuant to Rule 68 of the Federal Rules of Civil Procedure. Once a defendant makes such an offer, he is not liable for plaintiff's costs and attorney's fees if plaintiff does not ultimately recover the amount of the offer. Through such a device a defendant can place on the plaintiff much of the financial risk involved in litigation.

Finally, the policy of discouraging the filing of questionable claims must be balanced against the policy underlying the Truth in Lending Act itself. That Act embodies the national policy that economic stabilization and competition will be enhanced if consumers are given accurate and meaningful disclosure of credit. See 15 U.S.C. §1601. Enforcement of this policy was placed primarily on the private sector through suits for civil penalties. A provision for attorney's fees helps assure that enforcement will take place. But such a provision is rendered meaningless unless attorneys for successful parties are given reasonably adequate compensation for their services.

The need for adequate compensation is particularly important since the statutory penalty is now limited to $1,000 per transaction. If a presumption is imposed that a successful attorney is allowed only that amount recovered by his client—as apparently was done here—creditors can effectively stop the filing of all Truth in Lending actions. By refusing to negotiate even reasonable claims and by litigating every case, creditors can soon force a plaintiff to terminate the litigation, not because his claim is invalid, but because it is no longer economically feasible for his attorney to continue the case. This case is a prime example. I dare say few attorneys will handle a Truth in Lending case when they learn that they may earn only $5.71 an hour.

QUOTES FOR THE ATTORNEY'S ARSENAL: "CLASS ACTIONS AND TIL"

If the purpose of the Act . . . in these cases of technical violations with no actual damages was to secure compliance with the Act's disclosure requirements rather than to punish the unheeding violator, then this Court believes maintenance of the class action (at least at this time) is an unnecessary overreaction to the violation here.

Watkins v. Simmons & Clark, Inc., 618 F.2d 398, 403 (6th Cir. 1980) (quoting district court opinion). Congress has made it more difficult to win TIL class actions; see the Truth In Lending Class Action Relief Act of 1995, Pub. L. No. 104-121, 109 Stat. 161 (1995), which added TILA §§130(i) and 139.

C. Creditor Defenses

1. Reliance on Board

As mentioned in Chapter 7 at the beginning of the discussion of TILA, the United States Supreme Court has instructed the federal courts to give great deference to the opinions of the Federal Reserve Board. Congress has done better than that. Section 130(f) of the Truth in Lending Act completely insulates creditors from liability if they act in reliance on the Board's rules, regulations, or interpretations. The Board has promulgated model forms (and published them as an Appendix to Regulation Z), and reliance on these forms, without substantial change, protects creditors from disclosure violations. The Board has published an Official Staff Interpretation of Regulation Z, and it has the force of law. In close questions, it should be consulted carefully.

2. Bona Fide Error

PROBLEM 127

Octopus National Bank sent its loan officers to a two-day school to teach them compliance with TILA and Regulation Z. But some of these people were more attentive to their lessons than others. One, Rudolph Slow, never understood the rules and routinely filled out his TIL statements incorrectly. You are the bank's new attorney. When the attorney you are replacing showed you around, she mentioned Slow's inability to master TILA. You asked whether she was worried about the bank being sued, but she replied that any mistakes he makes are mere clerical errors; since the statute contains a bona fide error defense, she isn't worried about liability. You get back to the quiet of your office and decide to have a glance at the exact wording of TILA §130(c). What do you advise your client?

MIRABAL v. GENERAL MOTORS ACCEPTANCE CORP.[5]
United States Court of Appeals, Seventh Circuit, 1976 537 F.2d 871

SPRECHER, Circuit Judge.
This appeal primarily concerns interpretations of certain provisions of the Truth in Lending Act, 15 U.S.C. §§1601 et seq., and regulations

---

5. Footnotes in the case have been renumbered for clarity.

promulgated thereunder by the Federal Reserve Board, 12 C.F.R. §§226.1 et seq. (Regulation Z).

I

The plaintiffs in this action, John and Sharon Mirabal, bought a new 1971 Buick Skylark from one of the defendants, Ed Murphy Buick-Opel, Inc., in July of 1971. The cash price for the car including service, accessories and taxes totalled $4,497.65. The Mirabals financed their purchase through General Motors Acceptance Corporation (GMAC), the other defendant to this action. The Mirabals made a down payment of $2,296.65 including $600.00 in trade for their 1964 Rambler. The retail installment contract which the defendants provided the Mirabals required that they buy $259.00 of physical damage insurance for a total amount financed after deduction of the down payment of $2,460.00. A $511.80 finance charge was imposed on this and the total deferred payment price of $2,971.80 was to be paid in 36 monthly installments of $82.55 each. The installment contract disclosed the annual percentage rate on this transaction as 11.08 percent and contained a voluminous quantity of detailed requirements on its back, including provisions detailing the seller's rights upon default.

About one week after the transaction was consummated, GMAC sent a letter to the plaintiffs informing them that the annual percentage rate disclosed in the transaction had been understated by 1.75 percent and stating that the contract be corrected to provide for an annual percentage rate of 12.83 percent. The plaintiffs denied that they received any such letter. The trial court made no finding of fact on this issue.

In late 1971, the Mirabals filed this action charging numerous violations of the Truth in Lending Act, the Illinois Motor Vehicle Retail Installment Sales Act, Ill. Rev. Stat., ch. 12½, §§561 et seq. (1967) and the Illinois Sales Finance Agency Act, Ill. Rev. Stat., ch. 121½, §§401 et seq. (1967) in connection with the transaction. The district court in a trial without a jury found that the defendants had violated the Truth in Lending Act in a number of ways, and had also violated both Illinois acts.

The district court found seven specific violations of Truth in Lending requirements in the transaction. For each violation of the Truth in Lending Act the court assessed damages of $1,000 against the defendants.[6] Along with the damages under both Illinois acts, the plaintiffs won a judgment of

---

6. [A later amendment to §130 added (g) to make it clear that multiple violations of TILA do not, as the district court here held, given rise to more than one allowance of the statutory damages imposed as a penalty under the Act—ED.]

more than $8,000. From this judgment, the defendants appealed and the plaintiffs cross-appealed. . . .

III

The facts are not in question in regard to the plaintiff's major claim concerning a disclosure error under the Truth in Lending Act. The annual percentage rate disclosed in the contract was 11.08 percent. As all parties agree, this understated by 1.75 percent the annual percentage rate properly applicable to the finance charge, amount financed, and term of the Mirabals' contract. Thus, the defendants disclosed an erroneous annual percentage rate.

The defendants contend that the error resulted from a bona fide mistake and claim exemption from liability under 15 U.S.C. §1640(c). This section provides:

> A creditor may not be held liable in any action brought under this section for violation of this part if the creditor shows by a preponderance of evidence that the violation was not intentional and resulted from a bona fide error notwithstanding the maintenance of procedures reasonably adapted to avoid any such error.

Thus, we must determine whether the defendants have met the burden of section 1640(c).[7]

---

7. The section does not require proof as to exactly what happened with regard to the error in the transaction in question. This, however, does not mean as the defendants seem to suggest that the plaintiffs must prove exactly what happened either. The defendants contended in their reply brief that the "plaintiffs submitted no evidence . . . that the defendants failed to use proper charts and tables." They went on to assert that "no witness identified what particular chart or table was used in preparing the instant Contract." They blandly concluded by suggesting that the "plaintiffs . . . had the burden of proof on the issue."

Nothing could be further from the truth. The statute, 15 U.S.C. §1640(c), specifically requires the *creditor* to show by a preponderance of the evidence that he maintained procedures that were reasonably adapted to avoid errors. This means that the creditor has the burden of proof not only to show that the procedures existed, but also to show that they were in effect and consistently followed during the time in question. It bodes ill for the defendants that they can assert in their brief that "[t]he witnesses were not sure which particular chart was used. But they were sure that some chart had been used." Certainly, as noted above, the witnesses do not have to testify to or remember the particular events in question. However, they must testify that during the period in which the transaction took place, they *always* used particular tables, or they *always* followed certain procedures which included reference to particular tables, or they *always* followed certain procedures which included reference to particular tables or particular computations. In other words, if the defendants were to meet this burden of proof, their witnesses should have been able to testify that during the period in question they always followed a certain procedure which included taking the annual rate from a certain chart, and thus that that chart must have been used.

Under that provision, the creditors must prove first, that the error was an unintentional, bona fide error and second, that they maintained procedures reasonably adapted to avoid any such error. The first part of the test is met. Even the plaintiffs admit that the error was unintentional and that the defendants had no motive to understate the annual percentage rate. Clearly, the defendants' good faith is not in question.

In regard to the second part of the test, we will take the defendants' contentions on brief before this court as true. The defendants laid out their procedures in this manner:

> Defendant dealer had specially trained office personnel to assist salesmen in determining annual percentage rates for installment contracts. Those office personnel had been trained in the preparation of Truth in Lending disclosure statements at educational meetings that defendant GMAC held with each GM dealer before the Act went into effect. At these meetings, GMAC used a chart easel presentation to explain full disclosure, the new type of contracts, the establishment of rates, and how to arrive at rates. GMAC held classes at the premises of every one of the 48 GM dealers in the area in June 1969 to prepare the dealers to work under the Act. In addition, GMAC sent to all General Motors dealers materials and a form of contract designed to aid compliance under the Truth in Lending Act. These materials included rate charts and tables which were less awkward to use than those provided by the Federal Reserve Board. GMAC prepared these materials after extensive consultation with the Federal Reserve Board and Federal Trade Commission. A manual sent by GMAC to all GM dealers emphasized the need for the accurate statement of annual percentage rates:
>
> > These terms [including annual percentage rate] have been called the "common denominators" of consumer credit. If comparison shopping for credit terms is to become a feature of the consumer credit business, federal authorities believe that these two disclosures will make it possible regardless of the type of credit extended. The federal effort is to make such disclosures clearly visible in every consumer transaction.

The defendants concluded by suggesting that the error in the disclosure statement arose in copying numbers from an interest conversion table.

These efforts, as outlined by the defendants, are impressive. Clearly, they indicate that the defendants established procedures designed to correctly calculate the figures required. However, this does not answer the question. We must decide whether this showing meets the requirements of §1640(c), whether the defendants have shown that they maintained procedures reasonably adapted to avoid bona fide errors.

Congress had no intention of having the consumer bear the burden of a creditor's negligence. As was noted in the Senate hearings on the Act, the philosophy behind its passage was not "let the buyer beware" but "let the seller make full disclosure." In a similar vein, the fifth circuit has noted that the policy in the area of consumer credit has shifted from one of *caveat emptor* to one of *caveat vendor*.[8] Moreover, as courts have noted on numerous occasions, the Act should be interpreted liberally in favor of the consumer to effectuate its broad remedial purpose. With this in mind we can examine the provision.

As we have already noted, the provision for our purposes has basically two requirements, that the error be a bona fide error and that the creditor maintain procedures reasonably adapted to avoid such errors. A bona fide error is an error made in the course of a good faith attempt at compliance.[9] The statute says that these errors are the precise errors which must be avoided. Therefore, the statute requires a higher burden than merely good faith compliance. In other words, Congress required more than just the maintenance of procedures which were designed to provide proper disclosure calculations. Rather, it required procedures designed to avoid and prevent the errors which might slip through procedures aimed at good faith compliance. This means that the procedures which Congress had in mind were to contain an extra preventative step, a safety catch or a rechecking mechanism. Congress left the exact nature of the preventative mechanism undefined. It is clear, however, that Congress required more than just a showing that a well-trained and careful clerk made a mistake. On the other hand, a showing that the first well-trained clerk's figuring was checked by a second well-trained clerk or that one clerk made the calculations on an adding machine and then checked this by looking up the figures on a table would satisfy Congress' requirements. We save for

---

8. In Thomas v. Meyers Dickson Furniture Co., 479 F.2d 740, 748 (5th Cir. 1973), the fifth circuit wrote:

> The result we reach today is consistent with the statute's goal of creating a system of "private attorney generals" who will be able to aid the effective enforcement of the Act. Section 1640 is intended to allow aggrieved consumers to participate in policing the Act, . . . and its language should be construed liberally in light of its broadly remedial purpose. . . . The domain of consumer credit with its allied commercial practices is no longer in the *laissez faire* era of *caveat emptor*. That doctrine is increasingly relegated to its proper place as a historical relic without modern applications. The regulatory scheme forcefully expounds an emerging ethic of "caveat vendor," and we will not strain to avoid giving effect to the Federal Consumer Credit *Protection* Act (italics in original).

9. Clearly, an error could not be made in good faith when no good faith attempt to comply with the statute was made. Thus, when no procedures are set up to provide correct disclosure calculations, or when untrained employees are left to calculate disclosure figures, errors made do not even rise to the level of bona fide errors.

future determination what procedures, other than rechecking, might also satisfy this requirement.[10]

Congress required not only that procedures designed to avoid bona fide errors be established by creditors if they seek exemption under this section but also, that these procedures be maintained. This means that the creditor must show that the proper procedures were followed time in and time out. As we noted in an earlier opinion, the exemption was provided to avoid imposing "strict liability" for unavoidable clerical errors upon creditors. Haynes v. Logan Furniture Mart, Inc., 503 F.2d 1161, 1167 (7th Cir. 1974). In the face of a showing that procedures containing a rechecking mechanism or other preventative device existed and were maintained consistently by a creditor, a court could conclude that whatever error occurred was unavoidable and that the congressional policy of requiring creditors to do everything reasonably possible to avoid disclosure errors was fulfilled.

In the present case the defendants made neither of these showings. Their procedures, although probably designed to provide correct disclosures, did not contain any type of preventative mechanism for catching disclosure errors. Moreover, the defendants did not show that these procedures were maintained consistently. Indeed, in the present instance the defendants do not seem to know what procedures were followed in generating the figures for the Mirabals' contract. Therefore, since the defendants did not meet the burden of establishing their right to an exemption under section 1640(c), they are liable for the inaccurate disclosure of the annual percentage rate in the Mirabals' contract. . . .

Judgment affirmed as modified and cause remanded for further proceedings.

---

10. The defendant admits on brief that the error "would [not] be obvious when it occurred." Certainly, if this is true, and it is true whenever the rates differ by only small amounts, rechecking is the only way to avoid mistakes. Even the most highly trained person makes mistakes. The only way to catch such mistakes is by rechecking, in some way, the computation. This is not a great burden on a creditor, as checking a chart takes only seconds and doing the computations on an adding machine cannot take more than a minute.

It is clear from this case that rechecking does bring errors to light. GMAC when it received the contract recalculated the annual percentage rate and immediately found the error.

QUOTES FOR THE ATTORNEY'S ARSENAL:
"THE UNFOCUSED ATTORNEY"

His method of advocacy could best be described as the "sieve approach," i.e., indiscriminately throwing legal gravel upon a sieve hoping that some would not filter through, never giving any hint to the Court as (to mix a metaphor) how to separate the wheat from the chaff. One of the ten claims thus hurled did turn out to be meritorious; hence his present application [for attorney's fees].

Kramer v. Marine Midland Bank, 577 F. Supp. 999, 1000 (S.D.N.Y. 1984) (the court reduced the application for $38,634.75 to an awarded figure of $2,000, the amount involved with the successful claim).

PROBLEM 128[11]

The head of the collections department of Big Department Store brings you the following legal questions about TIL lawsuits.

a. If the consumer sues the store in the federal courts, when the store files its answer, should it counterclaim for the amount of the outstanding debt that the consumer owes? Or must it bring suit in state courts at a later time? Rephrase the question to yourself like this: is the suit on the debt a permissive or compulsory counterclaim? (See footnote.) Compare Plant v. Blazer Fin. Serv., Inc., 598 F.2d 1357 (5th Cir. 1979) (compulsory), with Maddox v. Kentucky Fin. Co., 736 F.2d 380 (6th Cir. 1984) (permissive).

b. If the store brings the original lawsuit in state court and the consumer fails to raise TILA claims in defense, are such claims *res judicata*, so that the consumer may not later sue on them? See White v. World Fin. of Meridian, 653 F.2d 147 (5th Cir. 1981); Albano v. Norwest Fin. Haw., Inc., 244 F.3d 1061 (9th Cir. 2001).

---

11. A little reminder on some federal civil procedure. A *compulsory* counterclaim is one that must be brought in the original lawsuit or it is lost forever. A *permissive* counterclaim may be brought in the same lawsuit only if independent federal jurisdiction is present. The test on compulsory/permissive is whether the subject of the counterclaim arises from the same transaction: if so, it is compulsory; if not, then it is permissive. See Fed. R. Civ. P. 13(a).

For an Annotation on the permissive/compulsory counterclaim dichotomy, see 51 A.L.R. Fed. 509 (1981).

PROBLEM 129

When his practice was rather slow, attorney Sam Ambulance would drum up a little work for himself by applying for small loans from lenders whose forms he had examined and determined were in violation of both TILA and the Equal Credit Opportunity Act. He would sue under these statutes and ask for actual damages (which were always small—in one case $2.76), punitive damages, and attorney's fees. The lenders would defend by arguing that he was not deceived by the misdisclosures since he was an expert in the field and was, in effect, setting them up. Sam replied that he thought of himself as the "Truth in Lending Enforcer," sort of a private attorney general, and the fact that he was not personally misled didn't excuse their noncompliance with the law. How should this come out?

3. Arbitration

GREEN TREE FINANCIAL CORP. v. RANDOLPH[12]
Supreme Court of the United States, 2000
531 U.S. 79

CHIEF JUSTICE REHNQUIST delivered the opinion of the Court.

In this case we first address whether an order compelling arbitration and dismissing a party's underlying claims is a "final decision with respect to an arbitration" within the meaning of §16 of the Federal Arbitration Act, 9 U.S.C. §16, and thus is immediately appealable pursuant to that Act. Because we decide that question in the affirmative, we also address the question whether an arbitration agreement that does not mention arbitration costs and fees is unenforceable because it fails to affirmatively protect a party from potentially steep arbitration costs. We conclude that an arbitration agreement's silence with respect to such matters does not render the agreement unenforceable.

I

Respondent Larketta Randolph purchased a mobile home from Better Cents Home Builders, Inc., in Opelika, Alabama. She financed this purchase through petitioners Green Tree Financial Corporation and its wholly

---

12. Footnotes in this case have been renumbered for clarity.

owned subsidiary, Green Tree Financial Corp.-Alabama. Petitioners' Manufactured Home Retail Installment Contract and Security Agreement required that Randolph buy Vendor's Single Interest insurance, which protects the vendor or lienholder against the costs of repossession in the event of default. The agreement also provided that all disputes arising from, or relating to, the contract, whether arising under case law or statutory law, would be resolved by binding arbitration.[13]

Randolph later sued petitioners, alleging that they violated the Truth in Lending Act (TILA), 15 U.S.C. §1601 et seq., by failing to disclose as a finance charge the Vendor's Single Interest insurance requirement. She later amended her complaint to add a claim that petitioners violated the Equal Credit Opportunity Act, 15 U.S.C. §§1691-1691f, by requiring her to arbitrate her statutory causes of action. She brought this action on behalf of a similarly situated class. In lieu of an answer, petitioners filed a motion to compel arbitration, to stay the action, or, in the alternative, to dismiss. The District Court granted petitioners' motion to compel arbitration, denied the motion to stay, and dismissed Randolph's claims with prejudice. The District Court also denied her request to certify a class. 991 F. Supp. 1410 (MD Ala. 1997). She requested reconsideration, asserting that she lacked the resources to arbitrate and as a result, would have to forgo her claims against petitioners. See Plaintiff's Motion for Reconsideration, Record Doc. No. 53, p. 9. The District Court denied reconsideration. 991 F. Supp. at 1425-1426. Randolph appealed.

The Court of Appeals for the Eleventh Circuit first held that it had jurisdiction to review the District Court's order because that order was a final decision. 178 F.3d 1149 (1999). The Court of Appeals looked to §16 of

---

13. The arbitration provision states in pertinent part: "All disputes, claims, or controversies arising from or relating to this Contract or the relationships which result from this Contract, or the validity of this arbitration clause or the entire contract, shall be resolved by binding arbitration by one arbitrator selected by Assignee with consent of Buyer(s). This arbitration Contract is made pursuant to a transaction in interstate commerce, and shall be governed by the Federal Arbitration Act at 9 U.S.C. Section 1. Judgment upon the award rendered may be entered in any court having jurisdiction. The parties agree and understand that they choose arbitration instead of litigation to resolve disputes. The parties understand that they have a right or opportunity to litigate disputes through a court, but that they prefer to resolve their disputes through arbitration, except as provided herein. THE PARTIES VOLUNTARILY AND KNOWINGLY WAIVE ANY RIGHT THEY HAVE TO A JURY TRIAL EITHER PURSUANT TO ARBITRATION UNDER THIS CLAUSE OR PURSUANT TO A COURT ACTION BY ASSIGNEE (AS PROVIDED HEREIN). The parties agree and understand that all disputes arising under case law, statutory law, and all other laws, including, but not limited to, all contract, tort, and property disputes will be subject to binding arbitration in accord with this Contract. The parties agree and understand that the arbitrator shall have all powers provided by the law and the Contract." See Joint Lodging 37.

the Federal Arbitration Act (FAA), 9 U.S.C. §16, which governs appeal from a District Court's arbitration order, and specifically §16(a)(3), which allows appeal from "a final decision with respect to an arbitration that is subject to this title." The Court determined that a final, appealable order within the meaning of the FAA is one that disposes of all the issues framed by the litigation, leaving nothing to be done but execute the order. The Court of Appeals found the District Court's order within that definition.

The court then determined that the arbitration agreement failed to provide the minimum guarantees that respondent could vindicate her statutory rights under the TILA. Critical to this determination was the court's observation that the arbitration agreement was silent with respect to payment of filing fees, arbitrators' costs, and other arbitration expenses. On that basis, the court held that the agreement to arbitrate posed a risk that respondent's ability to vindicate her statutory rights would be undone by "steep" arbitration costs, and therefore was unenforceable. We granted certiorari, 529 U.S. 1052 (2000), and we now affirm the Court of Appeals with respect to the first conclusion, and reverse it with respect to the second.

II

[The Court first decided that the decision was appealable.]

III

We now turn to the question whether Randolph's agreement to arbitrate is unenforceable because it says nothing about the costs of arbitration, and thus fails to provide her protection from potentially substantial costs of pursuing her federal statutory claims in the arbitral forum. Section 2 of the FAA provides that "[a] written provision in any maritime transaction or a contract evidencing a transaction involving commerce to settle by arbitration a controversy thereafter arising out of such contract . . . shall be valid, irrevocable, and enforceable, save upon such grounds as exist at law or in equity for the revocation of any contract." 9 U.S.C. §2. In considering whether respondent's agreement to arbitrate is unenforceable, we are mindful of the FAA's purpose "to reverse the longstanding judicial hostility to arbitration agreements . . . and to place arbitration agreements upon the same footing as other contracts." Gilmer v. Interstate/Johnson Lane Corp., 500 U.S. 20, 24, 114 L. Ed. 2d 26, 111 S. Ct. 1647 (1991).

In light of that purpose, we have recognized that federal statutory claims can be appropriately resolved through arbitration, and we have enforced agreements to arbitrate that involve such claims. [Citations omitted.] We have likewise rejected generalized attacks on arbitration that rest on "suspicion of arbitration as a method of weakening the protections afforded in the substantive law to would-be complainants." Rodriguez de Quijas, supra, at 481. These cases demonstrate that even claims arising under a statute designed to further important social policies may be arbitrated because "'so long as the prospective litigant effectively may vindicate [his or her] statutory cause of action in the arbitral forum,'" the statute serves its functions. See Gilmer, supra, at 28 (quoting Mitsubishi, supra, at 637).

In determining whether statutory claims may be arbitrated, we first ask whether the parties agreed to submit their claims to arbitration, and then ask whether Congress has evinced an intention to preclude a waiver of judicial remedies for the statutory rights at issue. See Gilmer, supra, at 26; Mitsubishi, supra, at 628. In this case, it is undisputed that the parties agreed to arbitrate all claims relating to their contract, including claims involving statutory rights. Nor does Randolph contend that the TILA evinces an intention to preclude a waiver of judicial remedies. She contends instead that the arbitration agreement's silence with respect to costs and fees creates a "risk" that she will be required to bear prohibitive arbitration costs if she pursues her claims in an arbitral forum, and thereby forces her to forgo any claims she may have against petitioners. Therefore, she argues, she is unable to vindicate her statutory rights in arbitration. See Brief for Respondent 29-30.

It may well be that the existence of large arbitration costs could preclude a litigant such as Randolph from effectively vindicating her federal statutory rights in the arbitral forum. But the record does not show that Randolph will bear such costs if she goes to arbitration. Indeed, it contains hardly any information on the matter.[14] As the Court of Appeals recognized, "we

---

14. In Randolph's Motion for Reconsideration in the District Court, she asserted that "arbitration costs are high" and that she did not have the resources to arbitrate. But she failed to support this assertion. She first acknowledged that petitioners had not designated a particular arbitration association or arbitrator to resolve their dispute. Her subsequent discussion of costs relied entirely on unfounded assumptions. She stated "for the purposes of this discussion, we will assume filing with the [American Arbitration Association], the filing fee is $500 for claims under $10,000 and this does not include the cost of the arbitrator or administrative fees." Randolph relied on, and attached as an exhibit what appears to be informational material from the American Arbitration Association that does not discuss the amount of filing fees. She then noted "[The American Arbitration Association] further cites $700 per day as the average arbitrator's fee." For this proposition she cited an article in the Daily Labor Report, February 15, 1996, published by the Bureau of National Affairs, entitled Labor Lawyers at ABA Session Debate Role of American Arbitration Association. Plaintiff's Motion for Reconsideration, Record Doc. No. 53, pp. 8-9. The article contains a stray statement by an association executive that the average arbitral fee is $700 per day. Randolph plainly failed to make any factual showing that the American Arbitration Association would conduct the arbitration, or that, if it did, she would be charged the filing fee or arbitrator's fee that she identified. These unsupported

lack . . . information about how claimants fare under Green Tree's arbitration clause." 178 F.3d at 1158. The record reveals only the arbitration agreement's silence on the subject, and that fact alone is plainly insufficient to render it unenforceable. The "risk" that Randolph will be saddled with prohibitive costs is too speculative to justify the invalidation of an arbitration agreement.

To invalidate the agreement on that basis would undermine the "liberal federal policy favoring arbitration agreements." *Moses H. Cone Memorial Hospital*, 460 U.S. at 24. It would also conflict with our prior holdings that the party resisting arbitration bears the burden of proving that the claims at issue are unsuitable for arbitration. See *Gilmer*, supra, at 26; *McMahon*, supra, at 227. We have held that the party seeking to avoid arbitration bears the burden of establishing that Congress intended to preclude arbitration of the statutory claims at issue. See *Gilmer*, supra; *McMahon*, supra. Similarly, we believe that where, as here, a party seeks to invalidate an arbitration agreement on the ground that arbitration would be prohibitively expensive, that party bears the burden of showing the likelihood of incurring such costs. Randolph did not meet that burden. How detailed the showing of prohibitive expense must be before the party seeking arbitration must come forward with contrary evidence is a matter we need not discuss; for in this case neither during discovery nor when the case was presented on the merits was there any timely showing at all on the point. The Court of Appeals therefore erred in deciding that the arbitration agreement's silence with respect to costs and fees rendered it unenforceable.[15]

The judgment of the Court of Appeals is affirmed in part and reversed in part.

It is so ordered.

---

statements provide no basis on which to ascertain the actual costs and fees to which she would be subject in arbitration.

In this Court, Randolph's brief lists fees incurred in cases involving other arbitrations as reflected in opinions of other Courts of Appeals, while petitioners' counsel states that arbitration fees are frequently waived by petitioners. None of this information affords a sufficient basis for concluding that Randolph would in fact have incurred substantial costs in the event her claim went to arbitration.

15. We decline to reach respondent's argument that we may affirm the Court of Appeals' conclusion that the arbitration agreement is unenforceable on the alternative ground that the agreement precludes respondent from bringing her claims under the TILA as a class action. See Brief for Respondent 39-48. The Court of Appeals did not pass on this question, and we need not decide here issues not decided below. Roberts v. Galen of Va., Inc., 525 U.S. 249, 142 L. Ed. 2d 648, 119 S. Ct. 685 (1999) (per curiam).

Justice GINSBURG, with whom Justice STEVENS and Justice SOUTER join, and with whom Justice BREYER joins as to Parts I and Ill, concurring in part and dissenting in part. [Omitted.]

While arbitration agreements in consumer contracts have often been upheld, they have sometimes been successfully attacked as unconscionable or otherwise in violation of state public policy. A number of courts have held arbitration clauses unconscionable because they bind the consumer to arbitration in all cases, but do not so limit the creditor. See, e.g., Iberia Credit Bureau, Inc. v. Cingular Wireless LLC, 379 F.3d 159 (5th Cir. 2004).

In *Green Tree*, there is a footnote in which the Supreme Court holds that the consumer alleged but did not prove that the costs of arbitration would be an excessive burden on her. There are decisions finding arbitration clauses unconscionable for just this reason. See Porpora v. Gatliff Bldg. Co., 160 Ohio App. 3d 843, 828 N.E.2d 1081 (2005). In that case, according to the fee schedule published by the American Arbitration Association, the alleged damages claimed would have required the consumers to pay an initial fee of $2,750 upon filing their claims and an additional case-service fee of $1,250 if their case proceeded to an initial hearing. AAA Rule 50 does provide that the administrative fees may be deferred or reduced "in the event of extreme hardship on the part of any party." The rule makes clear, however, that such a deferral or reduction is entirely within the discretion of the AAA. Moreover, the rule does not provide for a waiver of the fees. Lastly, the initial filing fee of $2,750 and the case-service fee of $1,250 do not reflect additional costs that will be incurred by the parties during the course of arbitration. AAA Rule 51 explains that the parties are responsible for the expenses of the arbitrator, witnesses, and AAA representatives, as well as the arbitrator's compensation. See also Brower v. Gateway 2000, Inc., 246 A.D.2d 246, 676 N.Y.S.2d 569 (N.Y. App. Div. 1998) (holding unconscionable an agreement to make the New York consumer arbitrate in Chicago using the rules of the International Chamber of Commerce, which required an up-front fee of $4,000, half of which was non-refundable, winner to pay the loser's attorney's fees); see also Tillman v. Commercial Credit Loans, Inc., 362 N.C. 93, 655 S.E.2d 362 (2008) (the first appellate decision in North Carolina history finding any contract unconscionable).

The Court in *Green Tree* refused to consider the question of whether TILA class action claims could be arbitrated, but there have been a large number of cases addressing the issue as one of unconscionability. See Muhammad v. County Bank of Rehoboth Beach, Delaware, 189 N.J. 1, 912

A.2d 88 (2006) (class waivers unconscionable in arbitration clauses); McKee v. AT&T Corp., 164 Wash. 2d 372, 191 P.3d 845 (2008) (mandatory arbitration clauses forbidding class actions are "essentially exculpatory clauses in disguise"). The next case has a variation on that issue.

DISCOVER BANK v. SUPERIOR COURT
Supreme Court of California, 2005
36 Cal. 4th 148, 113 P.3d 1100, 30 Cal. Rptr. 3d 76

MORENO, J.

This case concerns the validity of a provision in an arbitration agreement between Discover Bank and a credit cardholder forbidding classwide arbitration. The credit cardholder, a California resident, alleges that Discover Bank had a practice of representing to cardholders that late payment fees would not be assessed if payment was received by a certain date, whereas in actuality they were assessed if payment was received after 1:00 p.m. on that date, thereby leading to damages that were small as to individual consumers but large in the aggregate. Plaintiff filed a complaint claiming damages for this alleged deceptive practice, and Discover Bank successfully moved to compel arbitration pursuant to its arbitration agreement with plaintiff.

Plaintiff now seeks to pursue a classwide arbitration, which is well accepted under California law. (See Keating v. Superior Court (1982) 31 Cal. 3d 584, 613-614, 183 Cal. Rptr. 360, 645 P.2d 1192 (Keating), overruled on other grounds in Southland Corp. v. Keating (1984) 465 U.S. 1, 104 S. Ct. 852, 79 L. Ed. 2d 1 (Southland).) But plaintiff's arbitration agreement with Discover Bank has a clause forbidding classwide arbitration. Moreover, the agreement has a Delaware choice-of-law provision. Discover Bank argues that Delaware law allows contracting parties to waive class action remedies. The trial court ruled that the class arbitration waiver was unconscionable and enforced the arbitration agreement with the proviso that plaintiff could seek classwide arbitration. The Court of Appeal, without disputing that such class arbitration waivers may be unconscionable under California law and without addressing the choice-of-law issue, nonetheless held that the Federal Arbitration Act (FAA) (9 U.S.C. §1 et seq.) preempts the state law rule that class arbitration waivers are unconscionable.

As explained below, we conclude that, at least under some circumstances, the law in California is that class action waivers in consumer contracts of adhesion are unenforceable, whether the consumer is being asked to waive the right to class action litigation or the right to classwide arbitration. We further conclude that the Court of Appeal is incorrect that the FAA preempts California law in this respect. Finally, we will remand to the Court of Appeal to decide the choice-of-law issue.

I. FACTUAL AND PROCEDURAL BACKGROUND

The following undisputed facts are largely drawn from the Court of Appeal opinion. Plaintiff Christopher Boehr obtained a credit card from defendant Discover Bank in April 1986. The Discover Bank cardholder agreement (agreement) governing plaintiff's credit card account contained a choice-of-law clause providing for the application of Delaware and federal law.

When plaintiff's credit card was issued, the agreement did not contain an arbitration clause. Discover Bank subsequently added the arbitration clause in July 1999, pursuant to a change-of-terms provision in the agreement. Relying on the change-of-terms provision, Discover Bank added the arbitration clause by sending to its existing cardholders (including plaintiff) a notice that stated in relevant part: "NOTICE OF AMENDMENT . . . WE ARE ADDING A NEW ARBITRATION SECTION WHICH PROVIDES THAT IN THE EVENT YOU OR WE ELECT TO RESOLVE ANY CLAIM OR DISPUTE BETWEEN US BY ARBITRATION, NEITHER YOU NOR WE SHALL HAVE THE RIGHT TO LITIGATE THAT CLAIM IN COURT OR TO HAVE A JURY TRIAL ON THAT CLAIM. THIS ARBITRATION SECTION WILL NOT APPLY TO LAWSUITS FILED BEFORE THE EFFECTIVE DATE."

In addition, the arbitration clause precluded both sides from participating in classwide arbitration, consolidating claims, or arbitrating claims as a representative or in a private attorney general capacity: ". . . NEITHER YOU NOR WE SHALL BE ENTITLED TO JOIN OR CONSOLIDATE CLAIMS IN ARBITRATION BY OR AGAINST OTHER CARDMEMBERS WITH RESPECT TO OTHER ACCOUNTS, OR ARBITRATE ANY CLAIM AS A REPRESENTATIVE OR MEMBER OF A CLASS OR IN A PRIVATE ATTORNEY GENERAL CAPACITY."

The arbitration agreement also stated that the FAA would govern the agreement: "Your Account involves interstate commerce, and this provision shall be governed by the Federal Arbitration Act (FAA)." "The arbitrator shall follow applicable substantive law to the extent consistent with the FAA and applicable statutes of limitations and shall honor claims of privilege recognized at law." Existing cardholders were notified that if they did not wish to accept the new arbitration clause, they must notify Discover

Bank of their objections and cease using their accounts. Their continued use of an account would be deemed to constitute acceptance of the new terms. Plaintiff did not notify Discover Bank of any objection to the arbitration clause or cease using his account before the stated deadline.

On August 15, 2001, Boehr filed a putative class action complaint in superior court against Discover Bank. Plaintiff alleged two causes of action—breach of contract and violation of the Delaware Consumer Fraud Act (Del. Code Ann., tit. 6, §§2511-2527). The latter act in part prohibits misrepresentations "of any material fact with intent that others rely upon such concealment, suppression or omission in connection with the sale, lease or advertisement of any merchandise." (Id., §2513.) He alleged that Discover Bank breached its cardholder agreement by imposing a late fee of approximately $29 on payments that were received on the payment due date, but after Discover Bank's undisclosed 1:00 p.m. "cut-off time." Discover Bank also allegedly imposed a periodic finance charge (thereby disallowing a grace period) on new purchases when payments were received on the payment due date, but after 1:00 p.m. The complaint acknowledged that the contract with Discover Bank provided that the contract was "governed by federal law and the law of Delaware." Plaintiff alleged, however, that "this choice of law provision applies only to plaintiff's substantive claims and not to other issues related to the contract, which plaintiff contends are governed by California or other applicable law."

Discover Bank moved to compel arbitration of plaintiff's claim on an individual basis and to dismiss the class action pursuant to the arbitration agreement's class action waiver.

Plaintiff opposed the motion, contending among other things that the class action waiver was unconscionable and unenforceable under California law. Discover Bank, on the other hand, argued that the FAA requires the enforcement of the express provisions of an arbitration clause, including class action waivers. Discover Bank contended that under section 2 of the FAA, arbitration agreements should not be singled out for suspect status under state laws applicable only to arbitration provisions.

[The trial court held that under California law an arbitration class action waiver is unconscionable and, thus, unenforceable. The trial court further conducted a choice-of-law analysis and concluded that enforcing the class action waiver under Delaware law would violate a fundamental public policy under California law. The Court of Appeals reversed, holding that the FAA preempted the California unconscionability rule on point.]

II. DISCUSSION

A. CLASS ACTION LAW SUITS AND CLASS ACTION ARBITRATION

Before addressing the questions at issue in this case, we first consider the justifications for class action lawsuits. These justifications were set forth in Justice Mosk's oft-quoted majority opinion in Vasquez v. Superior Court (1971) 4 Cal. 3d 800, 808, 94 Cal. Rptr. 796, 484 P.2d 964 (*Vasquez*): "Frequently numerous consumers are exposed to the same dubious practice by the same seller so that proof of the prevalence of the practice as to one consumer would provide proof for all. Individual actions by each of the defrauded consumers is often impracticable because the amount of individual recovery would be insufficient to justify bringing a separate action; thus an unscrupulous seller retains the benefits of its wrongful conduct. A class action by consumers produces several salutary by-products, including a therapeutic effect upon those sellers who indulge in fraudulent practices, aid to legitimate business enterprises by curtailing illegitimate competition, and avoidance to the judicial process of the burden of multiple litigation involving identical claims. The benefit to the parties and the courts would, in many circumstances, be substantial." . . .

These same concerns were acknowledged by the United States Supreme Court: "'The policy at the very core of the class action mechanism is to overcome the problem that small recoveries do not provide the incentive for any individual to bring a solo action prosecuting his or her rights. A class action solves this problem by aggregating the relatively paltry potential recoveries into something worth someone's (usually an attorney's) labor.'" (Amchem Products, Inc. v. Windsor (1997) 521 U.S. 591, 617, 117 S. Ct. 2231, 138 L. Ed. 2d 689.)

B. THE ENFORCEABILITY OF CLASS ACTION WAIVERS

* * *

"To briefly recapitulate the principles of unconscionability, the doctrine has "'both a 'procedural' and a 'substantive' element," the former focusing on "'oppression'" or "'surprise'" due to unequal bargaining power, the latter on "'overly harsh'" or "'one-sided'" results.' [Citation.] The procedural element of an unconscionable contract generally takes the form of a contract of adhesion, "'which, imposed and drafted by the party of superior bargaining strength, relegates to the subscribing party only the opportunity to adhere to the contract or reject it.'" . . . [¶] Substantively unconscionable terms may take various forms, but may generally be described as unfairly one-sided." (Little v. Auto Stiegler, Inc. (2003) 29 Cal. 4th 1064, 1071, 130 Cal. Rptr. 2d 892, 63 P.3d 979 (Little), cert. den. sub nom. Auto Stiegler, Inc. v. Little (2003) 540 U.S. 818, 124 S. Ct. 83, 157 L. Ed. 2d 35.)

We agree that at least some class action waivers in consumer contracts are unconscionable under California law. First, when a consumer is given an amendment to its cardholder agreement in the form of a "bill stuffer" that he would be deemed to accept if he did not close his account, an element of procedural unconscionability is present. (*Szetela*, supra, 97 Cal. App. 4th at p. 1100, 118 Cal. Rptr. 2d 862.) Moreover, although adhesive contracts are generally enforced (Graham v. Scissor-Tail, Inc. (1981) 28 Cal. 3d 807, 817-818, 171 Cal. Rptr. 604, 623 P.2d 165), class action waivers found in such contracts may also be substantively unconscionable inasmuch as they may operate effectively as exculpatory contract clauses that are contrary to public policy. As stated in Civil Code section 1668: "All contracts *which have for their object, directly or indirectly, to exempt anyone from responsibility for his own fraud, or willful injury* to the person or property of another, or violation of law, whether willful or negligent, are against the policy of the law." (Italics added.)

Class action and arbitration waivers are not, in the abstract, exculpatory clauses. But because, as discussed above, damages in consumer cases are often small and because "'[a] company which wrongfully exacts a dollar from each of millions of customers will reap a handsome profit'" (*Linder*, supra, 23 Cal. 4th at p. 446, 97 Cal. Rptr. 2d 179, 2 P.3d 27), "'the class action is often the only effective way to halt and redress such exploitation.'" (Ibid.) Moreover, such class action or arbitration waivers are indisputably one-sided. "Although styled as a mutual prohibition on representative or class actions, it is difficult to envision the circumstances under which the provision might negatively impact Discover [Bank], because credit card companies typically do not sue their customers in class-action lawsuits." (*Szetela*, supra, 97 Cal. App. 4th at p. 1101, 118 Cal. Rptr. 2d 862.) Such one-sided, exculpatory contracts in a contract of adhesion, at least to the extent they operate to insulate a party from liability that otherwise would be imposed under California law, are generally unconscionable.

We acknowledge that other courts disagree. Some courts have viewed class actions or arbitrations as a merely procedural right, the waiver of which is not unconscionable. (See, e.g., Strand v. U.S. Bank National Association ND (N.D. 2005) 693 N.W.2d 918, 926 (Strand); Blaz v. Belfer (5th Cir. 2004) 368 F.3d 501, 504-505; Johnson v. West Suburban Bank (3d Cir. 2000) 225 F.3d 366, 369; Champ v. Siegel Trading Co., Inc. (1995)

55 F.3d 269, 277; but see Leonard v. Terminix Intern. Co. L.P. (Ala. 2002) 854 So. 2d 529, 538 [class action waiver together with limitation of damages clause in adhesive consumer arbitration agreement deprives plaintiffs of a "meaningful remedy" and is therefore unconscionable]; State v. Berger (2002) 211 W. Va. 549, 567 S.E.2d 265, 278 [holding contract provision limiting class action rights unconscionable]; Powertel v. Bexley (Fla. Dist. Ct. App. 1999) 743 So. 2d 570, 576 [same].) But as the above cited cases of this court have continually affirmed, class actions and arbitrations are, particularly in the consumer context, often inextricably linked to the vindication of substantive rights. Affixing the "procedural" label on such devices understates their importance and is not helpful in resolving the unconscionability issue. . . .

We do not hold that all class action waivers are necessarily unconscionable. But when the waiver is found in a consumer contract of adhesion in a setting in which disputes between the contracting parties predictably involve small amounts of damages, and when it is alleged that the party with the superior bargaining power has carried out a scheme to deliberately cheat large numbers of consumers out of individually small sums of money, then, at least to the extent the obligation at issue is governed by California law, the waiver becomes in practice the exemption of the party "from responsibility for [its] own fraud, or willful injury to the person or property of another." (Civ. Code, §1668.) Under these circumstances, such waivers are unconscionable under California law and should not be enforced.

C. FAA PREEMPTION OF CALIFORNIA RULES AGAINST CLASS ACTION WAIVERS

1. The Court of Appeal Opinion

The Court of Appeal did not dispute the conclusions of AOL and Szetela that, at least under some circumstances, a class action waiver would be unconscionable or contrary to public policy. The court concluded, however, that when class action waivers are contained in arbitration agreements, California law prohibiting such waivers is preempted by section 2 of the FAA (9 U.S.C. §2). We conclude the Court of Appeal erred.

We begin by reviewing some basic principles pertaining to the enforcement of arbitration agreements. "California law, like federal law, favors enforcement of valid arbitration agreements. [Citation.] . . . Thus, under both federal and California law, arbitration agreements are valid, irrevocable, and enforceable, save upon such grounds as exist at law or in equity for the revocation of any contract." (*Armendariz*, supra, 24 Cal. 4th at pp. 97-98, 99 Cal. Rptr. 2d 745, 6 P.3d 669, fn. omitted; see also 9 U.S.C.

§2; Code Civ. Proc., §1281.) In other words, although under federal and California law, arbitration agreements are enforced "in accordance with their terms" (Volt Info. Sciences v. Leland Stanford Jr. U. (1989) 489 U.S. 468, 109 S. Ct. 1248, 103 L. Ed. 2d 488 (*Volt*)), such enforcement is limited by certain general contract principles "at law or in equity for the revocation of any contract."

At the outset of our discussion, we note that the FAA is silent on the matter of class actions and class action arbitration. Indeed, not only is classwide arbitration a relatively recent development, but class action litigation for damages was for the most part unknown in federal jurisdictions at the time the FAA was enacted in 1925. (Act of Feb. 12, 1925, ch. 213, 43 Stat. 883.) The Congress that enacted the FAA therefore cannot be said to have contemplated the issues before us. Accordingly, our conclusions with respect to FAA preemption must come from the United States Supreme Court's articulation of general principles regarding such preemption. . . .

"[U]nder section 2 of the FAA, a state court may refuse to enforce an arbitration agreement based on 'generally applicable contract defenses, such as fraud, duress, or unconscionability.'" (*Little*, supra, 29 Cal. 4th at p. 1079, 130 Cal. Rptr. 2d 892, 63 P.3d 979, quoting Doctor's Associates, Inc. v. Casarotto (1996) 517 U.S. 681, 687, 116 S. Ct. 1652, 134 L. Ed. 2d 902.) In the present case, the principle that class action waivers are, under certain circumstances, unconscionable as unlawfully exculpatory is a principle of California law that does not specifically apply to arbitration agreements, but to contracts generally. In other words, it applies equally to class action litigation waivers in contracts without arbitration agreements as it does to class arbitration waivers in contracts with such agreements. (See *AOL*, supra, 90 Cal. App. 4th at pp. 17-18, 108 Cal. Rptr. 2d 699.) . . .

The Court of Appeal in the present case concluded that, unlike in *Volt*, the imposition of class action arbitration despite a class action waiver in the arbitration agreement would defeat the purpose of the FAA because it would not be enforcing the arbitration agreement according to its terms. We disagree. *Volt*'s dictum that the primary purpose of the FAA is to "ensur[e] that private agreements to arbitrate are enforced according to their terms" (*Volt*, supra, 489 U.S. at p. 479, 109 S. Ct. 1248) was intended to explain why the procedural rules provided in arbitration agreements should be enforced, rather than imposing the rules contained in the FAA. (Id. at pp. 478-479, 109 S. Ct. 1248.) Nothing in *Volt*, nor any other Supreme Court case, however, suggests that state courts are obliged to enforce contractual terms even if those terms are found to be unconscionable or contrary to public policy under general contract law principles. As discussed, section 2 of the FAA and cases interpreting it make clear that state courts have no such obligation. Agreements to arbitrate may not be used to "harbor terms, conditions and practices" that undermine public policy. (*Little*, supra, 29 Cal. 4th at p. 1079, 130 Cal. Rptr. 2d 892, 63 P.3d 979.) . . .

The Court of Appeal opinion below also relied on the supposed short-comings of arbitration to bolster its conclusion that a class action waiver is enforceable under the FAA. As the court stated: "Although California courts have recognized the consumer protection value of classwide arbi-tration, that is not the sole consideration. Courts should also consider the 'California rule which prevents reweighing the merits of an arbitrator's decision.' [Citation.] The FAA does not preempt this rule. [Citation.] As judicial review of the merits of an arbitrator's decision may not be had under California law, a multi-million dollar class arbitration award entered on nothing more than mere whim cannot be corrected under California law."

Far from holding that the invalidation of a class action waiver dis-criminates against arbitration, the Court of Appeal below reasoned in effect that arbitration is an inferior forum and therefore cannot be entrusted with classwide claims. The court's conclusion regarding the unsuitability of arbitration to class actions reflects, as we stated in the context of another proposed limitation on arbitration, "the very mistrust of arbitration that has been repudiated by the United States Supreme Court." (*Armendariz*, supra, 24 Cal. 4th at p. 120, 99 Cal. Rptr. 2d 745, 6 P.3d 669.) Moreover, as explained below, there is nothing to indicate that class action and arbitration are inherently incompatible. . . .

Discover Bank argues that Green Tree Financial Corp. v. Bazzle (2003), 539 U.S. 444, 123 S. Ct. 2402, 156 L. Ed. 2d 414 (*Bazzle*), issued after the filing of the Court of Appeal opinion, supports the position that a state law rule against class arbitration waivers is preempted by the FAA. We disagree. . . .

The *Bazzle* court addressed a narrow question: Green Tree disputed whether the arbitration clause was silent on classwide arbitration, arguing that the contract language in fact prohibited such arbitrations. As the court's plurality framed the issue: "[W]e must deal with that argument at the outset, for if it is right, then the South Carolina court's holding is flawed on its own terms; that court neither said nor implied that it would have authorized class arbitration had the parties' arbitration agreement forbidden it." (*Bazzle*, supra, 539 U.S. at p. 450, 123 S. Ct. 2402 (plur. opn. of Breyer, J.).)

Even on this narrow issue, *Bazzle* produced no majority opinion. A plurality of four justices held that the question whether the contract was in fact silent on arbitration was for the arbitrator to decide, and remanded for an arbitral determination. As the plurality stated: "In certain limited circumstances, courts assume that the parties intended courts, not arbitrators, to decide a particular arbitration-related matter (in the absence of 'clea[r] and unmistakabl[e]' evidence to the contrary). [Citation.] These limited instances typically involve matters of a kind that 'contracting parties would likely have expected a court' to decide. [Citation.] They include certain gateway matters, such as whether the parties have a valid arbitration agreement at all or whether a concededly binding arbitration clause applies to a certain type of controversy. [Citations.] [¶] The question here whether—the contracts forbid class arbitration—does not fall into this narrow exception. It concerns neither the validity of the arbitration clause nor its applicability to the underlying dispute between the parties." (*Bazzle*, supra, 539 U.S. at p. 452, 123 S. Ct. 2402.) . . .

More significant than *Bazzle*'s holding, for purposes of the present case, is what it did not decide. The court did not address whether a state court can, consistent with the FAA, hold a class action waiver appearing in a contract of adhesion for arbitration unconscionable or contrary to public policy, as part of an arbitration-neutral law that finds all such waivers unenforceable. . . .

Nor did the court address the question whether that determination of unconscionability should be made by a court or an arbitrator. The court was in general agreement that courts should be left to decide certain "gateway matters" (*Bazzle*, supra, 539 U.S. at p. 452, 123 S. Ct. 2402 (plur. opn. of Breyer, J.)) or "fundamental" matters such as the validity and scope of the arbitration agreement (id. at pp. 456-457, 123 S. Ct. 2402 (dis. opn. of Rehnquist, C.J.)). Under California law, the question whether "grounds exist for the revocation of the [arbitration] agreement" based on "grounds as exist for the revocation of any contract" is for the courts to decide, not an arbitrator. (Code Civ. Proc., §1281.2; see Engalla v. Permanente Medical Group, Inc. (1997) 15 Cal. 4th 951, 973, 64 Cal. Rptr. 2d 843, 938 P.2d 903.) This includes the determination of whether arbitration agreements or portions thereof are deemed to be unconscionable or contrary to public policy. [Citing cases.] Nothing in *Bazzle* is to the contrary. . . .

The judgment of the Court of Appeal is reversed, and the cause is remanded for proceedings consistent with this opinion.

[The dissenting opinion of Baxter, J., joined by Chin and Brown, JJ., is omitted.]

Is the consumer better off in arbitration as opposed to the courtroom? There are advantages and disadvantages.

Advantages include the fact that no attorney is required (though many consumers still hire one for arbitration proceedings), arbitration is faster in all ways than a lawsuit (over quickly, no appeal, immediate closure of the dispute), and the procedure in arbitration is simpler, with the rules of evidence relaxed. The arbitrator is often favorable to the consumer and less inclined to buy the technical defenses the seller/creditor urges ("We can't afford to recognize the consumer's rights/problems"). The decision of the arbitrator is confidential.

The disadvantages, however, are substantial. The arbitration agreement is typically worded so that the company gets as much as possible: forum selection, choice of which arbitration rules apply, etc. The consumer cannot negotiate as to these things. The arbitration fees can be daunting. While the ICC fees mentioned above are $4,000 for small disputes, more typically the fees are closer to $500, plus payment for the arbitrator's time (usually billed at between $200 and $300 an hour for a day or two of work), often split between the parties unless the seller/creditor agrees to bear it all. Some courts have invalidated arbitration agreements where the consumer is forced to bear these amounts. See, e.g., Armendariz v. Foundation Health Psychcare Serv., Inc., 24 Cal. 4th 83 (Cal. 2000). Also troubling is that the arbitrator is not required to follow the law in the same way that a judge must (so that technical violations of TILA, for example, might be treated lightly), and there is no transcript or written opinion in the usual case, and thus no precedential value from the proceeding even if the consumer prevails.

The National Consumer Disputes Advisory Committee has promulgated a Consumer Due Process Protocol which sets out general guidelines for protecting consumers in arbitration, and it might be useful in arguments about the conscionability of any given arbitration agreement.

As to all of this, see Stephen Goldberg, Frank E.A. Sander, Nancy H. Rogers, and Sarah R. Cole, Dispute Resolution (5th ed. 2007).

II. HOME EQUITY LENDING AND RESCISSION

A. Home Equity Lending

As consumers came to appreciate the fact that they were sleeping in their most valuable asset, they began to contemplate giving a second mortgage on the house or using their equity in the house as security for an open-end line of credit. Of course there are risks in putting one's home up as collateral, but that risk may not be well appreciated when the loan is negotiated. Losing one's home is such a dire consequence that our law is sensitive to the plight of consumers who have too carelessly taken the step of betting the family home.

From its very beginning in 1968, the Truth in Lending Act gave consumers a right of rescission whenever they put their home on the line in situations other than its original construction or acquisition. In recent years, however, TILA has been much amended to provide even greater rights to consumers who are using their home as collateral for non-home-related debts. Effective November 7, 1989, the Home Equity Loan Consumer Protection Act of 1988 was grafted onto the Truth in Lending Act. Generally it provides for disclosures to the consumer of all the terms of the home equity loan, including both general disclosures (such as advice to consult a tax lawyer about whether interest payments are deductible) and specific disclosures about the transaction (such as up-front costs, repayment schedules, the APR and its method of calculation). Some disclosures must be made at the time the consumer applies for the home equity loan; others must be given at the time the account is opened. Compare Reg. Z §226.5b(b) (application disclosures) with §226.6(e) (initial disclosures at opening of account). For closed-end transactions, a good faith estimate of all disclosures must be given to the consumer prior to consummation of the transaction, or mailed within three days after the creditor receives the consumer's written application (whichever is earlier); Reg. Z §226.19(a). The Home Equity Act also gives the consumer certain substantive rights, which are explored in the following Problem.

PROBLEM 130

The directors of Nightflyer Finance Company have come up with a plan, called internally the "Your House Is Our House" plan, by which to start home equity lending. You are the lawyer for Nightflyer, and it wants your blessing on this proposal. Under the plan, the consumer will receive an advertisement like this:

WRITE A CHECK ANYTIME YOU WANT, AND WE'LL CASH IT IF YOU WILL PUT UP YOUR HOUSE AS COLLATERAL! INTEREST PAYMENTS ON THE RESULTING LOANS WILL BE TAX DE-DUCTIBLE! PAYMENTS ARE LOW, LOW, LOW! NO ANNUAL FEE! CALL (800) 555-5911 FOR DETAILS!

Nightflyer plans to make loans for up to 75 percent of the consumer's equity in his or her home, with the interest rate being variable and set by reference to the in-house rate established by Nightflyer to achieve maximum possible return.[16] The plan also provides that the consumer pay a minimum of only $100 each month—no matter how high the interest rate surges—with the balance being added to the loan (thus the debt increases even though payments are being made, a so-called negative amortization). The contract will provide that whenever the debt to Nightflyer has increased to the point where the consumer has exhausted more than 75 percent of his or her equity in the home, the entire amount comes due (a "balloon" payment); if the consumer cannot make the payment within 30 days, Nightflyer forecloses the loan. Look at Reg. Z §226.5b and decide whether you will approve this plan. Does the advertisement cause trouble? See Reg. Z §226.16(d).

FRANK AND ERNEST reprinted by permission of Newspaper Enterprise Association, Inc.

Home equity loans can be either open-end or closed-end. A closed-end loan involves the advancement of a set amount. In an open-end home equity loan, like the one in Problem 130, the consumer is given the ability to get loan after loan from the lender, with the consumer's home standing as collateral for this series of advances and their repayment. Sometimes in these latter transactions the consumer is given a special checkbook in order to obtain the needed monies from the lender (on whom the checks are drawn). In other open-end cases the consumer is issued a credit card, with the credit extensions being protected by the creditor's mortgage interest in the consumer's home.

1. High Rate/High Fee Mortgages

The 1980s were a grand time for rapacious lenders. In the 1987 movie "Wall Street," Gordon Gekko, the character played by actor Michael

---

16. Review page 557 for a discussion of the meaning of the terms used in variable-rate financing.

Douglas, set the tone by pontificating that "greed is good." Just as banks and other lending institutions pulled out of minority and poor areas, the federal government greatly slackened its enforcement of fair housing laws, and the tax code was changed so as to encourage second mortgage lending by making the interest payments tax deductible. Deregulation also played a part, allowing unscrupulous entities to enter the lending business and go after those who had equity in their homes but who otherwise could not attract the attention of legitimate lenders (particularly the uneducated and the elderly). "Subprime" lending of this stripe was a $140 billion industry by 2000 (and currently constitutes 13 percent of all home loans), leading to predatory loans made at outrageously high interest rates or to "packing" the deal with unwanted extras (such as very high credit insurance) and extra-high closing costs known in the trade as "garbage fees" or "junk charges."[17] Often, dilapidated homes are purchased at a low price and then resold at exorbitant rates to unsophisticated buyers, a process called "flipping."[18]

Congress responded to these so-called high rate/high fees mortgages with the Home Ownership and Equity Protection Act of 1994 (HOEPA), which amended the Truth in Lending Act by adding §129; Regulation Z reflects the statutory changes in §226.32. Generally these sections require special disclosures and prohibit certain distasteful practices whenever the interest rate is 10 percent (8 percent for first-time borrowers) higher than the current Treasury bill rate, or if the total points and fees paid by the borrower at the closing exceed 8 percent of the loan amount or $400, whichever is greater. These amounts are subject to annual adjustment (with a 2009 figure of $583). At the same time, Congress upped the statutory penalties for violating the provisions of this statute, see §130(a)(4) ("all finance charges and fees paid by the consumer" awarded as punitive damages, in addition to the usual penalties), and provided that the inclusion in the contract of a prohibited term (see below) is a material misdisclosure and gives rise to a three-year right of rescission; TILA §129(j). For all closed-end credit transactions secured by a dwelling, the usual numbers in §130(a) (minimum of $100, cap of $1,000) increase to $400 and $4,000, respectively.

---

17. Some of these practices were successfully attacked in class actions, see Rodash v. AIB Mortgage Co., 16 F.3d 1142 (11th Cir. 1994), leading Congress to pass the Truth in Lending Class Action Relief Act of 1995, Pub. L. No. 104-121, 109 Stat. 161 (1995), making TIL class actions tougher to bring and win; see TILA §§130(i) and 139.

18. For loans insured by the Federal Housing Administration, there are some FHA guidelines designed to prevent flipping. See 24 C.F.R. §203.37a.

Note also that the definition of "creditor" is expanded for HOEPA to include any lender who makes two or more qualifying loans a year. See footnote 3 to Reg. Z.

However, in spite of these efforts, predatory lending gained in strength as unscrupulous lenders engaged in *asset-based lending* (relying on the property to repay the loan, not caring about whether the debtor will have the ability to repay the debt), planning on what is called "equity stripping." These lenders are known to lie to the consumer, flagrantly violate the consumer laws, and trample all pretense of fairness as they go after the consumer's home, selling the resulting mortgages in packages ("securitization") to respectable financial institutions hoping to escape the stench of the unsavory underlying deals. See Christopher L. Peterson, Predatory Structured Finance, 28 Cardozo L. Rev. 2185 (2007); Kathleen C. Engel and Patricia A. McCoy, Turning a Blind Eye: Wall Street Finance of Predatory Lending, 75 Fordham L. Rev. 2039 (2007). Some states have adopted a model statute that deals more stringently with the HOEPA issues: the Home Loan Protection Act, created by the AARP Public Policy Institute.[19]

In 2008, the Federal Reserve Board amended Regulation Z to add §226.35, which regulates what are called "higher-price mortgages," defined as those that exceed the prime rate by 1.5 or more percentage points (3.5 for subordinate liens on a dwelling). At the same time, the Board created §226.36, which applies to *all* mortgages (not just those with high rates/high fees or higher prices). Use these sections (§§226.32 to 226.36) to resolve the following Problems.

PROBLEM 131

Nightflyer Loan Company has decided to make loans to people owning homes in the poorer part of town, charging them very high interest rates and then selling their mortgages to other institutions (which will possibly qualify as holders in due course, and thus take free of the borrower's defenses). You are Nightflyer's attorney and are asked what the company can get away with.

a. Will you put your imprimatur on the following practices?

---

19. As of this writing the adopting states are Illinois, Massachusetts, New York, North Carolina, Texas, and Virginia.

1. A large ("balloon") payment at the end of the loan that the consumer is unlikely to be able to meet, which would thus allow Nightflyer to foreclose, buy the property cheaply at the foreclosure sale, and sell it at a nice profit to a later purchaser. See Reg. Z ¶226.32(d)(1)(i).

2. A payment schedule in which the payments are not large enough to cover the interest rate in full each month, with any shortage added to the principal due. See Reg. Z ¶226.32(d)(2).

3. A clause forbidding prepayment. See Reg. Z ¶226.32(d)(6) and (7); ¶226.35(b)(2).

4. A practice of making loans only to those who are so poor that they are highly likely to default. See Reg. Z ¶¶226.34(a)(4), 226.35(b)(1).

b. Nightflyer has a favorite contractor who steers much business its way, and the two sometimes inflate the charges and split the extra money. Advise Nightflyer how to keep the consumer from knowing the actual amounts paid to the contractor. See Reg. Z §226.32(e)(2).

c. Are the subsequent purchasers of the mortgages going to be able to take free of the consumers' defenses as holders in due course normally would? See Reg. Z §226.32(e)(3) and TILA §131(d).

d. Could you get away with these practices if this were an open-end loan, where the consumers would give Nightflyer a second mortgage on their homes in return for a line of credit against which they could make periodic draws? See Reg. Z §226.32(a)(2)(iii).

PROBLEM 132

Before lenders agree to make a home mortgage loan, it is routinely required that the property's value be appraised by an independent entity. Nightflyer Loan Company has been making subprime loans to people whose creditworthiness is suspicious, and having them sign promissory notes for more than the worth of property they are buying. The appraiser must go along with this, of course, by appraising the property at more than its true market value. It is Nightflyer's usual practice to tell the appraiser ahead of time what the amount of the loan will be and to broadly hint that if the appraiser should deem the property not to be worth such a loan, Nightflyer will never use the services of that appraiser again, and will funnel its business to one who is more sensitive to the business necessities of the situation. Is this kind of pressure legal? Could Nightflyer get away with it by using winks and nods to convey the same idea without actually dictating the appraisal amount to the appraiser? See §226.36(b).

2. The Foreclosure Crisis

The collapse of the housing market in the middle of the first decade of the 21st century was a direct consequence of the greedy and unwise business practices discussed above. Gullible consumers were encouraged to take out mortgages they could not afford on property that turned out to be worth far less than the mortgage indebtedness. The subprime lenders frequently sold the mortgages (and the promissory notes that went with them) to other financial institutions, and these mortgages were then bundled into a mass, placed in a trust, and used as the assets backing the issuance of bonds by the trust (a "securitization"). Things went fine until real property stopped appreciating in value and its worth dropped to alarmingly low levels, with a recession that engulfed the country and, indeed, the world. Not just subprime borrowers were affected; the recession reduced the value of almost all property, and perfectly responsible mortgagors (many of whom were also laid off from their jobs) began to struggle to make payments and avoid foreclosure.

Scams abounded. For a high up-front fee (followed by the agent's quick disappearance), foreclosure rescue companies would offer help to distressed homeowners, only to add to their problems when the promised rescue never took place. Some of these schemes involved the homeowner's signing title to the property over to the scammer. Not only do such practices amount to common law fraud, it is a violation of the Truth in Lending Act for a lender to tell consumers that it is helping them refinance their home when it is actually buying the home and turning the consumers into renters; see Moore v. Cycon Enterprises, Inc., 2006 WL 2375477 (W.D. Mich. 2006). It is also a violation of state laws; see Eicher v. Mid America Financial Inv. Corp. 270 Neb. 370, 702 N.W.2d 792 (2005). In these situations the consumers do not realize at the closing that they are signing away their ownership rights as they put their signatures on the mass of documents presented to them across the table. When the lender subsequently resells the home, the consumers are evicted, often with little or no compensation for the loss of their principal dwelling.

Securitization also resulted in the mortgages/promissory notes being held by impersonal entities with little incentive to help the mortgagors who faced financial difficulties and wanted to renegotiate the terms of their mortgages. Frequently it was difficult to identify the true owner of the mortgage debt at any given moment, making such negotiations impossible. The bundled mortgages/notes in the securitization trusts sometimes changed hands in complicated refinancing deals, and/or the entities holding the notes went under, leading to distress sales of the notes to others and creating a murky mess of transfers and assumptions.

There was a bright spot in all this for homeowners, however. When they stopped paying the mortgage amounts, and the current owners of the mortgages/notes tried to foreclose on the property, the rules of Article 3 of the Uniform Commercial Code unexpectedly came to the aid of the debtors. UCC §3-301 states that the only entity that is allowed to sue on a promissory note is a "person entitled to enforce the instrument." That in turn is defined as a holder of the instrument who takes through a valid series of negotiations or, even if the note was not properly endorsed by the payee, who can demonstrate a clear chain of title to the note in its possession.

PROBLEM 133

Octopus National Bank purchased a large number of home mortgages (and the promissory notes that went with them) that were being sold in a bankruptcy foreclosure sale by the trustee for the bankrupt entity, Wizard Securities, Inc. It was unclear from whom Wizard Securities had purchased the mortgages/notes. ONB was pleased to snap up the mortgages/notes at bargain prices, and it has now given you, the bank's attorney, the job of contacting the debtors, securing payment, and foreclosing on the properties if payment is not forthcoming. When you look at the notes, you observe that the original mortgagee-payees frequently failed to endorse them at all, so that the notes were transferred from one entity to another without the necessary signatures for a valid negotiation. Even worse, some of the notes that should accompany the mortgages are missing, and no one seems to know what happened to them. Getting out your copy of the UCC, you discover a section that allows a creditor to sue on missing notes if the creditor can prove good title to the notes; U.C.C. §3-309.

When you contact the homeowners, you discover that they are now being represented by a legal aid society, which claims that without valid endorsements or proof of a chain of transfers clearly establishing ONB as the true owner of the notes, no foreclosure is possible. In fact, the legal aid society points to U.C.C. §3-602(a), which says that if the debtor pays the wrong entity, it will still owe the money to the "person entitled to enforce the instrument."

This all sounds like technical gobbledygook to you (you wrote off the Commercial Paper course in law school as too dull to be worthy of consideration). You do have the mortgages themselves in your possession, and, for most of them, the promissory notes with the missing endorsements. Will that be enough to allow a foreclosure action to succeed? If not, what legal steps can you suggest to your boss at the bank? See In re Foreclosure Cases, 2007 WL 3232430 (N.D. Ohio 2007).

3. Reverse Mortgages

The high rate/high fee mortgage rules are not applicable to what are called *reverse mortgages*—see Reg. Z §226.32(a)(2)(ii)—but these transactions are subject to Reg. Z §226.33. In a reverse mortgage—typically used by elderly individuals who have no fixed income and wish to live off of the equity they have built up in their home—the lending institution in effect *buys* the homeowner's equity in the property by making a loan or series of loans, with the agreement that the homeowner has *no personal liability* for repaying the debt (this is called a "nonrecourse" loan). Instead, the lender will be repaid from the sale of the property when the homeowner dies, resells the property, moves, or defaults. See Jean Reilly, Reverse Mortgages: Backing into the Future, 5 Elder L.J. 17 (1997).[20] Reverse mortgage payouts come in three forms: a single lump-sum payment, a line of credit, or monthly annuity payments for the life of the mortgagor. When the mortgagor dies or moves out, the loan must be repaid along with the interest thereon (and the closing costs as well, which can be substantial but are, of course, not emphasized in the mortgagee's sales pitch). All of this is in the nature of a bet: the homeowner comes out on top if he/she lives longer than expected; otherwise the bank gets the better deal. For reverse mortgages Reg. Z §226.33 requires certain descriptive disclosures designed to warn the borrowers what they are in for. Financial counseling is required by HUD before a homeowner can obtain a federally insured reverse mortgage, but the counseling is free and is provided by federally approved agencies.

4. Canceling Mortgage Insurance

Private mortgage insurance (PMI) protects the lender by paying off the loan if the mortgagor dies. However, the rates can be high, and the

---

20. The Association for the Advancement of Retired Persons (AARP) has a web site to help borrowers understand reverse mortgages. See www.aarp.org/money/revmort/revmort_basics/.

mortgagee's risk becomes low as the loan is repaid and the equity in the property exceeds the remaining debt. In the late 1990s Congress finally became aware that consumers were paying far too much for unnecessary coverage.

Under the Homeowners Protection Act of 1998, 12 U.S.C. §4901 et seq., lenders are required to cancel private mortgage insurance on most home mortgage loans. Cancellation occurs automatically when amortization has reduced the loan balance to 78 percent of the value of the property at the time the loan was made. However, mortgagees must also cancel the insurance at the borrower's request when the loan balance hits 80 percent of the original value. The law does take account of the appreciation in value of the property, which adds to the equity, and which ought to allow cancellation of PMI even earlier.

B. Rescission Rights

The complex issue in second mortgage lending to consumers is the difficulty of taking the steps necessary to comply with the rescission rights granted the consumer by the Truth in Lending Act. The statute and its supplementary regulation, Regulation Z, provide a three-day cooling-off period following the execution of the second mortgage in which the consumer-debtor (and all those having an ownership interest in the realty) may cancel the transaction. During this three-day period, the lender is not supposed to advance any money or perform any services (such as putting on aluminum siding). Contractor-creditors sometimes deliberately disobey this mandate, performing services during the rescission period—a process called "spiking"—with the belief that the consumer is less likely to cancel once performance has begun (or the contractor may even lie and tell the consumer that rescission is only allowed pre-performance).

Even where the lender is playing fair, the law is so complicated that many lenders misunderstand what is required and fail to comply with the technicalities of the regulation. The net effect of this is that the consumer has *three years* in which to cancel, a bad situation for the lending institution. The basic rules for compliance are detailed below.[21]

---

21. In Chapter 2 we covered the FTC "door-to-door sales" Regulation, which gives the consumer a three-day cooling-off period in which to cancel certain sales taking place away from the seller's fixed place of business. That Regulation provides that it does *not* apply to transactions subject to rescission under TILA. Thus, where the creditor in a door-to-door sale takes a security interest in the consumer's residence, the TIL rules we are currently exploring, and not the usual FTC Regulation, will govern.

1. Scope of the Regulation

The right of rescission is given to all consumers having an ownership interest in the property if that ownership will be subject to the security interest. Reg. Z §226.23.

In closed-end transactions, the right to rescind does not apply to a residential mortgage transaction (one in which a mortgage is taken in the consumer's principal dwelling to finance the acquisition or initial construction of the dwelling, i.e., a first mortgage), a refinancing of the same, or one in which a state agency is a creditor. Reg. Z. §226.23(f). For open-end transactions, the Regulation Z provision is §226.15, where the rules vary only slightly from those described below. For example, the right to rescind arises when the plan is opened, at each credit extension exceeding a previously established credit limit, at any increase in the credit limit, and when a security interest is added or increased to secure an existing plan. The material disclosures are different. See Reg. Z n.36.

2. The Cancellation Period

The consumer may exercise the right to cancel until midnight of the third business day following consummation, delivery of the required notice (see below for the form of the notice), or delivery of all material disclosures, whichever occurs last. To rescind, the consumer must mail the notice of rescission (or send a telegram) before this deadline. It need only be *sent* within the three-day period.

If the required notices or material disclosures are not properly given to the consumer, the consumer has *three years* from consummation in which to rescind, though this three-year period is cut short by the sale of the property within the three-year period. Reg. Z §226.23(a). A cancellation by one consumer is effective as to all having the right to cancel. Reg. Z §226.23(a)(4). Thus, if the wife cancels, the rescission also is effective in favor of the husband.[22] The courts have shown a marked hostility to allowing TIL rescission *class actions*. See Andrews v. Chevy Chase Bank, 545 F.3d 570 (7th Cir. 2008).

---

22. If the consumer files for bankruptcy, the right to rescind passes to the bankruptcy trustee. In re Crevier, 820 F.2d 1553 (9th Cir. 1987).

3. Common Mistakes in Documentation

a. Consummation

Most lenders assume that consummation means the date of the loan and that three days later the right to rescind has expired. Technically, "consummation" means the close of the offer and acceptance process (i.e., the moment when the loan contract between the parties becomes effective). The three-day period, however, runs from the *later* of three days after consummation, the giving of a proper notice, or the delivery of all material disclosures.

Consummation is typically not much of a problem, but the other two requirements are very tricky, and if the lender makes a mistake with them, the cancellation period becomes three years, not three days.

JENKINS v. LANDMARK MORTGAGE CORP. OF VIRGINIA
United States District Court, Western District of Virginia, 1988
696 F. Supp. 1089

MICHAEL, District Judge.

This matter is before the court on plaintiff's motion for declaratory judgment under 28 U.S.C. §2201 (1988). Plaintiff seeks to have this court declare that her June 22, 1988, rescission of a credit transaction governed by the federal Truth in Lending Act ("TILA"), 15 U.S.C. §§1601, et seq., was valid. For the reasons elaborated below, this court finds that the provisions of TILA empower plaintiff to rescind the consumer credit transaction into which plaintiff entered on August 25, 1987.

I. BACKGROUND

On August 25, 1987, plaintiff and her son went to the law office of W. Dale Houff, Esq., in order to close a consumer credit transaction whereby First American Mortgage and Loan Association of Virginia ("First American") gained a security interest in plaintiff's home. Complaint ¶6. On September 4, 1987, plaintiff was notified that defendant Landmark Mortgage had purchased her note and deed of trust from First American. Complaint ¶27.

Houff ("the attorney") merely acted as an agent for the original lender in order to complete the closing process and to convey to plaintiff the necessary TILA disclosures. At the closing, plaintiff and her son signed the "Acknowledgment of Receipt" appearing at the bottom of the TILA disclosure statement. The closing attorney testified that it was his usual practice to explain the contents of the disclosure statement to obligors, but that he could not recall the details of that particular transaction. Plaintiff testified that the documents were not explained or summarized to her. The attorney testified that it was his usual practice to ask consumer[s] if they wished to take a copy of the TILA disclosure form with them or to have it mailed to them, along with the other loan documents. Plaintiff testified that neither she nor her son were [sic] offered a copy of the disclosure form at the closing but, instead, simply told that a copy would be mailed to them. Regardless of the apparent conflict in the testimony between the attorney and plaintiff, it is clear that plaintiff and her son left the office without the TILA disclosure form in their possession.

Plaintiff did sign, date, and take with her the creditor's copy of the "Notice of Right to Cancel." That notice correctly sets out the three alternate *terminus post quem* events which could establish the expiration date of the consumer's right to rescind the credit transaction. The consumer has the right "to cancel this transaction without cost, within three business days from whichever of the following events occurs last: 1) the date of the transaction, which is August 25, 1987; or 2) the date you received your Truth in Lending disclosures; or 3) the date you received this notice of your right to cancel." As indicated, the transaction occurred August 25, 1987. That is the date plaintiff and son signed the instrument which encumbered her home. Clearly, since plaintiff and son signed the notice of the right to cancel on August 25, 1987, and took it with them that same day, that date must be considered the date upon which condition (3), described supra, occurred. The threshold question in this matter is when the effective receipt of the item described in (2) supra, the Truth in Lending disclosures, occurred.

Plaintiff was advised that her right to rescind expired on Friday, August 28, 1987, and, further, the attorney testified that he believed that he told her that her notice of rescission would need to be received by the lender by midnight of that date in order to be effective. While in the office on August 25, 1987, plaintiff and her son also signed a "Statement of Non-Rescission," purporting to indicate that plaintiff and her son had not rescinded the transaction as of August 28, 1987. The attorney testified that his normal practice was to offer to have the consumer sign and post-date that document while in his office so that, if they decided not to rescind within that three-day period, they would not need to make an additional trip to his office. His policy in post-dating the "Statement of Non-Rescission" was to void that statement in the event that the consumer exercised his right to rescind in a timely fashion. The closing attorney signed off on this document to the effect that it had been received by him on August 31, 1987.

On August 26, 1987, a complete set of the loan documents, including the TILA disclosure statement, was mailed to plaintiff. In addition, a cover letter was enclosed, stating, in relevant part,

> Please let me know if you have any questions and as I discussed with you at closing if you desire to cancel this transaction you must do so by Friday night [August 28, 1987], but that will not mean that you are relieved of all fees or expenses associated with the transaction as it has advanced to this point.

Neither plaintiff nor her son rescinded the transaction before midnight on August 28, 1987.

Plaintiff has admittedly defaulted in her payments on the note. Complaint, ¶28. Defendant Evans, as trustee of the Deed of Trust, proceeded to arrange for a foreclosure sale of plaintiff's house and notified plaintiff to that effect by a letter of May 19, 1988. On June 21, 1988, plaintiff, through her counsel, indicated in a letter to defendants that she wished to rescind the transaction of the prior August.

II. THE STATUTORY AND REGULATORY STRUCTURE

The rights which plaintiff seeks to invoke are wholly statutory creatures. The Truth in Lending Act clearly establishes the right of a consumer to rescind the credit transaction within a given time period. 15 U.S.C. §1635(a) (1982); 12 C.F.R. §226.23 (1988). The period for rescission is normally that circumscribed by the latest of the series of events listed in the "Notice of Right to Cancel" supra. 12 C.F.R. §226.23(a)(3). However, certain omissions in notification or failures of disclosure can trigger a longer rescission period.

> If the required notice or material disclosures are not delivered, the right to rescind shall expire three years after consummation, upon transfer of all of the consumer's interest in the property, or upon sale of the property, whichever occurs first.

Id.; 15 U.S.C. §1635(f). Most important for this matter, the statute provides that these rights should be "clearly and conspicuously" disclosed to the consumer. 15 U.S.C. §1635(a); 12 C.F.R. §226.23(b).

Not only are the statutory provisions extensive in the protection they provide for the consumer, but judicial interpretation of those provisions has only buttressed the paternalistic rationale of the TILA scheme. See, e.g., Sellers v. Wollman, 510 F.2d 119, 122 (5th Cir. 1975). The few cases which seem to undercut or pare back on the borrower's shield of TILA are readily distinguishable from the instant matter on a clear factual basis. For example, when a district court in the Eastern District of Pennsylvania held that there was no violation of the disclosure requirements of TILA, it did so within the context of a transactional history where the mortgagors had the representation of counsel at all stages of the proceeding. McCarrick v. Pollonia Federal Savings & Loan Assn., 502 F. Supp. 654, 657 (E.D. Pa. 1980).

The protective posture of this legislation is also reflected in the legal standard to which lenders are held. "The purposes of the act are further demonstrated through a standard of strict liability against creditors who fail to make mandated disclosures." Curry v. Fidelity Consumer Discount Co., 656 F. Supp. 1129, 1131 (E.D. Pa. 1987) (citation omitted). Technical defects in the disclosure process, even the solely oral transmission of information which must be disclosed in writing, are matters of which a court must take cognizance. Dryden v. Lou Budke's Arrow Finance Co., 661 F.2d 1186, 1190 (8th Cir. 1981). Such a strict standard of interpretation may well be more Draconian than Solomonic, especially in its effect on lenders. But there can be no doubt that the resemblance in TILA to the regime of Draco was intentional.

III. DEFECTS IN THE CREDIT TRANSACTION

First, the court finds that there was a failure of delivery in regard to the TILA disclosure statement. The "Notice of Right to Cancel" was accurate and correctly delivered to plaintiff at the closing on August 25, 1987. Plaintiff was advised orally and in the cover letter of August 26, 1987, that the deadline for rescission was midnight Friday, August 28, 1987. Had proper delivery of all the mandated forms been made on the day of the closing, August 25, 1987, then plaintiff's right of rescission would have run only until August 28, 1987, because the transaction date, date of delivery of the TILA disclosure materials, and the delivery of the "Notice of Right to Cancel" would all have occurred on August 25, 1987. However, plaintiff did not take the TILA disclosure statement with her and only received it in the mail on or about August 27, 1987.

Given the overt, undeniable policy of TILA virtually to force-feed information to the credit consumer and, therefore, reading the relevant statutory provisions as a consistent scheme, it is apparent that "delivery" of the TILA disclosure form only occurred when plaintiff received that form in the mail, not on August 25, 1987, when plaintiff and her son signed the form and returned it to the attorney. 15 U.S.C. §1635(a); 12 C.F.R. §226.17(a)(1). On the transaction date, August 25, 1987, plaintiff only signed and returned the original; she did not have a copy she could keep and take with her at that time. Since plaintiff did not receive a copy of the TILA disclosure form she could keep until August 27, 1987, she would have had until August 31, 1987, to rescind.[23]

Plaintiff's acknowledgment of receipt of the TILA disclosure statement does not mean that delivery to her of the disclosure statement was effectuated at the date of closing. Acknowledgment of receipt of the TILA disclosure statement creates only a rebuttable presumption of delivery, a presumption which cannot stand in the face of the testimony that plaintiff left the attorney's office without the TILA disclosure form and did not actually receive it in a form she could keep until August 27, 1987. 15 U.S.C. §1635(c); §1641(b), (c).

Furthermore, it is not credible to maintain that plaintiff waived her rescission rights. In order for those rights to have been waived in a legally cognizable fashion, it would have required a more prescient and deliberate process of renunciation than can possibly be recreated from the actual series of events. 12 C.F.R. §226.15(e).

Thus, the oral representations of the attorney and his cover letter of August 26, 1987, advising plaintiff of an August 28, 1987, rescission deadline were erroneous and misled plaintiff regarding the duration of the actual rescission period.[24] Plaintiff was also misinformed in regard to other material aspects of her rights in the transaction under the TILA scheme. The attorney testified he had indicated to plaintiff that, if she were to attempt to rescind the transaction, the lender would have to be notified in writing by midnight, Friday, August 28, 1987. However, the regulations do not require that the lender receive the letter of rescission by midnight of the final day of the rescission period. Instead, the regulations establish that "notice [of rescission] is considered given when mailed, when filed for telegraphic transmission or, if sent by other means, when delivered to the creditor's designated place of business." 12 C.F.R. §226.23(a)(2). To make even more tediously explicit what is already sufficiently plain, the Federal Reserve Board's Official Staff Interpretation of these regulations explains that "the consumer must place the rescission notice in the mail . . . within that period to exercise the right." Official Staff Interpretations, 12 C.F.R. §226

---

23. Sunday, August 30, 1987, would not have counted as a day for measuring the rescission period. 12 C.F.R. §226.2(a)(6).

24. This court wants to take care to note that there is absolutely nothing in the record which indicates or even suggests that any of the misleading statements made to plaintiff were the result of an intent to mislead or confuse. On the contrary, it is clear to this court that Mr. Houff attempted to discharge conscientiously his responsibilities as closing attorney and this court is convinced that the defects in the transaction were solely the result of inadvertence.

Supp. I at 285 (1988).[25] Thus, plaintiff was materially misled not only about the actual termination date of the rescission period, but also about what would have had to have taken place within that period in order for the rescission to be efficacious. The effect of the statements made to plaintiff was that a letter of rescission would have had to have been received by the lender before midnight of the third day of the rescission period, but the rescinding borrower actually need only postmark the rescission letter by that time.

The oral explanation given to plaintiff of what must occur by midnight of the final day of the rescission period (actual receipt of rescission letter by the lender) and the regulation's requirement (posting the rescission letter) substantially differ. The "right" suggested by the oral representations is a toothless creature compared to the rather more robust right contemplated by the regulations. As the regulations describe the right to rescind, one has three full days to reflect upon the transaction and to decide whether to rescind. The ostensible chronology outlined orally to plaintiff hardly would give the would-be rescinder three days. Since, under that interpretation, actual receipt by mail is required by midnight of the final day, a consumer cognizant of the inevitable vagaries of postal service would surely feel compelled to act as if he had only one or two days to rescind.[26] The point is that the conflicting oral description of the legal requirements of rescission could lead a borrower to believe that his rescission rights were more severely constricted than they actually are and are a serious, material misrepresentation.

---

25. The Supreme Court has held that "a high degree of deference" is due these "administrative" interpretations of TILA provisions. Ford Motor Credit Co. v. Milhollin, 444 U.S. 555, 557, 100 S. Ct. 790, 792, 63 L. Ed. 2d 22 (1980).

26. There are three pertinent responses to those who would argue that a credit consumer could easily avoid the constrictive effects of the chronology represented orally to plaintiff by "stretching" the rescission period through the use of a faster medium of written communication. First, the oral interpretation fails to state accurately the law with regard to rescission by telegraph which requires only that the message be filed by the end of the rescission period. 12 C.F.R. §226.23(a)(2). Second, while a rescinding consumer certainly has the option to employ media other than the mail, it would be disingenuous in the extreme virtually to force them to use such media in order to secure the benefit of the statutorily created rescission period. After all, rescission by mail is an option clearly contemplated by the regulations. To require a borrower to choose a more expensive medium of communication in order to have use of a rescission period which is not truncated would be to place a burden on the borrower clearly not envisioned by the regulatory scheme. Finally, to amputate a portion of the rescission period through that sort of misreading of the regulations runs directly counter to the basic rationale for a rescission, "to give the debtor an opportunity to reflect in the quiet of his home" without undue pressure. Rudisell v. Fifth Third Bank, 622 F.2d 243, 249 n.9 (6th Cir. 1980); Curry v. Fidelity Consumer Discount Co., 656 F. Supp. 1129, 1131 (E.D. Pa. 1987).

Plaintiff was also misinformed regarding the effects of a rescission. The pertinent regulation states that "when a consumer rescinds a transaction, the security interest giving rise to the right of rescission becomes void and the consumer shall not be liable for any amount, including any finance charge." 12 C.F.R. §226.23(d)(1). The "notice of right to cancel" also informed plaintiff that

> You have a legal right under federal law to cancel this transaction, without cost . . . and we must return to you any money or property you have given to us or to anyone else in connection with this transaction.

Yet the cover letter of August 26, 1987, told plaintiff that even if she rescinded in a timely manner, the rescission would "not mean that you are relieved of all fees or expenses associated with the transaction as it has advanced to this point." It is unnecessary for the court to investigate thoroughly the subtle and, in this setting, academic, question of whether a credit consumer could still be potentially liable for some expenses incurred outside of the credit transaction which nevertheless were incurred because of that credit transaction. See Official Staff Interpretations, 12 C.F.R. §226.26(d)(1). It is evident that the quoted statement is, at best, misleading and effectively contradictory to the pertinent federal regulations, for plaintiff clearly was not liable for expenses incurred within the context of the credit transaction.

IV. CONSEQUENCES OF THE DISCLOSURE DEFECTS

Lenders are required to "clearly and conspicuously disclose . . . to any obligor in a transaction subject to this section the rights of the obligor under this section." 15 U.S.C. §1635(a). If such a clear and conspicuous disclosure is not made, then the rescission period can extend up to three years after the transaction. 15 U.S.C. §1635(f). Since this court finds that plaintiff was misinformed about the contours of her rights under TILA in several material aspects, the "clear and conspicuous" standard of disclosure was not met and this transaction was subject to the three-year rescission period.

One additional question regarding the potential consequences of materially insufficient disclosures must be addressed. Defendants allege that there is no evidence that plaintiff was actually misled or confused by the information disclosed to her. While the record presently before the court does not contain sufficient data for a clear resolution of the defendants' allegation, this allegation, even if true, would be legally irrelevant. The legal inquiry about the quality of disclosure is not directed at whether the credit consumer was actually confused or misled. Nor does it matter whether the consumer would have rescinded the transaction had a "clear and conspicuous" disclosure taken place. The court must engage only in an objective inquiry into the violation of specific provisions of TILA requirements. Powers v. Sims and Levin, 542 F.2d 1216, 1219 (4th Cir. 1976).

There is no place here for an appeal to a subjective standard of what a given consumer knew, actually found confusing, or even would have done had the disclosure been adequate. The imputed conclusions of counterfactual propositions is a wholly inapposite inquiry in this matter.

Furthermore, violations of TILA cannot be explained away as merely "technical" and, thus, *de minimis.* Mars v. Spartanburg Chrysler Plymouth, 713 F.2d 65 (4th Cir. 1983); Huff v. Stuart-Gwinn Furniture Co., 713 F.2d 67 (4th Cir. 1983). In *Mars*, the Fourth Circuit interpreted TILA to require a standard which was both strict and objective. The Fourth Circuit concluded that

> We disagree with the district court's analysis that a technical violation of the Act without actual harm imposes no liability. . . . To insure that the consumer is protected, as Congress envisioned, requires that the provisions of the Act and the regulations implementing it be absolutely complied with and strictly enforced.

Mars, 713 F.2d at 67. Therefore, this court need only look to see if there was a violation of the specific disclosure requirements. It is evident to this court that there was such a violation.

V.   CONCLUSION

The conversion of the three-day rescission period into the three-year period for this plaintiff was the result of a sequence of events. Failure to deliver the TILA disclosure statement on August 25, 1987, standing alone, did not convert the rescission period from three days to three years. If delivery of the forms by mail had taken place without the misleading statements of the cover letter or the oral gloss which was provided in addition to that cover letter, then the rescission period would have expired on August 31, 1987. However, in his role as agent for the lender, the attorney conveyed information which contradicted both the statutory and regulatory provisions and the disclosure forms which he transmitted to plaintiff. Since plaintiff was not provided with a clear and conspicuous disclosure of her rights under TILA, the three-year rescission period was operative and plaintiff's rescission of June 21, 1988, was both timely and effective. Plaintiff's motion for declaratory judgment is granted.

An appropriate Order shall this day issue.

b. The Rescission Note

Contents. The rescission notice must be on a separate document and, according to Reg. Z §226.23(b), shall state the following clearly and conspicuously:[27]

> (1) the retention or acquisition of a security interest in the consumer's principal dwelling;
> (2) the consumer's right to cancel;
> (3) how to exercise that right, with a form for that purpose, designating the address of the creditor's place of business;
> (4) the effects of rescission, as described in Reg. Z §226.23(d) (see below); and
> (5) the date the rescission period expires.

What could go wrong here? Well, the Federal Reserve Board has promulgated model forms for the rescission notice, and using such a form is the better part of wisdom. No lender using such a form can be liable for content violations of the statute. But the chief mistake made by creditors is in filling out the form.

PROBLEM 134

Say that the date of consummation of the loan agreement is Monday, September 15. The consumer was also given a proper TIL statement and notice describing the right to rescind on that date. On midnight of what day will the consumer's right to rescind expire?

The notice must contain a reprint of Reg. Z §226.23(d), which you should read carefully. We will explore its rather complicated meaning in the materials that follow.

PROBLEM 135

Mr. and Mrs. Suburb went to Octopus National Bank to borrow money in a closed-end transaction, and the bank took a second mortgage on their home. At the loan closing the bank official gave them two copies of a correctly completed TIL rescission notice and

---

27. If the notice were filled out illegibly, this "clear and conspicuous" requirement would be violated.

one copy of an accurate TIL statement. A week later the Suburbs decided they wanted to rescind and they are now in your office. Is it too late? See Reg. Z §§226.23(b) and 226.17(d); Davison v. Bank One Home Loan Serv., 2003 WL 124542 (D. Kan. 2003).

c. Material Disclosures

The three-day rescission period is also delayed until three days after all *material* disclosures have been given to the consumer. What does this mean? Reg. Z §226.23(a) n.48, dealing with closed-end transactions, explains:

> 48. The term "material disclosures" means the required disclosures of the annual percentage rate, the finance charge, the amount financed, the total of payments, and the payment schedule.

Hence, if the TIL statement is wrong on any of these required disclosures, the consumer would have three years in which to cancel. Since it is all too easy to make a TIL disclosure error of this sort, these disclosures must be carefully checked for accuracy lest they lead to an extension of the normal three-day rescission period.

4. Waiver

The consumer's right to rescind can be waived whenever the consumer determines that the credit is necessary to meet a "bona fide personal financial emergency." Reg. Z §226.23(e). To do so, the consumer must give the creditor a dated written statement that describes the emergency, specifically modifies or waives the right to rescind, and is signed by all consumers entitled to rescind. The Regulation forbids the use of printed waiver forms.

RODASH v. AIB MORTGAGE CO.
United States Court of Appeals, Eleventh Circuit, 1994
16 F.3d 1142

JOHNSON, Senior Circuit Judge:
The appellant, Martha Rodash, appeals the district court's denial of her motion for summary judgment regarding violations of the federal Truth in

Lending Act ("TILA") and its grant of the appellees' cross-motion for summary judgment. Because we conclude that TILA was violated, we hold that the district court's orders were erroneous as a matter of law. We therefore reverse the district court.

I. STATEMENT OF THE CASE

A. FACTUAL BACKGROUND

The material facts in this case are not disputed. On January 18, 1991, Rodash obtained a home equity mortgage on her principal residence with appellee AIB Mortgage Company ("AIB") to pay for medical treatment for her multiple sclerosis. Rodash executed (1) a Promissory Note in favor of AIB evidencing an obligation to repay $102,000 and (2) a mortgage securing repayment of the Note to AIB. Later that day, AIB assigned its interest to appellee Empire of America Realty Credit Corporation ("Empire"). At the loan closing, the appellees gave Rodash the following four documents: (1) a federal Truth-in-Lending Disclosure Statement, (2) a Mortgage Settlement Statement, (3) a Notice of Right to Cancel, which stated that Rodash had three days to rescind the mortgage, and (4) an Acknowledgment of Receipt of Notice of Right to Cancel and Election Not to Cancel. The Settlement Statement reflected itemized charges of $22 for Federal Express delivery, $204 for intangible Florida taxes, and $6 for assignment of the mortgage. These charges were itemized under the "amount financed" in the transaction. Rodash signed the Election Not to Cancel on January 18, 1991, and the loan proceeds were distributed sometime after January 23, 1991. Rodash stopped making her mortgage payments as of July 1, 1991, and on December 26, 1991, Rodash's counsel wrote the appellees, stating she was rescinding the transaction under TILA and seeking cancellation of the security interest therein. Empire accelerated the balance due under the Note and filed a foreclosure action in state court.

B. PROCEDURAL HISTORY

On February 13, 1992, Rodash filed an action against the appellees under TILA, 15 U.S.C.A. §§1601-1641 (West 1982 & Supp. 1993), and the Act's accompanying regulation, Regulation Z, 12 C.F.R. §226 (1993), seeking rescission of the transaction and statutory penalties. In April 1992, the district court denied the appellees' motions to dismiss the case or, in the alternative, for a stay pending the outcome of the state court foreclosure action. That same April, Rodash moved for summary judgment. The appellees jointly cross-motioned for summary judgment in June 1992. In

December 1992, the district court entered an order of final summary judgment in favor of the appellees and against Rodash, holding that TILA had not been violated and that, as a matter of law, Rodash was not entitled to relief thereunder. . . .

II. ANALYSIS

According to Rodash, the district court erred by finding that (1) the appellees provided clear and conspicuous disclosure of her right to rescind the transaction and (2) the appellees did not understate the finance charge. After setting out general principles, we address each of these contentions in turn.

A. GENERAL PRINCIPLES

Congress designed TILA to promote the informed use and awareness of the cost of credit by consumers. Shroder v. Suburban Coastal Corp., 729 F.2d 1371, 1380 (11th Cir. 1984). The Act ensures a meaningful disclosure of credit terms to enable consumers to compare readily the various credit terms available in the marketplace. Id. Congress intended the statute to create a system of private attorneys general to aid its enforcement; thus, to further its remedial purpose, we liberally construe its language in favor of the consumer. McGowan v. King, Inc., 569 F.2d 845, 848 (5th Cir. 1978). Accord Smith v. Fidelity Consumer Discount Co., 898 F.2d 896, 898 (3rd Cir. 1990). Additionally, creditors must strictly comply with TILA's requirements. *Shroder,* 729 F.2d at 1380 (The creditor's disclosures must be in "the proper technical form and in the proper locations on the contract, as mandated by the requirements of TILA and Regulation Z. Liability will flow from even minute deviations from requirements."). Moreover, the consumer may sue for enforcement even if she is not actually deceived or harmed. Zamarippa v. Cy's Car Sales, 674 F.2d 877, 879 (11th Cir. 1982) ("An objective standard is used to determine violations of the TILA, based on the representations contained in the relevant disclosure documents; it is unnecessary to inquire as to the subjective deception or misunderstanding of particular consumers.").

B. RODASH'S RESCISSION OF THE TRANSACTION

On the closing date of January 18, 1991, the appellees provided Rodash the Notice of the Right to Cancel. On a separate, single sheet of paper, the appellees provided an acknowledgment that the Notice of Right to Cancel was received and provided an Election Not to Cancel, a pre-printed waiver of that right.[28] Beneath the waiver provision, Rodash signed the sole signature line on the paper. The appellees maintain that by signing this document Rodash waived her right to rescind the contract. Rodash, who rescinded the agreement in December 1991, contends that Empire's provision of the Election Not to Cancel on January 18 violated TILA because she had an unqualified right to rescind the transaction within three business days. Rodash also contends that the appellees violated TILA because they did not clearly disclose her right to rescind as required by the Act.

As part of TILA, Congress provided the consumer with the right to rescind a credit transaction by notifying the creditor within set time limits of the consumer's intent to rescind. *Williams,* 968 F.2d at 1139. See 12 C.F.R. §226.23(a) (restating consumer's right of rescission). TILA specifically permits a consumer borrower to rescind a loan transaction that results in the creditor taking a security interest in the consumer's principal dwelling. In re Porter, 961 F.2d 1066, 1073 (3d Cir. 1992); see 15 U.S.C.A. §1635(a). The consumer has an absolute right to rescind the agreement for three business days following the closing of the transaction. 15 U.S.C.A. §1635(a); 12 C. F. R. §226.23(a)(3). In addition, the consumer's ability to rescind an agreement may be extended for up to three years if the creditor fails to make all material disclosures to the borrower, including disclosure of the right to rescind. 12 C.F.R. §226.23(a)(3).

The purpose of the three-day waiting period is "to give the consumer the opportunity to reconsider any transaction which would have the serious consequence of encumbering the title to his [or her] home." S. Rep. No. 368, 96th Cong., 2d Sess. 28 (1980), *reprinted in* 1980 U.S.C.C.A.N. 236, 264. Thus, the sole instance in which the statute and its implementing regulations allow the consumer to waive her right to rescind within three days is where the consumer believes that a bona fide emergency necessitates an immediate extension of credit, in which case the consumer must sign a dated, handwritten statement that describes the emergency. 12 C.F.R. §226.23(e). Printed forms may not be used for this purpose. Id. Here, the appellees attempted to modify the rescission by having Rodash sign a pre-printed waiver of her right to rescind. This is prohibited. See id. Hence, we

---

28. The sheet of paper read in its entirety:

The undersigned hereby acknowledges and affirms that on or before <u>January 18, 1991</u>, each of us received two copies of the annexed "Notice of Right to Cancel." Furthermore, the undersigned hereby acknowledges and affirms that each of us have [sic] elected not to cancel the transaction to which the annexed Notice relates. /s/ <u>Martha Rodash.</u>

The underlined portions were handwritten, while the remainder of the page was typewritten boilerplate.

find the putative waiver to be invalid. Accordingly, our inquiry is whether the appellees' Notice of Right to Cancel is deficient, as Rodash's attempt to rescind came after the three-day cancellation period following the transaction but before three years had passed.

Under the Act, the creditor must "clearly and conspicuously disclose" the consumer's right to rescind the transaction. 15 U.S.C.A. §1635(a); see 12 C.F.R. §226.23(b)(2) ("Notice [of right to rescind] shall be on a separate document that identifies the transaction and shall clearly and conspicuously disclose . . . the consumer's right to rescind the transaction."). To determine whether the notice given Rodash was confusing or misleading, this Court must scrutinize the circumstances of the transaction. See *In re Porter*, 961 F.2d at 1076 (determination of clear and conspicuous notice of rescission rights under TILA is intensely fact-based). As noted supra, the creditor's subjective intent is irrelevant to this determination; rather, notice of the right to rescind must be objectively conspicuous and apparent. *Zamarippa*, 674 F.2d at 879. The issue, then, is whether the appellees' provision of the Election Not to Rescind on January 18, 1991 prevented clear and conspicuous notice of Rodash's right to rescind within three days. We hold that it did. It is without question that this boilerplate provision precluded clear and conspicuous disclosure to Rodash that she had the right to rescind the agreement within three days of entering the mortgage purchase. Rather, it is far more likely that the primary effect of the appellees' providing Rodash the Election Not to Cancel at the closing was to confuse Rodash about her right.

Several considerations compel this conclusion. First, the appellees' proffering of the Election Not to Cancel during the transaction would confuse any reasonable borrower because it implies, incorrectly, that waiver is generally possible within the three-day cooling off period. Indeed, the presentation of the waiver form on the day of the transaction contradicted the very purpose of the cooling off period: to give the consumer time to consider the terms of her financial commitments. Second, by having Rodash sign a certificate of non-rescission on the date of the transaction, the appellees suggested that she had foreclosed her right of rescission. Thus, if Rodash had changed her mind the next day and wished to rescind the transaction, it would have been reasonable for her not to have exercised that right as a direct result of the improper furnishing of the Election Not to Cancel. Third, the appellees' practice of placing the acknowledgment and the waiver on the same page—indeed, in the same boilerplate paragraph— is confusing because an objective borrower may not understand what she is signing. Finally, we find that the appellees' practice of handing the consumer a waiver form the same day as the mortgage and Note is a misleading one, as the consumer, here Rodash, could reasonably think that she had to sign that form—as she must sign other forms—to consummate the mortgage transaction.[29]

Considered together, the Notice of Right to Cancel and the Election Not to Cancel do not constitute a "clear and conspicuous" disclosure of the three-day right to rescission under TILA. The Notice announces that there are three business days to rescind, but it is accompanied by the Election announcing in boilerplate that rescission has been declined at the outset such that no rescission period exists. These contradictory documents preclude the possibility of "clear" disclosure. Accordingly, the appellee violated TILA, and the district court erred as a matter of law by denying Rodash's summary judgment motion and granting the appellees' motion. On this ground alone, we reverse the district court. Nonetheless, in part III.C, we also reverse the district court on the ground that the appellees violated TILA by understating the finance charge.

C.   THE APPELLEES' NONDISCLOSURE OF ALL FINANCE FEES

Rodash contends that the appellees did not make all required material disclosures because they included the Federal Express charge of $22 and the intangible state tax of $204 in the "amount financed" instead of the "finance charge." Rodash asserts that AIB understated the finance charge by omitting these two charges and thus violated the Act. We agree.

TILA requires the lender to disclose to the borrower, among other things, the "amount financed" and the "finance charge." 15 U.S.C.A. §1638. In transactions such as this one, the "amount financed" and the "finance charge" are mutually exclusive and together constitute the "total of payments." §1638(a)(5). The Act defines "finance charge" as "the sum of all charges, payable directly or indirectly by the person to whom the credit is extended, and imposed directly or indirectly by the creditor as an incident to the extension of credit." Id. §1605(a). The Act then illustrates examples

---

29. The appellees' two main contentions are that (1) the Election Not to Cancel was on a separate piece of paper than the Notice of Right to Cancel, and (2) early provision of an election not to rescind is a reasonable, convenient practice for creditors to disburse the funds quickly to the borrower after expiration of the three-day period. These arguments are specious and without merit. First, the regulation states that the notice of the right to cancel "shall be on a separate document that identifies the transaction and shall clearly and conspicuously disclose the consumer's right to rescind." 12 C.F.R. §226.23(b)(3). The appellees' contradictory presentment of the waiver form immediately after its presentment of the right to rescind form completely obviates clear and conspicuous disclosure. Second, the early provision serves no purpose. It does not allow the creditor to do anything that the creditor could not have done otherwise, as the Election Not to Cancel had no legal effect and was not binding on the consumer.

of finance charges. Id. TILA and Regulation Z also provide examples of exclusions from the finance charge. See 15 U.S.C.A. §1605(d) & (e); 12 C.F.R. §§226.4(c)(7) & (e). Moreover, the definition of "finance charge" includes charges imposed on the consumer by someone other than the creditor for services required by the creditor even if the creditor does not retain the charges. See Johnson v. Fleet Finance, 4 F.3d 946, 949 (11th Cir. 1993) (per curiam) (non-required broker's fees are not included in finance charge); First Acadiana Bank v. Federal Deposit Ins. Corp., 833 F.2d 548, 550-51 (5th Cir. 1987) (required lawyer's fees should be included in finance charge). Congress strictly requires creditors to disclose all finance charges to prohibit creditors from circumventing TILA's objectives and burying the cost of credit in the price of goods sold. Mourning v. Family Publications Serv., 411 U.S. 356, 366, 93 S. Ct. 1652, 1658, 36 L. Ed. 2d 318 (1973).

1. $22 Federal Express Charge

AIB incurred $22 in Federal Express charges during the transaction, treating this cost within the amount financed rather than within the finance charge. AIB incurred this charge to pay off Rodash's then-existing mortgage held by another creditor named Centrust and to return the original loan documents to Empire. Only those charges payable by the consumer "directly or indirectly by the creditor as an incident to . . . the extension of credit" fall within the general definition of finance charge. 15 U.S.C.A. §1605(a); see also 12 C.F.R. §226.4(a). We hold that, under the Act's definition, the Federal Express fee is undoubtedly part of the finance charge. "Finance charges" include "service, transaction, activity, and carrying charges." 12 C.F.R. §226.4(b)(2). Here, the complete transaction included the appellees' providing a home equity loan. Part-and-parcel of the fulfillment of the transaction was AIB's paying off the consumer's previous mortgage by delivery of a check to Centrust. Thus, the Federal Express fee can be viewed as a "transaction charge"—without mailing the check to Centrust, the home equity transaction would not have been consummated.

In addition, the finance charge also includes "charges imposed on a creditor by another person for purchasing or accepting a consumer's obligation." 12 C.F.R. §226.4(b)(6). We view the Federal Express fee as just such a charge. The consumer was obligated to pay Centrust for an existing loan. The appellees accepted the consumer's obligation. In accepting the payment from the appellees, Centrust imposed the burden—in other words, the cost—of transporting the check to AIB, who had the option of selecting the method of transportation. Rodash then paid this cost to the appellees incident to receiving credit. Accordingly, we hold that the Federal Express fee constituted a finance charge that was improperly included in the amount financed because the Federal Express charge was "imposed directly or indirectly by the creditor as an incident to the extension of credit."[30]

Our conclusion is buttressed by public policy. The purpose of TILA is to make various credit terms available to consumers, so they can more easily compare such terms between banks and other financial institutions. Consequently, financial institutions may not bury any costs of credit as such indirection would hinder consumers in comparing credit terms and making the best informed decision on the use of credit. Cf. *Mourning,* 411 U.S. at 377, 93 S. Ct. at 1664 ("Some may claim that it is a relatively easy matter to calculate the total payments to which petitioner was committed by her contract with respondent; but at the time of sale, such computations are often not encouraged . . . or performed."). Consequently, the appellees violated TILA as a matter of law by failing to disclose as part of the finance charge the charge imposed upon Rodash for payment of the Federal Express delivery.

2. *Intangible Tax*

Rodash paid the appellees a $204 Florida intangible tax on the Note securing the loan. AIB included this tax in the amount financed rather than the finance charge. Because the intangible tax is a charge payable by the consumer "directly or indirectly . . . as an incident to the extension of credit," it is a finance charge, unless it falls within an exclusion. Given that state intangible taxes are not specifically excluded, the only potentially relevant exclusions are as follows:

(1) "A tax imposed by a state . . . on the credit transaction that is payable by the consumer (even if the tax is collected by the creditor)" when the charge is imposed on the consumer by someone other than the creditor. F.R.B. Commentary on 12 C.F.R. §226.4(a), Comment 3, reprinted in 12 C.F.R. pt. 226, Supp. I;

(2) "charges for filing or recording security agreements, mortgages, . . . and similar documents." F.R.B. Commentary on 12 C.F.R. §226.4(e), Comment 12, reprinted in 12 C.F.R. Pt. 226, Supp. I; and

(3) "taxes and fees prescribed by law that actually are or will be paid to public officials for . . . perfecting . . . a security interest." 12 C.F.R. §226.4(e)(1).

We hold that the Florida tax should have been included in the finance charge because it was a charge paid by the consumer directly for the extension of credit and no exclusion applies. First, the plain language of

---

30. The appellees maintain that a Federal Express charge is analogous to a courier fee and that neither charge is included in the finance charge. We need not address this unsupported assertion, noting only that the appellees' own action in this case undercuts this claim as they in fact treated a courier fee as part of the finance charge.

TILA evinces no explicit exclusion of an intangible tax from the finance charge. Second, the intangible tax does not fall under the first listed exclusion because it is imposed on the creditor—not the consumer—for holding the Note, an intangible asset. See Fla. Stat. Ann. §199.135(1) (West 1989) (nonrecurring tax is imposed on person recording note); First Nat'l Bank v. Department of Revenue, 364 So. 2d 38, 39 (Fla. Dist. Ct. App. 1978) (noting that intangible property tax is assessed against creditor), *appeal dismissed*, 368 So. 2d 1366 (Fla. 1979) (Table, No. 55880). Third, contrary to the appellees' contention, the intangible tax does not fall under the second exclusion because it is not a recording fee; rather, recording fees are imposed under a wholly different statute. See Fla. Stat. Ann. §28.24 (West 1988) (setting charge for recording fees). Finally, the purpose of the tax is most likely revenue enhancement, not perfection of a security interest, which concerns the proper recordation of the instrument, and therefore the third exclusion is equally inapplicable. Thus, the Florida intangible tax was improperly excluded from the TILA finance charge, and Rodash had the legal right to rescind the transaction in December 1991.[31]

III. CONCLUSION

The Truth in Lending Act, now a quarter of a century old, manifested a change in federal policy from a philosophy of "Let the buyer beware" to one of "Let the seller disclose." *Mourning,* 411 U.S. at 377, 93 S. Ct. at 1664. The burdens imposed on creditors are minimal, especially when compared to the harms that are avoided. The appellees' actions in this case disregarded that policy. Consequently, the district court erred as a matter of law in holding that TILA had not been violated and granting the appellees' cross-motion for summary judgment. The court also erred as a matter of law in denying Rodash's motion for summary judgment. The court's orders must be, and are, therefore, REVERSED, and the case is REMANDED for a disposition consistent with this decision. On remand, we instruct the district court to consider the issue of statutory damages.

5. Rescission Tactics

In theory, the rescission procedure is simple. Read Reg. Z §226.23(d), which makes it all appear mechanical. The consumer gives the notice of

---

31. We do not discuss Rodash's argument that TILA was violated by an alleged failure of the appellees to respond to Rodash's December 26, 1991 letters of rescission.

rescission; the creditor has 20 days to return the consumer's money and cancel the mortgage; the consumer then tenders back the money or property received; the creditor takes it within 20 days of this tender or forfeits the right to ever receive it. The difficulty is that no one behaves like this. Typically, the consumer sends the notice of rescission and the creditor ignores it. Now what? The courts have said that the creditor forfeits nothing because the consumer has not triggered the second 20-day period by tendering back the money or the property. The consumer's only remedy is to go to court and get a decision that he or she is entitled to cancel. The following case illustrates the difficulty. It was decided under the wording of the statute prior to the Truth in Lending Simplification Act in 1980, but the only relevant change made by Simplification was to raise the time period for creditor response from 10 days to 20 days. With that difference, this case is still good law.

GERASTA v. HIBERNIA NATIONAL BANK
United States Court of Appeals, Fifth Circuit, 1978
575 F.2d 580

JAMES C. HILL, Circuit Judge.

The case on appeal raises the question of the appropriate remedy for a creditor's failure to comply with 15 U.S.C. §1635 [§125], the rescission provision of the Truth in Lending Act. The district court held that the defendant-creditor in the case on appeal forfeited its rights to recover the property it had delivered to the obligor because the creditor did not perform those duties prescribed in §1635(b). We reverse this holding.

The plaintiffs-appellees, Joseph E. Gerasta and Josefina E. Gerasta, received a home improvement loan from the defendant-appellant, Hibernia National Bank. The loan was secured by a second mortgage on the Gerastas' property. Approximately six months after receiving the loan, the Gerastas discovered that the Bank had not made all the material disclosures required by the Act, and they exercised their statutory right to rescind the transaction pursuant to §1635(a). Within ten days after receipt of the notice of rescission, the Bank was statutorily required to return to the Gerastas all money received from them and to take all necessary actions to reflect the termination of the security interest created by the second mortgage in the Gerastas' property. 15 U.S.C. §1635(b). If the Bank had performed these duties within ten days, the Gerastas then would have been required to tender the loan proceeds to the Bank. The Bank, however, took no action after receipt of the Gerastas' rescission notice. Therefore, the Gerastas did not tender the loan proceeds to the Bank, and they filed this suit.

The district court held that the loan to the Gerastas fell within the ambit of the Truth in Lending Act and that the Bank had not made all the statutorily prescribed material disclosures, thereby entitling the Gerastas to rescind the loan transaction pursuant to §1635. After a careful review of the record, we affirm these holdings. See Powers v. Sims and Levin, 542 F.2d 1216, 1219 (4th Cir. 1976); Simmons v. American Budget Plan, Inc., 386 F. Supp. 194, 200 (E.D. La. 1974). We must reverse and remand, however, on the issue of damages. In accordance with §1635, the district court entered a judgment recognizing the Gerastas' rescission of the loan agreement and recognizing their right to a complete refund of the money they had already paid to the Bank, plus interest. The district court also entered judgment for the Gerastas for costs and a reasonable attorney's fee and for the cancellation of any inscription in the public records of the second mortgage on the Gerastas' property. The district court also held, however, that the Gerastas are entitled to retain the loan proceeds without any obligation to the Bank, because the Bank did not perform those duties imposed by §1635.

This court has recognized that the Truth in Lending Act provides "detailed remedial machinery" to redress violations of the Act. Sosa v. Fite, 498 F.2d 114, 117 (5th Cir. 1974). Therefore, courts should apply those remedies provided in the Act. Burgess v. Charlottesville Savings and Loan Association, 477 F.2d 40, 45 (4th Cir. 1973); Jordan v. Montgomery Ward & Co., 442 F.2d 78, 81, 82 (8th Cir.), cert. denied, 404 U.S. 870, 92 S. Ct. 78, 30 L. Ed. 2d 114 (1971). Section 1635 does not expressly provide a remedy for the situation in which the creditor fails to take any action upon receipt of a rescission notice and the consumer does not tender the creditor's property. Section 1640(a) [130], however, provides the remedy for a creditor's failure to comply with "any requirement" imposed by certain provisions of the Act, including §1635.

Section 1635 and §1640 are not mutually exclusive remedies; a consumer may be entitled to both rescission pursuant to §1635 and damages pursuant to §1640. See Mourning v. Family Publications Service, Inc., 411 U.S. 356, 376, 93 S. Ct. 1652, 36 L. Ed. 2d 318 (1973); Sellers v. Wollman, 510 F.2d 119, 123 (5th Cir. 1975). That Congress intended the §1640 liability provision to apply to creditors' violations of §1635 is confirmed by the 1974 amendment of §1640. Before amendment, §1640(a) provided that it applied only when a creditor failed "to disclose to any person any information required under this part to be disclosed to that person. . . ." As stated, §1640 now expressly applies whenever a creditor fails to comply with "any requirement" imposed by certain provisions of the Act, including §1635. Although the amended version of §1640 did not become effective until after the present cause of action arose, the amended version of §1640 is applicable to the case on appeal. Mirabel v. General Motors Acceptance Corp., 537 F.2d 871, 875-76 (7th Cir. 1976). See also Gore v. Turner, 563 F.2d 159, 163 (5th Cir. 1977).

Section 1640 does not provide for forfeiture of the creditor's property. It provides in relevant part for an award of actual damages, a reasonable attorney's fee, and twice the amount of any finance charge in an amount up to $1,000 and not less than $100. Application of §1640 thus serves the congressional purpose of restoring the parties to the status quo ante and is consistent with the Act's remedial character. Murphy v. Household Finance Corp., 560 F.2d 206, 208-11 (6th Cir. 1977); Binnick v. Avco Financial Services of Nebraska, Inc., 435 F. Supp. 359, 364-66 (D. Neb. 1977); Porter v. Household Finance Corp. of Columbus, 385 F. Supp. 336, 340-43 (S.D. Ohio 1974). If, after a hearing, the court determines that the consumer is entitled to rescind, the consumer will be recompensed for any additional damages and costs he has incurred as a result of the litigation.

The statement of law contained in this opinion may be usefully illustrated by its application to the facts involved in the case on appeal. The Gerastas determined that the defendant Bank had violated the disclosure provisions of the Act. Therefore, the Gerastas notified the Bank of their intention to rescind the loan transaction pursuant to §1635. The Bank did not perform its statutorily prescribed duties within ten days, allegedly because the Gerastas' rescission was equivocal and because the Bank was uncertain whether the transaction came within the ambit of the disclosure and rescission provisions of the Truth in Lending Act. The Bank's noncompliance exposed the Bank to the possibility of increased liability pursuant to §1640(a).

It has now been judicially determined that the Gerastas were entitled to rescind their transaction with the Bank and that the Gerastas' notice of rescission was valid. Therefore, the Bank now must return to the Gerastas any money or property that it has received from them in connection with this transaction. The Bank also must take any action necessary to reflect the termination of any security interest created in the Gerastas' property by the transaction. Upon the Bank's performance of its duties, the Gerastas must tender the loan proceeds to the Bank. They should be given a reasonable time within which to do so. Unless the Bank fails to take possession within ten days of tender, its interest will not be forfeited.

This court's decision in Sosa v. Fite, 498 F.2d 114 (5th Cir. 1974), does not require a different result. In *Sosa,* as in the case on appeal, the creditors did not perform their statutorily prescribed duties after receiving the consumer's notice of rescission. In *Sosa,* however, the consumer's notice of rescission was accompanied by the consumer's express offer to return the creditor's property. The court in *Sosa* emphasized that the consumer's obligation to restore the creditor to the status quo ante was discharged by the tender. In the case on appeal, on the other hand, the Gerastas stated in their rescission notice that they refused to tender the loan proceeds until the Bank performed its statutorily prescribed duties.

On remand, the district court should award the Gerastas the amount of damages to which they are entitled pursuant to §1640(a). The award should include a reasonable attorney's fee for the services rendered on this appeal because the suit was a "successful action." See Powers v. Sims and Levin, 542 F.2d 1216, 1222 (4th Cir. 1976); Sosa v. Fite, 498 F.2d 114, 122 (5th Cir. 1974); 15 U.S.C. §1640(a)(3). In determining an appropriate fee, the district court should consider the factors stated in Johnson v. Georgia Highway Express, Inc., 488 F.2d 714 (5th Cir. 1974). McGowan v. King, Inc., 569 F.2d 845 (5th Cir. 1978). The district court judgment also should make clear that the Bank is entitled to a return of the loan proceeds, though the debt is no longer secured by a second mortgage on the Gerastas' property and though the Bank's duties are in no way conditional upon the Gerastas' tender of the loan proceeds. . . .

Affirmed in part, and reversed and remanded in part.

ALVIN B. RUBIN, Circuit Judge, concurring.

The opinion is so thorough that I concur completely. I add simply what may be a personal gloss: the forfeiture provision contained in Section 1635 (b) is still a part of the statute; it should be enforced as written in an appropriate case; but, in the absence of the tender by the obligor that the Section specifically requires, it is not applicable.

In the leading case of Sosa v. Fite, 498 F.2d 114 (5th Cir. 1974), the consumer made the unusual move of tendering back the creditor's property at the same time that the consumer sent the notice of rescission. The court held that this triggered *both* 20-day periods (actually, the periods were each 10 days at the time of the *Sosa* decision), and that if the creditor did not accept the tendered property within that period, the creditor forfeited any right to ever claim it.

PROBLEM 136

Nightflyer Loan Company was astounded when the mail one morning brought a letter of rescission of the second mortgage transaction it had entered into with Mr. and Mrs. Suburb, who contended that NLC had failed to give the Suburbs the correct number of copies of the rescission notice (assume this proves to be true). Enclosed with the letter of rescission was the Suburbs' check for the loan amount, marked "VOID IF NOT CASHED WITHIN 20 DAYS." Worried about this, the president of NLC calls you, the company attorney, and asks what should be done to preserve the company's rights. See Reg. Z §226.23(d)(4). If the Suburbs fail to give a notice of rescission for three years, can they still use their rescission rights as a matter of recoupment when Nightflyer sues them for failure to make the required payments? See TILA §125(i); Beach v. Ocwen Fed. Bank, 523 U.S. 410 (1998).

PROBLEM 137

Original National Bank failed miserably in its attempts to comply with the disclosure requirements of TILA when taking a second mortgage on the home of Mr. and Mrs. Suburb. The Suburbs sent the bank a rescission notice, but did not tender back the money that the bank had loaned to them. Instead, they demanded that the bank first remove the mortgage from their house and return to them the two payments they had given to the bank prior to their valid cancellation. Must the bank do this, or can it admit liability but then subtract the payments from the much greater amount that the Suburbs will owe the bank when they must return the amount it lent them? May a court order that the security interest remain attached to the Suburbs' home until they repay the amount loaned? See American Mortgage Network, Inc. v. Shelton, 486 F.3d 815 (4th Cir. 2007).

PROBLEM 138

Big Department Store sold attorney Portia Moot a new roof and had its workers install it on her home. The store took a security interest in the roof as a fixture, U.C.C. §9-334. This seemed wrong to Portia because she didn't think the roof was a fixture, see U.C.C. §9-334(a), but she signed the contract anyway, and the store filed a financing statement in the real property records.

a. Does this transaction require a TIL rescission notice? See Reg.Z §226.23(a)(1) and the definition of "security interest" in §226.2(a)(25).

b. State law frequently gives a mechanic's lien on realty for work performed thereon (or materials incorporated into the building) in favor of those who did the work. This *statutory lien* arises automatically when the mechanic remains unpaid, and permits the mechanic to foreclose on the realty after going through certain steps. When Big Department Store installed the roof, assume that it made Portia sign a contract to pay for the roof but that it did not take a security interest in the roof, nor did it file anything in the real property records. Is it nonetheless required to give her a TIL rescission notice?

c. If Portia sues and convinces the court that the store had failed to respond to a proper TIL rescission notice *and* that the TIL disclosure statement contained material errors, can she get *double* punitive damages under §130? See Mayfield v. Vanguard Sav. & Loan Assn., 710 F. Supp. 143 (E.D. Pa. 1989).

d. Does she have to tender back the roof? See Reg. Z §226.23(d)(3).

III. THE ULTIMATE PENALTY

Section 112 of the Truth in Lending Act makes it a crime for a creditor willfully and knowingly to violate the statute. By itself this probably doesn't mean much. Federal district attorneys are busy people, and they have more than enough to do without ferreting out TIL criminals.

Toothless as the penalty is for criminal convictions, §112 is nonetheless of some use in civil actions. Why? Remember the case of Bennett v. Hayes, Chapter 2 supra, which we studied when covering deceptive practices? It highlighted the common law rule that those guilty of entering into "illegal" contracts are not only stripped of their right to sue on that contract but deprived of quasi-contractual relief as well. An illegal contract is one that is void because it is against public policy.

Couldn't it be argued that a creditor who is seriously out of compliance with TILA is just this sort of outlaw? Section 112 tells us that Congress thought willful and knowing noncompliance serious enough to be a crime.

PROBLEM 139

In 1969, Octopus National Bank was careful to comply with the then-new requirements of TILA and Regulation Z. As time rolled by and the pro-consumer movement faded, ONB worked less at compliance; after all, no one was suing any more—not federal agencies, not consumers. By 2010 ONB's forms were seriously flawed, but the bank kept using them anyway. In that year the bank made an $80,000 first mortgage loan to Portia Moot, a recent law school graduate. She was astounded when she read through the TIL statement and saw how many disclosure violations it contained. She promptly brought suit under §130 of the Act and added a count under state law contending that the bank was the guilty party in an illegal contract. Thus she asked the court to rule that she was entitled to at least $4,000, costs, and attorney's fees under §130, and to declare that she did not have to repay one penny of the $80,000. Now alert and working at it, the bank's attorney pored over TILA, looking for a defense. He came up with §111(d). How should this come out? See Hernandez v. Kerry Buick, Inc., Consumer Cred. Guide (CCH) ¶98,094 (N.D. Ill. 1977); American Buyers Club v. Grayling, 53 Ill. App. 3d 611, 368 N.E.2d 1057 (1977); and Conrad v. Beneficial Fin. Co., 57 A.D.2d 91, 394 N.Y.S.2d 923 (1977).

PEOPLES TRUST & SAVINGS BANK v. HUMPHREY
Court of Appeals of Indiana, 1983
451 N.E.2d 1104

ROBERTSON, Presiding Judge.

The plaintiff-appellant, Peoples Trust and Savings Bank (Bank) appeals a judgment which denied its complaint to foreclose a mortgage given by the defendants-appellees, Jerry W. and Carolyn L. Humphrey (Humphreys), as security for a realty installment loan. The trial court also granted Humphreys' counterclaim for misrepresentation and awarded them $1,000 in compensatory damages and $40,000 in punitive damages. Additionally, the trial court reformed the loan, thus fixing the interest rate at 8½% annually and deleting a demand clause. . . .

We affirm.

Humphreys approached the Bank in February, 1978, seeking a construction loan for a house. Construction costs were to be $60,000 and Humphreys were seeking a $35,000 loan. They intended to finance the balance with money from the sale of their former home. Humphreys explained to Bennett, the Bank's vice-president whom they had dealt with previously, that the Bank's president, Waldo Hendrickson, had promised them a good deal on their next loan because of their dissatisfaction with charges for a prior loan. Bennett told them that he would discuss the loan with Hendrickson. On February 28, 1978, the Bank made a verbal commitment for a $35,000 loan at an 8½% annual interest repayable over 20 years. No documents were executed at that time.

Humphreys began construction and expended all their funds. On June 8, 1978, they signed a promissory note with the Bank for the balance of their construction funds, a total of $35,482. This was a 4 month note with an annual interest rate of 8½%, an annual percentage rate of 8½% based on a 20 year payoff and a finance charge of $1507.99. The note contained a "demand clause." Humphreys also executed a mortgage to secure the note.

According to Humphreys, no discussion took place when this note was executed nor were they informed that the note was payable on demand. A variable interest rate was not mentioned and no disclosure statements, other than the note itself, were given to Humphreys. Humphreys believed that they had a 20 year loan at 8½% interest.

On October 11, 1978, Humphreys executed a renewal note which contained the same terms as the original note except that it was a 90 day note rather than a 4 month note. Neither interest charges nor the demand clause were discussed. Construction was completed prior to expiration of the 90 day period and on November 28, 1978, Humphreys returned to the Bank where they executed a third note which was titled a "Realty Installment Note."

The Realty Installment Note provided for repayment by 240 monthly payments of $308.00 each, which were due on the fifth of each month beginning in January, 1979. The note provided for an interest charge of 8½% annually. The note also contained a variable interest rate clause, which provided that "the rate of interest per annum may be 4% more than the bank pays on any time deposit," and a demand clause. The Humphreys were also given a Truth In Lending disclosure statement to sign which reflected the note's terms except the demand clause.

At trial, Humphreys explained that when they arrived at the Bank to sign the third note, Bennett was busy and instead, they dealt with Mr. Bender. All the documents had been completed except for their signatures. They did not read the documents in their entirety, but they did scan them to verify the number and amount of monthly payments and the amount of the loan. Upon seeing the variable interest provision, Humphreys asked Bender about it and were told that the Bank had raised rates once before, but probably would not do so again and that they should not worry about it. Humphreys signed the note and disclosure statement. Thereafter, they began making their monthly payments.

In October, 1979, Humphreys received a letter from the Bank notifying them that the interest rate on their loan would be increased to 9½% annually effective December 1, 1980 [sic, 1979?]. Jerry Humphrey called the Bank and talked with President Hendrickson. He reminded Hendrickson of the Bank's promises of a better deal. Hendrickson responded that the increase was in keeping with the Bank's policy for years and that the Bank would continue to pursue it. The conversation became heated and Hendrickson called Humphrey's attention to the demand provision in the loan, threatening to foreclose the mortgage if Humphrey made trouble. The next week, Humphreys received a copy of their Realty Installment Loan with the demand provision underlined.

Humphreys made their monthly payments and the controversy languished until February, 1980. Humphreys retained counsel, who wrote the Bank alleging that it had violated Truth In Lending disclosure regulations and state law. The letter sought to fix the interest rate at 8½%. In response, the Bank demanded full payment of the loan. Humphreys' counsel requested negotiations and the Bank again demanded full payment. The Bank instructed its tellers to refuse any tendered payments except full payment. Humphreys then tendered their March 5, 1980, payment; the Bank kept their check and again wrote them saying that anything less than full payment would be unacceptable. Humphreys' counsel responded that his clients would not be threatened into making full payment. Humphreys tendered the April 5, 1980, payment and the Bank again retained the check without crediting their account. On April 11, 1980, the Bank filed its foreclosure action. . . .

The Bank's argument in support of its motion, both at trial and on appeal, also sets the tone for the balance of its case. The Bank asserts that the counterclaim alleged *only* a Truth In Lending claim.

Although 15 U.S.C.A. §1640(e) does place a one year statute of limitations on affirmative recoveries under the act, the trial court did not err by denying judgment on the pleadings. Contrary to the Bank's view, Humphreys' counterclaim was not solely based upon a Truth In Lending violation. Simply because Humphreys asserted that a federal question was present in their removal petition does not mean that it was the only theory in their counterclaim. Drawing inferences in their favor, the counterclaim also presented a claim for misrepresentation or fraud. . . .

We now turn to the Bank's related arguments that Truth In Lending violations do not affect the underlying contract and that the Truth In Lending Act provides the Humphreys' exclusive remedy.

The Truth In Lending Act at 15 U.S.C.A. §1610 [§111] discusses its effect on state laws.

Subsection (d) states:

Contract or other obligations under State or Federal law

(d) Except as specified in sections 1635, 1640, and 1666e of this title, this sub-chapter and the regulations issued thereunder *do not affect the validity or enforce-ability of any contract or obligation under State or Federal law.* (Emphasis added.)

The Bank interprets this subsection to mean that an institution's failure to disclose terms pursuant to the act cannot affect the enforceability of the underlying contract. Thus, the Bank reads 15 U.S.C.A. §1640, which pro-vides civil penalties for violations of the act, as providing exclusive rem-edies to debtors.

The Bank's interpretation is erroneous and neglects the emphasized language in subsection (d). The validity or enforceability of credit contracts is still to be determined by applicable state and federal law. The subsection merely provides that a disclosure violation does not void a contract; it does not limit the application of state law. Piatchek v. Fairview Reliable Loan, Inc. (S.D. Ill. 1979) 474 F. Supp. 622; Hobbiest Financing Corporation v. Spivey, (1975) 135 Ga. App. 353, 217 S.E.2d 613.

In the following cases, the courts held a debtor has alternative remedies under state law and §1640. These cases also support the conclusion that state law determines the validity of a contract although the facts reveal Truth In Lending violations. Ninth Liberty Loan Corp. v. Hardy, (1977) 53 Ill. App. 3d 601, 11 Ill. Dec. 363, 368 N.E.2d 971; Public Finance Corp. v. Riddle, (1980) 83 Ill. App. 3d 417, 38 Ill. Dec. 712, 403 N.E.2d 1316; Ballew v. Associates Financial Serv. Co. of Neb., Inc. (D. Neb. 1976), 450 F. Supp. 253; Cantrell v. First National Bank of Euless, (1978) Tex. App., 560 S.W.2d 721.

In summary, to the extent that the Bank's appeal is based upon the arguments that Humphreys pled only a Truth In Lending claim, that the Truth In Lending Act is an exclusive remedy and that the act precludes the application of Indiana law to determine the contract's validity, the appeal fails. . . .

The Bank raises numerous issues challenging the trial court's findings of fact and conclusions of law. Essentially, the Bank is attacking the evi-dentiary basis for the trial court's findings, particularly its findings con-cerning intentional misrepresentation and unconscionability, and the resulting relief granted.

We first note that we may not reverse a trial court's decision and its related findings unless they are clearly erroneous, Indiana Industries, Inc. v. Wedge Products, (1982) Ind. App., 430 N.E.2d 419; Ind. Rules of Proce-dure Trial Rule 52(A). Furthermore, we may not reweigh the evidence or judge the witnesses' credibility. Id. It is also important to recall the elements of misrepresentation.

> To sustain an action for fraud it must be proven that a material representation of a past or existing fact was made which was untrue and known to be untrue by the party making it or else recklessly made and that another party did in fact rely on the representation and was induced thereby to act to his detriment.

Fleetwood v. Mirich, (1980) Ind. App., 404 N.E.2d 38, 42.

Additionally, and particularly relevant to this case, when parties to a contract have a prior understanding about the contract's terms, and the party responsible for drafting the contract includes contrary terms and then allows the other party to sign it without informing him of changes, the drafter's conduct is fraudulent. McNair v. Public Sav. Ins. Co. of America, (1928) 88 Ind. App. 386, 163 N.E. 290.

In McNair, the court discussed the party's duty to disclose stating:

> *Concealment becomes fraudulent only when it is the duty of the party having knowledge of the facts to discover them to the other; and this brings back the question, When does such duty rest upon either party to any transaction: All the instances in which the duty exists, and in which a concealment is therefore fraudulent, may be reduced to three distinct classes.* These three classes are, in general clearly distinct and separate, although their boundaries may sometimes overlap, or a case may fall within two of them. . . . 2. *The second class embraces those instances in which there is no existing special fiduciary relation between the parties, and the transaction is not in its essential nature fiduciary, but it appears that either one or each of the parties, in entering into the contract or other transaction expressly reposes a trust and confidence in the other; or else from the circumstances of the case, the nature of their dealings, or their position towards each other, such a trust and confidence in the particular case is necessarily implied. The nature of the transaction is not the test in this class. Each case must depend upon its own circumstances.* The trust and confidence, and the consequent duty to disclose, may expressly appear by the very language of the parties, or they may be necessarily implied from their acts and other circumstances. (Emphasis added, citations omitted.)

163 N.E. at 293.

With these concepts in mind, we cannot find the trial court's findings clearly erroneous. Humphreys approached the Bank seeking a construction loan which was to be secured by a mortgage. The Bank represented that the loan would be at 8½% annually and would be repayable over 20 years. Ultimately, the actual loan agreement provided for variable interest and payment on demand, provisions which were contrary to the parties' original understanding of the contract.

The Bank makes a great deal of the facts that Humphreys had prior loans with it, that the demand provision was contained in all three notes, that three separate loan agreements were executed and that Humphreys read the variable interest provision in the third note, the Realty Installment Note. The Bank argues Humphreys' prior transactions put them on notice about the variable interest provision because a prior loan contained a variable interest clause. It claims Humphreys were not obligated to ultimately finance the long term note with it, and it asserts the notes were separate transactions.

We disagree. The Bank disregards its construction loan policy and statements made by the employees. Bennett explained the Bank's policy for construction loans. Short term demand notes were executed to cover the construction period and thus provide the Bank with additional security. The Bank would distribute the loan proceeds on a monthly basis to cover construction costs by either paying bills directly or depositing an appropriate amount in the borrower's account. Also during construction, the Bank supervised the work and made periodic appraisals to insure its security interest was adequate. Bennett further explained that if the property was not sold upon completion, the debt would be converted to a long term installment note.

This procedure was followed in Humphreys' case. In fact, Bennett explained the second note, the 90 day note, was executed because construction wasn't completed on schedule. Once construction was completed, the debt was converted to the long term installment note. Therefore, the Bank itself viewed the three notes as a continuous transaction which would culminate in a long term loan. Indeed, the Bank actively participated in the progression of events. Humphreys' potential awareness of the demand clause in the first two notes would not have put them on notice that the final note would be a demand-installment note because of the Bank's own procedures. The fact that Humphreys had a prior loan with a variable interest clause does not undermine their claim. Humphreys were specifically promised a "better deal" than their last prior loan. The Bank's contention that Humphreys were not obligated to long term financing with it views events from an erroneous perspective. Instead, the proper focal point is Humphreys' perspective that if they had a long term loan with the Bank, it would be according to their previously negotiated understanding. Reaching that stage was merely a matter of renewing the interim notes as a permanent installment note, *according to the Bank's normal procedures for construction loans.*

Likewise, the fact that Humphreys read the variable interest provision in the Realty Installment Note does not defeat their claim. They questioned

Bender, in Bennett's absence, about the variable interest provision and were told not to worry about it. Taken in context, they were justified in assuming the variable interest provision was not applicable.

Drawing inferences favorable to the judgment, the Bank represented one set of contract terms to Humphreys; then it drafted other more odious terms; it allowed Humphreys to execute notes and a mortgage based upon their original understanding, but containing the latter terms; and then the Bank tried to apply the unfair terms, particularly the demand clause. The trial court's findings are not clearly erroneous.

The Bank challenges the sufficiency of the evidence to support the trial court's award of $1,000 in actual damages to Humphreys. This issue is related to the Bank's argument about punitive damages because it asserts without actual damages, punitive damages are improper.

The facts reveal the Bank held two of Humphreys' payments totaling $608.00 for over a year without crediting their account or returning their checks. Additionally, the Bank clouded Humphreys' title by its foreclosure action when their monthly payments were current. This evidence is sufficient to support the award of actual damages. Shelby Federal Sav. and Loan Assn. v. Doss, (1983) Ind. App., 431 N.E.2d 493. To the extent this issue is related to punitive damages, the punitive damages are also appropriate.

Two issues remain concerning punitive damages: (1) is it proper for the Bank to be subjected to punitive damages when it is also potentially subject to criminal penalties under the Truth In Lending Act? and (2) does the evidence supporting punitive damages satisfy the "clear and convincing" standard of proof required by our supreme court in Travelers Indem. Co. v. Armstrong, (1982) Ind., 442 N.E.2d 349? . . .

The supreme court in *Travelers* was concerned with the assessment of punitive damages in cases of good faith contract disputes. The court determined "clear and convincing" evidence is necessary to support punitive damages in a contract dispute. Explaining this standard, the court stated:

> [P]unitive damages should not be allowable upon evidence that is merely consistent with the hypothesis of malice, fraud, gross negligence or oppressiveness. Rather some evidence should be required that is *inconsistent with the hypothesis that the tortious conduct was the result of a mistake of law or fact, honest error of judgment, over-zealousness, mere negligence or other such noniniquitous human failing.* (Emphasis added.)

442 N.E.2d at 362.

In the case at bar, evidence inconsistent with the hypothesis of human failing is present. As we have recounted, the Bank represented one set of terms to Humphreys, but included others in the notes. Humphreys were left in the position of having expended their loan receipts and having their newly completed home subject to foreclosure on demand even though their monthly payments were current. Even more damning, the Bank invoked the demand clause only after Humphreys questioned their contract. Humphreys introduced evidence that the Bank had threatened another borrower in a similar situation with foreclosure if he sought legal advice. We find this scenario inconsistent with "noniniquitous human failing," *Travelers,* supra. Punitive damages were appropriate.

The Bank argues reformation was erroneous, relying on its previously raised argument that misrepresentation and unconscionability were not at issue, but conceding reformation is appropriate when unconscionability and misrepresentation are involved. Consistent with the award of punitive damages, unconscionability and misrepresentation were at issue and reformation was appropriate.

The trial court's judgment is affirmed.

CHAPTER 9

Consumer Leasing

More and more consumers are leasing personal property. It is now estimated that more than one-third of all new automobiles are leased instead of bought. A number of different statutes arguably apply to these transactions.

I. ARTICLE 2A OF THE UNIFORM COMMERCIAL CODE

During much of the last century, both consumers who leased personal property and their lessors received little guidance regarding their rights under state law. In the late 1980s, however, the states adopted Article 2A of the Uniform Commercial Code (Leases), which applies to commercial leases of goods as well as giving some special rights to consumer lessees (those leasing cars or furniture, for example).

A "consumer lease" is defined in §2A-103(1)(e) as a "lease that a lessor regularly engaged in the business of leasing or selling makes to a lessee, except an organization, who takes under the lease primarily for a personal, family, or household purpose, if the total payments to be made under the lease contract, excluding payments for options to renew or buy, do not exceed $25,000." The reason for the exclusion of leases of more than $25,000 is that in such big-ticket transactions the lessee is likely to be sophisticated and without need of special protection (though as automobile prices skyrocket upward, luxury cars leased by perfectly ordinary consumers might routinely exceed this figure). Some states enacting Article 2A removed these caps altogether.

Article 2A contains an unconscionability provision, modeled on a similar one in Article 2 (§2-302) of the Code, but allowing for the consumer's recovery of attorney's fees in the event of a successful unconscionability argument, §2A-108(4).

If the lessor is a financial institution that merely has purchased the leased item and then leased it to the lessee (called a "finance lease" in §2A-103(1)(g)), the lessee is given the benefit of any warranties the original seller (called a "supplier" in the statute) gave to the lessor,

§2A-209. The Article 2A warranties are modeled on Article 2 warranties and are found in §§2A-210 to 2A-216. If the lessor defaults, §2A-508 lists the lessee's remedies, which include the ability to withhold payment, §2A-508(6). If the lessee is in default, the lessor is given various rights, including the right to repossess the leased item if this can be done without a breach of the peace, §2A-525.

II. RENT-TO-OWN STATUTES

People in poverty of course have a difficult time buying consumer goods on credit. An increasingly popular way around this difficulty is for the consumer to lease the goods on a short-term, renewable basis, with a contractual understanding that after a certain number of lease payments are made, the goods become the property of the lessee. These rent-to-own transactions (RTOs) have a couple of problems. If the consumer were able to pay cash for the goods or even had the credit to buy the goods on time, the cost of the goods would be dramatically less than the amount paid in the RTO. In one case holding that rent-to-own agreements were usurious under the Minnesota usury statute, a court found that in some RTOs consumers were paying an APR of 746 percent! See Fogie v. Thorn Am., Inc., 95 F.3d 645 (8th Cir. 1996); see also Perez v. Rent-a-Center, 188 N.J. 215, 902 A.2d 1232 (2006). Additional problems include failure to disclose the terms of the agreement in a manner the consumer can understand, outrageous extra charges (repossessing, reinstating the lease, etc.), failure to protect the equity the consumer begins to have in items that have been leased for a long time, and out-and-out lies by the lessor as to what the RTO entails. See James Nehf, Effective Regulation of Rent-to-Own Contracts, 52 Ohio St. L.J. 751 (1991).

Article 2A of the Uniform Commercial Code, described above, applies to RTO contracts, and that statute (particularly its treatment of unconscionability) may be very useful in regulating the actions of the lessor. Often state consumer protection statutes apply to the lease of goods as well as the sale thereof, so relief from harsh practices may be had by resort to these; see Annot., 89 A.L.R.4th 854. Finally, many states have enacted special statutes regulating RTOs and addressing the most frequent abuses. Use your state statutes to resolve the following Problem.

PROBLEM 140

Hannah Smith had a clerical job at a large company. It didn't pay much, and she struggled to pay her bills. One day she became fascinated by a TV ad showing beautiful furniture that was available from Temporary Possessions, a rent-to-own company. She went down to their showroom, was very impressed with a living room suite she saw, and signed an agreement to lease the suite for three months at $100 a month. The salesman had her sign a contract, which provided that when she had made 20 payments, the suite would be hers to keep.

"What would it cost to buy this suite?" she asked.

"I don't know," the salesman said. "Oh, there's also this." He pointed to a sign on the wall that said, "REPOSSESSION FEE $50." She said nothing.

Payments were due on the first of every month.

Hannah made the February payment on time but, after being laid off from her job, was late on the March payment by two weeks. She sent them the full amount at that time. She failed to make the April payment, and the furniture was repossessed from the apartment in which she lives on April 4.

On June 3, Hannah is sitting in your office. She wants the furniture back, even if it means she must start all over in terms of building any equity in it. She's worried that the company will have leased her furniture to someone else. She has found a new job and is sure she can make all future payments. A friend who is in the furniture business tells her that she is crazy—this same set can be purchased for $800 retail, but she can't afford that much money up front.

You look at the lease agreement she originally signed. One of its provisions says, "Lessee hereby authorizes lessor and its agents to enter into lessee's home after any default and repossess the leased goods, even if lessor entry onto the premises is accomplished by forced means and while lessee is not at home." You ask her about this, and she says that when they repossessed the suite in April, she in fact was not home, and they had picked the lock before taking the furniture (kindly locking the door behind them when they left).

Advise her. See Article 2A of the Uniform Commercial Code, §§2A-108, and 2A-525, and whatever other state statutes seem relevant.

III. CONSUMER LEASING ACT

Although the Truth in Lending Act has always applied to a credit sale disguised as a lease, see Reg. Z §226.2(a)(16), a true lease of goods was not regulated by the original statute. In 1976, Congress enacted the Consumer Leasing Act and made it Part E of the Truth in Lending Act, 15 U.S.C.

§§1667 et seq., and the Federal Reserve Board adopted Regulation M, 12 C.F.R. §213, to flesh out the statutory language.

PROBLEM 141

The lease for a new car that Portia Moot signed provided that she would make monthly payments of $350 to the lessor for four years. At the end of the lease period the car would automatically become hers without any further payments. Assume that the car's original value was $15,000. Does Regulation Z or Regulation M govern this transaction? See Reg. Z §226.2(a)(16) and Reg. M §213.2(e)'s definition of "consumer lease."

Notice that under the Regulation M definition of "consumer lease," before the Regulation applies at all, the lease must last more than four months and not exceed $25,000 in payments. The four-month requirement keeps most RTO agreements from being covered by the Consumer Leasing Act, since RTOs typically have a renewable lease period measured week by week or month by month.

PROBLEM 142

When Joseph Armstrong rented an apartment, he also rented the furniture therein. Is this transaction subject to Regulation M? See §213.2(e)(3). If the apartment were unfurnished when he rented it, but he then leased furniture from a rental company, would Regulation M apply?

Advertising.   Normally, as we have seen, TIL advertising violations do not give rise to civil liability. When it comes to consumer leasing advertising, however, §213.7 regulates the content of that advertising, and §§184 and 185(b) provide for civil liability to the extent that the consumer can prove *actual* damages from the failure to comply.

Disclosures.   Section 213.4 of Regulation M contains the mandatory disclosure rules. In any action involving a consumer lease, the careful attorney on each side will examine the lease to determine whether the disclosures have been made as required.

PROBLEM 143

The Facade Motors automobile lease required customers to give a security deposit of $550 to the lessor, who agreed to return this amount when the lease ended, assuming the vehicle had been properly maintained. Facade, however, did not pay any interest on this security deposit. Is it required to disclose this fact in the lease? See Reg. M §213.4(b), (d), and (e). Compare Demitropoulos v. Bank One Milwaukee, N.A., 924 F. Supp. 894, 30 U.C.C. Rep. Serv. 2d 337 (N.D. Ill. 1996), with Gaydos v. Huntington Nat. Bank, 941 F. Supp. 669 (N.D. Ohio 1996).

PROBLEM 144

When lawyer Sam Ambulance leased a computer for his personal use at home, the lessor did not provide any of the required disclosures mandated by Regulation M. Sam's law practice had not been going so well, so he decided to look into whether this mistake could get him some money. Look at TILA §130 and decide. Since there will be no finance charge in the lease of goods, how does he measure any punitive damages? See TILA §130(a)(2).

The major complication with consumer leases comes in connection with an open-end lease. Consumer leases may provide that the lessee will lease the product for a set period, and at the end of that period the product is returned to the lessor and the lessee has no further liability. This is sometimes called a *closed-end lease*. Contrast that with the open-end lease described in the next Problem.

PROBLEM 145

The new car that Jay Eastriver leased was worth $24,000 at the start of the two-year lease. The lease contract required monthly payments of $300 and provided that at the end of the lease the car would be sold. The lease contained a provision by which the parties agreed that the value of the car at lease termination was predicted to be $15,000. When the car was sold, if it brought more than $15,000, Jay Eastriver would keep the excess. If it brought less than $15,000, Jay would pay the difference to the lessor.

a. How should the lessor disclose this part of the contract? See Reg. M §213.4(k) to (m).

b. When the lease ended, the car was sold for $10,000, and Jay was faced with a balloon payment of $5,000. He is in your office. Does he have to pay this large amount? See §213.4(m)(2).

c. Assume that you are representing the lessor in this last situation. What risks does the lessor run by suing Jay Eastriver for the money? What if it is possible to show that the car brought so little because Jay drove it hard and fast, wrecked it twice, and never took it in for maintenance? What if he took good care of the car, and it brought so little when sold because of government regulations on gas-gulping automobiles (like this one), which greatly depress their value?

CURRY CORP. v. MOORO
Court of Appeals of Georgia, 1990
195 Ga. App. 184, 393 S.E.2d 33

COOPER, Judge.

Appellant leased a car to appellee and sued after appellee returned the car and terminated the lease agreement. Appellee defended and counter-claimed on the ground that appellant violated the Federal Consumer Leasing Act (15 U.S.C. §§1667 et seq.) by not making certain disclosures. Specifically, appellee claimed that the lease did not disclose the following: the amount paid for registration fees, certificate of title, or taxes; the amount of other charges not included in the periodic payments; the warranties and guaranties made by the manufacturer or lessor; the fair market value of the car at the inception of the lease; and the aggregate cost of the lease at the expiration of the lease. Both parties filed motions for summary judgment. The trial court granted appellee's motion for summary judgment on the main claim, liability under the lease agreement, but held that appellee's counterclaim was barred by the applicable statute of limitations. The court denied appellant's motion on the main claim. This appeal follows.

1. Appellant first contends that the trial court erred in granting summary judgment to appellee. The grant of summary judgment is proper when the pleadings, depositions, answers to interrogatories, and admissions on file, together with affidavits show that there is no genuine issue as to any material fact and that the moving party is entitled to a judgment as a matter of law. OCGA §9-11-56(c). Neither party disputes the genuineness of the lease agreement or the disclosure statement, both of which are in the record,

and appellee's contentions regarding the nonexistence of various disclosures in these documents can be ascertained from the record. Furthermore, the uncontroverted affidavit of appellee shows that he signed an agreement to pay $337 per month for the lease of a car, but he was actually charged $350.48 per month. Appellant argues, however, that appellee failed to prove that the violations were intentional and did not result from bona fide error; therefore, summary judgment to appellee was error.

15 U.S.C. §1640(c) expressly provides that a creditor may not be held liable for a violation "if the creditor or assignee shows by a preponderance of evidence that the violation was not intentional and resulted from a bona fide error . . . " We have reviewed the pleadings together with the affidavit and find that they do not raise an issue of intentional conduct or bona fide error. Appellant did not respond to appellee's counterclaim, raising the defense that the alleged violations were unintentional. Nor did appellant, either in its motion for summary judgment or in response to appellee's motion, submit any affidavit which stated that the failure to make certain disclosures was not intentional or was the result of bona fide error. Had there been any fact question about intentional conduct versus bona fide error, appellee, as the movant, would have had the burden of proving that the violation was intentional and did not result from bona fide error. First Citizens Bank, etc. v. Owings, 151 Ga. App. 389(2), 259 S.E.2d 747 (1979). However, inasmuch as no such issue was raised, it was not error to grant summary judgment to appellee.

2. Appellant contends that the trial court erred in finding that the lease was void and unenforceable due to violations of the Federal Consumer Leasing Act. Appellant relies on First Citizens Bank, etc. v. Owings, supra, a case arising under the Federal Truth in Lending Act. In *Owings*, the bank brought an action seeking to foreclose on certain automobiles under the terms of two security agreements, and we held that violations of the Truth in Lending Act did not invalidate the contract and were no defense to the foreclosure proceedings. Unlike *Owings*, where the default was separate and distinct from the violation, in the case at bar, there has been no default, and the violations are directly related to the provisions of the contract which appellant seeks to enforce. The lease shows that appellee's monthly payments were to be $337, but appellee's affidavit establishes that he was actually charged $350.48 per month. Also, the disclosure statement shows that several disclosures were not made with respect to fees and taxes, other charges, warranties, and end of term liability. We have held that "'[w]here the terms of a contract directly involve the infraction of a civil statute not enacted for the purpose of raising revenue, and such infraction is penalized by a fine, or imprisonment or both, the contract is void and unenforceable.'

[Cit.]" Couch v. Blackwell & Assoc., 150 Ga. App. 739(1), 258 S.E.2d 552 (1979). We do not hold that a lessee can default under the lease, refuse to return the car, and hide behind the lessor's failure to make certain disclosures under the Consumer Leasing Act. In such a case, the lessor would not be prevented from seeking a writ of possession. However, here the provisions of the lease, which the lessor seeks to enforce, are directly related to the disclosures it failed to make, and the lessor cannot maintain the action. Therefore, we find no error with the trial court's finding that the lease contract was void and unenforceable.

For the foregoing reasons, we find no error with the trial court's denial of summary judgment to appellant.

Judgment affirmed.

IV. THE UNIFORM CONSUMER LEASES ACT

In August, 2001, the National Conference of Commissioners on Uniform State Laws (NCCUSL) approved and sent to the states for adoption the Uniform Consumer Leases Act (UCLA—famous initials in another context). As of this writing, early 2009, the proposed statute had been adopted only in Connecticut. The Act applies to the leases of consumer goods for a greater length than four months (thus cutting out rent-to-own transactions) and for a total lease amount of less than $150,000. It adopts the disclosure rules of the federal Consumer Leasing Act, but then goes much further in the required disclosures (including a disclosure to guarantors) and adds a number of substantive provisions regulating certain practices (such as forbidding wage assignments, confession of judgment clauses, security interests in non-leased items, and the imposition of "gap liability" when goods are destroyed). It also creates a right to cure defaults, while setting standards for various fees and charges. Particularly important is a provision copied from the federal Magnuson-Moss Act that forbids the disclaimer of implied warranties as part of the lease. The consumer is given a reciprocal right to attorney's fees if the lessor contracts for them, and in any event imposes civil liability for violations of its rules, including actual damages, statutory damages, costs, and attorney's fees. For an on-point article by one of the primary drafters, see Ralph J. Rohner, Leasing Consumer Goods: The Spotlight Shifts to the Uniform Consumer Leasing Act, 35 Conn. L. Rev. 647 (2003).

CHAPTER 10

Retail Installment Sales and Loans

I. INSTALLMENT SALES

A. *Rebates and the Rule of 78*

All states have a statute regulating consumer sales contracts, and of course these statutes vary widely. The Uniform Consumer Credit Code (fondly known as the "U Triple-C," or, sometimes, "U3C") has not been widely adopted,[1] and even in the states where it is in force, it has been much amended. Use your state statute or, in default thereof, the UCCC to resolve the following Problems.

PROBLEM 146

Joe Armstrong picked out the car of his dreams at Facade Motors and signed an installment sale contract to pay for it. The TIL statement on the contract revealed that he was paying a 15 percent APR over a five-year period on a car that he purchased for $24,000.

a. When Joe returned home that evening, his wife Yolanda was furious that he had gone into so much debt without discussing it with

---

1. The states that have adopted the UCCC are Colorado, Idaho, Indiana, Iowa, Kansas, Maine, Oklahoma, South Carolina, Utah, and Wyoming. No state has adopted the UCCC since 1974. Utah repealed its adoption effective in 1985, and Idaho substantially rewrote its version of the Code in 1983. The original 1968 version of the UCCC was rewritten in 1974, but only Iowa, Kansas, and Maine adopted it (with variations). The Idaho statute is based on the 1974 version, and South Carolina's statute is a combination of both Official Final Drafts of the UCCC. Wisconsin's statute on point is based largely on the 1968 UCCC. All citations in this chapter are to the 1974 version of the Code.

her first. She pointed out that a home equity loan on their house could raise the $24,000 he needed to buy the car at a much lower interest rate (and the interest payments would be deductible to boot). The next day the Armstrongs took out such a loan. Joe rushed the $24,000 down to the car dealership, but the manager told him that he had no right to pay off the loan before it was due. Is this right? See U.C.C.C. §2.509.

b. After a phone call to the dealership's lawyer, the manager of Facade Motors told Joe that he could pay off the car loan early only if he paid all the finance charge in addition to the principal. Joe was astounded by this. The loan had been outstanding for only one day, and Joe figured that the dealership ought to rebate some of the unearned interest. What amount is appropriate? See U.C.C.C. §2.510, and if that doesn't lay to rest all your questions, consult the discussion below.

c. If Joe had paid on the car loan for three years and had then prepaid the balance, how much of the interest would the dealership have earned?

As we saw in the discussion of usury in Chapter 7, a creditor is most at risk early in the loan when the largest amount of money is outstanding. Thus, it follows that the creditor really earns most of the interest charged during the beginning period of the loan. Consumers (particularly those making home mortgage payments) are frequently surprised to discover that their payments are first imposed against the interest due and then after it is paid, a smaller portion of the payment is used to reduce the principal. Only late in the loan period are the consumer's payments making substantial reductions in the principal amount. Phrased another way, the early mortgage payments reduce the interest debt, but do not create much equity in the property. If the consumer wants to repay a debt, as in the last Problem, the amount of the rebate of unearned interest is also affected by the theory that the creditor earns the interest early in the loan. The following quotation explains why.

QUOTES FOR THE ATTORNEY'S ARSENAL: "THE RULE OF 78"

Some people assuming the responsibility of speaking for consumers seem never to have gone beyond the simple assumption that if a 12-month installment contract is paid in full at the end of 6 months, only one half of the "finance charge" has been earned and the other half should be rebated. Since credit agencies apply a different standard known as "the Rule of 78," which produces a lesser rebate, consumer groups are quick in their denunciation of the Rule.

But if one makes the slight effort required to understand the Rule, the denunciation must stop. Let us [consider the] case of the $1200 balance on a used car, payable in 12 monthly installments.

As a first simplification, it is apparent that during the first month of the credit the buyer has the use of his 12 $100 bills. After he makes the first payment, he still has the use of 11 $100 bills for another month; after the second payment he has the use of 10 $100 bills; and so on. Over 12 months of the contract he has the use of 78 $100-months, and the finance charge must pay for this use. In the first month of a 12-month contract, the creditor, therefore, earns 12/78 of the finance charge; the second month he earns 11/78; and so on. At the end of the six months, the creditor has earned 57/78 of the finance charge. . . . This is the Rule of 78. The denominator is 171 for 18 months; 300 for 24 months; 666 for 36 months. The same [amount] would be found if you computed 12% per annum or 1% per month interest on the $100 bills in use during each month. Obviously, more interest or finance charge is earned in the early months when more money is in use than in later months. The foregoing is only an approximation of a true actuarial calculation, but it is a remarkably close approximation.

Homer Kripke, Consumer Credit Regulation: A Creditor-Oriented Viewpoint, 68 Colum. L. Rev. 445, 454-455 (1968).[2]

At the end of the above quotation, Professor Kripke states that the actuarial rate is different from but similar to the Rule of 78. This is because a true actuarial rate would apply the payments first to the interest accrued and then to principal, and these amounts would vary over the life of the loan, while the Rule of 78 assumes repayment of an identical amount of principal each month. In loans of small duration, this difference does not matter much, so that statutes on point typically permit the use of either the Rule of 78 (sometimes called the "sum of the balances" or "sum of the digits" method) or an actuarial method of rebate, though in some states the statute limits the creditor to the use of one or the other. In longer loans, those of four years or greater, the actuarial rate produces a significantly larger rebate than does the Rule of 78, and it is in such loans that use of the latter calculation is most subject to criticism. For articles on point, see Hunt, The Rule of 78: Hidden Penalty for Prepayment in Consumer Credit Transactions, 55 B.U. L. Rev. 331 (1975); Comment, Computing Interest Rebates Under the Rule of 78ths: A Formula for Usury upon Default in Maximum-Interest Precomputed Credit Transactions, 10

---

2. Copyright © 1968 by the Directors of the Columbia Law Review Association, Inc. All rights reserved. This article originally appeared at 68 Colum. L. Rev. 3 (1968). Reprinted by permission.

St. Mary's L.J. 94 (1978). The UCCC does not permit the Rule of 78 to be used in loans longer than 48 months, but does allow it for shorter credit extensions. See U.C.C.C. §2.510(1), (4), and (5). Helpful charts for computing the Rule of 78 can be found in the CCH Consumer Credit Guide, or online (see www.hughchou.org/calc/rule78.cgi).

PROBLEM 147

After Joe Armstrong had been making car payments for one year on the car that he had purchased from Facade Motors, he became involved in financial difficulties, and he stopped sending in money. Facade Motors repossessed the car and then sued Joe for the entire balance of the debt. Is this allowed? See U.C.C.C. § 5.103. Is Joe entitled to a rebate of unearned interest in this situation? See U.C.C.C. §2.510(7).

The federal government has rules involving prepayment and the Rule of 78 grafted onto the Truth in Lending Act by the Housing and Community Development Act of 1992, 15 U.S.C. §1615(d). It allows prepayment of any consumer credit loan as defined in TILA and forbids the used of the Rule of 78 for calculating the rebate in loans exceeding 61 months. In such a loan it requires a method of calculation "at least as favorable to the consumer as the actuarial method."

B. Security Interests and Payment Terms

The typical state installment sales law contains basic regulation of the permissible terms of the contract. First of all, such a statute will set the legal interest rate (so it is a usury statute), and will then detail other charges that are allowed to be imposed. Does the consumer make a payment late? Then the statute will limit the amount of the late charge.[3]

---

3. Whether the state statute does so or not, the Federal Trade Commission Credit Practices Rule, see Chapter 2 supra, forbids the pyramiding of late charges. Thus, if the consumer makes one late payment for which the creditor imposes a late charge, and the consumer then makes the next payment on time but does not also remit the amount of the late charge, the creditor may not take the late charge out of the new payment and then impose a new late charge because the new payment is not now in the full amount. The typical way this result is reached in consumer statutes is to say that payments shall be credited first to currently due obligations and not to those past due (thereby avoiding the creation of new late charges). See U.C.C.C. §2.502(3).

Does the consumer want to skip a payment and make it up at the end? The statute will place a cap on the permissible *deferral* charge. Is the creditor allowed to make the consumer agree to pay the creditor's attorney's fees in the event of a dispute? The statute will speak to this issue, see, e.g., U.C.C.C. §2.507, as well as establish remedies for violations of the statute, see, e.g., U.C.C.C. §5.201. Such statutes also usually apply to assignees of the contract, so that the finance company that purchases the consumer's obligation also will take subject to the consumer's defenses even if the finance company would normally qualify as a holder in due course. See U.C.C.C. §3.404.

PROBLEM 148

Heatwave, Inc. manufactured and marketed hot tubs for installation on a consumer's property. The hot tub could be placed on any solid surface and then connected to the water lines. Mr. and Mrs. Suburb decided to purchase Heatwave's top of the line: the Tsunami (retail cost: $ 13,000). Their first payment was due on April 1, 2012, and thereafter on the first of every month.

a. The Suburbs much enjoyed their hot tub and the other amenities they purchased to attain their creature comforts. Their style of living, however, exploded their budget, and they fell behind in payments. One month they missed the payment to Heatwave by six days. Can the company legally declare a default and repossess the Tsunami? See U.C.C.C. §§2.502(2) and 5.110(1).

b. The contract contained a clause that said that the creditor could declare a default "at will" and then accelerate the debt so that the unpaid balance was all due at once, so Heatwave did this. Surely this clause is unenforceable. See U.C.C. § 1-208. Is there no regulation of acceleration clauses in consumer law? See U.C.C.C. §5.109.

c. Heatwave sent the Suburbs a letter stating that it was not only repossessing the hot tub but also foreclosing a mortgage it held on their house. Startled, the Suburbs call you, the attorney who handled the closing on their house, and ask if they are going to lose their home. As you examine the paperwork, you notice that the contract between Heatwave and your clients claims a security interest in not only the Tsunami but also the house in which it was installed. Apparently the Suburbs also signed a mortgage, because you find one recorded in the real property records. Answer the question your clients asked you. See U.C.C.C. §3.301. Is there other paperwork that you need to search for? See TILA §125.

d. Assume, instead of all the above, that the Suburbs made all their payments on time until they reached the last payment. The prior payments had all been exactly $ 230, but they were dismayed to discover that the contract calls for a final payment of $ 1,500, and they can't afford to make such a large payment (usually called a balloon payment) all at once. What can they do? See U.C.C.C. §3.308.

PROBLEM 149

In one of the most famous unconscionability cases of all time, Mrs. Williams bought a series of appliances from the Walker-Thomas Furniture Company over a number of years. The total of all the purchases was $ 1,800, but she made timely payments as she went. Though she never reduced the debt to zero, at the time of default she owed only about $ 500. A clause in the contract stated that all items purchased would stand as security for all other items purchased, and "all payments now and hereafter made by the purchaser shall be credited pro rata on all outstanding leases, bills and accounts due." Thus, when she defaulted, the company repossessed not only the latest item purchased but every appliance she had bought over the years. The court in Williams v. Walker-Thomas Furniture Co., 350 F.2d 445 (D.C. Cir. 1965), held this clause unconscionable under both the common law and U.C.C. §2-302. Assume for a moment that the unconscionability doctrine is unavailable as a theory, so that only statutory remedies remain.

a. Does the law permit the seller to use purchased items as collateral for earlier or later debts (a process called "cross-collateralization")? See U.C.C.C. §3.302.

b. Does the law permit the "add-on" repossession that the contractual language was designed to allow? See U.C.C.C. §3.303.

The doctrine of unconscionability, which you undoubtedly covered in your contracts course, is a valuable consumer protection argument. Section 2-302 of the Uniform Commercial Code often has been wielded as a weapon on behalf of consumers, even though it contains no definition of the word "unconscionability." See, however, Leff, Unconscionability and the Code—The Emperor's New Clause, 115 U. Pa. L.

Rev. 485 (1967), a famous article arguing that a contract must be both *procedurally* (referring to unfairness in the bargaining process) and *substantively* (referring to a harsh term in the resulting contract) unconscionable before a court should grant relief. The Uniform Consumer Credit Code has a more complicated definition of "unconscionability." See U.C.C.C. §5.108.

II. LOANS TO THE CONSUMER

Most states have a wealth of statutes pertaining to consumer loans. These statutes typically exempt the lender from compliance with the general usury statute if the lender procures a license and follows the statutory guidelines. The CCH Consumer Credit Guide has a state-by-state listing of all such statutes. The Uniform Consumer Credit Code specifically deals with consumer loans, treating them on a par with sales to a consumer, and most states have enacted special statutes that regulate payday lenders (entities that allow consumers to borrow early on their future salary payments). Finally, as we have seen, in addition to sales, the Truth in Lending Act's coverage also includes loans to the consumer.

BESTA v. BENEFICIAL LOAN CO.[4]
United States Court of Appeals, Eighth Circuit, 1988
855 F.2d 532

BEAM, Circuit Judge.

Betty L. Besta appeals from an order of the district court dismissing her claim that her loan agreement with Beneficial Finance Company of Iowa (BFC) is unconscionable. We reverse.

BACKGROUND

The loan at issue (Loan II) was written on May 2, 1983, and in part refinanced an earlier loan made in 1981 (Loan I). The loans were structured in the following manner:

---

4. Footnotes in this case have been renumbered for clarity.

	Loan I	Loan II
Amount Requested	$ 1000.00	$ 500.00
Cash Advanced	$ 1249.33	$ 1442.23[5]
Insurance Premiums	$ 214.02	$ 972.00
Recording Fees	$ 15.00	$ 184.00
Loan Principal	$ 1478.35	$ 2598.23

	Loan I	Loan II
Length of Loan	36 months	72 months
Annual Percentage Rate	24%	28.09%
Amount per Payment	$ 58.00	$ 75.00
Amount of Interest to Be Paid	$ 609.65	$ 2801.77
Total Amount to Repay	$ 2088.00	$ 5400.00

David Mootz, an employee of BFC, negotiated both loans.

Besta made 18 of the 36 payments due on Loan I. At that time, she needed $ 500.00 to finish her basement. She contacted Dial Finance, who, in turn, called BFC to check on Besta's BFC Loan.

David Mootz asked Dial Finance how much money Besta was requesting. Mootz then telephoned Besta at her home and "explained to her that if she wanted to come to Beneficial, that, you know, [he would] be glad to see if [he] could work up something for her to get her the money she needed." Record at 35. All of the terms for Loan II were discussed over the telephone, and on May 2, 1983, Besta went to BFC to sign the prepared documents. Dial Finance never responded to Besta with regard to her loan inquiry.

---

5. $877.76 of this amount was the unpaid balance from Loan I. It is unclear from the record whether this amount reflects any credit given for refund of any part of the $214.02 in insurance premiums charged in conjunction with Loan I even though, as indicated infra, only one half of the payments under Loan I had come due at the time of the refinancing.

Besta was laid off from her job soon after Loan II was made. She fell in arrears. To prevent BFC from foreclosing on her assets, she filed this rescissionary action. BFC counterclaimed for the amount then owing—$ 2986.86. The district court found in BFC's favor on both claims.

STANDARD OF REVIEW

Iowa courts review unconscionability determinations de novo. Home Fed. Sav. & Loan Assn. v. [Campney], 357 N.W.2d 613, 615 (Iowa 1984). Unconscionability is something that courts usually find as a matter of law. Iowa Code Annot. §537.5108(1). At the same time, it is evident that factual findings must be made in order to determine whether or not the transaction at issue meets the statutory standard. Such cases present mixed questions of law and fact. See Hill v. Blackwell, 774 F.2d 338, 343 (8th Cir. 1985); see also Mullan v. Quickie Aircraft, 797 F.2d 845, 850 (10th Cir. 1986). . . .

THE STATE LAW QUESTION

Katherine Keest, an expert witness, presented undisputed testimony that the Besta loan if paid over 36 months instead of 72 months would have cost Besta a total of $2541.88 instead of $5400.00—and her installment payments would have been $ 5.00 per month less. The question before us, then, is whether Iowa law was correctly applied when the district court concluded that it was not unconscionable for BFC to arrange to finance Loan II over a six-year period without informing Besta of a more advantageous three-year option.

The district court concluded that all of the insurance charges under Loan II were lawful. For a six-year loan, the court was correct. However, the thrust of Keest's testimony—she was a consumer lending specialist—was that lending $1442.23 over six years, with the insurance premiums necessary for a six-year loan, was an arrangement no fair person would propose. Record at 437.

Her testimony was that the longer the loan period, the higher the insurance premiums. By adding the increased premiums to the cash advanced, BFC propelled the loan principal to an ever higher amount, and in this case, made the principal amount exceed $2000.00.

With the loan principal greater than $2000.00, the lender could then take a valid mortgage on the borrower's home. (Iowa Code Annot. §537.2307 corroborates Keest's testimony on this point.) The real estate mortgage allegedly necessitated the charging of additional recording and other fees with regard to the security taken.[6] These fees were, in turn, added to the principal amount which then required the payment of still higher insurance premiums. Interest, of course, runs for six years on this entire amount.

The following chart illustrates the effect of Loan II being stretched to six years when compared to the terms calculated by Keest under a three-year agreement (Exh. 69). The terms for Loan I, a BFC loan that was for three years, substantiates [sic] the accuracy of Keest's figures.

	Loan I	Loan II	Exh. 69
Amount Requested	$ 1000.00	$ 500.00	$ 500.00
Cash Advanced	$ 1249.33	$ 1442.23	$ 1444.46[7]
Disability Insurance	$ 79.34	$ 275.40	$ 96.59
Life Insurance	$ 40.72	$ 210.60	$ 49.57
Household Contents Insurance	$ 93.96	$ 486.00	$ 114.38
Recording Fees	$ 15.00	$ 184.00	$—
Amount Financed	$ 1478.35	$ 2598.23	$ 1705.00
Annual Percentage Rate	24%	28.09%	28.09%
Number of Payments	36	72	36
Amount per Payment	$ 58/mo.	$ 75/mo.	$ 70.61/mo.
Amount of Interest to Pay	$ 609.65	$ 2801.77	$ 836.88
Total Amount to Repay	$ 2088.00	$ 5400.00	$ 2541.88

UNCONSCIONABILITY

The Iowa Consumer Credit Code permits a court to refuse enforcement of an unconscionable agreement or to enforce the agreement without the unconscionable terms. Iowa Code Annot. §537.5108(1). The contract must have been unconscionable at the time it was made. Id. To aid in making this

---

6. The total of the recording and other fees under Loan II was $184.00. Under Loan I, BFC also took and filed a mortgage on the real estate, which mortgage was apparently invalid under Iowa law. The recording and other fees under Loan I were, however, only $15.00.

7. This amount also includes the unpaid principal from Loan I.

determination, a court may consider the setting, purpose, and effect of the agreement. Id. at § 537.5108(3). Additionally, the existence and amount of separate charges for insurance are to be considered by a court when testing the agreement for unconscionability. Id. at § 537.5108(4)(d). A court is also to consider other indicia of unconscionability as applicable. See id. at §537.5108(4).[8]

Iowa courts have considered as factors unfair surprise, lack of notice, disparity of bargaining power and substantive unfairness. *Campney*, 357 N.W.2d at 618. Courts find that a bargain is unconscionable "if it is such as no man in his senses and not under delusion would make on the one hand, and as no honest and fair man would accept on the other." Smith v. Harrison, 325 N.W.2d 92, 94 (Iowa 1982). While we think Loan II was substantively unfair because there was no reasonable basis for writing the loan for a six-year period, we need not base our decision on such a finding. Instead, we hold that not telling Besta that she could have repaid the same loan with lower monthly payments in one-half the time deprived her of fair notice and amounted to unfair surprise—clearly no person in her senses would have accepted the more expensive term.[9] This constituted, at least, procedural unconscionability.

Similarly, we see no reasonable social or economic reason for structuring Loan II for six years with its attendant higher costs without first explaining and comparing the costs of a three-year loan. This is not a case, for example, like *Campney*, where the court held that due on sale clauses are not substantively unconscionable. In that case, the Iowa Supreme Court expressly found that such clauses were standard provisions. 357 N.W.2d at 618. Applying *Campney* to this case, one might find that the failure to explain how a three-year loan would operate when compared to a six-year

---

8. Other provisions in the Consumer Code mandate rules and express policies and practices, which if not obeyed or furthered in a transaction, might warrant a finding of unconscionability. See, e.g., Iowa Code Annot. §537.1102(2)(c)-(e) (liberal construction of Code to promote consumer understanding of credit transactions; obtaining credit at a reasonable cost; protecting against unfair practices); id. at §537.2308 (prohibiting a loan term greater than 37 months where the amount financed is less than $ 1000.00); id. at §537.2307 (making void security interests in borrower's home where the amount financed in certain loans is $ 2000.00 or less).

9. This holding of unfair surprise is not based upon any notion of a "quasi-fiduciary" duty to disclose potentially disadvantageous contract terms. The existence of such a duty was clearly rejected by the Iowa Supreme Court in *Campney*, 357 N.W.2d at 619. Here, however, even a careful reading of the contract by Besta would not have disclosed the advantages of an alternative proposition. Also, the intertwining of the obligations of Loan I with the new requirements of Loan II made contract comparison difficult, if not impossible, for the average borrower and, thus, removed this situation from the rationale advanced in *Campney*.

loan would not be unconscionable were six-year loans the norm. Here, however, there was testimony that consumer loans for a period longer than 36 months are rarely made. Record at 381. The district court made no finding to the contrary.

Moreover, finding Loan II unconscionable will not run afoul of one of the concerns expressed in *Campney*, namely, that finding the due on sale clause unconscionable would adversely affect the supply of lendable funds by limiting a lender's ability to protect his loan portfolio. See *Campney*, 357 N.W.2d at 618. No evidence was offered or claim made that BFC would not have made Besta a loan under a three-year agreement with only her personal property and motor vehicle as collateral. Indeed, the evidence is contrary. While we have been unable to locate testimony or a document showing the amount at which BFC estimated the value of the personal property, Besta's valuation of personal property form (Exh. 3) lists her household contents at a worth of $2775.00 for insurance purposes. The value of her motor vehicle is unknown. Therefore, the inescapable conclusion is that a real estate mortgage was not necessary to persuade BFC to make Besta the loan.

Additional evidence of this is the fact that the amount financed under Loan I was $1478.35 and BFC had only the household goods and automobile as security for the transaction. This suggests that BFC would have considered itself secure had it extended Besta the loan calculated by Keest—$1705.00 for three years.

BFC also insists that Besta was not required to buy insurance as a condition for obtaining Loan II. See Record at 498-504. Using Keest's hypothetical loan as an example of a loan made without insurance, the amount financed under a three-year plan would have been $1444.46 ($564.47 cash advanced to finish basement plus $877.76 used to pay off the outstanding balance from Loan I). This amount is less than the amount financed under Loan I—$1478.35—when BFC felt itself to be adequately secured through the use of Besta's personal property as collateral.

Applying the same reasoning to the six-year loan that was actually extended, we again must conclude that BFC would have made a loan using only Besta's personal property as security. If Besta had not purchased the insurance listed under Loan II (and BFC says she did not have to), the amount financed would have been only $1442.23, an amount less than that financed under Loan I. Thus, there is no basis under which we should enforce an agreement that BFC could never have negotiated had it made full and fair disclosure.

We do recognize that by structuring Loan II for six years BFC was able to obtain a security interest in Besta's house. For some borrowers, this may have been the only way to obtain a loan. In those cases, though, there would have been no more advantageous terms to disclose. Such is not what occurred in this case. Mootz stated in his deposition that BFC was, in fact, oversecured on Loan I, and he based that assessment on Besta's work history and payment record. See Deposition at 67. Therefore, there is no reason to conclude that BFC set up Loan II in this manner because it would have been imprudent, creditwise, to lend an amount less than $2000.00 and not have a mortgage in Besta's house. And, the district court did not so conclude.

Considering the Code policies and the circumstances surrounding Loan II, executing this loan for six years without disclosure of the three-year option was an unconscionable practice—both under Iowa common law and the Iowa Consumer Credit Code. We reverse the district court and remand for rescissionary relief—but direct that BFC may collect on its judgment as if a three-year loan had been written, and find that BFC should have recourse to only those assets which would have been available as security under a three-year loan. As further relief, the district court should award Besta her reasonable attorney fees pursuant to section 537.5108(6) of the Iowa Consumer Credit Code.

CONCLUSION

We recognize the deference owed the trial judge who has observed witnesses and gauged credibility. And, we have not overturned a single finding of fact to the extent that such finding applies to a fairly negotiated six-year loan. However, we are uncomfortable with the fact that a lender would call up a borrower at home, tell her he could get her the money she needs, and then set up a loan that is exorbitantly expensive while failing to tell her that she could get everything she wants for less money and at a lower monthly payment. To the extent that the district court's decision did not address this matter, its decision that the loan in question was not unconscionable was an incorrect interpretation of the Iowa Code.

Accordingly, the order appealed from is reversed and remanded for the granting of the relief specified in this opinion.

CHAPTER 11
Debt Collection

I. THE COMMON LAW

The collection of debts brings out the ugliness in people. The usage of trade apparently permits almost any tactic this side of the law (and not infrequently far on the other side). The debt collector's justification for outrageous behavior is that the debtor is, after all, a deadbeat, the sort who likely will not pay his or her debts unless scared into it, and who therefore deserves whatever happens. Legal Services attorneys routinely testify in legislative hearings as to the abuse suffered by their clients, ranging from bizarre statements that play on people's worst fears ("You'll lose your children if you don't pay this debt") to violence (for example, bomb threats).When Congress was considering the adoption of the statute described in the next section, it heard testimony from a professional debt collector (he testified while wearing a ski mask!) who said that a debt collector is not considered really good unless able to collect a debt that is not owed at all.[1]

Courts (and juries), sympathetic to the debtor when the more atrocious cases came to trial, have dealt out punishment through the use of a number of tort theories. Assault and battery have successfully been used when the debt collector goes too far, and defamation (libel or slander) is available when the debt collector starts spreading stories to third parties (neighbors, relatives, babysitters, credit bureaus). The problem with defamation, as we noted earlier, is that truth is a defense, and the cagey debt collector avoids the tort by telling the literal truth about the debt. The most popular tort theory has proved to be invasion of privacy.

---

1. For a splendid discussion on point, see Arthur Leff, Injury, Ignorance, and Spite—The Dynamics of Collection, 80 Yale L.J. I (1970), and the symposium thereon in 33 U. Pitt. L. Rev. 66 (1972).

NORRIS v. MOSKIN STORES, INC.
Supreme Court of Alabama, 1961
132 So. 2d 321

STAKELY, Justice.

Nealus E. Norris (appellant) brought an action for damages against Moskin Stores, Inc. and Morris Nathan (appellees). Counts 1 and 3 of the complaint, as amended, seek damages for invasion of plaintiff's privacy. Count 4 of the amended complaint avers "an intentional interference" by defendants with plaintiff's "marital contract and marital relations." Count 2, which set forth a cause of action for slander, was stricken and is not involved on this appeal. The defendants separately and severally demurred to the complaint as amended and separately and severally to each count thereof. The trial court sustained the demurrers and, on motion of plaintiff, granted a nonsuit. From this order plaintiff has appealed, assigning as error the ruling of the trial court on the demurrers.

The gist of plaintiff-appellant's cause for invasion of privacy is contained in the allegations of Count 3, which are as follows:

[D]efendants were operating a commercial and mercantile business in the City of Birmingham, attempting to collect money allegedly owed by plaintiff to Moskin Stores, Inc. Plaintiff avers that an agent, servant, or employee of the defendants, while acting within the line and scope of her employment as such agent, servant, or employee in the course of said commercial and mercantile business, in attempting to collect money allegedly owed by plaintiff, by the use of the telephone, called plaintiff's wife on two occasions at the place where she was employed and stated, in substance, that the person calling was "Doris," that she had met the plaintiff in Indiana, that she had dated him, that she had to get in touch with plaintiff on a matter of importance, that said Doris wanted to meet with plaintiff alone and without plaintiff's wife being present, and said agent, servant, or employee as aforesaid left a telephone number, which number plaintiff was to call; plaintiff further avers that on the same date, an agent, servant, or employee of the defendants, while acting within the line and scope of her employment as such agent, servant, or employee, in the course of said commercial and mercantile business, in attempting to collect money allegedly owed by plaintiff, called plaintiff's sister-in-law inquiring as to plaintiff's whereabouts and his place of employment, that she (Doris) was "in trouble" and had to get in touch with plaintiff, inquiring as to whether plaintiff was married, and upon being advised in the affirmative she stated that "he (meaning the plaintiff) told me he wasn't married"; that said person, in the course of the aforesaid telephone conversations, and in an effort to locate plaintiff's employment, led persons to whom she was speaking into believing that plaintiff had engaged, or was engaging, in activities contrary to the recognized conventions of his marital status.

Plaintiff avers that the aforesaid inquiries and statements made over the telephone by an agent, servant, or employee of the defendants, while acting within the line and scope of her employment as such agent, servant, or employee, in the cause of said commercial and mercantile business, in attempting to collect money allegedly owed by plaintiff as aforesaid; violated plaintiff's right of privacy, and as a proximate consequence thereof plaintiff suffered the following injuries and damages; he was humiliated and embarrassed; his marital relations and homelife were disrupted; his wife parted from him for a short time; he was caused to suffer mental anguish; and his character and reputation were damaged and injured, for all of which plaintiff claims damages.

The State of Alabama is among those states which recognize that a man has a right of privacy the violation of which may be actionable. Smith v. Doss, 251 Ala. 250, 37 So. 2d 118. The particular application of the principles of the right of privacy which these appellants seek to make is, however, as yet novel to this jurisdiction. The earlier cases decided by this court have concerned situations in which it was claimed that the defendant had given unwarranted and intrusive publicity to the private affairs of the plaintiff, Smith v. Doss, supra, and Abernathy v. Thornton, 263 Ala. 496, 83 So. 2d 235, or had made unauthorized use of plaintiff's name for commercial purposes. Birmingham Broadcasting Co. v. Bell, 259 Ala. 656, 68 So. 2d 314; 263 Ala. 355, 82 So. 2d 345. But nothing in the foregoing cases shows that the action for invasion of privacy is necessarily limited to those situations alone. For example, a cause of action for invasion of privacy has been held to lie for unwarranted intrusion by means of a listening device (McDaniel v. Atlanta Coca-Cola Bottling Co., 60 Ga. App. 92, 2 S.E.2d 810, 811; Roach v. Harper, W. Va., 105 S.E.2d 564), for persistent shadowing (Schultz v. Frankfort Marine, Acci. & P.G. Ins. Co., 151 Wis. 537, 139 N.W. 386, 43 L.R.A., N.S., 520), and for a shop manager's angrily and roughly accosting a female customer and searching her coat and purse (Bennett v. Norban, 396 Pa. 94, 151 A.2d 476, 71 A.L.R.2d 803).

It is suggested in Prosser, Law of Torts 637-39 (2d ed. 1955), that the invasion of privacy tort consists in fact of four distinct wrongs, (1) "the intrusion upon the plaintiff's physical solitude or seclusion," (2) "publicity which violates the ordinary decencies," (3) "putting the plaintiff in a false but not necessarily defamatory position in the public eye," and (4) "the appropriation of some element of the plaintiff's personality for a commercial use." We think this analysis fundamentally consistent with our statement in the *Doss* case and reaffirmed in the *Abernathy* case, adopted from 41 Am. Jur. 925, that the right of privacy is "'the right of a person to be free from unwarranted publicity,' or 'the unwarranted appropriation or exploitation of one's personality, the publicizing of one's private affairs with which the public has no legitimate concern, or *the wrongful intrusion into one's private activities in such manner as to outrage or cause mental suffering, shame or humiliation to a person of ordinary sensibilities.*'" [Emphasis added.]

We think that there may be circumstances under which the actions of a creditor in regard to his debtor fall within Dean Prosser's first category of actionable wrong, or, in the words of the *Doss* case, constitute an outrageous "wrongful intrusion."

The mere efforts of a creditor, in this case the appellees, to collect a debt cannot without more be considered a wrongful and actionable intrusion. A creditor has and must have the right to take reasonable action to pursue his debtor and collect his debt. But the right to pursue the debtor is not a license to outrage the debtor. The problem of defining the scope of the right of privacy in the debtor-creditor situation is the problem of balancing the interest of the creditor in collecting his debt against that of the debtor in his own personality. Some courts appear to have struck that balance on the so-called "rule of reason." Thus in the recent case of Housh v. Peth, 99 Ohio App. 485, 135 N.E.2d 440, 449, affirmed 165 Ohio St. 35, 133 N.E.2d 340, the Ohio appellate courts asserted that "a creditor has a right to take reasonable action to pursue his debtor and persuade payment, although the steps taken may result to a certain degree in the invasion of the debtor's right of privacy," but that the debtor has a cause of action for injurious conduct on the part of the creditor which exceeds the bounds of reasonableness. We approve this statement.

The phrase "reasonable action" is of course not one for which exact legal definition can be prescribed. What constitutes "reasonable" action must depend largely on the facts of the particular case. In Housh v. Peth, supra, the creditor-defendant "deliberately initiated a systematic campaign of harassment of the plaintiff, not only in numerous telephone calls to the plaintiff herself every day for a period of three weeks, some of which were late at night, but also calls to her superiors over the telephone, informing them of the debt. . . ." Plaintiff "was called out of the classroom in the public schools where she was employed three times within 15 minutes; . . . she lost a roomer at her rooming house because of the repeated calls, and was threatened with loss of employment unless the telephone calls ceased." Housh v. Peth, 135 N.E.2d 440, 449.

The *Housh* decision is supported by Barnett v. Collection Service, 214 Iowa 1303, 242 N.W. 25, and LaSalle Extension University v. Fogarty, 126 Neb. 457, 253 N.W. 424, 91 A.L.R. 1491. These cases involved harassment of the plaintiff-debtor by the defendant-creditor by means of coarse, inflammatory, threatening, or malicious letters producing mental pain and anguish on the part of the plaintiff, which the Iowa and Nebraska courts held actionable. These cases have in common with the *Housh* case the element of intentional "systematic campaign of harassment." See also, Brents v. Morgan, 221 Ky. 765, 299 S.W. 967, 55 A.L.R. 964; Clark v.

Associated Retail Credit Men of Washington, D.C., 70 App. D.C. 183, 105 F.2d 62; Quina v. Robert's et al., La. App., 16 So. 2d 558; Western Guaranty Loan Co. v. Dean, Tex. Civ. App., 309 S.W.2d 857.

On the other hand, the case of Gouldman-Taber Pontiac Inc. v. Zerbst, 213 Ga. 682, 100 S.E.2d 881, consistent with dictum in *Housh*, and we think correctly, held that a single letter written by the defendant-creditor to the plaintiff-debtor's employer merely notifying him of the debt did not constitute an actionable invasion of plaintiff's privacy.

> The right of privacy is not absolute but is qualified by the rights of others. . . . A recluse who completely extricated himself from society might well expect no interference whatever from the outside world. But one who, like the plaintiff, is employed by a large corporation, who is an active participant in the business world, who has an automobile and drives it upon the highways, has it serviced and repaired, and obtains credit for goods and services used in repairing her car, may expect reasonable conduct on the part of those with whom she does business and from whom she gets credit. . . . When she accepts the credit, she impliedly consents for her creditor to take all reasonable and necessary action to collect the bill. Writing to her employer, as this creditor did, was in our opinion a reasonable exercise of his rights and constituted no unwarranted or unreasonable interference with her right of privacy. Gouldman-Taber Pontiac v. Zerbst, 100 S.E.2d 881, 883.

Following the *Zerbst* case, the recent case of Tollefson v. Safeway Stores, Colo., 351 P.2d 274, 276, concerned the activities of a defendant bill collector who informed plaintiff's wife that if the debt, on a dishonored check, were not paid, plaintiff's job would be in jeopardy, and who contacted plaintiff's superiors, seeking to bring pressure on plaintiff to pay. The Colorado court held that on these facts plaintiff had no cause of action for invasion of privacy, pointing out that "there was no campaign of continuous harassment, no attempt to vilify or expose plaintiff to public ridicule, and no effort to cause plaintiff to lose his position. . . ." "It is not an invasion of privacy," according to that court, "to remind one of his obligations be they legal or moral."

Similarly, relief was denied in Patton v. Jacobs, 118 Ind. App. 358, 78 N.E.2d 789 (two letters to employer concerning the debt); Lewis v. Physicians and Dentists Credit Bureau, Wash., 177 P.2d 896 (single telephone call to wife's employer advising of unpaid bill and of intent to start garnishment proceedings).

In the case at bar, assuming as we must that the allegations of the complaint are true, it may be difficult to construe the three telephone calls, compared for example with the numerous calls in the *Housh* case, supra, as a "systematic campaign" of harassment. Furthermore, the calls in the instant case were made to members of appellant's family, so that there may be here lacking part of the element of humiliating publicity present in some of the cases. On the other hand, according to the pleadings, it does not appear that the caller suggested or attempted to urge payment, or indeed that any reference whatever was made to the existence of the alleged debt. If the allegations of the complaint are true, the alleged telephone calls were but a vicious attempt to coerce payment. This course of conduct cannot be justified as reasonably related to a legitimate effort to collect the debt. The defendants did not choose to put themselves in the position of creditor when they, through their agent, made these calls. They cannot seek to invoke that protection now. In view of the nature of these telephone conversations, which a jury could find outrageous and humiliating to a person of ordinary sensibilities, we must conclude that the complaint sets forth sufficient "harassment" and that the activities of the defendants fall beyond the realm of reasonable action and into the area of wrongful and actionable intrusion.

Appellees contend, however, that there can be no actionable invasion of privacy for spoken, as opposed to written, words. Dicta to this effect appear in Brents v. Morgan, 221 Ky. 765, 299 S.W. 967, 55 A.L.R. 964; Cason v. Baskin, 155 Fla. 198, 20 So. 2d 243, 168 A.L.R. 430, and Melvin v. Reid, 112 Cal. App. 285, 297 P. 91. We think this proposition is incorrect. To exclude actions for oral invasion of privacy would, for example, be to ignore the dangerous potential of the modern media of mass communication. Furthermore, our acceptance of this proposition would be inconsistent with, if not to overrule, our decision in the *Doss* case, supra, which involved the spoken word.

In the *Abernathy* case, supra, we quoted with general approval an extensive paragraph, outlining the general theory of the right to privacy, from Dean Hepburn's Cases on Torts, which contains the statement that "The right of privacy can only be violated by printings, writings, pictures, or other printed publications or reproductions, and not by word of mouth." Hepburn, Cases on Torts 504. But we consider that our concern in the *Abernathy* case was more with other aspects of the quoted paragraph, and particularly with the situation wherein one "becomes an actor in an occurrence of public or general interest." Certainly nothing in the *Abernathy* case turned on whether the allegedly objectionable words were written or not. Nor was there any attempt or intention in the *Abernathy* case to overrule the *Doss* case, supra. The *Abernathy* opinion cites *Doss* and rests in part on it. *Abernathy* cannot be taken as authority for the proposition here urged.

We note that the cases which contain language purporting to limit the action to written words or printings appear to base their position on the original article from which the action is generally conceded to originate. Warren and Brandeis, The Right to Privacy, 4 Harv. L. Rev. 193 [1890].

The "Hepburn" statement is from one of those cases, Melvin v. Reid, supra.

We observe that the statement actually made by Warren and Brandeis is that "The Law would *probably* not grant any redress for the invasion of privacy by oral publication *in the absence of special damages*." 4 Harv. L. Rev. 217. [Emphasis added.] While a requirement of special damages for oral invasion of privacy may have been occasionally suggested in later writings (see 41 Am. Jur. 950), we find no indication that it has received general acceptance. Indeed, in Smith v. Doss, supra [251 Ala. 250, 37 So. 2d 120], we pointed out that unlike libel, "in actions for infringement of the right of privacy . . . it is never necessary to allege or prove special damages."

In Roach v. Harper, W. Va., 105 S.E.2d 564, the West Virginia court stated that

> Courts which have followed the doctrine of the existence of the right of action have had no difficulty in reaching the conclusion that an allegation of special damages is not necessary to the validity of the pleading. We think the conclusion logical. The invasion of the right, the tort committed, gives right to the action, the right to recover damages. "Publication or commercialization may aggravate, but the individual's right to privacy is invaded and violated nevertheless in the original act of intrusion." McDaniel v. Atlanta Coca-Cola Bottling Co., supra. Questions of special damages, of course, may arise so as to enhance recovery. Also, circumstances may arise which would mitigate the damages. . . . The same reasoning leads to the conclusion that a declaration in such an action, to be sufficient against demurrer, need not allege publication of information or results obtained through the invasion. 105 S.E.2d at page 568.

We note that Warren and Brandeis gave us their reason for the limitation, reasoning by way of analogy to the law of libel and slander, that "The injury resulting from such oral communications would ordinarily be so trifling that the law might well, in the interest of free speech, disregard it altogether." 4 Harv. L. Rev. at 217. The Warren-Brandeis article was published in 1890, long before the advent of the modern methods of mass communication to which we have already alluded. While it may have been possible seventy years ago to dismiss all oral communications as "trifling" in effect, such a conclusion would today be contrary to modern realities. Therefore, if we have not already done so in Smith v. Doss, supra, we must now reject the view, if such exists, that special damages must be shown where the invasion of privacy is by spoken words.

We conclude that the complaint states a good cause of action for invasion of privacy and that the demurrers to Counts 1 and 3 should have been overruled. . . .

Reversed and remanded.

PROBLEM 150

Caspar Milquetoast borrowed $1,000 from Webster Loan Company, agreeing to pay it back in six months. In addition to a promissory note, Webster presented Caspar with a blank check for $1,125 payable to the order of Webster and dated six months in the future. The loan officer asked him to sign it on the drawer's line. Caspar protested that it was drawn on a bank at which he had no account. The loan officer reassured him that there was no plan to cash the check; it was simply extra collateral, and signing it was a mere formality. Relieved by this explanation, Caspar signed the check. Six months later Caspar was having financial troubles, and he failed to pay the Webster loan on the date it was due. Two days later Caspar was horrified when he was arrested for passing a bad check. It seems that Webster had cashed the check after all, and when it bounced, had Caspar prosecuted under a bad check law. This law permits the payee to recover not only the amount of the check but also 10 percent penalty, plus costs and attorney's fees. You are the criminal lawyer whom Caspar calls from jail. Can you help him?

There may be some relief here in the tort of abuse of process, which requires the wrongful use of legal proceedings. Other theories include the intentional infliction of emotional distress, see the Restatement (Second) of Torts §46(1) and MacDermid v. Discover Fin. Servs., 488 F.3d 721 (6th Cir. 2007) (mentally ill woman committed suicide when creditor threatened criminal action for failure to pay a credit card debt); or, if Webster had merely threatened to prosecute him, blackmail (which is statutorily controlled). Malicious prosecution—the bringing of groundless suits with malice—is also a possibility. See W. Prosser, Torts ch. 22 (4th ed. 1971). Some states have created their own special remedy. Texas recognizes a tort called "unreasonable collection efforts," see, e.g., Southwestern Bell Tel. Co. v. Wilson, 768 S.W.2d 755 (Tex. App. 1988) (award of $5 million upheld).

Bankruptcy and the Automatic Stay.   One important rule everyone should be aware of is this: the filing of a bankruptcy petition stops all creditor collection activity other than the filing of a claim in the bankruptcy proceeding. Section 362 of the Bankruptcy Code creates an *automatic stay* of acts to collect, enforce, or recover the debtor's property and gives a remedy of actual damages, punitive damages, and attorney's fees to any individual injured by the violation of the automatic stay. The operation of the stay does not depend on formal notice to the creditor of the filing of the bankruptcy petition, so that if the creditor takes action that *unknowingly* violates the stay the creditor must immediately undo that action or be in contempt of court. *Any* true information that a bankruptcy has been filed, coming from whatever source, that reaches the creditor means that creditors must cease any further collection activities. Creditors who continue collection efforts of any kind thereafter risk the civil remedy just mentioned in addition to an angry bankruptcy judge holding the creditor in contempt.

II. FAIR DEBT COLLECTION PRACTICES ACT

Effective March 20, 1978, the Fair Debt Collection Practices Act, 15 U.S.C. §1692, became Title VIII of the Consumer Credit Protection Act. Read FDCPA §802. The Federal Trade Commission is given charge of administrative enforcement of the Act, but is specifically forbidden the power to promulgate trade regulation rules having the force of law, FDCPA §814(d). This stern decree has not, however, prevented the FTC from issuing a "General Policy of Interpretation Staff Commentary" on point, 53 Fed. Reg. 50,097 (Dec. 13, 1988), and any attorney practicing in this field would be well advised to write to the FTC, obtain a copy, and study it carefully. This commentary, while persuasive, does not have the force of law. See Jordan v. Kent Recovery Servs., Inc., 731 F. Supp. 652 (D. Del. 1990). The introduction to the Commentary specifically says this, noting that

> it is a guideline intended to clarify the staff interpretations of the statute, but does not have the force or effect of statutory provisions. It is not a formal trade regulation rule or advisory opinion of the Commission, and thus is not binding on the Commission or the public.

A. Scope

As the Act regulates "debt collectors," the meaning of that term is crucial. For an annotation on point, see Annot., "What Constitutes 'Debt' and 'Debt Collector' for Purposes of Fair Debt Collection Practices Act," 62 A.L.R. Fed. 552. Study §803(6) and use it to solve the following Problems.

PROBLEM 151

Big Department Store had a prize-winning collection department, the envy of all the debt collectors in town. It always communicated with debtors by postcards with the word DEADBEAT written in large letters across the front, and this message on the reverse side: "Pay up or our employee Bruno will drop by to explain the company's usual procedures on being stiffed." Does this conduct violate the FDCPA? See §§806, 808(7), and 803(6). If the company uses a phony letterhead to pretend that the collection letter is from the nonexistent "Dunner Collection Agency," is it now covered by the Act? See Catencamp v. Cendant Timeshare Resort Group—Consumer Finance, Inc., 471 F.3d 780 (7th Cir. 2006).

As the FDCPA doesn't regulate creditors who are collecting their own debts (and who account for the vast majority of collection activity), what does? The common law theories discussed at the start of this chapter are still in play, of course. The Federal Trade Commission has indicated that it is a violation of the Commission's rules against "unfair and deceptive practices" (§5 of the FTC Act) for creditors to engage in reprehensible collection activity, and that in deciding this issue the Commission will look to the rules of FDCPA for examples of forbidden behavior.

1. The Meaning of "Debt Collector"

Returning to the Fair Debt Collection Practices Act, the statutory definition of "debt collector" in §803(6) includes two broad categories: independent professional debt collection businesses, and persons "who regularly collect . . . directly or indirectly, debts owed or due or asserted to be owed or due another," unless one of the six exceptions then listed applies. This is trickier than it at first looks.

PROBLEM 152

Facade Motors sold all its customers' accounts to Octopus National Bank, which proceeded to try to collect the debts. The bank found that debtors were more likely to pay debts if they were willing to talk to the debt collector. Debtors who ducked all conversations with debt collectors, either over the phone or in person, rarely paid a cent voluntarily. To make debtors anxious to discuss the debt, ONB's first dunning letter greatly exaggerated the actual debt ("Our records show that you owe $816," when the true debt was $387, for example). ONB found that this outraged and frightened the debtors, so that they would immediately place an indignant call to the bank. At this point the bank's loan officer would seduce the debtor with a gentle apology ("Our records were in error and we are so sorry") and then talk the debtor into a payment plan. Does this collection practice violate the Act? See §807(2)(A); for an annotation on the meaning of §807, see Annot., 67 A.L.R. Fed. 974. Is an assignee of the debt, like ONB, a "debt collector," or is it collecting its *own* debt? See McKinney v. Cadleway Properties, Inc., 548 F.3d 496 (7th Cir. 2008).

PROBLEM 153

Mr. and Mrs. Suburb financed the purchase of their home through Octopus National Bank, which had the first mortgage thereon. Shortly after the closing, the bank forwarded the debt to the Proper Mortgage Corporation for servicing. Proper Mortgage was a mortgage service company, which means that it handled the administration of the mortgage as agent for the bank. Thus, it sent the consumer monthly bills, collected the money, and, if necessary, engaged in foreclosure. The Suburbs made their payments regularly for five years, sending the money to Proper Mortgage (which deducted its fee and remitted the excess to ONB). Then Mrs. Suburb became very ill and her medical expenses consumed their income. They stopped paying all creditors for two months. Proper Mortgage Corporation sent a collection letter that contained an insert purporting to be from the Internal Revenue Service and addressed to the Suburbs. It stated, in part:

> You have been claiming interest on your mortgage debt as a tax-deductible expense. We understand you have ceased paying your mortgage, and, unless we hear otherwise shortly, will begin an investigation of you for tax fraud.

You are an attorney who has been doing the Suburbs' taxes for the last three years, so they naturally bring this letter to you. You know that the IRS did not send the enclosed threat. Is this pretense a violation of the FDCPA? See §807(9). Is Proper Mortgage Corp. a "debt collector"? See §803(6)(F)(iii) and Coppola v. Connecticut Student Loan Found., 1989 WL 47419 (D. Conn. Mar. 21, 1989).

PROBLEM 154

Facade Motors, as we saw in Problem 152, frequently sold its customers' accounts to Octopus National Bank. These accounts represented the sale of vehicles, and the dealership naturally had taken a security interest in the vehicles at the time of purchase. When the accounts were sold, Facade Motors assigned its interest in the collateral to the bank and agreed to help the bank collect the accounts if the consumers involved proved difficult. When the dealership follows through on this promise, is it a "debt collector"? See §803(6)(F)(ii).

PROBLEM 155

Facade Motors borrowed money from Octopus National Bank under an agreed line of credit, using all of its accounts receivable as collateral for the various loans. When Facade defaulted on its re- payment schedule, the bank began collecting the accounts owed to Facade by contacting the dealership's customers and demanding payment directly to the bank. In this situation is the bank a "debt collector"? See §803(6)(F)(iv).

When Congress realized that there were more attorneys engaged in full- time debt collection than there were debt collection agencies,[2] it amended the statute in 1986 so that some attorneys were included in the definition of "debt collector."

PROBLEM 156

Sam Ambulance was an attorney who was on retainer to the Permanent Temporary Company, which supplied temporary work- ers to businesses. Sam's debt collection was limited to writing let- ters on behalf of Permanent Temporary Company whenever its business clients did not pay their bills on time. This happened about three times a year. Last week Permanent asked him to collect $200 it was owed by Barbara Shipek, who had hired one of their laborers

---

2. The numbers were 5,000 to 4,500. H.R. Rep. No. 405, 99th Cong., 2d Sess. (1985), *reprinted in* 1986 U.S. Code & Admin. News 1752.

as a maid for a swank party she threw. Sam wrote Ms. Shipek a letter asking her to pay the debt and telling her that if she did not, Sam would see to it that she went to jail. Ms. Shipek, who is sure that she paid this bill, is very upset. She calls you, the attorney who lives in the house across the street from her, and asks for advice. Has Sam violated the Act? See §807(4). Is Sam a "debt collector"? See the Supreme Court case below. If Sam threatens to take legal action to collect the debt, but in fact has never filed suit in connection with the hundreds of letters he has sent on behalf of the Permanent Temporary Company, does this violate §807? See *United States v. National Fin. Servs.*, 98 F.3d 131 (4th Cir. 1996) (FTC action in which magazine distributor and its attorney hit with $550,000 fine for sending millions of debt collection letters threatening lawsuits when none were actually ever filed); *Boyd v. Wexler*, 275 F.3d 642 (7th Cir. 2001) (attorney claimed to personally review each of 439,606 dunning letters sent out in nine-month period); *Brown v. Card Service Center*, 464 F.3d 450 (3d Cir. 2006) (letter saying nonpayment "could" result in lawsuit violated FDCPA if such suits were never filed).

When an attorney collecting debts on behalf of a client contacts the debtor, in addition to complying with FDCPA, the attorney must be very careful not to pretend to be disinterested or give the debtor legal advice supposedly to protect his/her interests. This is forbidden by Rule 4.3 of the Model Rules of Professional Conduct ("Dealing with Unrepresented Person"), which elaborates in its Official Comment:

> An unrepresented person, particularly one not experienced in dealing with legal matters, might assume that a lawyer is disinterested in loyalties or is a disinterested authority on the law even when the lawyer represents a client. During the course of a lawyer's representation of a client, the lawyer should not give advice to an unrepresented person other than the advice to obtain counsel.

QUOTES FOR THE ATTORNEY'S ARSENAL: "THREATS BY AN ATTORNEY"

> Abuses by attorney collectors are more egregious than those of lay collectors because a consumer reacts with far more duress to any attorney's improper threat of legal action than to a debt collection agency committing the same practice. A debt collection letter on an attorney's letterhead conveys authority and credibility.

Crossley v. Lieberman, 868 F.2d 566, 570 (3d Cir. 1989).

HEINTZ v. JENKINS
United States Supreme Court, 1995
514 U.S. 291

Justice BREYER delivered the opinion of the Court.

The issue before us is whether the term "debt collector" in the Fair Debt Collection Practices Act, 91 Stat. 874, 15 U.S.C. §§1692-1692o (1988 ed. and Supp. V), applies to a lawyer who "regularly," *through litigation*, tries to collect consumer debts. The Court of Appeals for the Seventh Circuit held that it does. We agree with the Seventh Circuit and we affirm its judgment.

The Fair Debt Collection Practices Act prohibits "debt collector[s]" from making false or misleading representations and from engaging in various abusive and unfair practices. The Act says, for example, that a "debt collector" may not use violence, obscenity, or repeated annoying phone calls, 15 U.S.C. §1692d; may not falsely represent "the character, amount, or legal status of any debt," §1692e(2)(A); and may not use various "unfair or unconscionable means to collect or attempt to collect" a consumer debt, §1692f. Among other things, the Act sets out rules that a debt collector must follow for "acquiring location information" about the debtor, §1692b; communicating about the debtor (and the debt) with third parties, §1692c(b); and bringing "[l]egal actions," §1692i. The Act imposes upon "debt collector[s]" who violate its provisions (specifically described) "[c]ivil liability" to those whom they, e.g., harass, mislead, or treat unfairly. §1692k. The Act also authorizes the Federal Trade Commission to enforce its provisions. §1692l(a). The Act's definition of the term "debt collector" includes a person "who regularly collects or attempts to collect, directly or indirectly, debts owed [to] . . . another." §1692a(6). And, it limits "debt" to consumer debt, i.e., debts "arising out of . . . transaction[s]" that "are primarily for personal, family, or household purposes." §1692a(5).

The plaintiff in this case, Darlene Jenkins, borrowed money from the Gainer Bank in order to buy a car. She defaulted on her loan. The bank's law firm then sued Jenkins in state court to recover the balance due. As part of an effort to settle the suit, a lawyer with that law firm, George Heintz, wrote to Jenkins's lawyer. His letter, in listing the amount she owed under the loan agreement, included $4,173 owed for insurance, bought by the bank because she had not kept the car insured as she had promised to do.

Jenkins then brought this Fair Debt Collection Practices Act suit against Heintz and his firm. She claimed that Heintz's letter violated the Act's prohibitions against trying to collect an amount not "authorized by the agreement creating the debt," §1692f(1), and against making a "false representation of . . . the . . . amount . . . of any debt," §1692e(2)(A). The loan agreement, she conceded, required her to keep the car insured "against loss or damage" and permitted the bank to buy such insurance to protect the car should she fail to do so. App. to Pet. for Cert. 17. But, she said, the $4,137 substitute policy was not the kind of policy the loan agreement had in mind, for it insured the bank not only against "loss or damage" but also against her failure to repay the bank's car loan. Hence, Heintz's "representation" about the "amount" of her "debt" was "false"; amounted to an effort to collect an "amount" not "authorized" by the loan agreement; and thus violated the Act.

Pursuant to Rule 12(b)(6) of the Federal Rules of Civil Procedure, the District Court dismissed Jenkins's Fair Debt Collection lawsuit for failure to state a claim. The court held the Act does not apply to lawyers engaging in litigation. However, the Court of Appeals for the Seventh Circuit reversed the District Court's judgment, interpreting the Act to apply to litigating lawyers. Jenkins v. Heintz, 25 F.3d 536 (1994). The Seventh Circuit's view in this respect conflicts with that of the Sixth Circuit. See Green v. Hocking, 9 F.3d 18 (1993) (per curiam). We granted certiorari to resolve this conflict. 513 U.S.—, 115 S. Ct. 416, 130 L. Ed. 2d 332 (1994). And, as we have said, we conclude that the Seventh Circuit is correct. The Act does apply to lawyers engaged in litigation.

There are two rather strong reasons for believing that the Act applies to the litigating activities of lawyers. *First*, the Act defines the "debt collector[s]" to whom it applies as including those who "regularly collec[t] or attemp[t] to collect, directly or indirectly, [consumer] debts owed or due or asserted to be owed or due another." §1692a(6). In ordinary English, a lawyer who regularly tries to obtain payment of consumer debts through legal proceedings is a lawyer who regularly "attempts" to "collect" those consumer debts. See, e.g., Black's Law Dictionary 263 (6th ed. 1990) ("To collect a debt or claim is to obtain payment or liquidation of it, either by personal solicitation or legal proceedings.").

Second, in 1977, Congress enacted an earlier version of this statute, which contained an express exemption for lawyers. That exemption said that the term "debt collector" did not include "any attorney-at-law collecting a debt as an attorney on behalf of and in the name of a client." Pub. L. 95-109, §803(6)(F), 91 Stat. 874, 875. In 1986, however, Congress repealed this exemption in its entirety, Pub. L. 99-361, 100 Stat. 768, without creating a narrower, litigation-related, exemption to fill the void. Without more, then, one would think that Congress intended that lawyers be subject to the Act whenever they meet the general "debt collector" definition.

Heintz argues that we should nonetheless read the statute as containing an implied exemption for those debt-collecting activities of lawyers that consist of litigating (including, he assumes, settlement efforts). He relies primarily on three arguments.

First, Heintz argues that many of the Act's requirements, if applied directly to litigating activities, will create harmfully anomalous results that Congress simply could not have intended. We address this argument in light of the fact that, when Congress first wrote the Act's substantive provisions, it had for the most part exempted litigating attorneys from the Act's coverage; that, when Congress later repealed the attorney exemption, it did not revisit the wording of these substantive provisions; and that, for these reasons, some awkwardness is understandable. Particularly when read in this light, we find Heintz's argument unconvincing.

Many of Heintz's "anomalies" are not particularly anomalous. For example, the Sixth Circuit pointed to §1692e(5), which forbids a "debt collector" to make any "threat to take action that cannot legally be taken." The court reasoned that, were the Act to apply to litigating activities, this provision automatically would make liable any litigating lawyer who brought, and then lost, a claim against a debtor. *Green,* supra, at 21. But, the Act says explicitly that a "debt collector" may not be held liable if he "shows by a preponderance of evidence that the violation was not intentional and resulted from a bona fide error notwithstanding the maintenance of procedures reasonably adapted to avoid any such error." §1692k(c). Thus, even if we were to assume that the suggested reading of §1692e(5) is correct, we would not find the result so absurd as to warrant implying an exemption for litigating lawyers. In any event, the assumption would seem unnecessary, for we do not see how the fact that a lawsuit turns out ultimately to be unsuccessful could, by itself, make the bringing of it an "action that cannot legally be taken."

The remaining significant "anomalies" similarly depend for their persuasive force upon readings that courts seem unlikely to endorse. For example, Heintz's strongest "anomaly" argument focuses upon the Act's provisions governing "[c]ommunication in connection with debt collection." §1692c. One of those provisions requires a "debt collector" not to "communicate further" with a consumer who "notifies" the "debt collector" that he or she "refuses to pay" or wishes the debt collector to "cease further communication." §1692c(c). In light of this provision, asks Heintz, how can an attorney file a lawsuit against (and thereby communicate with) a nonconsenting consumer or file a motion for summary judgment against that consumer?

We agree with Heintz that it would be odd if the Act empowered a debt-owing consumer to stop the "communications" inherent in an ordinary lawsuit and thereby cause an ordinary debt-collecting lawsuit to grind to a halt. But, it is not necessary to read §1692c(c) in that way—if only because that provision has exceptions that permit communications "to notify the consumer that the debt collector or creditor may invoke" or "intends to invoke" a "specified remedy" (of a kind "ordinarily invoked by [the] debt collector or creditor"). §§1692c(c)(2), (3). Courts can read these exceptions, plausibly, to imply that they authorize the actual invocation of the remedy that the collector "intends to invoke." The language permits such a reading, for an ordinary court-related document does, in fact, "notify" its recipient that the creditor may "invoke" a judicial remedy. Moreover, the interpretation is consistent with the statute's apparent objective of preserving creditors' judicial remedies. We need not authoritatively interpret the Act's conduct-regulating provisions now, however. Rather, we rest our conclusions upon the fact that it is easier to read §1692c(c) as containing some such additional, implicit, exception than to believe that Congress intended, silently and implicitly, to create a far broader exception, for all litigating attorneys, from the Act itself.

Second, Heintz points to a statement of Congressman Frank Annunzio, one of the sponsors of the 1986 amendment that removed from the Act the language creating a blanket exemption for lawyers. Representative Annunzio stated that, despite the exemption's removal, the Act still would not apply to lawyers' litigating activities. Representative Annunzio said that the Act

> regulates debt collection, not the practice of law. Congress repealed the attorney exemption to the act, not because of attorney[s'] conduct in the courtroom, but because of their conduct in the backroom. Only collection activities, not legal activities, are covered by the act. . . . The act applies to attorneys when they are collecting debts, not when they are performing tasks of a legal nature. . . . The act only regulates the conduct of debt collectors, it does not prevent creditors, through their attorneys, from pursuing any legal remedies available to them.

132 Cong. Rec. 30842 (1986). This statement, however, does not persuade us.

For one thing, the plain language of the Act itself says nothing about retaining the exemption in respect to litigation. The line the statement seeks to draw between "legal" activities and "debt collection" activities was not necessarily apparent to those who debated the legislation, for litigating, at first blush, seems simply one way of collecting a debt. For another thing, when Congress considered the Act, other Congressmen expressed fear that repeal would limit lawyers' "ability to contact third parties in order to facilitate settlements" and "could very easily interfere with a client's right to pursue judicial remedies." H.R. Rep. No. 99-405, p.11 (1985) (dissenting views of Rep. Hiler). They proposed alternative language designed to keep litigation activities outside the Act's scope, but that language was not enacted. Ibid. Further, Congressman Annunzio made his statement not during the legislative process, but after the statute became law. It therefore is not a statement upon which other legislators might have relied in voting for or against the Act, but it simply represents the views of one informed person on an issue about which others may (or may not) have thought differently.

Finally, Heintz points to a "Commentary" on the Act by the Federal Trade Commission's staff. It says: "Attorneys or law firms that engage in traditional debt collection activities (sending dunning letters, making collection calls to consumers) are covered by the [Act], but *those whose practice is limited to legal activities are not covered.*" Federal Trade Commission—Statements of General Policy or Interpretation Staff Commentary on the Fair Debt Collection Practices Act, 53 Fed. Reg. 50097, 50100 (1988) (emphasis added; footnote omitted). We cannot give conclusive weight to this statement. The Commentary of which this statement is a part says that it "is not binding on the Commission or the public." Id., at 50101. More importantly, we find nothing either in the Act or elsewhere indicating that Congress intended to authorize the FTC to create this exception from the Act's coverage—an exception that, for the reasons we have set forth above, falls outside the range of reasonable interpretations of the Act's express language. See, e.g., Brown v. Gardner, 513 U.S.—,—, 115 S. Ct. 552, 555, 130 L. Ed. 2d 462 (1994) (slip op., at—,—); see also Fox v. Citicorp Credit Servs., Inc., 15 F.3d 1507, 1513 (CA9 1994) (FTC staff's statement conflicts with Act's plain language and is therefore not entitled to deference); Scott v. Jones, 964 F.2d 314, 317 (CA4 1992) (same).

For these reasons, we agree with the Seventh Circuit that the Act applies to attorneys who "regularly" engage in consumer-debt-collection activity, even when that activity consists of litigation. Its judgment is therefore

Affirmed.

Following the decision in this last case, Congress amended the Fair Debt Collection Practices Act to make it clear that the §807(11) notifications need not be given in a formal pleading made in connection with a legal action.

THOMAS v. LAW FIRM OF SIMPSON & CYBAK
United States Court of Appeals, Seventh Circuit, *en banc*, 2004
392 F.3d 914

WILLIAMS, Circuit Judge.

Frank Thomas appeals from the district court's dismissal of his suit which alleged that General Motors Acceptance Corporation ("GMAC"), the law firm Simpson & Cybak ("Simpson"), and their employees failed to send him a debt validation notice advising him of his rights as a debtor within five days of their initial communication with him, as is required by the Fair Debt Collection Practices Act ("FDCPA"), 15 U.S.C. §§1692-1692o. Two principal questions are raised in this appeal: whether a creditor's letter to a debtor and whether a debt collector's initiation of a lawsuit in state court constitute "initial communications" within the meaning of the FDCPA. In dismissing Thomas's case for failure to state a claim, the district court determined that the creditor's letter to the debtor constituted an "initial communication," while the debt collector's initiation of the lawsuit did not. We disagree with both conclusions. Accordingly, we reverse the district court's decision to dismiss Thomas's claim against Simpson, and we remand for further proceedings.

I. BACKGROUND

In January 1998, Frank Thomas purchased a Chevrolet Blazer from Apple Chevrolet under an installment contract immediately assigned to GMAC. Around January 20, 2000, shortly after Thomas lost his job with GMAC, he received a default letter from GMAC operations manager Kay Candiano on GMAC letterhead informing him that his payment on the vehicle was past due.

On March 27, 2000, GMAC, through its attorneys, Simpson & Cybak, sued Thomas in Illinois state court to recover the vehicle. Kathleen Haggerty, a Simpson lawyer, signed the complaint. The complaint included a statement that, "[p]ursuant to the [FDCPA], you are advised that this law firm is a debt collector attempting to collect a debt, and any information obtained will be used for that purpose." The summons included similar language.

Thomas filed suit against GMAC and Simpson under the FDCPA, claiming that neither party sent him a debt validation notice advising him of his rights as a debtor. See 15 U.S.C. §1692g(a). The district court granted both defendants' motions to dismiss pursuant to Rule 12(b)(6) of the Federal Rules of Civil Procedure. Thomas now appeals.

II. *ANALYSIS*

We review de novo the district court's dismissal of Thomas's complaint for failure to state a claim, accepting as true the well-pleaded allegations in Thomas's complaint and drawing all reasonable inferences in his favor. Porter v. DiBlasio, 93 F.3d 301, 305 (7th Cir. 1996).

The FDCPA requires that "within five days after the initial communication with a consumer in connection with the collection of any debt, a debt collector" must send the debtor a written validation notice containing certain information. 15 U.S.C. §1692g(a). The notice must inform the debtor of the amount of the debt, the name of the creditor, and state that the debt will be assumed valid if the debtor does not dispute its validity within 30 days of the receipt of the notice. Id. §1692g(a)(1)-(3). Furthermore, the notice must include a statement that if the debtor disputes the debt within 30 days of the notice, the debt collector will obtain and send the debtor verification of the debt and, upon written request, send the debtor the name and address of the current creditor, if different from the original creditor. Id. §1692g(a)(4)-(5).

Thomas argues that neither GMAC nor Simpson notified him of these debt validation rights. Thomas primarily contends that the summons and complaint Simpson filed initiating state court litigation against him constituted an "initial communication" under the FDCPA, and Simpson was therefore required to notify him of his validation rights within five days of the service of that communication.

As an initial matter, we must decide whether GMAC's January 20, 2000 default letter to Thomas constitutes an "initial communication" for purposes of the FDCPA. Despite the district court's finding to the contrary, all parties to this appeal now concede that the letter does not constitute an "initial communication" regarding a debt under the FDCPA.

The FDCPA defines a "communication" broadly: "the conveying of information regarding a debt directly or indirectly to any person through any medium." 15 U.S.C. §1692a(2). But, because the Act regulates debt collectors rather than creditors, Schlosser v. Fairbanks Capital Corp., 323 F.3d 534, 536 (7th Cir. 2003), GMAC's letter to Thomas—a letter from a creditor—does not qualify as an "initial communication" under the Act. Because the FDCPA makes debt collectors, but not creditors, responsible for notifying debtors of their validation rights, see 15 U.S.C. §1692g(a), finding that a letter from a creditor constitutes an "initial communication" could create significant unintended obligations for debt collectors. For example, if a letter from a creditor constitutes an "initial communication," debt collectors would be responsible for notifying debtors of their debt validation rights within five days of an "initial communication" that the debt collector did not send, or for one communicated even before the creditor retained the debt collector. Nothing in the FDCPA suggests that Congress intended creditors' unilateral actions to obligate debt collectors to inform debtors of their rights; rather, the Act is intended to deter debt collectors from employing their own abusive tactics. Because we decide that GMAC's letter to Thomas does not constitute an initial communication for FDCPA purposes, no obligation to inform Thomas of his validation rights arose upon the sending of the letter.

The principal question remains, whether Simpson's service of a summons and complaint, filed in state court, was an "initial communication" within the meaning of the FDCPA, such that its service triggered an obligation to notify Thomas of his validation rights within five days. Simpson concedes that it is a debt collector as defined in §1692a(6), but argues that pleadings do not constitute "communications." . . .

By its terms, as stated above, the FDCPA's broad definition of a "communication" encompasses the service of a summons and complaint. When Simpson served the summons and complaint, it conveyed information regarding Thomas's debt. The plain language of a statute "should be conclusive 'except in the rare cases [in which] the literal application of a statute will produce a result demonstrably at odds with the intentions of its drafters.'" Castellon-Contreras v. INS, 45 F.3d 149, 153 (7th Cir. 1995) (quoting United States v. Ron Pair Enter., Inc., 489 U.S. 235, 242, 109 S. Ct. 1026, 103 L. Ed. 2d 290 (1989)). This is not such a case; rather, viewing the service of a summons and a complaint as an "initial communication" is consistent with the drafters' intent.

The statute was intended to "protect consumers from a host of unfair, harassing, and deceptive debt collection practices . . . " S. Rep. No. 382, 95th Cong. 2d. Sess. 4, 1, U.S. Code Cong. & Admin. News 1977 at pp. 1695, 1696. Our interpretation of the statute furthers this objective because it helps ensure that debtors will be informed about their validation rights and that debt collectors, knowing that they are obliged to advise debtors of these rights, will investigate claims before initiating litigation to collect debts. Defendants' argument that state courts offer sufficient protections to guard against abusive debt collection tactics during litigation is unpersuasive. The FDCPA affords different protections than state court; debt collectors who violate its provisions may be subject to civil liability. See 15 U.S.C. §1692k.

Furthermore, to except the service of pleadings from the definition of "communication" would erode the §1692g requirement to inform debtors of their validation rights; debt collectors could avoid their obligation to advise debtors of their validation rights altogether by initiating litigation. Such a loophole, creating an end-run around the validation notice requirement, is inconsistent with the drafters' intention of protecting debtors from "unfair, harassing, and deceptive" collection tactics, especially because many debtors cannot afford to hire attorneys to represent them in collection actions. Congress was careful to except pleadings from the definition of "communication" where it so intended. Section 1692e(11) provides that a debt collector must disclose in its initial communication with the debtor that "the debt collector is attempting to collect a debt and that any information obtained will be used for that purpose," except that the provision does "not apply to formal pleading[s] made in connection with a legal action." 15 U.S.C. §1692e(11). No such pleadings exception exists in §1692g.

Defendants contend that we should ignore the FDCPA's plain language because deeming the service of a summons and complaint an "initial communication" would interfere with litigation by making debt collection lawsuits more cumbersome for attorneys. In Heintz v. Jenkins, 514 U.S. 291, 115 S. Ct. 1489, 131 L. Ed. 2d 395 (1995), the Supreme Court considered and, in light of the FDCPA's plain language, rejected similar arguments. . . .

Nonetheless, some of defendants' concerns warrant further discussion, as they claim our holding will create a host of practical difficulties; however, these practical difficulties can be overcome. Section 1692g(b) directs debt collectors to cease their collection efforts if within 30 days of receiving the debt validation notice, the consumer seeks verification of the debt. Thus, a consumer could potentially halt a lawsuit by requesting verification of the debt. This problem is not insurmountable. A debt collector need not make the summons and complaint its first communication with the debtor; rather, it can have its initial communication with the debtor upwards of 30 days before it intends to initiate litigation. After the thirty-day verification period has expired, the debt collector can then initiate litigation without fear that the debtor will "interfere" with the suit by seeking verification of the debt.

Sending the notice in advance also avoids other complications. Some states prohibit the inclusion of other documents with the summons and complaint. A debt collector avoids running afoul of such a rule by sending the notice separately, either in advance or within five days of the initial communication. After all, the FDCPA does not require debt collectors to notify debtors of their rights in the initial communication itself. See 15 U.S.C. §1692g(a).

Sending the notice along with the pleadings, or shortly thereafter, might also confuse the debtor. A debtor must comply with deadlines imposed by court rules and judges, even if that debtor has requested verification of the debt. While the §1692g notice indicates that the debtor has 30 days to dispute his debt, in federal court a defendant must answer a complaint within 20 days of its filing. Fed. R. Civ. P. 12(a)(1)(A). Failing to timely file an answer could result in a default judgment. Fed. R. Civ. P. 55(a). Thus, the validation notice could potentially give a debtor the false impression that it has 30 days before it is required to take any action in the lawsuit.

Nonetheless, there may be instances when a debt collector believes delay in initiating a lawsuit is unwise, such as when it fears the debtor will dissolve assets. Given the potential for confusion, a debt collector who chooses to send the validation notice either with the summons and complaint or shortly thereafter should take care to phrase its notice so as to not mislead. It should make clear that the advice contained in the §1692g validation notice in no way alters the debtor's rights or obligations with respect to the lawsuit, emphasizing that courts set different deadlines for filings.

As we have in cases addressing other FDCPA provisions, . . . we think it helpful to suggest explanatory language for debt collectors to use. A debt collector who chooses to send the §1692g validation notice with the summons or complaint or shortly thereafter can send a carefully worded notice, such as one containing the following language, to comply with the FDCPA without disrupting the litigation process:

> This advice pertains to your dealings with me as a debt collector. It does not affect your dealings with the court, and in particular it does not change the time at which you must answer the complaint. The summons is a command from the court, not from me, and you must follow its instructions even if you dispute the validity or amount of the debt. The advice in this letter also does not affect my relations with the court. As a lawyer, I may file papers in the suit according to the court's rules and the judge's instructions.

We note that an additional potential complication exists under §1692c (a)(2), which prohibits debt collectors from communicating with a debtor it knows to be represented by counsel. If pleadings are "communications" under the FDCPA, in any jurisdiction in which a defendant must be personally served, a debtor could arguably thwart service by simply retaining an attorney. But other exceptions within §1692c could be read to allow for service. For instance, §1692c(a) permits communication with debtors represented by attorneys with the express permission of the court. Court rules permitting service could be interpreted as granting such express permission.

The above-referenced practical difficulties are not insurmountable and, thus, do not warrant overriding the Act's plain language. . . . Accordingly, we hold that Simpson's service of the summons and complaint was an "initial communication," which triggered its obligation to notify Thomas of his validation rights. In so holding, we recognize that we part company from the Eleventh Circuit, which reached a contrary result. See Vega, 351 F.3d at 1337. But the Eleventh Circuit relied principally on non-binding Federal Trade Commission ("FTC") staff commentary issued before *Heintz,* see Federal Trade Commission, Staff Commentary on the Fair Debt Collection Practices Act, 53 Fed. Reg. 50097, 50108 (1988), to which we do not give significant weight. See *Heintz,* 514 U.S. at 298, 115 S. Ct. 1489 (declining to give much weight to FTC staff commentary discussing the FDCPA's application to attorneys). Indeed, the FTC itself, in a more recent Advisory Opinion letter issued in 2000 noted the following: "In light of *Heintz,* the Commission concludes that, if an attorney debt collector serves on a consumer a court document 'conveying information regarding a debt,' that court document is a 'communication' for purposes of the FDCPA." Federal Trade Commission, Staff Opinion Letter of March 31, 2000, at 3, available at http://www.ftc.gov/os/2000/04/fdcpaadvisoryopinion.htm. The FTC may think it wise to issue advisory opinions providing guidance for the many variations that lawyers may encounter in their roles as statutory debt collectors, and 15 U.S.C. §1692k(e) provides that no liability results from good faith reliance on such opinions.

Because we have concluded that the service of a summons and complaint by a debt collector constitutes an "initial communication" under the FDCPA, Thomas has stated a viable claim for violation of 15 U.S.C. §1692g.

III. CONCLUSION

For the foregoing reasons, we REVERSE the district court's dismissal under Rule 12(b)(6) of Thomas's claim against Simpson and REMAND for further proceedings consistent with this opinion.

TERENCE T. EVANS, Circuit Judge, joined by COFFEY, MANION, and KANNE, Circuit Judges, dissenting.

I agree that the FDCPA's definition of "communication" could be read to encompass the filing of a summons and complaint by a lawyer. But I don't think it should be read that way. To do so, I submit, leads to a result that is not consistent with the purpose of the FDCPA, nor with the traditional view of what lawyers must do when they take a pivotal step in their relationship with a client—instituting formal legal proceedings in a court of law.

No doubt, lawyers can be "debt collectors" when they act like them—by engaging in the kind of "unfair, harassing and deceptive debt collection practices" that the FDCPA is designed to protect against. See Avila v. Rubin, 84 F.3d 222 (7th Cir. 1996) (lawyer sending out dunning letters is a "debt collector" subject to the FDCPA). But in this case, the lawyers were not sending dunning "communications" to Mr. Thomas. Instead, they were doing what lawyers traditionally do—filing a lawsuit in state court on behalf of their client. To hold that they must include in their court pleadings all the notice/validation, etc. information required by the FDCPA seems very odd indeed. And it will also be very confusing—"you have 20 days to answer the complaint" and "30 days to dispute the validity and request verification of the debt." All of which will make even a sophisticated defendant scratch his head and say "Huh?" . . .

PROBLEM 157

Attorney Sam Ambulance had a practice representing small businesses. Occasionally he would dun consumers on behalf of his clients, but only 2 percent of his overall practice consisted of any debt collection cases, and most of these involved dunning other businesses rather than consumers. When he takes on the occasional collection against a consumer, may he ignore the requirements of the FDCPA? Goldstein v. Hutton, Ingram, Yuzek, Gainen, Carroll & Bertolotti, 374 F.3d 56 (2nd Cir. 2004).

2. The Meaning of "Debt"

The Fair Debt Collection Practices Act only applies if the debt collector is attempting to collect a "debt" as that term is defined by §803(5). Look at that section to resolve the following issues.

PROBLEM 158

a. Howard Hacker rigged up a satellite dish and pirated television signals from a television company's satellite. When the company found this out, it hired a debt collector to try to make him pay for the transmissions he had received. Does the Act apply here? See Zimmerman v. HBO Affiliate Group, 834 F.2d 1163 (3d Cir. 1987).

b. Sally Quickfingers shoplifted 87 items from Big Department Store. If the store sends a debt collector after her, will FDCPA apply? See Shorts v. Palmer, 155 F.R.D. 172 (S.D. Ohio 1994).

c. Portia Moot gave a check for $213 to Cornucopia Grocery Store, and when the check bounced, the store turned the collection of the check over to its lawyer. Does the statute apply here? See F.T.C. v. Check Investors, Inc., 502 F.3d 159 (3rd Cir. 2007).

d. On behalf of his client, landlord Simon Mustache, attorney Sam Ambulance sent Tuesday Tenant a letter demanding that she pay back rent, and threatening eviction if she did not. Is this a FDCPA matter? See Romea v. Heiberger & Assoc., 163 F.3d 111 (3rd Cir. 1998).

e. When Mr. and Mrs. Suburb failed to pay their county property tax, the county turned the overdue tax obligations to Trash Collection Agency. Is a tax obligation a "debt" under FDCPA? See Pollice v. National Tax Funding, L.P., 225 F.3d 379 (3rd Cir. 2000).

MILLER v. McCALLA, RAYMER, PADRICK, COBB, NICHOLS & CLARK, L.L.C.

United States Court of Appeals, Seventh Circuit, 2000
214 F.3d 872

POSNER, Chief Judge

This is a suit under the Fair Debt Collection Practices Act, 15 U.S.C. §§1692 et seq., against two related law firms engaged in debt collection. The plaintiff (the debtor) claims that the defendants violated the Act by failing to state "the amount of the debt" in the dunning letter of which he complains. See sec. 1692g(a)(1). They reply that they did state the amount and that anyway the letter is outside the scope of the Act because they were trying to collect a business debt rather than a consumer debt, and the Act is limited to the collection of consumer debts. §1692a(5); First Gibraltar Bank, FSB v. Smith, 62 F.3d 133 (5th Cir. 1995). The district court granted summary judgment for the defendants on the latter ground, and let us start there.

The plaintiff bought a house in Atlanta in 1992, and took out a mortgage. He lived in the house until 1995, when he accepted a job in Chicago; from then on, he rented the house. He received the dunning letter from one of the defendant law firms on behalf of the mortgagee in 1997. By this time, renting the property to strangers, the plaintiff was making a business use of the property and so the mortgage loan was financing a business rather than a consumer debt. But the plaintiff argues that the relevant time for determining the nature of the debt is when the debt first arises, not when collection efforts begin. The defendants riposte that since the Act under which the plaintiff is suing, unlike the Truth in Lending Act, governs debt *collection,* the relevant time is when the attempt at collection is made. Oddly, there are no reported appellate decisions on the issue, though it was assumed in Bloom v. I.C. System, Inc., 972 F.2d 1067, 1068-69 (9th Cir. 1992), that the relevant time is when the loan is made, not when collection is attempted.

The language of the statute favors this interpretation. "Debt" is defined as "any obligation or alleged obligation of a consumer to pay money arising out of a transaction in which the money, property, insurance, or services which are the subject of the transaction are primarily for personal, family, or household purposes." §1692a(5). The defendants don't deny that the plaintiff is a "consumer," even though he is in the "business" of renting his house (they can't deny this, because "the term 'consumer' means any natural person obligated or allegedly obligated to pay any debt," §1692a(3)), and the antecedent of the first "which" in the clause "in which the money, property, insurance, or services which are the subject of the transaction are primarily for personal, family, or household purposes" is, as a matter of grammar anyway, the transaction out of which the obligation to repay arose, not the obligation itself; and that transaction was the purchase of a house for a personal use, namely living in it. Grammar needn't trump sense; the purpose of statutory interpretation is to make sense out of statutes not written by grammarians. But we cannot say that it is senseless to base the debt collector's obligation on the character of the debt when it arose rather than when it is to be collected. The original creditor is more likely to know whether the debt was personal or commercial at its incipience than either the creditor or the debt collector is to know what current use the debtor is making of the loan (in this case, the plaintiff is using the loan, in effect, to generate income from the house that secures the loan).

Against this the defendants argue that the plaintiff's interpretation creates a loophole. Suppose the plaintiff had bought the house to use as an office, and later converted it to personal use; on the plaintiff's interpretation of the Act the debt collector would not have to give him the statutory warnings. But this makes perfect sense. The Act regulates the debt collection tactics employed against personal borrowers on the theory that they are likely to be unsophisticated about debt collection and thus prey to unscrupulous collection methods. See S. Rep. No. 382, 95th Cong., 1st

Sess. 2 (1977); Keele v. Wexler, 149 F.3d 589, 594 (7th Cir. 1998); McCartney v. First City Bank, 970 F.2d 45, 47 (5th Cir. 1992). Businessmen don't need the warnings. A businessman who converts a business purchase to personal use does not by virtue of that conversion lose his commercial sophistication and so acquire a need for statutory protection. And we agree with the plaintiff's concession that if a borrower for a personal use were to assign the loan that financed that use to a business, the debt would then arise out of the assignment, rather than out of the original loan, and so the Act would be inapplicable—rightly so since the recipient of the dunning letter would be a businessman, not a consumer.

So the Act is applicable and we move to the question whether the defendants violated the statutory duty to state the amount of the loan. 15 U.S.C. §1692g(a)(1). The dunning letter said that the "unpaid *principal* balance" of the loan (emphasis added) was $178,844.65, but added that "this amount does not include accrued but unpaid interest, unpaid late charges, escrow advances or other charges for preservation and protection of the lender's interest in the property, as authorized by your loan agreement. The amount to reinstate or pay off your loan changes daily. You may call our office for complete reinstatement and payoff figures." An 800 number is given.

The statement does not comply with the Act (again we can find no case on the question). The unpaid principal balance is not the debt; it is only a part of the debt; the Act requires statement of the debt. The requirement is not satisfied by listing a phone number. It is notorious that trying to get through to an 800 number is often a vexing and protracted undertaking, and anyway, unless the number is recorded, to authorize debt collectors to comply orally would be an invitation to just the sort of fraudulent and coercive tactics in debt collection that the Act aimed (rightly or wrongly) to put an end to. It is no excuse that it was "impossible" for the defendants to comply when as in this case the amount of the debt changes daily. What would or might be impossible for the defendants to do would be to determine what the amount of the debt might be at some future date if for example the interest rate in the loan agreement was variable. What they certainly could do was to state the total amount due—interest and other charges as well as principal—on the date the dunning letter was sent. We think the statute required this.

In a previous case, in an effort to minimize litigation under the debt collection statute, we fashioned a "safe harbor" formula for complying with another provision of the statute. Bartlett v. Heibl, 128 F.3d 497, 501-02 (7th Cir. 1997); see also Herzberger v. Standard Ins. Co., 205 F.3d 327, 331 (7th Cir. 2000). We think it useful to do the same thing for the "amount of debt" provision. We hold that the following statement satisfies the debt collector's duty to state the amount of the debt in cases like this where the amount varies from day to day: "As of the date of this letter, you owe $[the exact amount due]. Because of interest, late charges, and other charges that may vary from day to day, the amount due on the day you pay may be greater. Hence, if you pay the amount shown above, an adjustment may be necessary after we receive your check, in which event we will inform you before depositing the check for collection. For further information, write the undersigned or call 1-800-[phone number]" A debt collector who uses this form will not violate the "amount of the debt" provision, provided, of course, that the information he furnishes is accurate and he does not obscure it by adding confusing other information (or misinformation). E.g., Marshall-Mosby v. Corporate Receivables, Inc., 205 F.3d 323, 326 (7th Cir. 2000); Bartlett v. Heibl, supra, 128 F.3d at 500. Of course we do not hold that a debt collector *must* use this form of words to avoid violating the statute; but if he does, and (to repeat an essential qualification) does not add other words that confuse the message, he will as a matter of law have discharged his duty to state clearly the amount due. No reasonable person could conclude that the statement that we have drafted does not inform the debtor of the amount due. Cf. Walker v. National Recovery, Inc., 200 F.3d 500, 503 (7th Cir. 1999)....

The judgment in favor of the defendants is reversed and the case is remanded to the district court for further proceedings consistent with this opinion.

Reversed and Remanded.

B. Locating the Debtor

PROBLEM 159

"Are you the creeps who taught their daughter it was okay to stiff her creditors?" Thus began the phone call that Trash Collection Agency made to the home of Mr. and Mrs. Moot, parents of law school student Portia Moot, who was having some trouble with her credit card bills. "If so, maybe you can give me her phone number at work," continued the caller. Is this a violation of the statute? See §§804, 806, and 803(7). Can anyone other than the debtor sue for violations of the Act? See §813; Whatley v. Universal Collection Bureau, Inc. (Fl.), 525 F. Supp. 1204 (N.D. Ga. 1981).

C. Communications with the Debtor

RUTYNA v. COLLECTION ACCOUNTS TERMINAL
United States District Court, Northern District of Illinois, 1979
478 F. Supp. 980

McMILLEN, District Judge.

This is an action for violations of the Fair Debt Collection Practices Act, 15 U.S.C. §§1692 et seq. (the F.D.C.P.A.). The F.D.C.P.A. was enacted by Congress to eliminate abusive, deceptive, and unfair debt collection practices and became effective on March 20, 1978. This court has subject-matter jurisdiction, without regard to the amount in controversy, under §1692k(d) of the Act.

The facts of this case are undisputed, except where noted herein. Plaintiff is a 60 year old widow and Social Security retiree. She suffers from high blood pressure and epilepsy. In December 1976 and January 1977, she incurred a debt for medical services performed by a doctor with Cabrini Hospital Medical Group. Her belief was that Medicare or other, private, medical insurance had paid in full this debt for medical treatment. She contends that in July 1978, an agent of defendant telephoned her and informed her of an alleged outstanding debt for $56.00 to Cabrini Hospital Medical Group. When she denied the existence of this debt, the voice on the telephone responded, "you owe it, you don't want to pay, so we're going to have to do something about it." In its brief, defendant denies that it ever telephoned the plaintiff but states that plaintiff did telephone defendant on several occasions. There is no evidentiary support in the record for defendant's contention.

On or about August 10, 1978, plaintiff received a letter from defendant which supplies the basis for her complaint. It stated:

> You have shown that you are unwilling to work out a friendly settlement with us to clear the above debt.
>
> Our field investigator has now been instructed to make an investigation in your neighborhood and to personally call on your employer.
>
> The immediate payment of the full amount, or a personal visit to this office, will spare you this embarrassment.

The top of the letter notes the creditor's name and the amount of the alleged debt. The letter was signed by a "collection agent." It is attached as exhibit B to the plaintiff's memorandum. The envelope containing that letter presented a return address that included defendant's full name: Collection Accounts Terminal, Inc.

Upon receiving this letter from defendant, plaintiff alleges that she became very nervous, upset, and worried, specifically that defendant would cause her embarrassment by informing her neighbors of the debt and about her medical problems. In its brief, defendant states its lack of knowledge concerning plaintiff's reaction to the letter.

Plaintiff wishes to reserve certain of her F.D.C.P.A. allegations for trial should this court deny her summary judgment motion. But three of her alleged violations regarding defendant's liability are ripe for disposition by summary judgment. If plaintiff prevails, a hearing will be appropriate to determine a damage award. §1692k provides for actual and statutory damages, and a reasonable attorney's fee.

(1) Harassment or abuse (§1692d). The first sentence of §1692d provides: "A debt collector may not engage in any conduct the natural consequence of which is to harass, oppress, or abuse any person in connection with the collection of a debt." This section then lists six specifically prohibited types of conduct, without limiting the general application of the foregoing sentence. The legislative history makes clear that this generality was intended:

> In addition to these specific prohibitions, this bill prohibits in general terms any harassing, unfair or deceptive collection practice. This will enable the courts, where appropriate, to proscribe other improper conduct which is not specifically addressed. 1977 U.S. Code Cong. & Admin. News at p.1698.

Plaintiff does not allege conduct which falls within one of the specific prohibitions contained in §1692d, but we find that defendant's letter to plaintiff does violate this general standard.

Without doubt defendant's letter has the natural (and intended) consequence of harassing, oppressing, and abusing the recipient. The tone of the letter is one of intimidation, and was intended as such in order to effect a collection. The threat of an investigation and resulting embarrassment to the alleged debtor is clear and the actual effect on the recipient is irrelevant. The egregiousness of the violation is a factor to be considered in awarding statutory damages (§1692k(b)(1)). Defendant's violation of §1692d is clear.

(2) Deception and improper threats (§1692e). §1692e bars a debt collector from using any "false, deceptive, or misleading representation or means in connection with the collection of any debt." Sixteen specific practices are listed in this provision, without limiting the application of this general standard. §1692e(5) bars a threat "to take any action that cannot legally be taken or that is not intended to be taken." Defendant also violated this provision.

Defendant's letter threatened embarrassing contacts with plaintiff's employer and neighbors. This constitutes a false representation of the actions that defendant could legally take. §1692c(b) prohibits communication by the debt collector with third parties (with certain limited exceptions not here relevant). Plaintiff's neighbors and employer could not legally be contacted by defendant in connection with this debt. The letter falsely represents, or deceives the recipient, to the contrary. This is a deceptive means employed by defendant in connection with its debt collection. Defendant violated §1692e(5) in its threat to take such illegal action.

(3) Unfair practice/return address (§1692f(8)). The envelope received by plaintiff bore a return address, which began "COLLECTION ACCOUNTS TERMINAL, INC." §1692f bars unfair or unconscionable means to collect or attempt to collect any debt. §1692f specifically bars:

> (8) Using any language or symbol, other than the debt collector's address, on any envelope when communicating with a consumer by use of the mails or by telegram, except that a debt collector may use his business name if such name does not indicate that he is in the debt collection business.

Defendant's return address violated this provision, because its business name does indicate that it is in the debt collection business. The purpose of this specific provision is apparently to prevent embarrassment resulting from a conspicuous name on the envelope, indicating that the contents pertain to debt collection.

On the subject of the return address on the envelope, defendant cites §1692k(c), which provides:

> A debt collector may not be held liable in any action brought under this subchapter if the debt collector shows by a preponderance of the evidence that the violation was not intentional and resulted from a bona fide error notwithstanding the maintenance of procedures reasonably adapted to avoid any such error.

Defendant states that it was "unaware that the return address could be considered a violation of any statute." Memorandum in opposition, at 4. No affidavit is offered. §1692k(c) does not immunize mistakes of law, even if properly proven (as this one is not). §1692k(c) is designed to protect the defendant who intended to prevent the conduct which constitutes a violation of this Act but who failed even though he maintained procedures reasonably adapted to avoid such an error. Defendant here obviously *intended* the conduct which violates the Act in respect to the return address, but it simply failed to acquaint itself with the pertinent law. This is similar to a provision in the Truth in Lending Act, providing a defense by establishing the facts, not by claiming ignorance of the law. Haynes v. Logan Furniture Mart, Inc., 503 F.2d 1161 (7th Cir. 1974).

It is therefore ordered, adjudged and decreed that judgment is entered in favor of plaintiff on the issue of liability.

PROBLEM 160

Trash Collection Agency's employee of the month, Ski Mask, has recently learned that the Fair Debt Collection Practices Act applies to him. Worried that it might contain things that affect his professional advancement, he contacts you, TCA's attorney, and asks you to look over his collection letters. (He has them all on his computer—a series of seven sent to debtors, each more interesting than the last—so he'll just run them off for you.) You should let him know whether the Act will require him to make some changes. The first letter in the collection series is as follows:

> Dear Debtor:
> Get this clearly in mind: YOU ARE GOING TO PAY THIS DEBT! The only question is how long it will take and how expensive, embarrassing, and ugly life will be for you in the meantime. We're tough and we're rough and we have the law on our side. Your car, your home, your most cherished possessions—kiss 'em goodbye! How would you like it if we filed an involuntary bankruptcy against you next week?
> Or you could pay the debt.
> To discuss your repayment schedule, call Ski Mask at 864-5911.
> Now.
> Sincerely,
> Ski Mask

You are a bit worried about this, so you have a good look at the statute and decide that a redraft is in order. Write it and be prepared to read yours aloud in class. See §§805,809. You should know that the courts have held that the disclosures mentioned in the statute are mandatory and are not excepted merely because the creditor has no intention of engaging in the practices being regulated, Emanuel v. American Credit Exch., 870 F.2d 805 (2d Cir. 1989).

BARTLETT v. HEIBL
United States Court of Appeals, Seventh Circuit, 1997
128 F.3d 497

POSNER, Chief Judge.

The Fair Debt Collection Practices Act, 15 U.S.C. §§1692-1692o, provides that within five days after a debt collector first duns a consumer debtor, the collector must send the debtor a written notice containing specified information. The required information includes the amount of the debt, the name of the creditor, and, of particular relevance here, a statement that unless the debtor "disputes the validity of the debt" within thirty days the debt collector will assume that the debt is valid but that if the debtor notifies the collector in writing within thirty days that he is disputing the debt, "the debt collector will obtain verification of the debt [from the creditor] . . . and a copy of [the] verification . . . will be mailed to the consumer." §§1692g(a)(1)-(4). A similar provision requires that the debtor be informed that upon his request the debt collector will give him the name and address of his original creditor, if the original creditor is different from the current one. §1692g(a)(5). If the debtor accepts the invitation tendered in the required notice, and requests from the debt collector either verification of the debt or the name and address of the original creditor, the debt collector must "cease collection of the debt . . . until the [requested information] is mailed to the consumer." §1692g(b). These provisions are intended for the case in which the debt collector, being a hireling of the creditor rather than the creditor itself, may lack first-hand knowledge of the debt.

If the statute is violated, the debtor is entitled to obtain from the debt collector, in addition to any actual damages that the debtor can prove, statutory damages not to exceed $1,000 per violation, plus a reasonable attorney's fee. §1692k(a).

A credit-card company hired lawyer John Heibl, the defendant in this case, to collect a consumer credit-card debt of some $1,700 from Curtis Bartlett, the plaintiff. Heibl sent Bartlett a letter, which Bartlett received but did not read, in which Heibl told him that "if you wish to resolve this matter before legal action is commenced, you must do one of two things within one week of the date of this letter": pay $316 toward the satisfaction of the debt, or get in touch with Micard (the creditor) "and make suitable arrangements for payment. If you do neither, it will be assumed that legal action will be necessary." Under Heibl's signature appears an accurate, virtually a literal, paraphrase of section 1692g(a), advising Bartlett that he has thirty days within which to dispute the debt, in which event Heibl will mail him a verification of it. At the end of the paraphrase Heibl adds: "suit may be commenced at any time before the expiration of this thirty (30) days." . . .

The letter is said to violate the statute by stating the required information about the debtor's rights in a confusing fashion. Finding nothing confusing about the letter, the district court rendered judgment for the defendant after a bench trial. The plaintiff contends that this finding is clearly erroneous. The defendant disagrees, of course, but also contends that even if the letter is confusing this is of no moment because Bartlett didn't read it. That would be a telling point if Bartlett were seeking actual damages, for example as a consequence of being misled by the letter into surrendering a legal defense against the credit-card company. He can't have suffered such damages as a result of the statutory violation, because he didn't read the letter. But he is not seeking actual damages. He is seeking only statutory damages, a penalty that does not depend on proof that the recipient of the letter was misled. E.g., Tolentino v. Friedman, 46 F.3d 645, 651 (7th Cir. 1995); Harper v. Better Business Services, Inc., 961 F.2d 1561, 1563 (11th Cir. 1992); Clomon v. Jackson, 988 F.2d 1314, 1322 (2d Cir. 1993); Baker v. G.C. Services Corp., 677 F.2d 775, 780-81 (9th Cir. 1982). All that is required is proof that the statute was violated, although even then it is within the district court's discretion to decide whether and if so how much to award, up to the $1,000 ceiling. E.g., Tolentino v. Friedman, supra, 46 F.3d at 651; Clomon v. Jackson, supra, 988 F.2d at 1322.

If reading were an element of the violation, then Bartlett would have to prove that he read the letter. But it is not. The statute, so far as material to this case, requires only that the debt collector "send the consumer a written notice containing" the required information. §1692g(a). It is unsettled whether "send" implies receipt or just mailing. Compare, e.g., Bates v. C & S Adjusters, Inc., 980 F.2d 865, 868 (2d Cir. 1992) (receipt), with, e.g., Maloy v. Phillips, 64 F.3d 607, 608 (11th Cir. 1995) (mailing). No matter; Bartlett did receive the letter. Sending a letter doesn't imply that the letter is read; there is no contradiction in saying, "I received your letter but I never read it."

Before coming to the central issue, concerning the likelihood of confusion, we must remark the fatuity of Bartlett's naming "John A. Heibl" and "John A. Heibl, Attorney at Law," as separate defendants. If Heibl were being sued for conduct within the scope of his agency or employment as a partner or an associate of a law firm, the firm could be named along with him as a defendant, because it would be liable jointly with him for that conduct. E.g., Old Republic Ins. Co. v. Chuhak & Tecson, P.C., 84 F.3d 998, 1002 (7th Cir. 1996); Dinco v. Dylex Ltd., 111 F.3d 964, 969 (1st Cir. 1997); Entente Mineral Co. v. Parker, 956 F.2d 524 (5th Cir. 1992); Grotelueschen v. American Family Mutual Ins. Co., 171 Wis. 2d 437, 492 N. W.2d 131, 136-37 (1992). Apparently he is not being sued in such a capacity; in any event "John A. Heibl, Attorney at Law" is not the name of a firm but merely the name of an individual and the identification of his profession. For the plaintiff to try to split Heibl into an individual and a lawyer and sue both is the equivalent of, in a medical malpractice suit, suing

"John Smith" and "Dr. John Smith," or of suing a sole proprietor in both his personal and his business capacity. A sole proprietorship ("John A. Heibl, Attorney at Law") is not a suable entity separate from the sole proprietor. Patterson v. V & M Auto Body, 63 Ohio St. 3d 573, 589 N.E.2d 1306, 1308 (1992).

The main issue presented by the appeal is whether the district judge committed a clear error in finding that the letter was not confusing. The statute does not say in so many words that the disclosures required by it must be made in a nonconfusing manner. But the courts, our own included, have held, plausibly enough, that it is implicit that the debt collector may not defeat the statute's purpose by making the required disclosures in a form or within a context in which they are unlikely to be understood by the unsophisticated debtors who are the particular objects of the statute's solicitude. E.g., Avila v. Rubin, 84 F.3d 222, 226 (7th Cir. 1996); Terran v. Kaplan, 109 F.3d 1428, 1431-34 (9th Cir. 1997); Russell v. Equifax A.R.S., 74 F.3d 30, 34-35 (2d Cir. 1996); Graziano v. Harrison, 950 F.2d 107, 111 (3d Cir. 1991); Miller v. Payco-General American Credits, Inc., 943 F.2d 482, 484 (4th Cir. 1991).

Most of the cases put it this way: the implied duty to avoid confusing the unsophisticated consumer can be violated by contradicting or "overshadowing" the required notice. E.g., Chauncey v. JDR Recovery Corp., 118 F.3d 516, 518 (7th Cir. 1997); United States v. National Financial Services, Inc., 98 F.3d 131, 139 (4th Cir. 1996); Russell v. Equifax A.R.S., supra, 74 F.3d at 34; Graziano v. Harrison, supra, 950 F.2d at 111. This sounds like two separate tests, one for a statement that is logically inconsistent with the required notice and the other for a statement that while it doesn't actually contradict the required notice obscures it, in much the same way that static or cross-talk can make a telephone communication hard to understand even though the message is not being contradicted in any way. The required notice might be "overshadowed" just because it was in smaller or fainter print than the demand for payment. United States v. National Financial Services, Inc., supra, 98 F.3d at 139.

As with many legal formulas that get repeated from case to case without an effort at elaboration, "contradicting or overshadowing" is rather unilluminating—even, though we hesitate to use the word in this context, confusing. The cases that find the statute violated generally involve neither logical inconsistencies (that is, denials of the consumer rights that the dunning letter is required to disclose) nor the kind of literal "overshadowing" involved in a fine-print, or faint-print, or confusing-typeface case. In the typical case, the letter both demands payment within thirty days and explains the consumer's right to demand verification within thirty days. These rights are not inconsistent, but by failing to explain how they fit together the letter confuses. E.g., id.; Chauncey v. JDR Recovery Corp., supra, 118 F.3d at 518-19; Avila v. Rubin, supra, 84 F.3d at 226; Russell v. Equifax A.R.S., supra, 74 F.3d at 35; Miller v. Payco-General American Credits, Inc., supra, 943 F.2d at 484; Swanson v. Southern Oregon Credit Service, Inc., 869 F.2d 1222, 1225-26 (9th Cir. 1988) (per curiam).

It would be better if the courts just said that the unsophisticated consumer is to be protected against confusion, whatever form it takes. A contradiction is just one means of inducing confusion; "overshadowing" is just another; and the most common is a third, the failure to explain an apparent though not actual contradiction—as in this case, which is indistinguishable from our recent *Chauncey* decision, as well as from most of the other cases we have cited. On the one hand, Heibl's letter tells the debtor that if he doesn't pay within a week he's going to be sued. On the other hand, it tells him that he can contest the debt within thirty days. This leaves up in the air what happens if he is sued on the eighth day, say, and disputes the debt on the tenth day. He might well wonder what good it would do him to dispute the debt if he can't stave off a lawsuit. The net effect of the juxtaposition of the one-week and thirty-day crucial periods is to turn the required disclosure into legal gibberish. That's as bad as an outright contradiction.

Although the question whether a dunning letter violates the Fair Debt Collection Practices Act does not require evidence that the recipient was confused—or even, as we noted earlier, whether he read the letter—the issue of confusion is for the district judge to decide, subject to light review for "clear error." The cases, however, leave no room to doubt that the letter to Bartlett was confusing; nor as an original matter could we doubt that it was confusing—we found it so, and do not like to think of ourselves as your average unsophisticated consumer. So the judgment must be reversed. But we should not stop here. Judges too often tell defendants what the defendants cannot do without indicating what they can do, thus engendering legal uncertainty that foments further litigation. The plaintiff's lawyer takes the extreme, indeed the absurd, position—one that he acknowledged to us at argument, with a certain lawyerly relish, creates an anomaly in the statutory design—that the debt collector cannot in any way, shape, or form allude to his right to bring a lawsuit within thirty days. That enforced silence would be fine if the statute forbade suing so soon. But it does not. The debt collector is perfectly free to sue within thirty days; he just must cease his efforts at collection during the interval between being asked for verification of the debt and mailing the verification to the debtor. 15 U.S.C. §1692g(b). In effect the plaintiff is arguing that if the debt collector wants to sue within the first thirty days he must do so without advance warning. How this compelled surprise could be thought either required by the statute, however imaginatively elaborated with the aid of the concept of "overshadowing," or helpful to the statute's intended beneficiaries, eludes us.

The plaintiff's argument is in one sense overimaginative, and in another unimaginative—unimaginative in failing to see that it is possible to devise a form of words that will inform the debtor of the risk of his being sued without detracting from the statement of his statutory rights. We here set forth a redaction of Heibl's letter that complies with the statute without forcing the debt collector to conceal his intention of exploiting his right to resort to legal action before the thirty days are up. We are not rewriting the statute; that is not our business. Jang v. A.M. Miller & Associates, 122 F.3d 480, 484 (7th Cir. 1997). We are simply trying to provide some guidance to how to comply with it. We commend this redaction as a safe harbor for debt collectors who want to avoid liability for the kind of suit that Bartlett has brought and now won. The qualification "for the kind of suit that Bartlett has brought and now won" is important. We are not certifying our letter as proof against challenges based on other provisions of the statute; those provisions are not before us. With that caveat, here is our letter:

Dear Mr. Bartlett:

I have been retained by Micard Services to collect from you the entire balance, which as of September 25, 1995, was $1,656.90, that you owe Micard Services on your MasterCard Account No. 5414701617068749.

If you want to resolve this matter without a lawsuit, you must, within one week of the date of this letter, either pay Micard $316 against the balance that you owe (unless you've paid it since your last statement) or call Micard at 1-800-221-5920 ext. 6130 and work out arrangements for payment with it.

If you do neither of these things, I will be entitled to file a lawsuit against you, for the collection of this debt, when the week is over.

Federal law gives you thirty days after you receive this letter to dispute the validity of the debt or any part of it. If you don't dispute it within that period, I'll assume that it's valid. If you do dispute it—by notifying me in writing to that effect—I will, as required by the law, obtain and mail to you proof of the debt. And if, within the same period, you request in writing the name and address of your original creditor, if the original creditor is different from the current creditor (Micard Services), I will furnish you with that information too.

The law does not require me to wait until the end of the thirty-day period before suing you to collect this debt. If, however, you request proof of the debt or the name and address of the original creditor within the thirty-day period that begins with your receipt of this letter, the law requires me to suspend my efforts (through litigation or otherwise) to collect the debt until I mail the requested information to you.

Sincerely,

John A. Heibl

We cannot require debt collectors to use "our" form. But of course if they depart from it, they do so at their risk. Debt collectors who want to avoid suits by disgruntled debtors standing on their statutory rights would be well advised to stick close to the form that we have drafted. It will be a safe haven for them, at least in the Seventh Circuit.

The judgment is reversed and the case is remanded with instructions to enter judgment for the plaintiff and compute the statutory damages, costs, and attorneys' fees to which he is entitled.

REVERSED AND REMANDED.

A number of commentators have pointed out deficiencies in the letter Judge Posner proposes. For example, it does not contain the statement mandated by §807(11) that requires that all communications with the debtor disclose not only that the debt collector is attempting to collect a debt but also that any information obtained will be used for that purpose.

PROBLEM 161

Now fully versed in the ways of the FDCPA, Ski Mask is working very hard to comply. At 8:59 p.m., he phoned Mrs. Shoe, who owed money to one of his agency's clients, and told her that she had better pay her debt. She replied that she hadn't any money and that she was turning over her affairs to Angelina Barth, a bankruptcy attorney. She told him that she had to hang up now because she needed to get to work (she was assigned to the night shift). Mask told her she would hear from him later. The next day, Mask phoned the Barth law offices and left a message asking that his call be returned. Hearing nothing the rest of that day, Mask felt it was all right to call Mrs. Shoe the next day at 8:01 a.m., which, of course, woke her up. She told him to quit calling her, but he just laughed and said, "You're going to hear from me every day until you pay up." Two days later he sent her a proper §809 validation notice. Mrs. Shoe, who was upset by the morning phone calls Mask made each day, called Angelina Barth and asked her if anything could be done to stop the calls. Has Ski Mask violated the law? See §805(a).

PROBLEM 162

Assume that when Ski Mask first called Mrs. Shoe, she told him that some mistake had obviously been made. She denied owing the debt. Must Ski Mask stop collection efforts until he has complied with §809(b)? See §805(c). Can Ski Mask comply with §809 by phoning her and giving her an oral verification of the debt? See Johnson v. Statewide Collections, Inc., 778 P.2d 93 (Wyo. 1989).

PROBLEM 163

When Ski Mask called Mrs. Shoe at home, he got her answering machine. If he leaves a message about the debt, must he state that the call is from a debt collector? May he leave a message about the debt on the answering machine if it is used by others? See Foti v. NCO Fin. Syst., Inc., 424 F. Supp. 2d 643 (S.D.N.Y. 2006).

PROBLEM 164

When he contacted her, Mrs. Shoe told Ski Mask that she did owe one of the two debts he was attempting to collect, and was willing to pay it, but she denied any liability on the other. When she sent him a payment, Ski Mask applied it to the disputed debt, and then continued to press her for payment of the debt she admitted owing. Can he do this? See §810. If he sues her, can he take advantage of a clause in the contract she signed with the creditor specifying that all litigation would take place in the state of California? Mrs. Shoe lives in West Virginia. See §811.

PROBLEM 165

The vice president in charge of collection for Big Department Store has an idea. It has been his experience that debtors are more likely to pay a debt if they think it has been turned over to a collection agency than if the original creditor is the only one involved. On the other hand, collection agencies take a substantial bite out of the monies they collect, and the vice president would like to avoid that expense. His idea is to have stationery printed up with the letterhead of a nonexistent debt collection agency and use it to collect BDS's accounts. He told the company's printer what he wanted, and the head of the printing department and the vice president together created the phony letterhead. Just before he used it, the v.p. thought he'd better run this through the legal department, so it has landed on your desk. Do you give the project your blessing? See FDCPA §812. If you approve this ruse, who can be sued?

The vice president has stumbled upon a practice called *flat-rating*. There actually are enterprises that will design such stationery for creditors and sell it to them for a "flat rate" (as opposed to a percentage of the collected accounts). The drafters of §812 explain:

> Another common collection abuse is known colloquially as "flat-rating." A "flat-rater" is one who sells to creditors a set of dunning letters bearing the letterhead of the flat-rater's collection agency and exhorting the debtor to pay the creditor at once. The creditor sends these letters to his debtors, giving the impression that a third party debt collector is collecting the debt. In fact, however, the flat-rater is not in the business of debt collection, but merely sells dunning letters. . . . The prohibition on furnishing such forms does not apply, however, to printers and custom stationery sellers who innocently print or sell such forms without knowledge of their intended use.

From the legislative history of §812, *reprinted in* 1977 U.S. Code Cong. & Admin. News 1699.

D. Civil Actions

PROBLEM 166

Ski Mask became so angry at Mrs. Shoe when she sassed him on the phone and questioned his parentage, that he phoned her all night every night on the hour for two days, put up a billboard near her home stating "Helen Shoe Stiffs Her Creditors!," and sent her a postcard stating that he was going to plant a bomb in her car if she didn't pay the $550 debt she owed his client. Assume that she really does owe this debt. Can she sue under FDCPA §813 and recover punitive damages for each of his violations of the statute? Compare §§813 and 814; Wright v. Financial Serv. of Norwalk, Inc., 22 F.3d 647 (6th Cir. 1994).

Section 813 creates a civil action in favor of any person injured by a violation of the statute. Section 813, modeled as it is on the consumer statutes that came before it, is remarkable only because §813(a)(3) permits the *defendant* to recover attorney's fees if the court finds that the consumer brought a §813 action in bad faith or for purposes of harassment. Only the Electronic Fund Transfer Act has a similar feature. Do you think it wise?

PROBLEM 167

You are a newly elected representative to your state legislature. Your platform included a pro-consumer stance, and now it is being put to the test. A bill has been introduced that would amend all state consumer laws to provide that the non-prevailing party—whether creditor or consumer—should pay the attorney's fees of the winner. The sponsor of the bill justifies it by pointing to the large number of baseless suits that consumers bring, causing needless expense to banks, department stores, automobile dealerships, insurance companies, and other creditors. How will you vote on this bill?

III. GARNISHMENT

Title III of the Consumer Credit Protection Act of 1968 puts limits on the abilities of creditors to garnish wages, 15 U.S.C. §1671. Read §301 of the Act, which explains the policy considerations underlying the enactment of the statute.

To creditors, the debtor's paycheck is a fertile source of repayment, so, on winning a judgment, they arrange to have a court issue a garnishment order requiring the employer (the garnishee) to send a portion of the amount due to the garnishor (the judgment creditor). The state garnishment procedures vary widely and are not our subject here. Instead, the issue is the percentage of an employee's paycheck that is vulnerable to creditor process.[3]

A. The Garnishment Exemption

The Act places restrictions on the amount of a person's wages that are available for creditor garnishment. In computing this amount (yes, law

---

3. The Secretary of Labor has issued regulations supplementing the Act. See 29 C.F.R. pt. 870.

students, again the time has come for computations) it is important to understand the concept of "disposable earnings." Read §302(b). Once you have determined the amount of "disposable earnings," §303 commands that two additional calculations be accomplished and compared:

(1) 25 percent of the disposable earnings, and
(2) the amount by which disposable earnings exceed 30 times the current federal minimum wage ($7.25 as of July 24, 2009; thus 30 × 7.25 = $217.50).

The lesser of these two amounts is the amount of the paycheck subject to garnishment by creditors.

PROBLEM 168

Joe Lunchpail's weekly pay is $350. State and federal taxes took $62, Social Security took $15, and Joe arranged to have $5 taken out every week and put in the company's credit union so that he could save some money for Christmas. When he failed to pay his tab down at the local department store, the store sued him, recovered judgment, and garnished his wages. What is the maximum amount that the store can reach per week?

Support orders for a former spouse or dependents are not restricted by the above, but instead by §303(b)(2). Plans formulated in Chapter 13 of the Bankruptcy Code are also exempted from the restrictions of Title III, see §303(b)(1)(B), as are all tax debts, §303(b)(1)(C).

PROBLEM 169

Joe Lunchpail took his paycheck and deposited it into the account he carried with Octopus National Bank. Prior to the deposit the account balance was zero. One hour later the local department store garnished the account and seized the entire amount of the paycheck. Joe is in your law office asking if Title III protects him here. What do you think? See Usery v. First Nat'l Bank of Ariz., 586 F.2d 107 (9th Cir. 1978); John O. Melby & Co. Bank v. Anderson, 276 N.W.2d 274 (Wis. 1979).

B. Priorities

Both tax garnishments and those for alimony and support are senior to the garnishments of ordinary creditors, even if the ordinary creditor garnishment is prior in time. This policy-oriented result causes an interesting issue to arise in the construction of §303. The next case, in which the matter was first decided, reaches the same conclusion since achieved by all later courts.

MARSHALL v. DISTRICT COURT FOR THE 41b JUDICIAL DISTRICT OF MICHIGAN[4]
United States District Court, Eastern District of Michigan, 1978
444 F. Supp. 1110

GUY, District Judge.

The plaintiff, Secretary of Labor, United States Department of Labor, having filed his complaint; and the defendants having appeared; and all the parties having entered into an agreement providing for the entry of these findings of fact and conclusions of law and dismissal of this action without the entry of a prospective injunction; and the court having been fully advised in the premises; now therefore, on motion of the plaintiff, the court hereby makes and enters its findings of fact and conclusions of law as follows:

FINDINGS OF FACT

1. This is an action by the Secretary of Labor, United States Department of Labor, hereinafter called the Secretary, brought to enforce the provisions of section 303 of Title III of the Consumer Credit Protection Act, as enacted May 29, 1968, effective July 1, 1970, and as amended by Public Law 95-30 on May 23, 1977, effective June 1, 1977 (15 U.S.C. 1671, et seq.), hereinafter called the Act.

2. Defendant Sears, Roebuck & Co. (hereinafter called Sears) is and at all times hereinafter mentioned was a corporation having its principal office and place of business at Sears Tower, Chicago, Illinois; and it is and at all times hereinafter mentioned was engaged in the sale of goods in its nationwide chain of department stores and through its nationwide catalogue operations.

3. Defendant Ford Motor Company (hereinafter called Ford) is and at all times hereinafter mentioned was a corporation having its principal office

---

4. Footnote in this case has been renumbered for clarity.

and place of business at Ford World Headquarters, Dearborn, Michigan; and it is and at all times hereinafter mentioned was engaged in the manufacture and sale of automobiles, trucks, and other goods of various kinds.

4. Defendant District Court for the Forty-first-b Judicial District of the State of Michigan, Mount Clemens Division (hereinafter called the State Court) is and at all times hereinafter mentioned was a court of the State of Michigan having, pursuant to Michigan Statutes Annotated, Sections 27A.8122, 27A.8301, 27A.8306, and 27A.4011 [M.C.L.A. §§600.4011, 600.8122, 600.8301, 600.8306] original jurisdiction in the City of Mount Clemens in the County of Macomb, Michigan, to adjudicate claims that do not exceed $10,000 and, among other things, to subject the earnings of judgment debtors to garnishment in order to satisfy the judgments.

5. Defendant John G. Roskopp (hereinafter called Judge Roskopp) is and at all times hereinafter mentioned was a duly elected and functioning judge of the State Court.

6. Defendant Dolores Wiskirch (hereinafter called Clerk Wiskirch) is and at all times hereinafter mentioned was the Clerk of Court for the State Court.

7. Mr. Norman Jones (hereinafter called Mr. Jones), from time to time over a period well in excess of a year, made various purchases of various goods from Sears for his use; and Mr. Jones used a charge account, pursuant to a charge account agreement he had with Sears, to obtain some or all of said goods on credit.

8. Upon failure of Jones to pay Sears in full the total of the purchase prices they had agreed upon for such goods as purchased by and delivered to Mr. Jones by Sears, together with finance charges provided for in the charge account agreement entered into between them, Sears on or about August 28, 1974, filed a civil action (Docket Number MC 74-8389) in the State Court against Mr. Jones for $1,164.89, the unpaid balance due thereon; and as a result, on or about November 25, 1974, Sears obtained a judgment (hereinafter called the principal judgment) against Mr. Jones for $1,164.89, plus $20.00 in court costs, for a total of $1,184.89, substantially all of which remained unpaid at all times material hereto except for the $34.81 withheld by Ford and paid to Sears from the earnings of Mr. Jones for the weekly pay period ending March 30, 1975 (hereinafter called the weekly pay period in question), as hereinafter described.

9. On or about September 30, 1974, in Sylvia Jones v. Norman Jones, Docket Number D73-6905 in the Circuit Court for the County of Macomb, Michigan, a Divorce Judgment (hereinafter called the Divorce Judgment) was entered against Mr. Jones in a divorce action brought on December 31, 1973, by his then wife. The Divorce Judgment granted the divorce sought

and ordered Mr. Jones to pay $32.00 per week in child support for each of his three children of the marriage there ended, for a total of $96.00 per week in child support payments.

10. Mr. Jones failed to voluntarily make the child support payments called for by the Divorce Judgment. Accordingly, on or about November 29, 1974, the court which entered the Divorce Judgment entered an "Order for Wage Assignment" (hereinafter called the Order for Wage Assignment) which ordered Mr. Jones to direct his employer to withhold from his earnings each week the sum of $96.00 to meet the child support provisions of the Divorce Judgment and pay amounts so withheld directly to the Friend of the Court of the Macomb County Circuit Court (16th Judicial Circuit) (hereinafter called the Friend of the Court) to be used for the support of the children of the marriage ended by the Divorce Judgment; the Order for Wage Assignment further provided that upon Mr. Jones' failure to so direct, the order be served on Mr. Jones' employer and itself be effective to direct the employer to make such withholdings and payments.

11. During the period from on or about September 1, 1964 on or about November 4, 1975, Mr. Jones was employed by Ford.

12. When Mr. Jones failed to direct Ford to withhold and pay the child support payments as required by the Order for Wage Assignment, the Order for Wage Assignment was served on Ford, which thereupon began making and continuously thereafter each weekly pay period made the withholdings and resulting payments as required by the Order for Wage Assignment.

13. When Mr. Jones failed to pay the principal judgment in favor of Sears in the State Court, Sears sought a writ of garnishment in the State Court; and on or about March 24, 1975, a writ of garnishment directed to Ford (hereinafter called the garnishment order in question) was issued by the State Court. The garnishment order in question was served on Ford on or about March 27, 1975, and pursuant to State law impacted on the earnings of Mr. Jones from Ford for the weekly pay period in question and none other.

14. In the weekly pay period in question, Mr. Jones earned from Ford for work performed by Mr. Jones in the course of his employment by Ford, the gross amount of $350.01, payable on April 3, 1975, after appropriate deductions. For the weekly pay period in question, Mr. Jones' earnings from Ford, after subtraction of the federal Social Security tax (employee portion only), the federal withholding tax, and the State withholding tax due thereon, were $235.23. From the $235.23, Ford subtracted, and paid to the Friend of the Court, $96.00 in child support payments pursuant to the Order for Wage Assignment.

15. Pursuant to State law and the requirements of the garnishment order in question, Ford responded to the garnishment order in question by serving

on Sears and filing with the State Court a "Disclosure" (hereinafter called the Disclosure). In its Disclosure, Ford claimed that the disposable earnings of Mr. Jones from Ford for the weekly pay period in question were $235.23 and that Ford's liability to Sears under the garnishment order in question was zero because the $96.00 in child support withheld and paid pursuant to the Order for Wage Assignment exceeded 25% of $235.23.

16. Thereafter, Sears sought from the State Court a ruling that the child support withheld by Ford pursuant to the Order for Wage Assignment: (1) was an amount required by law to be withheld, within the meaning of section 302(b) of the Act, which should be subtracted to arrive at disposable earnings, within the meaning of the Act; and (2) was not a garnishment which absorbs disposable earnings for purposes of applying the general restrictions to the garnishment order in question.

17. When Ford learned that Sears was seeking such a ruling, Ford, knowing the position taken by the Secretary on these issues was to the contrary, notified the Secretary and asked the Secretary to take steps to vindicate the position taken by the Secretary on these issues.

18. Thereafter on May 21, 1975, attorneys for the Secretary wrote to the State Court, attention of Judge Roskopp before whom the matter was then pending, with carbon copies to Sears and Ford, stating that it was the position of the Secretary as the responsible enforcement agency under the Act, that: (1) an amount withheld pursuant to a support order was not an amount required by law to be withheld (within the meaning of section 302(b) of the Act) which could be deducted to arrive at disposable earnings (within the meaning of section 302(b) of the Act); and (2) an amount withheld pursuant to a support order absorbed disposable earnings for purposes of the application of the general restrictions, notwithstanding the fact that a court order for the support of any person was itself exempt from the general restrictions.

19. Thereafter on June 18, 1975, the State Court with Judge Roskopp presiding at a hearing held in open court and attended by Sears and Ford but not the Secretary who declined to intervene as a party in the State Court proceeding, granted the aforesaid ruling sought by Sears and ordered Ford to withhold from Mr. Jones and pay to Sears the amount of $34.81 from Mr. Jones' earnings for the weekly pay period in question, calculating that $235.23 less the $96.00 in child support yields $139.23 found by the State Court to be Mr. Jones' disposable earnings for the weekly pay period in question, and that 25% of $139.23 is $34.81 found by the State Court to be the amount withholdable for payment to Sears (over and above the $96.00 in child support withheld pursuant to the Order for Wage Assignment) without violating the general restrictions. Thereafter on July 29, 1975, the State Court entered a final "Judgment Against Garnishee" (hereinafter

called the Judgment Against Garnishee) effectuating the ruling by so construing and enforcing the garnishment order in question.

20. Ford withheld from Mr. Jones and paid to Sears the $34.81, as so ordered by the State Court.

21. Judge Roskopp made the aforesaid ruling sought by Sears and on July 29, 1975, made, approved, and ordered to be entered on the docket of the State Court the Judgment Against Garnishee.

22. Clerk Wiskirch entered on the docket of the State Court the orders and rulings of the State Court, and, pursuant to the standing orders or rules of procedure of the State Court, made and entered on the said docket the garnishment order in question when originally issued on March 24, 1975.

23. Each of the defendants has represented, and the Secretary has not challenged the representation, that the actions of that defendant in the State Court proceeding, as referred to in numbered paragraphs 13 through 22 hereof, were based on interpretations of the Act by that defendant on questions of law, not theretofore resolved by the Courts, which interpretations that defendant reached in good faith and that that defendant took said actions in good faith without intent to violate the Act.

24. Throughout the State Court proceedings, as referred to in paragraphs 13 through 22 hereof, Sears was represented by outside counsel. Sears has represented, and the Secretary has not challenged the representation, that in acting in that proceeding at variance with the Secretary's interpretation of the Act, the outside counsel proceeded without the prior knowledge of responsible officials of Sears itself.

25. Subsequent to the filing of this federal court action by the Secretary, Sears has tendered to the Secretary the $34.81, which was withheld by Ford and paid to Sears by Ford pursuant to the garnishment order in question as construed and enforced by the Judgment Against Garnishee, so that said sum can be disbursed to Mr. Jones, or if not so disbursed, deposited with the Clerk of this Court pursuant to 28 U.S.C. §2041. Thereafter, Sears succeeded in paying the $34.81 directly to Mr. Jones, and the Secretary returned to Sears the $34.81 Sears had tendered to the Secretary.

CONCLUSIONS OF LAW

26. Prior to June 1, 1977,[5] section 303(b) of the Act exempted certain orders from the general restrictions, as follows:

---

5. Since the 1977 amendment, effective June 1, 1977, section 303(b) has read as follows:

(b)(1) The restrictions of subsection (a) do not apply in the case of

(b) The restrictions of subsection (a) do not apply in the case of

(1) any order of any court for the support of any person.

(2) any order of any court of bankruptcy under Chapter XIII of the Bankruptcy Act.

(3) any debt due for any State or Federal tax.

27. Section 302(b) of the Act defines "disposable earnings" as follows:

(b) The term "disposable earnings" means that part of the earnings of any individual remaining after the deduction from those earnings of any amounts required by law to be withheld.

For the purposes of this definition, "amounts required by law to be withheld" includes the amount of deductions for federal Social Security taxes (employee portion only) and withholding taxes (whether imposed by federal, State, or local government) which are taxes due on the earnings from which the deductions are made; but it does not include any amount withheld pursuant to any order for the support of any person, within the meaning of section 303(b)(1) of the Act as enacted (section 303(b)(1)(A) of the Act since the 1977 Amendment effective June 1, 1977). The fact that an order, such as an order for the support of any person, is an order exempted by the Act from the general restrictions does not provide a lawful basis for classifying deductions made pursuant to it as "amounts required by law to be withheld" subtractable from earnings to arrive at "disposable earnings" within the meaning of section 302(b) of the Act.

(A) any order of any court for the support of any person.

(B) any order of any court of bankruptcy under chapter XIII of the Bankruptcy Act;

(C) any debt due for any State or Federal tax.

(2) The maximum part of the aggregate disposable earnings of an individual for any workweek which is subject to garnishment to enforce any order for the support of any person shall not exceed—

(A) where such individual is supporting his spouse or dependent child (other than a spouse or child with respect to whose support such order is used), 50 percentum of such individual's disposable earnings for that week; and

(B) where such individual is not supporting such a spouse or dependent child described in clause (A), 60 percentum of such individual's disposable earnings for that week;

except that, with respect to the disposable earnings of any individual for any workweek, the 50 percentum specified in clause (A) shall be deemed to be 55 percentum, if and to the extent that such earnings are subject to garnishment to enforce and [sic] support order with respect to a period which is prior to the twelve week period which ends with the beginning of such workweek.

28. Section 302(c) of the Act defines "garnishment" as follows:

(c) The term "garnishment" means any legal or equitable procedure through which the earnings of any individual are required to be withheld for payment of any debt.

Any order which meets the definition of "garnishment" order contained in section 302(c) of the Act, including any order for the support of any person meeting that definition of "garnishment" order, is a garnishment order for all purposes under the Act. The fact that an order, such as an order for the support of any person, is an order exempted by the Act from the general restrictions does not provide a lawful basis for not classifying it as a "Garnishment" order, within the meaning of the definition contained in section 302(c) of the Act.

29. Any order for the support of any person within the scope of section 303(b)(1) of the Act as enacted (or section 303(b)(1)(A) of the Act as amended effective June 1, 1977) is an order falling within the definition of "garnishment" order contained in section 302(c) of the Act if, pursuant to it, the earnings of any individual are required to be withheld to meet the requirements of the order.

30. The Order for Wage Assignment referred to in paragraph number 10 hereof was a garnishment order within the meaning of the definition of "garnishment" in section 302(c) of the Act.

31. Any order which orders or coerces a principal defendant to consent to withholding by a garnishee-defendant or prospective garnishee-defendant, or to allegedly consent voluntarily to such withholding, is for purposes of the Act the same as an order which itself directly requires withholding.

32. Whenever earnings are withheld pursuant to the requirements of any garnishment order, disposable earnings are absorbed. The question is whether in a particular case such absorption violates any of the restrictions contained in the Act, not whether such absorption takes place.

33. Since the Order for Wage Assignment, entered by the court which entered the Divorce Judgment, was a "garnishment" order within the meaning of section 302(c) of the Act, the withholding of earnings of Mr. Jones pursuant to it absorbed disposable earnings for purposes of the application of the general restrictions in section 303(a) of the Act, even though pursuant to section 303(b)(1) of the Act (section 303(b)(1)(A) of the Act as amended effective June 1, 1977), it was not itself subject to the general restrictions.

34. Establishing the order of priority between or among garnishment orders as to their claim to earnings which may be withheld pursuant to

"garnishment" within the meaning of section 302(c) of the Act, without violating the restrictions contained in the Act, is not governed by the Act and is governed by State law in the absence of a controlling federal law; but in all events, any restrictions the Act places on the amount of earnings which may be withheld pursuant to garnishment must be adhered to.

35. Prior to the 1977 Amendment, effective June 1, 1977, section 303(c) of the Act provided that:

> (c) No court of the United States or any State may make, execute, or enforce any order or process in violation of this section.

36. Under the supremacy clause in Article VI of the federal Constitution, federal law, when within the scope of the powers delegated to the federal government by the federal Constitution, takes precedence over State law; and State courts, just as much as the federal courts, must follow and give precedence to such federal law, especially where the law includes a command expressly running to such courts, as is true under section 303(c) of the Act.

37. Where a garnishment order(s) exempted by the Act from the general restrictions is entitled to priority over a garnishment order not exempted from the general restrictions, as was the case under applicable Michigan law in the garnishment proceeding in the State Court as described herein where the child support was entitled to priority over the price of sold goods constituting the principal judgment against Mr. Jones in favor of Sears, nothing may be withheld pursuant to the non-exempt garnishment order unless, and except to the extent that, the exempted order(s) having such priority leave(s) the "maximum part" specified in the general restrictions not fully absorbed.

38. This Court having entered these Findings of Fact and Conclusions of Law and the Secretary having accepted the representation tendered by each of the defendants that that defendant has made changes in its policies and procedures so that in all activities of that defendant, that defendant will comply with the Act as interpreted in the conclusions of law stated herein, including refraining from making, executing, enforcing, or seeking or knowingly accepting the benefits of the making, execution or enforcement of any order or process violative of the Act, as so interpreted, and including the public defendants revising the writ of garnishment form used, so as, as to that public defendant, to affirmatively prevent garnishee-defendants from making disclosures and withholdings of earnings violative of the Act, as so interpreted, and all the parties having agreed that this action may be

dismissed on those terms without the entry of a prospective injunction, this Court will so order.

PROBLEM 170

You handled Joe Lunchpail's divorce for him last year, and now he is back in your office with a problem. It seems that Big Department Store has garnished his wages. With what is left for him after this garnishment, it is hard for Joe to make the child support payments to his ex-wife. Joe is proud of the fact that he has never missed a single payment. Can you do anything to help Joe? Does your advice cause you any ethical dilemmas? See Comment, Federal Wage Garnishment: Inadequate Protection for Dependents, 64 Iowa L. Rev. 1000 (1979).

C. Discharge from Employment

PROBLEM 171

When Joe Lunchpail's boss received the notice of garnishment, he decided that he didn't much like the idea of dividing up Joe's paycheck and paying a part to Joe and a part to the garnishing creditor. In addition, the employer evaluated Joe as no better than an average worker. He called Joe into his office and fired him and then hired the next person who came through the door as Joe's replacement. Is this a violation of the Act? See §304. What remedy does the Act give to Joe? See LeVeck v. Skaggs Companies, Inc., 701 F.2d 777 (9th Cir. 1983). Would it be a defense to the employer that Joe's wages were garnished once before by a different creditor (three years ago)?

IV. REPOSSESSION AND RESALE

KLINGBIEL v. COMMERCIAL CREDIT CORP.[6]
United States Court of Appeals, Tenth Circuit, 1971
439 F.2d 1303

JOHN R. BROWN, Circuit Judge.

---

6. Footnotes in this case have been renumbered for clarity.

When Vern Klingbiel (Purchaser), went outside his home in St. Louis, Missouri, on the morning of June 22, 1966 he found his brand new (1966) Ford Galaxie 500 gone. Later he was to learn that in the dark of night and with skillful stealth the car—despite its being fully locked—had been taken away, not by some modern auto rustler, but by an anonymous representative of the Automobile Recovery Bureau acting for Commercial, the installment finance company, which was described with remarkable accuracy as a "professional firm." Little did he know that with this sudden, unexplained disappearance of an automobile, which—with all its chrome and large mortgage—was still his, so much had been unleashed. First, of course, was his anguish at his loss. More significant for us, time, tide, litigation, trial, victory and appeal was to instruct him in the intricacies of the fine print of the purchase mortgage contract he signed and, perhaps to his awe, the Uniform Commercial Code.

A Kansas jury, under the Judge's careful instructions, which we find to be unexceptionable, did not think much of this treatment and by its verdict awarded some small actual damages plus punitive damages in a sum almost twice the purchase price of the car.

Fleeing from this judgment as a matter of principle, if not principal, Commercial quite naturally and properly seeks a haven in the terms of the contract[7] and, as an anchor to windward, the acceleration[8] and good

---

7. For convenience of reference the bracketed numbers are inserted (e.g., [i] [a] [b] [c] etc.); "This Mortgage may be assigned by Seller [Dealer], and when assigned, all rights of Seller shall vest in its assignee [Commercial] and this Mortgage shall be free from any claims or defenses whatsoever which Purchaser may have against Seller. . . . [i] If Purchaser [a] defaults on any obligation or breaches any agreement or warranty under this Mortgage, or [b] if Seller should feel itself or Vehicle insecure, [c] the unpaid portion of the Time Balance and any expense (including taxes) shall without notice, at the option of Seller, become due forthwith. [ii] Purchaser agrees in any such case [a] to pay said amount to Seller, upon demand, or [b] at the election of Seller, to deliver Vehicle to Seller. [iii] This Mortgage may be foreclosed [a] in any manner provided by law, or [b] Seller may, without notice or demand for performance or legal process, except such as may be required by law, lawfully enter any premises where Vehicle may be found, and take possession of it. [iv] Seller may retain all payments made by Purchaser as compensation for the use of the Vehicle while in Purchaser's possession. [v] Any personal property in Vehicle at the time of repossession which has not become a part thereof may be held temporarily by Seller for Purchaser, without liability therefor. . . . All rights and remedies hereunder are cumulative and not alternative."

8. "84-1-208. Option to accelerate at will. A term providing that one party or his successor in interest may accelerate payment of [sic] performance or require collateral or additional collateral 'at will' or 'when he deems himself insecure' or in words of similar import shall be construed to mean that he shall have power to do so only if he in good faith believes that the prospect of payment or performance is impaired. The burden of establishing lack of good faith is on the party against whom the power has been exercised." K.S.A. §84-1-208.

faith[9] provisions of the Kansas Uniform Commercial Code. We find the attack unavailing and affirm.

WHAT HAPPENED

The case was tried largely on stipulated facts. On May 26, 1966 Vern Klingbiel, a resident of St. Louis, Missouri, entered into an installment contract with Dealer for the purchase of a new Ford Galaxie automobile. This installment contract showed a time sale price of $4,907.56. Purchaser made a down payment of $400.00, tendering to Dealer a personal check in the amount of $300.00 and a second check in the amount of $100.00, the latter being signed in his wife's name. This left a time balance of $4,504.56, to be paid in 36 equal, successive monthly installments of $125.21, the payments to commence on June 26, 1966, under the mortgage contract containing the acceleration and enforcement provisions. Commercial shortly became the assignee, on a dealer recourse basis, for the consideration of $3,400.00.

Subsequently, but before Purchaser's first monthly installment became due, Commercial felt itself insecure, and it directed the Automobile Recovery Bureau of St. Louis, Missouri to repossess the automobile. On June 22, 1966—four days before Purchaser's first monthly installment was due and at a time when he was not in default—the repossessing professionals, without notice, demand, communication, or correspondence with Purchaser, removed his locked automobile from the front of his house in the dead of night, and delivered it to Commercial[10] along with Purchaser's personal property. . . .

---

9. "84-1-201(19). 'Good faith' means honesty in fact in the conduct or transaction concerned." K.S.A. §84-1-201(19).

10. Purchaser did not have the slightest idea that his car had been repossessed. He notified the police that it was missing, in the belief that it had been stolen, and it was the police who finally uncovered what had actually transpired.

Even the austere stipulation vividly portrays Commercial's conduct and presages its predicament:

> On June 22, 1966, Automobile Recovery Bureau, St. Louis, Missouri, at the telephone direction and request of Commercial Credit Corporation, without any notice, demand, communication or correspondence with plaintiff, some time during the night, took the locked 1966 Ford Galaxie automobile off the street in front of plaintiff's home, and delivered the car to Commercial Credit Corporation at St. Louis, Missouri. Commercial Credit Corporation had no communication either written or oral, with plaintiff prior to taking the automobile. Commercial Credit Corporation requested, ordered, authorized and directed the repossession of the 1966 Ford Galaxie 500 automobile from Vern Klingbiel because it felt itself, or vehicle, insecure.

Out of the Verbal Wilderness

The skillful Trial Judge having been aware that this contract was not written for those who run to read discerned its true meaning by recognizing its true sequential structure. Unlike Commercial which assumes that the right to accelerate without notice or demand is synonymous with the right to repossess without notice or demand, the Judge carefully distinguished between the two. Acceleration, he charged, was permissible without notice or demand. But upon acceleration Commercial then had to make demand or give notice to Purchaser so that the admitted failure of notice/demand made Commercial's repossession an unlawful conversion.

The Court's instruction tracked the terms of the contract correctly. Though under clause [i] [b] "Time Balance" might from acceleration become due at any time without notice, if Commercial felt itself insecure, the very next provision in the contract provides "[ii] Purchaser agrees in any such case [a] to pay said amount to Seller, *upon demand*, or, [b] at the election of Seller, to deliver vehicle to Seller." (Emphasis added.) Clause [ii] [a] [b] with its alternative stated in the disjunctive does not speak in terms of rights which Commercial has. Rather it speaks in terms of *actions* which Purchaser must take depending on the choice opted by Commercial. It could require Purchaser to pay off in full or it could require redelivery. But before Purchaser was bound to do either Commercial had first to indicate which course was required. The two words, "upon demand," are not only conspicuous, they are unavoidable.

Not yet overborne, Commercial would further have us construe the contract so as to declare that no notice was necessary prior to repossession by falling back on clause [iii] [b] which provides: "[iii] This mortgage may be foreclosed [a] . . . or [b] Seller may, without notice or demand for performance or legal process, . . . lawfully enter any premises where Vehicle may be found, and take possession of it."

This is equally unavailing. At the onset, this clause follows—does not precede—but follows clause [ii] which, [a] [b] as we have held, calls for notice/demand before Purchaser is required to act upon a declared acceleration. Equally important, in the sequential structure of the contract this refers only to a *foreclosure*. This means that there must be a default on the part of the Purchaser. This can take the form of Purchaser's failure to perform as in [i] [a] or an acceleration under [i] [b]. Certainly in the case of predefault acceleration, as a result of the manner in which this contract is constructed, clause [ii] [b] in effect calls for notice/demand to precipitate a default. The failure or refusal of Purchaser after such notice/demand would of course, be a [i] [a] default, thus setting in train the foreclosure provisions of [iii] [a] or [b], including *at that stage* even the most stealthy repossession by night riders. But this privilege is not available by skipping from [i] [b] to [iii] [b] over the head of [ii] [a] [b]. . . .

We think there was evidence, if believed by the jury, to warrant the inference of more than simple inadvertence or a technical conversion. There was first the circumstance of the stealthy retaking without notice of any kind, although notice clearly was called for as we have held. At that time Purchaser was not in default. Further, Purchaser's own personal property was taken along with the automobile. This was never returned to him, nor did he receive recompense for it. In fact, Commercial never even contacted Purchaser to inform him of the repossession. He had to find it out through his own effort and investigation. There are many other factors unnecessary to catalogue which sustain the punitive damage finding.

This leaves only the objection to the Court's instruction on actual damages. Clearly there was sufficient evidence to cover the three elements submitted by the Court for the loss of value of the automobile, purchaser's personal property, and the loss of use of the vehicle for an intervening period.

The objection is pointed at the term "actual value" rather than market value of the car. Assuming, but not deciding that it was error, such error was harmless. The "actual" damages awarded totalled $770.00. Of this sum $120.00 was for the loss of Purchaser's personal property, which Commercial fully concedes is correct. Purchaser's testimonial estimate of the loss from the loss of use of the car, which clearly is a permissible element of damages, was approximately $500.00. Thus this leaves only $150.00 for the loss of value of the automobile itself. This modest recovery does not demonstrate any harm.

Affirmed.

Article 9 of the Uniform Commercial Code (which was significantly rewritten in 1999) regulates creditor conduct in the repossession of collateral. Section 9-609 of the Code permits the creditor to engage in "self-help" repossession if this can be done without a *breach of the peace*. Your state Retail Installment Sales Act (RISA) may also contain provisions regulating creditor repossession and resale. Use both the UCC and RISA (or in default thereof, the Uniform Consumer Credit Code) to resolve the following.

PROBLEM 172

When two repo men who worked for Octopus National Bank came to her house to take her car, Mrs. Shoe began crying. She told them that she needed the car for transportation and she begged them not to take it away. They laughed at her tears, told her to stand back from the car, then hot-wired it and drove off. You are the attorney who represented her when she was injured in a car accident last year, so she calls you and asks what she can do. See U.C.C. §9-625; U.C.C.C. §5.112. Are there any common law theories that might give relief?

GRIFFITH v. VALLEY OF THE SUN RECOVERY AND ADJUSTMENT BUREAU

Arizona Court of Appeals, 1980
613 P.2d 1283

OGG, C.J.

This is a negligence action based on a shooting that occurred during an attempted repossession of an automobile. The appellant-plaintiff, Norman Griffith, an innocent bystander, was injured by the accidental discharge.

In their complaint, Norman and Hannelore Griffith alleged that the appellees, a collection and repossession agency, its owners, and its employee, Donald Gorney, had attempted to repossess an automobile in such a careless and reckless fashion as to have precipitated the shooting. The appellees' motion for summary judgment was granted and this appeal followed.

The pertinent facts indicate that A-Able Adjusters had been contacted by American National Bank & Trust Co. regarding the repossession of a 1973 Lincoln Continental. The bank sent a letter to the adjuster which indicated that the car belonged to Miroslav Marsalek but was being driven by Bob Williams and Linda Marsalek. Don Gorney was employed by A-Able Adjusters. He was authorized by American National Bank & Trust to repossess the automobile. Employees of A-Able had previously attempted to take possession of the car. However, their efforts were apparently frustrated by a car burglar alarm.

The deposition testimony of those present at the time of the shooting indicates that Mr. Gorney was aware of the prior attempts to repossess the car. Mr. Gorney was also aware of a violent confrontation that had occurred during one of the prior attempts. Nevertheless, he unscrewed the spotlight that lighted the area where the automobile was parked and then set off the alarm on the car sometime after 4:00 on the morning of April 30, 1977. He anticipated that the owner would then be forced to deactivate the alarm. The alarm aroused the neighbors and the police were called. Both Williams and Griffith noted that someone had unscrewed the light bulb and had tampered with the lock on the automobile.

Mr. Gorney then waited out of sight until the neighbors and police had left the scene. He then returned to take possession of the car. The alarm was still active and went off. As a result, Gorney's efforts to repossess were met with a great deal of verbal and physical resistance. A neighbor responding to what appeared to be an attempt to steal the car arrived at the scene armed with a shotgun. Williams shouted for the gun and as the neighbor passed the gun to Williams, it accidentally discharged and severely injured Norman Griffith.

I. NEGLIGENCE PER SE

The appellants raise three issues on appeal. They initially argue that the appellees were negligent per se because they instigated a breach of the peace in contravention of A.R.S. §44-3149 [U.C.C. §9-503[11]], which provides in part that

> In taking possession a secured party may proceed without judicial process *if this can be done without breach of the peace* or may proceed by action (emphasis added).

However, negligence per se applies when there has been a violation of a *specific* requirement of a law or an ordinance. See generally W. Prosser, The Law of Torts 36 (4th ed. 1971).

In Salt River Valley Water Users' Association v. Compton, 39 Ariz. 491, 8 P.2d 249 (1932), the Arizona Supreme Court stated:

> Where a valid statute, enacted for the public safety, or governmental regulations made in pursuance thereof, provide that *a certain thing* must or must not be done, if a failure to comply with the regulations is the proximate cause of injury to another, such failure is actionable negligence per se (emphasis added).

39 Ariz. at 496, 8 P.2d at 251. Similarly, in Deering v. Carter, 92 Ariz. 329, 376 P.2d 857 (1962), the court stated that:

> When, as here, the statute *does not proscribe certain or specific acts*, but defines a standard of conduct against which the jury must measure the party's conduct, a

---

11. [Now §9-609—ED.]

finding that the party violated the statutory standard is a finding that the party was *negligent*. The words "per se" add nothing to the word negligent in this case, and are better reserved to describe those instances where certain acts or omissions constitute negligence without further inquiry into the circumstances or reasonableness of their occurrence.

Id. at 333, 376 P.2d at 860 (emphasis added). See Brand v. J. H. Rose Trucking Co., 102 Ariz. 201, 427 P.2d 519 (1967); Cobb v. Salt River Valley Water Users' Assn., 57 Ariz. 451, 114 P.2d 904 (1941).

Other jurisdictions have also limited the application of negligence per se to statutes which express rules of conduct in specific and concrete terms as opposed to general or abstract principles. See Northern Lights Motel, Inc. v. Sweaney, 561 P.2d 1176 (Alaska 1977); Sego v. Mains, 578 P.2d 1069 (Colo. App. 1978); Smith v. Cook, 361 N.E.2d 197 (Ind. App. 1977); Koppleman v. Springer, 157 Ohio St. 117, 104 N.E.2d 695 (1952).

A.R.S. §44-3149 simply authorizes repossession "if this can be done without breach of the peace." It does not proscribe certain or specific acts. "[T]he facts of each individual case must be evaluated to determine if a breach of the peace has occurred." Walker v. Walthall, 121 Ariz. 121, 122, 588 P.2d 863, 864 (App. 1978). Consequently, we believe it would be inappropriate to apply the concept of negligence per se to a violation of the statute.

The official comments to U.C.C. §9-503 (A.R.S. §44-3149) and to Article 9 in general also indicate that the concept of negligence per se should not be applied to A.R.S. §44-3149. The comments to §9-503 only discuss the protection offered *to the security holder* while the comment to §9-101 states that:

> This Article sets out a comprehensive scheme for the regulation of security interests in personal property and fixtures. . . . The aim of this Article is to provide a simple and unified structure within which the immense variety of present-day secured financing transactions can go forward *with less cost and with greater certainty* (emphasis added).

Self help repossession "has been recognized as an essential ingredient in commercial financing and serves to benefit both the creditor and the debtor." Mikolajczyk, Breach of the Peace and Section 9-503 of the Uniform Commercial Code—A Modern Definition for an Ancient Restriction, 82 Dickinson L. Rev. 351, 351-52 (1977-78). The various creditor advantages inherent in self help also benefit consumers in general by making credit available at lower costs. Id. See White, The Abolition of Self-Help Repossession: The Poor Pay Even More, 1973 Wis. L. Rev. 502, 522-23;

Mentschikoff, Peaceful Repossession under the Uniform Commercial Code: A Constitutional and Economic Analysis, 14 Wm. and Mary L. Rev. 767, 772, 779 (1973).

A.R.S. §44-2202(A) [U.C.C. §1-102(1)] requires that "this chapter shall be *liberally construed* and applied to promote its *underlying purposes and policies*" (emphasis added). Since an "underlying purpose" of Article 9 is to promote financial transactions "with less cost," a liberal construction of the statutes indicates that the application of negligence per se to violations of A.R.S. §44-3149 would be an unwarranted constraint upon creditors seeking to assert their remedy of self help. Such a holding would be contrary to the aims of Article 9 as a whole and to the specific purpose of A.R.S. §44-3149.

We therefore hold that a repossessor is not negligent per se simply because a breach of the peace has occurred. However, once a breach of the peace has occurred, a repossessor is no longer protected by the provisions of §44-3149.

> [W]hen appellee's agents . . . committed a breach of the peace . . . [they] lost the protective application of that section, and thereafter stood as would any other person who unlawfully refuses to depart from the land of another.

Morris v. First National Bank and Trust Company of Ravenna, 21 Ohio St. 2d 25, 30, 254 N.E.2d 683, 686-87 (1970). While the appellees had the right to peacefully repossess their property, they are "responsible for any tortious acts committed during the repossession." Whisenhunt v. Allen Parker Company, 119 Ga. App. 813, 819, 168 S.E.2d 827, 831 (1969).

II.   COMMON LAW DUTY

The appellants also argue that even if the appellees were not negligent per se, they owed a common law duty to Mr. Griffith and are liable for his injuries. Appellees contend that the injury was unanticipated and unforeseeable and consequently was outside of any duty owed to Griffith.

In the first instance, the determination of the duty (foreseeability of harm) issue is always a question of law for the court. If a reasonable person could not foresee the harm, then the trial court has a duty to dismiss the case. City of Scottsdale v. Kokaska, 17 Ariz. App. 120, 495 P.2d 1327 (1972). However, if reasonable minds could differ and there is a debatable question on the foreseeability of harm, then such an issue is ordinarily a question for the jury. City of Scottsdale v. Kokaska; Paul v. Holcomb, 8 Ariz. App. 22, 442 P.2d 559 (1968).

Similarly, in Arizona Public Service Co. v. Brittain, 107 Ariz. 278, 486 P.2d 176 (1971), the Arizona Supreme Court stated that:

> In a case such as this where the establishment of the duty, i.e., foreseeability of harm, *varies as a result of factual distinctions*, we have held what is or is not negligence or what is foreseeable *is a question for the trier of fact*. Barker v. Gen. Petroleum Corp., 72 Ariz. 187, 232 P.2d 390 (1951); Seifert v. Owen, 10 Ariz. App. 483, 460 P.2d 19 (1969). Id. at 280, 486 P.2d at 178 (emphasis added).

In the instant case, previous efforts to take possession of the car were frustrated by the car burglar alarm. Gorney was aware of the violent confrontation (involving attack dogs) that had occurred in a prior attempt. Gorney's actions in setting off the car alarm around 4:00 a.m., unscrewing the spotlight and then hiding while police investigated what appeared to be a burglary, created an explosive atmosphere in the immediate neighborhood. His persistence in again setting off the burglar alarm and his attempts to remove the car amid the created confusion set the stage for the resulting injury. Since this is a case in which reasonable minds could differ and in which the "foreseeability of harm varies as a result of factual distinctions," we hold that a jury question was presented as to whether a reasonable man could have foreseen that his actions were creating a confrontation where someone could be injured.

III. SUPERSEDING CAUSE

In their final argument, appellants contend that, contrary to the assertions of the appellees, the discharge of the firearm was not a superseding cause. We agree. In analyzing the concepts of intervening force and superseding cause in Zelman v. Stauder, 11 Ariz. App. 547, 466 P.2d 766 (1970), this court stated that:

> A review of the Arizona cases reveals that their holdings are consistent with the position taken by Restatement (Second) of Torts, that *where defendant's negligent course of conduct (as distinguished from the risk of harm created) actively continues up to the time the injury is sustained, then any outside force which is also a substantial factor in bringing about the injury is a concurrent cause of the injury and never an "intervening" force.* Worthington v. Funk, 7 Ariz. App. 595, 442 P.2d 153 (1968); Restatement (Second) of Torts Sec. 439 (1965). On the other hand, where the defendant's negligent *course of conduct* has terminated and only the *risk of harm* created by his prior negligent conduct is present at the time of injury then any outside force which is a substantial factor in bringing about the injury may be referred to as an intervening force. This distinction has variously been referred to in terms of "dynamic-static" negligence and "active-passive" negligence. Salt River Valley Water Users' Association v. Cornum, [49 Ariz. 1, 63 P.2d 639 (1937)]; Herzberg v.

White, [49 Ariz. 313, 66 P.2d 253 (1937)]; Molloy, Jury Instructions in Negligence Cases, 6 Ariz. L. Rev. 27, 32 (1964). This conceptual distinction is more than one of semantics for *the question of "superseding cause" arises only where the facts disclose that an intervening force is present. Thus, if under the facts of a case the outside force was a concurrent cause of the injury, the issue of "superseding cause" is never reached* and defendant's negligence will always remain a proximate cause of the injury. This does not mean, however, that all intervening forces are superseding causes. City of Phoenix v. Schroeder, 1 Ariz. App. 510, 405 P.2d 301 (1965); Herzberg v. White, supra. Id. at 550, 466 P.2d at 769 (emphasis added).

The repossessor, Donald Gorney, testified in his deposition as follows:

Q: So you were trying different procedures for starting this car at the time this conversation between you and Mr. Williams and Mrs. Williams yelling back and forth about what you were doing?

A: Right.

Q: Then what happened?

A: I looked over on the passenger side because I saw something moving, and there was a guy standing there in his underwear with a 12-gauge [sic] shotgun pointed at me.

Q: Where was he standing?

A: Directly outside the passenger door.

Q: So you would look—

A: To my right.

Q: Directly to your right. And he would be right in the passenger window?

A: That's correct.

Q: Right front seat?

A: Right.

Q: How close was he to the car?

A: He had the gun up against the glass.

Q: Was it actually pointed right at you?

A: Yes, it was.

The deposition testimony of various witnesses differs as to what then transpired. However, it is clear that Donald Gorney did not leave the scene until after Mr. Griffith had been shot.

In light of the reasoning in *Zelman*, we conclude that "the issue of superseding cause is never reached" because the conduct continued "up to the time the injury [was] sustained." We therefore hold that the trial judge erred in granting summary judgment on behalf of the defendants, and we remand this action for a trial on the merits.

Credit Insurance and Default.   If the debtor has died or become ill or disabled, so that the credit insurance should pay the debt, there is authority for the proposition that the secured creditor must look first to the credit insurance before repossessing. Owens v. Walt Johnson Lincoln Mercury,

Inc., 281 Or. 287, 574 P.2d 642 (1978); Corbin v. Regions Bank, 574 S.E.2d 616, 49 U.C.C. Rep. Serv. 2d 1328 (Ga. App. 2002).

PROBLEM 173

Octopus National Bank's collection department sent a letter to Mrs. Shoe after it had repossessed her car, telling her that it was planning to keep the car and forget the rest of the debt (a practice called "strict foreclosure"). This upset Mrs. Shoe since she had almost paid off the entire car loan before she got ill and missed the last two payments. She calls you again. What can she do? See U.C.C §§9-620(a)(1), 9-623.

PROBLEM 174

When Mrs. Shoe tried to exercise her right of redemption, U.C.C. §9-623, the bank pointed to a clause in the original loan agreement by which Mrs. Shoe waived this right in the event of repossession. Is this clause valid? See U.C.C. §9-602; U.C.C.C. §5.111. One of the maxims of the common law was that "nothing can clog the equity of redemption."

PROBLEM 175

Assume instead that the bank plans to sell the car, apply the proceeds of the resale to the debt, and sue Mrs. Shoe for the deficiency. Look at RISA and U.C.C. §9-610, and advise the bank what steps, if any, it needs to take to make sure that it is in compliance with the law (see U.C.C. §5.110). What happens if it ignores the debtor's rights? See U.C.C. §9-625 (§9-626, which regulates this issue in commercial repossessions, does not apply to the resale of consumer goods). If the consumer disputes the suspiciously low amount brought at a consumer goods repossession sale (and worries about the huge amount still due), the consumer may utilize the procedures in §§9-615(f) and 9-616 to make sure nothing funny is going on.

PROBLEM 176

You are about to close up your law office and call it a day when the phone rings. It is Joe Armstrong and he wants to know what he can do about Big Department Store. It seems that BDS sold him a new furnace on credit two years ago, took a security interest in the furnace by means of a fixture filing in the real property records, and has been collecting his money monthly ever since. Three weeks ago Armstrong paid the debt in its entirety, and now he is planning to sell the house. He wrote BDS a letter with the last payment, telling them it was important that they clear up the real property records immediately so he could remove the cloud on his title. He has heard nothing from them. Can you help? See U.C.C. §9-513.

CHAPTER 12
Consumers in Cyberspace

There is, of course, a revolution going on as the Internet takes over the commercial world. As businesses begin skipping the middlemen and contracting directly with one another—the so-called B2B ("business to business") model—products get cheaper as efficiency cuts down costs. Small markets can now find their buyers in a way never before possible, and large entities can engage in mass marketing on a scale never imagined.

The consumer can take advantage of all these new, exciting possibilities, but can also get lost in the maze that includes a bewildering number of choices but almost nothing in the way of bargaining power, and, because of the global nature of the Internet, with little government protection from fraud or recourse in the event of a dispute. The Federal Trade Commission, using its Section 5 power to attack unfair and deceptive practices in interstate commerce, has prosecuted some Net fraud—those selling miracle cures for AIDS, for example, or spammers who collect personal information by telling victims that they have to supply the data or lose access to the Internet—but the FTC has so far resisted establishing specific regulations for cybercommerce.

This changing world also presents a problem for a casebook writer dealing with consumer law. One ought to say something about this brave new world, but what and how much? Consider the issue of privacy. Internet companies are using tracking devices called "cookies" (much like Hansel and Gretel's path-marking method) to follow their customers and learn their preferences, and those who log on to sites and purchase something risk having their identities or credit information stolen or sold. Identity theft is a major concern, causing huge damage to the victim, but is hard to control in spite of the attempts of a number of states (who hardly have jurisdiction over the entire Internet). Then there are issues of inappropriate marketing: selling to children or the unwanted distribution of pornography.

The various statutes already explored in this book will almost always apply to Internet transactions in which the consumer is in the United States. Thus, for example, the credit/debit card laws (Chapter 5) limiting the consumer's liability for unauthorized use will give some relief to misappropriation of card numbers by cyberthieves. Warranty laws for the sale of goods (Chapters 3 and 4) still apply, as do the proscriptions against fraud (Chapter 1) and deceptive practices (Chapter 2). But finding a solvent defendant amenable to civil process can be a problem, and, as with many consumer disputes, the amount involved may make an effort at redress more trouble than giving in and living with the problem.

There is not a great deal of cyberlaw in the area of civil relief, a chief focus of this book, but there are some early legal maneuvers, and it is these that are explored below.

I. ELECTRONIC DISCLOSURES

At both the federal and state levels, statutes have been enacted to facilitate electronic commerce as civilization moves from the world of paper into cyberspace. The states acted first, with most of them adopting the Uniform Electronic Transactions Act (UETA), and the federal government followed with the similar Electronic Signatures in Global and National Commerce Act, 15 U.S.C. §7001, commonly known as "E-Sign." The latter statute applies only in the few jurisdictions not adopting UETA. Both statutes should be in your statute book.

The basic thrust of these statutes is to allow electronic records in most commercial transactions even if other statutes, such as the Statute of Frauds, require a written signature. See, e.g., D'Arrigo v. Alitalia, 192 Misc. 2d 188, 745 N.Y.S.2d 816 (City Civ. Ct. 2002) (entry of passenger's complaint on a computer by carrier's employee met written notification requirement of the Warsaw Convention). In addition, with certain exceptions (utility cut-off notices, notices of default, repossession, foreclosure, and eviction, insurance cancellations, etc.), almost all legal notices can now be delivered electronically. These include the various disclosures required by the consumer laws studied in this book. There are a number of unsettled issues.

Both of the statutes mentioned above require that the consumer have *agreed* to electronic disclosures, but it is unclear exactly what this means. The federal statute is broader, requiring that there be electronic agreement or confirmation of agreement, and this agreement must be "affirmative"; 15 U.S.C. §7001(c)(1)(C)(ii). This means that the consumer must have agreed electronically to receive electronic records or have confirmed this consent electronically. UETA is less clear about this, though Comment 4 to §5 indicates that the consumer's agreement to receive electronic communications must be actual and not imposed unconscionably as part of the fine print in a written contract.

There is also no consensus on what electronic communication means. Is it sufficient for the required information to be posted on a web site (the so-called "Come and Get It" notice) that the consumer must periodically access (which, of course, most won't do) to keep informed? In the 1990s AOL posted rate changes only on its web site, making customers agree that this was sufficient notice of any hike in the rate, only to back down when 19 Attorneys General objected that the practice was unfair and deceptive. What about email notification? Must it be highlighted in such a way that the consumer will recognize its importance and not delete it as "spam"? If the consumer has switched email addresses, then what? Must the sender do something with bounced-back messages? These issues and others will have to await case resolution.

For a summary of the consumer issues and suggested resolutions, see Jean Braucher, Rent-Seeking and Risk-Fixing in the New Statutory Law of Electronic Commerce: Difficulties in Moving Consumer Protection Online, 2001 Wis. L. Rev. 527.

II. CONTRACTING IN CYBERSPACE

HILL v. GATEWAY 2000, INC.
United States Court of Appeals, Seventh Circuit, 1997
105 F.3d 1147

EASTERBROOK, Circuit Judge.

A customer picks up the phone, orders a computer, and gives a credit card number. Presently a box arrives, containing the computer and a list of terms, said to govern unless the customer returns the computer within 30 days. Are these terms effective as the parties' contract, or is the contract term-free because the order-taker did not read any terms over the phone and elicit the customer's assent?

One of the terms in the box containing a Gateway 2000 system was an arbitration clause. Rich and Enza Hill, the customers, kept the computer more than 30 days before complaining about its components and performance. They filed suit in federal court arguing, among other things, that the product's shortcomings make Gateway a racketeer (mail and wire fraud are said to be the predicate offenses), leading to treble damages under RICO for the Hills and a class of all other purchasers. Gateway asked the district court to enforce the arbitration clause; the judge refused, writing that "the present record is insufficient to support a finding of a valid arbitration agreement between the parties or that the plaintiffs were given adequate notice of the arbitration clause." Gateway took an immediate appeal, as is its right. 9 U.S.C. §16(a)(1)(A).

The Hills say that the arbitration clause did not stand out: they concede noticing the statement of terms but deny reading it closely enough to discover the agreement to arbitrate, and they ask us to conclude that they therefore may go to court. Yet an agreement to arbitrate must be enforced "save upon such grounds as exist at law or in equity for the revocation of any contract." 9 U.S.C. §2. Doctor's Associates, Inc. v. Casarotto, 134 L. Ed. 2d 902, 116 S. Ct. 1652 (1996), holds that this provision of the Federal Arbitration Act is inconsistent with any requirement that an arbitration clause be prominent. A contract need not be read to be effective; people who accept take the risk that the unread terms may in retrospect prove unwelcome. Carr v. CIGNA Securities, Inc., 95 F.3d 544, 547 (7th Cir. 1996); Chicago Pacific Corp. v. Canada Life Assurance Co., 850 F.2d 334 (7th Cir. 1988). Terms inside Gateway's box stand or fall together. If they constitute the parties' contract because the Hills had an opportunity to return the computer after reading them, then all must be enforced.

ProCD, Inc. v. Zeidenberg, 86 F.3d 1447 (7th Cir. 1996), holds that terms inside a box of software bind consumers who use the software after an opportunity to read the terms and to reject them by returning the product. Likewise, Carnival Cruise Lines, Inc. v. Shute, 499 U.S. 585, 113 L. Ed. 2d 622, 111 S. Ct. 1522 (1991), enforces a forum-selection clause that was included among three pages of terms attached to a cruise ship ticket. *ProCD* and *Carnival Cruise Lines* exemplify the many commercial transactions in which people pay for products with terms to follow; *ProCD* discusses others. 86 F.3d at 1451-52. The district court concluded in *ProCD* that the contract is formed when the consumer pays for the software; as a result, the court held, only terms known to the consumer at that moment are part of the contract, and provisos inside the box do not count. Although this is one way a contract could be formed, it is not the only way: "A vendor, as master of the offer, may invite acceptance by conduct, and may propose limitations on the kind of conduct that constitutes acceptance. A buyer may accept by performing the acts the vendor proposes to treat as acceptance." Id. at 1452. Gateway shipped computers with the same sort of accept-or-return offer ProCD made to users of its software. *ProCD* relied on the Uniform Commercial Code rather than any peculiarities of Wisconsin law; both Illinois and South Dakota, the two states whose law might govern relations between Gateway and the Hills, have adopted the UCC; neither side has pointed us to any atypical doctrines in those states that might be pertinent; *ProCD* therefore applies to this dispute.

Plaintiffs ask us to limit *ProCD* to software, but where's the sense in that? *ProCD* is about the law of contract, not the law of software. Payment preceding the revelation of full terms is common for air transportation, insurance, and many other endeavors. Practical considerations support allowing vendors to enclose the full legal terms with their products. Cashiers cannot be expected to read legal documents to customers before ringing up sales. If the staff at the other end of the phone for direct-sales operations such as Gateway's had to read the four-page statement of terms before taking the buyer's credit card number, the droning voice would anesthetize rather than enlighten many potential buyers. Others would hang up in a rage over the waste of their time. And oral recitation would not avoid customers' assertions (whether true or feigned) that the clerk did not read term X to them, or that they did not remember or understand it. Writing provides benefits for both sides of commercial transactions. Customers as a group are better off when vendors skip costly and ineffectual steps such as telephonic recitation, and use instead a simple approve-or-return device. Competent adults are bound by such documents, read or unread. For what little it is worth, we add that the box from Gateway was crammed with software. The computer came with an operating system, without which it was useful only as a boat anchor. See Digital Equipment Corp. v. Uniq Digital Technologies, Inc., 73 F.3d 756, 761 (7th Cir. 1996). Gateway also included many application programs. So the Hills' effort to limit *ProCD* to software would not avail them factually, even if it were sound legally—which it is not.

For their second sally, the Hills contend that *ProCD* should be limited to executory contracts (to licenses in particular), and therefore does not apply because both parties' performance of this contract was complete when the box arrived at their home. This is legally and factually wrong: legally because the question at hand concerns the *formation* of the contract rather than its *performance*, and factually because both contracts were incompletely performed. *ProCD* did not depend on the fact that the seller characterized the transaction as a license rather than as a contract; we treated it as a contract for the sale of goods and reserved the question whether for other purposes a "license" characterization might be preferable. 86 F.3d at 1450. All debates about characterization to one side, the transaction in *ProCD* was no more executory than the one here: Zeidenberg paid for the software and walked out of the store with a box under his arm, so if arrival of the box with the product ends the time for revelation of contractual terms, then the time ended in *ProCD* before Zeidenberg opened the box. But of course ProCD had not completed performance with delivery of the box, and neither had Gateway. One element of the transaction was the warranty,

which obliges sellers to fix defects in their products. The Hills have invoked
Gateway's warranty and are not satisfied with its response, so they are not
well positioned to say that Gateway's obligations were fulfilled when the
motor carrier unloaded the box. What is more, both ProCD and Gateway
promised to help customers to use their products. Long-term service and
information obligations are common in the computer business, on both
hardware and software sides. Gateway offers "lifetime service" and has a
round-the-clock telephone hotline to fulfill this promise. Some vendors
spend more money helping customers use their products than on developing
and manufacturing them. The document in Gateway's box includes promises of future performance that some consumers value highly; these
promises bind Gateway just as the arbitration clause binds the Hills.

Next the Hills insist that *ProCD* is irrelevant because Zeidenberg was a
"merchant" and they are not. Section 2-207(2) of the UCC, the infamous
battle-of-the-forms section, states that "additional terms [following acceptance of an offer] are to be construed as proposals for addition to a
contract. Between merchants such terms become part of the contract unless. . . ." Plaintiffs tell us that *ProCD* came out as it did only because
Zeidenberg was a "merchant" and the terms inside ProCD's box were not
excluded by the "unless" clause. This argument pays scant attention to
the opinion in *ProCD*, which concluded that, when there is only one form,
"§2-207 is irrelevant." 86 F.3d at 1452. The question in *ProCD* was not
whether terms were added to a contract after its formation, but how and
when the contract was formed—in particular, whether a vendor may propose that a contract of sale be formed, not in the store (or over the phone)
with the payment of money or a general "send me the product," but after the
customer has had a chance to inspect both the item and the terms. *ProCD*
answers "yes," for merchants and consumers alike. Yet again, for what
little it is worth we observe that the Hills misunderstand the setting of
ProCD. A "merchant" under the UCC "means a person who deals in goods
of the kind or otherwise by his occupation holds himself out as having
knowledge or skill peculiar to the practices or goods involved in the
transaction," §2-104(1). Zeidenberg bought the product at a retail store, an
uncommon place for merchants to acquire inventory. His corporation put
ProCD's database on the Internet for anyone to browse, which led to the
litigation but did not make Zeidenberg a software merchant.

At oral argument the Hills propounded still another distinction: the box
containing ProCD's software displayed a notice that additional terms were
within, while the box containing Gateway's computer did not. The difference
is functional, not legal. Consumers browsing the aisles of a store can look at
the box, and if they are unwilling to deal with the prospect of additional terms

can leave the box alone, avoiding the transactions costs of returning the package after reviewing its contents. Gateway's box, by contrast, is just a shipping carton; it is not on display anywhere. Its function is to protect the product during transit, and the information on its sides is for the use of handlers ("Fragile!" "This Side Up!") rather than would-be purchasers.

Perhaps the Hills would have had a better argument if they were first alerted to the bundling of hardware and legal-ware after opening the box and wanted to return the computer in order to avoid disagreeable terms, but were dissuaded by the expense of shipping. What the remedy would be in such a case—could it exceed the shipping charges?—is an interesting question, but one that need not detain us because the Hills knew before they ordered the computer that the carton would include *some* important terms, and they did not seek to discover these in advance. Gateway's ads state that their products come with limited warranties and lifetime support. How limited was the warranty—30 days, with service contingent on shipping the computer back, or five years, with free onsite service? What sort of support was offered? Shoppers have three principal ways to discover these things. First, they can ask the vendor to send a copy before deciding whether to buy. The Magnuson-Moss Warranty Act requires firms to distribute their warranty terms on request, 15 U.S.C. §302(b)(1)(A); the Hills do not contend that Gateway would have refused to enclose the remaining terms too. Concealment would be bad for business, scaring some customers away and leading to excess returns from others. Second, shoppers can consult public sources (computer magazines, the Web sites of vendors) that may contain this information. Third, they may inspect the documents after the product's delivery. Like Zeidenberg, the Hills took the third option. By keeping the computer beyond 30 days, the Hills accepted Gateway's offer, including the arbitration clause.

The Hills' remaining arguments, including a contention that the arbitration clause is unenforceable as part of a scheme to defraud, do not require more than a citation to Prima Paint Corp. v. Flood & Conklin Mfg. Co., 388 U.S. 395, 18 L. Ed. 2d 1270, 87 S. Ct. 1801 (1967). Whatever may be said pro and con about the cost and efficacy of arbitration (which the Hills disparage) is for Congress and the contracting parties to consider. Claims based on RICO are no less arbitrable than those founded on the contract or the law of torts. Shearson/ American Express, Inc. v. McMahon, 482 U.S. 220, 238-42, 96 L. Ed. 2d 185, 107 S. Ct. 2332 (1987). The decision of the district court is vacated, and this case is remanded with instructions to compel the Hills to submit their dispute to arbitration.

This case and similar ones, particularly ProCD, Inc. v. Zeidenberg, 86 F.3d 1447 (7th Cir. 1996), have generated much controversy. Among the complaints is that Judge Easterbrook is ignoring how people actually behave: the number of consumers who read the legal limitations, understand them, reject them, and then go to the trouble of returning the product to the manufacturer is so small as to not be worth considering. Most buyers of software will use it and only then discover the defects/limitations that may reduce or destroy its usefulness to them. Further, the various remedies given by existing law, mainly the Uniform Commercial Code, are available in most jurisdictions only against the retail seller, and not the manufacturer (with whom the consumer is not in privity). The retailer typically will not take back software once it has been opened.

SPECHT v. NETSCAPE COMMUNICATIONS CORP.

United States District Court, Southern District of New York, 2001
150 F. Supp. 2d 585

ALVIN K. HELLERSTEIN, U.S.D.J.:

Promises become binding when there is a meeting of the minds and consideration is exchanged. So it was at King's Bench in common law England; so it was under the common law in the American colonies; so it was through more than two centuries of jurisprudence in this country; and so it is today. Assent may be registered by a signature, a handshake, or a click of a computer mouse transmitted across the invisible ether of the Internet. Formality is not a requisite; any sign, symbol or action, or even willful inaction, as long as it is unequivocally referable to the promise, may create a contract.

The three related cases before me all involve this timeless issue of assent, but in the context of free software offered on the Internet. If an offeree downloads free software, and the offeror seeks a contractual understanding limiting its uses and applications, under what circumstances does the act of downloading create a contract? On the facts presented here, is there the requisite assent and consideration? My decision focuses on these issues.

In these putative class actions, Plaintiffs allege that usage of the software transmits to Defendants private information about the user's file transfer activity on the Internet, thereby effecting an electronic surveillance of the user's activity in violation of two federal statutes, the Electronic Communications Privacy Act, 18 U.S.C. §2510 et seq., and the Computer Fraud and Abuse Act, 18 U.S.C. §1030. Defendants move to compel arbitration and stay the proceedings, arguing that the disputes reflected in the Complaint, like all others relating to use of the software, are subject to a binding arbitration clause in the End User License Agreement ("License Agreement"), the contract allegedly made by the offeror of the software and the party effecting the download. Thus, I am asked to decide if an offer of a license agreement, made independently of freely offered software and not expressly accepted by a user of that software, nevertheless binds the user to an arbitration clause contained in the license.

I.   FACTUAL AND PROCEDURAL BACKGROUND

Defendant Netscape, a provider of computer software programs that enable and facilitate the use of the Internet, offers its "SmartDownload" software free of charge on its web site to all those who visit the site and indicate, by clicking their mouse in a designated box, that they wish to obtain it. SmartDownload is a program that makes it easier for its users to download files from the Internet without losing their interim progress when they pause to engage in some other task, or if their Internet connection is severed. Four of the six named Plaintiffs—John Gibson, Mark Gruber, Sean Kelly and Sherry Weindorf—selected and clicked in the box indicating a decision to obtain the software, and proceeded to download the software on to the hard drives of their computers. The fifth named Plaintiff, Michael Fagan, allegedly downloaded the software from a "shareware"[1] web site operated by a third party. The sixth named Plaintiff, Christopher Specht, never obtained or used SmartDownload, but merely maintained a web site from which other individuals could download files.

Visitors wishing to obtain SmartDownload from Netscape's web site arrive at a page pertaining to the download of the software. On this page, there appears a tinted box, or button, labeled "Download." By clicking on the box, a visitor initiates the download. The sole reference on this page to the License Agreement appears in text that is visible only if a visitor scrolls down through the page to the next screen. If a visitor does so, he or she sees the following invitation to review the License Agreement:

---

1. Various companies and individuals maintain "shareware" web sites containing libraries of free, publicly available software. The ZDNet site library included SmartDownload. The pages that a user would see in downloading SmartDownload from ZDNet, however, differ from the pages that a user would see in downloading SmartDownload directly from the Netscape web site. Notably, there is no reference to the License Agreement on the ZDNet pages, merely a hypertext link to "more information" about SmartDownload, which, if clicked, takes the user to a Netscape web page which, in turn, contains a link to the License Agreement. In other words, an individual could obtain SmartDownload from ZDNet without ever seeing a reference to the License Agreement, even if he or she viewed all of ZDNet's web pages.

Please review and agree to the terms of the Netscape SmartDownload software license agreement before downloading and using the software.

Visitors are not required affirmatively to indicate their assent to the License Agreement, or even to view the license agreement, before proceeding with a download of the software. But if a visitor chooses to click on the underlined text in the invitation, a hypertext link takes the visitor to a web page entitled "License & Support Agreements." The first paragraph on this page reads in pertinent part:

The use of each Netscape software product is governed by a license agreement. You must read and agree to the license agreement terms BEFORE acquiring a product. Please click on the appropriate link below to review the current license agreement for the product of interest to you before acquisition. For products available for download, you must read and agree to the license agreement terms BEFORE you install the software. If you do not agree to the license terms, do not download, install or use the software.

Below the paragraph appears a list of license agreements, the first of which is "License Agreement for Netscape Navigator and Netscape Communicator Product Family (Netscape Navigator, Netscape Communicator and Netscape SmartDownload)." If the visitor then clicks on that text, he or she is brought to another web page, this one containing the full text of the License Agreement.

The License Agreement, which has been unchanged throughout the period that Netscape has made SmartDownload available to the public, grants the user a license to use and reproduce SmartDownload, and otherwise contains few restrictions on the use of the software. The first paragraph of the License Agreement describes, in upper case print, the purported manner in which a user accepts or rejects its terms.

BY CLICKING THE ACCEPTANCE BUTTON OR INSTALLING OR USING NETSCAPE COMMUNICATOR, NETSCAPE NAVIGATOR, OR NETSCAPE SMARTDOWNLOAD SOFTWARE (THE "PRODUCT"), THE INDIVIDUAL OR ENTITY LICENSING THE PRODUCT ("LICENSEE") IS CONSENTING TO BE BOUND BY AND IS BECOMING A PARTY TO THIS AGREEMENT. IF LICENSEE DOES NOT AGREE TO ALL OF THE TERMS OF THIS AGREEMENT, THE BUTTON INDICATING NON-ACCEPTANCE MUST BE SELECTED, AND LICENSEE MUST NOT INSTALL OR USE THE SOFTWARE.

The License Agreement also contains a term requiring that virtually all disputes be submitted to arbitration in Santa Clara County, California.

> Unless otherwise agreed in writing, all disputes relating to this Agreement (excepting any dispute relating to intellectual property rights) shall be subject to final and binding arbitration in Santa Clara County, California, under the auspices of JAMS/EndDispute, with the losing party paying all costs of arbitration.

All users of SmartDownload must use it in connection with Netscape's Internet browser, which may be obtained either as an independent product, Netscape Navigator, or as part of a suite of software, Netscape Communicator. Navigator and Communicator are governed by a single license agreement, which is identical to the License Agreement for SmartDownload. By its terms, the Navigator/Communicator license is limited to disputes "relating to this Agreement."

II. APPLICABLE LAW

The Federal Arbitration Act expresses a policy strongly favoring the enforcement of arbitration clauses in contracts.

> A written provision in . . . a contract evidencing a transaction involving commerce to settle by arbitration a controversy thereafter arising out of such contract or transaction, or the refusal to perform the whole or any part thereof . . . shall be valid, irrevocable, and enforceable, save upon such grounds as exist at law or in equity for the revocation of any contract.

9 U.S.C. §2. The interpretation of an arbitration agreement is governed by the federal substantive law of arbitration. See, e.g., In re Salomon Inc. Shareholders' Derivative Litigation, 68 F.3d 554, 559 (2d Cir. 1995) ("We have long held that once a dispute is covered by the [FAA], federal law applies to all questions of interpretation, construction, validity, revocability, and enforceability.") (citation omitted). On this basis, Defendants argue that this motion properly is analyzed using the federal common law regarding the arbitrability of disputes, and that such federal common law "simply 'comprises generally accepted principles of contract law.'" McPheeters v. McGinn, Smith & Co., 953 F.2d 771, 772 (2d Cir. 1992) (citations omitted).

However, Defendants' approach elides the distinction between two separate analytical steps. First, I must determine whether the parties entered into a binding contract. Only if I conclude that a contract exists do I proceed to a second stage of analysis: interpretation of the arbitration clause and its applicability to the present case. The first stage of the analysis—whether a contract was formed—is a question of state law. If, under the law, a contract is formed, the interpretation of the scope of an arbitration clause in the contract is a question of federal law.

[The court then determined that California law governed the transaction.]

By its terms, Article 2 of the Uniform Commercial Code "applies to transactions in goods." See Cal. Com. Code §2102. The parties' relationship essentially is that of a seller and a purchaser of goods. Although in this case the product was provided free of charge, the roles are essentially the same as when an individual uses the Internet to purchase software from a company: here, the Plaintiff requested Defendant's product by clicking on an icon marked "Download," and Defendant then tendered the product. Therefore, in determining whether the parties entered into a contract, I look to California law as it relates to the sale of goods, including the Uniform Commercial Code in effect in California.

III.   DID PLAINTIFFS CONSENT TO ARBITRATION?

Unless the Plaintiffs agreed to the License Agreement, they cannot be bound by the arbitration clause contained therein. My inquiry, therefore, focuses on whether the Plaintiffs, through their acts or failures to act, manifested their assent to the terms of the License Agreement proposed by Defendant Netscape. More specifically, I must consider whether the web site gave Plaintiffs sufficient notice of the existence and terms of the License Agreement, and whether the act of downloading the software sufficiently manifested Plaintiffs' assent to be bound by the License Agreement. I will address separately the factually distinct circumstances of Plaintiffs Michael Fagan and Christopher Specht.

In order for a contract to become binding, both parties must assent to be bound. "Courts have required that assent to the formation of a contract be manifested in some way, by words or other conduct, if it is to be effective." E. Allan Farnsworth, Farnsworth on Contracts §3.1 (2d ed. 2000). "To form a contract, a manifestation of mutual assent is necessary. Mutual assent may be manifested by written or spoken words, or by conduct." Binder v. Aetna Life Ins. Co., 75 Cal. App. 4th 832, 850, 89 Cal. Rptr. 2d 540, 551 (Cal. Ct. App. 1999) (citations omitted). "A contract for sale of goods may be made in any manner sufficient to show agreement, including conduct by both parties which recognizes the existence of such a contract." Cal. Com. Code §2204.

These principles enjoy continuing vitality in the realm of software licensing. The sale of software, in stores, by mail, and over the Internet, has resulted in several specialized forms of license agreements. For example, software commonly is packaged in a container or wrapper that advises the purchaser that the use of the software is subject to the terms of a license agreement contained inside the package. The license agreement generally explains that, if the purchaser does not wish to enter into a contract, he or she must return the product for a refund, and that failure to return it within a certain period will constitute assent to the license terms. These so-called "shrink-wrap licenses" have been the subject of considerable litigation.

In ProCD, Inc. v. Zeidenberg, for example, the Seventh Circuit Court of Appeals considered a software license agreement "encoded on the CD-ROM disks as well as printed in the manual, and which appears on a user's screen every time the software runs." 86 F.3d 1447, 1450 (7th Cir. 1996). The absence of contract terms on the outside of the box containing the software was not material, since "every box containing [the software] declares that the software comes with restrictions stated in an enclosed license." Id. The court accepted that placing all of the contract terms on the outside of the box would have been impractical, and held that the transaction, even though one "in which the exchange of money precedes the communication of detailed terms," was valid, in part because the software could not be used unless and until the offeree was shown the license and manifested his assent. Id. at 1451-52.

> A vendor, as master of the offer, may invite acceptance by conduct, and may propose limitations on the kind of conduct that constitutes acceptance. A buyer may accept by performing the acts the vendor proposes to treat as acceptance. And that is what happened. ProCD proposed a contract that a buyer would accept by using the software after having an opportunity to read the license at leisure. This Zeidenberg did. He had no choice, because the software splashed the license on the screen and *would not let him proceed without indicating acceptance.*

Id. at 1452 (emphasis added). The court concluded that "shrinkwrap licenses are enforceable unless their terms are objectionable on grounds applicable to contracts in general (for example, if they violate a rule of positive law, or if they are unconscionable)." Id. at 1449.[2]

The Seventh Circuit expanded this holding in Hill v. Gateway 2000, Inc., 105 F.3d 1147 (7th Cir. 1997), *cert. denied*, 522 U.S. 808 (1997). In *Hill*, a customer ordered a computer by telephone; the computer arrived in a box also containing license terms, including an arbitration clause, "to

---

2. In a breach-of-warranty suit involving software, the Supreme Court of Washington, en banc, enforced a license agreement that, like the agreement at issue in ProCD, was presented on the user's computer screen each time the software was used, and also was located on the outside of each diskette pouch and on the inside cover of the instruction manuals. See M.A. Mortenson Co., Inc. v. Timberline Software Corp., 140 Wn. 2d 568, 998 P.2d 305 (Wash. 2000).

govern unless the customer returned the computer within 30 days." Id. at 1148. The customer was not required to view or expressly assent to these terms before using the computer. More than 30 days later, the customer brought suit based in part on Gateway's warranty in the license agreement, and Gateway petitioned to compel arbitration. The court held that the manufacturer, Gateway, "may invite acceptance by conduct," and that "by keeping the computer beyond 30 days, the Hills accepted Gateway's offer, including the arbitration clause." Id. at 1149, 1150. Although not mentioned in the decision, the customer, by seeking to take advantage of the warranty provisions contained in the license agreement, thus could be fairly charged with the arbitration clause as well. It bears noting that unlike the plaintiffs in *Hill* and *Brower*, who grounded their claims on express warranties contained in the contracts, the Plaintiffs in this case base their claims on alleged privacy rights independent of the License Agreement for SmartDownload.

Not all courts to confront the issue have enforced shrink-wrap license agreements. In Klocek v. Gateway, Inc., the court considered a standard shrink-wrap license agreement that was included in the box containing the computer ordered by the plaintiff. 104 F. Supp. 2d 1332 (D. Kan. 2000). The court held that Kansas and Missouri courts probably would not follow *Hill* or *ProCD*, supra. The court held that the computer purchaser was the offeror, and that the vendor accepted the purchaser's offer by shipping the computer in response to the offer. Under Section 2-207 of the Uniform Commercial Code, the court held, the vendor's enclosure of the license agreement in the computer box constituted "[a] definite and seasonable expression of acceptance . . . operating as an acceptance even though it stated terms additional to or different from those offered or agreed upon, unless acceptance [was] expressly made conditional on assent to the additional or different terms." Id. (quoting K.S.A. §84-2-207). The court found that the vendor had not made acceptance of the license agreement a condition of the purchaser's acceptance of the computer, and that "the mere fact that Gateway shipped the goods with the terms attached did not communicate to plaintiff any unwillingness to proceed without plaintiff's agreement to the [license terms.]" Id. at 1340. Therefore, the court held, the plaintiff did not agree to the license terms and could not be compelled to arbitrate. Id. at 1341.

For most of the products it makes available over the Internet (but not SmartDownload), Netscape uses another common type of software license, one usually identified as "click-wrap" licensing. A click-wrap license presents the user with a message on his or her computer screen, requiring that the user manifest his or her assent to the terms of the license agreement by clicking on an icon.[3] The product cannot be obtained or used unless and until the icon is clicked. For example, when a user attempts to obtain Netscape's Communicator or Navigator, a web page appears containing the full text of the Communicator/Navigator license agreement. Plainly visible on the screen is the query, "Do you accept all the terms of the preceding license agreement? If so, click on the Yes button. If you select No, Setup will close." Below this text are three button [sic] or icons: one labeled "Back" and used to return to an earlier step of the download preparation; one labeled "No," which if clicked, terminates the download; and one labeled "Yes," which if clicked, allows the download to proceed. Unless the user clicks "Yes," indicating his or her assent to the license agreement, the user cannot obtain the software. The few courts that have had occasion to consider click-wrap contracts have held them to be valid and enforceable. See, e.g., In re RealNetworks, Inc. Privacy Litigation, 2000 U.S. Dist. LEXIS 6584, No. 00 C 1366, 2000 WL 631341 (N.D. Ill. May 8, 2000); Hotmail Corp. v. Van Money Pie, Inc., 1998 U.S. Dist. LEXIS 10729, No. C98-20064, 1998 WL 388389 (N.D. Cal. April 16, 1998).

A third type of software license, "browse-wrap," was considered by a California federal court in Pollstar v. Gigmania Ltd., No. CIV-F-00-5671, 2000 WL 33266437 (E.D. Cal. Oct. 17, 2000). In *Pollstar*, the plaintiff's web page offered allegedly proprietary information. Notice of a license agreement appears on the plaintiff's web site. Clicking on the notice links the user to a separate web page containing the full text of the license agreement, which allegedly binds any user of the information on the site. However, the user is not required to click on an icon expressing assent to the license, or even view its terms, before proceeding to use the information on the site. The court referred to this arrangement as a "browse-wrap" license. The defendant allegedly copied proprietary information from the site. The plaintiff sued for breach of the license agreement, and the defendant moved to dismiss for lack of mutual assent sufficient to form a contract. The court, although denying the defendant's motion to dismiss, expressed concern about the enforceability of the browse-wrap license:

> Viewing the web site, the court agrees with the defendant that many visitors to the site may not be aware of the license agreement. Notice of the license agreement is provided by small gray text on a gray background. . . . No reported cases have ruled on the enforceability of a browse wrap license. . . . While the court agrees with [the defendant] that the user is not immediately confronted with the notice of the license

---

3. In this respect, click-wrap licensing is similar to the shrink-wrap license at issue in *ProCD,* supra, which appeared on the user's computer screen when the software was used and could not be bypassed until the user indicated acceptance of its terms. See *ProCD,* 86 F.3d at 1452.

agreement, this does not dispose of [the plaintiff's] breach of contract claim. The court hesitates to declare the invalidity and unenforceability of the browse wrap license agreement at this time.

Id. at *5-6.

The SmartDownload License Agreement in the case before me differs fundamentally from both click-wrap and shrink-wrap licensing, and resembles more the browse-wrap license of *Pollstar*. Where click-wrap license agreements and the shrink-wrap agreement at issue in *ProCD* require users to perform an affirmative action unambiguously expressing assent before they may use the software, that affirmative action is equivalent to an express declaration stating, "I assent to the terms and conditions of the license agreement" or something similar. For example, Netscape's Navigator will not function without a prior clicking of a box constituting assent. Netscape's SmartDownload, in contrast, allows a user to download and use the software without taking any action that plainly manifests assent to the terms of the associated license or indicates an understanding that a contract is being formed.

California courts carefully limit the circumstances under which a party may be bound to a contract. "An offeree, regardless of apparent manifestation of his consent, is not bound by inconspicuous contractual provisions of which he was unaware, contained in a document whose contractual nature is not obvious. . . . This principle of knowing consent applies with particular force to provisions for arbitration." Windsor Mills, Inc. v. Collins & Aikman Corp., 25 Cal. App. 3d 987, 993, 101 Cal. Rptr. 347 (Cal. Ct. App. 1972). . . .

Netscape argues that the mere act of downloading indicates assent. However, downloading is hardly an unambiguous indication of assent. The primary purpose of downloading is to obtain a product, not to assent to an agreement. In contrast, clicking on an icon stating "I assent" has no meaning or purpose other than to indicate such assent. Netscape's failure to require users of SmartDownload to indicate assent to its license as a precondition to downloading and using its software is fatal to its argument that a contract has been formed.

Furthermore, unlike the user of Netscape Navigator or other click-wrap or shrink-wrap licensees, the individual obtaining SmartDownload is not made aware that he is entering into a contract. SmartDownload is available from Netscape's web site free of charge. Before downloading the software, the user need not view any license agreement terms or even any reference to a license agreement, and need not do anything to manifest assent to such a license agreement other than actually taking possession of the product.

From the user's vantage point, SmartDownload could be analogized to a free neighborhood newspaper, readily obtained from a sidewalk box or supermarket counter without any exchange with a seller or vender. It is there for the taking.

The only hint that a contract is being formed is one small box of text referring to the license agreement, text that appears below the screen used for downloading and that a user need not even see before obtaining the product:

> Please review and agree to the terms of the Netscape SmartDownload software license agreement before downloading and using the software.

Couched in the mild request, "Please review," this language reads as a mere invitation, not as a condition. The language does not indicate that a user must agree to the license terms before downloading and using the software. While clearer language appears in the License Agreement itself, the language of the invitation does not require the reading of those terms or provide adequate notice either that a contract is being created or that the terms of the License Agreement will bind the user.

The case law on software licensing has not eroded the importance of assent in contract formation. Mutual assent is the bedrock of any agreement to which the law will give force. Defendants' position, if accepted, would so expand the definition of assent as to render it meaningless. Because the user Plaintiffs did not assent to the license agreement, they are not subject to the arbitration clause contained therein and cannot be compelled to arbitrate their claims against the Defendants.

Defendants further contend that even if the arbitration clause in the SmartDownload License Agreement is not binding, the license agreement applicable to Netscape Communicator and Navigator applies to this dispute. As discussed earlier, the Communicator and Navigator agreement is a conventional click-wrap contract; it prevents any use of the software unless and until the user clicks an icon stating his or her assent to the terms of the license. The agreement contains a clause requiring arbitration of "all disputes relating to this Agreement." Assuming arguendo that it is enforceable, the Communicator/Navigator license agreement is a separate contract governing a separate transaction; it makes no mention of SmartDownload. Plaintiffs' allegations involve an aspect of SmartDownload that allegedly transmits private information about Plaintiffs' online activities to Defendants. These claims do not implicate Communicator or Navigator any more than they implicate the use of other software on Plaintiffs' computers. Resolution of this dispute does not require interpretation of the parties' rights or obligations under the license agreement for Netscape Communicator and Navigator. Defendants were free to craft broader language for the Communicator/Navigator license, explicitly making later applications such as SmartDownload subject to that click-wrap agreement. They did not do so. Therefore, I reject Defendants' argument that the arbitration clauses in the Communicator and Navigator license agreements mandate arbitration of this dispute. . . .

VI. CONCLUSION

For the reasons stated, I deny Defendants' motion to compel arbitration. The parties shall appear for a status conference on July 26, 2001 at 11:00 a.m., and shall prepare and bring to the conference a Civil Case Management Plan addressing, inter alia, a motion for class certification.
SO ORDERED.

PROBLEM 177

When Alice Bluegown ordered a new sofa online from the website of Ponzi, Inc., the order form contained a blue hyperlink to the company's "Terms and Conditions of Sale." She never activated the hyperlink, but if she had, she would have been told that these terms included a binding arbitration clause. When the sofa arrived, Alice discovered it was torn. Ponzi, Inc., did not respond to her complaint in any way, so she filed suit against it in the local state court. Ponzi, Inc., immediately moved to compel her to submit to binding arbitration, and Alice contended that this requirement was not part of the contract at all. Is the hyperlink sufficient to include the arbitration clause in the contract the two parties formed? See In re Jet Blue Airways Corp. Private Litig.__F. Supp. 2d__(E.D.N.Y. 2005); Hubbert v. Dell Corp., 835 N.E.2d 113 (Ill. App. 2005). If Alice had gone to Ponzi, Inc.'s web site and if the entire contract was displayed on the site but was complicated, would she be bound by its terms if she skipped reading them and just clicked the "I Agree to These Terms" icon, which she was required to do in order to buy the sofa? Compare Riensche v. Cingular Wireless, LLC, 2006 WL 3827477 (W.D. Wash. 2006) (no unconscionability if consumer clicked on "I Agree" icon), with Bragg v. Linden Research, Inc., 487 F. Supp. 2d 593 (E.D. Pa. 2007) (finding unconscionability in spite of consumer's clicking "I Agree" icon).

PROBLEM 178

Portia Moot was amazed to learn that her telephone service provider, Deadspot, Inc., had added new service charges to her monthly bill. When she inquired about these, she was told that notice of the new charges had been posted on the company's web site, though she was otherwise given no notice of the changes. Is she bound by them? See Douglas v. U.S. Dist. Court for Cent. Dist. of California, 495 F.3d 1062 (9th Cir. 2007).

III. THE UNIFORM COMPUTER INFORMATION TRANSACTIONS ACT

Judges in the two opinions above were given no statutory guidance on the resolution of cyberspace issues, but some clarity may be provided by a new state uniform statute on point: the Uniform Computer Information Transactions Act (UCITA), a very controversial proposal. Initially written as proposed new Article 2B to the Uniform Commercial Code, it was rejected in that format by the American Law Institute because it contained insufficient consumer protection. The National Conference of Commissioners on Uniform State Laws (the other body that creates additions to the Uniform Commercial Code) then promulgated it on its own and sent it out to the states for adoption. Because of its scant consumer protection, UCITA was opposed by numerous entities, including the Federal Trade Commission and 26 Attorneys General, but to date it has been enacted (albeit with some consumer protections added) in both Maryland and Virginia. Four states have enacted so-called "bombshelter" statutes forbidding UCITA as a choice of law in transactions with their in-state consumers. See Iowa Code §554D.104, N.C. Gen. Stat. §66-329, W. Va. Code §55-8-15, and 9 Vt. Stat. Ann. §2463(a).

Use UCITA, which will be found in your statute book, to resolve the Problems below.

PROBLEM 179

Hank Glasses visited the web site of Adhesion World, Inc., and, after clicking on a button by which he agreed to various legal matters that he did not bother to read, he downloaded BUGBAN, a virus protection program that was advertised on the site as "the best in the world," for which he authorized a charge to his VISA card. The first time he turned on his computer after BUGBAN had been installed, his computer crashed and all of his files were corrupted. It had been four months since he last copied his files to a floppy disk, so he had lost everything since that backup. Moreover, his computer would no longer boot up, so he will have to buy a new one. For the first time he has now (using a friend's computer) gone back to the Adhesion World web site and read the legal disclaimer carefully. It contains the following interesting provisions. Decide which ones bind Hank and which do not.

a. "The law of Virginia will apply to this transaction." Hank lives in Kansas, and Adhesion World has its corporate headquarters in California. The only connection to Virginia that can explain this clause is that it is one of the few states that has adopted UCITA. See UCITA §110.

b. "There are no warranties express or implied, particularly not the warranty of MERCHANTABILITY that apply to this transaction." UCITA §§400-406, particularly §406.

c. "Clicking on the button below is an agreement to all terms herein." UCITA §§209, 211, 112, 208. Would the same legal result obtain if Hank had purchased the software program in a computer store and the box had warned him that removal of the plastic wrapping would be an agreement to all terms of the license contained therein? What if he sees the license and then doesn't want to go forward? See Official Comment 5b to §209, and §613.

d. "By clicking on the button below buyer agrees that all further upgrades to this program may be sent to the consumer without further contact and charged to the credit card supplied, and the buyer further agrees to have charged to said card all manuals created by BUGBAN now and in the future concerning virus protection." UCITA §111.

PROBLEM 180

When Portia Moot out of curiosity visited a site that sold new automobiles online, she saw the very expensive car of her dreams and, while exploring its features, accidentally hit the "BUY NOW" button. Panicked, she calls you, the attorney who is her best friend, for advice. See UCITA §214.

PROBLEM 181

Luke Kautz was an amateur chef, very proud of his cooking abilities. One night while logged onto the Internet, he entered a chat room called "Cooking Secrets" and, as others were doing, posted his favorite recipe, "Grandma's Backhand Surprise," to the occupants of the room. He was considerably startled six months later to see his recipe, called by the same name, in a book titled "Chat Room Cooks Tell All," published by the company that was his service provider. Can the provider get away with this? UCITA §207. When Luke protested to the company and threatened to sue it for allowing this sort of thing, the company decided to cancel his account and did so without notice. Is this allowed? UCITA §§701, 814, and 816.

PROBLEM 182

The next month, using a new service provider, Luke visited a private web site called "Kitchen Magic Made Easy," which offered a program for training amateur cooks in the complexities of formal dinners. He clicked on a button that informed him that he could download the program for $20, which would be charged to his service provider bill. What he didn't know was that the web site creator was an evil genius who had programmed the site so that whenever anyone clicked the order button, the site would read the visitor's computer and download much of the information on it, including the password used to log on to service provider's site. The evil genius then used this information to order all sorts of merchandise and services, which it then shipped to itself. Luke was very upset when he received a monthly bill for $9,000. Must he pay it? UCITA §§212 and 213.

Table of Cases

Table of Statutes and Regulations

Index